Fiscal Policy after the
Financial Crisis

**A National Bureau of
Economic Research
Conference Report**

Fiscal Policy after the Financial Crisis

Edited by **Alberto Alesina and Francesco Giavazzi**

The University of Chicago Press

Chicago and London

ALBERTO ALESINA is the Nathaniel Ropes Professor of Political Economy at Harvard University, and a research associate and director of the Political Economy Program at the National Bureau of Economic Research. FRANCESCO GIAVAZZI is professor of economics at Bocconi University, Italy, and visiting professor of economics at the Massachusetts Institute of Technology. He is a research associate of the National Bureau of Economic Research.

The University of Chicago Press, Chicago 60637
The University of Chicago Press, Ltd., London
© 2013 by the National Bureau of Economic Research
All rights reserved. Published 2013.
Printed in the United States of America

22 21 20 19 18 17 16 15 14 13   1 2 3 4 5
ISBN-13: 978-0-226-01844-7 (cloth)
ISBN-13: 978-0-226-01858-4 (e-book)

Library of Congress Cataloging-in-Publication Data

Fiscal policy after the financial crisis / edited by Alberto Alesina and
    Francesco Giavazzi.
        pages ; cm. — (National Bureau of Economic Research
    conference report)
    Includes bibliographical references and index.
    ISBN 978-0-226-01844-7 (cloth : alkaline paper) —
    ISBN 978-0-226-01858-4 (e-book)   1. Fiscal policy—Congresses.
    2. Fiscal policy—United States—Congresses.   I. Alesina, Alberto.
    II. Giavazzi, Francesco.   III. Series: National Bureau of Economic
    Research conference report.
    HJ192.5.F5687 2013
    339.5'2—dc23
                                                        2012028694

Relation of the Directors to the Work and Publications of the National Bureau of Economic Research

1. The object of the NBER is to ascertain and present to the economics profession, and to the public more generally, important economic facts and their interpretation in a scientific manner without policy recommendations. The Board of Directors is charged with the responsibility of ensuring that the work of the NBER is carried on in strict conformity with this object.

2. The President shall establish an internal review process to ensure that book manuscripts proposed for publication DO NOT contain policy recommendations. This shall apply both to the proceedings of conferences and to manuscripts by a single author or by one or more co-authors but shall not apply to authors of comments at NBER conferences who are not NBER affiliates.

3. No book manuscript reporting research shall be published by the NBER until the President has sent to each member of the Board a notice that a manuscript is recommended for publication and that in the President's opinion it is suitable for publication in accordance with the above principles of the NBER. Such notification will include a table of contents and an abstract or summary of the manuscript's content, a list of contributors if applicable, and a response form for use by Directors who desire a copy of the manuscript for review. Each manuscript shall contain a summary drawing attention to the nature and treatment of the problem studied and the main conclusions reached.

4. No volume shall be published until forty-five days have elapsed from the above notification of intention to publish it. During this period a copy shall be sent to any Director requesting it, and if any Director objects to publication on the grounds that the manuscript contains policy recommendations, the objection will be presented to the author(s) or editor(s). In case of dispute, all members of the Board shall be notified, and the President shall appoint an ad hoc committee of the Board to decide the matter; thirty days additional shall be granted for this purpose.

5. The President shall present annually to the Board a report describing the internal manuscript review process, any objections made by Directors before publication or by anyone after publication, any disputes about such matters, and how they were handled.

6. Publications of the NBER issued for informational purposes concerning the work of the Bureau, or issued to inform the public of the activities at the Bureau, including but not limited to the NBER Digest and Reporter, shall be consistent with the object stated in paragraph 1. They shall contain a specific disclaimer noting that they have not passed through the review procedures required in this resolution. The Executive Committee of the Board is charged with the review of all such publications from time to time.

7. NBER working papers and manuscripts distributed on the Bureau's web site are not deemed to be publications for the purpose of this resolution, but they shall be consistent with the object stated in paragraph 1. Working papers shall contain a specific disclaimer noting that they have not passed through the review procedures required in this resolution. The NBER's web site shall contain a similar disclaimer. The President shall establish an internal review process to ensure that the working papers and the web site do not contain policy recommendations, and shall report annually to the Board on this process and any concerns raised in connection with it.

8. Unless otherwise determined by the Board or exempted by the terms of paragraphs 6 and 7, a copy of this resolution shall be printed in each NBER publication as described in paragraph 2 above.

Contents

Acknowledgments

This project was made possible by a generous grant from the Smith Richardson Foundation to the NBER. We thank Jim Poterba for his encouragement, support, and substantive comments throughout this project.

For their well-known impeccable efficiency, we thank the conference department of the NBER and in particular Carl Beck, Helena Fitz-Patrick, and Rob Shannon. We also thank Università Bocconi and its (then) rector, Guido Tabellini, for providing the venue for the conference in December 2011. Laura Salini at Bocconi performed her usual miracles to run an extremely smooth conference.

Two referees greatly helped us improve the introduction of the volume to make it more coherent. We are grateful to the University of Chicago Press and in particular David Pervin for help throughout the publication process.

Introduction

Alberto Alesina and Francesco Giavazzi

Fiscal policy is at the forefront of political debates on both sides of the Atlantic. The recent Great Recession has raised (once again) several fundamental questions: Should aggressive fiscal policy be used to counteract business cycle fluctuations? At what level do public debts start being a source of concern, and how can they be reduced? Is the current generation leaving an excessive debt burden to future ones? What are the political constraints that governments face in reducing deficits and are there legislative or constitutional rules that may help?

On the first question, regarding countercyclical stabilization policy, many economists would support the "tax smoothing" principle. This theory implies stable tax rates over the cycle, allowing deficits to accumulate during recessions, when tax revenues fall, to be compensated by surpluses during expansions, when tax revenues recover. But the agreement stops here. Economists disagree about the value of more aggressive discretionary tax and spending policies to counteract the cycle.

The second set of questions relates to long-term issues. Is our generation building an intergenerational time bomb above and beyond the deficits induced by the Great Recession? In other words, are we following policies that are inherently unsustainable and will lead to a drastic reduction of the standard of living of future generations of Americans and Europeans?

Alberto Alesina is the Nathaniel Ropes Professor of Political Economy at Harvard University, and a research associate and director of the Political Economy Program at the National Bureau of Economic Research. Francesco Giavazzi is professor of economics at Bocconi University, Italy, and visiting professor of economics at the Massachusetts Institute of Technology. He is a research associate of the National Bureau of Economic Research.

For acknowledgments, sources of research support, and disclosure of the authors' material financial relationships, if any, please see http://www.nber.org/chapters/c12631.ack.

The third set of questions relates to how to chip away at accumulated deficits. Will this occur by raising taxes or cutting spending? What taxes (if any) should we raise and which spending programs (if any) should we cut? Would some inflation help? Are we heading toward sovereign debt defaults, orderly or less so?

Finally, one has to recognize that fiscal policy is highly charged politically: we cannot ignore politics and institutional arrangements when discussing it. For instance, how willing is the current generation of voters to reduce deficits? Are there rules that should be adopted in national constitutions like balanced budget amendments?

There is much that we do not know about all these questions. In the area of monetary policy, academic research and the practice of central banking have joined forces in aiming to make monetary policy scientific. Research in monetary economics has deeply affected policymaking. During the Great Moderation we thought that we had solved most of the problems regarding monetary policy. The recent crisis has made our profession reconsider this conclusion, in particular with the lack of attention to the financial sector, which characterized previous research on optimal monetary policy in Dynamic General Equilibrium Models.

Fiscal policy has experienced a similar fate, perhaps starting from an even lower level of agreement between economists even before the Great Recession. In fact, researchers are still deeply divided on some crucial issues such as the size (and sometimes also the sign) of fiscal multipliers. Also, fiscal policy is much more politicized than monetary policy. Policymakers have been willing to delegate monetary policy to technocrats (central bankers), but they keep fiscal policy close to their chest. This is because spending programs and tax rates are the bread and butter of what politics is all about: politicians build coalitions within generations and across generations. Politicians rarely, if ever, are willing to delegate fiscal policy.

This book sheds some light on these issues, drawing from the best research available. Hopefully it will help make the practice of fiscal policy a bit more "scientific."

Discretionary Countercyclical Fiscal Policy

The first question pertains to the need for aggressive discretionary fiscal policy during recessions like the one we have just experienced. Is it a good idea to engage in expansionary tax and spending policies during recessions?

This question has very different answers in models with a neo-Keynesian flavor or in full-employment models of the business cycle, like real business cycle models with no role for aggregate demand to stimulate output. In the latter type of model it makes no sense to advocate expansionary spending policies to stimulate output. Generally speaking, they would have the opposite effect by implying higher taxes in the future. Thus, if one does not believe that downturns can be caused by insufficient aggregate demand, and, conversely, that stimulation of aggregate demand can facilitate the end of recessions, asking about spending multipliers is meaningless.

If one instead thinks that when aggregate demand is lacking fiscal policy can have a role, then it makes sense to ask when and how discretionary fiscal policy can help reduce business fluctuations. The answer to this question depends, among other things, on the size of spending and tax multipliers. A spending multiplier measures by how much GDP increases for a one-dollar increase in government spending, and an analogous definition holds for tax multipliers. There are two difficulties of calculating these multipliers. First, government spending, taxes, and GDP are deeply correlated and move together. Movements in policy variables like spending and taxes affect GDP, but movements in GDP in turn affect tax revenues and certain spending programs (think of unemployment compensation). How does one establish a direction of casualty? The second difficulty is that fiscal policy does not act in isolation, and when evaluating the effects of, say, an increase in spending, one has to take into account what other factors were at work at the same time: monetary policy, the exchange rate, the international business cycle, and so on. Not an easy task.

Chapter 1 by Valerie A. Ramey and the accompanying discussion by Roberto Perotti illustrate these difficulties well and also effectively summarize what we know about spending multipliers. The bottom line seems to be that based upon US data, spending multipliers are most likely between 0.4 and 1.5. This is a very large interval. If the "true" multiplier were close to 0.4 it would be impossible to advocate an aggressive spending policy to stimulate the economy. In fact, such a multiplier would imply that for each dollar spent by the government, the private sector spends half a dollar less. If one then factors in the future cost of taxation needed to cover the additional spending, it is hard to imagine that this policy would be welfare-improving. The argument would be quite different if the multiplier were close to 1.5 instead.

Valerie A. Ramey and Roberto Perotti would probably agree on this wide range. Narrowing it should be high on the fiscal policy research agenda. But before moving forward, two methodological points of great importance need to be solved. On both issues the two economists sharply disagree. Ramey argues that the best way to isolate movements in spending, which are exogenous to the state of the economy, is to use defense spending as the "exogenous" component of federal spending. Defense spending is dictated by foreign policy needs, which are most likely uncorrelated with the state of the business cycle. In addition, changes in military spending during and after major wars are large and thus can provide much needed variability in the policy variables. Perotti instead believes that using military spending relies on too few wartime observations. In addition, he argues, in those war years many other confounding factors were at work, like the prohibition of purchasing durables for consumers, or "patriotic" effects on people's behavior.

However, it is a priori unclear whether these "war induced" behaviors and laws would bias the estimated multipliers up or down. The second methodological disagreement is on how important it is to distinguish on whether or not changes in government spending are anticipated by the private sector. Ramey thinks that it is important, but Perotti disagrees. The point is vital because if shifts in fiscal policy were anticipated, then the statistical techniques that are sometimes used to identify "exogenous" policy shifts (for example, imposing restrictions on a vector autoregression) would be invalid, and the multipliers thus estimated meaningless.

In her chapter, Valerie A. Ramey also investigates the effects of exogenous changes in government spending on employment. She finds that virtually all of the increase in employment comes from new government hires; that is, from the jobs directly created by the federal and local governments. The induced effect on private employment is very small or even absent. This is interesting in light of the recent discussion of the employment effect of the US stimulus package, because so far unemployment has remained stubbornly high in the United States. Ramey's results would suggest that this is because private employment does not respond much to government spending. Others would argue instead that the stimulus package was simply too small.

A common thread in some recent research is that there is no such thing as a "single" fiscal multiplier; that is, a single number policymakers could use to inform their fiscal actions. Chapter 2 by Alan J. Auerbach and Yuri Gorodnichenko shows that spending multipliers do not need to be the same in every period: their size may depend on other features of the economy. The kind of multipliers estimated by Ramey (and others) of, say, slightly less than one, is an average of larger multipliers during recessions and smaller ones during booms. This insight has important policy implications, since it suggests that during deep recessions spending multipliers are especially large.

A related argument concerns the effectiveness of fiscal policy when the zero lower bound on nominal interest rates binds. (Correia et al. 2011, for example, show that when monetary policy can no longer provide appropriate stimulus, tax policy can deliver it at no cost and in a time-consistent manner.) The results in this chapter are also relevant for a discussion of fiscal policy at the "zero bound," namely, in situations where interest rates cannot fall any more and monetary policy has almost exhausted its role as a stimulus to the economy. We say "almost" because during the recent Great Recession, several Central Banks have used nontraditional forms of interventions, which have made it a bit less obvious what the zero lower bound is as in the traditional liquidity trap of a Keynesian nature.

In chapter 3, Francesco Giavazzi and Michael McMahon come to a similar conclusion by following a different approach based on micro data. They study how individual heads of households respond to a particular type of government spending: military contracts awarded by the Pentagon. Their way to identify "exogenous" shifts in government spending uses the variation of spending not across time, but across US states—a strategy that allows them to control for other factors that were at work at the same time as fiscal policy was changing: monetary policy, the exchange rate, the international business cycle, all summarized in "time fixed effects." That is, they hold constant everything that varied over time and focus on comparing different states in the same year. Similar to Auerbach and Gorodnichenko, they also find significant differences in the effects of government spending, depending on the state-specific unemployment rate. In states with relatively low unemployment, government spending could have insignificant or even negative effects on private consumption. On the contrary, private consumption increases in high-unemployment states, suggesting that in such states the multiplier is likely to be positive. They also find that fiscal policy can have important distributional effects, since there is significant heterogeneity in households' responses to shifts in government spending. For instance, lower-income households and households where the head works relatively few hours per week following an increase in spending tend to reduce consumption. Heads who on average work relatively few hours, differently from those working full time, also respond to an increase in spending by working more—a result that confirms that fiscal policy can have important supply-side effects.

Recognizing that the effects of fiscal policy are heterogeneous is important not only when considering the consequences of fiscal action at different points along the business cycle, but also when considering their effects in different countries. Favero, Giavazzi, and Perego (2011), for example, find that the effect of fiscal policy on output is different across countries. They find that the response of output to a fiscal retrenchment ranges from significantly contractionary in Belgium and France, to not significantly different from zero in the United Kingdom and Italy, to initially zero and then slightly expansionary in Canada and the United States, to significantly expansionary in Japan and in Sweden, at least on impact. Interestingly, one example of expansionary contractions is Japan, the country with the highest debt ratio in the Organization for Economic Cooperation and Development (OECD), suggesting that the level of the debt is important in determining the sign of fiscal multipliers.

And what about tax multipliers? A widely cited paper by Romer and Romer (2010) identifies several episodes of large shifts in taxes in the United States and argues that tax multipliers are quite large, in the order of three. This number seems unreasonably large, particularly when confronted with the results of previous research, such as Blanchard and Perotti (2002), who find a multiplier close to one. Recent research by Perotti (2012) and Favero and Giavazzi (2012) has suggested that tax multipliers could be much smaller: the impact of a shift in taxes on output growth rarely exceeds one, although it could be larger than spending multipliers, contrary to the basic

Keynesian model. Confirming the results on heterogeneity, they also point to the instability of the tax multiplier, at least in the United States, before and following 1980: larger before 1980, smaller in the following decades where it is not significantly different from zero.

In summary, what can one conclude about fiscal multipliers? The very basic textbook Keynesian argument is that spending multipliers should be (much) larger than one, and tax multipliers should be smaller. The evidence seems mixed at best. Spending multipliers appear to be smaller than tax multipliers and most estimates of tax multipliers place them not too far from one. The Keynesian argument in favor of aggressive spending policies may have a bigger bite during deep recessions. One also has to take very seriously the notion that multipliers might be different in different states of the economy (recessions versus expansions, low versus high debt). There is still a lot of uncertainty about the size of multipliers, but one needs to allow for them being different if we want to make progress in understanding the role of discretionary fiscal policy. Even though multipliers might be larger in recessions, one has to take into account two caveats. First, one has to keep in mind the "long and variable lags" argument by Milton Friedman. Namely, by the time an expansionary fiscal package has been decided, approved, implemented, and spent, it may come into action too late and thus be useless or even counterproductive. The second caveat is how to evaluate the future costs of reducing the accumulated deficits generated by aggressive spending programs, an issue to which we now turn to. In fact, by and large the literature on fiscal multipliers is silent regarding the long-run effects of expansionary fiscal policy (although Favero, Giavazzi, and Perego [2011] show that the size of spending multipliers depends on how the government is expected to meet its intertemporal budget constraint). In other words, one may believe that fiscal multipliers are relatively large and therefore engage in deficit spending during recessions. This may help during the recessions, but what are the medium term long-run costs of such a policy? What are the costs associated with debt accumulation? This problem is made even worse if one adds political economy considerations here. A deficit accumulated during a recession could be relatively easily eliminated by allowing surpluses during expansions, retrenching the expansionary measures introduced during the recession. However, experience shows that policymakers are eager to embrace the deficit spending side of the equation, but reluctant to embrace the other side. Surpluses are almost never large enough during expansions. The result is a series of deficit spending during recessions, which lead to ever-growing debt levels. These potential costs are not incorporated in these measures of fiscal multipliers. A different way of putting it is that we know very little about welfare. Even assuming that spending multipliers are relatively large (say, above one), do we know if aggressive spending policy during recessions raises overall welfare when we take their long-run effects into account?

The problem is made even worse by the aging of the population and the shrinking of the number of taxpayers relative to the beneficiaries of government transfers, an issue we address in the next several chapters.

Long-Term Accumulation of Debt

The recent Great Recession has generated a very large increase in government indebtedness, both in the United States and in Europe. But this could only be the tip of the iceberg: debt problems in advanced economies could be even deeper than what has been caused by the Great Recession. Their roots are structural.

Chapter 4 by William Easterly makes a simple but important point. He argues that advanced economies did not adjust their fiscal policy to a secular decline in their rate of growth. Such secular decline is "normal": richer countries are expected to grow less as they become richer according to many, although not all, models of long-term development. Governments in those countries have not adjusted their fiscal policies to this basic fact, and debt over GDP ratios have kept increasing simply because the denominator of this ratio was growing less while the growth of the numerator was not adjusted accordingly. A different way of putting it is that many OECD economies mistook (perhaps strategically for short-term attitudes of various governments) a secular decline of their rate of growth for a temporary one. While a temporary one would not require a structural fiscal adjustment, a permanent one would. Yet in other words many OECD economies tried to "fight" a secular downturn in growth with temporary expansionary spending policies that were largely ineffective. This is why many countries, when hit by the Great Recession, were in an already weak fiscal position with large accumulated debts. A perfect example is Italy, where a decade-long decline of growth started in the early nineties and led to an increasing debt over GDP ratio, even with relatively small current deficits.

This problem is compounded, according to chapter 5 by Richard W. Evans, Laurence J. Kotlikoff, and Kerk L. Phillips, by an underestimation of the liability of the current generation versus future ones. According to this chapter, the current generation is following policies that will lead to an exceptionally high burden for future ones. Indeed, projection of Medicare and Social Security spending with unchanged policies look definitively unsustainable for the United States and similar consideration applies to many other countries. This chapter suggests that if a generation introduces unsustainable policies the problem compounds very quickly, leading to disaster—namely, to the inability of the government to fulfill its obligations. Chapter 5 is a reminder of how dangerous it can be to rely on conventional measures of deficits, which often disguise intergenerational obligations that escape such measures. This chapter is a sobering reminder of the importance of a careful analysis of what true government liabilities to future generations really are; in other words, of the importance of the so-called "generational accounting" principle. Often the budget deficit, as conventionally measured, is just the tip of the iceberg of the liabilities that the current generation is banqueting to future ones. In addition, measures that reduce current deficits as conventionally measured are simply a rewriting of the book to borrow even more from the future.

In this regard chapter 6 by Mathias Trabandt and Harald Uhlig raises an additional warning flag. European countries, and to a lesser extent the United States, have reached levels of government spending and taxation approaching 50 percent of GDP, and in a few cases even more. When considering further increases in government spending, one should start worrying about whether they would imply levels of taxation approaching the maximum that can be extracted from an economy. In other words, the question is how far various economies are from the top of their Laffer curve. Obviously the answer depends upon the various assumptions that the authors use to estimate Laffer curves. However, under the assumptions of the model, the picture that emerges is somewhat worrisome; many countries are not too far from the top of the Laffer curve. This raises the question of how much additional space tax increases have to solve the debt problems of OECD economies.

What should we expect given this worrisome scenario? If substantial tax increases are not feasible (as argued in chapter 5), and large spending cuts are difficult to implement, is inflation the way out, or will widespread defaults occur? This is the topic addressed in chapter 7 by Eric M. Leeper and Todd B. Walker. In a famous article, Sargent and Wallace (1981) argued that if primary deficits are impossible to reduce, then monetary policy loses its ability to control inflation. In such a situation the economy falls into a regime of "fiscal dominance": politicians set the rules and the central bank has no choice but to raise inflation to generate the seigniorage revenue necessary to avoid a default. In the current world the inflation solution—and thus the Sargent-Wallace argument—often look unrealistic, both because in many countries the independence of the central bank is protected by law, or even by a constitution (such as for the European Central Bank), and because in the midst of a world recession it is hard to envisage a surge in inflation. This chapter argues that there is a subtler way for the central bank to monetize the debt, one that does not necessarily require a large increase in inflation. The reason is that not all government bonds are real, that is, indexed to the price level, as the Treasury Inflation-Protected Securities (TIPS) issued by the US Treasury. Recognizing that most government bonds are nominal introduces a direct channel from fiscal policy to inflation, which does not rely on seigniorage. Instead, it springs from the fact that a nominal bond is a claim to a *nominal* payoff—dollars, euros, or pounds—and that the *real* value of the payoff depends on the price level. Higher nominal debt may be backed by real resources—real primary surpluses and seigniorage—or it may be backed only by *nominal* cash flows. When real resources fully back the debt, the Sargent-Wallace intuition holds and fiscal policy is inflationary only if the central bank monetizes deficits. But when the government cannot or will not raise the necessary real backing, the fiscal theory creates a direct link between current and expected deficits and inflation: it is fiscal, not monetary policy, that determines the level of prices in the economy. The bottom line is that the concern for a monetization of the debt could be more serious than it is often thought to be.

In summary, the message from this set of chapters is very sobering and should make policymakers pause. The fiscal problem of OECD countries may be substantially deeper than the short-term one caused by the Great Recession. Our generation may have followed policies that are inherently unsustainable and need radical changes above and beyond the short-term fiscal adjustments, which are on the books of current governments on both sides of the Atlantic. This point leads us directly into the next issue—namely, how do we reduce budget deficits and chip away at accumulated debts?

How Do We Reduce Deficits?

Given that virtually everyone agrees that sooner rather than later OECD countries will need to reduce deficits and debt over GDP ratios, the next question is how to do it and how costly it will be in terms of induced recessions. This is a topic that, not surprisingly, has received an enormous amount of attention in recent months. There are two critical questions. First, if one needs to reduce deficits, is it better to do it on the spending side or on the tax side? Second, is it possible to achieve large budget consolidations limiting or even eliminating the short-term recessionary costs implied by the basic Keynesian model?

The connection with the first set of chapters of this book is obvious, since the size of fiscal multipliers is a central issue in answering the first question. Chapter 8 by Roberto Perotti, however, follows a different methodology, analyzing in great detail case studies of a few large fiscal adjustments. This allows us to understand in much more detail the policy packages that are more likely to be successful. This chapter is the latest installment in a long series of papers, which, one way or the other, have looked at case studies of large fiscal adjustments. The first in this series was by Giavazzi and Pagano (1990). That paper studied the experience of Denmark in the early 1980s and Ireland at the end of the same decade and argued that these episodes represent clear cases of expansionary fiscal adjustments. The argument was that an increase in consumers' and investors' confidence, associated with the drastic fiscal change and reflected in a sharp fall in long-term interest rates, compensated the Keynesian effect of tax hikes and spending cuts. A large literature has followed that paper, making two points: spending-based adjustments are less contractionary and are more likely to lead to a permanent stabilization or a reduction of the debt GDP ratio. Second, in some cases spending-based adjustments have been associated with no recession at all, even in the short run, thus producing expansionary fiscal adjustments. A survey of this literature is found in Alesina and Ardagna (2010).

One difficult issue in this literature is how to identify episodes of large discretionary policy changes. Until recently the identification criteria was based on observed outcomes: a large fiscal adjustment was one where the cyclically adjusted deficit over GDP ratio fell by a certain amount (normally at least 1.5 percent of GDP). The idea was that such a large adjustment in the cyclically adjusted deficit was unlikely to be driven by the business cycle and was instead an indication of a discretionary active fiscal adjustment package. Assuming that the cyclical adjustment was reasonably done, that did not seem a bad assumption to make. Alesina and Ardagna (2010) confirmed the results of many other papers along the same line: in OECD economies with close to 50 percent of government spending as a fraction of GDP, spending-based adjustments are very likely to be less costly than tax-based ones. A large fiscal consolidation accompanied by a menu of other policies (income policies leading to wage moderation and an accommodating monetary policy leading to a weaker exchange rate) can be much less costly than we normally think, not only in the medium run but also in the short run. In some cases fiscal adjustments can even be expansionary.

A recent paper by economists at the IMF (2010) suggested a different way of identifying large, exogenous fiscal adjustments. Following the narrative approach pioneered by Romer and Romer (2010), they picked cases that (according to their criteria) were discretionary attempts by governments to reduce deficits aggressively. Although the presentation of that paper emphasized the differences with earlier work, the findings were essentially in line with the results summarized by Alesina and Ardagna (2010) in the sense that both agree that spending-based adjustments are superior to tax-based adjustments in terms of their effects on the economy. The IMF study finds that on average, in the episodes their identification technique picks up, adjustment cause modest recessions in the short run. The IMF findings, however, will have to be revisited since a later IMF paper (Devries et al. 2011)[1] using the same methodology came up with a slightly different set of fiscal stabilization episodes (see Favero, Giavazzi, and Perego [2011] for a comparison of the results obtained using the two sets of data).

Chapter 8 sums up this debate. It argues that fiscal adjustments are multiyear complex policy packages and that one can learn a lot from detailed case studies. One lesson is that several accompanying policies favor the success of a fiscal adjustment and can moderate the effects on the economy. For instance, income policies (wage agreements) help, and such policies are helped by fiscal programs that slow down the dynamics of public sec-

---

1. The data set is available at www.imf.org/external/pubs/cat/longres.aspx?sk=24892.0.

tor wages. Wage moderation, and sometimes exchange-rate devaluation (induced by an accommodating monetary policy) help competitiveness, inducing a temporary export boom that can compensate a slowdown in domestic demand. The behavior of private investment is sometimes central if entrepreneurs react positively to a change in fiscal stance. The bottom line is that this chapter provides a healthy warning against oversimplification in the description of policy packages, which are often complex, multifaceted affairs.

One observation made by many papers that have examined fiscal adjustments, especially in European countries, is that there are two key spending items that need to be tackled by governments who seriously want to chip away at large debts: the government wage bill and public pensions.

Chapter 9, by Pierre Cahuc and Stéphane Carcillo, examines government wages. The interesting finding of this chapter is that what matters for a country's fiscal sustainability is not the size of the public sector per se, and thus its overall wage bill, but the transparency of the government and the freedom of the press. Two countries exemplify this. Greece is a typical example of a country where weak transparency and lack of freedom of the press induce drifts of the public wage bills during booms and election years that governments have no incentive to counteract when economic difficulties arise, with the result that public sector wages eventually result in large overall deficits. At the opposite end of the spectrum, in Denmark the public sector wage bill is higher than in Greece (17 percent of GDP on average between 1996 and 2008, compared with 11 percent in Greece), but the transparency of public institutions and the freedom of the press put pressure on governments to avoid deficit-financed increases in public wage bills. Chapter 9 stresses that it is transparency and freedom of the press that prevent unsustainable increases in the public wage bill. From the standpoint of fiscal balance, it is not the size of the public sector, but whether it contributes to an overall budget deficit, that is the key consideration.

The main message of chapter 10 by Axel H. Börsch-Supan—which provides a careful and very useful review of the state of pension systems in the major OECD countries—is similar. There is no single optimal pension policy since initial conditions (culture, history, and political preferences, all of which have shaped the design of the welfare state) differ so much among countries. Some general lessons can still be drawn from the attempt of several countries at controlling their pension expenditures. The introduction of notional defined contribution (NDC) systems reduces fiscal strain when implemented early and consistently, such as in Sweden and (to some extent) in Italy. It failed, however, in Germany, where, as Börsch-Supan notes, the taste of a funded system seems unpalatable. Automatic stabilizers, such those introduced in the NDC systems in Sweden, Italy, and Poland, and the indexation of pension benefits to the dependency ratio introduced in Germany, may also help to put pension systems on a long-run fiscally sustainable path since they are sheltered from day-to-day political opportunism. One may want to introduce similar automatic rules for the retirement age, such as a proportionality rule that keeps the ratio of time spent in retirement to time spent working constant. The sheltering effect, of course, goes only so far. In Germany, for example, the sustainability factor in the benefit formula has been set out of force through a "pension benefit guarantee," which rules out any nominal benefit reduction, and parts of the dynamic increase in the retirement age have been offset by the introduction of new duration-of-service rules. By and large, however, pension reforms introducing automatic stabilizers have worked better than those without such mechanisms.

What about taxes? How can tax reform help reduce debt and deficits? Chapter 11 by Ruud de Mooij and Michael Keen discusses the tax side of fiscal adjustments. It first explores the idea, prominent in troubled Euro area countries, of a "fiscal devaluation"—that is, shifting from social contributions to the value added tax (VAT) as a way to mimic a nominal devaluation. An excellent theoretical discussion of fiscal devaluations can be found in Gopinath, Farhi, and Itskhoki (2011). The empirical evidence presented shows that in Euro area countries fiscal devaluations could improve the trade balance quite sizably in the short run, though the effects will eventually disappear. The paper then assesses the wider scope for using a VAT to achieve a fiscal consolidation. It is sometimes argued (see, e.g., Gale and Harris 2011) that in the United States and Japan the introduction of a VAT could go a long way toward solving the countries' fiscal problems. But VAT reform faces strong political opposition from two quite different quarters. The argument on the left is that the VAT is regressive. The argument on the right is that it makes raising revenue much easier, thus creating an incentive to inflate government expenditure (see, e.g., Holtz-Eakin 2011). The popular perception of the VAT as inherently regressive is hard to dismantle, impeding both base-broadening in Europe and rate-raising or introduction in Japan and the United States. It would be comforting to believe that resistance of this kind will be overcome by good analysis communicated effectively. But these points have been well-known, to key policymakers at least, for many years and yet no real progress has been made.

In summary, one can draw a few relatively sound conclusions from these chapters. Large fiscal adjustments have occurred in the past. When implemented mostly on the spending side and accompanied by an appropriate mix of policies, their recessionary effect can be minimized or much attenuated. An interesting question is which are the desirable accompanying policies in the current situation. For instance, devaluations are not feasible for individual members of the Euro area, but a devaluation of the Euro itself would help. On the other hand, wage moderation supported by public wage restraint is a feasible avenue to follow. A possibly worrisome feature of the current situation is the fact that contrary to previous experiences of large fiscal consolidation that occurred in individual economies, in the next few years many countries will have to follow restrictive fiscal policies at the same time, on both sides of the Atlantic.

Politics and Institutions

Fiscal policy is much politicized because it has very obvious and large redistributive consequences, both within a generation and across generations. While policymakers have been willing to delegate monetary policy to independent institutions (national central banks or even a super national independent central bank like the ECB), they have kept fiscal policy very close to their chest and thus to day-to-day politics. Delegation of fiscal prerogatives to EU institutions like the Stability and Growth Pact has not worked well because it has proven impossible to force national governments to stick by it. France and (remarkably) Germany were the two countries that first violated it.

An interesting question, then, is whether it is possible for national governments to follow rules of behavior and therefore keep fiscal policy at arms' length from day-to-day politics. There are two key questions. First, which rules should a government adopt? Second, can a supranational entity, like the EU, impose to a national sovereign a rule? Chapter 12 by Charles Wyplosz begins by arguing that national governments do need to be constrained by fiscal rules to correct the externality introduced by the power of interest groups that lead to a deficit bias. The question is, which rules? Unfortunately the simplest one may not be the most efficient, and the most complicated one may not be easily enforceable. The simplest possible rule is a balanced budget law stating that the budget has to be balanced every period. This rule is easy to verify, but it does not allow the necessary budgetary flexibility over the cycle. A cyclically adjusted balanced budget rule would allow such flexibility, but it would be hard to verify. How would we agree on the correct cyclical adjustment? Each government would always try to justify that a deficit is due to a cyclical slowdown. Another rule often discussed is the "golden rule." This is a balanced budget rule that allows deficit financing for public investment. While the general principle that governments, like private corporations, should be allowed to amortize investment expenditure is obviously correct, the point is whether lack of growth throughout the OECD is primarily the result of a lack of public investment. We do not think it is (see Leduc and Wilson 2012). Another arrangement sometimes adopted is fiscal boards. These are independent bodies of economists and public servants that offer opinions on the sustainability of national fiscal policies and sometimes (as in the Netherlands) of political platforms ahead of general elections. Their views should serve as a constraint on governments. The chapter's wise conclusion is that rules are neither necessary nor sufficient to achieve fiscal discipline, yet they help. Similarly, fiscal institutions are neither necessary nor sufficient to achieve fiscal discipline, but they help. In this case we face a delicate balance. Institutions must bind the policymakers without violating the democratic requirement that elected officials have the power to decide on budgets. This argues against assigning wide discretionary powers to fiscal institutions, but it is fully compatible with giving them either the authority to apply legal rules or to act as official watchdogs.

One of the arguments for rules is that a government has a hard time reducing deficits because any such policy would lead to an immediate political defeat in the next election. Chapter 13 by Alberto Alesina, Dorian Carloni, and Gianpaolo Lecce looks at the evidence about this so-called conventional wisdom—namely, that deficit-reducing policies are the kiss of death (electorally speaking) for fiscally conservative governments. This chapter shows that the empirical evidence on this point is much less clear cut than the conviction with which this conventional wisdom is held. The authors find no evidence that governments that reduce budget deficits even decisively are systematically voted out of office. In some cases they are, in some (more often) they are not. The authors address as carefully as possible the issue of reverse causality, namely the possibility that only "strong and popular" governments can implement fiscal adjustments and thus they are not voted out of office despite having reduced the deficits. Even taking this possibility into account the authors find no evidence that fiscal adjustments, even decisive ones, systematically (on average) imply electoral defeats. But then, if fiscal adjustments do not lead systematically to electoral defeats, why do they often seem so politically difficult? The reason is that the political game played around a fiscal adjustment goes above and beyond one-person-one-vote elections. Strikes, contributions from powerful lobbies, and press campaigns are all means by which various groups can use to enforce (or block) policies above and beyond voting at the polls. For example, imagine a public sector union that goes on strike to block a reduction of the public wage bill. They may create disruptions with consequences that may be too costly to bear for a government. Public sector unions may have connections with parts of the incumbent coalition and block fiscal adjustments. Similar considerations may lead to postponements of pension reforms. In many countries pensioners developed a strong political support even within workers' unions. Alesina and Drazen (1990) provide a model that explains delays on deficit stabilization policies not relying on electoral defeats of governments.

In summary, the politics of fiscal policy are complex. National government may have incentives to run excessive deficits and then find it hard to reduce them. If there is a deficit bias in national government policies, then fiscal rules may help. But one must be careful not to oversell what one can achieve with rules. To begin with, the choice of whether or not to adopt a tight fiscal rule is endogenous. That is, societies where an agreement for fiscal tightness is solid are more likely to adopt such rules; societies that have not reached such consensus will not adopt the rules even though these would be precisely the societies that need their hands to be tied by rules. So, paradoxically, more prudent governments will choose to impose rules on themselves and not the other way around! In addition, it is very difficult to impose from abroad fiscal rules on national sovereigns, as the failure of the Stability and Growth Pact highlights. What can be said, we believe, is that a fiscal rule can help a well-intentioned government to hold a fiscally responsible policy, but it will hardly prevent a different type of government from breaking the rule directly or implicitly with some creative accounting. Without a deeply held national political commitment to fiscal responsibility, no rules will be a deus ex machina.

The desirability of fiscal rules has been at the forefront of discussions in the European Union. The rapid accumulations of deficits and debt within the EU have led to an impasse. Northern European countries (Germany above all) feel that any movement toward a centralization of government liabilities (such as introducing Eurobonds) would imply that the German taxpayers would be stuck with the bills arising from the profligacy of Southern European countries. Any rule that would effectively constrain new emissions of fresh debt would not solve the problem of the stock of accumulated debt in countries like Greece or Italy.

To what extent can fiscal policy be coordinated within the European Union to avoid future crises, exploding spreads, default risks, and so on? The answer is not easy, for the reasons discussed previously. Member countries are not ready to give up fiscal independence for two reasons. First, national politicians want to keep domestic fiscal discretion to achieve policy goals sometimes dictated more by politics than good economics. Second, Europe is not a unified country. While in the United States it is relatively accepted that citizens of certain states doing better at a certain point in time (say, Texas) have to redistribute through the federal government to citizens of less successful states (say, Nevada), we are quite far from this situation in Europe. While German taxpayers might have been convinced to help the Greeks in order to save German banks, it is unclear what would have happened if German banks had been less exposed to Greece. Redistributions across national borders remain difficult in Europe. Any attempts at setting up fiscal rules that ignore this fact are unlikely to command the needed popular support.

But perhaps the crisis raises even bigger issues regarding the coordination of fiscal policies above and beyond Europe. Has the crisis highlighted a need for a stronger coordination between major areas to avoid fiscal and commercial imbalances? What rules should we adopt to achieve such an objective? Is it realistic to strive for this goal? These are some of the issues that many economist and policymakers struggle with.

Conclusions

There is much that we do not know about fiscal policy. We believe that this book makes a contribution at taking stock of what we know and making progress in many directions, but many questions are still open regarding both the theory and the practice of fiscal policy.

One important open question regards the size of multipliers. Quite apart from narrowing down their size, we need to know more about welfare. How far above one does a spending multiplier have to be in order for a countercyclical spending policy to be welfare improving? How does one evaluate the costs of accumulated deficits and future taxation versus the benefit of reducing unemployment in the short run? There is a vague sense that multipliers greater than one call for aggressive countercyclical policy, while multipliers smaller than one call for the opposite. We need to deepen our understanding of this point.

Assuming that discretionary countercyclical fiscal policy is needed, is it better to act on the tax side or the spending side? What variables would influence this choice?

A further set of questions relate to whether or not we are underestimating the size of the problem of accumulated debt. How much are we missing by not considering more carefully the accumulated liabilities of this generation versus future ones? Are we truly sitting on a time bomb and kidding ourselves with commonly used data that (although worrisome by themselves) are unable to capture the intergenerational dimension of fiscal policy? Should we expect widespread defaults and inflation, or are public debts manageable? Is there enough room to raise taxes in countries approaching 50 percent of GDP tax burden? If raising taxes is becoming more and more difficult what is the alternative? Can fiscal rules prevent the aggravation of an already dire situation?

We need to better understand how to design fiscal adjustment programs so as to minimize the cost for the economy and maximize the probability of success, defined as a reduction of the debt over GDP ratio. In our view, the literature on this point has reached two relatively solid conclusions: first, cutting spending is less recessionary than raising taxes in OECD economies with already large public sectors. The second is that a well-designed policy package can minimize or, under the same circumstances, even eliminate the recessionary effects of budget cuts in the short run. We need to know more about what can feasibly be cut, how to design the policy package, and how to minimize the possible negative effects on income inequality. We do not know enough about the distributive costs of large fiscal adjustments. The commonly held view is that budget cuts typically hurt the poor, but is this really true in countries with 50 percent public spending over GDP? Presumably the answer depends on how well targeted the welfare system is: it may be possible to reduce spending and the tax burden, preserving welfare coverage for the truly needy.

Finally, and related to the previous point, there are many political economy questions regarding fiscal policy. The most commonly held view is that citizens blindly prefer spending increases and tax cuts and this introduces a deficit bias in democracies. Reality might be a bit more complex. Certain governments have been able to be fiscally responsible and be reelected. What explains, then, the tendency of governments to postpone fiscal adjustments? What is the role of specific lobbying pressures versus the risk of electoral defeats? How do the design fiscal adjustments and their fairness affect the popularity of governments?

References

Alesina, Alberto, and Silvia Ardagna. 2010. "Large Changes in Fiscal Policy: Taxes versus Spending." In *Tax Policy and the Economy,* vol. 24, edited by Jeffrey R. Brown, 35–68. Chicago: University of Chicago Press.

Alesina, Alberto, and Allan Drazen. 1990. "Why Are Stabilizations Delayed?" *American Economic Review* 81 (5): 1170–88.

Blanchard, Oliver, and Roberto Perotti. 2002. "An Empirical Characterization of the Dynamic Effects of Changes in Government Spending and Taxes on Output." *Quarterly Journal of Economics* 117 (4): 1329–68.

Correia, Isabel, Emmanuel Farhi, Juan Pablo Nicolini, and Pedro Teles. 2011. "Unconventional Fiscal Policy at the Zero Bound." NBER Working Paper no. 16758. Cambridge, MA: National Bureau of Economic Research, February.

Devries, P., J. Guajardo, D. Leigh, and A. Pescatori. 2011. "A New Action-Based Dataset of Fiscal Consolidation." IMF Working Paper no. 11/128. Washington, DC: International Monetary Fund.

Favero, Carlo, and Francesco Giavazzi. 2012. "Measuring Tax Multipliers: The Narrative Method in Fiscal VARs." *American Economic Journal: Economic Policy* 4 (2): 69–94.

Favero, Carlo, Francesco Giavazzi, and Jacopo Perego. 2011. "Country Heterogeneity and the International Evidence on the Effects of Fiscal Policy." *IMF Economic Review* 59:652–82. Washington, DC: International Monetary Fund.

Gale, William G., and Benjamin H. Harris. 2011. "A VAT for the United States: Part of the Solution." *Tax Analysts,* 64–82.

Giavazzi, Francesco, and Marco Pagano. 1990. "Can Severe Fiscal Contractions Be Expansionary? Tales of Two Small European Countries." In *NBER Macroeconomics Annual 1990,* vol. 5, edited by Olivier Jean Blanchard and Stanley Fischer, 75–122. Cambridge, MA: MIT Press.

Gopinath, Gita, Emmanuela Farhi, and Oleg Itskhoki. 2011. "Fiscal Devaluations." NBER Working Paper no. 17662. Cambridge, MA: National Bureau of Economic Research, December.

Holtz-Eakin, Douglas. 2011. "The Case Against VAT." *Tax Analysts,* 96–101.

International Monetary Fund (IMF). 2010. "Will It Hurt? Macroeconomic Effects of Fiscal Consolidation." *World Economic Outlook,* chapter 3, October. Washington, DC: International Monetary Fund.

Leduc, Sylvain, and Daniel Wilson. 2012. "Roads to Prosperity or Bridges to Nowhere? Theory and Evidence on the Impact of Public Infrastructure Investment." NBER Working Paper no. 18042. Cambridge, MA: National Bureau of Economic Research, May.

Perotti, Roberto. 2012. "The Effects of Tax Shocks On Output: Not So Large, But Not Small Either." *American Economic Journal: Economic Policy* 4 (2): 214–37.

Romer, Christina, and David H. Romer. 2010. "The Macroeconomic Effects of Tax Changes: Estimates Based on a New Measure of Fiscal Shocks." *American Economic Review* 100:763–801.

Sargent, T. J., and N. Wallace. 1981. "Some Unpleasant Monetarist Arithmetic." *Federal Reserve Bank of Minneapolis Quarterly Review* 5:1–17.

1
Government Spending and Private Activity

Valerie A. Ramey

1.1 Introduction

The potential stimulus effects of fiscal policy have once again become an active area of academic research. Before the Great Recession, the few researchers who estimated the effects of government spending did so in order to understand which macroeconomic models were the best approximation to the economy. Rather than analyzing differences in estimated multipliers, most of the literature debated whether the movements of key variables, such as real wages and consumption, were more consistent with Keynesian or neoclassical views of fiscal policy (e.g., Rotemberg and Woodford 1992; Ramey and Shapiro 1998; Blanchard and Perotti 2002; Burnside, Eichenbaum, and Fisher 2004; and Perotti 2008). Starting with the stimulus debate, however, the focus shifted to empirical estimates of multipliers. In Ramey (2011b), I surveyed the growing recent literature that estimates government spending multipliers in aggregate national data as well as in state panel data. Reviewing that literature, I found that the range of estimates of the GDP multiplier is often as wide within studies as it is across studies. I concluded that the multiplier for a deficit-financed temporary increase in

Valerie A. Ramey is professor in and chair of the Department of Economics at the University of California, San Diego, and a research associate of the National Bureau of Economic Research.

This is a revised version of a paper presented at the NBER conference, "Fiscal Policy after the Financial Crisis," in Milan in December 2011. I am grateful to Roger Farmer, Garey Ramey, and David Romer for discussions that led to the questions analyzed in this chapter and to Alberto Alesina, Francesco Giavazzi, Roberto Perotti, and participants in the conference for their comments. I thank Jonas Fisher for sharing the Fisher-Peters defense excess returns variable. For acknowledgments, sources of research support, and disclosure of the author's material financial relationships, if any, please see http://www.nber.org/chapters/c12632.ack.

government spending probably lies somewhere between 0.8 and 1.5, but could be as low as 0.5 or as high as 2.

Two of the key questions for deciding whether policymakers should use government spending for short-run stabilization policy are: (1) Can an increase in government spending stimulate the economy in a way that raises private spending? and (2) Can an increase in government spending raise employment and lower unemployment? With respect to the first question, if an increase in government spending raises GDP without raising private sector spending, then private welfare does not necessarily rise. With respect to the second question, most economists and policymakers would agree that job creation is at least as important a goal as stimulating output. In theory, one can use Okun's law to translate GDP multipliers to unemployment multipliers. However, because of variations in the parameters of this "law" over time, the advent of jobless recoveries, and the frictions involved in creating and filling jobs, the translation of output multipliers to employment or unemployment multipliers is not straightforward. Thus, it makes sense to devote as much attention to the employment effects of government spending as to the output effects.

This chapter empirically studies the effect of government spending on private spending, unemployment, and employment. I define private spending to be GDP less government spending. I show that whether one uses structural vector autoregressions (SVARs) or expectational vector autoregressions (EVARs), whether the sample includes World War II and Korea or excludes them, an increase in government spending never leads to a significant rise in private spending. In fact, in most cases it leads to a significant fall. These results imply that the government spending multiplier is more likely below one rather than above one.

These estimates are based on samples in which part of the increase in government spending is financed by an increase in tax rates, so the multipliers are not necessarily the ones applicable to current debates on deficit-financed stimulus packages. I thus explore two different ways to adjust for the increase in taxes in order to determine a deficit-financed government spending multiplier. One method uses the VARs to create counterfactuals and the other uses more structural instrumental variables estimates. Surprisingly, both methods suggest that the behavior of marginal tax rates does not have a significant effect on the size of the spending multiplier.

In the final part of the chapter I investigate the effects of government spending on unemployment and employment. I begin by conducting a case study of labor markets during the World War II period. I then use the VAR methods on various samples and find that an increase in government spending lowers unemployment. However, I find the surprising result that in the great majority of time periods and specifications, all of the increase in employment after a positive shock to government spending is due to an increase in government employment, not private employment. There is only one exception. These results suggest that the employment effects of government spending work through the direct hiring of workers, not stimulating the private sector to hire more workers.

1.2 Background

1.2.1 Output Multipliers

There has been a dramatic increase in research on the output multiplier in the last few years. The aggregate studies that estimate the multiplier fit in two general categories. The first are the studies that use long spans of annual data and regress the growth rate of GDP on current and one lag of defense spending, or government spending instrumented by defense spending (e.g., Hall 2009; Barro and Redlick 2011). These studies tend to find multipliers that are less than one. The second type are the VARs estimated on quarterly data, such as those used by Ramey and Shapiro (1998), Blanchard and Perotti (2002), Mountford and Uhlig (2009), Fisher and Peters (2010), Auerbach and Gorodnichenko (2012), and Ramey (2011c). Some of these papers calculate the multipliers based on comparing the peak of the government spending response to the peak of the GDP response. Others compare the area under the two impulse response functions. As I discuss in my forum piece for the *Journal of Economic Literature* (Ramey 2011b), the range of multiplier estimates are often as wide within studies as across studies. An interesting, but unnoticed, pattern arises from this literature. In particular, the Blanchard-Perotti style SVARs yield smaller multipliers than the expectational VARs (EVARS), such as the ones used in my work. This result is intriguing because the SVARs tend to find rises in consumption whereas the EVARs tend to find falls in consumption in response to an increase in government spending. Overall, most output multiplier estimates from the aggregate literature tend to lie between 0.5 and 1.5.

There are also numerous papers that use cross-sections or panels of states to estimate the effects of an increase in government spending in a state on that state's income. These papers typically find multipliers of about 1.5. However, translating these state-level multipliers to aggregate multipliers is tricky, as discussed in Ramey (2011b).

While the explicit instrumental variables frameworks with few dynamics provide statistical confidence bands around the implied multipliers, the VAR-based literature does not. Typically, the VAR literature provides separate impulse responses of government spending, GDP, and the spending subcomponents, and then calculates an implied multiplier by either comparing the peak response of GDP to the peak response of government spending, or comparing the integral under the two impulse response functions. As I will show later, a simple permutation of the VAR makes it easy to provide confidence intervals of the multiplier relative to unity.

1.2.2   Labor Market Effects of Government Spending

A few of the older papers and a growing number of recent papers have studied government spending effects on labor markets. Most of the studies that exploit cross-state or locality variation focus on employment as much as income. For example, Davis, Loungani, and Mahidhara (1997) and Hooker and Knetter (1997) were among the first to study the effects of defense spending shocks on employment in a panel of states. Nakamura and Steinsson (2011) study similar effects in updated data. Fishback and Kachanovskaya (2010) analyze the effects of various New Deal programs during the 1930s on states and localities. Chodorow-Reich et al. (2012) and Wilson (2012) estimate the effects of the recent American Recovery and Reinvestment Act (ARRA) on employment using cross-state variation. As summarized by Ramey (2011b), on average these and related studies produce estimates that imply that each $35,000 of government spending produces one extra job. However, some of these studies, such as by Wilson (2012), find that the jobs disappear quickly.

At the aggregate level, the recent paper by Monacelli, Perotti, and Trigari (2010) analyzes the effects of government spending shocks on a number of labor market variables. In particular, they use a standard structural VAR to investigate the effects of government spending shocks on unemployment, vacancies, job-finding rates, and separation rates in the post-1954 period. Their point estimates suggest that positive shocks to government spending lower the unemployment rate and the separation rate, and increase vacancies and the job finding rate. However, their estimates are imprecise, so most of their points estimates are not statistically different from zero at standard significance levels. On the other hand, Brückner and Pappa (2010) study the effects of fiscal expansions on unemployment in a sample of Organization for Economic Cooperation and Development (OECD) countries using quarterly data. Whether they use a standard SVAR, sign restrictions, or the Ramey-Shapiro military dates, they find that a fiscal expansion often *increases* the unemployment rate. In most cases, these increases are statistically significant at the 5 percent confidence level.

In sum, the studies using state or local panel data find more robust positive effects of government spending on employment than the aggregate studies. As discussed earlier, translating state-level multipliers to the aggregate is not straightforward.

1.2.3   The Distinction between Government Purchases and Government Value Added

To understand why there is not a one-to-one correspondence between output multipliers and private employment multipliers, it is useful to consider the distinction between government spending on private goods versus government output. In the National Income and Product Accounts (NIPA), government purchases (*G*) includes both government *purchases of goods* from the private sector, such as aircraft carriers, and government *value added,* which is comprised of compensation of government employees, such as payments to military and civilian personnel, and consumption of government capital. Rotemberg and Woodford (1992) made this distinction in their empirical work by examining shocks to total defense spending after conditioning on lags of the number of military personnel. Wynne (1992) was the first to point out the theoretical distinction between government spending on purchases of goods versus compensation of government employees. He used comparative statistics in a neoclassical model to demonstrate the different effects. Finn (1998) explored the issue in a fully dynamic neoclassical model. She showed that increases in *G* resulting from an increase in government employment and increases in *G* resulting from an increase in purchases of goods from the private sector have opposite effects on private sector output, employment, and investment. Other authors exploring this distinction include Cavallo (2005), Pappa (2009), and Gomes (2010).

Figure 1.1 shows the two ways of dividing the output of the economy. The top panel shows the usual way of dividing goods and services according to which entity purchased the goods. Variable *G* is the usual NIPA category of "Government Purchases of Goods and Services." The rest of the output is purchased by the private sector, either as consumption, investment, or net exports. The middle panel divides the economy according to who produces the goods and services. Production by the government occurs when it directly hires workers and buys capital stock. The value added is counted as production by this sector. Examples include education services, police services, military personnel services, and other general government activities.[1] All other production is done by the private sector. The third panel superimposes these two ways of dividing the economy. As the panel illustrates, government purchases (*G*) consist of the value added of government (Y^{Gov}), which the government itself produces and essentially "sells" to itself, and government purchases of goods and services from the private sector (G^{Priv}). During the typical military buildup, the government hires more military personnel, resulting in more government production, and buys tanks from the private sector. Thus, both components of *G* rise.

To see why different types of government spending can have different effects, consider the following key equations from an augmented neoclassical model. Consider first the production function for private value added:

$$(1) \qquad Y^{\text{Priv}} = F(N^{\text{Priv}}, K^{\text{Priv}}),$$

1. The output of government enterprises, such as post offices of the US Postal Service, are included in the private business sector.

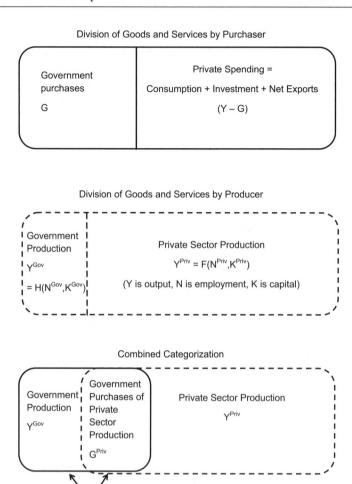

Division of Goods and Services by Purchaser

| Government purchases G | Private Spending = Consumption + Investment + Net Exports (Y − G) |

Division of Goods and Services by Producer

Government Production Y^{Gov} = H(N^{Gov},K^{Gov})

Private Sector Production Y^{Priv} = F(N^{Priv},K^{Priv}) (Y is output, N is employment, K is capital)

Combined Categorization

Government Production Y^{Gov}

Government Purchases of Private Sector Production G^{Priv}

Private Sector Production Y^{Priv}

$G = Y^{Gov} + G^{Priv}$

Fig. 1.1   Government spending versus government output distinction
Notes: The region sizes are not to scale.

where Y^{Priv} is private value added, N^{Priv} is private employment, and K^{Priv} is the private capital stock. The number of workers available for private employment is determined by the labor resource constraint:

(2) $N^{Priv} = \bar{T} - N^{Gov} - L,$

where $\bar{T}$ is the time endowment, N^{Gov} is government employment, and L is leisure. Thus, one way that the government draws resources from the private sector is through the labor resource constraint. Another way that the government draws resources from the private sector is through its purchases of private goods. In this case, the affected resource constraint is the one for private output, given by:

(3) $$Y^{\text{Priv}} = C + I + NX + G^{\text{Priv}},$$

where G^{Priv} is government purchases from the private sector. Total G from the NIPA is:

(4) $$G = G^{\text{Priv}} + Y^{\text{Gov}},$$

where Y^{Gov} is government value added, created by combining government employment with government capital as follows:

(5) $$Y^{\text{Gov}} = H(N^{\text{Gov}}, K^{\text{Gov}}).$$

Under reasonable assumptions about labor markets and production functions, the relative price of private and government output is one, so total GDP is given by:

(6) $$Y = Y^{\text{Priv}} + Y^{\text{Gov}}.$$

In the context of this type of model, an increase in government spending raises total employment. However, the extent to which government spending raises private employment depends on whether the increase in G is due more to an increase in purchases of private sector output or more to an increase in government output and employment. We would expect private sector employment to rise in the first case but to fall in the second case. Thus, a rise in overall employment does not necessarily imply a rise in private sector employment, so it is important to distinguish private versus government employment in the data.

1.3   The Effects on Private Spending

In most studies using aggregate data and VARs, government spending multipliers are usually calculated by comparing the peak of the output response to the peak of the government spending response or by comparing the integral under the impulse response functions up to a certain horizon. Usually, no standard errors are provided, but given the wide standard error bands on the output and government spending components, the standard error bands on the multipliers are assumed to be large. Studies of the subcomponents of private spending, such as nondurable consumption or nonresidential fixed investment, often give mixed results with wide error bands.

As I will now show, a simple permutation of the variables in a standard VAR can lead to more precise estimates for the relevant policy question: on average does an increase in government spending raise private spending? To answer this question, I will use a standard set of VAR variables employed

by many in the literature with one modification: I will use private spending
($Y - G$) rather than total GDP. Since previous VAR studies have shown that
the peak of government spending and the peak of total GDP are roughly
coincident in the impulse response functions, I do not distort the results by
considering only the contemporaneous multiplier.

1.3.1   Econometric Framework

To study the effects of government spending shocks on private spending,
I will estimate the following VAR system:

$$(7) \qquad\qquad X_t = A(L)X_{t-1} + U_t,$$

where X_t is a vector of variables that includes the log of real per capita
government spending on goods and services (G), the log of real per capita
private spending ($Y - G$), the Barro-Redlick average marginal tax rate, and
the interest rate on three-month Treasury bills, as well as key variables for
identification that I will discuss shortly. The interest rate and tax variables
are used as controls for monetary and tax policy, and $A(L)$ is a polynomial
in the lag operator. As is standard, I include four lags of all variables, as well
as a quadratic time trend.

I consider several of the main identification schemes used in the literature.
These are as follows:

1. *Ramey News EVAR:* Concerned that most changes in government
spending are anticipated, Ramey and Shapiro (1998) used a dummy variable
for military events that led to significant rises in defense spending as the
exogenous shock. In more recent work in Ramey (2011c), I extended this
idea and used sources such as *Business Week* to construct a series of changes
in the expected present discounted value of government spending caused by
military events. I divided this series by the previous quarter's GDP to create a
"news" series. This series augments the list of variables in the X matrix in the
previous VAR and the shock is identified as the shock to this series, using a
standard Choleski decomposition with the news series ordered first. Perotti
(2011) has termed VARs that incorporate news "Expectational VARs" or
"EVARs."

2. *Blanchard-Perotti SVAR:* Blanchard and Perotti (2002) identify the
shock to government spending with a standard Choleski decomposition
with total government spending ordered first. No news series are included
in the VAR.

3. *Perotti SVAR:* Perotti (2011) claims that the structural VAR (SVAR)
equivalent to my news EVAR is one that replaces the news series with defense
spending or federal spending. Shocks are then identified as shocks to this
variable ordered first. (Total government spending is also included in the
VAR.) As my reply argues (Ramey 2011a), there is little difference between
the impulse response functions generated by this scheme and the original

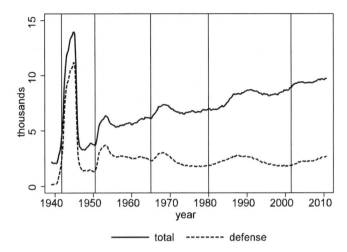

thousands

——— total   -------- defense

Fig. 1.2   Real government spending per capita, 1939:Q1–2010:Q4
Notes: Data from the NIPA and the Census. Amounts are stated in 2010 dollars.

BP scheme. For the sake of argument, however, I will also show the results from this scheme, where I augment the system with defense spending. Since the results are so similar to the Blanchard-Perotti SVAR, these results are shown in the data appendix.

4. *Fisher-Peters EVAR:* Fisher and Peters (2010) develop an alternative measure of anticipated increases in government spending based on stock returns. They use the cumulative excess returns on stocks of defense contractors relative to the rest of the stock market as an indicator of anticipated increases in defense spending. This series is available for 1958 to 2008. Thus, this specification is the same as the first one, but with the Fisher-Peters news variable replacing the Ramey news variable.

While some, such as Blanchard and Perotti (2002), have argued that one should omit World War II and the Korean War from the sample, Hall (2009), Ramey (2011c), and Barro and Redlick (2011) argue that there is not enough variation in government spending after 1954 to identify the effects of government spending. Consider figure 1.2, which updates the figure shown in numerous other papers. It is clear that the movements in government spending during World War II and the Korean War are orders of magnitude greater than any other movements. The notion that there is much less information in the post-1954 period is also supported by statistical analysis. As I demonstrate in Ramey (2011c), the first-stage F-statistic for my news series is well above the Staiger and Stock (1997) safety threshold of 10 for samples that include either World War II or Korea. However, the F-statistic is very low for samples that exclude both periods. Fisher and

Peters' (2010) excess returns measure has a first-stage F-statistic of 5.5 for defense spending, but only 2.3 for total government spending. Both are below the Staiger-Stock safety threshold. An additional concern about the Fisher-Peters measure of news is raised in Ramey (2011c). Because exports of military goods constitute part of the profits of defense companies, the Fisher-Peters' variable might be capturing news about exports as well as news about future US government spending.

Given the debate on this issue, I estimate the first three specifications on three samples each: 1939:1 to 2008:4, 1947:1 to 2008:4, and 1954:1 to 2008:4. The Fisher-Peters EVAR is estimated from 1958:1 to 2008:4. In all cases, the shock is normalized so that the peak of government spending is 1 percent of GDP. The response of private spending is converted to percentage points of total GDP. The standard error bands are 95 percent bands based on bootstrap standard errors.

1.3.2   VAR Results

Figure 1.3 shows results from the EVAR using my news variable. In the first two samples, government spending rises significantly and peaks at around six quarters. The delayed response of actual government spending to the news variable is consistent with my hypothesis that government spending changes are anticipated at least several quarters before they happen. In the 1939 to 2008 sample, private spending rises slightly on impact, but then falls significantly below zero, troughing at around 0.5 percent of GDP. In the 1947 to 2008 sample, private spending rises significantly on impact, to about 0.5 percent of GDP, but then falls below zero within a few quarters. These results are consistent with the effects of anticipations discussed in the theoretical section of Ramey (2009b). As that paper showed, in a simple neoclassical model, news about future increases in government spending lead output to rise immediately, even though government spending does not rise for several quarters. Thus, the theory predicts that private output should jump on impact and then fall. In addition, as discussed as well in Ramey (2011c), the Korean War is influential in the post–World War II sample. As observed in the consumer durable expenditure data and discussed in the press at that time, the start of the Korean War led to panic buying of durable goods in the United States because many feared rationing (such as during World War II) was imminent. This is another likely source of the positive impact effect. For the post–Korean War period, the low first-stage F-statistic of my news variables means that any results for that sample are questionable. Nevertheless, they are shown for completeness. The standard error bands are much larger for this sample. Private spending falls, but the estimates, though large, are not statistically different from zero.

Figure 1.4 shows the responses based on the Blanchard-Perotti SVAR. In contrast to the EVAR, this specification implies that government spending jumps up immediately in all three samples. Private spending declines

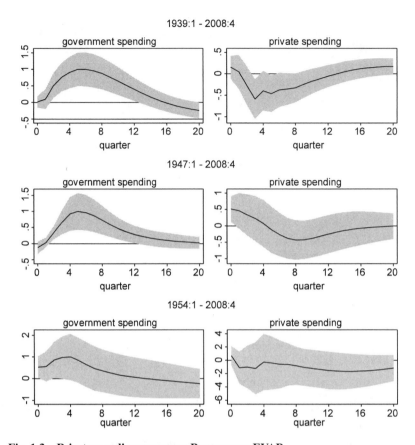

Fig. 1.3   Private spending responses: Ramey news EVAR

Notes: The government spending shock is identified as the shock to the news variable, ordered first. The shock is normalized so that government spending peaks at 1 percent of GDP. Private GDP is denoted as a percent of total GDP. The standard error bands are 95 percent bands based on bootstrap standard errors.

significantly in response to a rise in government spending in the first two samples. The declines are sizeable, suggesting multipliers well below one. In the post–Korean War sample, private spending falls slightly below zero, but is not statistically significant. Appendix figure 1A.1 shows that the results of the augmented SVAR advocated by Perotti (2011) are essentially the same.

Figure 1.5 shows the responses based on the Fisher-Peters type of SVAR, where government spending shocks are identified as shocks to the excess stock returns for defense contractors. In contrast to the three previous specifications in which government spending peaks around quarter six and returns to normal between twelve and fourteen quarters, this shock leads to a more sustained increase in government spending. Government spending barely falls from its peak, even after twenty quarters. Private

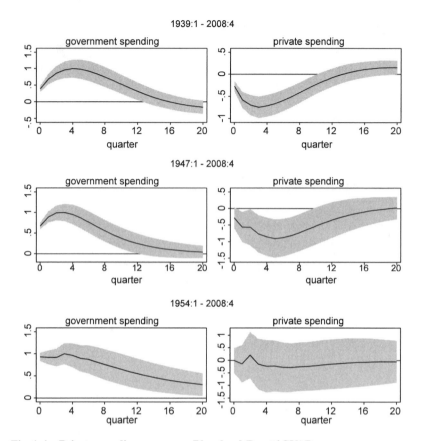

Fig. 1.4   Private spending responses: Blanchard-Perotti SVAR

Notes: The government spending shock is identified as the shock to total government spending, ordered first. The shock is normalized so that government spending peaks at 1 percent of GDP. Private GDP is denoted as a percent of total GDP. The standard error bands are 95 percent bands based on bootstrap standard errors.

spending oscillates around zero, but it only becomes statistically different from zero when it becomes negative at longer horizons.

Thus, the SVAR specifications give essentially the same answer to the question posed as do the EVAR specifications: a rise in government spending does not appear to stimulate private spending. In fact, in many samples and specifications, it reduces private spending.

An interesting point to note is that the VAR results imply a time-varying multiplier that shrinks as government spending hits its peak. This result is consistent with Gordon and Krenn's (2010) finding of a higher multiplier in samples ending in mid-1941, when the increase in government spending was more modest than in samples ending later.

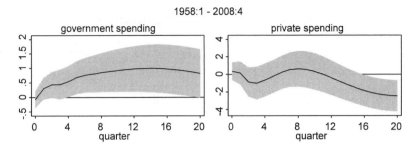

Fig. 1.5   Private spending responses: Fisher-Peters news EVAR

Notes: The government spending shock is identified as the shock to excess stock returns of top defense contractors, ordered first. The shock is normalized so that total government spending peaks at 1 percent of GDP. Private GDP is denoted as a percent of total GDP. The standard error bands are 95 percent bands based on bootstrap standard errors.

1.3.3   The Effects of Taxes and Implications for Multipliers

These results imply that for the types of changes in government spending identified by the various schemes, the total GDP multiplier lies below unity. In every case, there is evidence that government spending crowds out private spending. On average, though, these increases in government spending were financed partly by a rise in distortionary taxes. Figure 1.6 shows the impulse responses of the Barro and Redlick (2011) average marginal tax rate for the various samples for both the Ramey News EVAR and Blanchard-Perotti SVAR specifications. In five of the six cases, the tax rate rises significantly. It rises much more in the Ramey News EVAR.

Romer and Romer (2010) construct a measure of exogenous tax shocks using a narrative approach that summarizes tax legislation. They show that the reduced-form effect of a tax shock equal to 1 percent GDP leads to a multiyear decline in GDP equal to 2.5 to 3 percent of GDP by the end of the third year. These estimates suggest that the multiplier could potentially be greater for a deficit-financed increase in government spending than for one in which taxes rise.

To gauge how much the rise in taxes dampens the spending multiplier, I conduct two different kinds of experiments. The first one uses the estimated VARs to conduct counterfactual analysis and the second uses instrumental variables estimation of a more structural model. In the first method, using the estimated VARs, I compare the actual estimated impulse response to one in which I assume counterfactually that the tax rate did not change. That is, I set all of the coefficients in the tax rate equation to zero. I then compute the alternative impulse response based on a dynamic simulation using the actual estimated coefficients from the other equations and the zero coefficients from the tax rate equation.

Figure 1.7 shows the results for government spending and private output.

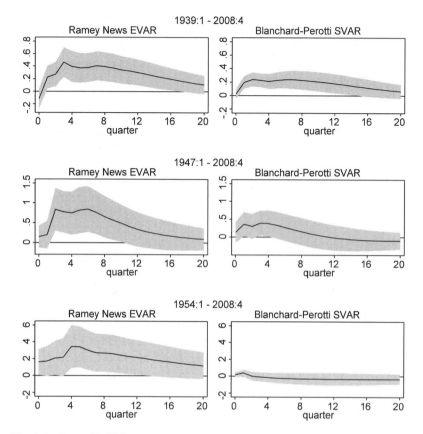

Fig. 1.6   Barro-Redlick tax rate responses

Notes: The shock is normalized so that government spending peaks at 1 percent of GDP. The response of taxes is shown in percentage points. The standard error bands are 95 percent bands based on bootstrap standard errors.

In both the Ramey News EVAR and the Blanchard-Perotti SVAR, the response of neither government spending nor private output changes much. The fact that the paths change little implies that the coefficients on tax rates in the equations for the other variables are not economically different from zero.

Because VARs are essentially reduced-form relationships, it is difficult to make structural interpretations. Thus, my second method uses instrumental variables to estimate the separate effects of government spending and taxes on private output. I specify the following baseline quarterly model, which is similar in structure to the one used by Barro and Redlick (2011) on their long sample of annual data:

(8) $$\frac{\Delta S_t^{\text{Priv}}}{Y_{t-1}} = \beta_0 + \beta_1 \frac{\Delta G_t}{Y_{t-1}} + \beta_2 \Delta_4 \text{tax}_t + \beta_3 \text{News}_t + \varepsilon_t,$$

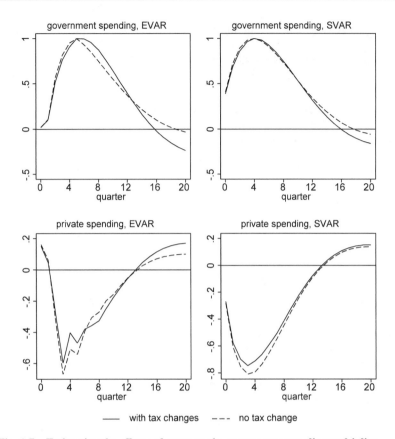

Fig. 1.7   Estimating the effects of taxes on the government spending multiplier, 1939:Q1–2008:Q4

Notes: In the EVAR the government spending shock is identified as the shock to the news variable, ordered first. In the SVAR, the government spending shock is identified as the shock to total government spending, ordered first. The line labeled "with tax changes" is the estimated effect of a government spending shock, allowing taxes to change as estimated. The line labeled "no tax change" is the computed counterfactual response in which taxes are not allowed to change.

where S^{Priv} is real private spending $(Y - G)$, Y is real GDP, G is real government spending (deflated by the GDP deflator), *tax* is a measure of the tax rate, *News* is from Ramey (2011c) and is equal to the change in the expected present discounted value of government purchases caused by military events, and ε is an error term. The four-quarter difference of tax rates is used because the Barro-Redlick variable only changes once per year. It is potentially important to include the current value of the news variable as a control. According to the argument made in my earlier work, private agents respond to news about future government spending before the spending even occurs. My earlier work emphasized the negative wealth effect, but other possible factors include building up capital in anticipation of future government spending because of investment adjustment costs and buying consumer goods because of fears of future rationing.

Because both government spending and taxes are potentially affected by the state of the economy, which also impacts private spending, we would expect these fiscal variables and tax rates to be correlated with the error term ε. Thus, estimation calls for instrumental variables. A natural instrument for the tax variable is the Romer and Romer (2010) narrative series on exogenous tax changes. This variable calculates the annualized change in tax liabilities due to legislation based on either deficit concerns or long-run growth promotion. Thus, the identification assumption I am making is that the tax legislation changes affect the economy only through changes in tax rates. Because the Romer-Romer tax instruments are available only from 1945 to 2007, the estimation must exclude the World War II sample. For government spending, I use *lags* of my news variable as an instrument. Because the current value of news is an included variable, my identification assumption is that while current news can independently affect private spending, lagged values of news affect the economy only through current changes in government spending. This assumption might be questionable if there are additional lags in the effects. Thus, I will assess the robustness of the results to adding lags of spending growth, government spending, and taxes to the specification. Using the period 1948 to 2007, I explored various lags of the two instruments up to twelve lags. I use four lags of each instrument since this number of lags maximized the Cragg and Donald (1993) statistic.

Table 1.1 shows the estimates from the model presented in equation (8). The top panel shows the results when the tax rate is measured with the Barro-Redlick average marginal tax rate and the bottom panel shows the results when the tax rate is measured as the ratio of current tax receipts to GDP. The first column shows the results when tax rate changes are excluded from the equation. The estimated effect of a change in government spending on private output is –0.7, with a standard error of 0.26. This estimate implies a multiplier on total GDP of only 0.3. In contrast, news about future government spending increases current private spending. An increase in the expected present discounted value of future government spending of one dollar raises current private spending by about five cents. The effect of this variable is estimated precisely. The high Cragg and Donald (1993) statistics imply that we can reject the null hypothesis of weak instruments at any relative bias level.

The second column shows the results of the baseline model when tax rates are included. For both tax rate specifications, the coefficient on government spending implies that a one dollar increase in government spending lowers private spending by 55 cents. The news variable continues to be positive and significant, while the tax variable is negative, but is not statistically different

Table 1.1   Instrumental variables regressions for private spending

Specification	No tax	Tax-1	Tax-2	Tax-3
		Dependent variable: $\Delta S_t^{Private}/Y_t$		
		Barro-Redlick average marginal tax rate		
$\Delta G_t/Y_{t-1}$	−0.705***	−0.539*	−0.506*	−1.057*
	(0.259)	(0.284)	(0.268)	(0.548)
$\Delta G_{t-1}/Y_{t-2}$				0.632
				(0.535)
News$_t$	0.056***	0.059***	0.038**	0.042***
	(0.016)	(0.017)	(0.016)	(0.017)
$\Delta_4\tau_t$		−0.097	−0.057	0.215
		(0.116)	(0.109)	(0.435)
$\Delta_4\tau_{t-1}$				−0.293
				(0.388)
$\Delta S_{t-1}^{Private}/Y_{t-2}$			0.319***	0.346***
			(0.060)	(0.069)
Cragg-Donald Wald F-statistic	51.80	8.13	8.16	0.98
		Average tax rate		
$\Delta G_t/Y_{t-1}$		−0.548**	−0.483*	−0.770
		(0.278)	(0.263)	(0.540)
$\Delta G_{t-1}/Y_{t-2}$				0.294
				(0.521)
News$_t$		0.067***	0.043**	0.045**
		(0.020)	(0.018)	(0.018)
$\Delta_4\tau_t$		−0.194	−0.153	−0.271
		(0.196)	(0.183)	(0.417)
$\Delta_4\tau_{t-1}$				0.129
				(0.393)
$\Delta S_{t-1}^{Private}/Y_{t-2}$			0.353***	0.380***
			(0.073)	(0.082)
Cragg-Donald Wald F-statistic		7.25	8.08	2.14

Notes: All regressions contain 240 quarterly observations, estimated from 1948:Q1 to 2007:Q4. Variable $S^{Private}$ denotes real private spending, Y denotes real GDP, G denotes real government spending (deflated by the GDP deflator), and τ denotes the tax rate. The average tax rate is calculated as the ratio of current tax receipts divided by GDP. Variable Δ_4 denotes the four-quarter difference. Current values of government spending are instrumented with four lagged values of Ramey news and current values of tax rate changes are instrumented with the current value and four lags of the Romer-Romer exogenous tax shock. When lags are included, an extra lag of the instruments is used. Standard errors are reported in parentheses.
***Significant at the 1 percent level.
**Significant at the 5 percent level.
*Significant at the 10 percent level.

from zero. The Cragg and Donald (1993) statistics, ranging from seven to eight, imply that we can reject the null hypothesis of weak instruments for a 15 percent maximal relative bias, according to the Stock and Yogo (2005) critical values for instrument relevance. Thus, controlling for taxes reduces the magnitude of the negative effect of government spending on private spending by 0.15, from –0.7 to –0.55. Given the size of the standard errors, however, the change is probably not statistically significant.

I also investigated the effect of omitting the current value of the news variable as a regressor and instead including it as an instrument for government spending (results not shown in the table). When the Barro-Redlick tax rate is used, the coefficient on government spending is estimated to be –0.64, with a standard error of 0.29. Thus, the negative effect of government spending on private spending becomes even more negative if the news variable is omitted. The coefficient on the tax variable becomes slightly positive but not different from zero.

The third column of table 1.1 explores the effect of controlling for the lagged growth of private spending. This variable is statistically significant, but it lowers the magnitude of the government spending coefficient only slightly, to about 0.5. Finally, the last column also adds lags of government spending and taxes. This results in imprecise estimates for a number of the coefficients and leads to unacceptably low Cragg-Donald statistics. Not shown in the table are the results of other explorations, which either replace the four-quarter difference of tax rates with the one-quarter difference of tax rates or replace the one-quarter difference of government spending with the four-quarter difference, or substitute the change in real tax receipts relative to lagged GDP for the Barro-Redlick tax rate. The results do not change in any meaningful way in these alternative specifications, except to become more imprecise and/or have inferior first-stage statistics.

My survey of the estimates in the literature in Ramey (2011b) concluded that the multiplier for a deficit-financed short-run increase in government spending was probably between 0.8 and 1.5, but that reasonable people could argue for multipliers as low as 0.5 or as high as 2. The main reason that I placed the lower end of the probable range at 0.8 was my belief, based on the Romer and Romer (2010) reduced-form results, that the tax effects on GDP were large. The results of this section suggest otherwise. The counterfactuals constructed from the VAR estimates imply that accounting for current tax rates has no impact on the estimated government spending multiplier. The instrumental variables estimates imply that controlling for changes in tax rates raises the multiplier slightly, by about 0.15 to 0.2. The instrumental variables estimates imply a government spending multiplier on total GDP of about 0.5. This is very close to the estimate obtained using annual data by Barro and Redlick (2011).

1.4   The Effects of Government Spending on Unemployment and Employment

As we saw in the last section, no matter which identification scheme or which sample period was used, an increase in government spending did not lead to an increase in private sector spending. In most cases, it led to a significant decrease. Even in the face of this result, however, policymakers might still want to use stimulus packages to reduce unemployment. There is substantial microeconomic evidence that long spells of unemployment lead to persistent losses of human capital. Thus, even if government spending cannot stimulate private spending, it might still have positive effects by raising employment.

This section studies several aspects of the labor market. It begins with a case study of the labor market during World War II because the dramatic changes of this era highlight some useful points. In the second subsection, I use the VARs from earlier to study the effects of government spending shocks on unemployment. In the third subsection, I study their effects on private versus government employment.

1.4.1   A Case Study of the Labor Market during World War II

World War II is especially interesting from a labor market point of view because the economy went from an unemployment rate of 12 percent (18 percent if one includes emergency workers as unemployed) at the start of 1939 to an unemployment rate of less than 1 percent by 1944. Thus, it is useful to conduct a case study before moving on to the formal statistical analysis. To review the history briefly, Germany invaded Poland on September 1, 1939, and Britain and France declared war on September 3, 1939. Initially, the US stock market increased, as exports to the belligerents increased business profits. The stock market started to decline in spring 1940, as Germany took Norway in April 1940, invaded the low countries in May 1940, and took Paris in June 1940. As discussed in Ramey (2009a), the United States began gearing up for war well before Pearl Harbor, which occurred on December 7, 1941. Figure 1.8 shows Gordon and Krenn's (2010) monthly interpolated data on real government spending (in 1937 dollars) from 1938 to 1945. Between January 1938 and September 1940 when the draft was enacted, real government spending rose by 18 percent (measured in log differences), or by 2.6 percent of initial January 1938 GDP. Between September 1940 and December 1941, real government spending increased 89 percent (in log differences), or by 20 percent of initial September 1940 GDP. It increased another 113 percent (in log differences), or 56 percent of December 1941 GDP, between December 1941 and its peak in May 1945.

Consider the labor market at the start of World War II. Based on new labor market data that I have compiled for this period, we can track the flows of individuals between various labor market states. I use September 1940 as the starting point, since that is when the draft was instituted and because government spending started rising in the fourth quarter of 1940. Figure 1.9 shows the behavior of various employment components around this time and table 1.2 presents the net changes. The first feature to note from the figure is that, despite the fact that government spending rose by only 2.6 percent of initial GDP, total employment rose by 8 percent from 1938 to

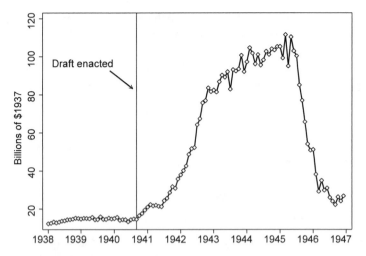

Fig. 1.8   Real government spending during World War II
Notes: Data from gordon.krenn-2010-nber.

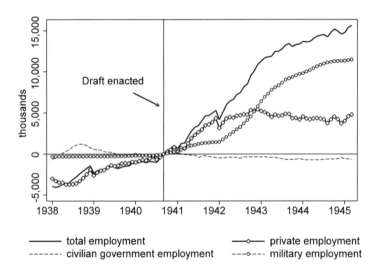

Fig. 1.9   Decomposition of employment changes during World War II
Notes: Each employment component has been normalized to zero in September 1940. Numbers are in thousands. Employment data based on data compiled by V. Ramey. See data appendix for details.

September 1940, and that most of the increase in total employment was due to an increase in private employment. As the table shows, from September 1940 to the peak in March 1945, total employment rose by 15.6 million, a 27 percent increase in log differences. Most of the rise was due to the rise in military employment, however. Government civilian employment (including

Table 1.2   **Labor market changes during World War II: September 1940 to March 1945**

Component	Change (in millions)
Total employment	15.6
Military employment	11.5
Population ages 14+	5.4
Labor force	11.1
Unemployment	−4.5
Emergency workers	−2.5

Source: Data compiled by the author. See data appendix for details.

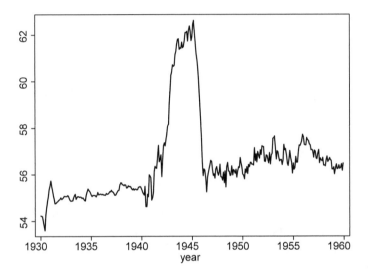

Fig. 1.10   Labor force participation rate
Notes: Labor force participation rate of population ages fourteen and above. Based on data compiled by V. Ramey. See data appendix for details.

New Deal emergency workers) declined slightly during this period. As the figure shows, private employment rose robustly from 1938 through most of 1941, but then leveled off.

Over this same time period, the population ages fourteen and above rose by 5.4 million, but the labor force rose by 11.1 million. Figure 1.10 shows the dramatic increase in the labor force participation rate. Decennial data from before 1930 suggests a typical labor force participation rate of around 56 percent. It was a little lower during the 1930s because of the Great Depression. As the graph shows, during World War II, the participation rate was 6 percentage points higher than it was before or in the decade after. Thus, 70 percent of the increase in employment during World War II is accounted for by the rise in the labor force, with a large part of that increase due to an increase in the participation rate. It is likely that an important part of that rise was due to the effects of the draft and patriotism. The number in the military rose by 11.5 million during World War II. The rise was only 2.2 million during the Korean War.

Over this same period from 1940 to 1945, the number unemployed fell by 4.5 million. Thus, the remaining 30 percent of the increase in employment was due to flows from unemployment to employment.

These numbers omit one other important flow of workers. My unemployment numbers do not include emergency workers, who were workers employed by the various New Deal government programs. Like Darby (1976) and Weir (1992), I included those workers in the "employed" category rather than unemployed. The number of individuals employed as emergency workers decreased from 2.5 million in September 1940 to zero by mid-1943. Thus, these workers represented an additional 2.5 million workers available for other sectors.

While total employment rose by 27 percent, real GDP rose by 58 percent (in log points), meaning that labor productivity rose by 31 percent. Thus, during the five-year period from 1940 to 1945, labor productivity rose at an average annualized rate of 7 percent. This rate of growth is substantially greater than the growth of productivity in the decade before or the decade after. For example, from 1947 to 1960, labor productivity growth was about 3.3 percent. In their study of the behavior of the economy during World War II, McGrattan and Ohanian (2010) find that the neoclassical model can explain the data only if one also assumes large positive productivity shocks.

Since the GDP multiplier is intimately linked to the effect of government spending on employment and productivity, the combination of the unprecedented rise in the labor force participation rate and the exceptionally high rate of productivity growth most likely raised the GDP multiplier during World War II relative to more normal times. Some researchers, such as Hall (2009), Gordon and Krenn (2010), and Perotti (2011), have argued that the multiplier estimated from samples that include World War II may be lower because of price controls and rationing. While there is no denying that price controls and rationing distorted allocations, their argument only makes sense if the price controls and rationing depressed employment and productivity *more* than the other factors, such as conscription and patriotism, raised it. The extraordinary increases in labor force participation rates, employment, and productivity that I have just documented suggest that this argument is implausible.

1.4.2   The Effects of Government Spending on Unemployment

Given the previous case study, it is interesting to use more formal analysis to determine the effect of government spending on unemployment. To do this, I estimate the following modification of the VARs described in equation (7) in the earlier section. First, I revert to using total GDP rather than just

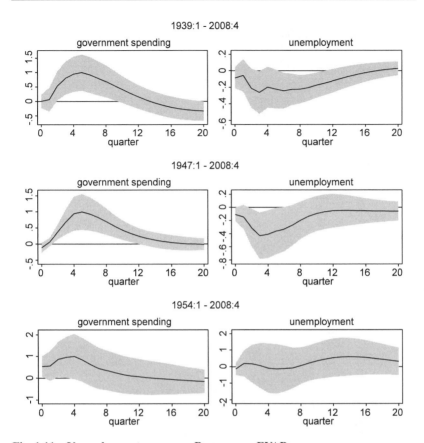

Fig. 1.11   Unemployment responses: Ramey news EVAR

Notes: The government spending shock is identified as the shock to the news variable, ordered first. The shock is normalized so that government spending peaks at 1 percent of GDP. Unemployment is denoted as a percent of the civilian labor force. The standard error bands are 95 percent bands based on bootstrap standard errors.

private GDP, as is common in the literature. Second, I add the log of per capita unemployment to the VARs. For the impulse response functions, I rescale unemployment so that it has the same scale as the civilian unemployment rate, based on a long-run average unemployment rate of 5.5 percent.

Figures 1.11 through 1.13 show the impulse response functions. For the various identification schemes and samples, the point estimates suggest that an increase in government spending leads to a fall in unemployment. The fall is always statistically significant in the period from 1939 to 2008 and is sometimes significant in the other periods for a number of the specifications. Most estimates imply that an increase in government spending that peaks at 1 percentage point of GDP lowers the unemployment rate by between 0.2 and 0.5 percentage points. The exception is the EVAR that uses the Fisher-

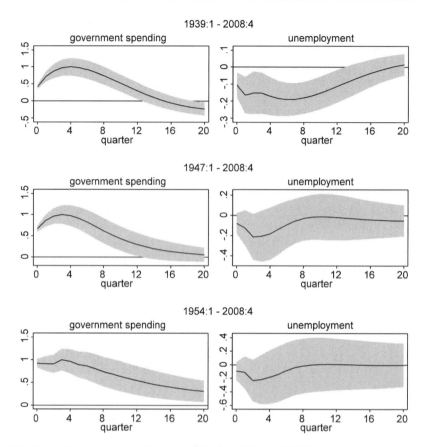

Fig. 1.12   Unemployment responses: Blanchard-Perotti SVAR

Notes: The government spending shock is identified as the shock to total government spending, ordered first. The shock is normalized so that government spending peaks at 1 percent of GDP. Unemployment is denoted as a percent of the civilian labor force. The standard error bands are 95 percent bands based on bootstrap standard errors.

Peters stock market variable. In this case, the unemployment rate falls by a full percentage point.

As noted previously, the Fisher-Peters experiment appears to involve a much more sustained increase in government spending. However, even comparing the ratio of the integral of unemployment to the integral of government spending over the five-year period, the Fisher-Peters specification implies a much larger effect on unemployment. In contrast, the Blanchard-Perotti SVAR implies the smallest effect.

1.4.3   The Effects of Government Spending on Employment

The bulk of evidence just presented suggests that a rise in government spending tends to lower the unemployment rate. Given the earlier discussion

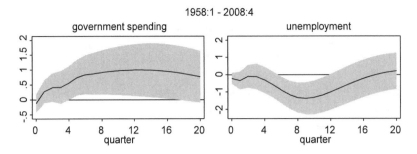

Fig. 1.13   Unemployment responses: Fisher-Peters news EVAR

Notes: The government spending shock is identified as the shock to excess stock returns of top defense contractors, ordered first. The shock is normalized so that total government spending peaks at 1 percent of GDP. Unemployment is denoted as a percent of the civilian labor force. The standard error bands are 95 percent bands based on bootstrap standard errors.

about how much of government spending is actually compensation of government employees, it is useful to decompose the employment effects into rises in government employment versus rises in private employment.

To study this issue, I estimate the following modification of the VARs presented in the last section. In each of the VARs, I omit the unemployment variable and instead include both the log of per capita government employment and the log of per capita private employment. Government employment includes civilian government workers and armed forces employment, as well as emergency worker employment during the late 1930s and early 1940s. The four identification schemes are the same ones discussed before. In all cases, the employment numbers are converted so that they are a percent of total employment.

Figure 1.14 shows the results from the specification with my defense news variable. In the full sample from 1939:1 to 2008:4, a rise in government spending equal to 1 percent of GDP leads to a rise in government employment of close to 0.5 percent of total employment. Private employment rises by about 0.2 percent of total employment, but is never significantly different from zero at the 5 percent level. The story for the 1947:1 to 2008:4 sample is the same. For the post–Korean War sample, the estimates are even less precise (note the change in scale). It appears that private employment initially dips, then rises, but there is much uncertainty about that path.

Figure 1.15 shows the responses based on the Blanchard-Perotti SVAR. Private employment falls in the first two sample periods for this specification. In the third sample period it rises, but the standard errors bands are very wide.[2]

Figure 1.16 shows the responses based on the Fisher-Peters type of SVAR. In contrast to the previous cases, this identification and sample suggests

---

2. The Perotti SVAR gives very similar results. The graphs are shown in the data appendix.

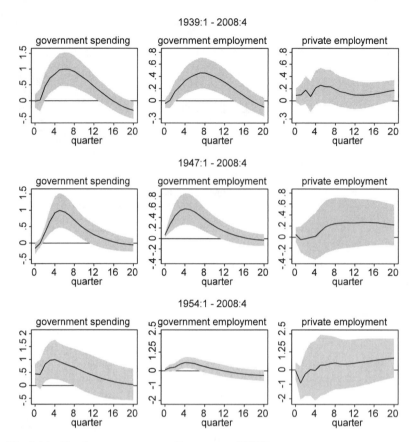

Fig. 1.14   Employment responses: Ramey news EVAR

Notes: The government spending shock is identified as the shock to the news variable, ordered first. The shock is normalized so that government spending peaks at 1 percent of GDP. Each employment response is rescaled to represent a percentage of total employment. The standard error bands are 95 percent bands based on bootstrap standard errors.

that increases in government spending raise both government employment and private employment. Although government spending rises steeply throughout the first six quarters after the shock, private employment does not begin to rise until after the fourth quarter. It peaks during the third year at about 1.5 percent of total employment. Since this identification scheme seems to pick up more persistent movements in government spending, it might be the case that only sustained increases in government spending raise private sector employment. More research on this issue is required.

To summarize, the EVAR using my defense news variable and the Blanchard-Perotti SVARs suggest that for the most part, increases in government spending raise government employment but not private

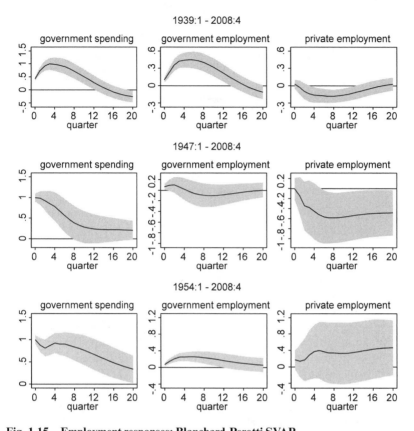

Fig. 1.15   Employment responses: Blanchard-Perotti SVAR

Notes: The government spending shock is identified as the shock to total government spending, ordered first. The shock is normalized so that government spending peaks at 1 percent of GDP. Each employment response is rescaled to represent a percentage of total employment. The standard error bands are 95 percent bands based on bootstrap standard errors.

employment. In contrast, the Fisher-Peters identification scheme suggests that government spending shocks that lead to sustained rises in government spending also raise private employment significantly, even more so than government employment. One should be mindful of the caveat discussed earlier: since exports of military goods have been an important part of profits of defense companies during some time periods, the Fisher-Peters' variable might be capturing news about exports as well as news about future US government spending. Because an increase in export demand would be expected to increase private sector employment, some of the increase might be due to this factor.

A question of interest is whether the employment effects depend on if it is government purchases of private goods or government value added that

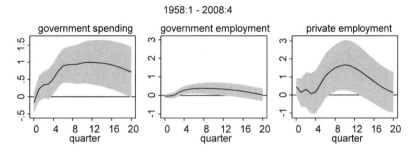

Fig. 1.16   Employment responses: Fisher-Peters news EVAR

Notes: The government spending shock is identified as the shock to excess stock returns of top defense contractors, ordered first. The shock is normalized so that total government spending peaks at 1 percent of GDP. Each employment response is rescaled to represent a percentage of total employment. The standard error bands are 95 percent bands based on bootstrap standard errors.

increases. As shown earlier in the chapter, both components of government spending typically increase at the same time. Because separate shocks to each cannot be identified with my one news instrument, I explore the effects of separate shocks using only the Blanchard-Perotti SVAR. In particular, I estimate a system with the (log per capita) values of real government purchases of private goods, real government value added, real GDP, government employment, private employment, the three-month Treasury bill rate, and the Barro-Redlick average marginal tax rate. The shocks are normalized so that in each case the shock is equal to 1 percent of GDP. The employment responses shown are rescaled to indicate the percentage of total employment.

Figure 1.17 shows the responses to the two types of shocks for the period 1939 to 2008 and figure 1.18 shows the responses for the period 1947 to 2008. Consider first the period from 1939 to 2008. It is clear that shocks to government purchases of private goods also raise government value added and vice versa. Thus, the data do not allow us to disentangle the separate effects. In response to both shocks, government employment rises, whereas private employment falls. The exception is the shock to government value added, which leads private employment to fall in the short-run, but then rise in the long-run, even after the government spending variable has returned to normal. In the post–World War II period, the results differ in a few ways. First, a shock to government purchases does not appear to raise government value added. Second, a shock to government value added has a positive effect on private employment, but the effect is never close to being statistically significant. Thus, separating the shocks into the two components does not paint a different picture from that presented earlier.

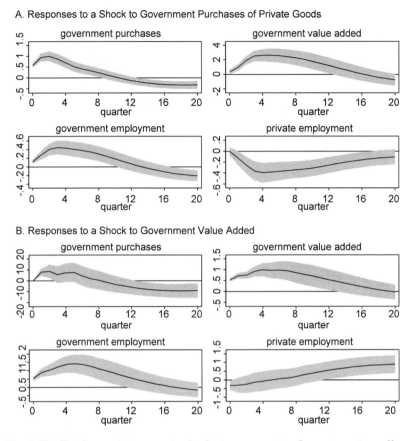

Fig. 1.17   Employment responses to shocks to components of government spending: 1939:1–2008:4

Notes: The SVAR uses the Blanchard-Perotti methodology. The government purchases shock is identified as the shock to real government purchases, ordered first. The government value added shock is identified as the shock to real government value added, ordered second. The shocks are normalized so that the government spending component peaks at 1 percent of GDP. Each employment response is rescaled to represent a percentage of total employment. The standard error bands are 95 percent bands based on bootstrap standard errors.

1.5   Conclusion

This chapter has investigated the effects of government spending on private spending, unemployment, and employment. For the most part, it appears that a rise in government spending does not stimulate private spending; most estimates suggest that it significantly lowers private spending. These results imply that the government spending multiplier is below unity. Adjusting the implied multiplier for increases in tax rates has only a small effect. The results imply a multiplier on total GDP of around 0.5.

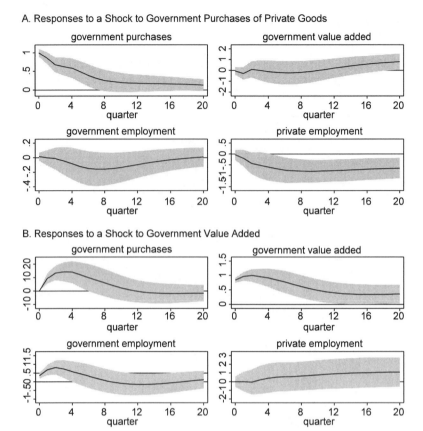

Fig. 1.18   Employment responses to shocks to components of government spending: 1947:1–2008:4

Notes: The SVAR uses the Blanchard-Perotti methodology. The government purchases shock is identified as the shock to real government purchases, ordered first. The government value added shock is identified as the shock to real government value added, ordered second. The shocks are normalized so that the government spending component peaks at 1 percent of GDP. Each employment response is rescaled to represent a percentage of total employment. The standard error bands are 95 percent bands based on bootstrap standard errors.

Increases in government spending do reduce unemployment. For all but one specification, however, it appears that all of the employment increase is from an increase in government employment, not private employment. The only exception is in the specification using the Fisher-Peters measure of defense news for the 1958 to 2008 period. This specification implies that a sustained increase in government spending has a robust positive effect on private employment. On balance, though, the results suggest that direct hiring of workers by the government may be more effective than relying on multiplier effects of government purchases.

Data Appendix
Quarterly GDP Data

The quarterly GDP data from 1939 to 1946 are the same that were constructed in my earlier work Ramey (2011c). The data from 1947 to the present are from www.bea.gov. The only difference from the earlier work is that I deflated total government and defense spending by the GDP deflator, rather than specific deflators, so that the multiplier is easier to interpret. Private spending is defined as nominal GDP less nominal government spending, and the result is deflated by the GDP deflator. All variables are converted to a per capita basis by dividing by total population, including the armed forces overseas.

Tax Data

The Barro-Redlick average marginal tax rate is from Barro and Redlick (2011). Annual values are repeated for each quarter in the year. The average tax rate is calculated by dividing current tax receipts from table 3.1, line 2, by nominal GDP.

Instruments

The defense news variable is discussed in Ramey (2011c). The excess returns on defense stocks are described in Fisher and Peters (2010). The data series were kindly provided by Jonas Fisher. The Romer-Romer exgenous tax series is the variable labeled *EXOGENRRATIO* in the Romer and Romer (2010) online data file.

Employment and Unemployment Data

The various employment and unemployment components are from monthly data and are converted to quarterly. The Conference Board data are from the 1941 to 1942 and 1945 to 1946 editions of *The Economic Almanac* published by the Conference Board (see Conference Board 1941 and Conference Board 1945.)

Civilian Employment Data. The data from 1930 through 1940 are based on employment data from the Conference Board. I seasonally adjusted these data using the default X-12 features of Eviews. I then used the twelve-month moving average of the ratio of the annual average of Weir's (1992) civilian employment series to the annual average of these series to make the monthly series match Weir's (1992) data. From 1941 to 1947, I used the monthly series published in the 1947 and 1949 *Supplement to the Survey of Current Business.* Again, I adjusted them so that the annual averages matched Weir (1992). Data from 1948 to the present are from the Bureau of Labor Statistics (BLS) Current Population Survey.

Civilian Government Employment. The series from 1930 to 1938 are interpolated from the annual series from the BLS' establishment survey. The monthly data from 1939 to the present were from the establishment survey and were downloaded from www.bls.gov.

Armed Forces Employment. The series from 1930 to 1937 was interpolated from the annual series from the 1942 *Supplement to the Survey of Current Business.* From 1938 to 1941, the series was reported monthly in the 1942 *Supplement to the Survey of Current Business.* From 1942 to 1947, the numbers from the 1947 and 1949 *Supplement to the Survey of Current Business* were spliced (using the difference in 1948:1) to the unpublished BLS quarterly employment numbers (provided by Shawn Sprague), that are available from 1948 to the present. (The 1947 and 1949 *Supplement* numbers that were spliced to match the newer BLS numbers matched the older 1942 *Supplement* numbers very closely at the overlap.)

Emergency Workers. Monthly data are from the Conference Board.

Unemployment. Monthly data from 1930 to February 1940 are from the Conference Board, and are available from the NBER Macrohistory Database. These data were rescaled to match Weir's (1992) annual series (with emergency workers added, to be consistent). Data from March 1940 through 1946 were from the Bureau of the Census. Both the Conference Board and Census data were seasonally adjusted with Eviews. (For the case of the Conference Board unemployment data, the results using the default multiplicative seasonal factors looked odd, so I used additive factors instead.)

Population. Total population was the same as used in my earlier work. The population aged 14 and older was interpolated from annual data.

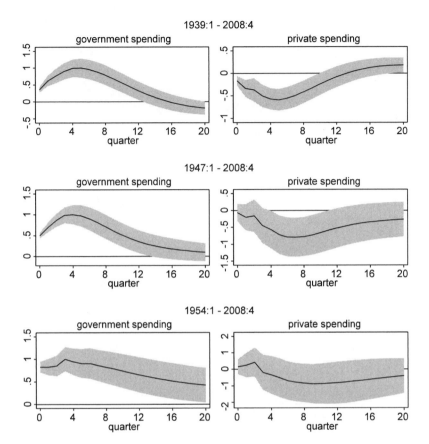

Fig. 1A.1   Private spending responses: Perotti SVAR

Notes: The government spending shock is identified as the shock to defense spending, ordered first. The shock is normalized so that total government spending peaks at 1 percent of GDP. Private GDP is denoted as a percent of total GDP. The standard error bands are 95 percent bands based on bootstrap standard errors.

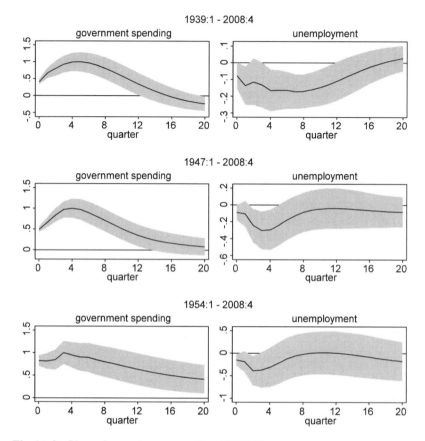

Fig. 1A.2   Unemployment responses: Perotti SVAR

Notes: The government spending shock is identified as the shock to defense spending, ordered first. The shock is normalized so that total government spending peaks at 1 percent of GDP. Unemployment is denoted as a percent of the civilian labor force. The standard error bands are 95 percent bands based on bootstrap standard errors.

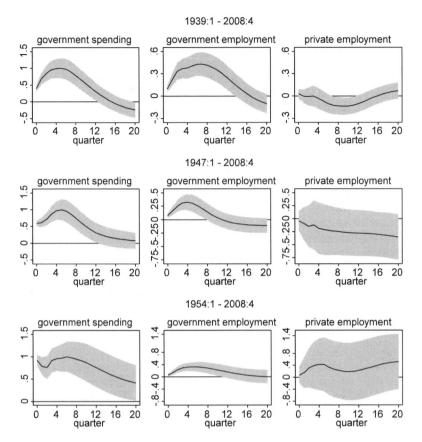

Fig. 1A.3   Employment responses: Perotti SVAR

Notes: The government spending shock is identified as the shock to defense spending, ordered first. The shock is normalized so that total government spending peaks at 1 percent of GDP. Each employment response is rescaled to represent a percentage of total employment. The standard error bands are 95 percent bands based on bootstrap standard errors.

References

Auerbach, Alan, and Yuriy Gorodnichenko. 2012. "Measuring the Output Responses to Fiscal Policy." *American Economic Journal: Economic Policy* 4 (2): 1–27.

Barro, Robert J., and Charles J. Redlick. 2011. "Macroeconomic Effects from Government Purchases and Taxes." *Quarterly Journal of Economics* 126 (1): 51–102.

Blanchard, Olivier, and Roberto Perotti. 2002. "An Empirical Characterization of the Dynamic Effects of Changes in Government Spending and Taxes on Output." *Quarterly Journal of Economics* 117 (4): 1329–68.

Brückner, Markus, and Evi Pappa. 2010. "Fiscal Expansions Affect Unemployment,

But They May Increase It." Working Paper DP7766. London: Centre for Economic Policy Research.

Burnside, Craig, Martin Eichenbaum, and Jonas D. M. Fisher. 2004. "Fiscal Shocks and Their Consequences." *Journal of Economic Theory* 115 (1): 89–117.

Cavallo, Michele P. 2005. "Government Employment and the Dynamic Effects of Fiscal Policy Shocks." Working Papers in Applied Economic Theory 2005-16. Federal Reserve Bank of San Francisco.

Chodorow-Reich, Gabriel, Laura Feiveson, Zachary Liscow, and William Gui Woolston. 2012. "Does State Fiscal Relief during Recessions Increase Employment? Evidence from the American Recovery and Reinvestment Act." *American Economic Journal: Economic Policy* 4 (3): 118–45.

Conference Board. 1941. *The Economic Almanac 1941–42.* New York: National Industrial Conference Board Inc.

———. 1945. *The Economic Almanac 1945–46.* New York: National Industrial Conference Board Inc.

Cragg, J. G., and S. G. Donald. 1993. "Testing Identifiability and Specification in Instrumental Variables Models." *Econometric Theory* 9:222–40.

Darby, Michael R. 1976. "Three-and-a-Half Million US Employees Have Been Mislaid: Or, an Explanation of Unemployment, 1934–1941." *Journal of Political Economy* 84 (1): 1–16.

Davis, Steven J., Prakash Loungani, and Ramamohan Mahidhara. 1997. "Regional Labor Fluctuations: Oil Shocks, Military Spending, and Other Driving Forces." Working Paper 578. Board of Governors of the Federal Reserve System.

Finn, Mary G. 1998. "Cyclical Effects of Government's Employment and Goods Purchases." *International Economic Review* 39 (3): 635–57.

Fishback, Price V., and Valentina Kachanovskaya. 2010. "In Search of the Multiplier for Federal Spending in the States during the New Deal." NBER Working Paper no. 16561. Cambridge, MA: National Bureau of Economic Research, November.

Fisher, Jonas D. M., and Ryan Peters. 2010. "Using Stock Returns to Identify Government Spending Shocks." *The Economic Journal* 120:414–36.

Gomes, Pedro. 2010. "Fiscal Policy and the Labour Market: The Effects of Public Sector Employment and Wages." IZA Discussion Paper 5321. Bonn: Institute for the Study of Labor (IZA).

Gordon, Robert J., and Robert Krenn. 2010. "The End of the Great Depression 1939–41: VAR Insight on the Roles of Monetary and Fiscal Policy." NBER Working Paper no. 16380. Cambridge, MA: National Bureau of Economic Research, September.

Hall, Robert E. 2009. "By How Much Does GDP Rise If the Government Buys More Output?" *Brookings Papers on Economic Activity* Fall:183–236. Washington, DC: Brookings Institution.

Hooker, Mark A., and Michael M. Knetter. 1997. "The Effects of Military Spending on Economic Activity: Evidenced from State Procurement Spending." *Journal of Money, Credit and Banking* 29 (3): 400–21.

McGrattan, Ellen R., and Lee E. Ohanian. 2010. "Does Neoclassical Theory Account for the Effects of Big Fiscal Shocks: Evidence from World War II." *International Economic Review* 51 (2): 509–32.

Monacelli, Tommaso, Roberto Perotti, and Antonella Trigari. 2010. "Unemployment Fiscal Multipliers." *Journal of Monetary Economics* 57 (5): 531–53.

Mountford, Andrew, and Harald Uhlig. 2009. "What Are the Effects of Fiscal Policy Shocks?" *Journal of Applied Econometrics* 24:960–92.

Nakamura, Emi, and Jón Steinsson. 2011. "Fiscal Stimulus in a Monetary Union: Evidence from US Regions." Working Paper. Columbia University.

Pappa, Evi. 2009. "The Effects of Fiscal Shocks on Employment and the Real Wage." *International Economic Review* 50 (217–243): 400–21.

Perotti, Roberto. 2008. "In Search of the Transmission Mechanism of Fiscal Policy." In *NBER Macroeconomics Annual 2007,* edited by Daron Acemoglu, Kenneth Rogoff, and Michael Woodford, 169–226. Chicago: University of Chicago Press.

———. 2011. "Expectations and Fiscal Policy: An Empirical Investigation." Working Paper. Bocconi University.

Ramey, Valerie A. 2009a. "Defense News Shocks, 1939–2008: Estimates Based on News Sources." Working Paper. University of California, San Diego.

———. 2009b. "Identifying Government Spending Shocks: It's All in the Timing." NBER Working Paper no. 15464. Cambridge, MA: National Bureau of Economic Research, October.

———. 2011a. "A Reply to Roberto Perotti's 'Expectations and Fiscal Policy: An Empirical Investigation.'" Unpublished Paper. University of California, San Diego.

———. 2011b. "Can Government Purchases Stimulate the Economy?" *Journal of Economic Literature* 49 (3): 673–85.

———. 2011c. "Identifying Government Spending Shocks: It's All in the Timing." *Quarterly Journal of Economics* 126 (1): 51–102.

Ramey, Valerie A., and Matthew D. Shapiro. 1998. "Costly Capital Reallocation and the Effects of Government Spending." *Carnegie-Rochester Conference Series on Public Policy* 48:145–94.

Romer, Christina D., and David H. Romer. 2010. "The Macroeconomic Effects of Tax Changes: Estimates Based on a New Measure of Fiscal Shocks." *American Economic Review* 100 (3): 763–801.

Rotemberg, Julio J., and Michael Woodford. 1992. "Oligopolistic Pricing and the Effects of Aggregate Demand on Economic Activity." *Journal of Political Economy* 100 (6): 1153–207.

Staiger, Douglas, and James H. Stock. 1997. "Instrumental Variables Regression with Weak Instruments." *Econometrica* 65 (3): 557–86.

Stock, James H., and M. Yogo. 2005. "Testing for Weak Instruments in Linear IV Regression." In *Identification and Inference for Econometric Models: Essays in Honor of Thomas Rothemberg,* edited by Donald W. K. Andrews and James H. Stock, 80–108. New York: Cambridge University Press.

Weir, David R. 1992. "A Century of US Unemployment, 1890–1990: Revised Estimates and Evidence for Stabilization." In *Research in Economic History,* edited by Roger L. Ransom, 301–46. Greenwich, CT: JAI Press.

Wilson, Daniel. 2012. "Fiscal Spending Jobs Multipliers: Evidence from the 2009 American Recovery and Reinvestment Act." *American Economic Journal: Economic Policy* 4 (3): 251–82.

Wynne, Mark. 1992. "The Analysis of Fiscal Policy in Neoclassical Models." Working Paper 9212. Federal Reserve Bank of Dallas.

Comment   Roberto Perotti

This is the usual work by Valerie Ramey—insightful, careful, and with a clear message: regardless of the methodology used, shocks to *total* government spending on goods and services increase GDP, but at the cost of depressing private economic activity and private employment.

Still, I disagree with this conclusion. In my view, the correct conclusion is: shocks to *defense* expectations (in EVARs) and to *defense* government spending on goods and services (in SVARs) lead to a decline in private GDP and employment. Shocks to *nondefense* government spending on goods and services, on the other hand, have positive effects on private GDP and private employment.

Ramey (2011a) argues that EVARs and the Blanchard-Perotti SVAR deliver the same results because they essentially use two different instruments for the only government spending variable that appears in these two specifications, *total* government spending:

> An SVAR can always be interpreted as an instrumental variables (IV) regression. Viewed in this context, the exercise I performed consists of comparing two instruments for total government spending, the first instrument being the VAR shock to total government spending using a Choleski decomposition and the second being the shock to the military date variable. Defense spending is not included in either VAR. In both VARs, I compare the response of all variables when the peak rise in total government spending has been normalized to the same number. Since there is no significant feedback of other variables to the news variable, in essence I am simply comparing the effects of the same size increase in total government spending on variables of interest, using two different instruments for the same measure of government spending." (Ramey 2011a, 2)[1]

Roberto Perotti is professor of economics at IGIER–Bocconi University and a research associate of the National Bureau of Economic Research.

Prepared for the IGIER-NBER conference, "Fiscal Policy after the Financial Crisis," held in Milan in December 2011. This chapter was produced as part of the project Growth and Sustainability Policies for Europe (GRASP), a collaborative project funded by the European Commission's Seventh Research Framework Programme, contract number 244725. For acknowledgments, sources of research support, and disclosure of the author's material financial relationships, if any, please see http://www.nber.org/chapters/c12633.ack.

1. Readers of Ramey (2011b) might be a bit puzzled by the approach and conclusions of the present chapter. The point of Ramey (2011b) was twofold. First, a Blanchard-Perotti SVAR, in which shocks to total government spending are identified via a simple Choleski decomposition, leads to biased estimates of impulse responses to total government spending shocks when there are anticipation effects. Suppose we live in a neoclassical world, so that shocks to government spending on goods and services cause a decline in private consumption and the real wage via a wealth effect; however, because changes to government spending are often known in advance, SVARs tend to exhibit spurious positive responses of private consumption and the real wage total government spending shocks (some might want to call these typical neo-Keynesian results, although so-called neo-Keynesian models deliver a bewildering array of responses depending on the specific assumptions). Second, EVARs are immune from this problem, and indeed they

This argument is correct if defense and nondefense government spending have the same effects. But if they do not—and surely this is not a crazy hypothesis—then both the EVAR and the Blanchard-Perotti SVAR are misspecified: instead of total government spending, one should have both defense and civilian government spending in the EVARs and the SVARs. Now the "source" of the shock—whether to defense or nondefense spending—matters a great deal. A shock to the defense news variable in the EVAR or to defense spending in the SVAR is likely to be associated with a large response of defense spending, while a shock to nondefense spending in an SVAR is likely to be associated with a large response of nondefense spending. The fact that in all these cases one normalizes the total government response to 1 percent of GDP is useful to interpret the results but does not change the substance, because to each of the two types of shocks there corresponds a different "defense spending intensity" of the response of total government spending. Of course, this all depends on whether we can identify defense and nondefense shocks separately in an SVAR. I will show that we can, and that they give widely different answers.

To this end, I estimate exactly the same EVAR and SVAR estimated by Ramey, except that I have both the log of per capita defense spending and the log of per capita civilian spending whenever she has the log of per capita total government spending. So I estimate the reduced forms

$$(1) \qquad\qquad X_t = A(L)X_{t-1} + U_t,$$

where in the EVAR case the vector X_t includes the defense news variable, the log of defense spending on goods and services, the log of civilian government spending on goods and services, the log of private GDP (all three last variables are in real, per capita terms), the Barro-Redlick average margined tax rate, the three-month interest rate, the log of government employments, and the log of private employment. In the SVAR case, the vector X_t includes the same variables except that the defense news variable is omitted. The regressions are in levels, with four lags or each variable, a constant, and linear and quadratic trends in each equation. All the data were kindly provided by Valerie Ramey.

In the SVAR, it is meaningful to talk about defense and civilian government spending shocks only if the reduced-form residuals of the defense and

---

tend to show that private consumption and the real wage fall in response to defense news shocks (the neoclassical response).

In the present chapter, these differences between EVARs and SVARs have disappeared. Ramey reaches the same conclusion as Perotti (2011), namely that, when estimated on the same sample and in response to the same types of shocks (to be defined more precisely later), EVARs and SVARs give essentially the same answers. Hence, in these comments I will not dwell much on the question of whether SVAR shocks do capture something structural, an issue I discuss in Perotti (2011). Given that SVARs have the same status as EVARs in the present chapter (in the last section Ramey tests an hypothesis using only an SVAR), I will consider myself authorized to treat SVARs as meaningful objects.

civilian government spending equations are nearly uncorrelated, so that the ordering of the two variables in a Choleski decomposition does not matter. Empirically, this is indeed the case. As a convention, when I present the response to a shock that variable is ordered first, but the opposite ordering gives virtually identical results.

For brevity, I will focus on the sample starting in 1947:1. Although the analysis of World War II is insightful and interesting as usual, most researchers would be unconvinced by any conclusion based on that period. World War II was obviously by far the largest shock to defense spending and total spending in the sample (and probably in the history of the United States). It could be a great experiment in fiscal policy. Unfortunately, it was also accompanied by things like price controls, production controls, rationing, the draft, and patriotism: to disentangle the role of these factors on variables like labor supply, the real wage, private consumption, and private investment is impossible. For example, Hall (2009) argues that the combined effect of these factors on GDP and labor supply was probably negative; Barro and Redlick (2011) argue that it was probably positive. Unfortunately, as they openly recognize, their conclusions are based exclusively on intuition.

However, given the extensive production controls and rationing, it is hard to see how consumption of goods and some components of private investment could go anywhere but down.[2] It is interesting to note that, as I show in Perotti (2011), the consumption of services that were not subject to rationing increased instead during World War II. For all these reasons, I will focus on the post–World War II period.

Column (1) of figure 1C.1 displays the median (out of 1,000 bootstrap replications) responses to the defense news shock in an EVAR in the sample starting in 1947:1. The responses of national income aggregates are expressed as percentage points of total GDP by multiplying the log responses by the average share of that variable in GDP. Similarly, the responses of the employment variables are expressed as percentage points of total employment. All responses are normalized so that the peak response of total government spending (the sum of defense and civilian purchases of goods and services) is 1 percent of total GDP, 95 percent standard error bands are displayed.

---

2. In addition, there are accounting issues that can explain the decline in investment and consumption. As Gordon and Krenn (2010, 11) argue, the war and its preparation mechanically reduced private consumption of nondurables, as recorded in the national income accounts, "since it excludes the food and clothing provided to the 10 percent of the population that served in the military, as these were counted as government rather than consumption expenditures." Similar accounting issues arise with private investment, another item that displays a decline in the EVAR responses: "Yet much of this new investment in plant and equipment was not counted as investment in the national accounts. . . . [T]he ongoing attempt to double plant capacity was being financed by the government, not by the company's own funds. . . . Since investment in war-related plant expansion was counted as government spending rather than private investment in the national accounts, the surge of war-related investment during 1941 occurred simultaneously with a decline in measured private investment in the last half of 1941."

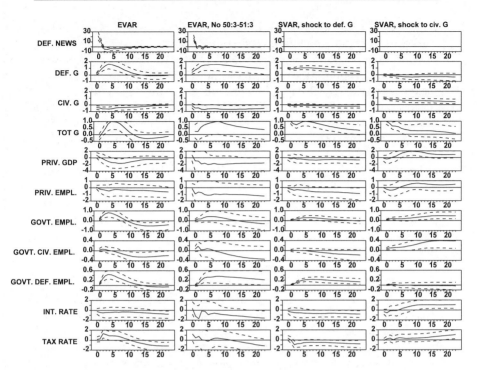

Fig. 1C.1   Responses to various shocks, EVAR and SVAR

Obviously the responses of column (1) are virtually identical to those reported by Ramey in her figures 1.3, 1.6, and 1.14: private GDP and private employment fall. Note, however, an important feature of these responses that could not be detected in the Ramey specification: defense spending increases, but civilian spending falls; hence, if the two types of government spending have different effects, this is not really a clean experiment. The response of private employment is flat; government employment increases, but, not surprisingly, it is only military employment that increases: civilian government employment is flat.[3]

Column (2) of figure 1C.1 checks the robustness of these results to one key quarter, 1950:3, when the defense news variable takes a value of 63 percent of GDP, the largest value during the Korean War. The next largest revisions during the Korean War were 41 percent in 1950:4, and then –2.02 percent in 1953:1 and –3.06 percent in 1953:3; the next largest revision in the post–Korean War sample is 6.4 percent in 1980:1. Column (2) shows that omitting 1950:3[4] causes the standard errors to increase drastically. The

---

3. The responses of civilian and military government employment are obtained from specifications in which each of these two variables replaces the government employment variable in turn.

4. In practice, this is achieved by including a dummy variable for 1950:3 and its four lags.

response of private GDP is now insignificant; only the response of military employment remains significant. Of course, whether one wants to discard any information is largely a philosophical question that will never be solved; still, it is important for the reader to be aware to what extent the results of the defense news EVAR depend on just one quarter of the sample.

Now turn to the SVAR responses. As it turns out, they are very robust, to the exclusion of 1950:3. For brevity, I will focus on the sample with 1950:3 excluded. Column (3) displays responses to a defense spending shock. Note that this is a "pure" defense shock: the response of civilian spending is flat at all horizons. All responses are virtually identical to the responses to a defense news shock in the EVAR: private GDP falls and government employment increases, but only because of an increase in military employment. Now both private employment and the short-term interest rate fall significantly, while their response was insignificant in the EVAR case. The Barro-Redlick tax rate also falls after several quarters.

Column (4) displays the responses to a civilian government spending shock. Note that this too is a pure shock: the response of defense spending is flat at all horizons. The responses are almost symmetrical relative to those in column (3). Private GDP increases by about 2 percentage points of total GDP, and private employment increases, even though the standard errors are larger. Of course, government employment also increases; but now obviously it is civilian government employment that increases.

The short-term interest rate and the Barro-Redlick tax rate increases in response to civilian spending shocks; in contrast, they decline in response to defense spending shocks. To the extent that these are policy variables, one must conclude that civilian spending shocks have positive effects on private activity despite the unfavorable monetary and tax policies that accompany them.

Column (1) of figure 1C.2 displays the median difference, out of 1,000 replications, between the EVAR responses and the SVAR responses to a defense news shock. As it was obvious even from a visual inspection of the impulse responses, these differences are minimal, and never statistically significant. Column (2) displays the median difference or the response between SVAR shocks to nondefense spending and SVAR shocks to defense spending. These differences are large and statistically significant.

In conclusion, the evidence suggests that shocks to defense spending on goods and services have diametrically opposite effects to shocks to civilian spending on goods and services, despite the fact that the latter were on average associated with stricter monetary and tax policies. Ramey's conclusions are based on the effects of defense spending shocks; they would have been the opposite if she had looked at nondefense spending shocks. Defense spending shocks display the typical neoclassical features of fiscal policy; nondefense shocks display what some might want to call Keyensian features.

In these comments, I have just presented the facts; I do not have a rigorous explanation. But I believe these results are relevant not only from a theoretical

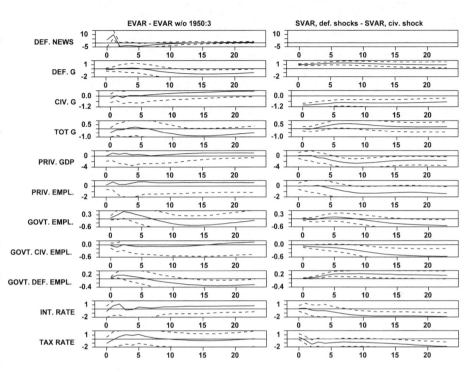

Fig. 1C.2   Significance of differences of responses

perspective. They are relevant also for the policy debate in the United States; and they are of interest for non-US countries, where defense spending is a much smaller part of total government spending, and has exhibited smaller variation over time.

References

Barro, R., and C. J. Redlick. 2011. "Macroeconomic Effects from Government Purchases and Taxes." *Quarterly Journal of Economics* 126 (1): 51–102.
Gordon, R., and R. Krenn. 2010. "The End of the Great Depression 1939–41: VAR Insight on the Roles of Monetary and Fiscal Policy." NBER Working Paper no. 16380. Cambridge, MA: National Bureau of Economic Research, September.
Hall, R. 2009. "By How Much Does GDP Rise If the Government Buys More Output?" *Brookings Papers on Economic Activity* Fall:183–231. Washington, DC: Brookings Institution.
Perotti, R. 2011. "Expectations and Fiscal Policy: An Empirical Investigation." Technical Report. Bocconi University.
Ramey, V. 2011a. "A Reply to Roberto Perotti's 'Expectations and Fiscal Policy: An Empirical Investigation.'" Unpublished Paper. University of California, San Diego.
———. 2011b. "Identifying Government Spending Shocks: It's All in the Timing." *Quarterly Journal of Economics* 126 (1): 51–102.

2

Fiscal Multipliers in Recession and Expansion

Alan J. Auerbach and Yuriy Gorodnichenko

2.1 Introduction

A key issue coming out of recent economic events is the size of fiscal multipliers when the economy is in recession. In a recent paper (Auerbach and Gorodnichenko 2012), we extended the standard structural vector autoregression (SVAR) methodology in three ways to shed light on this issue. First, using regime-switching models, we estimated effects of fiscal policies that can vary over the business cycle, finding large differences in the size of spending multipliers in recessions and expansions with fiscal policy being considerably more effective in recessions than in expansions. Second, we estimated multipliers for more disaggregate spending variables that behave differently in relation to aggregate fiscal policy shocks, with military spending having the largest multiplier. Third, we showed that controlling for real-time predictions of fiscal variables tends to increase the size of the multipliers in recessions.

In this chapter, we extend our previous analysis in three important ways. First, we estimate multipliers for a large number of Organization for Economic Cooperation and Development (OECD) countries, rather than just for the United States, again allowing for state dependence and controlling

Alan J. Auerbach is the Robert D. Burch Professor of Economics and Law and director of the Robert D. Burch Center for Tax Policy and Public Finance at the University of California, Berkeley, and a research associate of the National Bureau of Economic Research. Yuriy Gorodnichenko is assistant professor of economics at the University of California, Berkeley, and a faculty research fellow of the National Bureau of Economic Research.

This chapter was prepared for the NBER conference, "Fiscal Policy after the Financial Crisis," held in Milan, December 2011. We thank conference participants, particularly our discussant, Robert Hall, for comments on earlier drafts. For acknowledgments, sources of research support, and disclosure of the authors' material financial relationships, if any, please see http://www.nber.org/chapters/c12634.ack.

for information provided by predictions. Second, we adapt our previous methodology to use direct projections rather than the SVAR approach to estimate multipliers, to economize on degrees of freedom, and to relax the assumptions on impulse response functions imposed by the SVAR method. Third, we estimate responses not only of output but also of other macroeconomic aggregates. Our findings confirm those of our earlier paper. In particular, multipliers of government purchases are larger in a recession, and controlling for real-time predictions of government purchases tends to increase the estimated multipliers of government spending in recession.[1]

2.2 Methodology

Before developing our current approach, we review the one taken in our earlier paper. We developed what we referred to there as a smooth transition vector autoregression (STVAR), based on the smooth transition autoregressive (STAR) models developed in Granger and Teräsvirta (1993); one important difference in our approach is that we allow not only differential dynamic responses but also differential contemporaneous responses to structural shocks. Our basic specification, without controlling for real-time predictions, was:

$$(1) \qquad \mathbf{X}_t = (1 - F(z_{t-1}))\mathbf{\Pi}_E(L)\mathbf{X}_{t-1} + F(z_{t-1})\mathbf{\Pi}_R(L)\mathbf{X}_{t-1} + \mathbf{u}_t$$

$$(2) \qquad \mathbf{u}_t \sim N(\mathbf{0}, \mathbf{\Omega}_t)$$

$$(3) \qquad \mathbf{\Omega}_t = \mathbf{\Omega}_E(1 - F(z_{t-1})) + \mathbf{\Omega}_R F(z_{t-1})$$

$$(4) \qquad F(z_t) = \frac{\exp(-\gamma z_t)}{1 + \exp(-\gamma z_t)}, \gamma > 0,$$

where $\mathbf{X}_t = [G_t \ T_t \ Y_t]'$ is a vector of the logarithms of real government purchases (G_t), taxes net of transfers (T_t), and real gross domestic product (GDP, Y_t), observed at a quarterly frequency;[2] z is an indicator of the state of the economy, normalized to have zero mean and unit variance; and the matrices $\mathbf{\Pi}_i(L)$ and $\mathbf{\Omega}_i(L)$ represent the VAR coefficients and variance-covariance matrix of disturbances in two regimes, recession ($i = R$) and expansion ($i = E$). The weights assigned to each regime for a given observation by weight-

1. We focus here, as in our previous paper, on the effects of government purchases rather than those of taxes and transfer payments, which we have argued are more difficult to identify and estimate using simple time series models.

2. Hall (2009), Barro and Redlick (2012), and others normalize changes in government spending by the lagged level of output so that an estimated coefficient can be directly interpreted as a multiplier. In contrast, the coefficients we estimate are elasticities. One can, however, easily convert elasticities into multipliers at sample averages by multiplying the elasticities by the mean ratio of output to government spending. While there are pros and cons for each specification, in our sample the choice makes little difference since the ratio of output to government spending is fairly constant over time and cross-sectional variation in this ratio is absorbed into country fixed effects.

ing function $F(\cdot)$ vary between 0 and 1 according to the contemporaneous state of the economy, z, which we took to be a moving average of real GDP growth.[3]

In our earlier paper, we considered a variety of approaches to extend this basic model to take account of real-time information regarding expectations of fiscal variables and GDP, available from a variety of sources. One of these approaches, which we will use in this chapter, was to include a direct measure of the unanticipated component of government purchases, equal to the difference between actual purchases G_t and the forecast of this variable one period earlier, $G_{t|t-1}$. This forecast is typically taken from a survey of professional forecasters, projections prepared by government or international agencies (e.g., Greenbook forecasts prepared by the Federal Reserve staff) or other credible sources (e.g., financial markets). Specifically, we estimated the SVAR for $\hat{\mathbf{X}}_t = [FE_t^G \ G_t \ T_t \ Y_t]'$ where FE_t^G is the forecast error computed as the difference between forecast series and actual, first-release series of the government spending growth rate.[4] By stacking FE_t^G first in the SVAR, we could then estimate directly from the SVAR coefficients the multipliers for unanticipated government purchases.[5]

In contrast to Auerbach and Gorodnichenko (2012) focusing only on the US macroeconomic time series, in this chapter we use data on multiple countries available from the OECD, for which consistent measures of actual and forecast values are available only at a semiannual frequency, rather than quarterly. This lower frequency of observations, in conjunction with the availability of data starting at a later date than our data for the United States, substantially reduces the number of observations we have for any particular country. For such short time series, our original approach, which involves highly nonlinear estimation of a large number of parameters, would be very challenging. Therefore, we modify our approach in two ways. First, we use panel estimation, allowing intercepts to vary by country but constraining other coefficients to be the same. Second, rather than estimating the entire system of equations in the STVAR and using these to estimate impulse response functions (IRFs), we estimate the IRFs directly by projecting a variable of interest on lags of variables entering the VAR, or more generally, variables capturing information available in a given time period. This single-equation approach has been advocated by Jorda (2005), Stock and Watson (2007), and others as a flexible alternative that does not impose dynamic restrictions implicitly embedded in VARs and that can conveniently

---

3. In our earlier paper as well as the present chapter, we abstract from other potential non-linearities such as asymmetric responses to increases and decreases in government spending and nonlinear responses in size of government spending shocks.

4. We compare forecasts to contemporaneous measures to take account of subsequent data revisions.

5. Because this SVAR includes a forecast of a variable in addition to standard macroeconomic variables, this approach is also known as the expectations-augmented VAR, or EVAR.

accommodate nonlinearities in the response function. For example, when we use GDP as the dependent variable, the response of Y at the horizon h is estimated from the following regression:

$$(5) \qquad Y_{i,t+h} = \alpha_{i,h} + F(z_{i,t-1})\Pi_{R,h}(L)Y_{i,t-1} + (1 - F(z_{i,t-1}))\Pi_{E,h}(L)Y_{i,t-1}$$
$$+ F(z_{i,t-1})\Psi_{R,h}(L)G_{i,t-1} + (1 - F(z_{i,t-1}))\Psi_{E,h}(L)G_{i,t-1}$$
$$+ F(z_{i,t-1})\Phi_{R,h}FE_{it}^{G} + (1 - F(z_{i,t-1}))\Phi_{E,h}FE_{it}^{G} + u_{it},$$

$$\text{with } F(z_{i,t-1}) = \frac{\exp(-\gamma z_{i,t-1})}{1 + \exp(-\gamma z_{i,t-1})}, \gamma > 0,$$

where i and t index countries and time, α_i is the country fixed effect, $F(\cdot)$ is the transition function, $z_{i,t-1}$ is a variable measuring the state of the business cycle, and FE_{it}^{G} is the forecast error for the growth rate of government spending in the forecasts prepared by professional forecasters at time $t - 1$ for period t. Note that all coefficients vary with the horizon h; that is, a separate regression is estimated for each horizon.

We interpret FE_{it}^{G} as the surprise government spending shock. This treatment of what constitutes a shock is consistent with Ramey (2011) and Auerbach and Gorodnichenko (2012), where changes in spending are projected on professional forecasts to construct a series on unanticipated innovations in spending. Observe that by controlling for information contained in lags of Y and G we purify FE_{it}^{G} of any predictable component that would have been eliminated had the professional forecaster run a VAR. The fact that we include the government spending shock FE_{it}^{G} dated by time t is consistent with the recursive ordering of government spending first in the VARs.

In the STVAR or standard VAR analysis of how government spending shocks affect the economy, the impulse response is constructed in two steps. First, the contemporaneous responses are derived from a Cholesky decomposition of Ω_t in equation (3), with government spending ordered first. In Auerbach and Gorodnichenko (2012) we allowed contemporaneous responses to vary since Ω_t can change over the business cycle. Second, the propagation of the responses over time is obtained by using estimated coefficients in the lag polynomials such as $\Pi_R(L)$ and $\Pi_E(L)$ in equation (1) applied to the contemporaneous responses from the first step. The direct projection method effectively combines these two steps into one.

Note that the lag polynomials $\{\Pi_{R,h}(L), \Psi_{R,h}(L), \Pi_{E,h}(L), \Psi_{E,h}(L)\}$ in equation (5) are used to control for the history of shocks rather than to compute the dynamics. The dynamics are constructed by varying the horizon h of the dependent variable so that we can directly read the impulse responses off estimated $\{\Phi_{E,h}\}_{h=0}^{H}$ for expansions and $\{\Phi_{R,h}\}_{h=0}^{H}$ for recessions. For horizon $h = 0$, the impulse response constructed with this approach recovers the response constructed with a STVAR where FE_{it}^{G} is ordered first. At longer horizons, however, there is potentially a difference between the approaches.

To simplify the argument, suppose that the STVAR has just one lag $\mathbf{\Pi}_R$ in $\mathbf{\Pi}_R(L)$. Then this STVAR imposes that dynamics at short and long horizons are described by the same matrix $\mathbf{\Pi}_R$ (or, more generally, with a handful of matrixes like $\mathbf{\Pi}_R$) while direct projections do not impose such a restriction.

One can think of the direct projection approach as constructing a moving average representation of a series: the lag polynomial terms control for initial conditions while $\{\mathbf{\Phi}_{E,h}\}_{h=0}^{H}$ and $\{\mathbf{\Phi}_{R,h}\}_{h=0}^{H}$ describe the behavior of the system in response to a structural, serially uncorrelated shock. Indeed, if we abstract from variation in initial conditions at time t, we effectively regress a variable of interest at time $t + h$ on a shock in a given regime at time t and thus we obtain an average response of the variable of interest h periods after the shock, which is precisely the definition of an impulse response.[6]

This estimation method has several advantages over our earlier approach. First, it involves only linear estimation, if one fixes (as we have throughout our work) the parameter γ in expression (4). Second, it obviates the need to estimate the equations for dependent variables other than the variable of interest (e.g., GDP) and thus we can significantly economize on the number of estimated parameters. Third, it does not constrain the shape of the IRF, rather than imposing the pattern generated by the SVAR. (Under the maintained assumption that the SVAR is correctly specified, the patterns should be the same.) Fourth, the error term in equation (5) is likely to be correlated across countries. This correlation would be particularly hard to handle in the context of nonlinear STVARs but is easy to address in linear estimation by using, for example, Driscoll-Kraay (1998) standard errors or clustering standard errors by time period. Fifth, we can use specification (5) to construct impulse responses for any macroeconomic variable of interest as we are not constrained by the VAR's curse of dimensionality. Finally, because the set of regressors in (5) does

---

6. The following example can help to contrast the direct-projection approach and the conventional approach to computing impulse responses. Consider an AR(1) data generating process $y_t = \alpha y_{t-1} + \varepsilon_t + \text{error} = \Sigma_s \alpha^s \varepsilon_{t-s} + \text{error}$, where ε_t is a structural shock and "error" is a collection of unidentified innovations. The conventional approach estimates the model $y_t = \alpha y_{t-1} + \varepsilon_t$ + error and computes the impulse response function (IRF) as IRF = $\{1, \hat{\alpha}, \hat{\alpha}^2, \ldots, \hat{\alpha}^h\}$. In contrast, direct projections are a series of regressions for each horizon $j = 0, \ldots, h$:

$$j = 0:\ y_t = \phi_0 y_{t-1} + \beta_0 \varepsilon_t + \text{error} = \alpha y_{t-1} + \varepsilon_t + \text{error}$$

$$j = 1:\ y_{t+1} = \phi_1 y_{t-1} + \beta_1 \varepsilon_t + \text{error} = \alpha^2 y_{t-1} + \alpha \varepsilon_t + \varepsilon_{t+1} + \text{error}$$

$$j = 2:\ y_{t+2} = \phi_2 y_{t-1} + \beta_2 \varepsilon_t + \text{error} = \alpha^3 y_{t-1} + \alpha^2 \varepsilon_t + \alpha \varepsilon_{t+1} + \varepsilon_{t+2} + \text{error}$$

$$\cdots$$

$$j = h:\ y_{t+h} = \phi_h y_{t-1} + \beta_h \varepsilon_t + \text{error} = \alpha^{h+1} y_{t-1} + \alpha^h \varepsilon_t + \Sigma_{s=0}^{h-1} \alpha^s \varepsilon_{t+h-s} + \text{error}.$$

Note that $\varepsilon_{t+1} + \text{error}$, $\alpha \varepsilon_{t+1} + \varepsilon_{t+2} + \text{error}$, $\ldots$, $\Sigma_{s=0}^{h-1} \alpha^s \varepsilon_{t+h-s} + \text{error}$ are all orthogonal to y_{t-1} and ε_t by assumption and thus each of these regressions can be estimated by ordinary least squares (OLS). The IRFs are computed as IRF = $\{\hat{\beta}_0, \hat{\beta}_1, \hat{\beta}_2, \ldots, \hat{\beta}_h\}$. Note that under the null hypothesis $\{\hat{\beta}_0, \hat{\beta}_1, \hat{\beta}_2, \ldots, \hat{\beta}_h\}$ are estimates of $\{1, \alpha, \alpha^2, \ldots, \alpha^h\}$ and thus that direct projections recover the same IRFs as the conventional approach. However, the direct projections do not impose that the IRFs are tied together by α and thus are more flexible. This becomes a crucial advantage in the context of nonlinear models.

not vary with the horizon h, the impulse response incorporates the average transitions of the economy from one state to another. In other words, we do not have to separately model how z changes over time. If government spending shocks systematically affect the state of the economy (e.g., an unanticipated increase in government spending during a recession pushes the economy into expansion and thus z changes from a negative value to a positive value), this systematic effect will be absorbed into estimated $\{\Phi_{E,h}\}_{h=0}^{H}$ and $\{\Phi_{R,h}\}_{h=0}^{H}$ (e.g., $\Phi_{R,h}$ will be lower if the response of output to government spending shocks is smaller during expansions than during recessions). In contrast, using the system in (1) requires that we explicitly model the dynamics of z.

Similar to our earlier paper, z_{it} is based on the (standardized) deviation of the output growth rate (moving average over 1.5 years) from the trend. However, in contrast to the earlier paper, we allow the trend to be time-varying because several counties exhibit low frequency variations in the growth rates of output. Specifically, we extract the trend using the Hodrick-Prescott filter with a very high smoothing parameter ($\lambda = 10,000$) so that the trend is very smooth.[7] Because identification of the curvature in the transition function $F(\cdot)$ is based on highly nonlinear moments and thus is potentially sensitive to a handful of unusual observations, we follow our earlier approach and calibrate $\gamma = 1.5$ so that a typical economy spends about 20 percent of the time in a recessionary regime, which is consistent with the fraction of recessionary periods in the United States.[8]

The linear analogue of specification (5) is given by

$$(5')\qquad Y_{i,t+h} = \alpha_{i,h} + \Pi_{Lin,h}(L)\,Y_{i,t-1} + \Psi_{Lin,h}(L)G_{i,t-1} + \Phi_{Lin,h}FE_{it}^{G} + u_{it},$$

where the response of Y is constrained to be the same for all values of z_{it}: that is, $\Pi_{Lin,h}(L) = \Pi_{E,h}(L) = \Pi_{R,h}(L)$, $\Psi_{Lin,h}(L) = \Psi_{E,h}(L) = \Psi_{R,h}(L)$, and $\Phi_{Lin,h} = \Phi_{E,h} = \Phi_{R,h}$ for all L and h.

2.3   Data

The macroeconomic series we use in our analyses come from the OECD's Statistics and Projections database. There are several benefits of using these data. First, macroeconomic series and forecasts for these series are prepared using a unified methodology so that series are comparable across countries. Second, the OECD prepares semiannual forecasts for key macroeconomic

7. We prefer this value of the smoothing parameter to $\lambda = 400$, which is a more conventional value in the literature for semiannual data, because a larger value ensures that the trend in the Hodrick-Prescott filter does not follow cyclical fluctuations in the series. For example, with $\lambda = 400$, the Great Recession does not look like a deep contraction, as the trend significantly falls along with the actual output. In contrast, $\lambda = 10,000$ does not produce this counterintuitive result. In any case, our qualitative and, to a large extent, quantitative results are insensitive to the choice of λ.

8. This magnitude of γ is also in line with estimates we obtain in logit regressions on US data where the dependent variable is the dummy variable equal to one for recessions identified by the NBER and the regressor is our measure of z.

variables such as GDP and government spending in June and December of each year. The OECD's forecasts are available for a broad array of variables. Third, these forecasts have "reality checks," as the OECD exploits its local presence in the member countries and holds extensive discussions on the projections and related analyses with local government experts and policymakers. Thus, the OECD's forecasts incorporate a great deal of local knowledge and information about future policy changes. Fourth, in recent assessments of the OECD's forecasts, Vogel (2007) and Lenain (2002) report that these forecasts have a number of desirable properties and perform at par with the forecasts prepared by the private sector. More information on these forecasts is available on the OECD's website.[9]

The OECD's forecasts are consistently available since 1985 for "old" members of the OECD (e.g., the United States) and since the mid-1990s for newer members (e.g., Poland). The downside of using the OECD projections is that, for most of the available sample, they are available only at the semi-annual frequency rather than the quarterly frequency more commonly used in the SVAR literature. Our sample ends in 2008.

Consistent with the OECD definitions and the previous literature on fiscal multipliers, our government spending series is the sum of real public consumption expenditure and real government gross capital formation. That is, it does not include imputed rent on the government capital stock, as is now the convention in the US national income accounts. In addition to the standard real GDP series, we will examine responses of other key macroeconomic variables to government spending shocks. First, we document responses of other components of GDP: real private consumption, real private gross capital formation, and real exports and imports. Second, we investigate the behavior of the variables describing the labor market: total employment in the economy, employment in the private sector, the unemployment rate, and the real compensation rate in the private sector. This last series is our measure of real wages. Finally, we explore how prices, measured by the consumer price index (CPI) and the GDP deflator, respond to government spending shocks. All variables except the unemployment rate enter specification (5) in logs.

2.4   Results

2.4.1   Impulse Responses in a VAR and Direct Projections Method

As a first pass through the data, we examine how our approach of direct projections compares with the more conventional approach of using VARs to construct impulse responses. Figure 2.1 contrasts the impulse response of output to a 1 percent increase in government spending in a linear bivariate VAR—which includes real GDP and real government spending as endog-

9. http://www.oecd.org/faq/0,3433,en_2649_33733_1798284_1_1_1_1,00.html

Panel A: Full sample, 1960–2010

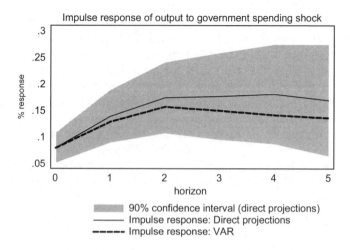

Panel B: Sample for which OECD forecasts are available, 1985–2010

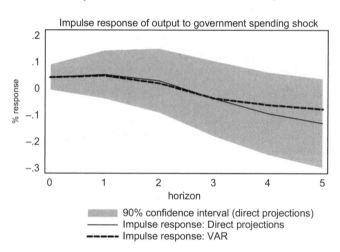

Fig. 2.1   Comparison of impulse responses from VAR and direct projection

enous variables and country fixed effects with slopes assumed to be the same across countries—with the impulse response of output to the same shock in government spending in the specification given by (5′), which is restricted to have the same responses and dynamics in recessions and expansions. Note that, since the linear VAR uses a Cholesky decomposition, the contemporaneous responses have to be the same in these two approaches. However, even when we extend the horizons, the responses are remarkably similar across

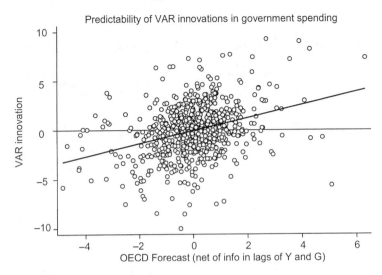

Fig. 2.2   Predictability of VAR shocks to government spending
Note: Correlation is 0.36.

approaches and thus we can be more confident that our subsequent results are not driven by using an alternative approach to construct impulse responses.

2.4.2   Predictability of VAR Shocks

A key assumption in the construction of fiscal multipliers is that shocks to government spending are not forecastable. The VARs try to ensure unforecastability of shocks by including sufficiently many lags of endogenous variables so that the error term is orthogonal to information contained in the past values of macroeconomic variables. However, as has been discussed extensively in the literature (see, e.g., Ramey 2011), many changes in fiscal variables are anticipated and lagged values of the few variables included in the VAR may fail to capture these anticipated future changes.

To assess the extent to which VAR shocks are forecastable, we perform the following exercise. First, we project growth rates of government spending predicted by the OECD forecasts on the lags of endogenous variables in the VAR to remove the component of government spending growth that is predictable on the basis of information contained in the VAR. Second, we compute the error term in the government spending equation in the VAR with the same number of lags of endogenous variables—the standard VAR shocks. Third, we check the correlation between these two series, which should be zero if the OECD forecasts do not have systematically better information than is contained in the lagged variables of the VAR. In fact, we find (figure 2.2) that the VAR shocks are predicted by professional forecasters to a significant degree: the correlation between the two series is

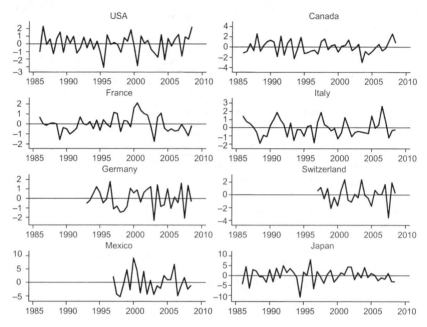

Fig. 2.3   Time series of government spending shocks for selected countries

0.36. In other words, a considerable part of the VAR shocks to government spending is anticipated by the OECD forecasts. This suggests that estimates of impulse responses in the conventional VAR approach may be seriously biased, as the responses to anticipated and unanticipated shocks, in theory, can be radically different.

To minimize the contamination of government spending shocks with predictable changes, we will project the forecast errors of the OECD government spending forecasts on the lags of output (or any other endogenous variable of interest, e.g., private consumption) and government spending and take the residual from this projection as a government spending shock; that is, FE_{it}^G in specification (5). Figure 2.3 presents time series of constructed government spending shocks for selected countries. In line with previous evidence on properties of government spending shocks, our shocks have persistent effects on government spending.

2.4.3   State-Dependent Impulse Responses

Figure 2.4 presents impulses responses of key macroeconomic variables to an unanticipated 1 percent increase in government spending. Each panel in this figure has two subpanels showing responses (black, thick line) in a recessionary regime (z has a large negative value; the response is given by $\{\hat{\Phi}_{R,h}\}_{h=0}^H$) and an expansionary regime (z has a large positive value; the response is given by $\{\hat{\Phi}_{E,h}\}_{h=0}^H$). Because the data are semiannual, the time

Panel A. Real GDP

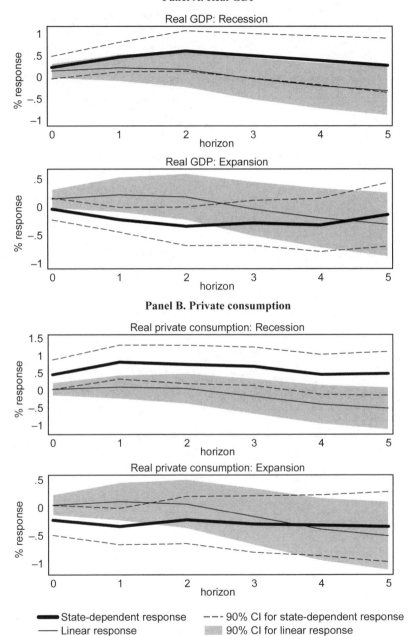

Real GDP: Recession

Real GDP: Expansion

Panel B. Private consumption

Real private consumption: Recession

Real private consumption: Expansion

━━━ State-dependent response   --- 90% CI for state-dependent response
——— Linear response   ▨ 90% CI for linear response

Fig. 2.4   State-dependent versus linear responses

Notes: Each panel reports impulse responses for the linear model (5′) and the state-dependent model (5) to an unanticipated 1 percent government spending shock.

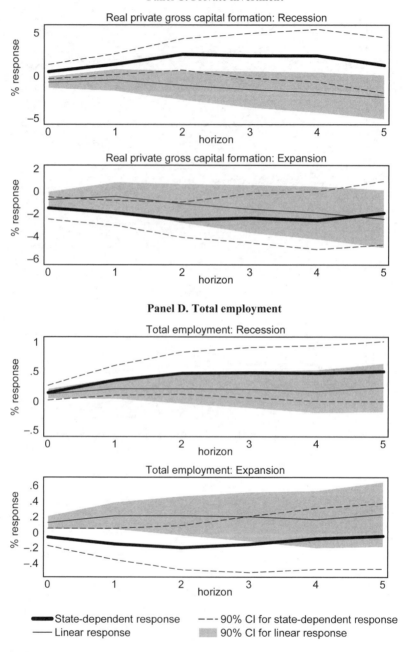

Panel C. Private investment

Real private gross capital formation: Recession

Real private gross capital formation: Expansion

Panel D. Total employment

Total employment: Recession

Total employment: Expansion

━━━ State-dependent response   ─ ─ ─ 90% CI for state-dependent response
──── Linear response   90% CI for linear response

Fig. 2.4   (cont.)

Panel E. Private sector employment

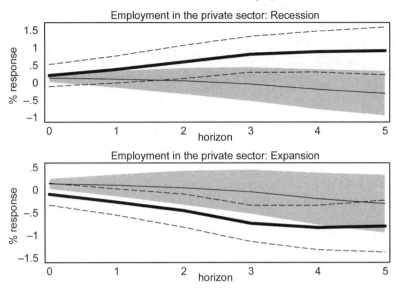

Panel F. Unemployment rate

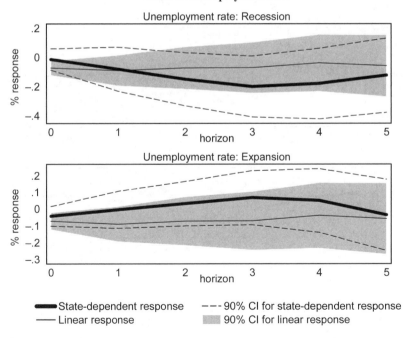

Fig. 2.4 (cont.)

Panel G. Real compensation rate of the private sector

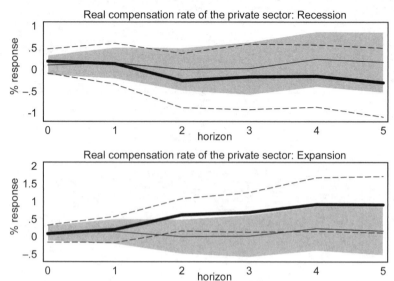

Panel H. Real exports

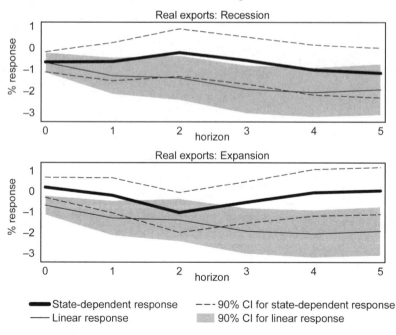

Fig. 2.4 (cont.)

Panel I. Real imports

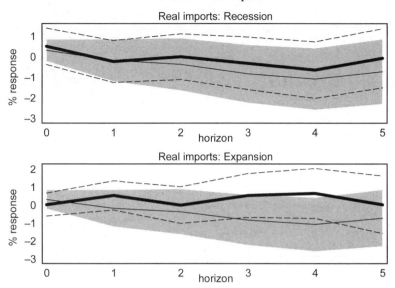

Panel J. Consumer price index

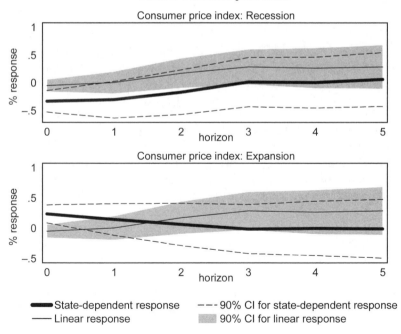

Fig. 2.4   (cont.)

Panel K. GDP deflator

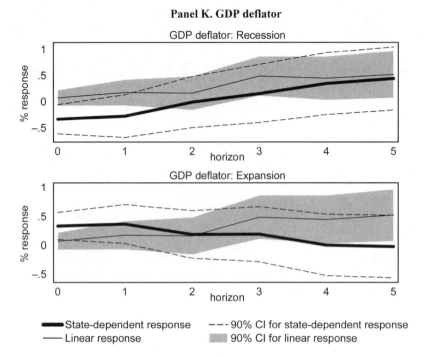

Fig. 2.4   (cont.)

horizons are in half-year increments. The thin, dashed lines indicate the 90 percent confidence bands, which are based on Driscoll-Kraay (1998) standard errors that allow arbitrary correlations of the error term in specification (5) across countries and time. As a point of comparison, each subpanel also reports the response in the linear model (5′) (thin line) and associated 90 percent confidence bands (shaded region), which are also based on Driscoll-Kraay (1998) standard errors.[10]

The responses of output (panel A) are remarkably different across regimes and models. In the linear model, only the contemporaneous response is positive and marginally statistically significant. For the next two periods, the response is positive but not statistically different from zero and then the point estimates of the response turn negative although we cannot reject the null that these responses are zero. In contrast, the response of output in the recessionary regime is robustly positive up to two years. If we use the sample-period US average ratio of output to government purchases (≈ 5.12) to convert percentage changes into dollar changes, the maximum size of the government spending multiplier is about 3.5, with the 90 percent confidence

---

10. The responses are normalized so that the government spending response to a shock in FE_{it}^G is equal to unity.

interval being (0.6, 6.3). The average government spending multiplier over three years is about 2.3. The response of output in the expansionary regime is much weaker, in fact negative at some horizons, but generally we cannot reject the null that the response is zero for most horizons. This result is consistent with our earlier work for the United States where we estimated the spending multiplier to be approximately zero in expansions and about 1.5 to 2.0 in recessions. This finding is also consistent with estimates reported in the nascent literature that explores cyclical variation of fiscal multipliers. For example, Gordon and Krenn (2010) document that the government spending multiplier was about two just before the start of World War II, when the US economy had a considerable degree of slack. Bachmann and Sims (2012) report that the spending multiplier is approximately zero in expansions and approximately 3 in recessions. Using state-level variation in government spending, Shoag (2010) finds that the multiplier is approximately 3.0 to 3.5 when labor markets have a slack, which could be interpreted as a recessionary regime, and only approximately 1.5 when there is no slack, which could be interpreted as an expansionary regime.[11] Finally, government spending shocks in the linear model have some effect on output. Consistent with Blanchard and Perotti (2002) and the literature that followed, the multiplier is about 1 if we continue to use the US average ratio of government purchases to output ratio as before. It is clear, however, that the linear model can considerably underestimate the stimulating power of government spending in recessions and overstate it in expansions.

One may be concerned that we find a strong response of output to government spending shocks in recessions because these shocks systematically occur in periods when an economy starts to recover so that one can find a positive correlation between output growth and government spending shocks. Note that we use professional forecasts to purge predictable movements in government spending. Thus, if there is any systematic pattern in how government spending reacts to the state of the economy, we remove this correlation. We also find no statistically or economically significant correlation between our government spending shocks and measures of the state of a business cycle (e.g., $F(z_{it})$) or changes in that state (e.g., $\Delta F(z_{it})$). In other words, when the economy is in a recession or is starting to move into an expansion, a contractionary government spending shock is as probable as an expansionary government spending shock. Therefore, it is unlikely that our results are driven by a particular timing of government spending shocks.

The first rows of tables 2.1 and 2.2 present estimates of the output response

---

11. There are also studies that find no evidence of time variation in the size of fiscal multipliers (e.g., Pereira and Lopes 2010) or produce estimates that are too imprecise to conclusively establish whether multipliers have cyclical variation (e.g, Barro and Redlick 2012). These studies, however, tend to use data with lower frequencies (e.g., annual data in Barro 2011) or to model variation in multipliers as random walks rather than as a function of the business cycle (e.g., Pereira and Lopes 2010).

Table 2.1 Mean and maximum response to an unanticipated 1 percent government spending shock

	Mean response			Max response		
	Recession $\frac{1}{1+H}\sum_{h=0}^{H}\Phi_{R,h}$ (1)	Expansion $\frac{1}{1+H}\sum_{h=0}^{H}\Phi_{E,h}$ (2)	Linear $\frac{1}{1+H}\sum_{h=0}^{H}\Phi_{Lin,h}$ (3)	Recession $\max_h\Phi_{R,h}$ (4)	Expansion $\max_h\Phi_{E,h}$ (5)	Linear $\max_h\Phi_{Lin,h}$ (6)
Real GDP	0.46*	−0.20	0.14	0.68**	0.04	0.19*
	(0.26)	(0.22)	(0.10)	(0.34)	(0.09)	(0.11)
Real private consumption	0.60***	−0.17	0.22*	0.80***	−0.07	0.34***
	(0.24)	(0.29)	(0.13)	(0.24)	(0.34)	(0.13)
Real private gross capital formation	1.92*	−1.79	0.32	2.76	−0.70	0.48
	(1.17)	(1.10)	(0.43)	(1.96)	(0.45)	(0.49)
Total employment	0.45**	−0.06	0.20**	0.57*	−0.01	0.29***
	(0.20)	(0.18)	(0.09)	(0.33)	(0.28)	(0.12)
Employment in the private sector	0.60***	−0.53***	−0.07	0.88***	−0.09	0.02
	(0.20)	(0.14)	(0.09)	(0.31)	(0.07)	(0.03)
Unemployment rate	−0.14*	0.01	−0.07	−0.21**	−0.06**	−0.09*
	(0.07)	(0.07)	(0.04)	(0.11)	(0.03)	(0.05)
Real compensation rate of the private sector	0.02	0.64*	0.31	0.23*	1.14**	0.56
	(0.26)	(0.36)	(0.22)	(0.12)	(0.55)	(0.34)

Real exports	-0.57	-0.40	-0.45***	-0.01	0.01	-0.26*
	(0.49)	(0.44)	(0.18)	(0.83)	(0.23)	(0.14)
Real imports	0.01	0.33	0.16	0.55	0.67	0.25
	(0.53)	(0.69)	(0.29)	(0.53)	(1.00)	(0.18)
Consumer price index	-0.12	0.07	-0.02	0.06	0.24***	0.04
	(0.18)	(0.20)	(0.09)	(0.25)	(0.08)	(0.13)
GDP deflator	0.05	0.16	0.11	0.47	0.38	0.21
	(0.19)	(0.24)	(0.12)	(0.32)	(0.23)	(0.17)
Government receipts	0.26	-0.45	-0.54*	0.61	0.08	-0.19
	(0.78)	(0.64)	(0.29)	(0.80)	(1.21)	(0.16)
Memorandum						
Real GDP (no control for professional forecasts)	0.31	-0.20	-0.02	0.43	0.06	0.12***
	(0.33)	(0.27)	(0.11)	(0.38)	(0.08)	(0.05)

Notes: The table reports percent responses of variables indicated in the left column. The estimated specification is given by equations (5) and (5′). For unemployment, columns (4) through (6) show the minimal response. Mean and maximum responses are calculated over three years. Government receipts are nominal. Robust standard errors are reported in parentheses.

***Significant at the 1 percent level.

**Significant at the 5 percent level.

*Significant at the 10 percent level.

Table 2.2   Mean and maximum response to an unanticipated 1 percent government spending shock, control for year fixed effects

	Mean response			Max response		
	Recession $\frac{1}{1+H}\sum_{h=0}^{H}\Phi_{R,h}$ (1)	Expansion $\frac{1}{1+H}\sum_{h=0}^{H}\Phi_{E,h}$ (2)	Linear $\frac{1}{1+H}\sum_{h=0}^{H}\Phi_{Lin,h}$ (3)	Recession $\max_h \Phi_{R,h}$ (4)	Expansion $\max_h \Phi_{E,h}$ (5)	Linear $\max_h \Phi_{Lin,h}$ (6)
	0.43*	−0.19	0.18*	0.67**	0.05	0.26**
	(0.26)	(0.19)	(0.10)	(0.32)	(0.09)	(0.11)
Real private consumption	0.60***	−0.24	0.24**	0.78***	−0.13	0.37***
	(0.22)	(0.26)	(0.12)	(0.23)	(0.15)	(0.11)
Real private gross capital formation	1.63*	−2.05**	0.09	2.27	−0.89**	0.26
	(0.90)	(0.93)	(0.48)	(1.54)	(0.42)	(0.54)
Total employment	0.39**	−0.16	0.15	0.46	−0.03	0.18*
	(0.19)	(0.18)	(0.10)	(0.32)	(0.05)	(0.09)
Employment in the private sector	0.33**	−0.53***	−0.05	0.48**	−0.07	0.06
	(0.15)	(0.14)	(0.10)	(0.24)	(0.06)	(0.06)
Unemployment rate	−0.12*	0.06	−0.04	−0.19**	−0.02	−0.07**
	(0.07)	(0.07)	(0.04)	(0.10)	(0.05)	(0.03)
Real compensation rate of the private sector	−0.13	0.56*	0.23	0.13	0.92*	0.36
	(0.32)	(0.32)	(0.21)	(0.13)	(0.54)	(0.35)

Real exports	-0.04	-0.39	-0.15	0.67	0.04	-0.04
	(0.34)	(0.28)	(0.16)	(0.61)	(0.66)	(0.24)
Real imports	0.62	0.01	0.40**	0.88*	0.41	0.56**
	(0.47)	(0.53)	(0.21)	(0.50)	(0.56)	(0.26)
Consumer price index	-0.06	-0.01	-0.02	0.07	0.18***	0.02
	(0.16)	(0.17)	(0.08)	(0.20)	(0.06)	(0.12)
GDP deflator	-0.00	0.12	0.08	0.33	0.35	0.13
	(0.18)	(0.23)	(0.12)	(0.33)	(0.23)	(0.15)
Government receipts	-0.08	-0.51	-0.56***	0.30	-0.09	-0.14
	(0.48)	(0.36)	(0.24)	(0.51)	(0.68)	(0.17)
Memorandum						
Real GDP (no control for professional forecasts)	0.27	-0.05	0.10	0.48	0.10	0.16***
	(0.32)	(0.24)	(0.08)	(0.38)	(0.44)	(0.05)

Notes: The table reports percent responses of variables indicated in the left column. The estimated specification is given by equations (5) and (5'). For un-employment, columns (4) through (6) show the minimal response. Mean and maximum responses are calculated over three years. Robust standard errors are reported in parentheses.

***Significant at the 1 percent level.
**Significant at the 5 percent level.
*Significant at the 10 percent level.

to government spending shocks over the three-year horizon. The tables report two statistics: the mean response computed as $\sum_{h=0}^{H} Y_h/(1 + H)$, and the maximum response computed as $\max_{h=0,\ldots,H} Y_h$ with $H = 5$, which corresponds to three years. The last rows of the tables show the estimates of the output response when we use VAR residuals rather than forecast errors of professional forecasts as a measure of government spending shocks. Although the difference between the estimates in the first and last rows is not statistically different from zero, the point estimates based on VAR residuals are consistently lower by 0.1 to 0.2 (or about 50 cents to a dollar if we use the ratio of output to government spending in the US) in recessionary periods than the point estimates based on the forecast errors of professional forecasters. Thus, controlling for predictable movements in government spending raises the size of the output responses, which is consistent with the theoretical implications of how output should respond to anticipated and unanticipated changes in government spending.

These differential responses of output naturally raise the questions about the channels of amplification and propagation of government spending shocks through the economies. To get a sense of the basic mechanisms behind these responses, we examine in tables 2.1 and 2.2 and figure 2.4, which corresponds to table 2.1, the responses of various macroeconomic variables to government spending shocks.

Panel B of figure 2.4 shows that private consumption appears to be crowded out in expansions and to be stimulated in recessions by government spending shocks. If we take the ratio of private consumption to government spending for the United States (≈ 3.5), a dollar increase in government spending in recessions can increase consumption up to $2.8 with a 90 percent confidence interval of (1.4, 4.2). Although some may consider this multiplier as too large to be plausible, note that it applies to a very deep recession and that the average response over three years is about $2. Also observe that the linear model predicts that the maximum response of consumption to a dollar increase in government spending would be approximately $1, which is not small economically but in statistical terms is marginally significantly different from zero. Although we do not have data to explore further the sources of these consumption multipliers, Bachmann and Sims (2012) argue that an important ingredient for stimulating consumption in recessions is the response of consumer confidence to government spending shocks. Bachmann and Sims note that government spending shocks may have pure sentiment effects (i.e., one can think of "animal spirits" shifted by changes in government spending) and news effects when changes in government spending provide signals about future changes in output and productivity. In the US context, Bachmann and Sims find that it is the latter effect that stimulates confidence and hence consumption.

The countercyclical pattern of crowding-out and stimulatory effects of government spending are particularly apparent in the responses of private investment (panel C). Over three years, a dollar increase in government spending increases investment in recessions by approximately \$1.5 and decreases investment in expansions by approximately \$1.4 if we use the ratio of private investment to government spending in the United States (≈ 0.8). In contrast, the linear model would predict that investment does not respond to government spending shocks. Thus, imposing the same responses in recessions and expansions can mask a great deal of heterogeneity in responses over the business cycle.

Panels D, E, and F show the responses of total employment, employment in the private sector, and the unemployment rate. In the recessionary regime, increased government spending leads to more total employment. This increase in employment comes to a large extent from the increase in private sector employment. For example, after 2.5 years, total employment increases by 0.5 percent while private employment increases by 0.9 percent in response to a 1 percent increase in government spending, given that the economy is in a recession. Consistent with the employment responses, the unemployment rate shrinks after a government spending shock in a recession. On the other hand, the response of employment (or the unemployment rate) to a government spending shock in an expansion is anemic at best: it is generally close to zero and not statistically different from zero.

To have a better sense of what the percentage changes mean in terms of jobs, we can use the ratio of private employment to real government spending for the United States (≈ 49 thousands/billion) to find that a one billion dollar increase in government spending creates approximately 44,000 jobs; the 90 percent confidence interval is fairly wide and ranges from 2,000 to 88,000 jobs per a billion dollar increase in government spending. One can also interpret this magnitude as stating that it takes about \$23,000 to create a job in a recession. Although it is hard to come by a comparable estimate of employment multipliers during recessions in the literature, a few recent studies use the state- or county-level variation in government spending due to fiscal stimulus in the United States during the 2009 to 2010 period to estimate how many jobs were saved or created due to the fiscal stimulus. For example, Wilson (2012) reports that a billion-dollar increase in government spending raises employment by about 25,000 jobs, with a standard error of 9,000 jobs; that is, an incremental job costs \$39,200, with the 90 percent confidence interval ranging between \$25,000 and \$96,000. Chodorow-Reich et al. (2012) estimate that a \$100,000 increase in spending increases employment by about 3.5 jobs, with a standard error of 1.7 jobs or, alternatively, an additional job costs approximately \$28,000. Thus, our estimates of employment multipliers in a recession are broadly in line with alternative estimates in this literature.[12]

---

12. It should be kept in mind that these other recent estimates are based on cross-section variation and therefore cannot take into account the possible positive or negative spillovers that spending in one state might have on employment changes in another state.

We can get further insight into the workings of the labor market by examining the responses of real wages in expansions and recessions (panel G). We find that real wages remain largely unchanged in response to government spending shocks when the economy is in a recession. In contrast, government spending shocks appear to spur an increase in real wages in the expansionary regime. These results, taken together with the responses of employment, suggest that government spending shocks are probably absorbed into higher wages in expansions and into higher employment in recessions, which is consistent with the differences in our output multipliers across regimes.

Panels H and I show the responses of real exports and real imports. By and large, we find only weak reactions of these variables to government spending shocks. Only the contemporaneous response of exports (negative) and imports (positive) are marginally significant in the recessionary regime. The pattern of the contemporaneous responses is consistent with short-term appreciation of the domestic currency, which could in turn be triggered by an increase in interest rates caused by a strengthening economy and/or the response of the monetary authorities to counteract spending shocks.

Finally, panels J and K show the response of the price level as measured by the CPI and GDP deflator, respectively. Generally, government spending shocks lead to inflationary contemporaneous responses in expansions and deflationary responses in recessions. At the longer horizons we cannot reject the null that the response of the price level is zero in either of the regimes. These responses are largely consistent with the idea that prices may be relatively inflexible in the short run and most of the adjustment occurs via quantities.

2.4.4   Robustness and Sensitivity Analysis

In the baseline formulation of the empirical model, we use a moving average of the output growth rate to measure the state of the business cycle in a given economy. The key advantage of using this variable is that the growth rate of output is a coincident indicator. However, Keynesian theories rely on the notion of slack as a stock variable (e.g., how many workers are unemployed) rather than a flow variable (e.g., output growth rate or how many workers are hired or fired). In other words, it may be important to distinguish between recessions and slumps. Since the moving average is computed over 1.5 years and thus is cumulative, it should to some extent capture the output gap and thus the degree of slack in the economy, but one may want to verify that using more direct measures of slack yields similar results.

Table 2.3 reports estimates of the output response to government spending shocks when we use alternative indicators of slack: (a) the output gap computed as the deviation of log output from a trend; (b) the detrended unemployment rate; (c) the detrended log employment level; (d) the detrended change in the unemployment rate; and (e) the detrended change in employment. In all cases, we detrend series using the Hodrick-Prescott filter with

Table 2.3   **Alternative measures of business cycle conditions**

Variable measuring the state of the business cycle	Mean response		Max response	
	Recession $\frac{1}{1+H}\sum_{h=0}^{H}\Phi_{R,h}$ (1)	Expansion $\frac{1}{1+H}\sum_{h=0}^{H}\Phi_{E,h}$ (2)	Recession $\max_h \Phi_{R,h}$ (3)	Expansion $\max_h \Phi_{E,h}$ (4)
	A. Country fixed effects			
Recession vs. expansion				
6 quarter moving average of GDP growth rate (baseline)	0.46*	−0.20	0.68**	0.04
	(0.26)	(0.22)	(0.34)	(0.09)
Change in unemployment rate	1.03**	−0.88**	1.27**	−0.48*
	(0.47)	(0.45)	(0.58)	(0.27)
Growth rate of employment	0.92*	−0.74	1.15**	−0.34
	(0.51)	(0.48)	(0.59)	(0.28)
Slump vs. boom				
Output gap	0.45	−0.05	0.61	0.13
	(0.32)	(0.23)	(0.40)	(0.37)
Unemployment rate	0.41	−0.10	0.52**	0.06
	(0.25)	(0.23)	(0.26)	(0.35)
Employment gap	0.36	−0.09	0.50***	0.01
	(0.24)	(0.16)	(0.20)	(0.33)
	B. Country and time fixed effects			
Recession vs. Expansion				
6 quarter moving average of GDP growth rate (baseline)	0.43*	−0.19	0.67**	0.05
	(0.26)	(0.19)	(0.32)	(0.09)
Change in unemployment rate	0.75**	−0.50	0.87**	−0.27
	(0.37)	(0.32)	(0.43)	(0.27)
Growth rate of employment	0.48	−0.24	0.86**	0.11
	(0.46)	(0.40)	(0.44)	(0.58)
Slump vs. Boom				
Output gap	0.48*	−0.04	0.64**	0.10
	(0.27)	(0.18)	(0.30)	(0.21)
Unemployment rate	0.50**	−0.11	0.64***	0.05
	(0.22)	(0.15)	(0.27)	(0.10)
Employment gap	0.35*	−0.00	0.46***	0.12
	(0.20)	(0.16)	(0.18)	(0.18)

Notes: The table reports estimates of equation (5) for alternative choices of the variable z, which captures the state of the business cycle. "Output gap" and "Employment gap" are computed as deviation from Hodrick-Prescott filter with smoothing parameters $\lambda = 10{,}000$. "Change in unemployment rate" and "Growth rate of employment" are detrended from the Hodrick-Prescott filter with smoothing parameters $\lambda = 10{,}000$. All data are semiannual. Mean and maximum responses are calculated over three years. Robust standard errors are reported in parentheses.

***Significant at the 1 percent level.

**Significant at the 5 percent level.

*Significant at the 10 percent level.

smoothing parameter $\lambda = 10{,}000$. While the first three measures are explicitly stock variables (i.e., slumps), the last two measures are aimed to capture acceleration in an economy (i.e., recessions). Irrespective of which measure we use, the response in a recession or slump is larger than the response in an expansion or boom. Furthermore, we observe that the response tends to be somewhat stronger when we focus on the acceleration measures of the business cycle. In other words, the response of output seems to be larger when an economy starts to contract than when it reaches a bottom or stays in a slump. We conclude that cyclical variation in the output responses is robust across a variety of variables measuring the state of business cycle.

Since we have significant variation in macroeconomic characteristics across countries and time, we can explore how some key characteristics are correlated with the size of government spending multipliers. We will examine four characteristics: the level of government debt (as a percent of GDP), openness to trade (mean tariff), an index of the strength of collective relations laws, and an index of labor market regulations. Our approach will be based on the following modification of equation (5):

$$(6) \quad Y_{i,t+h} = \alpha_{ih} + F(z_{i,t-1})\Pi_{R,h}(L)Y_{i,t-1} + (1 - F(z_{i,t-1}))\Pi_{E,h}(L)Y_{i,t-1}$$

$$+ F(z_{i,t-1})\Psi_{R,h}(L)G_{i,t-1} + (1 - F(z_{i,t-1}))\Psi_{E,h}(L)G_{i,t-1}$$

$$+ F(z_{i,t-1})\Phi_{R,h}FE_{it}^{G} + (1 - F(z_{i,t-1}))\Phi_{E,h}FE_{it}^{G}$$

$$+ F(z_{i,t-1})\tilde{\Phi}_{R,h}FE_{it}^{G}Q_{it} + (1 - F(z_{i,t-1}))\tilde{\Phi}_{E,h}FE_{it}^{G}Q_{it} + \mu Q_{it} + u_{it},$$

where Q_{it} is a macroeconomic dimension we would like to study. Coefficients $\Phi_{R,h}$ and $\Phi_{E,h}$ describe the response of Y to a government spending shock FE_{it}^{G} when $Q_{it} = 0$ (e.g., the debt-GDP ratio is zero), while $(\Phi_{R,h} + \tilde{\Phi}_{R,h})$ and $(\Phi_{E,h} + \tilde{\Phi}_{E,h})$ describe the response of Y to a government spending shock FE_{it}^{G} when $Q_{it} = 1$ (e.g., the debt-GDP ratio is 1). Likewise, we estimate the linear analogue of specification (6) as follows:

$$(6') \quad Y_{i,t+h} = \alpha_{ih} + \Pi_{Lin,h}(L)Y_{i,t-1} + \Psi_{Lin,h}(L)G_{i,t-1} + \Phi_{Lin,h}FE_{it}^{G}$$

$$+ \tilde{\Phi}_{Lin,h}FE_{it}^{G}Q_{it} + \mu Q_{it} + u_{it}.$$

Table 2.4 reports mean responses for $\Phi_{R,h}$, $\Phi_{E,h}$, $\Phi_{Lin,h}$ and $(\Phi_{R,h} + \tilde{\Phi}_{R,h})$, $(\Phi_{E,h} + \tilde{\Phi}_{E,h})$, and $(\Phi_{Lin,h} + \tilde{\Phi}_{Lin,h})$ over the three-year horizon.[13]

Consistent with Perotti (1999) and others, we find that large government debt reduces the response of output to government spending shocks. Specifically, when the level of debt is equal to zero and an economy is in a deep recession, a 1 percent increase in government spending raises output by approximately 0.73 percent over the course of three years. In contrast, if the level of debt is 100 percent of GDP, then the response of output in a deep recession is just 0.09 percent. Furthermore, the cyclical variation in

---

13. We find similar results when all characteristics are included simultaneously.

Table 2.4   Variation in the mean response of output across countries

Macroeconomic characteristic	Response when characteristic is equal to zero percent			Response when characteristic is equal to 100 percent		
	Recession $\sum_{h=0}^{H}\frac{\Phi_{R,h}}{1+H}$ (1)	Expansion $\sum_{h=0}^{H}\frac{\Phi_{E,h}}{1+H}$ (2)	Linear $\sum_{h=0}^{H}\frac{\Phi_{Lin,h}}{1+H}$ (3)	Recession $\sum_{h=0}^{H}\frac{\Phi_{R,h}+\phi_{R,h}}{1+H}$ (4)	Expansion $\sum_{h=0}^{H}\frac{\Phi_{E,h}+\phi_{E,h}}{1+H}$ (5)	Linear $\sum_{h=0}^{H}\frac{\Phi_{Lin,h}+\phi_{Lin,h}}{1+H}$ (6)
Country fixed effects						
Level of government debt	0.84*** (0.32)	−0.58 (0.38)	0.22 (0.17)	0.05 (0.35)	0.26 (0.36)	0.04 (0.16)
Openness to trade	1.13** (0.51)	−0.34 (0.39)	0.04 (0.24)	0.97** (0.44)	−0.32 (0.35)	0.04 (0.21)
Protection of collective relations	−0.61 (0.59)	−0.33 (0.63)	−0.51** (0.23)	2.28*** (0.79)	−0.37 (0.64)	0.91** (0.41)
Labor market regulation	0.09 (0.47)	0.18 (0.44)	0.17 (0.18)	1.34** (0.59)	−0.99*** (0.36)	−0.01 (0.36)
Country and time fixed effects						
Level of government debt	0.90*** (0.34)	−0.61* (0.34)	0.24 (0.16)	−0.30 (0.30)	0.42 (0.33)	0.08 (0.15)
Openness to trade	1.10** (0.54)	−0.66* (0.38)	0.12 (0.20)	0.96** (0.45)	−0.58* (0.34)	0.11 (0.17)
Protection of collective relations	−0.20 (0.49)	−0.72 (0.46)	−0.43*** (0.13)	1.65** (0.74)	0.11 (0.57)	0.93*** (0.35)
Labor market regulation	−0.08 (0.35)	0.26 (0.30)	0.14 (0.20)	1.49*** (0.51)	−1.05*** (0.39)	0.16 (0.32)

Notes: The table reports estimates of equations (6) and (6'). "Level of government debt" is measured as percent of GDP (source: OECD). "Openness to trade" is the mean tariff measured in percent of value of traded goods (source: World Bank). "Protection of collective relations" is an index ranging from zero (weak protection of collective labor relations) to one (high protection). This index is from Botero et al. (2004). "Labor market regulation" is an index ranging from zero (low regulation) to one (high regulation). This index is also from Botero et al. (2004). Robust standard errors are reported in parentheses.

***Significant at the 1 percent level.

**Significant at the 5 percent level.

*Significant at the 10 percent level.

the size of the output multiplier vanishes as the level of debt approaches 100 percent.

Ilzetzki, Mendoza, and Végh (2010) report that the government spending multiplier is larger in closed economies than in open economies, which is consistent with textbook macroeconomics. Thus, one may have predicted that closed economies are more likely to have larger multipliers than open economies, but we do not find evidence for this prediction. We find that the size of tariffs does not appear to be correlated with the size of the government spending multipliers.[14] Two observations may help to reconcile this somewhat surprising result. First, the strength of the government spending multiplier depends on the exchange rate regime (floating vs. fixed, capital controls, etc.) in a country. Thus, one may need a more sophisticated set of controls to differentiate how various aspects of international flows of goods and capital influence the size of the multiplier. Second, small open economies with low tariffs (e.g., Belgium) are also more likely to run large fiscal deficits and to accumulate large government debt. To the extent high levels of government debt decrease the size of the fiscal multipliers, one may find that open economies have lower multipliers. Indeed, we find (not shown) that controlling for government debt tends to move the variation in the right direction, although it does not resolve the puzzle completely. Thus, a positive correlation between openness and the size of the fiscal multiplier in a recession may be driven by an omitted variable.

One may also expect that a high rigidity of labor markets is likely to lead to more rigid wages and hence amplified responses of output to demand shocks (e.g., Cole and Ohanian 2004; Gorodnichenko, Mendoza, and Tesar 2012). We use two measures of labor market rigidities constructed in Botero et al. (2004). The first is an index of protection of labor relations. This index aggregates various dimensions of union strength such as legislative rights to establish unions, to organize strikes, and to collectively bargain. The second index, which we call "labor market regulation," measures how easy it is to fire/hire workers, to increase/decrease hours of work, and to engage in alternative labor contracts (mainly use temporary and part-time workers). We find that as the rigidity in the labor market rises (i.e., either index increases), the output response in recession increases and the cyclical variation in the fiscal multiplier becomes more pronounced. This pattern is consistent with the view that more rigid labor markets can result in enhanced effectiveness of government spending shocks to stimulate output during a downturn.

Overall, we find that variation in the size of the fiscal multiplier is consistent with basic predictions of macroeconomic theory, although one should be careful in interpreting the results. Some correlations between macroeconomic dimensions and the size of the fiscal multiplier may be driven by

14. We find similar results for alternative measures of openness, for example, (exports + imports)/GDP.

omitted variables. One may also need a more nuanced view on what determines the size of fiscal multipliers.

2.4.5   Discussion

In general, the responses we estimate for key macroeconomic variables are remarkably consistent with the Keynesian view that the size of spending multipliers should vary over the business cycle, with fiscal policy being more effective (i.e., larger multipliers) in recessions than in expansions. Interestingly, Galí, López-Salido, and Vallés (2007) argue that New Keynesian models are typically unable to generate an increase in private consumption after a government spending shock. Furthermore, spending multipliers rarely exceed 1 even in New Keynesian models. In many respects, New Keynesian models are similar to neoclassical models that emphasize crowding out of private consumption by increased government spending. Recently, Woodford (2011) and Christiano, Eichenbaum, and Rebelo (2011) showed theoretically in New Keynesian models that government spending shocks can have large multipliers when the zero lower bound (ZLB) on nominal interest rates is binding. Using high-frequency data on interest, inflation, and exchange rates, Wieland (2011) provides some empirical support for the spending multipliers to exceed 1 when there is a binding ZLB. However, the upper bound on multipliers found by Wieland is typically about 1.5, which is considerably smaller than suggested by the theoretical results of Woodford (2011) and Christiano, Eichenbaum, and Rebelo (2011). Furthermore, binding ZLB episodes during recessions have been very rare in modern history and thus it is hard to extend this argument more generally to recessions.[15]

The discrepancy between the old and new Keynesian views on the effects of government spending shocks is striking. We conjecture that in part this discrepancy stems from the fact that the notion of slack is largely absent from the New Keynesian models. Indeed, despite having some frictions, New Keynesian models effectively impose clearing factor and product markets and thus there is no spare capacity (or slack) in these model economies. In contrast, old Keynesian models emphasized that markets may not clear at all times (and especially in recessions) so that crowding out of private consumption or investment by government spending increases in recession can be minimal.

Another source of the discrepancy is that workhorse macroeconomic models are approximately linear so that there is little, if any, variation in

15. Some observers suggest that one may use the World War II experience to study fiscal multipliers at the zero lower bound. However, as Robert Hall pointed out in a discussion of the present chapter, while nominal interest rates were stable and very low during this period, real interest rates fell dramatically and thus had a large stimulatory effect on the economy. In contrast, the present-day Fed controls inflation tightly and hence greatly limits changes in real interest rates.

marginal effects over the business cycle. One can anticipate that macro-economic models where nonlinearities are more important (e.g., models where net worth and leverage play an important role) are more likely to generate cyclical variation in fiscal multipliers. For example, Canzoneri et al. (2012) develop a theoretical model with financial frictions that lead to countercyclical government spending multipliers.

2.5   Concluding Remarks

During the Great Recession, countries around the world adopted expansionary fiscal policies aimed at counteracting the large negative shocks to their economies. These actions occurred in spite of skepticism among many economists about the potential of fiscal policy to stimulate economic activity. In the United States, at least, the stage for this active course for fiscal policy was already set by earlier policy developments, which showed a marked increase in fiscal policy activism earlier in the decade (Auerbach and Gale 2009).

The results in this chapter and those in our earlier one suggest that fiscal policy activism may indeed be effective at stimulating output during a deep recession, and that the potential negative side effects of fiscal stimulus, such as increased inflation, are also less likely under these circumstances. These empirical results call into question the results from the New Keynesian literature, which suggests that shocks to government spending, even when increasing output, will crowd out private economic activity. While there has been some recent progress in providing a rationale for large multipliers when economies confront a binding zero lower bound on interest rates, our findings apply to more general recessionary conditions, and thus present a challenge for the development of new models that, like the simple traditional Keynesian model, can encompass positive fiscal multipliers for private activity.

Appendix
Additional Tables

Table 2A.1   Mean and maximum response (over one-year horizon) to an unanticipated 1 percent government spending shock

	Mean response			Max response		
	Recession $\sum_{h=0}^{H}\frac{\Phi_{R,h}}{1+H}$ (1)	Expansion $\sum_{h=0}^{H}\frac{\Phi_{E,h}}{1+H}$ (2)	Linear $\sum_{h=0}^{H}\frac{\Phi_{Lin,h}}{1+H}$ (3)	Recession $\max_h \Phi_{R,h}$ (4)	Expansion $\max_h \Phi_{E,h}$ (5)	Linear $\max_h \Phi_{Lin,h}$ (6)
Real GDP	0.35** (0.18)	−0.09 (0.10)	0.14** (0.07)	0.53*** (0.22)	0.04 (0.09)	0.15* (0.08)
Real private consumption	0.62*** (0.22)	−0.18 (0.16)	0.21*** (0.08)	0.80*** (0.24)	−0.14 (0.15)	0.29*** (0.10)
Real private gross capital formation	0.96* (0.52)	−1.06** (0.47)	0.16 (0.30)	1.34** (0.58)	−0.70 (0.45)	0.23 (0.37)
Total employment	0.28*** (0.10)	−0.06 (0.08)	0.11*** (0.04)	0.39*** (0.13)	−0.02 (0.06)	0.15*** (0.06)
Employment in the private sector	0.26** (0.13)	−0.17* (0.09)	0.00 (0.05)	0.35** (0.18)	−0.09 (0.07)	0.02 (0.03)
Unemployment rate	−0.05 (0.04)	−0.04 (0.03)	−0.05** (0.03)	−0.08 (0.06)	−0.06** (0.03)	−0.06* (0.04)
Real compensation rate of the private sector	0.20 (0.18)	0.18 (0.22)	0.14 (0.12)	0.23* (0.12)	0.23 (0.29)	0.15 (0.14)
Real exports	−0.54* (0.31)	−0.28 (0.32)	−0.38** (0.17)	−0.47 (0.44)	0.01 (0.23)	−0.26* (0.14)

(continued)

Table 2A.1   (continued)

	Mean response			Max response		
	Recession $\frac{\sum_{h=0}^{H}\Phi_{R,h}}{1+H}$ (1)	Expansion $\frac{\sum_{h=0}^{H}\Phi_{E,h}}{1+H}$ (2)	Linear $\frac{\sum_{h=0}^{H}\Phi_{Lin,h}}{1+H}$ (3)	Recession $\max_{h}\Phi_{R,h}$ (4)	Expansion $\max_{h}\Phi_{E,h}$ (5)	Linear $\max_{h}\Phi_{Lin,h}$ (6)
Real imports	0.23	0.18	0.19	0.55	0.41	0.25
	(0.56)	(0.46)	(0.24)	(0.53)	(0.60)	(0.18)
Consumer price index	−0.32***	0.19	−0.05	−0.30*	0.24***	−0.03
	(0.13)	(0.12)	(0.05)	(0.18)	(0.08)	(0.04)
GDP deflator	−0.33**	0.37**	0.04	−0.30	0.38	0.06
	(0.16)	(0.19)	(0.09)	(0.20)	(0.23)	(0.11)
Government receipts	0.31	−0.41	−0.37*	0.47	−0.15	−0.19
	(0.45)	(0.35)	(0.20)	(0.62)	(0.26)	(0.16)

Notes: The table reports percent responses of variables indicated in the left column. The estimated specification is given by equation (5). For unemployment, columns (4) through (6) show the minimal response. Mean and maximum responses are calculated over three years. Government receipts are nominal. Robust standard errors are reported in parentheses.

***Significant at the 1 percent level.

**Significant at the 5 percent level.

*Significant at the 10 percent level.

Table 2A.2   Mean and maximum response (over one-year horizon) to an unanticipated 1 percent government spending shock, control for year fixed effects

	Mean response			Max response		
	Recession $\sum_{h=0}^{H}\frac{\Phi_{R,h}}{1+H}$ (1)	Expansion $\sum_{h=0}^{H}\frac{\Phi_{E,h}}{1+H}$ (2)	Linear $\sum_{h=0}^{H}\frac{\Phi_{Lin,h}}{1+H}$ (3)	Recession $\max_h \Phi_{R,h}$ (4)	Expansion $\max_h \Phi_{E,h}$ (5)	Linear $\max_h \Phi_{Lin,h}$ (6)
Real GDP	0.33*	−0.05	0.19***	0.48**	0.05	0.23***
	(0.18)	(0.09)	(0.07)	(0.22)	(0.09)	(0.09)
Real private consumption	0.60***	−0.18	0.24***	0.78***	−0.13	0.33***
	(0.22)	(0.15)	(0.08)	(0.23)	(0.15)	(0.09)
Real private gross capital formation	0.95**	−1.22***	0.11	1.18**	−0.89**	0.13
	(0.46)	(0.43)	(0.29)	(0.51)	(0.42)	(0.36)
Total employment	0.26***	−0.07	0.11***	0.36***	−0.03	0.15***
	(0.09)	(0.08)	(0.04)	(0.13)	(0.05)	(0.06)
Employment in the private sector	0.17	−0.13	0.06	0.20	−0.07	0.06
	(0.11)	(0.09)	(0.04)	(0.16)	(0.06)	(0.06)
Unemployment rate	−0.04	−0.04	−0.06**	−0.07	−0.02	−0.07**
	(0.05)	(0.03)	(0.03)	(0.06)	(0.05)	(0.03)
Real compensation rate of the private sector	0.09	0.22	0.15	0.13	0.26	0.15
	(0.18)	(0.19)	(0.11)	(0.13)	(0.25)	(0.10)
Real exports	−0.17	−0.24	−0.12	0.06	−0.03	−0.11
	(0.25)	(0.20)	(0.13)	(0.34)	(0.19)	(0.17)

Table 2A.2   (continued)

	Mean response			Max response		
	Recession $\sum_{h=0}^{H}\frac{\Phi_{R,h}}{1+H}$ (1)	Expansion $\sum_{h=0}^{H}\frac{\Phi_{E,h}}{1+H}$ (2)	Linear $\sum_{h=0}^{H}\frac{\Phi_{Lin,h}}{1+H}$ (3)	Recession $\max_{h}\Phi_{R,h}$ (4)	Expansion $\max_{h}\Phi_{E,h}$ (5)	Linear $\max_{h}\Phi_{Lin,h}$ (6)
Real imports	0.55	0.16	0.43***	0.73	0.41	0.48**
	(0.55)	(0.46)	(0.17)	(0.53)	(0.56)	(0.21)
Consumer price index	−0.22**	0.13	−0.04	−0.19	0.18***	−0.03
	(0.10)	(0.09)	(0.04)	(0.14)	(0.06)	(0.04)
GDP deflator	−0.32**	0.35*	0.03	−0.29	0.35	0.05
	(0.14)	(0.19)	(0.09)	(0.18)	(0.23)	(0.10)
Government receipts	0.25	−0.43	−0.30	0.30	−0.22	−0.14
	(0.42)	(0.28)	(0.20)	(0.51)	(0.27)	(0.17)

Notes: The table reports percent responses of variables indicated in the left column. The estimated specification is given by equation (5). For unemployment, columns (4) through (6) show the minimal response. Mean and maximum responses are calculated over three years. Robust standard errors are reported in parentheses.

***Significant at the 1 percent level.
**Significant at the 5 percent level.
*Significant at the 10 percent level.

References

Auerbach, Alan J., and William G. Gale. 2009. "Activist Fiscal Policy to Stabilize Economic Activity." Paper presented at the Federal Reserve Bank of Kansas City Conference on Financial Stability and Macroeconomic Policy. Jackson Hole, WY, August 20–22.

Auerbach, Alan J., and Yuriy Gorodnichenko. 2012. "Measuring the Output Responses to Fiscal Policy." *American Economic Journal: Economic Policy* 4 (2): 1–27.

Bachmann, Ruediger, and Eric Sims. 2012. "Confidence and the Transmission of Government Spending Shocks." *Journal of Monetary Economics* 59 (3): 235–49.

Barro, Robert, and Charles Redlick. 2012. "Macroeconomic Effects of Government Purchases and Taxes." Forthcoming in *Quarterly Journal of Economics*.

Blanchard, Olivier, and Roberto Perotti. 2002. "An Empirical Characterization of the Dynamic Effects of Changes in Government Spending and Taxes on Output." *Quarterly Journal of Economics* 117 (4): 1329–68.

Botero, Juan, Simeon Djankov, Rafael La Porta, Florencio Lopez-de-Silanes, and Andrei Shleifer. 2004. "The Regulation of Labor." *Quarterly Journal of Economics* 119 (4): 1339–82.

Canzoneri, Matthew, Fabrice Collard, Harris Dellas, and Behzad Diba. 2012. "Fiscal Multipliers in Recessions." Diskussionsschriften dp1204. Universitaet Bern, Departement, Volkswirtschaft.

Chodorow-Reich, Gabriel, Laura Feiveson, Zachary Liscow, and William Woolston. 2012. "Does State Fiscal Relief during Recessions Increase Employment? Evidence from the American Recovery and Reinvestment Act." *American Economic Journal: Economic Policy* 4 (3): 118–45.

Christiano, Lawrence, Martin Eichenbaum, and Sergio Rebelo. 2011. "When is the Government Spending Multiplier Large?" *Journal of Political Economy* 119 (1): 78–121.

Cole, Harold, and Lee Ohanian. 2004. "New Deal Policies and the Persistence of the Great Depression: A General Equilibrium Analysis." *Journal of Political Economy* 112 (4): 779–816.

Driscoll, J. C., and A. C. Kraay. 1998. "Consistent Covariance Matrix Estimation with Spatially Dependent Panel Data." *Review of Economics and Statistics* 80 (4): 549–60.

Galí, Jordi, J. David López-Salido, and Javier Vallés. 2007. "Understanding the Effects of Government Spending on Consumption." *Journal of the European Economic Association* 5 (1): 227–70.

Gordon, Robert J., and Robert Krenn. 2010. "The End of the Great Depression 1939–41: Policy Contributions and Fiscal Multipliers." NBER Working Paper no. 16380. Cambridge, MA: National Bureau of Economic Research, September.

Gorodnichenko, Yuriy, Enrique Mendoza, and Linda Tesar. 2012. "The Finnish Great Depression: From Russia with Love." *American Economic Review* 102 (4): 1619–44.

Granger, Clive W. J., and Timo Teräsvirta. 1993. *Modelling Nonlinear Economic Relationships.* New York: Oxford University Press.

Hall, Robert E. 2009. "By How Much Does GDP Rise if the Government Buys More Output?" *Brookings Papers on Economic Activity* 2009 (2): 183–231. Washington, DC: Brookings Institution.

Ilzetzki, Ethan, Enrique G. Mendoza, and Carlos A. Végh. 2010. "How Big (Small?) Are Fiscal Multipliers?" NBER Working Paper no. 16479. Cambridge, MA: National Bureau of Economic Research, October.

Jorda, Oscar. 2005. "Estimation and Inference of Impulse Responses by Local Projections." *American Economic Review* 95 (1): 161–82.

Lenain, Patrick. 2002. "What is the Track Record of OECD Economic Projections?" Paris: OECD.

Pereira, Manuel Coutinho, and Artur Silva Lopes. 2010. "Time-Varying Fiscal Policy in the US." Working Papers w201021, Banco de Portugal, Economics and Research Department.

Perotti, Roberto. 1999. "Fiscal Policy in Good Times and Bad." *Quarterly Journal of Economics* 114 (4): 1399–436.

Ramey, Valerie A. 2011. "Identifying Government Spending Shocks: It's All in the Timing." *Quarterly Journal of Economics* 126 (1): 1–50.

Shoag, Daniel. 2010. "The Impact of Government Spending Shocks: Evidence on the Multiplier from State Pension Plan Returns." Unpublished Manuscript. Harvard University.

Stock, James, and Mark Watson. 2007. "Why Has US Inflation Become Harder to Forecast?" *Journal of Money, Banking and Credit* 39 (1): 3–33.

Vogel, Lukas. 2007. "How Do the OECD Growth Projections for the G7 Economies Perform? A Post-Mortem." OECD Working Paper no. 573. Paris: OECD.

Wieland, Johannes. 2011. "Fiscal Multipliers in the Liquidity Trap: International Theory and Evidence." Unpublished Manuscript. University of California, Berkeley.

Wilson, Daniel J. 2012. "Fiscal Spending Multipliers: Evidence from the 2009 American Recovery and Reinvestment Act." *American Economic Journal: Economic Policy* 4 (3): 251–82.

Woodford, Michael. 2011. "Simple Analytics of the Government Expenditure Multiplier." *American Economic Journal: Macroeconomics* 3 (1): 1–35.

Comment   Robert E. Hall

Auerbach and Gorodnichenko provide impressive evidence about what happens in a panel of advanced economies when government purchases rise or fall. They find that changes in purchases in a weak economy have large effects in the same direction on output and employment. Their point estimate is that one added dollar of government purchases results in about $3.50 of added GDP when the economy is weak, with a 90 percent confidence interval running from 0.6 to 6.3. By contrast, in times of a strong economy, added government purchases *reduce* GDP, according to the point estimate. The confidence interval for that finding includes moderate positive values.

Auerbach and Gorodnichenko (henceforth, AG) identify weak and strong economies in two ways. One is the eighteen-month change in the departure of an activity measure (real GDP, unemployment, and others) from its slow-

Robert E. Hall is the Robert and Carole McNeil Joint Hoover Senior Fellow and professor of economics at Stanford University, and a research associate and director of the Economic Fluctuations and Growth Program at the National Bureau of Economic Research.

For acknowledgments, sources of research support, and disclosure of the author's material financial relationships, if any, please see http://www.nber.org/chapters/c12635.ack.

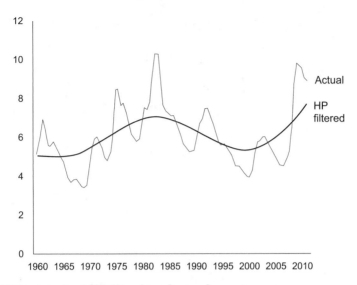

Fig. 2C.1   Actual and HP-filtered trend unemployment

moving trend. The second is the departure from trend itself. They think of these as rate-of-change and level measures, respectively. They measure the trend using the Hodrick-Prescott filter with a smoothing parameter of 10,000, well above the amount of smoothing conventionally used for semi-annual data. That said, it turns out that they remove quite a bit of the cyclical movement of the activity variables. Figure 2C.1 shows semiannual data for US unemployment over the period 1960 through 2011, along with its HP trend. According to the figure, unemployment only barely exceeded trend following the 2001 recession. More significantly, most of the high level of unemployment in late 2011 was the result of a high trend value. The signal from the variable that AG use is that the slump following the financial crisis of 2008 was practically over at that time, despite an unemployment rate of 8.9 percent. The HP filter is least reliable at the beginning and end of the data. Here, it plainly overstates the movement of the trend over the past five years.

One of the puzzles in the chapter is the similarity of the results for the rate-of-change specification of the variable z that signals the strength of the economy—the authors' favored one—and the alternative level specification. If the detrended activity variable were a sine wave and the rate of change not taken over an extended period (so it would be a cosine wave), the two measures would be out of phase and have a correlation of zero. One quarter of the time, both would be signaling strength (the second half of an expansion); one quarter of the time, activity would be positive but rate of change negative (the first half of a contraction); one quarter of the time, both would be signaling weakness (the second half of a contraction); and one quarter

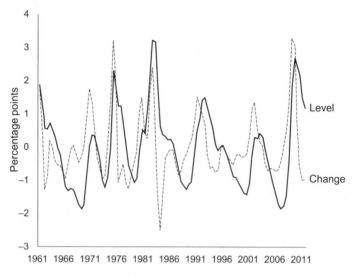

Fig. 2C.2   Change and level variables constructed from US unemployment, 1960–2011

of the time, activity would be negative but rate of change positive (the first half of an expansion).

AG's use of an eighteen-month period to measure growth radically changes the relation between the two measures. The fact that activity is not a pure sine wave does as well. Figure 2C.2 shows that the two measures used in the chapter are actually quite similar. As the authors note, the rate-of-change measure leads the level measure, but not by much, and otherwise the two variables are sending the same signal about the strength of the economy most of the time. The single big exception was the rapid improvement following the 1981 recession, when unemployment was high but falling rapidly.

The figure makes it clear that both measures rise rapidly at the beginning of a recession and then return to normal well before unemployment falls back to normal. The findings would not support the proposition that purchases policy would be unusually effective in, say, early 2012, four years after the beginning of the contraction at the end of 2007. Interestingly, Stock and Watson (2010) find that inflation responds in the same way to slack as does the purchases multiplier. Their preferred measure of slack in the economy for a simple Phillips curve is the difference between unemployment and its minimum over the prior three years, a variable that looks a lot like the ones in figure 2C.2.

I conclude that the chapter uncovers a proposition of great importance in macroeconomics—that the response to government purchases is substantially greater in weak economies than in strong ones. The finding is a true challenge to current thinking. The first thing to clear away is that the finding has little to do with the current thought that the multiplier is much higher when the interest rate is at its lower bound of zero. The authors do not appear to report the ending date of their sample period, but the sample surely includes only a few years when any country apart from Japan was near the lower bound.

Standard macro models have labor and product supply functions that are close to linear over the range of activity in the OECD post-1960 sample. The simple idea that output and employment are constrained at full employment is not reflected in any modern model that I know of. The cutting edge of general-equilibrium modeling—seen primarily in the dynamic stochastic general equilibrium models (DSGE) popular at central banks around the world—incorporates price and wage stickiness that makes supply quite elastic both above and below full employment, defined as the level of employment that would occur absent any price and wage frictions. A new development in this line of work (see Gertler, Sala, and Trigari 2008) embodies wage frictions in the Diamond-Mortensen-Pissarides framework, so unemployment is an explicit variable in the model. Such a model constrains unemployment to be nonnegative, so with enough expansionary policy, the nonlinearity of the unemployment response will come into play. But the models with this feature are still pretty close to linear around the normal level of unemployment and do not become visibly nonlinear over the range of variation seen in AG's data.

According to current macro thinking, the feature of the economy that controls the government purchases multiplier is not labor or product supply, but rather the response of monetary policy as expressed in the central bank's Taylor rule. The reason that an economy at its zero lower bound has a much higher multiplier is that, with the interest rate fixed at zero, the bank loses its power to offset a fiscal expansion. In normal times, higher government purchases raise inflation and output. The Taylor rule instructs the bank to raise the interest rate on both accounts. The higher rate inhibits activity and offsets a large part of the expansion that would otherwise occur.

Within the framework of current macro models, I conclude that the explanation for the findings of AG's chapter is a Taylor rule with some combination of the following features, all absent from the usual Taylor rule:

- *The response of the interest rate to unemployment is smaller when unemployment is high (nonlinear response).* The notion that the central bank is highly attentive to an overheated economy and raises the interest rate aggressively in that case (but is reluctant to stimulate by cutting the rate when the economy is slack) rings true. For example, commentators are quick to suggest high unemployment arises for "structural" reasons, but rarely suggest that unemployment is low for similar reasons.
- *The coefficient telling how much to raise the interest rate when inflation rises is smaller when unemployment is high.* This response might occur

if the central bank believes that higher inflation is more likely to be transitory in a slack economy than a strong one.

- *The Taylor rule ties the interest rate directly to government purchases; the tie is strong when unemployment is low and weak when it is high (another nonlinear response).* The central bank might behave this way if it believed that supply functions are nonlinear rather than accepting their economists' implicit beliefs that they are linear.

Because econometric identification of policy response functions is notoriously challenging, it will be hard to determine if the Taylor rule based explanations for the findings of this chapter are correct. Maybe we will have to reconsider our views about the linearity of labor and product supply. That would be a wrenching change for many of us macroeconomists.

The authors mention briefly that there is no correlation between government purchases and their measure of the economic activity. They do not pursue the point, but it illustrates a principle that recent US experience demonstrates remarkably: governments do not crank up purchases to cure a slack economy. Hall (2010) reviews the US data on this point. Notwithstanding the highly publicized attempts of the Obama administration, government purchases sagged below their established growth path following the financial crisis in 2008. The same principle applies, on average, among all the advanced economies of the OECD.

AG's chapter gives macroeconomists—especially those pursuing general-equilibrium aggregate models—a lot to chew on. We face a choice between discarding our belief in the near-linearity of product and labor supply, rethinking the Taylor rule, or something else that has escaped me so far. It will be interesting to see how the assimilation of the results of this chapter plays out.

References

Gertler, Mark, Luca Sala, and Antonella Trigari. 2008. "An Estimated Monetary DSGE Model with Unemployment and Staggered Nominal Wage Bargaining." *Journal of Money, Credit and Banking* 40 (8): 1713–64.
Hall, Robert E. 2010. "Fiscal Stimulus." *Daedalus* Fall:83–94.
Stock, James H., and Mark W. Watson. 2010. "Modeling Inflation after the Crisis." NBER Working Paper no. 16488. Cambridge, MA: National Bureau of Economic Research, October.

3

The Household Effects of Government Spending

Francesco Giavazzi and Michael McMahon

3.1 Introduction

This chapter provides new evidence on the effects of fiscal policy by studying (using household-level data) how households respond to a shift in government spending. Evidence based on micro data is interesting for three reasons. First, individual households' data allow us to identify how different groups (defined, for example, by their age, income, occupation, and the state of the labor market where they live) respond to the same shift in fiscal policy. For instance, Ercolani and Pavoni (2012), using Italian micro data, find that the response to shifts in government spending differs depending on the age of the head of household and on where the family lives (Northern or Southern Italy). Thus, if studies using aggregate data find that consumption does not respond to a shift in public spending, it could simply be the result of averaging across households who all respond significantly but with offsetting signs. Moreover, knowing how different groups respond to a shift in fiscal policy allows such shifts to be better designed and targeted to groups or

Francesco Giavazzi is professor of economics at Bocconi University, Italy, and visiting professor of economics at the Massachusetts Institute of Technology. He is a research associate of the National Bureau of Economic Research. Michael McMahon is assistant professor of economics at the University of Warwick and a research associate of the Centre for Economic Performance.

We are especially grateful to Jon Steinsson for making available the military procurement data and to Larry Christiano for his discussion of the chapter. We are grateful also for comments received from other participants at both the preconference held at the NBER Summer Institute in July 2011 and the main conference in Milan in December. Any remaining errors are those of the authors. For acknowledgments, sources of research support, and disclosure of the authors' material financial relationships, if any, please see http://www.nber.org/chapters/c12636.ack.

areas where they might be more effective. Second, if households' responses to fiscal shocks differ depending on their characteristics, multipliers would change over time depending on the composition—for instance, by age, occupation, or geographical distribution—of the population, or by the state of the labor market as pointed out in Auerbach and Gorodnichenko (2011). Finally, to the extent that responses to fiscal shocks differ across households, aggregation bias might impair analyses that use aggregate data (such as the consumption time series from the national accounts) to study households' response to fiscal shocks. The problems raised by the aggregation bias in consumer behavior are well-known, at least since Gorman's (1953) seminal contribution.[1]

We use data from the Panel Study of Income Dynamics (PSID) of US households. Theory suggests that households could respond to a shift in fiscal policy in two ways: by changing their consumption and/or by changing their labor supply. We use the information on hours worked contained in the PSID to estimate the response labor supply to fiscal shocks. To build household consumption, which is not collected in the PSID, we use the methodology proposed by Blundell, Pistaferri, and Preston (2008a, 2008b) that combines Consumer Expenditure Survey (CEX) and PSID data. The combined data set is a panel of up to nearly 3,000 US households covering the period from 1967 to 1992.

There are lively disagreements over the effects of fiscal policy on consumption, on labor supply, and, through changes in labor supply, on real wages, the third variable we analyze. They center on theory—the very different predictions of alternative models—and on the way the empirical evidence is analyzed. Starting from theory, the sharpest difference arises between the predictions of the textbook Keynesian model and of models based upon representative agents who base their choices on optimal intertemporal decisions. The first, as is well-known, predicts that a positive spending shock raises consumption and the real wage, while the model has no predictions for hours worked. Intertemporal models give the opposite result: the negative wealth effect associated with an increase in government spending lowers consumption and (if consumption and leisure are complements) raises hours worked; this in turn lowers the real wage. The sharp difference between these results is attenuated in optimizations models that allow for nominal rigidities, or introduce consumers subject to credit constraints: the latter is one case in which the response of consumption to a spending shock can be positive despite a negative wealth effect.

On the empirical front the main issue is how the shifts in fiscal policy

1. Among many others, Constantinides (1982), Atkeson and Ogaki (1996), and Maliar and Maliar (2003) make the point that household heterogeneity collapses into parameters of the representative agent model, modifying its stochastic properties—a result extended by Lopez (2010) to the case of incomplete markets.

are identified, whether through vector autoregression (VAR) techniques or the "narrative" approach. This chapter does not take a stand on this issue but follows a third path: like Nakamura and Steinsson (2011), the shifts in government spending we analyze are variations in military contracts across states. This allows us to control for time-specific aggregate effects (such as the stance of monetary policy—common across US states—that accompanies a shift in fiscal policy) and instead measure the fiscal shock as the state-specific variation in military contracts driven by aggregate changes in US military spending. Along with Nakamura and Steinsson (2011), this is, as far as we know, the only other attempt at estimating the effects of government spending controlling for time fixed effects; that is, holding constant everything that varied over time and focusing on comparing different states in the same year.

When the effects of government spending shocks are studied, identifying such shocks within a VAR, one typically finds that a positive spending shock raises consumption, hours worked, and real wages (see, e.g., Blanchard and Perotti 2002; Mountford and Uhlig 2009; Perotti 2008; Galí, López-Salido, and Vallés 2007). In contrast, analyses that use narrative spending shocks (typically shifts in defense spending) find that while government spending raises hours, it lowers consumption and the real wage (e.g., Ramey and Shapiro 1998; Edelberg, Eichenbaum, and Fisher 1999; and Burnside, Eichenbaum, and Fisher 2004). The difference between these two sets of results could be due to the fact that narrative shocks, as mentioned before, are mostly shocks to military spending, while shocks identified within a VAR refer to overall government spending. A comparison of the effects of military and nonmilitary spending shocks, both identified with a VAR, is reported in Blanchard and Perotti (2002): they find similar multipliers in both cases, suggesting that the difference seems to be related to the way shocks are identified. Event studies such as Giavazzi and Pagano's (1990) analysis of fiscal consolidations in two European countries and Cullen and Fishback's (2006) analysis of World War II spending on local retail sales in the United States generally show a negative effect of government spending on private consumption. Hall's (1986) analysis using annual data back to 1920 and also identifying government spending shocks through shifts in military spending, finds a slightly negative effect of government purchases on consumption.

The main advantage of our identification strategy—namely, as already mentioned, that it allows us to use time fixed effects and thus control for time-specific aggregate effects such as the stance of monetary policy—comes at the cost of limiting the interpretation of our results. If households expect that the Federal government will satisfy its intertemporal budget constraint by raising taxes on all US households, independently of where they live and other characteristics, the negative wealth effect associated with the increase in spending will be the same for all households and therefore it will be absorbed in the time fixed effect. This means that while we are able to estimate the *direct* effect of spending shocks on consumption, hours worked, and real wages, we may not be capturing the *indirect* effect arising from the reduction in wealth associated with the expectation of higher taxes in the future. As we shall discuss, this problem would be compounded if the negative wealth effect associated with higher government spending were to differ across households—for instance, if higher income households were expected to pay a larger fraction of the future taxes than lower-income households.

In a textbook Keynesian framework there are no wealth effects: thus, within such a framework, what we estimate is indeed the multiplier of shifts in government spending. But if wealth effects are important, what we estimate is the multiplier net of the wealth effect that is captured in the fixed effect. In the extreme case in which government spending is pure waste, the effect we estimate (shutting down the wealth channel) should be exactly zero. Thus the finding of a positive response of consumption to these spending shocks is uninformative on the size of the multiplier because the wealth effect could turn that positive response into a negative one. But the finding—which we do estimate for some groups—of a negative response of consumption indicates that the multiplier is unambiguously negative. The same holds for the response of hours worked: when we find that labor supply increases following a spending shock—as we also do for some groups—we can unambiguously conclude that spending shocks raise hours worked, since the wealth effect works in the same direction.[2]

We find evidence of significant heterogeneity in our estimates of households' responses to positive spending shocks. For instance, lower-income households and households where the head works relatively few hours per week tend to cut consumption: since these estimates shut down the wealth effect, the cut in consumption is unambiguous. Instead, households with relatively higher income and households where the head has a full-time job tend to increase consumption—a result that in this case could be turned around by the presence of a wealth effect. Heads who on average work relatively few hours respond to the spending shock by immediately increasing their hours while those working full time do not adjust hours for many years after the shock. Once again, since the wealth effect goes in the same direction, we can unambiguously conclude that the labor supply response of these groups to a spending shock is positive. We also find significant differences in the effect of military spending shocks across states, depending on the state-specific unemployment rate. In states with relatively low unemployment, spending shocks have insignificant effects on consumption, suggesting that once you allow for wealth effects the multiplier could be negative. On the contrary, we estimate a positive response of consumption in high-unemployment states,

---

2. An alternative way to interpret our results is to think of them as the multiplier associated with an exogenous shift in export demand, as shocks to exports imply no wealth effect.

suggesting that the multiplier could be positive for a small enough wealth effect.

Our estimates suggest that the effects of a shift in government spending might vary over time depending, among other factors, on the state of business cycle and, at a lower frequency, on the composition of employment—for instance, the share of workers on part-time jobs. Shifts in spending could also have important distributional effects that are lost when estimating an aggregate multiplier. Aggregate fiscal multipliers conceal this wealth of information on the effects of shifts in fiscal policy; they also hamper the design of fiscal policies that are appropriate given the state of the business cycle. Finally, the more diverse are the effects of a fiscal impulse across different groups in the population, the more likely is the possibility that an economy-wide multiplier suffers from an aggregation bias (see, e.g., Stoker 2008).

The risks of relying on a single multiplier have recently been emphasized in the literature. Auerbach and Gorodnichenko (2011), using regime-switching models, find large differences in the size of spending multipliers in recessions and expansions, with fiscal policy being considerably more effective in recessions than in expansions. Favero, Giavazzi, and Perego (2011) compare fiscal multipliers across countries and find that they differ depending on the country's degree of openness to international trade, its debt dynamics, and its local fiscal reaction function. Interestingly, such differences concern not only the size of the multiplier, but sometimes also its sign.

We begin section 3.2 by describing our data. Section 3.3 discusses how the fiscal shocks we analyze are identified. Our results are presented in sections 3.4 and 3.5. Section 3.6 concludes.

3.2   Combining Household and State Data

We first detail the data that we use. We discuss the household-level data and in particular the approach to construct consumption data. We then explore the state-level data, especially the military procurement that provides the basis for our fiscal shocks instrument.

3.2.1   Constructing the Data for Individual Consumption, Hours, and Real Wages

In order to construct the panel of individual household data on consumption, we follow the approach of Blundell, Pistaferri, and Preston (2008a). The primary source of data is the PSID, a long-running (since 1968) panel series that includes a large number of socioeconomic characteristics of US households. These include data on income, hours worked,[3] wealth, and taxes, as well as other household characteristics such as family size and levels of

---

3. The 1983 questionnaire asks, "*How many weeks did you work in your main job in 1982? And, on the average, how many hours a week did you work on your main job in 1982?*"

education. However, it does not include data on total household consumption; instead there are measures of household expenditure on food.[4]

The CEX, collected by the Bureau of Labor Statistics (BLS), provides high-quality information on the purchasing habits of US consumers. While these data include numerous household characteristics, they are not collected in the form of a panel; specifically, different households respond in each year of the survey. Nonetheless, Blundell, Pistaferri, and Preston (2008a) impute estimates of both aggregate consumption as well as consumption of nondurables in the PSID using information from the CEX.

Their approach is detailed in their paper and in an unpublished appendix (Blundell, Pistaferri, and Preston 2008b): here we outline their imputation procedure. They estimate a demand function for food consumption (a variable that is available both in the PSID and CEX surveys but was not collected in the 1988 and 1989 surveys) using a total consumption variable (such as nondurable consumption expenditure),[5] a variety of household characteristics, and the relative prices of food and other types of consumption as regressors. They allow this function to have time- and characteristic-varying budget elasticities,[6] and they allow for measurement error in the total consumption variable by instrumenting it with cohort, year, and education-level demeaned hourly wages for the husband and wife. They then invert this consistently estimated demand function to derive the imputed PSID consumption measures.

Before we can make use of these data, they need to be carefully combined and merged to ensure that the timing of the PSID data matches the fiscal data that we discuss later. In particular, the questions used to construct the hours and income variables are retrospective: in the 1983 survey, the household is asked to report their working hours and income for 1982. With this in mind, and as shown in figure 3.1, the responses to the questions reported by the household during their interview in 1983 are recorded as head of household i's income earned and hours worked in 1982; these are denoted $y_{i,82}$ and $h_{i,82}$.

The questions referring to food expenditure, described in note 3, are much less clear in terms of their timing. The questions ask about food expenditure in an average week and we follow Blundell, Pistaferri, and Preston (2008a)

4. Again, using 1983 as a typical year, the question asked is, *"In addition to what you buy with food stamps, how much do you (or anyone else in your family) spend on food that you use at home? How much do you spend on that food in an average week? Do you have any food delivered to the door which isn't included in that? How much do you spend on that food? About how much do you (and everyone else in your family) spend eating out not counting meals at work or at school?"*

5. Nondurable consumption is defined as food; alcohol, tobacco, and expenditure on other nondurable goods, such as services, heating fuel, public and private transport (including gasoline), personal care, and semidurables, defined as clothing and footwear. It excludes housing (furniture, appliances, etc.), health, and education.

6. The budget elasticity is the elasticity of the food expenditure measure to the aggregate spending measure.

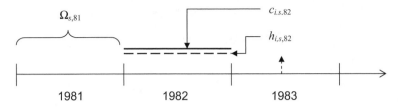

Fig. 3.1   A sample timeline of our data

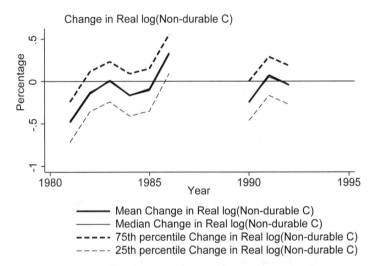

Fig. 3.2   The distribution of imputed household nondurable consumption growth

in assuming that this too refers to the previous calendar year. The imputed consumption variable, $c_{i,82}$, is therefore also the value from the 1983 survey.

Figure 3.2 shows a number of measures of the distribution of the (log growth) of the imputed nondurable consumption variable. We report the mean, median, 25th percentile, and 75th percentile for the cross-section in each year. As just discussed, the absence of the food expenditure variable for the years 1987 and 1988 (1988 and 1989 surveys) means that we lose the observations from those years. Additionally, the need to calculate a growth rate means we lose two further year's worth of observations: we lose the first year of data, as well as 1989 (the first year after the two-year break).

Figure 3.3 reports analogous statistics for the annual hours worked by the head of household. Three points are worth noting: (1) these data are continuous between 1967 and 1992 as the question was asked in each year of the PSID survey;[7] (2) the mean is below the median; (3) the median head

---

7. The survey started in 1968 but our retrospective treatment of the responses gives us data from 1967.

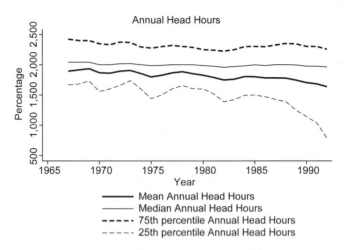

Fig. 3.3   The distribution of hours worked by head of household

of household works full time with about 2,000 hours per year (or nearly forty-two hours per week, based on forty-eight weeks of work), but there is a downside skew to the distribution caused by part-time and low-hours workers, as well those who do not work.

In order to explore the response of real wages, we take the real labor income of the head of household and divide it by annual hours. This gives us a measure of real labor income per hour worked, which we use as our measure of the real hourly wage. As with the hours data, this variable is available between 1967 and 1992. Overall, the sample contains between 1,500 households—for the early years in which we have only hours and real wage data—and nearly 3,000 households through the 1980s, when data for consumption can also be constructed. The time series of the number of observations per year, split between the hours and consumption variables, are displayed in figure 3.4. The main consumption regressions use 24,348 observations, while the hours and real wages regressions make use of 58,428 observations.

2.2.2   State-Level Data

In order to measure state-level fiscal shocks, we follow Nakamura and Steinsson (2011) and use state-level military spending data, which comes from the US Department of Defense's electronic database of military procurement (as reported in the DD-350 forms). They compiled these data for each state and year between 1966 and 2006. The spending covers all military purchases with value greater than $10,000 (from 1966 to 1983) and greater than $25,000 (1983 to 2006), and the form specifies the prime contractor as well as the location where the majority of the work was

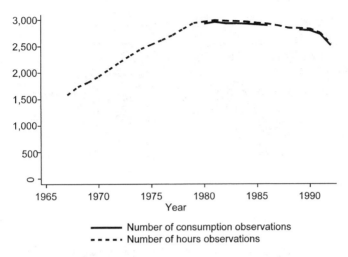

Fig. 3.4   **The number of households with hours and consumption data**

completed.[8] The DD-350 measure of government military spending in each state is denoted $G_{s,t}$, and it forms the basis of our fiscal policy instrument.

The macroeconomic literature generally agrees that aggregate military spending is exogenous to the economic decisions of US households and to the US business cycle (e.g., Ramey and Shapiro 1998). As such, a natural measure of the fiscal shock occurring in state s at time t, and resulting from changes in military spending in that state, is the percentage change in state military spending normalized by state GDP:

$$(1) \qquad \Omega_{s,t} \equiv \frac{\Delta G_{s,t}}{Y_{s,t}}.$$

In the next section we discuss issues related to the potential endogeneity of this variable.

We use Gross State Product (GSP) compiled by the US Bureau of Economic Analysis (BEA) as the measure of state output ($Y_{s,t}$) used to normalize the level of fiscal spending. To convert this and other variables to per capita values we use US Census Bureau state population data. Nominal variables are converted into real series using the state-level Consumer Price Index (CPI) data computed by Del Negro (2002) and constructed aggregating a

8. Nakamura and Steinsson (2011) deal with the potential concern that these data are mismeasured due to interstate subcontracting using a newly-digitized data set from the US Census Bureau's Annual Survey of Shipments by Defense-Oriented Industries. This is an alternative measure of state-level shipments from defense industries to the government. Though the alternative series only runs up to 1983, the two series are very closely correlated over the coincident time periods, suggesting that cross-border subcontracting plays little role in the $G_{s,t}$ variable.

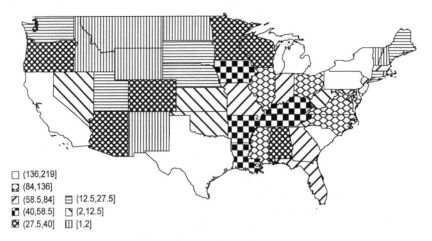

(136,219]
(84,136]
(58.5,84]   (12.5,27.5]
(40,58.5]   (2,12.5]
(27.5,40]   [1,2]

Fig. 3.5   The average number of households surveyed in each state per year

number of sources of state-level prices and costs of living. As these state-level data do not include CPI for the District of Columbia (DC), we assume that the price level there follows that of the overall United States in order to deflate nominal data from DC.

In terms of states, we use data from all fifty states as well as the District of Columbia. Of course, PSID sampling means that some states have much fewer households in each year. Figure 3.5 shows the median number of households per year in each state; to calculate this, we first calculate the total number of households in each state in each year and then calculate the median for each state. In figure 3.5 we show only the contiguous United States; this is simply to ensure that the map is easier to read. The median number of households per year is 4.5 in Alaska and 2.5 in Hawaii.

3.3   Econometric Identification of the Effects of Fiscal Shocks

The main advantage over aggregate studies of our use of state-level fiscal shocks is that we are able to control for those time effects that are common across states. Unfortunately this does not guarantee that we do not have endogeneity concerns: the variation in fiscal spending may not be completely random across states even if aggregate military spending is. Consider the possible factors that can drive the behavior of, for example, the change in hours of a head of household i who lives in state s at time t ($\Delta h_{i,s,t}$). As shown in equation (2), the movement of ($\Delta h_{i,s,t}$) will partly reflect factors that are common to all households at time t (for example, changes in monetary policy that affect the entire United States), factors common to all residents of state s (e.g., cross-state differences in working regulations), and then the idiosyncratic part related to household i. The latter two effects can be split into those effects that are time-invariant (such as the fact that certain people always work more hours than others) and those that are time-varying.

$$\Delta h_{i,s,t} = \overbrace{\delta_t}^{\text{Time } t \text{ Effects}} + \overbrace{\bar{\gamma}_s + \tilde{\gamma}_{s,t}}^{\text{State } s \text{ Effects}} + \overbrace{\bar{\alpha}_i + \tilde{\alpha}_{i,t}}^{\text{Household } i \text{ Effects}} .$$

(2)

In our analysis, we are interested in the effect of changes in state-level military spending, $\Omega_{s,t}$, on the behavior of households in those states. Our baseline equation, which we estimate for the three main dependent variables of interest (consumption, hours, and real wages) is:

$$\Delta z_{i,s,t} = \alpha_i + \gamma_s + \delta_t + \sum_{k=0}^{K} \beta_k \Omega_{s,t-k} + \phi X_{i,s,t} + \varepsilon_{i,s,t}$$

where z_{it} is (log) of household's i consumption/hours/real wages at time t, $\Omega_{s,t-k}$ is the k period lag of government military procurements from supplier companies located in state s in period t expressed as a percentage of state output, and X_{it} is a vector of control characteristics such as whether the head of household is employed or retired. Variables α_i, γ_s, and δ_t are, respectively, household, state, and time fixed-effects.[9]

In order to analyze the effects of shifts in fiscal policy, the fiscal shocks should be exogenous and so uncorrelated with the error term. Relating this regression equation to (2), and assuming that no controls and only the contemporaneous shock ($k = 0$) are included, the estimated equation is:

$$\Delta z_{i,s,t} = \delta_t + \bar{\gamma}_s + \bar{\alpha}_i + \beta_0 \Omega_{s,t} + \overbrace{\tilde{\gamma}_{s,t} + \tilde{\alpha}_{i,t}}^{\varepsilon_{i,s,t}}.$$

The key for unbiased estimates of the β_0 coefficient is that $\Omega_{s,t}$ is uncorrelated with $\varepsilon_{i,s,t}$, which incorporates state-time fixed effects that are not controlled for elsewhere. This may not be the case if the amount of state-level military spending is related to the state economic cycle. Even though aggregate military spending has been shown to be exogenous, we may still worry that the allocation of this spending across states is correlated with the state cycle; in other words, spending associated with an exogenous military build-up is directed toward those states with weaker local conditions following lobbying and the resulting political decision.[10] Therefore, like Nakamura and Steinsson (2011), we build state-level fiscal spending shocks instrumenting $\Omega_{s,t}$. Specifically, we shall use the same logic that Nekarda and Ramey (2011) applied to industry shares. The share that state s receives of overall military spending in year t is $\eta_{s,t} = G_{s,t}/G_t$ so that:

(3)
$$G_{s,t} = \eta_{s,t} G_t$$

---

9. Standard errors are clustered by household in all the household-level regressions.

10. For example, Mayer (1992) finds strong evidence of political business cycles in the distribution of military contracts, but suggests there is little evidence of the use of military contract awards for economic stimulus after 1965.

(4) $$\Rightarrow \dot{G}_{s,t} = \eta_{s,t}\dot{G}_t + \dot{\eta}_{s,t}G_t$$

(5) $$\frac{\dot{G}_{s,t}}{Y_{s,t}} = \frac{\eta_{s,t}\dot{G}_t}{Y_{s,t}} + \frac{\dot{\eta}_{s,t}G_t}{Y_{s,t}}$$

(6) $$\Rightarrow \Omega_{s,t} \approx \frac{\eta_{s,t}\Delta G_t}{Y_{s,t}} + \underbrace{\frac{\Delta\eta_{s,t}G_t}{Y_{s,t}}}_{\text{Endogenous?}}.$$

Equation (6) shows that the overall change in military spending in state s in year t can be split between the fact that aggregate spending has changed and a share of this goes to state s, and the fact that the share of aggregate spending going to state s has changed. If our worry is that states in which there are weaker economic conditions increase their share more ($\Delta\eta_{s,t} > 0$), then the second term on the right-hand-side equation (6) is potentially endogenous. Of course, some of $\Delta\eta_{s,t}$ may be exogenous variation and so excluding it we potentially reduce the variability in our shocks, which would lead to less tight standard errors. However, given that using an endogenous regressor will bias our estimates, we choose to purge the shocks of this potential correlation with the residual at the expense of potentially less precise estimates of effects of fiscal shocks. Doing this, we concentrate on the first term on the right-hand side of (6), which can be rewritten as:

$$\frac{\eta_{s,t}\Delta G_t}{Y_{s,t}} = \frac{\Delta G_t}{G_t}\frac{G_{s,t}}{Y_{s,t}}.$$

As a result of the GSP term in the denominator of $G_{s,t}/Y_{s,t}$, $(\eta_{s,t}\Delta G_t)/Y_{s,t}$ is likely to be correlated with the state business cycle even if $G_{s,t}$ and $\Delta G_t/G_t$ are exogenous. We thus need instrument fiscal shocks using, rather than $\Omega_{s,t}$,

(7) $$\widehat{\Omega}_{s,t}^{R} = \Delta\ln(G_t)\bar{\theta}_s,$$

where $\bar{\theta}_s$ is the time-average of the share of military spending in total output ($G_{s,t}/Y_{s,t}$) falling on state s.

Figure 3.6 shows, for four states, the raw shocks ($\Omega_{s,t}$) calculated according to equation (1) as well as the instrumented shocks ($\widehat{\Omega}_{s,t}^{R}$) as defined in (7). These data show, particularly in the case of Louisiana (top right frame), how the approach removes potential measurement error. The large spike up and then down in Louisiana in 1981 and 1982 is smoothed through when we use the instrumented approach. This noise seems to be less of an issue in some of the other states displayed. Comparing California (top left) to Wisconsin (bottom right) and New York (bottom left), it is clear that some states see much greater swings in the shock variable. In California the instrumented shocks are on average 0.14 percent of GSP and are as large (small) as 0.93 percent (–0.66 percent); in Wisconsin the mean is only .04 percent and the largest (smallest) shock was 0.25 percent (–0.18 percent) of GSP.

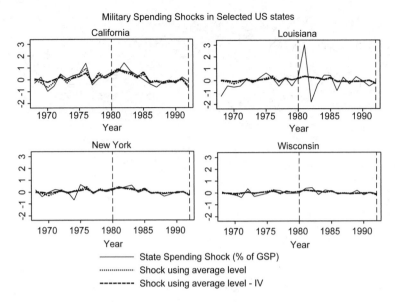

Fig. 3.6   State fiscal shocks in a selection of US states

Of course, figure 3.6 shows only a small sample of the states we use. To show the difference in variability across states in the main shock that we use, figure 3.7 shows the heat map (as in figure 3.5) of the interquartile range of $\widehat{\Omega}_{s,t}^{R}$;[11] California (0.7) is indeed one of the states with larger swings in military contracts. The most volatile are Missouri (1.0) and Connecticut (1.3). As before, we only show the contiguous United States; the interquartile range is 0.4 in Alaska and 0.5 in Hawaii.

As an alternative instrument, we also consider using Ramey's (2011) measure of defense news to instrument for aggregate US military spending. Specifically, we regress $\Delta \ln(G_t)$ on an annual sum of the news measure and generate $\widehat{\Delta \ln(G_t)}$ as the fitted value. We then create an alternative measure of our state-level shocks by applying the formula:

$$(8) \qquad \widehat{\Omega}_{s,t}^{IV} = \widehat{\Delta \ln(G_t)}\overline{\theta}_s.$$

This gives a very similar pattern as shown in figure 3.6; the correlation between the two shock series is over 0.9 across all time periods and states. In appendix A, we show that the main results are robust to using this alternative measure of fiscal shock.

---

11. As variability in $\widehat{\Omega}_{s,t}^{R}$ is driven by the aggregate growth in military spending, this map captures differences in average military intensity across states ($\overline{\theta}_s$).

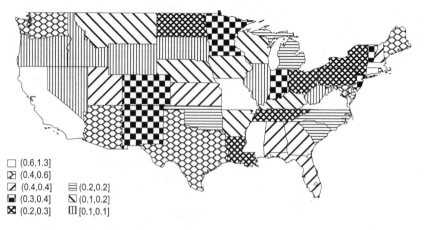

(0.6,1.3]
(0.4,0.6]
(0.4,0.4]   (0.2,0.2]
(0.3,0.4]   (0.1,0.2]
(0.2,0.3]   [0.1,0.1]

Fig. 3.7   The interquartile range of $\widehat{\Omega}_{s,t}{}^{R}$ by state

3.3.1   Household Heterogeneity

As mentioned before, an advantage of household data is that we can explore heterogeneity amongst households. Consider a simple dummy variable $D(A)_{i,s,t}$, which is 1 when the characteristic A applies to the head of household i in state s at time t. With this separation of households, we interact a particular set of household characteristics with the shock variables. The estimated regression is:[12]

$$\Delta z_{i,s,t} = \alpha_i + \gamma_s + \delta_t + \sum_{k=0}^{K} \beta_k \Omega_{s,t-k} + \sum_{k=0}^{K} \psi_k (D(A)_{i,s,t} \times \Omega_{s,t-k}) + \sigma D(A)_{i,s,t}$$

$$+ \phi X_{i,s,t} + \varepsilon_{i,s,t}.$$

In the remainder of the chapter we follow Romer and Romer (2010), who examine the effects of tax changes on the US economy, and choose a lag length that corresponds to three years ($K = 3$).

3.4   Results

Before describing our results it is useful to briefly summarize the predictions of a few models. In the (static) Investment-Saving/Liquidity Preference-Money supply (IS/LM) model an increase in government spending has no wealth effect and acts like a pure demand shock: because output is demand determined and prices do not respond, consumption increases, labor demand increases (although the model does not distinguish between

---

12. Where the characteristic is split into more than two groupings—for example, splitting the household into young, middle-aged, and older—we can use a similar but extended regression approach.

Table 3.1   **Effects of a positive spending shock in alternative models**

	Consumption	Labor supply	Real wages
Keynesian IS/LM model	+		+
Dynamic representative agent models	–	+	–
With nominal rigidities	–	+	+
With credit constrained consumers	+	+	+

an intensive and an extensive margin and thus has no predictions about the intensive margin), and so does the real wage.

Models based on a representative agent who makes optimal intertemporal decisions give the opposite result: the negative wealth effect associated with an increase in government spending lowers consumption and raises hours worked; this in turn lowers the real wage. The sharp difference between the results of the IS/LM and the intertemporal optimization models are attenuated in intertemporal models that allow for nominal rigidities, or introduce consumers subject to credit constraints: in the latter the response of consumption to a spending shock can be positive.[13] Table 3.1 summarizes these theoretical results.

When estimating the effects of a shift in fiscal policy one has two ambitions: (1) to control for anything that might have varied while fiscal policy was changing, so as to separate out the effects of other factors, such as shifts in monetary policy or the business cycle; (2) to construct an estimate of the total change in consumption (or hours worked, or the real wage) associated with the shift in fiscal policy. This will be the sum of the *direct* effect of the shift in fiscal policy, plus the indirect effect possibly arising from the change in wealth associated with the policy shift. In this chapter we achieve the first objective using time fixed effects and comparing the effects of shifts in government spending across different states in the same year. This, however, comes at the cost of shutting down the wealth channel—to the extent that one exists—that is, of overlooking any wealth effect associated with the shift in government spending. What we potentially estimate is simply the direct effect of the shift in government spending (i.e., excluding the wealth effect).

However, since we are interested in comparing the response of different households, we potentially run into an additional problem: the possibility that the wealth effect differs across households depending on their characteristics. For example, higher-income households might expect to pay a larger fraction of the future taxes than lower-income households. To understand what we estimate, the following might be useful.

---

13. See Leeper, Traum, and Walker (2011) for a detailed analysis of the multiplier implied by different models. The accompanying monetary policy obviously makes a difference, but remember that here we control for monetary policy that is the same across US states.

Assume the total wealth effect of the fiscal spending shock is, for a house-hold belonging to group i, $\bar{w} + w^i$. That is, the wealth effect is comprised of two components: the average wealth effect, $\bar{w} < 0$, plus the specific wealth effect, which varies by household characteristic. Overall, the wealth effect should be nonpositive for both groups (which means that the average effect $\bar{w}$ is nonpositive and also that $\bar{w} + w^i$ is nonpositive), but—for instance, if taxes are progressive—the rich could expect to have a larger negative wealth effect than the poor. In this case, their specific wealth effect w^R (which mea-sures the effect relative to the average), would be negative, while for the poor the specific effect would be positive, $w^P > 0$.

The response of interest, for testing between models and calculating mul-tipliers, is the total effect

$$\frac{dC_i}{dg} = x_i + \bar{w} + w^i.$$

However, our estimation procedure controls for time fixed effects which, as we said, capture common factors such as the US business cycle and Fed-eral Reserve policy stance, but also any common negative wealth effect that comes from the expected change in Federal taxes as a result of the spending shock. Therefore, we estimate:

- For the rich: $\beta^R = x^R + w^R$
- For the poor: $\beta^P = x^P + w^P$

Given that $\bar{w} < 0$, our estimate of the total effect is upward biased for both groups. If, however, we were interested in the direct effect, x^i, then if $w^R = w^P$ (i.e., if the two groups shared the same wealth effect), then our estimate of the direct effect would be unbiased. But it would not if instead $w^R < 0$, $w^P > 0$. In this case

- For the rich: $\beta^R < x^R$
- For the poor: $\beta^P > x^P$

In other words, if there are specific wealth effects as described earlier, these will cause us to overstate the x^P and understate x^R.

There are a few cases in which our results provide an upward bound for the total effect that is consistent with the intertemporal model. For instance, when, for consumption, we estimate $\beta^P < 0$ (that is, a negative response of consumption to the spending shocks—which we do for some groups, e.g., the relatively poor and part-time workers) our results are consistent with the intertemporal model because, for this group, our estimate of the direct effect is upward biased and $\bar{w} < 0$.

For hours, the analysis is similar except that the average wealth effect ($\bar{w} \geq 0$) and the specific wealth effects (relative to the average) under the progressive tax system described before, would be positive for the rich ($w^R \geq 0$) and negative for the poor ($w^P \leq 0$). Overall, the wealth effect should be

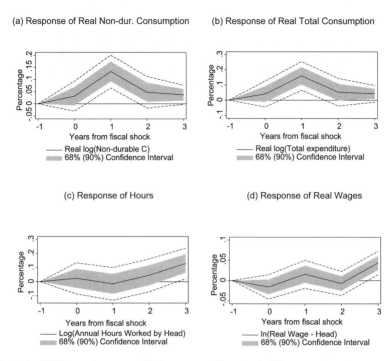

(a) Response of Real Non-dur. Consumption

(b) Response of Real Total Consumption

(c) Response of Hours

(d) Response of Real Wages

Fig. 3.8   IRFs to a 1 percent GDP state spending shock: The average response

nonnegative for both groups (they respond to the negative wealth effect by consuming less leisure) and, as aforementioned, the specific wealth effects reinforce the average wealth effect for the rich.

In this case, using similar logic, our estimates are downward biased estimates of the total effect for both groups, but we overstate the direct effect on hours and understate the direct effect on the poor. Where we estimate a positive response of hours for the rich ($\beta^R > 0$), we cannot conclude that the direct effect is positive, but we can state that the total effect is positive—since $\beta^R = x^R + w^R \geq x^R (w^R \geq 0$ and $\bar{w} \geq 0)$.

For the poor, where we find a negative ($\beta^P < 0$), as we do in the initial response, since $\beta^P = x^P + w^P \leq x^P (w^P \leq 0)$, we cannot conclude that the direct effect is negative nor can we conclude that the total effect is negative, as that depends on whether $|\bar{w}| > |\beta_P|$. If we estimate a positive effect ($\beta^P > 0$), as we do in the later years of the response, we can conclude that both the total effect and direct effect is positive.

We now illustrate our empirical findings. When we aggregate all households (figure 3.8) we find that following the increase in military spending, consumption increases right after the shock and remains higher for about two years; this is true for both durables and total consumption, which includes nondurables and services. (Given that the two categories of consumption seem to respond very similarly, in the rest of the chapter we only look at total consumption.) Hours worked and real wages initially do not move, although both increase significantly three years after the increase in spending: the long lag could be the result of off-setting positions by heterogeneous groups in the economy. Our estimates of the labor supply response focus on the intensive margin: longer hours by employed workers (we control for employment status in the regressions).[14] In section 3.5 we return to the issue of the extensive margin. The magnitude of these lagged effects is small. Since our shocks are equivalent to 1 percent of GDP, a point estimate of 0.16 for the percent change in aggregate consumption after the first year suggests that consumption increases by less than one-fifth, which is similar to the year-three response of hours, but four times as large as the percent change in real wages (0.04). In appendix A, we show that these results are unchanged if we use the alternative measure of the fiscal shock given by $\widehat{\Omega}_{s,t}^{IV}$ in equation (8).

As mentioned before, the evidence of a positive response of consumption is inconclusive, since it could be canceled or turned around by the presence of a wealth effect that our estimates capture in the time fixed effects.

As we mentioned, our data allow us to split the sample along a very large number of dimensions, although along some of them the resulting subsample included too few individuals. For instance, looking at splits based on the marital status of the head is problematic; over 70 percent of our more than 67,000 observations are married households (including permanently cohabiting), while only 11 percent are single and 19 percent are widowed, divorced, or separated. We thus have decided to look at six dimensions: the state of the local labor market, household income, workers in low-hours jobs, age, sector of employment, and gender.

3.4.1 The Effect of the State Cycle on Responses to Shocks

Using BLS data on state-level unemployment (available from 1976), we can derive measures of the state business cycle.[15] Auerbach and Gorodnichenko (2011) find that the effects of government purchases are larger in a recession: we can evaluate this with our data.

Our measure of the state cyclical conditions is the state unemployment gap, which we plot, along with the key components of the calculation, for the

---

14. All the regressions control for whether the head of household is employed or retired while the consumption regressions also control for real disposable income.

15. Using county-level unemployment data is problematic for two reasons. First, because many heads of household live outside the county in which they work and commute across county lines. Second, to protect the anonymity of respondents the PSID public-use files suppress the county identifier. As we wish to evaluate whether the local labor market is above or below its normal conditions, we cannot use the reported household measure of county unemployment because households may move to another county, meaning that the reported local unemployment rate can change with no meaningful change in labor market conditions relative to normal conditions.

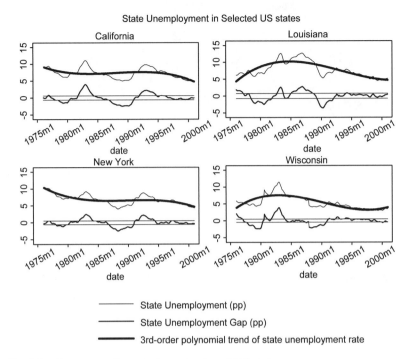

State Unemployment in Selected US states

Fig. 3.9   State unemployment in a selection of US states

same four states used previously to illustrate the military spending shocks in figure 3.9. The calculation proceeds as follows. First, we take the time-series of state-level unemployment and calculate a trend unemployment rate by fitting a third-order polynomial trend. Second, we calculate the state unemployment gap as the difference between state unemployment and this fitted trend—the lower line in figure 3.9. Finally, we look across time comparing, within each state, periods of high and low unemployment where we define "tight" ("loose") labor market conditions as periods when the state unemployment gap is in the lower (upper) quartile.[16] A tight labor market is therefore one in which the state unemployment is far below its trend. We then include these dummy variables, as well as the appropriate interactions, in our regression equation, as described before.

The results (see figure 3.10) are consistent with Auerbach and Gorodnichenko (2011). Spending shocks seem to have different effects in periods of high and low unemployment. When the local labor market is tight, our estimates suggest that neither consumption nor hours respond, implying that wealth effects could make the consumption multiplier negative and

16. The quartiles are marked in the figure by the parallel lines that cut through the unemployment gap.

(a) Response of Real Total Consumption

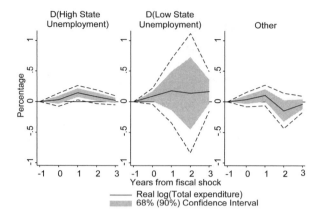

(b) Response of Hours

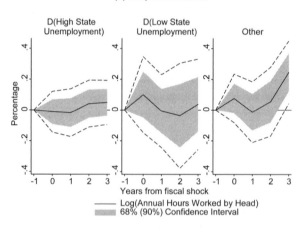

(c) Response of Real Wages

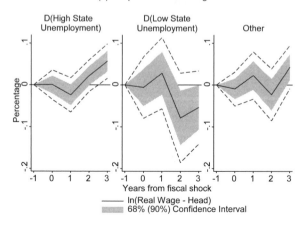

Fig. 3.10   IRFs to a 1 percent GDP state spending shock: The response by state labor conditions

the effect of hours worked positive. In periods of relatively high unemployment, we estimate a positive effect on consumption, which, however, could be canceled by the wealth effect.

3.4.2   Responses by Income Group

In order to examine whether relatively richer and relatively poorer households react differently to a spending shock, we define two dummy variables using the distribution of real disposable income:

$$D(\text{low income})_{ist} = \begin{cases} 1 & \text{if in lower quartile of year } t \text{ income distribution} \\ 0 & \text{otherwise} \end{cases}$$

$$D(\text{high income})_{ist} = \begin{cases} 1 & \text{if in upper quartile of year } t \text{ income distribution} \\ 0 & \text{otherwise} \end{cases}$$

Our definition means that a household i will be marked as a low (high) income household with $D(\text{low income})_{ist} = 1$ ($D(\text{high income})_{ist} = 1$) if the household has real disposable income in year t that is at or below (at or above) the twenty-fifth (seventy-fifth) percentile of the US income distribution in year t.

Figure 3.11 shows that there is an important difference between the response of higher- and lower-income households according to our definition of relative income. Lower-income households respond to the spending shock lowering consumption and raising (although with a three-year lag) hours worked. The presence of a group-specific wealth effect would make such responses even stronger; as described earlier for a progressive tax system, these results are consistent with lower-income households cutting consumption (the true direct effect is more negative than our estimates, which potentially include the specific wealth effect) and raising hours (both the total and direct effects would be larger than the estimates presented). Thus lower-income households appear to behave consistently with the predictions of intertemporal models where households derive no benefit from the increase in government spending, but realize they will eventually have to pay for it. Their real wages, however, do not change significantly (as those models predict): this could be because there are regulatory reasons that make their wages relatively sticky (such as minimum wage laws).

The response of high- and middle-income households, instead, is inconclusive: we estimate a positive and significant direct response of consumption, which, however, could be overturned by the wealth effect. If anything, however, the military contracts we analyze seem to favor relatively higher income households, perhaps because they are concentrated in firms with relatively high-skilled workers, or because higher-income households are more likely to own shares in such firms.

One concern with this analysis is that our dummy variable could simply

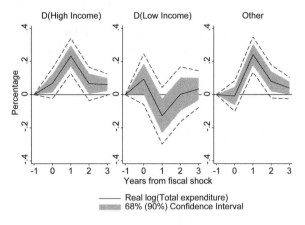

(a) Response of Real Total Consumption

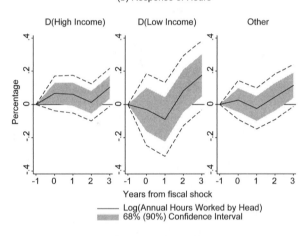

(b) Response of Hours

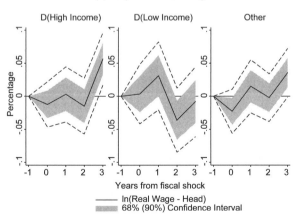

(c) Response of Real Wages

Fig. 3.11   IRFs to a 1 percent GDP state spending shock: The response by income relative to the US-wide distribution of income in period t

capture differences in levels of income across states: remember that we have identified those households with extreme (high or low) incomes within the entire distribution of income in the PSID in each year. Therefore, we repeat our analysis but use the following two alternative dummy variables:

$$D(\text{low income}^A)_{ist} = \begin{cases} 1 & \text{if in lower quartile of states, year } t \text{ income distribution} \\ 0 & \text{otherwise} \end{cases}$$

$$D(\text{high income}^A)_{ist} = \begin{cases} 1 & \text{if in upper quartile of states, year } t \text{ income distribution} \\ 0 & \text{otherwise.} \end{cases}$$

Now a household is a low (high) income household if the household has real disposable income in year t that is at or below (at or above) the twenty-fifth (seventy-fifth) percentile of the *state s* income distribution in year t. The potential worry about this approach is that some of the states, as just discussed, have relatively few households and therefore such a distribution is based on very few observations. Nonetheless, the results of the earlier analysis are little changed, as we show in figure 3.12.

3.4.3   Workers Who Work Low Hours

Heads of household working relatively few hours (most likely on part-time jobs) are likely to have more labor supply flexibility. In fact, in Giavazzi and McMahon (2010) we found that part-time German workers responded to an exogenous increase in uncertainty by working longer hours—a response we did not observe for workers in full-time employment. In order to check whether the response differs between full-time and part-time workers, we define a dummy variable:

$$D(\text{low hours})_{ist} = \begin{cases} 1 & \text{if the head regularly works less than 20 hours per week} \\ 0 & \text{otherwise.} \end{cases}$$

The choice of twenty hours per week is somewhat arbitrary. As aforementioned, we find that the median worker works about forty hours per week and so this number represents someone working about half the full-time worker's hours. We restrict the sample to heads of household who did not change their employment status during the year: since our data measure annual hours worked, if someone worked for six months and then lost their job and did not get a new one for the remainder of the year, their hours for the year would look like someone working about twenty hours a week but their position is not as a regular low hours worker.

Figure 3.13 shows that there is an important difference between the response of full-time and part-time workers. Heads working less than twenty hours per week initially respond to a spending shock increasing consumption, but they then soon reduce it (remember that these estimates likely over-

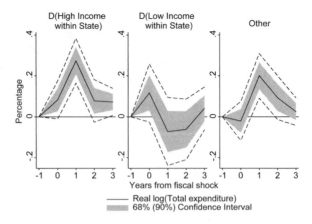

(a) Response of Real Total Consumption

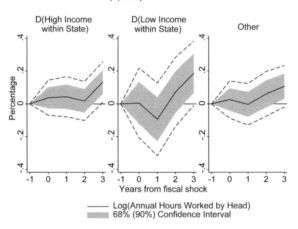

(b) Response of Hours

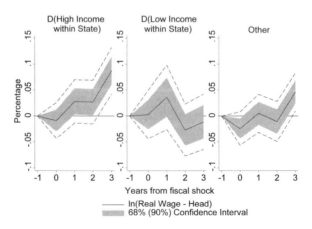

(c) Response of Real Wages

Fig. 3.12   IRFs to a 1 percent GDP state spending shock: The response by state income

(a) Response of Real Total Consumption

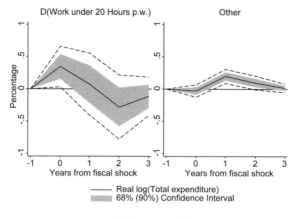

Real log(Total expenditure)
68% (90%) Confidence Interval

(b) Response of Hours

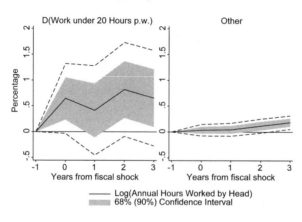

Log(Annual Hours Worked by Head)
68% (90%) Confidence Interval

(c) Response of Real Wages

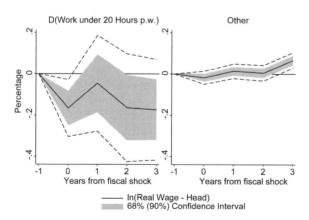

ln(Real Wage - Head)
68% (90%) Confidence Interval

Fig. 3.13   IRFs to a 1 percent GDP state spending shock: The response by part-time workers

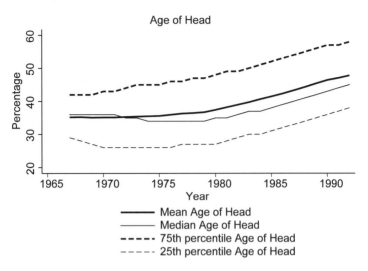

Fig. 3.14   Time series of the age distribution

state the multiplier). They also work longer hours, precisely as we observed for lower-income households. As in that case, our estimates understate the increase in hours because the average wealth effect would indicate an increase in hours, meaning that the hours of part-time workers unambiguously increase. And like the lower-income households, if they expect to pay less of the taxes, then the increase in hours and fall in consumption is further reinforced. Hours, which average about ten per week for this group, actually increase by between 50 and 75 percent, meaning the average worker would now work fifteen to eighteen hours per week. Finally, those working less than twenty hours also see their real wages fall, which is consistent with the increase in their labor supply.

The response of heads working more than twenty hours per week is instead closer to the response obtained using aggregate data.

3.4.4   Age

We have also looked at different age groups. In order to split the sample into different age groups, we do as we did for income and use the by-year distribution of ages as the point of reference. This is shown in figure 3.14 and we will define anyone above (below) the seventy-fifth (twenty-fifth) percentile in a given year as the high (low) age group:

$$D(\text{low age})_{ist} = \begin{cases} 1 & \text{if in lower quartile of age distribution in } t \\ 0 & \text{otherwise} \end{cases}$$

$$D(\text{high age})_{ist} = \begin{cases} 1 & \text{if in upper quartile of age distribution in } t \\ 0 & \text{otherwise.} \end{cases}$$

The response of older workers, relative to younger ones, should depend, in principle, on their life horizon and on the extent to which they internalize the well-being of their children. If they do not, and expect that someone else will bear the taxes that will be raised to pay for the additional spending, the negative wealth effect associated with the increase in government spending will be smaller. Instead, if they expect that some of these taxes will fall upon themselves, they will cut consumption and increase hours, the more so the fewer the active years they have left. However, because our time fixed effect captures the average wealth effect, any differential wealth effect should be reflected in the estimated response of the older workers.

The results are shown in figure 3.15. While all age groups seem to increase consumption (as in the aggregate response), the youngest workers tend to increase by the least. The response of hours is more striking: relatively young heads increase hours, while the oldest workers actually reduce their hours. These findings are consistent with the older workers experiencing a negative wealth effect that is smaller relative to the mean wealth effect captured in the time fixed effect; this (relative) positive wealth effect is reflected in the estimated response as more positive consumption and lower hours worked. Younger workers seem to experience a relatively larger negative wealth effect. Intriguingly, the middle-aged heads tend to both increase consumption and hours worked.

3.4.5   Responses by Workers from Different Industries

We are also able to follow which industry a head of household works for between 1976 to 1992. This is the response to a question in which the head is asked to report the "kind of business" that the head of household considers themselves to work in. The categorization uses the three-digit industry codes from the 1970 Census of Population Classified Index of Industries and Occupations. We use these data and classify workers according to two dummy variables, which we define only for those who are employed:[17]

$$D(\text{manufacturing})_{ist} = \begin{cases} 1 & \text{if head is employed in manufacturing industry} \\ 0 & \text{otherwise} \end{cases}$$

$$D(\text{services})_{ist} = \begin{cases} 1 & \text{if head is employed in services sector} \\ 0 & \text{otherwise.} \end{cases}$$

We use these two industries as Nekarda and Ramey (2011) discuss the effects of military spending on US manufacturing while services account for about 70 percent of the US economy; the residual includes "Agriculture,

17. Manufacturing industries include both durable and nondurable industries given by codes 139–169, 177–209, 219–238, 107–138, 239–259, 268–299, and 307–398. The "Services" sector is identified by codes 707–718, 757–759, 727–749, 769–798, 807–809, 338–389, 828–848, 857–868, 869–897, and 849.

(a) Response of Real Total Consumption

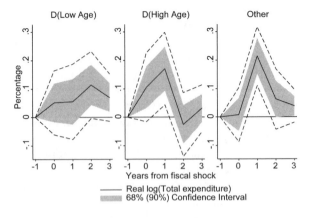

(b) Response of Hours

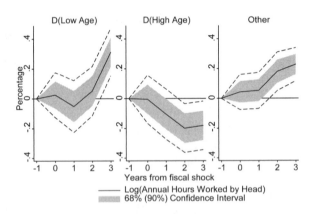

(c) Response of Real Wages

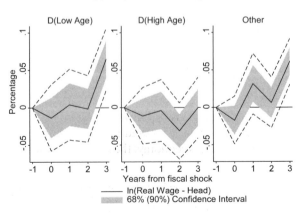

Fig. 3.15   IRFs to a 1 percent GDP state spending shock: The response by age

Forestry, and Fishing," "Mining and Extraction," "Construction," "Retail or Wholesale," "Transport, Communication & Utilities," and "Government" industries.

The results of our sectoral split are reported in figure 3.16. The sectoral response of consumption matches the aggregate response: there is no difference across sectors. But the (positive) response of hours is concentrated in the service sector, confirming what we had found looking at heads working less than twenty hours: flexibility is higher where part-time jobs are more frequent (3.2 percent of heads who work in the services sector work low hours compared with only 1.4 percent of those in other sectors).

We also compared government employees (including those working for states and cities) with heads of households working in the private sector. Interestingly, spending shocks have no effect on government employees: neither their consumption nor their hours move.

3.4.6   Gender Split

Finally, we look at whether there are differences in the reaction of households in which the head is a female. Such households make up 26 percent of all observations. While 12 percent of male heads are in the lower income quartile, 40 percent of female heads are. Female heads are disproportionately not employed; half of not employed heads are female. Of those female heads in employment, they are underrepresented (in the sense of less than 25 percent share) in all sectors of employment except for services; they make up 37 percent of the services sector.

Given this information, it is not surprising that their response to a spending shock matches that of heads working in the service industry (see figure 3.17). While the effect of the spending shock on consumption is independent of gender, the response of hours is concentrated on women. Also their real wages increase more than those of nonfemale heads.

3.4.7   In Sum

Our main findings from the various splits can be summarized as follows:

1. The spending shocks we have analyzed seem to have important distributional effects. There is a difference between the response of higher- and lower-income households. Lower-income households match the predictions of standard intertemporal representative agents models: they cut consumption (unambiguously because the wealth effect if anything reinforces our results) and work longer hours (also unambiguously), precisely as we would expect from households that receive no benefit from higher public spending but realize they will eventually have to pay for it. The response of higher-income households is more muted and we are unable to say whether the positive response of consumption we estimate is reversed by the wealth effect. Of course, our results may be specific to the military contracts that

(a) Response of Real Total Consumption

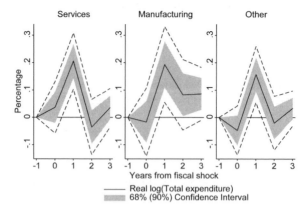

(b) Response of Hours

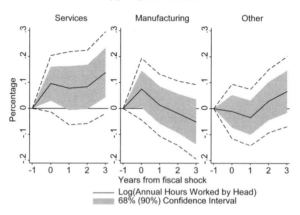

(c) Response of Real Wages

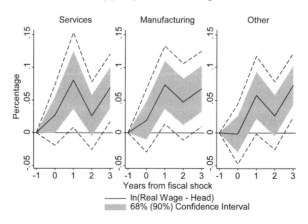

Fig. 3.16 **IRFs to a 1 percent GDP state spending shock: The response by industry**

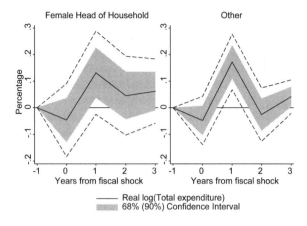

(a) Response of Real Total Consumption

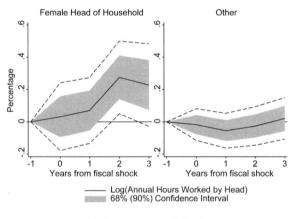

(b) Response of Hours

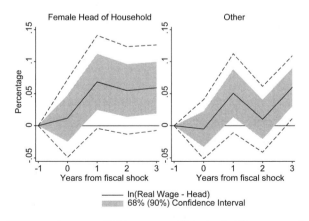

(c) Response of Real Wages

Fig. 3.17 IRFs to a 1 percent GDP state spending shock: The response by gender

we consider and so other types of fiscal spending may have very different distributional effects.

2. There is also an important difference between the response of full-time and part-time workers. Differently from full-time workers, part-timers respond to a spending shock cutting consumption, although perhaps not immediately. They also work longer hours, precisely as we observed for lower-income households. But differently from lower-income heads, those working less than twenty hours also see their real wages fall, which is consistent with the increase in their labor supply. Thus the response of part-time workers matches that predicted by a model in which households make optimal intertemporal decisions and government spending is pure waste, at least from their viewpoint.

3. Our results suggest that increases in military spending tend to be more effective in states with relatively high local unemployment. Although we cannot say whether in such states consumption increases, it certainly does not (and could very well decrease) in states with low local unemployment.

4. The positive response of hours worked to a spending shock is concentrated among households headed by a woman, among heads employed in the service sector, and among relatively younger workers).

5. There is not much our results can say about the aggregate effects of these spending shocks. At the aggregate level our estimates indicate an increase in consumption, which, however, could be overturned by the working of a wealth effect.

3.5   The Extensive Margin of Employment

So far we have analyzed the intensive labor supply margin: hours worked by employed workers. A separate question is the effect of the spending shocks on the extensive margins—employment. Specifically, we estimate a linear probability model and regress a dummy variable for whether the worker is employed on state, time, and household fixed effects. For this regression we include only those households in the labor force. The regression is analogous to those estimated before. For the aggregate results reported in figure 3.18 the estimated equation is:

$$D(\text{employed})_{i,s,t} = \alpha_i + \gamma_s + \delta_t + \sum_{k=0}^{K} \beta_k \Omega_{s,t-k} + \varepsilon_{i,s,t}.$$

While the point estimate is for an increase in the likelihood of employment for a household in a state receiving a positive fiscal spending shock, the result is only marginally significant after two years.

Figure 3.19 reports the results for a variety of the classifications just used; we cannot, obviously, do the industry breakdown as it is only classified for those that are employed. A positive spending shock increases the likelihood of employment for almost all households. Strikingly, households headed by relatively poorer workers see their probability of employment fall; this

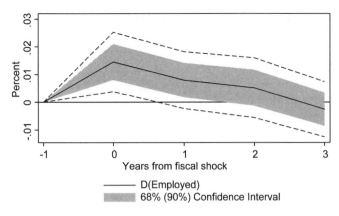

Fig. 3.18   Change in the probability of employment following a 1 percent fiscal shock

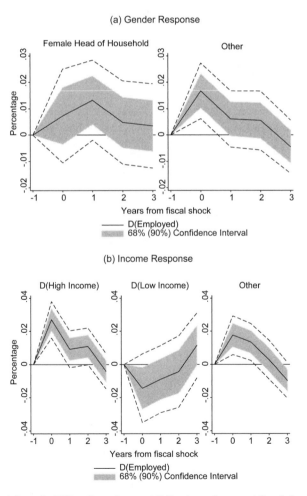

Fig. 3.19   Δ in probability of employment following a 1 percent fiscal shock

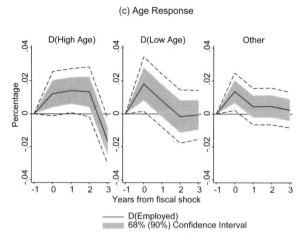

(c) Age Response

(d) Local Labor Market Response

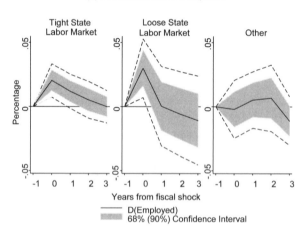

Fig. 3.19   (cont.)

effect tends to accentuate the relative decline in the intensive margin for these households. In periods of relatively high unemployment, spending shocks have no effect on hours worked nor on the likelihood of being employed.

3.6   Conclusion

Observing significant differences across the responses of various groups does not necessarily imply that aggregate estimates are biased: they could simply reflect the average of group-level responses. Aggregation theory suggests, however, that the large differences we have documented are likely to result in biased aggregate estimates. In our results there are no instances of a consistent response among all groups that disappears at the aggregate level, which would be clear evidence of an aggregation bias. If aggregation bias exists, it is likely to be attenuated.

Our results could be used to design the allocation of military contracts across states, so as to increase their macroeconomic effect: the answer here is simple—you want to spend in states with relatively high unemployment. They also suggest that military spending has significant distributional effects: the group more negatively hit appears to be part-time workers. They cut consumption, work longer hours, and see their real wages fall. Of course, it would also be interesting to explore the effects of other types of government spending, and so care should be taken in extrapolating from the identified fiscal spending shocks in this chapter to all other types of fiscal spending.

Finally our estimates, despite the potential problem of missing any wealth effect, can in some cases still allow us to discriminate between alternative models. We find it interesting that some groups (lower-income and low-hours workers in particular) appear to behave consistently with the predictions of models in which households respond to government spending shocks making optimal intertemporal decisions.

Appendix A
Robustness

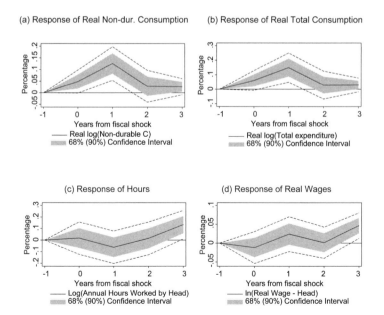

Fig. 3A.1   **IRFs to a 1 percent GDP state spending shock: The average response using the alternative measure of fiscal shock**

Appendix B
Robustness to Excluding Individual Years

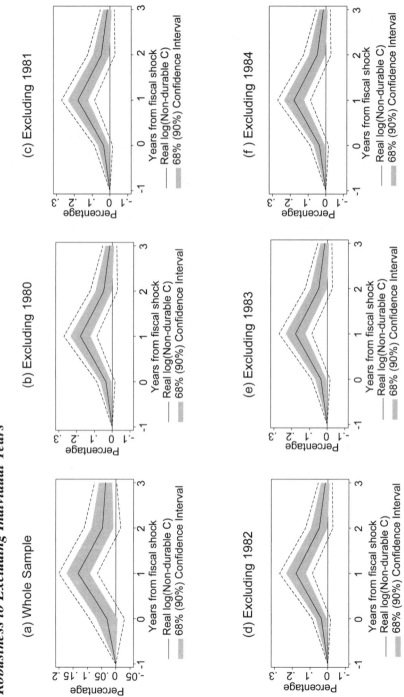

(a) Whole Sample

(b) Excluding 1980

(c) Excluding 1981

(d) Excluding 1982

(e) Excluding 1983

(f) Excluding 1984

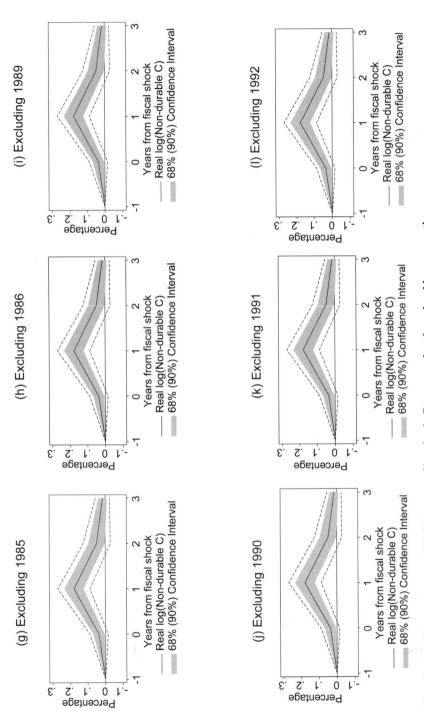

Fig. 3B.1   IRFs to a 1 percent GDP state spending shock: Response of real nondurable consumption

References

Atkeson, A., and M. Ogaki. 1996. "Wealth-Varying Intertemporal Elasticities of Substitution: Evidence from Panel and Aggregate Data." *Journal of Monetary Economics* 38 (3): 507–34.

Auerbach, A. J., and Y. Gorodnichenko. 2011. "Fiscal Multipliers in Recession and Expansion." NBER Working Paper no. 17447. Cambridge, MA: National Bureau of Economic Research, September.

Blanchard, O., and R. Perotti. 2002. "An Empirical Characterization of the Dynamic Effects of Changes in Government Spending and Taxes on Output." *Quarterly Journal of Economics* 117 (4): 1329–68.

Blundell, R., L. Pistaferri, and I. Preston. 2008a. "Consumption Inequality and Partial Insurance." *American Economic Review* 98 (5): 1887–921.

———. 2008b. "Full Web Appendix to 'Consumption Inequality and Partial Insurance' by Richard Blundell, Luigi Pistaferri, and Ian Preston." *American Economic Review* website. http://www.aeaweb.org/articles.php?doi=10.1257/aer.98.5.1887.

Burnside, C., M. Eichenbaum, and J. D. M. Fisher. 2004. "Fiscal Shocks and Their Consequences." *Journal of Economic Theory* 115 (1): 89–117.

Constantinides, G. M. 1982. "Intertemporal Asset Pricing with Heterogeneous Consumers and without Demand Aggregation." *Journal of Business* 55 (2): 253–67.

Cullen, J., and P. V. Fishback. 2006. "Did Big Government's Largesse Help the Locals? The Implications of WWII Spending for Local Economic Activity, 1939–1958." NBER Working Paper no. 12801. Cambridge, MA: National Bureau of Economic Research, December.

Del Negro, M. 2002. "Asymmetric Shocks among US States." *Journal of International Economics* 56 (2): 273–97.

Edelberg, W., M. Eichenbaum, and J. D. Fisher. 1999. "Understanding the Effects of a Shock to Government Purchases." *Review of Economic Dynamics* 2 (1): 166–206.

Ercolani, V., and N. Pavoni. 2012. "The Precautionary Effect of Government Expenditures on Private Consumption." Mimeo, IGIER-Bocconi University.

Favero, C., F. Giavazzi, and J. Perego. 2011. "Country Heterogeneity and the International Evidence on the Effects of Fiscal Policy." *IMF Economic Review* 59 (4): 652–82.

Galí, J., J. D. López-Salido, and J. Vallés. 2007. "Understanding the Effects of Government Spending on Consumption." *Journal of the European Economic Association* 5 (1): 227–70.

Giavazzi, F., and M. McMahon. 2010. "Policy Uncertainty and Precautionary Savings." *The Review of Economics and Statistics* 94 (2): 517–31.

Giavazzi, F., and M. Pagano. 1990. "Can Severe Fiscal Contractions Be Expansionary? Tales of Two Small European Countries." In *NBER Macroeconomics Annual 1990*, vol. 5, edited by Olivier Jean Blanchard and Stanley Fischer, 75–122. Cambridge, MA: MIT Press.

Gorman, W. M. 1953. "Community Preference Fields." *Econometrica* 21 (1): 63–80.

Hall, R. E. 1986. "The Role of Consumption in Economic Fluctuations." In *The American Business Cycle: Continuity and Change,* edited by Robert J. Gordon, 237–66. Chicago: University of Chicago Press.

Leeper, E. M., N. Traum, and T. B. Walker. 2011. "Clearing Up the Fiscal Multiplier Morass." NBER Working Paper no. 17444. Cambridge, MA: National Bureau of Economic Research, September.

Lopez, J. I. 2010. "Consumption and Labor Income Risk, Aggregation and Business Cycles." Mimeo, HEC, Paris.

Maliar, L., and S. Maliar. 2003. "The Representative Consumer in the Neoclassical Growth Model with Idiosyncratic Shocks." *Review of Economic Dynamics* 6 (2): 368–80.

Mayer, K. R. 1992. "Elections, Business Cycles and the Timing of Defense Contract Awards in the United States." In *The Political Economy of Military Spending in the United States,* edited by A. Mintz, 15–32. New York: Routledge.

Mountford, A., and H. Uhlig. 2009. "What Are the Effects of Fiscal Policy Shocks?" *Journal of Applied Econometrics* 24 (6): 960–92.

Nakamura, E., and J. Steinsson. 2011. "Fiscal Stimulus in a Monetary Union: Evidence from US Regions." NBER Working Paper no. 17391. Cambridge, MA: National Bureau of Economic Research, September.

Nekarda, C. J., and V. A. Ramey. 2011. "Industry Evidence on the Effects of Government Spending." *American Economic Journal: Macroeconomics* 3:36–59.

Perotti, R. 2008. "In Search of the Transmission Mechanism of Fiscal Policy." In *NBER Macroeconomics Annual 2007,* vol. 22, edited by Daron Acemoglu, Kenneth Rogoff, and Michael Woodford, 169–226. Chicago: University of Chicago Press.

Ramey, V. A. 2011. "Identifying Government Spending Shocks: It's All in the Timing." *The Quarterly Journal of Economics* 126 (1): 1–50.

Ramey, V. A., and M. D. Shapiro. 1998. "Costly Capital Reallocation and the Effects of Government Spending." *Carnegie-Rochester Conference Series on Public Policy* 48 (1): 145–94.

Romer, C. D., and D. H. Romer. 2010. "The Macroeconomic Effects of Tax Changes: Estimates Based on a New Measure of Fiscal Shocks." *American Economic Review* 100 (3): 763–801.

Stoker, T. M. 2008. "Aggregation (Econometrics)." In *The New Palgrave Dictionary of Economics,* 2nd edition, edited by S. N. Durlauf and L. E. Blume. New York: Palgrave Macmillan.

Comment   Lawrence J. Christiano

This is an excellent chapter on the effects of government spending that is well worth studying. Most of my discussion focuses on the background and motivation for the analysis. I begin by describing what it is about the current economic situation in the United States and other countries that motivates interest in the economic effects of government spending. Perhaps the natural place to look for information on the effects of government spending is the time series data. I review the information in the US time series data since 1940 using the different approaches taken by Ramey and Hall in this volume. I show that whatever information there is in the data about the effects of government spending primarily stems from the Korean War and World War II

Lawrence J. Christiano holds the Alfred W. Chase Chair in Business Institutions at Northwestern University and is a research associate of the National Bureau of Economic Research.
I am very grateful for discussions with Benjamin Johannsen. I am particularly grateful for his assistance on the computations for Valerie Ramey's vector autoregression, reported in this comment. For acknowledgments, sources of research support, and disclosure of the author's material financial relationships, if any, please see http://www.nber.org/chapters/c12637.ack.

episodes. I explain why the evidence on the government spending multiplier (i.e., the output effect of an increase in government spending) in these episodes is probably of limited value from the perspective of the current situation. This is why it is important to study other sources of evidence on the multiplier. Giavazzi and McMahon's chapter studies other such evidence by examining the response of consumption and labor in a cross-section of states in the United States. As the authors themselves emphasize, however, inferring information on the multiplier from the evidence they gather is problematic. Still, the work they do is important because it clarifies some of the channels by which government spending affects household decisions.

One Set of Reasons for Taking an Interest in the Effects of Government Spending

The authors' work can be appreciated from many different angles and I begin by describing one of them. There is widespread concern in the United States and other countries about the weak level of economic activity and high level of unemployment since 2008. One view is that the low level of activity reflects a failure of aggregate demand. A popular version of this view holds that the failure of aggregate demand stems from reduced spending by households and others as they struggle to reduce their levels of debt. In models of well-functioning markets, this kind of situation would trigger a fall in the relative price of current goods (i.e., the real interest rate), thus encouraging other people (e.g., the people who own the debt of the heavily indebted people) to shift expenditures away from future goods and toward present goods. In this way, the price mechanism minimizes what would otherwise be a waste of the resources available for current production. The aggregate demand failure view holds that, for various reasons, the fall in the real interest rate just described is prevented from occurring. To see why, consider the real rate of interest

$$\frac{R_t}{\pi^e_{t+1}}$$

where R_t denotes the gross nominal rate of interest and π^e_{t+1} denotes the public's expectation of inflation. In the United States and other countries, the nominal rate of interest is near its lower bound of unity. At the same time, π^e_{t+1} does not rise, presumably because of the credibility of central banks' commitment to low inflation. According to the aggregate demand failure view of the current slump, the inability of the real rate of interest to fall sufficiently is the cause of the low current rate of utilization of capital and labor.

Various policies have been proposed for addressing the problem of low aggregate demand. One set of policies would use various types of taxes to stimulate spending (see, e.g., Correia et al. 2010). Another set of policies would directly boost aggregate demand by increasing government spending (see, e.g., Christiano, Eichenbaum, and Rebelo 2011; Eggertsson 2011). Those who argue for government spending note that low utilization of resources suggests the benefits, net of the social cost, of additional spending is high. For example, unemployed teachers could be working to raise the human capital of children. Layed-off construction workers could be doing much-needed repairs to the crumbling US infrastructure. Proponents of government spending also note that financial markets are willing to lend funds to the US Federal government at virtually zero interest.

A key question in evaluating government spending as a way to help get us out of the current slump, is how much will it boost output? If for every bridge the government repairs, a factory somewhere else goes unbuilt, then it is not so obvious that government spending is desirable. A rise in government spending could in principle even have a negative effect on output if it creates large enough tax distortions, either through standard deadweight loss effects or by creating a climate of uncertainty.[1]

These considerations are what motivate interest in the size of the government spending multiplier, the ratio of the increase in output divided by the increase in government spending. The objective of this chapter is to shed light on the government spending multiplier using data and a minimum of economic assumptions. Of course, in this endeavor it is important that the evidence be drawn from circumstances that resemble our current situation. That is, we are interested in the effects of an increase in government spending that (a) must presumably be financed eventually, but not by an immediate rise in taxes; (b) is most likely temporary; and (c) is unlikely to be accompanied by a rise in the nominal rate of interest, since the zero bound on that rate appears to be very binding.

Time Series Evidence

The amount of relevant information in the time series about the government spending multiplier appears to be limited. Consider, for example, the vector autoregression (VAR) study in Valerie Ramey's contribution to this volume (chapter 1). The three panels in figure 3C.1 display the implications of her "News EVAR" for the government spending multiplier. For the purpose of these calculations, I define this multiplier as follows:

$$\text{multiplier} = \frac{\sum_{j=0}^{\infty} [1/(1+r)]^j \bar{Y}_{t+j}}{[1/(1+r)]^j \bar{G}_{t+j}}.$$

Here, $\bar{Y}_t$ and $\bar{G}_t$ denote the responses in GDP and government spending, respectively, to a government spending news shock. Also, the real interest rate, r, was set to 3.6 percent, at an annual rate.

---

1. See Baker, Bloom, and Davis (2011).

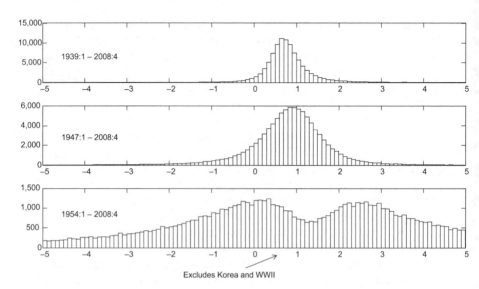

Fig. 3C.1   Posterior distribution of government spending multiplier implied by Ramey VAR

The calculations in figure 3C.1 were performed as follows. The vector of variables, y_t, in the VAR (kindly provided by Valerie Ramey) is defined as follows:

$$y_t = \left[\frac{PV_t}{GDP_{t-1}} \log G_t \log(GDP_t - G_t)R_t \text{ average marginal tax rate} \right]'.$$

Here, G_t denotes Federal, state, and local government purchases of goods and services, GDP_t denotes real gross domestic product in quarter t, R_t denotes the three-month Treasury bill rate, and the last variable is an estimate of the average marginal tax rate constructed by Barro and Redlick (2011). The variable PV_t is Ramey's measure of the present discounted value of government spending. Following Ramey, the VAR includes a constant, four lags of y_t, and a quadratic time trend. I compute the innovation to PV_t / GDP_{t-1} (the "news shock"), applying the approach in Ramey's "News EVAR" specification.[2] The posterior distribution of the multiplier using several sample periods is reported in figure 3C.1.[3] The top panel in figure

2. The average value of the private spending to government spending ratio, $(GDP_t - G_t) / G_t$, in the data set is 3.76. Then, $\bar{Y}_t = 3.76 \times \hat{y}_{3,t} + \hat{y}_{2,t}$ and $\bar{G}_t = \hat{y}_{2,t}$, $y_t = [y_{1,t}, y_{2,t}, y_{3,t}, y_{4,t}, y_{5,t}]$, and a hat over a variable indicates its impulse response to the news shock.

3. The posterior distribution was computed using the Markov chain Monte Carlo (MCMC) algorithm. The results in figure 3C.1 make use of a flat prior on the VAR parameters. The computations were also performed with a "Minnesota prior" and the results were virtually the same. Let θ denote the vector of VAR parameters. Corresponding to each MCMC draw of θ, impulse responses in $(\bar{Y}_t, \bar{G}_t)$ to a news shock were computed and these were used to compute

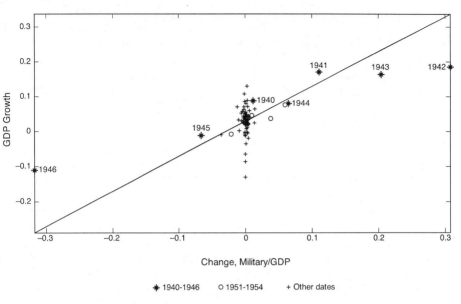

Fig. 3C.2   Hall's evidence on the multiplier

3C.1 displays the posterior distribution when the whole sample of data is used. The mode is below unity, and the distribution is moderately spread out. The middle distribution excludes the World War II period—note how the posterior distribution fans out substantially more. Finally, the distribution in the bottom panel drops both during the World War II and Korean episodes. Note that now the data are essentially completely uninformative about the multiplier. I conclude that the only information about the multiplier comes from the Korea and World War II episodes.[4]

My next time series evidence uses the methodology and annual data covering 1930 to 2008 used by Hall in his comment to chapter 2 in this volume.[5] The data are the annual change in military spending and the annual change in real GDP, each divided by lagged GDP. Let the military spending variable be denoted m_t and let GDP growth be denoted by y_t. The scatter plot of m_t and y_t is displayed in figure 3C.2. As a benchmark, I also display the curve, $y_t = a + m_t$, where a is the sample mean of y_t minus the sample mean of m_t. The data in figure 3C.2 are differentiated according to whether they belong to the World War II period, the period of the Korean War, or other periods.

---

the multiplier defined in the text (the infinite sum was truncated at horizon 500). A large number of θ's were drawn using the MCMC algorithm and the multiplier was computed in each case. Figure 3C.1 displays the resulting histogram of the multiplier.

4. A version of figure 3C.1 was computed using Ramey's "Blanchard-Perotti SVAR" approach, with similar results.

5. These were kindlly provided by Hall in an Excel file with the name, "Fig weights, Tables VARs and regs."

Table 3C.1   Least squares regression estimates of $y_t = a + bm_t$

$y_t \sim$ GDP growth, $m_t \sim$ (military spending$_t$ − military spending$_{t-1}$)/GDP$_{t-1}$

Sample period	a	b
Nonwar period	0.03	0.45
World War II	0.06	0.51
Korean War	0.02	0.90
Whole sample, 1930–2008	0.03	0.55

Note first that there is very little variation in military spending outside of the two war periods (see the observations indicated by a "+"). With so little variation, we do not expect to be able to get a precise measure of the multiplier, dy_t/dm_t, from these observations. Still, the least squares line computed using these data implies a very small multiplier, 0.45 (see table 3C.1). The observations indicated by circles in figure 3C.2 correspond to the Korean War. There is notably more variation in m_t during the Korean war period. Those observations generally lie along a line that is flatter than the 45 degree line, so those data suggest the multiplier is below unity. According to table 3C.1, the least squares estimate of the multiplier is 0.90. Finally, the greatest degree of variation in m_t is exhibited by the World War II data. Those observations lie along a line noticeably flatter than the benchmark curve. This is why, according to table 3C.1, the least squares estimate of the multiplier for that period is so small, 0.51.

The evidence in figure 3C.1 is consistent with the implications of the Ramey VAR analysis. Most of the information about the multiplier in the time series comes from World War II and the Korean War. Moreover, they do not provide much support for the notion that the multiplier is much larger than unity.

But is the evidence on the government spending multiplier from the two wars relevant to the current situation? Part of the answer can be seen in figure 3C.3. The top panel displays the Barro and Redlick (2011) tax data. Note that in both World War II and the Korean War, there was a sharp rise in taxes. Thus, those episodes do not share characteristic (a) in the current situation, that the rise in government spending is not likely to be accompanied by a rise in taxes right away. The top panel displays Hall's data on the log of real defense spending. Note that the expansion in military spending in the Korean War turned out to be essentially permanent. To the extent that people had a sense of this in real time—perhaps they interpreted Korea as the first battle in a long (mostly) cold war—they would have viewed the rise in military spending as being persistent. In this respect, the Korean War episode does not satisfy our characteristic (b) that it be temporary.[6] Finally,

6. It is not clear what the direction of bias might be. The impact of the persistence of government spending shocks on the spending multiplier is not robust across dynamic economic

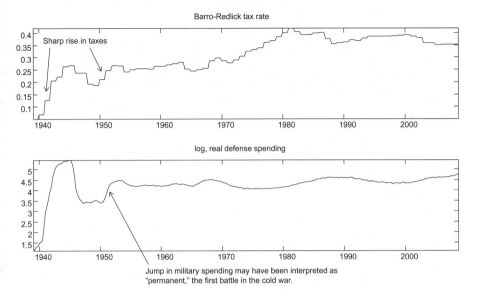

Fig. 3C.3   Government spending and tax data

rationing during World War II greatly biases estimates of the multiplier based on that period. Arithmetic requires that for the multiplier to be big, private spending must increase. But under rationing this possibility is ruled out by law. For these reasons, the US time series data beginning with World War II appear to have little information about the government spending multiplier that is relevant to the current situation.

Interestingly, Gordon and Krenn (2010) argue that the two years right before the entry of the United States into World War II do provide information about the government spending multiplier that is relevant to present circumstances. Military spending began to rise sharply "starting in June 1940, fully 18 months before Pearl Harbor" (Gordon and Krenn abstract). They note that the interest rate was roughly constant during that period, so that is it consistent with (c). Also, there was no rationing at that time and there was considerable slack in the economy, as there has been in the US economy in recent years. Gordon and Krenn (2010) argue that the quarterly data on this period warrant the conclusion that the multiplier is as high as 2.5. This is an important observation. Still, given the short sample on which it is based, it is important to find additional corroborating evidence.

---

models. According to a real business cycle model, the more persistent is the rise in government spending the greater is the government spending multiplier. This reflects the negative wealth effect of government spending on labor supply. The New Keynesian model deemphasizes labor supply. As a result, the more persistent is a government spending shock in that model, the smaller is the multiplier. This reflects the negative wealth effect on consumption. See Christiano, Eichenbaum, and Rebelo (2011) for further discussion.

Observations on the Chapter

The preceding observations make clear why the topic of this chapter is important. My brief summary of the time series evidence suggests that additional sources of information about the multiplier are needed. Exploiting one such source of information is the stated objective of this chapter.

The authors study the household consumption and labor supply response to a government spending shock. Identification proceeds as in Nakamura and Steinsson (2011). When government spending increases, its distribution across states in the United States is not completely predictable. States that receive an unexpectedly high share of government spending experience a positive spending shock and states that receive an unexpectedly low share of government spending receive a negative spending shock. Because of the richness of the authors' data set, they can identify how different types of households in a state respond to a state government spending shock and how their responses might vary over the business cycle. This type of information is of great interest for understanding how people respond to shocks.

As the authors themselves emphasize, it is not so clear whether the analysis sheds light specifically on the government spending multiplier, as discussed in the first section. For example, the positive spending shock received by a state under the authors' identification generates virtually no need for additional future taxes. The reason is that if one dollar of additional government spending finds its way into a particular state, the extra taxes to finance that extra dollar are paid by all states. As a result, one of the objectives of the research appears not to be infeasible. It is not possible to use the authors' analysis to determine whether the transmission mechanism for government spending implied by the IS/LM model corresponds better with the data than the mechanism implied by intertemporal models like the real business cycle model. A key difference between these models is that households in the former ignore future taxes, while households in the latter fully internalize them.

Perhaps a better way to think of the analysis in the chapter is to think of the states of the United States as separate, small open economies.[7] In effect, a rise in government spending in a particular state is equivalent to a rise in that state's exports. When a country experiences a rise in export demand, there is no sense in which the citizens expect to pay higher taxes in the future to finance those exports. Thinking of the analysis as shedding light on the effects of an export shock may also clarify some results that at first seem puzzling. For example, the authors find that low-income households respond to a rise in government spending shocks by working longer hours and consuming less. High-income households respond by consum-

---

7. This is an interpretation of this type of analysis stressed in Nakamura and Steinsson (2011).

ing more. Pursuing the small open economy idea, imagine that each state is a small open economy with a traded good and a nontraded good sector. Suppose that a state experiences a rise in government spending in the form of increased government purchases from the state's higher-income people. Suppose also that this increases the rent those people earn on their human and physical capital. Because the increased government spending raises their wealth, the higher-income people respond by purchasing more consumption goods, including nontradable consumption goods. This raises the price of nontradable consumption goods and, in effect, acts as a tax on the low-income people. This negative wealth effect suffered by poor people causes them to work harder and consume less.

References

Baker, Scott, Nicholas Bloom, and Steven J. Davis. 2011. "Measuring Economic Policy Uncertainty." Unpublished Manuscript. University of Chicago, Booth School of Business.

Barro, Robert, and Charles J. Redlick. 2011. "Macroeconomic Effects from Government Purchases and Taxes." *Quarterly Journal of Economics* 126:51–102.

Correia, Isabel, Emmanuel Fahri, Juan Pablo Nicolini, and Pedro Teles. 2010. "Unconventional Fiscal Policy at the Zero Bound." Unpublished Manuscript. Bank of Portugal.

Christiano, Lawrence, Martin Eichenbaum, and Sergio Rebelo. 2011. "When is the Government Spending Multiplier Large?" *The Journal of Political Economy* 119 (1): 78–121.

Eggertsson, Gauti. 2011. "What Fiscal Policy Is Effective at Zero Interest Rates?" *NBER Macroeconomic Annual 2010,* edited by Daron Acemoglu and Michael Woodford, 59–112. Chicago: University of Chicago Press.

Gordon, Robert J., and Robert Krenn. 2010. "The End of the Great Depression 1939–41: Policy Contributions and Fiscal Multipliers." NBER Working Paper no. 16380. Cambridge, MA: National Bureau of Economic Research, September.

Nakamura, Emi, and Jon Steinsson. 2011. "Fiscal Stimulus in a Monetary Union: Evidence from US Regions." NBER Working Paper no. 17391. Cambridge, MA: National Bureau of Economic Research, September.

4

The Role of Growth Slowdowns and Forecast Errors in Public Debt Crises

William Easterly

4.1 Introduction

It is very well known that growth rates play a role in debt dynamics. Despite this widespread knowledge, real world narratives of public debt crises often focus almost exclusively on budget deficits and neglect the role of growth. This chapter presents the simplest arithmetic possible to illustrate how growth slowdowns could contribute to rapid increases in public debt to GDP ratios. It shows that growth slowdowns have indeed played a role in a wide variety of well-known debt crises. It then considers the implications for precautionary fiscal policy, focusing in particular on conservative forecasts of future growth. Unfortunately, political economy incentives cause policymakers to violate such forecast practices, with a systematic tendency to excessive optimism about future growth.

This chapter updates an analysis in Easterly (2001) of the effect of growth slowdowns on the middle income debt crisis of the 1980s and 1990s, and on the low income debt crisis of the same period (Highly Indebted Poor Coun-

William Easterly is professor of economics at New York University, codirector of the NYU Development Research Institute, and a research associate of the National Bureau of Economic Research.

Thanks to Steven Pennings for superb research assistance and for helpful comments and suggestions. Thanks to the World Bank for kindly providing data on growth forecasts for many countries. Thanks to participants in the NBER conference, "Fiscal Policy after the Crisis," in Milan, December 12–13, 2011, and my discussant Indira Rajaraman This chapter expands greatly upon and draws partially upon an earlier paper, "Fiscal Policy, Debt Crises, and Economic Growth," "International Conference on Economic Policy in Emerging Economies, In Honor of Professor Vittorio Corbo," October 27–28, 2011, Santiago, Chile. Thanks to participants in that conference and my discussant Rodrigo Fuentes for useful suggestions and comments. For acknowledgments, sources of research support, and disclosure of the author's material financial relationships, if any, please see http://www.nber.org/chapters/c12640.ack.

tries, or HIPCs). Now that it is the rich countries having debt crises, the same methodology will, in this chapter, be applied to discuss the Eurozone debt crises and the debt crisis in the United States.

There are many things this chapter does NOT do. It does not present or test a well-developed theory of fiscal policymaking and policymakers' expectations formation, relying instead on simple arithmetic and descriptive analysis of outcomes. The focus is on medium-run to long-run growth, NOT on cyclical fluctuations or cyclicality of deficits or debt. This chapter does NOT consider managing business cycles. It also considers only the effects running from growth changes to public debt ratios. It does NOT consider any effects running the other way, from fiscal policy to growth. Obviously, these effects deserve consideration, but this chapter omits them to stay focused and a manageable length.

This chapter presents the simple arithmetic of the relationship between growth slowdowns and debt (section 4.2). It shows that this arithmetic indicates an important role for growth in past debt crises in the developing world (HIPC and Latin America in particular), and in the Eurozone and the United States more recently (section 4.3). Section 4.4 finds that when growth forecasts and fiscal policy do not adjust to growth slowdowns, the result is often large forecast errors and budget deficits. Section 4.5 concludes.

The treatment of fiscal arithmetic in section 4.2 considers two views of fiscal sustainability, the first relating to a constant debt-to-GDP ratio (Buiter 1985 and Blanchard 1990), and the second on the forward-looking solvency constraint of the government.[1] Using the latter approach, Mendoza and Oviedo (2004) find that lower growth rate assumptions can tip otherwise solvent countries in Latin America into insolvency. Huang and Xie (2008) use an endogenous growth model to calculate government solvency conditions, and find that in addition to debt-to-GDP, government expenditure-to-GDP is also needed to characterize fiscal sustainability.

There is a large literature that tests for biases in growth and budget forecasts. Frankel (2011) finds that official growth forecasts across thirty countries tend to be upward biased, and are more biased at longer horizons, during booms, and if the country is part of the Eurozone. For the United States, McNab, Rider, and Wall (2007) find that the US Government's one-year ahead, budget receipts forecasts for fiscal years 1963 through 2003 are biased and inefficient, and the errors are consistent with the political goals of the administration. Auerbach (1994) also finds evidence of bias, though using a longer sample Auerbach (1999) finds less evidence of overall bias (though still finds forecasts are inefficient). Moreover, he finds that official forecasts are no worse than private forecasts. Fredreis and Tatalovich (2000) find evidence of bias in official forecasts for different administrations, with Reagan and Bush administrations being particularly optimistic, and Kennedy, Johnson, and Clinton

---

1. See Chalk and Hemming (2000) for a review of fiscal sustainability.

being pessimistic.[2] Japanese official growth forecasts are biased upwards by 0.7 percentage points (Ashiya 2007), and depending on the period, growth forecasts are biased in either direction for Canada (Mühleisen et al. 2005).

The fiscal issues facing the Eurozone have spurred a series of papers that have found overoptimistic growth and budget forecasts. Strauch, Hallerberg, and von Hagen (2004) finds evidence of biases in some countries, with the cyclical position of the government, and its form of fiscal governance influencing the degree of the bias. Jonung and Larch (2004) find a tendency to overestimate the growth rates in Eurozone countries, with a large bias of about half a percentage point in Germany and Italy. The authors recommend forecasts by independent political bodies. Along these lines, Marinheiro (2011) compares the forecast accuracy of European Commission (EC) forecasts and national government forecasts. He finds that that EC's forecasts are often better (particularly for the year ahead), and argues EC forecasts can be used to reduce optimism bias of national forecasts.

4.2   Some Unpleasant Fiscal and Growth Arithmetic

This section considers the simple arithmetic by which debt crises may be provoked or worsened by growth slowdowns. This is meant to be an accounting of how high debt came about, not a theoretical analysis of policymakers' behavior.

4.2.1   Debt Dynamics

The simple arithmetic equation for the dynamics of public debt to GDP is extremely well-known. I repeat it here for ease of exposition, giving the version in continuous time.

D = Public debt in constant prices

Y = GDP in constant prices

F = Primary Fiscal Deficit in constant prices

r = Interest rate on government debt

g = growth of real GDP

(1) $$d = \frac{D}{Y}$$

(2) $$f = \frac{F}{Y}$$

(3) $$\Delta d = f + (r - g)d.$$

---

2. Fredreis and Tatalovich (2000) also find that Republican administrations overforecast inflation, and Democratic administrations overforecast unemployment.

Let f^* be the primary fiscal deficit that stabilizes the debt ratio at its current level d (which actually has to be negative in the long run, i.e., a primary surplus, because $r - g$ in the long run is positive). Substituting f^* for f in equation (3) will by definition make $\Delta d = 0$, so

(4) $$f^* = -(r - g)d.$$

The determination of f^* is still pure arithmetic. I do not mean to imply that it is automatically optimal to stabilize debt at its current level. Equations (3) and (4) hold even if we are considering very short-run debt dynamics, but in the short run, it is obviously necessary to have some discussion of cyclical policy on f. As mentioned before, this chapter does NOT consider managing business cycles. As a pure accounting matter, equation (3) still helps us decompose the rise in short-run debt to the part attributable to the primary deficit f and the part attributable to short-run growth g, but has nothing to say on whether the rise in debt is suboptimal.

At the other extreme, in the very long run, equations (3) and (4) help us address the well-known long-run budget constraint of the government. Suppose we take g now to be the steady state permanent growth rate, f is the permanent ratio of primary surplus to GDP, and d is the initial debt-to-GDP ratio at time zero. Then the long-run budget constraint is that the present value of primary surpluses in the future must be equal to or greater than the current debt:

(5) $$\int_0^\infty e^{-rt}(-f)e^{gt}dt \geq d.$$

When all variables g, r, f (as well as the initial, current debt ratio d) are constant in the steady state, the simple closed form solution to equation (5) is:

(6) $$\frac{-f}{r - g} \geq d.$$

Therefore, under these particular assumptions, equation (4) thus gives us the primary surplus $-f^*$ that will also satisfy the solvency condition (6). If it seems difficult politically or otherwise to attain this primary surplus, then there is a high risk of default on debt. This is, of course, what is usually meant by "debt crisis."

Now if the permanent growth rate should change, we can discuss how the primary surplus must change in the very long run to keep the government solvent. Note that we must assume in the long run that $r > g$ for the present value of primary surpluses in (5) to be finite.

Of course, how long a period corresponds to the long run is imprecise. I intend for this budget constraint discussion to be illustrative of the idea that the primary surplus must permanently increase in response to any permanent decrease in the growth rate. If it fails to do so, then the debt ratio will start increasing. Of course, the latter is still arithmetically true even if we are not sure about whether the long-run budget constraint is relevant.

The bottom line is that the identity (3) is always useful for descriptive accounting of changes in debt ratios and changes in growth rates, regardless of whether we are discussing the short run or long run. We can get closer to normative analysis of how the primary surplus should respond to changes in growth as we move toward the long run in which the solvency condition is relevant.

4.2.2   Effect of Growth Change if Fiscal Policy Unchanged

Now suppose that the growth rate g changes. Since we are assessing the possible role of growth rates on debt dynamics, let us go to the extreme case that fiscal policy f stays at its old value set in (4), which keeps the debt ratio stable for the OLD growth rate.

I assume the interest rate also does not change. This assumption is problematic in the final phase of a debt crisis when the market anticipates a risk of default and drives up sovereign borrowing rates. However, I am concentrating on how the debt crisis emerges in the long run, not its final phase of acute crisis.

The initial debt ratio of course does not immediately change either. So the only change in equation (3) is the growth change. Debt dynamics will now depart from the stable debt ratio achieved by (4) in the following amount:

(7) $$\Delta d = (-\Delta g)d.$$

This is the core equation in the chapter; it will form the basis for a number of charts that will have Δd on the vertical axis, and $(\Delta g)d$ on the horizontal axis. Given the previous assumptions, this (admittedly simplistic) unpleasant arithmetic of growth predicts a negative slope: that debt ratios will start rising for decreases in growth, and will fall for increases in growth. The larger is the initial debt ratio, the larger will be the rise in the debt ratio for a given change in growth.

In this thought experiment, the primary surplus had been set to the old growth rate to satisfy equation (4) for a stable debt ratio. To evaluate the rise in debt with a growth slowdown, it helps to set out three extreme cases: (a) the growth change was permanent, (b) the old growth rate was temporary but the new one is permanent, (c) the old growth rate was permanent but the new one is temporary. Remember again I am considering ONLY the role of fiscal policy in the long run to avoid debt crises and neglecting all other considerations, such as countercyclical policies. In case (a), the old fiscal policy was appropriate to stabilize the debt, but now must adjust to the new permanent growth rate. In case (b), the old fiscal policy was already incorrect because the old growth rate was not the permanent one, the new growth rate is permanent, and so fiscal policy should again adjust to the new growth rate. In case (c), if indeed the new growth rate is temporary, then there is no long-run reason to change fiscal policy.

Of course, in the real world, the new growth rate is unpredictable, and it is difficult to assess whether any growth rate is permanent or temporary. We will discuss evidence for permanent changes in growth using averages for as long a period as possible. We will also discuss mean reversion to consider temporary fluctuations in growth rates.

As already mentioned in the introduction, I am considering the effects of growth on debt crises, and not the reverse. Reverse causality in which debt crises decrease growth (such as the "lost decade" of growth often attributed to the Latin American debt crisis) would simply amplify the negative correlation already predicted in (5).

Even if this chapter abstracts from responses of policymakers, there are also mechanical effects of the growth slowdown on the primary surplus to consider. First, most obviously, if the growth change in the short run is a short-run cyclical phenomenon, there is the well-known effect of recessions increasing deficits and booms lowering them. This chapter is not focusing on such cyclical effects, but they may be too important in the data to ignore, especially in the crisis of 2008 to the present. Second, a growth slowdown may make private borrowers as well as public ones insolvent, possibly leading to bank bailouts with government money (as in the post-2007 crisis). More subtly and returning to thinking more in the medium to long run, if future spending plans were geared to the OLD growth rate (such as through forecasts geared to the old growth rate), while revenue reflects the actual NEW growth rate, then a growth slowdown would increase the deficit.[3] So this chapter will do some exercises looking at the primary surplus and growth slowdowns.

4.3   Public Debt Problems and Growth Slowdowns

This section looks at how much growth slowdowns can account for some well-known debt crises.

4.3.1   Previous Results: HIPCS and Middle Income Debt Crises of the 1980s

I showed in an earlier paper (Easterly 2001) that indeed growth slowdowns were strongly associated with rising debt ratios among all developing countries for 1975 to 1994. I reproduce here figure 3 from that paper illustrating those results (figure 4.1).

Figure 4.1 includes two different sets of debt crises—those of low-income

---

3. This effect is well known in the literature; I am grateful to Steven Pennings for suggesting it be included here.

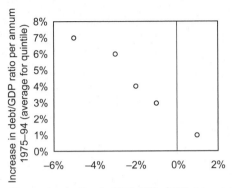

Change in growth rate 1960–75 to 1975–94, quintiles
sorted from most negative to most positive

Fig. 4.1   Change in growth and rise in public debt ratio to GDP
Source: Reproduction of figure 4.3 from Easterly (2001).

countries and those of middle-income countries (both in the 1980s and early
1990s). The low-income countries eventually got debt relief under the HIPC
program of bilateral and multilateral aid agencies. The old paper ran counterfactual exercises in which the debt ratios would have remained stable or
even declined if growth had continued at the 1960 to 1975 rate for cases as
diverse as Costa Rica, Côte d'Ivoire, Gabon, and Togo, and hence these
countries would not have become HIPCs or middle income debt crises. The
point is not that it was reasonable to expect the old growth to continue, but
that debt crises occurred partly because fiscal policy failed to adjust to the
new growth rate.

In the rest of this section, I consider new debt crises that have occurred
more recently. The most recent public debt problems are not among the poor
countries, but among the rich countries: the Eurozone countries (especially
Portugal, Ireland, Italy, Greece, and Spain, the unfortunately named group
PIIGS) and the United States.

4.3.2   Eurozone Debt Crises

There was indeed a growth slowdown in the Eurozone, as shown in the
Figure 4.2 with ten-year moving average growth.[4] Regarding the PIIGS
countries, Greece, Portugal, and Spain had the most severe growth slowdown, after growth in those countries was highest in the Eurozone in the
1960s and early 1970s. Italy went from one of the highest Eurozone growth
rates in the 1960s and early 1970s to the lowest in the 1990s and 2000s. Ire-

4. I omit more recent entrants into the Eurozone after 2001, which excludes Cyprus, Estonia,
Slovakia, and Slovenia.

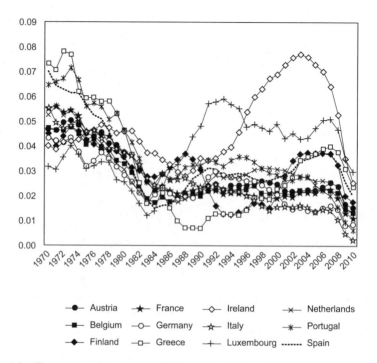

Fig. 4.2   Ten-year moving average GDP growth rate ending in year shown in Euro-zone countries

land is atypical, with a growth boom in the 1990s and a collapse in the 2000s. All of the Eurozone countries have a slowdown by 2010 of course, because of the deep crisis in 2007 to 2010, with Portugal and Italy at the bottom.

We can see more evidence for a permanent growth slowdown in a simple fixed effects panel regression for Eurozone countries, in table 4.1. To avoid any endogeneity to the choice of breakpoint, I choose the breakpoint that simply divides the period into two equal subperiods. The growth slowdown is statistically significant for each group, PIIGS and non-PIIGS. There seems to be a strong common element in the slowdown of each group, as we cannot reject the hypothesis of zero fixed effects within each group. The large standard deviation of the pure time-varying error term (assumed to be independent and identically distributed [i.i.d.] in this panel regression) is suggestive that mean reversion will be an important factor in the short to medium run.

Figure 4.3 looks at increases in the debt ratio per annum associated with the growth change from 1960 to 1985 to 1986 to 2010, based on equation (7). The vertical axis is Δd (per annum). Note from equation (7) that the larger is the initial debt ratio, the larger will be the predicted increase in the debt ratio associated with growth slowdowns. So the horizontal axis here is the change in growth times the initial debt ratio: $(\Delta g)\, d$. This graph gives more insight

Table 4.1   Fixed effects regressions for Eurozone annual growth rates, 1960–2010

	Variables: Growth					
Post-1985				-0.0130***	-0.0102***	-0.0170***
				(0.00223)	(0.00258)	(0.00392)
Constant	0.0320***	0.0296***	0.0354***	0.0385***	0.0347***	0.0439***
	(0.00114)	(0.00132)	(0.00203)	(0.00157)	(0.00183)	(0.00277)
Observations	600	350	250	600	350	250
Group	Eurozone	non-PIIGS	PIIGS	Eurozone	non-PIIGS	PIIGS
Number of countries	12	7	5	12	7	5
Standard error of time-varying error term	0.028	0.025	0.032	0.027	0.024	0.031
Significance level for fixed effects	0.045	0.334	0.167	0.032	0.307	0.140

Note: Standard errors in parentheses.

***$p < 0.01$.

**$p < 0.05$.

*$p < 0.1$.

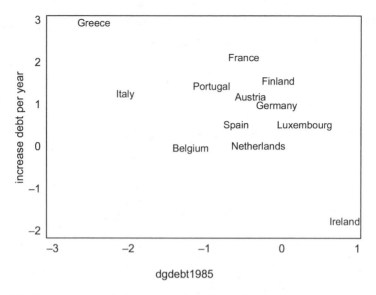

Fig. 4.3   Eurozone countries' growth change, 1960–1985 and 1986–2010 (interacted with initial debt ratio in 1985), and debt ratio increase per year, 1986–2010

into the longer-run debt problems of Greece, Italy, and Portugal among the PIIGS (as well as France!). Ireland actually had debt reduction over this period due to growth acceleration—we will see in the following graph that Ireland's debt changes only show up as associated with growth changes when broken down by decade. Spain did not experience as large a debt increase associated with the growth slowdown.

The previous regression is suggestive that the slowdown was permanent, which suggests a policy failure to adjust the primary balance to the new growth rate. Greece is the most notable example here.

Figure 4.4 looks at the Eurozone countries over the successive decades 1980s to 1990s to 2000s, again based on equation (7) relating Δd to $(\Delta g)d$. The horizontal axis thus shows the change in average GDP growth from one decade to the next (interacted with initial debt ratio at the beginning of each decade), and the vertical axis shows the increase in the public debt ratio per annum in the latter decade.

The way to think of these graphs is NOT as a test of significance of the correlation in this one sample alone (which only has twenty-two observations, not to mention the even fewer observations in the previous graph). We are doing debt accounting based on an arithmetic identity, not testing a statistical hypothesis. Rather, the location of points in the upper left-hand corner and lower right-hand corner show episodes where growth changes played an important role in debt changes.

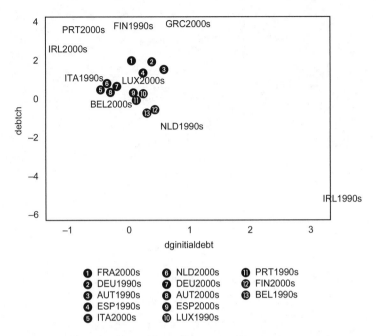

Fig. 4.4   **Annualized debt change related to growth change times initial debt, decades of 1990s and 2000s**

Portugal is an example of the recent debt crises in which there was a major growth slowdown from 1990 to 2000 to 2000 to 2010. Italy's debt accumulation was associated more with the growth slowdown in the 1990s. One non-PIIGS example of a growth slowdown associated with rising public debt ratios was Finland in the 1990s. With decade averages, there is less confidence about whether growth slowdowns are permanent or temporary.

Ireland is a special case where temporariness is more likely. The boom of the 1990s seems like a temporary deviation from a longer run average. Hence, allowing public debt ratios to fall during 1990 to 2000 with the boom, and then rise after the end of the boom, could be sensible policy as opposed to adjusting fiscal policy to a temporary growth rate. The extent of the public debt rise in 2000 to 2010 may still have been excessive if policymakers expected the high 1990s growth to partially persist; we will revisit this issue with data on projections later.

We suggested earlier that a growth slowdown could also affect the primary surplus. There is some evidence for this in figure 4.5, using five-year averages for growth (change from one five-year average to the next) and the average primary surplus to GDP ratio in the second five-year period. The year part of each point shows the year in which the second five-year period ended.

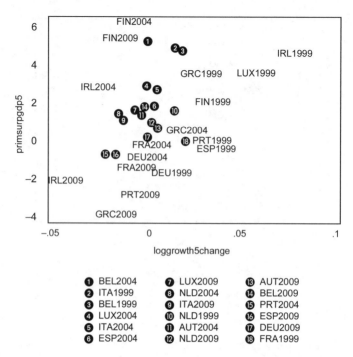

Fig. 4.5   Eurozone growth change and primary surplus/GDP, five-year averages

4.3.3   US Debt Crisis

Analysts of the recent crisis with US government debt usually focus on large deficits in the new millennium. Did growth slowdowns have any role in the United States, like they did for some Eurozone countries, the HIPCs, and the 1980s middle income debt crisis?

The federal debt ratio rose steadily for twenty years from 1975 to 1994 (figure 4.6) at the same time that US long-run growth (shown in figure 4.7 as a twenty-year moving average) was slowing down. A very different episode was the decline in the debt ratio during the Clinton years, as growth accelerated in the second half of the 1990s. Finally, the recent climb in US debt ratio corresponds to a collapse of the US growth rate in the new millennium. The 2008 to 2010 crisis was of course very important here, but the growth rate was already decelerating during the George W. Bush years before the crisis.

Next we will analyze growth forecasts made by the administration every year since 1975. These forecasts during most of this period have a six-year horizon, so I also present US data in the current section in rolling six-year averages.

Figure 4.8 shows the application of equation (7) to the US data, relating (Δd) to (Δg)d. The horizontal axis shows rolling averages for the average growth change from one six-year period to the next, interacted with the

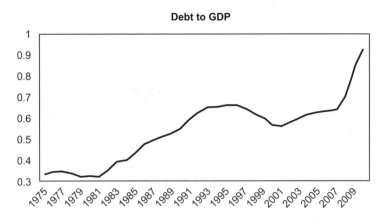

Fig. 4.6   US federal debt to GDP ratio, 1975–2010

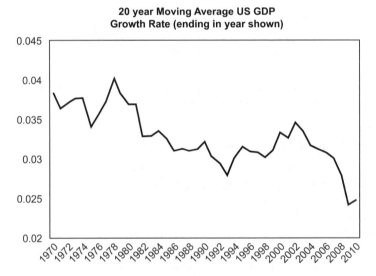

Fig. 4.7   Twenty-year moving average GDP growth rate, United States

initial public debt to GDP ratio at the start of each six-year period on the horizontal axis ((Δg)d). The vertical axis shows the public debt ratio increase per annum (Δd) in the second six-year period, beginning at the start date shown for each point in the graph. Again the purpose of this graph is not statistical testing (there are too few data points and they are not even independent because they are rolling averages) but an illustration of which years have the mechanical growth effect from equation (7) dominant. Growth accelerations in the late 1970s and mid-1990s show strong debt reduction, while growth slowdowns in the new millennium show strong debt increases.

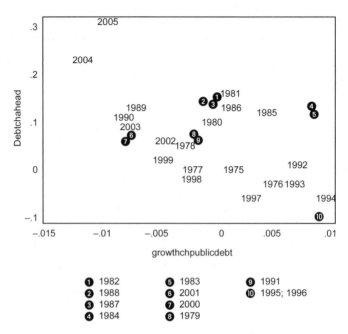

Fig. 4.8 US debt change per annum against change in growth*initial debt ratio, over six years, beginning with start date shown

4.4   Problems of Growth Projections

If debt crises can occur partly because of a growth slowdown to which fiscal policy fails to adjust, it may be because the changes are unanticipated or because the change year by year is considered temporary, when it is in fact permanent. We can study these possibilities with actual data we have on growth projections and outcomes. The sensitivity of debt crises to growth slowdowns makes it particularly important to have sound growth forecasting practices. This will give as much lead time as possible to precautionary fiscal policy to avoid debt crises. We will also consider some principles of sound forecasting, such as anticipating regression to the mean and making conservative forecasts when debt is high, and see whether they are observed in this section.

4.4.1   Association between Growth Changes and Forecast Errors

Our data on Eurozone growth forecasts comes from countries' budget ministries' submission of projections at the same time as they report budget plans. Unfortunately, these data are very time-consuming to collect and for this chapter it was only possible to collect data on the PIIGS countries in the Eurozone. The projections are for a period between three and five years forward, and began only in 1998. Hence, we have data on projections and

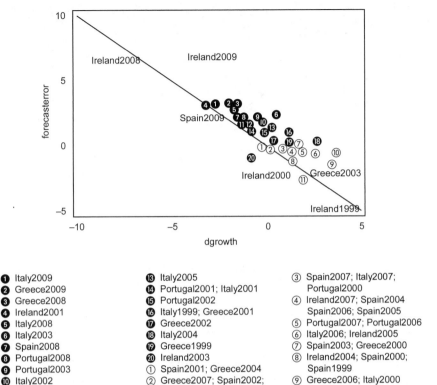

Fig. 4.9   PIIGS countries, change in growth and forecast error at horizon $t + 1$

actual outcomes for the period 1999 to 2010 for the PIIGS countries. The first thing to document is the unsurprising link between growth changes and forecast errors.

Figure 4.9 shows the association between forecast errors (projected GDP for $t + 1$ – actual GDP growth at $t + 1$) at horizon $t + 1$ and the change in growth from t to $t + 1$. There is indeed an association between declines in growth and positive forecast errors, as well as examples of negative forecast errors when growth accelerates. The slope will be –1 if the growth forecast was simply for the previous growth to continue (the graph shows a line with slope –1 for reference). In the presence of mean reversion (strongly confirmed by tests on growth rates in this sample and in others), predicting the same growth rate to continue fails to utilize information on mean reversion. If the current growth rate is above the long-run average, then forecasts should anticipate a movement back down toward the mean.

Figure 4.10 shows the growth changes and forecast errors for the time

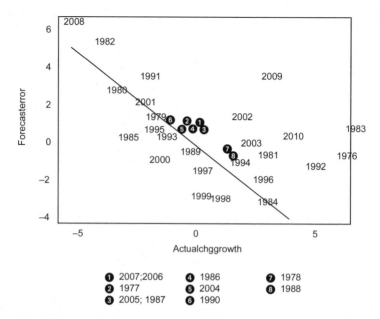

Fig. 4.10   US annual data, forecast error, and actual change in GDP growth at horizon *t* + 1

series for the United States for 1975 to 2010 for every year at horizon *t* + 1. Again, unsurprisingly, large growth changes produce forecast errors in the opposite direction. The line drawn shows the reference case of a slope of −1, in which the forecast is simply for the current growth to continue unchanged.

4.4.2   Association between Forecast Error and Debt Change and Deficits

Another way to show the role of growth changes in debt is to show the link directly from the forecast error to the change in the public debt ratio. Figure 4.11 shows positive forecast errors and negative forecast errors important for some debt changes for the PIIGS countries. A similar graph (figure 4.12) shows episodes of positive forecast errors associated with debt increases in the United States, while negative forecast errors are associated with debt decreases (here using the rolling six-year forward projections).

4.4.3   Sound Forecasting Practices and Reality

As previously suggested, countries that already have high debt are more sensitive to growth slowdowns. It makes sense that the higher is the initial debt, the more conservative should be the growth forecasts. In the Eurozone, the high debt countries should be more conservative about forecasts, and the United States should have been more conservative as the debt ratio got higher. We also have data on projections made for HIPC countries as an

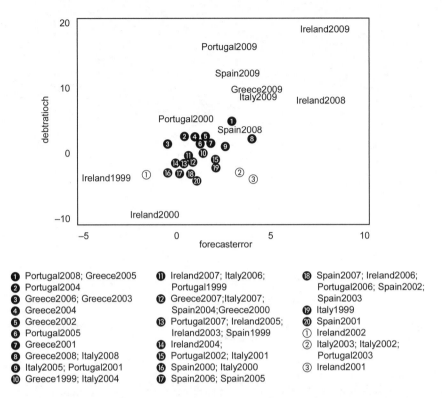

Fig. 4.11   **GDP growth forecast error for *t* + 1 and public debt to GDP ratio change in that year**

interesting post-debt-crisis example, where conservative forecasts could have helped to prevent reemergence of new debt crises.

The consideration of mean reversion should also play a role. High growth well above the countries' long-run average should not be expected to continue when projections are made. We have already seen in figures 4.9 and 4.10 a failure to utilize mean reversion.

Of course, projections are not made by disinterested parties. It may be tempting for politicians to use optimistic projections to disguise the reality of debt problems and postpone the need for fiscal adjustment. The HIPC example will show an unusual case of this. Politicians may find it tempting to treat low growth as temporary and high growth as permanent, and so may not sufficiently anticipate growth slowdowns from temporary highs.

HIPCs

Highly Indebted Poor Countries became HIPCs because in many cases they failed to adjust to the growth slowdown. In other cases, growth played

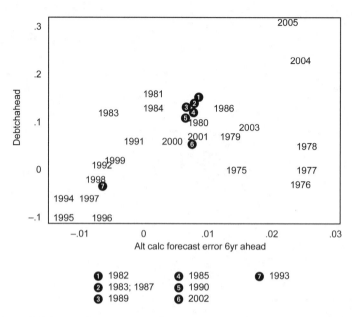

Fig. 4.12   US debt ratio change per annum and US GDP growth forecast error, over six years ahead, with start date shown

a smaller role or no role, and the HIPCs simply ran excessive deficits to accumulate high debt relative to GDP. In either case it would seem to suggest that the HIPCs would need to do fiscal adjustment along with receiving debt relief to prevent the emergence of new debt crises all over again.

However, the HIPC program was determined in part by an international political campaign to grant debt forgiveness to poor countries. This campaign applied pressure not only to forgive the debts but also to maintain the same flow of official financing to poor countries (which partly consisted of loans and not just grants) and to NOT otherwise reduce public spending, which implied NOT doing any major fiscal adjustment in HIPC countries. A fiscal policy unchanged from one that previously created a debt crisis would eventually result in the emergence of new debt problems. The World Bank and International Monetary Fund (IMF) analysts who designed HIPC debt relief packages were required to do long-run debt and growth forecasts to demonstrate that the HIPCs debt after relief was "sustainable"—that is, debt ratios would not increase again in the future.

How to reconcile these irreconcilable mandates? The answer appears in the next table: official HIPC programs prepared by IMF and World Bank staff exaggerated future growth prospects of the HIPCs. I gained access to a large database of growth forecasts in HIPC documents produced in the 1990s and early 2000s. I was also given growth forecasts made for non-HIPC countries for the same time periods by World Bank and IMF staff. Now that

Table 4.2   **Regression of annual growth forecast errors ("ForecastErr") and dummies for HIPC countries ("HIPC") and sub-Saharan Africa ("Africa"), 1995–2010**

	ForecastErr		
Variables	(1)	(2)	(3)
Africa	0.145		0.605
	(0.394)		(0.367)
HIPC	0.954**	1.022***	
	(0.380)	(0.343)	
Constant	−0.0416	0.0111	0.152
	(0.307)	(0.271)	(0.298)
Observations	156	156	156
R^2	0.055	0.054	0.018

Note: Robust standard errors in parentheses.
***$p < 0.01$.
**$p < 0.05$.
*$p < 0.1$.

I have access to actual growth data up through 2010, I can calculate the ex post forecast errors (ForecastErr in the regressions shown following) in both groups. There is a significant positive forecast error of HIPC countries of about 1 percentage point of growth relative to non-HIPC countries. These results are even more surprising when we consider the positive shocks to many HIPCs through commodity prices and growth rates in 2000 to 2010 that were at historic highs for other reasons. Although many HIPC countries are in Africa, the results are not a spurious consequence of excessive optimism about Africa (there is indeed no evidence for the latter (see table 4.2). To avoid the unpalatable expectation that debt ratios will start climbing again in the absence of fiscal adjustment in HIPCs (although from very low levels after debt forgiveness took effect in recent years), the analysts apparently resorted to high growth forecasts. A situation that called for conservative growth forecasts—countries with a long track record of fiscal mismanagement—instead generated the reverse.

PIIGS over 1999 to 2010

Were the PIIGS conservative on their growth forecasts because of their precarious debt situations? Or did they use optimistic growth forecasts as a way to cover up their fiscal problems? For example, the European Commission commented diplomatically on a Greek forecast in 2001:

> The macroeconomic projections included in the stability programme, indicating strong real GDP growth, are considered as ambitious, at the upper level of possibilities. ("Commission Assesses the 2000 Stability Pro-

Table 4.3   **Significance of forecast errors, annual data for PIIGS countries, 1999–2010**

Dependent Variable:	Forecast error for growth	Forecast error for growth	Forecast error for growth	Forecast error for growth
Average	1.286***	1.286***	1.286**	
	(0.182)	(0.25)	(0.426)	
Portugal				1.699***
				(0.271)
Ireland				1.367*
				(0.712)
Italy				1.731***
				(0.304)
Greece				1.142***
				(0.43)
Spain				0.434
				(0.299)
Observations	193	193	193	193
R^2				0.235
Standard errors clustered by	Country	Year forecast was made		

Note: Robust standard errors in parentheses.
***$p < 0.01$.
**$p < 0.05$.
*$p < 0.1$.

gramme for Greece (2000–2004)", European Commission press release, January 24, 2001, available at http://europa.eu/rapid/searchAction.do)

Table 4.3 shows the average forecast errors for the PIIGS sample over 1999 to 2010.

The forecast errors for the PIIGS over 1999 to 2010 were significantly positive on average. This result survives clustering the errors by the date of the forecast, or alternatively clustering by country. A simple sign test of whether forecast errors were positive also confirms the significance at the 1 percent level.

The result is not entirely driven by the crisis period 2008 to 2010. The PIIGS' average forecast error is much smaller (0.31 percentage point per annum) over 1999 to 2007, but both the average error test and the sign test are still significant at 5 percent for positive forecast errors (not shown). Moreover, even if the depth of the crisis was unusual, a recession at some point during a twelve-year period is NOT unusual, so it biases things the other way to endogenously exclude the bad years.

Looking at individual countries' forecast errors, those for Portugal, Italy, and Greece are large and statistically significant at the 1 percent level, Ireland is large but only significant at the 10 percent level, and Spain's forecast

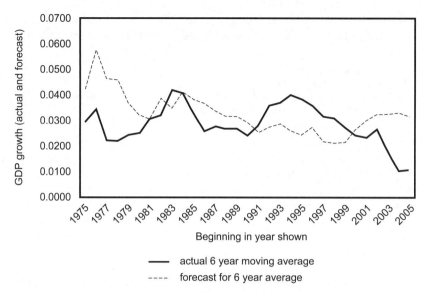

Fig. 4.13   Forecast and actual six-year moving average growth in United States

error is smaller and not statistically significant. The worst offenders against the maxim of being conservative when debt is already high were Italy and Greece, whose debt was already above 100 percent of GDP in 1998, yet forecasts over 1999 to 2010 were still too optimistic. Greece was also the worst offender against the principle of mean reverting forecasts, as the average growth projected for 1999 to 2010 was well above its previous long-run growth rate.

The United States during the New Millennium

Figure 4.13 shows the forecast and actual US GDP growth as six-year moving averages, going forward from the date shown. The excess optimism in the late 1970s was not that damaging because debt levels were not high. The conservative forecasts in the 1990s at higher debt levels contributed to the reduction in the debt ratio, as noted previously.

The final curious episode is the increase in projected growth even as the actual growth rate was falling, beginning at the new millennium (figure 4.13). This began before the effects of the financial crisis would be included in six-year-forward growth. This was the opposite of sound forecasting practice, which should have anticipated the reversion to the mean after the boom of the 1990s (that did, in fact, happen).

One possible interpretation is that negative fiscal shocks after 9/11—such as the spending associated with two new wars—led to anticipated increases in the deficit. To avoid showing a projected rise in debt ratios, the administration simply raised the projected growth rate. This was part of the complex of problems that contributed to the debt crisis the United States has today.

4.5   Conclusion

The unpleasant arithmetic of growth and public debt is that permanent growth slowdowns call for fiscal adjustments that (as in many examples shown here) politicians are unwilling or unable to make. As a result, debt crises often result in part from major growth slowdowns, a factor that has been underemphasized in the literature and in public discussion compared to the emphasis on budget deficits. This unpleasant arithmetic suggests the important benefits of forecasting of growth that acknowledges mean reversion and is more conservative the more precarious the debt situation. Unfortunately, political economy factors seem to result in analysts sometimes doing the reverse—making growth forecasts more optimistic to disguise the need for fiscal adjustment.

References

Ashiya, Mashahiro. 2007. "Forecast Accuracy of the Japanese Government: Its Year-Ahead GDP Forecast is Too Optimistic." *Japan and the World Economy* 19 (1): 68–85.

Auerbach, Alan J. 1994. "The US Fiscal Problem: Where We are, How We Got Here and Where We're Going." *NBER Macroeconomics Annual 1994,* vol. 9, edited by Stanley Fischer and Julio J. Rotemberg, 141–75. Cambridge, MA: MIT Press.

———. 1999. "On the Performance and Use of Government Revenue Forecasts." *National Tax Journal* 52 (4): 765–82.

Blanchard, Olivier J. 1990. "Suggestions for a New Set of Fiscal Indicators." OECD Working Paper no. 79. Paris: Organization for Economic Cooperation and Development.

Buiter, Willem H. 1985. "Guide to Public Sector Debt and Deficits." *Economic Policy: A European Forum 1* November:13–79.

Chalk, R., and R. Hemming. 2000. "Assessing Fiscal Sustainability in Theory and Practice." IMF Working Paper no. 00/81. Washington, DC: International Monetary Fund.

Easterly, William. 2001. "Growth Implosions and Debt Explosions: Do Growth Slowdowns Explain Public Debt Crises?" *Contributions to Macroeconomics* 1(1). http://williameasterly.files.wordpress.com/2010/08/29_easterly_growthimplosions anddebtexplosions_prp.pdf.

Frankel, J. 2011. "Over-optimism in Forecasts by Official Budget Agencies and Its Implications." NBER Working Paper no. 17239. Cambridge, MA: National Bureau of Economic Research, July.

Frendreis, John, and Raymond Tatalovich. 2000. "Accuracy and Bias in Macroeconomic Forecasting by the Administration, the CBO, and the Federal Reserve Board." *Polity* 32 (4): 623–32.

Huang, H., and D. Xie. 2008. "Fiscal Sustainability and Fiscal Soundness." *Annals of Economics and Finance* 9-2:239–51.

Jonung, Lars, and Martin Larch. 2004. "Improving Fiscal Policy in the EU: The Case for Independent Forecasts." European Commission Economic Paper no. 210.

Marinheiro, C. 2011. "Fiscal Sustainability and the Accuracy of Macroeconomic Forecasts: Do Supranational Forecasts Rather than Government Forecasts Make a Difference?" *Journal of Sustainable Economy* 3 (2): 185–209.

McNab, Robert M., Mark Rider, and Kent Wall. 2007. "Are Errors in Official US Budget Receipts Forecasts Just Noise?" Andrew Young School Research Paper Series Working Paper no. 07-22, April.

Mendoza, E., and P. M. Oviedo. 2004. "Public Debt, Fiscal Solvency and Macro-economic Uncertainty in Latin America: The Cases of Brazil, Colombia, Costa Rica, and Mexico." NBER Working Paper no. 10637. Cambridge, MA: National Bureau of Economic Research, July.

Mühleisen, Martin, Stephan Danninger, David Hauner, Kornélia Krajnyák, and Bennett Sutton. 2005. "How Do Canadian Budget Forecasts Compare with Those of Other Industrial Countries?" IMF Working Papers no. 05/66, April. Washington, DC: International Monetary Fund.

Strauch, R., M. Hallerberg, and J. von Hagen. 2004. "Budgetary Forecasts in Europe—The Track Record of Stability and Convergance Programs." European Central Bank Working Paper no. 307.

Comment   Indira Rajaraman

This chapter by William Easterly explores the possible contribution of technocratic error in growth projections toward the entire range of modern-day debt crises, from those in Latin American and Highly Indebted Poor Countries (HIPC) in the 1980s and 1990s, to the debt-stressed countries of the Eurozone today. The chapter is not about unforeseen adverse growth shocks. It is about systematic upward bias in official growth forecasts over the medium to long run, and is essentially descriptive in its linking of that bias to the fiscally unsustainable debt outcome, normalized by the (lower) realized GDP denominator.

The chapter adds to what is by now a fairly extensive literature on growth forecast error covering the United States, Canada, Japan, and the Eurozone. Systematic upward bias is reported in these prior studies for Japan (Ashiya 2007), and more generally for a set of thirty Organization for Economic Cooperation and Development (OECD) countries, with higher bias at longer horizons, and for membership of the Eurozone (Frankel 2011). A recent interesting paper by Marinheiro (2010) finds national forecasts of Eurozone members to be more biased upwards than European Commission forecasts.

I have five comments on the chapter by Easterly.

Indira Rajaraman is honorary visiting professor at the Indian Statistical Institute and a member of the Central Board of Directors and of the Technical Advisory Committee on Monetary Policy of the Reserve Bank of India.

For acknowledgments, sources of research support, and disclosure of the author's material financial relationships, if any, please see http://www.nber.org/chapters/c12641.ack.

First, in arguing that optimistic growth projections were what precipitated fiscal failure to adjust to the growth slowdown, the author presumes a compressible margin in public expenditure. In every country, there is a basic noncompressible core of public expenditure that is growth invariant, comprising at a minimum the sum of interest on accumulated debt, pensions, and salaries. To this can be added other constituents underpinned by statute, in the form of guarantees and entitlements. The residual compressible expenditure, after deduction of this core, could be essentially nonexistent in poorly managed fiscal regimes, which are typically characterized by bloated statutory entitlements. These entitlements, if underpinned by law, are not easily reversed or reduced. The compressible residual could also be very low in well-managed fiscal regimes, where irreversible entitlements of this kind are cut to the bone.

That being the case, the margin of compressibility, which determines the extent of ex ante fiscal compression possible, had growth been more correctly forecast, is not possible to ascertain except through a country-specific examination of the legal underpinnings of public expenditure constituents. The chapter could have made a very interesting contribution if the compressible margin had been quantified in a long time series going back fifty years, even if only for the stressed members of the Eurozone (Portugal, Italy, Ireland, Greece, and Spain). Of specific interest would be the impact of Eurozone membership as an event in that time series.

Second, suppose a country has an ex ante compressibility margin of zero, because of public entitlements protected in their entirety by law. In that case, there would be no reward to a correct growth forecast, since no fiscal adjustment is possible ex ante anyway. It is only a crisis that can transform expenditures that are noncompressible ex ante into compressibility ex post. A 10 percent salary cut, for example, is possible after a crisis, not before, no matter how correct the forecast of low growth, and how persuasive the expectation of its fiscal consequences if left uncorrected. Therefore, optimistic growth forecasts may be a politically strategic move rather than a result of technical incompetence.

Third, the central problem in the present Eurozone crisis is the need for fiscal cuts at a time of slow growth, whatever be the nature (cyclical or otherwise) of that slowdown. Had growth been correctly forecast, there would have actually been a need to provide for an increase in unemployment compensation, which is the automatic cyclical stabilizer built into the fiscal structure of the OECD world. So the failure to do prior fiscal correction should actually be calculated net of this added provision needed in public expenditure, had the growth slowdown been correctly foreseen.

Going forward, one strategy by which to resolve the impossible confluence of a low-growth trough, fiscal unsustainability, and political turbulence over expenditure cuts, might be to cap the sum of salaries and unemployment compensation. That renders transparent the need for salary containment, and calibrates the sacrifice required of those fortunate enough to have government jobs to the failure of the economy to provide jobs for all.

Fourth, within the compressible margin, the existence of which is what the chapter is predicated on, the growth impact of the different components amenable to compression would vary according to import content, and thereby the domestic multiplier specific to each, a critical consideration in a low-growth environment. At the same time, although this may be a consideration in emerging markets rather than in the Eurozone, spending on infrastructure, like transportation, for example, may simultaneously raise potential growth (Easterly and Rebelo 1993), and have a low domestic multiplier because of its high import content. So a composite scoring of components of compressible expenditure is needed, if the full benefit of accurate growth forecasts is to be reaped through ex ante fiscal containment with minimal growth costs.

My fifth and final point on the chapter has to do with the possible nature of the prior revenue side correction with an accurate forecast of a growth slowdown. The three possibilities here are higher tax rates to compensate for the decline in the taxable base; reduced avenues for tax avoidance, thus expanding the taxable base; and reduced avenues for evasion, thus expanding the reported taxable base. Of these, the first option of a rate increase could carry a high downward multiplier impact on growth, if the recent high estimates for the tax multiplier in the United States by Romer and Romer (2010) are generalizable to other countries. The second option of reduced avoidance, if attempted, for example, through elimination of investment incentives like accelerated depreciation, could carry a heavy growth cost. The third is the only option that carries a possible growth dividend, since evaded income usually flees out of the country.

References

Ashiya, Mashahiro. 2007. "Forecast Accuracy of the Japanese Government: Its Year-Ahead GDP Forecast is too Optimistic." *Japan and the World Economy* 19 (1): 68–85.

Easterly, William, and Sergio Rebelo. 1993. "Fiscal Policy and Economic Growth." *Journal of Monetary Economics* 32:417–58.

Frankel, Jeffrey. 2011. "Over-Optimism in Forecasts by Official Budget Agencies and Its Implications." NBER Working Paper no. 17239. Cambridge, MA: National Bureau of Economic Research, July.

Marinheiro, Carlos F. 2010. "Fiscal Sustainability and the Accuracy of Macroeconomic Forecasts: Do Supranational Forecasts Rather than Government Forecasts Make a Difference?" *Journal of Sustainable Economy* 3 (2): 185–209.

Romer, Christina D., and David H. Romer. 2010. "The Macroeconomic Effects of Tax Changes: Estimates Based on a New Measure of Fiscal Shocks." *American Economic Review* 100:763–801.

5

Game Over
Simulating Unsustainable
Fiscal Policy

Richard W. Evans, Laurence J. Kotlikoff,
and Kerk L. Phillips

5.1 Introduction

Most developed countries appear to be running unsustainable fiscal policies. In the United States, federal liabilities (official debt plus the present value of projected noninterest expenditures) exceed federal assets (the present value of projected taxes) by $211 trillion, or fourteen times GDP. Closing this fiscal gap requires an immediate and permanent 64 percent hike in all federal taxes.[1] Unlike official debt, the fiscal gap is a label-free and, thus, meaningful measure of fiscal sustainability.[2] But measuring the fiscal gap raises questions of how to properly discount risky future government purchases and the remaining lifetime net taxes of current and future generations—their generational accounts.

Our approach to assessing sustainability is to simulate a stochastic general equilibrium model and see how long it takes for unsustainable policy to produce game over—the point where the policies can no longer be maintained. Our framework is intentionally simple—a two-period overlapping generations (OLG) model with first-period labor supply and an aggregate productivity shock. The government redistributes a fixed amount H_t each

Richard W. Evans is assistant professor of economics at Brigham Young University. Laurence J. Kotlikoff is professor of economics at Boston University and a research associate of the National Bureau of Economic Research. Kerk L. Phillips is associate professor of economics at Brigham Young University.

This chapter has benefited from comments and suggestions from participants in the 2011 NBER "Fiscal Policy after the Financial Crisis" conference. For acknowledgments, sources of research support, and disclosure of the authors' material financial relationships, if any, please see http://www.nber.org/chapters/c12642.ack.

1. Calculation by authors based on Congressional Budget Office (June 2011) Alternative Fiscal Scenario long-term project of federal cash flows.
2. See Kotlikoff and Green (2009).

period from the young to the old. If times become sufficiently bad and the economy reaches game over (i.e., H_t exceeds the earnings of the young), we either let the government take all of the earnings of the young and give them to the old and thereby terminate the economy or start redistributing a fixed proportion of earnings from the young to the old.

Our simulations, calibrated to the US economy, produce an average duration to game over of about one century, with a 35 percent chance of reaching the fiscal limit in about thirty years. We also calculate our model's fiscal gap and equity premium. Our model's fiscal gaps are generally small and quite sensitive to the choice of discount rate. But for any choice of discount factors, the fiscal gaps are much larger when the economy is closer to game over, suggesting that this measure can provide early warning of unsustainable policy.

When post-game-over policy terminates the economy, initial period equity premia are about 6 percent—high enough to explain the equity premium puzzle. When game-over is followed by proportional redistribution, equity premiums are initially about 2 percent, but rise dramatically as the economy approaches game over.

When our economy reaches game over, the government is forced to default on its promised payment to the contemporaneous elderly. Thus, this chapter contributes to both the literatures on sovereign default[3] and fiscally stressed economies.[4]

Our model has no money, so it does not include the monetary and fiscal interactions described in Sargent and Wallace (1981) and highlighted in the recent fiscal limits research.[5] It does include sticky fiscal policy, examined in Alesina and Drazen (1991), as well as Auerbach and Hassett (1992, 2001, 2002, 2007) and Hassett and Metcalf (1999), and regime switching, surveyed in Hamilton (2008).

Section 5.2 presents the case that game over is followed by policy that kills the economy. Section 5.3 looks at the switch to policy with either permanently high or moderate intergenerational redistribution. Section 5.4 concludes.

5.2   Model with Shutdown

Consider a model with overlapping generations of two-period-lived agents in which the government redistributes a fixed amount $\bar{H} \geq 0$ from

---

3. See Yue (2010); Reinhart and Rogoff (2009); Arellano (2008); Aguiar and Gopinath (2006); Leeper and Walker (2011).
4. See Auerbach and Kotlikoff (1987); Kotlikoff, Smetters, and Walliser (1998a, 1998b, 2007); İmrohoroğlu, İmrohoroğlu, and Joines (1995, 1999); Huggett and Ventura (1999); Cooley and Soares (1999); De Nardi, İmrohoroğlu, and Sargent (1999); Altig et al. (2001); Smetters and Walliser (2004); and Nishiyama and Smetters (2007).
5. See also Cochrane (2011); Leeper and Walker (2011); Davig, Leeper, and Walker (2010, 2011); Davig and Leeper (2011a, 2011b); and Trabandt and Uhlig (2009).

the young to the old each period in which the transfer is feasible. When the transfer is not feasible, the government redistributes all of the available earnings of the young. In so doing, it leaves the economy with no capital in the subsequent period and makes game over economically terminal.

5.2.1   Household Problem

A unit measure of identical agents is born each period. They supply labor only when young and do so inelastically:

$$l_{1,t} = \bar{l} = 1 \quad \forall t,$$

where $l_{1,t}$ is labor supplied by age-1 workers at time t.

Young agents at time t have no wealth and allocate the earnings not extracted by the government between consumption $c_{i,t}$ and saving $k_{i+1,t+1}$ to maximize expected utility. Their problem is

$$\max_{c_{1,t}, k_{2,t+1}, c_{2,t+1}} u(c_{1,t}) + \beta E_t[u(c_{2,t+1})]$$

$$\text{where } c_{1,t} + k_{2,t+1} \leq w_t - H_t$$

$$\text{and } c_{2,t+1} \leq (1 + r_{t+1} - \delta)k_{2,t+1} + H_{t+1}$$

$$\text{and } c_{1,t}, c_{2,t+1}, k_{2,t+1} \geq 0$$

$$\text{and where } u(c_{i,t}) = \frac{(c_{i,t})^{1-\gamma} - 1}{1 - \gamma}.$$

Consumption in the second period of life satisfies

(1) $$c_{2,t+1} = (1 + r_{t+1} - \delta)k_{2,t+1} + H_{t+1}.$$

The nonnegativity constraint on consumption never binds because each term on the right-hand side of (1) is weakly positive. Consumption and saving when young, $c_{1,t}$ and $k_{2,t+1}$, are jointly determined by the first-period budget constraint and the Euler equation.

(2) $$c_{1,t} + k_{2,t+1} = w_t - H_t$$

(3) $$u'(c_{1,t}) = \beta E_t[(1 + r_{t+1} - \delta)u'(c_{2,t+1})]$$

From the right-hand side of (2), the nonnegativity constraints on $c_{1,t}$ and $k_{2,t+1}$ bind when $w_t \leq \bar{H}$. In these cases the government is only able to collect $H_t = w_t$. In so doing, it forces the consumption and saving of the young to zero and terminates the economy.

5.2.2   Firms' Problem

Firms collectively hire labor, L_t, at real wage, w_t, and rent capital, K_t, at real rental rate r_t. Output, Y_t, is produced via the Cobb-Douglas function,

(4) $$Y_t = A_t K_t^\alpha L_t^{1-\alpha} \quad \forall t,$$

where $A_t = e^{z_t}$ is distributed log normally, and z_t follows an AR(1) process.

(5) $$z_t = \rho z_{t-1} + (1 - \rho)\mu + \varepsilon_t$$

where $\rho \in [0,1)$, $\mu \geq 0$, and $\varepsilon_t \sim N(0,\sigma^2)$.

Profit maximization implies

(6) $$r_t = \alpha e^{z_t} K_t^{\alpha-1} L_t^{1-\alpha} \quad \forall t$$

(7) $$w_t = (1 - \alpha)e^{z_t} K_t^{\alpha} L_t^{-\alpha} \quad \forall t.$$

5.2.3   Market Clearing

In equilibrium, factor markets clear and national saving equals net investment

(8) $$L_t = l_1 = \overline{l} = 1 \quad \forall t$$

(9) $$K_t = k_{2,t} \quad \forall t$$

(10) $$Y_t - C_t = K_{t+1} - (1 - \delta)K_t \quad \forall t$$

where C_t in (10) is aggregate consumption; that is, $C_t \equiv \sum_{i=1}^{2} c_{i,t}$.

5.2.4   Solution and Calibration

A competitive equilibrium for a given $\bar{H}$ is defined as follows.

DEFINITION 1 (EQUILIBRIUM). *A competitive equilibrium with economic shutdown when $w_t < \bar{H}$ is defined as consumption, $c_{1,t}$ and $c_{2,t}$, and savings, $k_{2,t+1}$, allocations and a real wage, w_t, and real net interest rate, r_t, each period such that:*

1. *households optimize according to (1), (2) and (3),*
2. *firms optimize according to (6) and (7),*
3. *markets clear according to (8), (9), and (10).*

To solve the model, we rewrite (2) as

(11) $$k_{2,t+1} = w_t - H_t - c_{1,t},$$

and use this and the model's other equations to write the Euler equation as

(12) $$u'(c_{1,t}) = \beta E_{z_{t+1}|z_t}[(1 + \alpha e^{z_{t+1}}[(1 - \alpha)e^{z_t}k_{2,t}^{\alpha} - \bar{H} - c_{1,t}]^{\alpha-1} - \delta) \times \ldots$$
$$u'([1 + \alpha e^{z_{t+1}}([1 - \alpha)e^{z_t}k_{2,t}^{\alpha} - \bar{H} - c_{1,t}]^{\alpha-1} - \delta]([1 - \alpha)e^{z_t}k_{2,t}^{\alpha}$$
$$- \bar{H} - c_{1,t}) + H_{t+1})]$$

where

(13) $$H_t = \min\{w_t, \bar{H}\} = \min\{[1 - \alpha]e^{z_t}k_{2,t}^{\alpha}, \bar{H}\} \quad \forall t.$$

Table 5.1   **Calibration of two-period lived agent OLG model with promised transfer $\bar{H}$**

Parameter	Source to match	Value
β	Annual discount factor of 0.96	0.29
γ	Coefficient of relative risk aversion between 1.5 and 4.0	2
α	Capital share of income	0.35
δ	Annual capital depreciation of 0.05	0.79
ρ	AR(1) persistence of normally distributed shock to match annual persistence of 0.95	0.21
μ	AR(1) long-run average shock level	0
σ	Standard deviation of normally distributed shock to match the annual standard deviation of real GDP of 0.49	1.55
$\bar{H}$	Set to be 32 percent of the median real wage	0.11

Note: The appendix gives a detailed description of the calibration of all parameters.

Equations (12) and (13) determine $c_{1,t}$ when $w_t > \bar{H}$. Otherwise, $H_t = w_t$, leaving the young at t with zero consumption and saving ($c_{1,t} = k_{2,t+1} = 0$).

Given our calibration described in table 5.1, which treats one period as thirty years, we solve the previous two equations obtaining functions for $c_{1,t}$, $c_{2,t}$, $k_{2,t+1}$, Y_t, w_t, and r_t for any state ($k_{2,t}, z_t$).[6]

5.2.5   Simulation

To explore our model, we ran 3,000 simulations for each of nine combinations of the state variables and $\bar{H}$. For each of these simulations, we followed the economy through shutdown. The nine combinations includes three values of $\bar{H} = \{0.05, 0.11, 0.17\}$ and for three different values of $k_{2,0} = \{0.11, 0.14, 0, 17\}$.[7] In each simulation we set the initial value of z at its median value μ. Recall that $k_{2,0}$ references the capital held by the old (generation 2) at time zero. Also note that median values refer to the medians taken across all simulations for all periods in which the economy is still functioning.

Table 5.2 shows the median wage w_{med}, the median capital stock k_{med}, and the size of $\bar{H}$ and $k_{2,0}$ relative to the median wage w_{med} and the median capital stock k_{med}, respectively, for each of the nine combinations of $\bar{H}$ and $k_{2,0}$.

Table 5.3 provides four statistics on time to economic shutdown, that is, $w_t \le \bar{H}$. The middle row of table 5.3 corresponding to $\bar{H} = 0.11$ shows that this model economy has a greater than 50 percent chance of shutting down in sixty years (two periods) under a fiscal transfer system calibrated to be close to that of the United States. Table 5.3 also indicates what one would

---

6. MatLab code for the computation is available upon request.

7. The three values for each roughly correspond to low, middle, and high values. That is, $\bar{H} = 0.11$ is the value that is roughly equal to 32 percent of the median wage, and $k_{2,0} = 0.14$ is roughly equal to the median capital stock across simulations.

Table 5.2	Initial values relative to median values					
	$k_{2,0} = 0.11$		$k_{2,0} = 0.14$		$k_{2,0} = 0.17$	
	$\dfrac{w_{med}}{\bar{H}/w_{med}}$	$\dfrac{k_{med}}{k_{2,0}/k_{med}}$	$\dfrac{w_{med}}{\bar{H}/w_{med}}$	$\dfrac{k_{med}}{k_{2,0}/k_{med}}$	$\dfrac{w_{med}}{\bar{H}/w_{med}}$	$\dfrac{k_{med}}{k_{2,0}/k_{med}}$
$\bar{H} = 0.05$	0.3030	0.0992	0.3026	0.0996	0.3008	0.0991
	0.1650	1.1093	0.1652	1.4062	0.1662	1.7148
$\bar{H} = 0.11$	0.3445	0.1344	0.3433	0.1358	0.3474	0.1365
	0.3193	0.8187	0.3204	1.0311	0.3166	1.2457
$\bar{H} = 0.17$	0.2562	0.1043	0.2709	0.1090	0.2825	0.1134
	0.6635	1.0550	0.6275	1.2846	0.6018	1.4988

Note: w_{med} is the median wage and k_{med} is the median capital stock across all 3,000 simulations before economic shutdown.

Table 5.3	Periods to shutdown simulation statistics					
	$k_{2,0} = 0.11$		$k_{2,0} = 0.14$		$k_{2,0} = 0.17$	
	Periods	CDF	Periods	CDF	Periods	CDF
$\bar{H} = 0.05$						
min	1	0.1620	1	0.1543	1	0.1477
med	4	0.5370	4	0.5320	4	0.5283
mean	5.95	0.6704	6.00	0.6703	6.04	0.6694
max	45	1.0000	45	1.0000	45	1.0000
$\bar{H} = 0.11$						
min	1	0.3623	1	0.3480	1	0.3357
med	2	0.5653	2	0.5543	2	0.5433
mean	3.29	0.7060	3.35	0.7029	3.41	0.7022
max	24	1.0000	24	1.0000	25	1.0000
*$\bar{H} = 0.17$						
min	1	0.5203	1	0.4987	1	0.4807
med	1	0.5203	2	0.6833	2	0.6707
mean	2.42	0.7373	2.48	0.7336	2.54	0.7295
max	18	1.0000	18	1.0000	18	1.0000

Notes: The "min," "med," "mean," and "max" rows in the "Periods" column represent the minimum, median, mean, and maximum number of periods, respectively, in which the simulated time series hit the economic shutdown. The "CDF" column represents the percent of simulations that shut down in t periods or less, where t is the value in the "Periods" column. For the cumulative distribution function (CDF) value of the "mean" row, we used linear interpolation.

expect—that the probability of a near-term shutdown is very sensitive to the size of $\bar{H}$ given the size of the economy's time-zero capital stock and thus, initial wage.

5.2.6   Fiscal Gap and Equity Premium

Because actual receipts extracted from young workers are not always equal to the promised payment $H_t \leq \bar{H}$, we define the fiscal gap as the difference between the present value of all promised payments to current and future older generations and the present value of current receipts from current workers plus all future receipts obtained, on average, in each future period, from future workers. We express this difference as a percent of the present value of all current and future output realized, on average.

$$(14) \qquad \text{fiscalgap}_t = x_t \equiv \frac{\text{NPV}(\bar{H}) - \text{NPV}(H_t)}{\text{NPV}(Y_t)}.$$

This measure does not suffer from the economics labeling problem.

Define the discount factor in s periods from the current period as d_{t+s}, and write the net present values in the measure of the fiscal gap from (14) in terms of the discount factors and expected streams of transfers and income.

$$(15) \qquad x_t = \frac{\sum_{s=0}^{\infty} d_{t+s}\bar{H} - \sum_{s=0}^{\infty} d_{t+s}E[H_s]}{\sum_{s=0}^{\infty} d_{t+s}E[Y_s]}.$$

We present four measures of the fiscal gap using four sequences of discount factors d_{t+s}—two from our model and two from the literature. The first measure of the fiscal gap (fgap1) uses the prices of sure-return bonds that mature s periods from the current period t as the discount factors. Define $p_{t,j}$ as the price of an asset $B_{t,j}$ with a sure-return payment of one unit j periods in the future. If these assets can be bought and sold each period, then a household could purchase an asset that pays off after the household is dead and sell it before they die. Because each of these assets must be held in zero net supply, they do not change the equilibrium policy functions described in section 5.2.4. The equations characterizing the prices $p_{t,j}$ for all t and j are:[8]

$$(16) \qquad p_{t,j} = \begin{cases} 1 & \text{if } j = 1 \\ \beta \dfrac{E_t[u'(c_{2,t+1})p_{t+1,j-1}]}{u'(c_{1,t})} & \text{if } j \geq 1 \end{cases} \quad \forall t.$$

With the starting value of the sure-return price $p_{t,0}$ pinned down, the prices of the assets that mature in future periods can be calculated recursively using equation (16).

Table 5.4 shows the calculated sure-return prices at each maturity—which we use as our discount factors—and their corresponding net discount rates shown on an annual basis. The first column in each cell displays the prices of the different maturity s of sure-return bond $p_{t,t+s}$ computed using recursive equation (16). The second column in each cell represents the annualized version of the net return $r_{t,t+s}$APR, or net interest rate.[9]

---

8. We derive equation (16), as well as some other assets of interest, in detail in the appendix.

9. The return or yield of a sure-return bond should increase with its maturity in an economy that never shuts down. However, the increasing probability of the economy shutting down in each future period counteracts the increasing value of the sure return in the future. This is why the interest rates in the second column of each cell in table 5.3 seem to go toward an asymptote in the limit.

Table 5.4   Term structure of prices and interest rates

s	$k_{2,0}=0.11$		$k_{2,0}=0.14$		$k_{2,0}=0.17$	
	$p_{t,t+s}$	$r_{t,t+s}$ APR	$p_{t,t+s}$	$r_{t,t+s}$ APR	$p_{t,t+s}$	$r_{t,t+s}$ APR
$\bar{H}=0.05$						
0	1	0	1	0	1	0
1	1.5556	−0.0146	1.5897	−0.0153	1.6190	−0.0159
2	0.3115	0.0196	0.3466	0.0178	0.3782	0.0163
3	0.0385	0.0369	0.0441	0.0353	0.0493	0.0340
4	0.0088	0.0403	0.0096	0.0395	0.0099	0.0392
5	0.0049	0.0360	0.0063	0.0344	0.0063	0.0344
6	0.0014	0.0372	0.0025	0.0338	0.0024	0.0342
$\bar{H}=0.11$						
0	1	0	1	0	1	0
1	1.6771	−0.0171	1.7186	−0.0179	1.7673	−0.0188
2	0.1543	0.0316	0.1793	0.0291	0.2137	0.0261
3	0.0074	0.0560	0.0092	0.0535	0.0118	0.0506
4	0.0072	0.0420	0.0077	0.0414	0.0085	0.0405
5	0.0029	0.0397	0.0032	0.0390	0.0038	0.0379
6	4.3×10^{-4}	0.0440	5.0×10^{-4}	0.0431	5.9×10^{-4}	0.0421
$\bar{H}=0.17$						
0	1	0	1	0	1	0
1	1.5848	−0.0152	1.6811	−0.0172	1.7308	−0.0181
2	0.0092	0.0812	0.0156	0.0718	0.0359	0.0570
3	0.0010	0.0794	0.0031	0.0663	0.0038	0.0639
4	9.0×10^{-5}	0.0808	0.0046	0.0459	0.0049	0.0453
5	1.3×10^{-5}	0.0780	0.0010	0.0470	0.0011	0.0463
6	1.7×10^{-5}	0.0630	5.6×10^{-5}	0.0558	6.1×10^{-5}	0.0554

Notes: The first column in each cell is the price of the sure-return bond $p_{t,t+s}$ at different maturities s as characterized by equation (16). The second column in each cell is the net interest rate $r_{t,t+s}$APR implied by the sure-return rate and given in annual percentage rate (APR) terms according to equation (17). Full descriptions of the term structure of prices and interest rates for all calibrations and for up to $s = 12$ is provided in the appendix.

$$(17) \qquad r_{t,t+s} = \left(\frac{1}{p_{t,t+s}}\right)^{1/s30} - 1 \text{ for } s \geq 1.$$

The second fiscal gap measure (fgap 2) employs a constant discount rate, namely the current-period risky return on capital R_t. For example, the risky return on capital in period t is $R_t = 1.4971$ in the middle cell, in which $\bar{H} = 0.11$ and $k_{2,0} = 0.14$. So the discount factors are $d_{t+s} = (1.4971)^{-s}$. Our third fiscal gap measure (fgap 3) uses a constant discount rate taken from International Monetary Fund (2009, table 6.4). This study uses an annual discount factor of the growth rate in real GDP plus 1 percent to calculate the net present value of aging-related expeditures. This averages out across G-20 countries to be a discount rate of around 4 percent—for the United States, it is about 3.8 percent ($R_t \approx 3.1$). So the discount rates for fgap3 are $d_{t+s} = (3.05)^{-s}$. For the last measure of the fiscal gap (fgap4), we use the constant

Table 5.5   **Measures of the fiscal gap as percent of NPV(GDP)**

	$k_{2,0} = 0.11$		$k_{2,0} = 0.14$		$k_{2,0} = 0.17$	
	fgap 1	fgap 2	fgap 1	fgap 2	fgap 1	fgap 2
	fgap 3	fgap 4	fgap 3	fgap 4	fgap 3	fgap 4
$\bar{H} = 0.05$	0.0037	0.0078	0.0034	0.0096	0.0033	0.0118
	0.0033	0.0035	0.0030	0.0032	0.0028	0.0029
$\bar{H} = 0.11$	0.0192	0.0373	0.0175	0.0427	0.0164	0.555
	0.0168	0.0176	0.0152	0.0159	0.0140	0.0147
$\bar{H} = 0.17$	0.0474	0.0876	0.0421	0.1041	0.0385	0.1171
	0.0408	0.0426	0.0361	0.0378	0.0328	0.0344

Notes: Fiscal gap 1 uses the gross sure-return rates $R_{t,t+s}$ from table 5.4 as the discount rates for NPV calculation. Fiscal gap 2 uses the current period gross return on capital R_t from the model as the constant discount rate. Fiscal gap 3 uses the International Monetary Fund (2009) method of an annual discount rate equal to 1 plus the average percent change in GDP plus 0.01 (≈ 2.05). And fiscal gap 4 uses the Gokhale and Smetters (2007) method of an annual discount rate equal to 1 plus 0.0365 (≈ 1.93).

discount rate from Gokhale and Smetters (2007), who use an annual discount rate of 3.65 percent for their discount factors in their net present value (NPV) calculation. This is equivalent to a thirty-year gross discount rate of $R_t \approx 2.9$. So the discount rates for fgap4 are $d_{t+s} = (2.93)^{-s}$. The expectations for H_t and Y_t are simply the average values from the 3,000 simulations described in section 5.2.5.

Table 5.5 presents fiscal gaps for the nine different combinations of promised transfers $\bar{H}$ and initial capital stock $k_{2,0}$ as a percent of the net present value of output. By way of comparison, we note that the US fiscal gap is currently 12 percent of the present value of projected GDP. The figures in table 5.5 are generally much smaller. Importantly, though, given the initial capital stock, higher values of $\bar{H}$ are associated not just with much quicker time to shut down, but also substantially larger fiscal gaps regardless of the discount rates used.

Next we use the difference in the expected risky return on capital $E[R_{t+1}]$ and the riskless return on the one-period safe bond $R_{t,t+1}$ to calculate an equity premium. A large literature attempts to explain why the observed equity premium is so large.[10] Most recently, Barro (2009) has shown that incorporating rare disasters into an economic model produces realistic risk premia and risk-free rates. Our model features disaster in the form of economic shutdown, and it too (see table 5.6) produces realistic equity premia, ranging from 4.7 percent to as 7.3 percent, for a moderate-sized coefficient of relative risk aversion of $\gamma = 2$.

Table 5.6 presents Sharpe ratios as well as all of the components of the

10. See Shiller (1982); Mehra and Prescott (1985); Kocherlakota (1996); Campbell (2000); and Cochrane (2005, ch. 21) for surveys of the equity premium puzzle.

Table 5.6 Components of the equity premium in period 1

	$k_{2,0}=0.11$		$k_{2,0}=0.14$		$k_{2,0}=0.17$	
	30-year	Annual	30-year	Annual	30-year	Annual
$\bar{H}=0.05$						
$E[R_{t+1}]$	8.2070	1.0361	7.5150	1.0334	7.0113	1.0313
$\sigma(R_{t+1})$	23.3433	n/a	21.3222	n/a	19.8511	n/a
$R_{t,t+1}$	0.6428	0.9854	0.6291	0.9847	0.6177	0.9841
Equity premium $E[R_{t+1}] - R_{t,t+1}$	7.5641	0.0507	6.8859	0.0487	6.3936	0.0473
Sharpe ratio $\dfrac{E[R_{t+1}] - R_{t,t+1}}{\sigma(R_{t+1})}$	0.3240	n/a	0.3229	n/a	0.3221	n/a
$\bar{H}=0.11$						
$E[R_{t+1}]$	11.3042	1.0459	10.0769	1.0423	9.2241	1.0396
$\sigma(R_{t+1})$	32.3859	n/a	28.8049	n/a	26.3140	n/a
$R_{t,t+1}$	0.5963	0.9829	0.5819	0.9821	0.5658	0.9812
Equity premium $E[R_{t+1}] - R_{t,t+1}$	10.7080	0.0630	9.4950	0.0602	8.6582	0.0584
Sharpe ratio $\dfrac{E[R_{t+1}] - R_{t,t+1}}{\sigma(R_{t+1})}$	0.3306	n/a	0.3296	n/a	0.3290	n/a
$\bar{H}=0.17$						
$E[R_{t+1}]$	16.2082	1.0574	13.7520	1.0521	12.1889	1.0483
$\sigma(R_{t+1})$	46.7126	n/a	39.5389	n/a	34.9735	n/a
$R_{t,t+1}$	0.6310	0.9848	0.5948	0.9828	0.5778	0.9819
Equity premium $E[R_{t+1}] - R_{t,t+1}$	15.5772	0.0727	13.1572	0.0693	11.6112	0.0664
Sharpe ratio $\dfrac{E[R_{t+1}] - R_{t,t+1}}{\sigma(R_{t+1})}$	0.3335	n/a	0.3328	n/a	0.3320	n/a

Notes: The gross risky one-period return on capital is $R_{t+1} = 1 + r_{t+1} - \delta$. The annualized gross risky one-period return is $(R_{t+1})^{1/30}$. The expected value and standard deviation of the gross risky one-period return R_{t+1} are calculated as the average and standard deviation, respectively, across simulations. The annual equity premium is the expected value of the annualized risky return in the next period minus the annualized return on the one-period riskless bond.

equity premium. For the expected risky return $E[R_{t+1}]$, the one-period sure-return $R_{t,t+1}$, and the equity premium (the difference between the two), we report results for both one period from the model (thirty years) as well as the annualized (one-year) version. Our Sharpe ratios between 0.32 and 0.33 are in line with common estimates from the data.

Because the equity premium and the Sharpe ratio fluctuate from period to period, we report in table 5.7 the average equity premium and Sharpe ratio across simulations in the period immediately before the economic shutdown.

Table 5.8 compares three measures of the fiscal gap in the initial period to the fiscal gap in the period immediately before shutdown.[11] As with the

11. We exclude the calculation of measure of the fiscal gap that uses the current period marginal product of capital as the discount rate (fgap2) because the discount rate is often negative in the period immediately before shutdown. We exclude fgap3 because it is similar to fgap4.

Table 5.7 **Equity premium and Sharpe ratio in period immediately before shutdown**

	$k_{2,0} = 0.11$		$k_{2,0} = 0.14$		$k_{2,0} = 0.17$	
	Eq. prem.	Sharpe ratio	Eq. prem.	Sharpe ratio	Eq. prem.	Sharpe ratio
$\bar{H} = 0.05$						
Period 1	0.0507	0.3240	0.0487	0.3229	0.0473	0.3221
Before shutdown	0.0710	0.3356	0.0707	0.3337	0.0706	0.3370
Percent bigger	0.6617	0.5410	0.6843	0.5570	0.6960	0.5690
Percent smaller	0.1763	0.2970	0.1613	0.2887	0.1563	0.2833
$\bar{H} = 0.11$						
Period 1	0.0630	0.3306	0.0602	0.3296	0.0584	0.3290
Before shutdown	0.0679	0.3339	0.0667	0.3333	0.0664	0.3343
Percent bigger	0.3740	0.3760	0.4023	0.3970	0.4227	0.4153
Percent smaller	0.2637	0.2617	0.2497	0.2550	0.2417	0.2490
$\bar{H} = 0.17$						
Period 1	0.0727	0.3335	0.0693	0.3328	0.0664	0.3320
Before shutdown	0.0709	0.3353	0.0686	0.3354	0.0673	0.3348
Percent bigger	0.2027	0.2740	0.2253	0.2937	0.2543	0.3070
Percent smaller	0.2770	0.2057	0.2760	0.2077	0.2650	0.2123

Notes: The "Period 1" row represents the equity premium and Sharpe ratio in the initial period for each specification. The "Before shutdown" row represents the average equity premium and Sharpe ratio across simulations in the period immediately before shutdown for each specification. The "Percent bigger" and "Percent smaller" rows tell how many of the simulated ending values of the equity premium and Sharpe ratio were bigger than or less than, respectively, their initial period values. These percentages do not sum to one because the equity premium and Sharpe ratio do not change in the cases in which the economy shuts down in the second period.

equity premium and Sharpe ratio, the fiscal gap increases, on average, in the period immediately before shutdown relative to the initial period. In our baseline case of $\bar{H} = 0.11$ and $k_{2,0} = 0.14$, the fiscal gap nearly doubles in the period before shutdown. Tables 5.7 and 5.8 provide evidence that both the fiscal gap and the equity premium are good leading indicators of how close an economy is to its fiscal limit.

5.3 Model with Regime Change

We now assume that when the government defaults on its promised transfer $w_t \leq \bar{H}$, the regime switches permanently to one in which the transfer is simply τ percent of the wage each period $H_t = \tau w_t$. We solve the model for $\tau = 0.8$ and $\tau = 0.3$.

5.3.1 Regime Change to 80 Percent Wage Tax

Figure 5.1 illustrates the rule for the transfer H_t under regime 1 in which the transfer is $\bar{H}$ unless wages w_t are less than $\bar{H}$ and under regime 2 in which the transfer is permanently switched to the proportional transfer system $H_t = 0.8w_t$.

Table 5.8   **Fiscal gaps in period immediately before shutdown**

	$k_{2,0} = 0.11$		$k_{2,0} = 0.14$		$k_{2,0} = 0.17$	
	fgap1	fgap4	fgap1	fgap4	fgap1	fgap4
$\bar{H} = 0.05$						
Period 1	0.0037	0.0035	0.0034	0.0032	0.0033	0.0029
Before shutdown	0.0183	0.0187	0.0184	0.0187	0.0185	0.0191
Percent bigger	0.8940	0.8260	0.9100	0.8340	0.9220	0.8440
Percent smaller	0.1060	0.1740	0.0900	0.1660	0.0780	0.1560
$\bar{H} = 0.11$						
Period 1	0.0192	0.0176	0.0175	0.0159	0.0164	0.0147
Before shutdown	0.0339	0.0291	0.0337	0.0294	0.0356	0.0307
Percent bigger	0.7200	0.6940	0.7480	0.7060	0.7600	0.7160
Percent smaller	0.2800	0.3060	0.2520	0.2940	0.2400	0.2840
$\bar{H} = 0.17$						
Period 1	0.0474	0.0426	0.0421	0.0378	0.0385	0.0344
Before shutdown	0.0508	0.0447	0.0481	0.0429	0.0495	0.0414
Percent bigger	0.7180	0.6820	0.7340	0.6760	0.7500	0.6824
Percent smaller	0.2820	0.3180	0.2660	0.3240	0.2500	0.3180

Notes: The "Period 1" row represents the fiscal gap in the initial period for each specification. The "Before shutdown" row represents the average fiscal gap across simulations in the period immediately before shutdown for each specification. The "Percent bigger" and "Percent smaller" rows tell how many of the simulated ending values of the fiscal gap were bigger than or less than, respectively, their initial period values. Fiscal gap 1 uses the gross sure-return rates $R_{t,t+s}$ similar to table 5.4 as the discount rates for NPV calculation, and fiscal gap 4 uses the Gokhale and Smetters (2007) method of an annual discount rate equal to 1 plus 0.0365 (≈ 1.93).

Household Problem, Firm Problem, and Market Clearing

The characterization of the household problem remains the same as in equations (1), (2), and (3) from section 5.2.1. The only difference is in the definition of H_t in those equations. With the new regime-switching assumption, the transfer each period from the young to the old, H_t, is defined as follows

(18)
$$H_t = \begin{cases} \bar{H} & \text{if } w_s > \bar{H} \text{ for all } s \leq t \\ 0.8w_t & \text{if } w_s \leq \bar{H} \text{ for any } s \leq t. \end{cases}$$

The change is reflected in the expectations of the young of consumption when old $c_{2,t+1}$ in the savings decision (3).

The firm's problem and the characterization of output, aggregate productivity shock, and optimal net real return on capital and real wage are the same as equations (4) through (7) in section 5.2.2. The market-clearing conditions that must hold in each period are the same as (8), (9), and (10) from section 5.2.3.

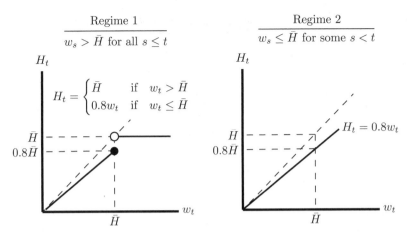

Fig. 5.1   Transfer program H_t under regime 1 and regime 2: 80 percent wage tax

Solution and Calibration

The competitive equilibrium with a transfer program regime switch is characterized in the same way as definition 1 with economic shutdown except that the transfer each period is characterized by equation (18). For the current young, this regime switch decreases the expected value of next period's transfer $H_{t+1} - 0.8w_t + 1$ instead of $w_t + 1$. Thus, the current period young will save more and bring more savings $k_{2,t+1}$ into old age than did the young in section 5.2. Once the regime has permanently switched to the high-rate proportional transfer program of $H_t = 0.8w_t$, allocations each period are determined by the following two equations,

$$(19) \qquad c_{2,t} = (1 + \alpha e^{z_t}k_{2,t}^{\alpha-1} - \delta)k_{2,t} + 0.8(1 - \alpha)e^{z_t}k_{2,t}^{\alpha}$$

$$(20) \qquad u'(c_{1,t}) = \beta E_{z_{t+1}|z_t}[(1 + \alpha e^{z_{t+1}}k_{2,t+1}^{\alpha-1} - \delta) \times \dots$$
$$u'([1 + \alpha e^{z_{t+1}}k_{2,t+1}^{\alpha-1} - \delta]k_{2,t+1} + 0.8(1 - \alpha)e^{z_{t+1}}k_{2,t+1}^{\alpha})]$$

where,

$$(21) \qquad k_{2,t+1} = 0.2(1 - \alpha)e^{z_t}k_{2,t}^{\alpha} - c_{1,t}$$

and in which we have substituted in the expressions for r_t and w_t from (6) and (7), respectively, and $H_t = 0.8w_t$.

We calibrate parameters as in table 5.1 for the economic shutdown model, with the exception of $\bar{H}$. We again calibrate $\bar{H}$ to be 32 percent of the median wage. However, we calculate the median wage from the time periods in the simulations before the regime switches (regime 1). Because the economy never shuts down, it is less risky in the long run. But the economy is actually

Table 5.9   **Initial values relative to median values from regime 1: 80 percent tax**

	$k_{2,0} = 0.0875$		$k_{2,0} = 0.14$	
	$\dfrac{w_{med}}{\bar{H}/w_{med}}$	$\dfrac{k_{med}}{k_{2,0}/k_{med}}$	$\dfrac{w_{med}}{\bar{H}/w_{med}}$	$\dfrac{k_{med}}{k_{2,0}/k_{med}}$
$\bar{H} = 0.09$	0.2827	0.0878	0.2883	0.0895
	0.3184	0.9967	0.3121	1.5642
$\bar{H} = 0.11$	0.2944	0.0886	0.3021	0.0899
	0.3736	0.9873	0.3641	1.5567

Note: w_{med} is the median wage and k_{med} is the median capital stock across all 3,000 simulations before the regime switch (in regime 1).

more risky to the current period young in that the expected value of their transfer in the next period is decreased by the potential regime switch. Higher precautionary saving induces a higher median wage and a higher promised transfer $\bar{H} = 0.09$ in order to equal 32 percent of the regime 1 median wage.

Simulation

We again simulate the regime-switching model 3,000 times with various combinations of values for the promised transfer $\bar{H} \in \{0.09, 0.11\}$ and the initial capital stock $k_{2,0} \in \{0.0875, 0.14\}$. As shown in table 5.9, our calibrated values of $\bar{H} = 0.09$ and $k_{2,0} = 0.0875$ correspond to 32 percent of the median real wage in regime 1 and the median capital stock in regime 1, respectively. In each simulation we again use an initial value of the productivity shock of its median value $z_0 = \mu$.

The upper left cell of table 5.9 is analogous to the middle cell of table 5.2 in that $\bar{H}$ is calibrated to be 32 percent of the regime 1 real wage and $k_{2,0}$ to equal the regime 1 median capital stock. However, the lower right cell of table 5.9 has the same $\bar{H}$ and $k_{2,0}$ as the middle cell of table 5.2. Notice that the median capital stock is higher in the regime-switching economy ($k_{med} = 0.1.5567$ for $\bar{H} = 0.11$ and $k_{2,0} = 0.14$ in regime-switching economy as compared to $k_{med} = 0.1.0311$ in the shutdown economy with the same $\bar{H}$ and $k_{2,0}$). This is because young households have an increased risk in the second period of life under the possibility of a regime switch because their transfer will be lower in the case of a default on $\bar{H}$.

Table 5.10 presents time to game over for this policy. Notice that the distribution of time until regime switch across simulations from the upper left cell of table 5.10 is very similar to the middle cell in table 5.3 from the shutdown economy. Higher precautionary savings extends the time until a regime switch, but increased promised transfers reduce that time.

Fiscal Gap and Equity Premium

For the model with regime switching to an 80 percent wage tax, we define the fiscal gap in the same way as in equation (14) from section 5.2.6. The

Table 5.10   **Periods to regime-switch simulation statistics: 80 percent tax**

	$k_{2,0} = 0.0875$		$k_{2,0} = 0.14$	
	Periods	CDF	Periods	CDF
$\bar{H} = 0.09$				
min	1	0.3677	1	0.3340
med	2	0.5727	2	0.5470
mean	3.25	0.7124	3.40	0.7066
max	24	1.0000	25	1.0000
$\bar{H} = 0.11$				
min	1	0.4517	1	0.4060
med	2	0.6430	2	0.6127
mean	2.78	0.7314	2.94	0.7244
max	24	1.0000	24	1.0000

Notes: The "min," "med," "mean," and "max" rows in the "Periods" column represent the minimum, median, mean, and maximum number of periods, respectively, in which the simulated time series hit the regime-switch condition. The "CDF" column represents the percent of simulations that switch regimes in t periods or less, where t is the value in the "Periods" column. For the CDF value of the "mean" row, we used linear interpolation.

discount factors used to calculate the net present values in the fiscal gap measures from the regime-switching model are calculated in the same way as described in section 5.2.6. Table 5.11 shows the calculated sure-return prices and their corresponding annualized discount rates for this regime-switching economy. Each cell represents the computed prices and interest rates that correspond to a particular promised transfer value $\bar{H}$ and initial capital stock $k_{2,0}$.

Table 5.12 shows our four measures of the fiscal gap as a percent of the net present value of GDP for each of our four combinations of $\bar{H}$ and $k_{2,0}$. Some of the fiscal gap measures are negative. This occurs because some of the discount factors decay more slowly than others (fgap 1 is the slowest) and because expected receipts are higher after the regime switch. Indeed, they can even end up higher than $\bar{H}$. Even though the impulse response of w_t decays to a lower level after the regime switch, the expected H_t can be high because of the high variance in productivity shocks. A median value would be lower. We therefore can get negative fiscal gap measures, even though $\bar{H}$ is big enough to trigger a regime switch in relatively few periods. Table 5.12 computes fiscal gaps as a percent of the present value of output as in equation (14) for the four combinations of values for the promised transfer $\bar{H}$ and the initial capital stock $k_{2,0}$.

Note also in table 5.12 that the fiscal gap measure fgap1 becomes even more negative as $\bar{H}$ increases. This is caused by the higher $\bar{H}$ shortening the periods until the regime switch or higher H_t values. In other words, the positive effect on the fiscal gap from a higher $\bar{H}$ in the preswitch periods is dominated by the negative effect on the fiscal gap from more periods of high

Table 5.11 — Term structure of prices and interest rates in regime-switching economy: 80 percent tax

s	$k_{2,0}=0.0875$		$k_{2,0}=0.14$	
	$p_{t,t+s}$	$r_{t,t+s}$ APR	$p_{t,t+s}$	$r_{t,t+s}$ APR
$\bar{H}=0.09$	1	0	1	0
0				
1	0.3269	0.0380	0.4645	0.0259
2	1.1607	−0.0025	2.5547	−0.0155
3	0.3534	0.0116	0.4138	0.0099
4	0.6753	0.0033	1.2121	−0.0016
5	0.4117	0.0059	0.2982	0.0081
6	0.1304	0.0114	0.4420	0.0045
$\bar{H}=0.11$	1	0	1	0
0				
1	0.2328	0.0498	0.3227	0.0384
2	1.3063	−0.0044	1.5334	−0.0071
3	2.5521	−0.0104	1.5811	−0.0051
4	0.2606	0.0113	0.8424	0.0014
5	1.7532	−0.0037	1.8832	−0.0042
6	0.3762	0.0054	0.4895	0.0040

Notes: The first column in each cell is the price of the sure-return bond $p_{t,t+s}$ at different maturities s as characterized by equation (16). The second column in each cell is the net interest rate $r_{t,t+s}$ APR implied by the sure-return rate and given in annual percentage rate terms according to equation (17). Full descriptions of the term structure of prices and interest rates for all calibrations and for up to $s = 12$ is provided in the appendix.

Table 5.12 — Measures of the fiscal gap with regime switching as percent of NPV(GDP): 80 percent tax

	$k_{2,0}=0.0875$		$k_{2,0}=0.14$	
	fgap 1 fgap 3	fgap 2 fgap 4	fgap 1 fgap 3	fgap 2 fgap 4
$\bar{H}=0.09$	−0.0519	0.0003	−0.0343	−0.0157
	0.0067	0.0066	0.0052	0.0051
$\bar{H}=0.11$	−0.0861	0.0057	−0.0749	−0.0075
	0.0130	0.0129	0.0103	0.0102

Notes: Fiscal gap 1 uses the sure-return rates $R_{t,t+s}$ from table 5.4 to form the discount factors used in its present value calculations. Fiscal gap 2 uses the current period gross return on capital R_t from the model as the constant discount rate. Fiscal gap 3 uses the International Monetary Fund (2009) method of an annual discount rate equal to 1 plus the average percent change in GDP plus 0.01 (≈ 2.05). And fiscal gap 4 follows Gokhale and Smetters (2007) in forming the discount factors using an annual discount rate equal to 1 plus 0.0365 (≈ 1.93).

Table 5.13   **Components of the equity premium with regime switching: 80 percent tax**

	$k_{2,0} = 0.0875$		$k_{2,0} = 0.14$	
	30-year	Annual	30-year	Annual
$\bar{H} = 0.09$				
$E[R_{t+1}]$	17.1319	1.0592	12.9708	1.0503
$\sigma(R_{t+1})$	49.4105	n/a	37.2570	n/a
$R_{t,t+1}$	3.0589	1.0380	2.1526	1.0259
Equity premium $E[R_{t+1}] - R_{t,t+1}$	14.0731	0.0213	10.8182	0.0244
Sharpe ratio $\dfrac{E[R_{t+1}] - R_{t,t+1}}{\sigma(R_{t+1})}$	0.2848	n/a	0.2904	n/a
$\bar{H} = 0.11$				
$E[R_{t+1}]$	22.1773	1.0678	16.0801	1.0572
$\sigma(R_{t+1})$	64.1466	n/a	46.3385	n/a
$R_{t,t+1}$	4.2960	1.0498	3.0985	1.0384
Equity premium $E[R_{t+1}] - R_{t,t+1}$	17.8813	0.0180	12.9816	0.0188
Sharpe ratio $\dfrac{E[R_{t+1}] - R_{t,t+1}}{\sigma(R_{t+1})}$	0.2788	n/a	0.2801	n/a

Notes: The gross risky one-period return on capital is $R_{t+1} = 1 + r_{t+1} - \delta$. The annualized gross risky one-period return is $(R_{t+1})^{1/30}$. The expected value and standard deviation of the gross risky one-period return R_{t+1} are calculated as the average and standard deviation, respectively, across simulations. The annual equity premium is the expected value of the annualized risky return in the next period minus the annualized return on the one-period riskless bond.

regime 2 H_t. For the other measures of the fiscal gap, the second effect dominates so the fiscal gap increases with the size of the promised transfer $\bar{H}$.

Finally, we caclulate the equity premium and Sharpe ratio for this regime-switching model using the difference in the expected risky return on capital one period from now $E[R_{t+1}]$ and the riskless return on the sure-return bond maturing one period from now $R_{t,t+1}$. In reference to the Barro (2009) result, our model with regime switching delivers equity premia that are significantly lower than the riskier model with shutdown from section 5.2.6 and do not match as closely observed equity premia and Sharpe ratios. As shown in table 5.13, our regime-switching model produces equity premia around 2 percent and Sharpe ratios around 0.28.

The interesting equity premium story in the model with the 80 percent regime switch is what happens to the equity premium as the economy approaches game one with respect to its initial policy. Table 5.14 reports the average equity premium and Sharpe ratio across simulations in the period immediately before the regime switch as compared to their respective values in the first period. The average equity premium and Sharpe ratio increase significantly from the initial period to the period right before the regime switch in each case.

Table 5.14   **Equity premium and Sharpe ratio in period immediately before regime switch: 80 percent tax**

| | $k_{2,0} = 0.0875$ | | $k_{2,0} = 0.14$ | |
	Eq. prem.	Sharpe ratio	Eq. prem.	Sharpe ratio
$\bar{H} = 0.09$				
Period 1	0.0213	0.2848	0.0244	0.2904
Before shutdown	0.0737	0.3231	0.0773	0.3272
Percent bigger	0.6287	0.5353	0.6600	0.5523
Percent smaller	0.0037	0.0970	0.0060	0.1137
$\bar{H} = 0.11$				
Period 1	0.0180	0.2788	0.0188	0.2801
Before shutdown	0.0637	0.3152	0.0675	0.3201
Percent bigger	0.5457	0.4770	0.5910	0.5180
Percent smaller	0.0027	0.0713	0.0030	0.0760

Notes: The "Period 1" row represents the equity premium and Sharpe ratio in the initial period for each specification. The "Before shutdown" row represents the average equity premium and Sharpe ratio across simulations in the period immediately before shutdown for each specification. The "Percent bigger" and "Percent smaller" rows tell how many of the simulated ending values of the equity premium and Sharpe ratio were bigger than or less than, respectively, their initial period values. These percentages do not sum to one because the equity premium and Sharpe ratio do not change in the cases in which the economy shuts down in the second period.

Table 5.15   **Initial values relative to median values from regime 1: 30 percent tax**

| | $k_{2,0} = 0.0875$ | | $k_{2,0} = 0.14$ | |
	$\dfrac{w_{med}}{\bar{H}/w_{med}}$	$\dfrac{k_{med}}{k_{2,0}/k_{med}}$	$\dfrac{w_{med}}{\bar{H}/w_{med}}$	$\dfrac{k_{med}}{k_{2,0}/k_{med}}$
$\bar{H} = 0.09$	0.2828	0.0864	0.2880	0.0885
	0.3183	1.0130	0.3125	1.5819
$\bar{H} = 0.11$	0.2963	0.0868	0.3051	0.0877
	0.3712	1.0082	0.3605	1.5970

Note: w_{med} is the median wage and k_{med} is the median capital stock across all 3,000 simulations before the regime switch (in regime 1).

5.3.2   Regime Change to 30 Percent Wage Tax

In this section, we show the effects of a less severe proportional wage tax of 30 percent $H_t = 0.3w_t$ in the case of a regime switch.

Simulation

As shown in table 5.15, our calibrated values of $\bar{H} = 0.09$ and $k_{2,0} = 0.0875$ again correspond to about 32 percent of the median real wage in regime 1 and close to the median capital stock in regime 1, respectively. Note that none of these regime 1 values change much from table 5.9 even though regime 2 entails switching to a very different policy when current policy fails.

Table 5.16   **Periods to regime switch simulation statistics: 30 percent tax**

	$k_{2,0} = 0.0875$		$k_{2,0} = 0.14$	
	Periods	CDF	Periods	CDF
$\bar{H} = 0.09$				
min	1	0.3677	1	0.3340
med	2	0.5697	2	0.5440
mean	3.28	0.7116	3.42	0.7054
max	24	1.0000	25	1.0000
$\bar{H} = 0.11$				
min	1	0.4517	1	0.4060
med	2	0.6390	2	0.6080
mean	2.80	0.7302	2.96	0.7228
max	24	1.0000	24	1.0000

Notes: The "min," "med," "mean," and "max" rows in the "Periods" column represent the minimum, median, mean, and maximum number of periods, respectively, in which the simulated time series hit the regime-switch condition. The "CDF" column represents the percent of simulations that switch regimes in t periods or less, where t is the value in the "Periods" column. For the CDF value of the "mean" row, we used linear interpolation.

In each simulation we use an initial value of the productivity shock of its median value $z_0 = \mu$.

The upper left cell of table 5.15 is analogous to the middle cell of table 5.2 in that $\bar{H}$ is calibrated to be 32 percent of the regime 1 real wage and $k_{2,0}$ to equal the regime 1 median capital stock. However, the lower right cell of table 5.15 has the same $\bar{H}$ and $k_{2,0}$ as the middle cell of table 5.2. Notice that the median capital stock is higher in the regime-switching economy ($k_{med} = 0.1.5970$ for $\bar{H} = 0.11$ and $k_{2,0} = 0.14$ in the regime-switching economy as compared to $k_{med} = 0.1.0311$ in the shutdown economy with the same $\bar{H}$ and $k_{2,0}$). This is because young households have an increased risk in the second period of life under the possibility of a regime switch because their transfer will be lower in the case of a default on $\bar{H}$.

Table 5.16 summarizes our findings on time to regime switch; that is, $w_t \leq \bar{H}$. Notice that the distributions of time until regime switch across simulations in all the cells of table 5.16 are very similar to the distributions in table 5.10, where the government takes 80 percent of wages when it can no longer take $\bar{H}$ Higher precautionary savings extends the time until a regime switch, but increased promised transfers reduce that time.

Fiscal Gap and Equity Premium

Table 5.17 shows the calculated sure-return prices and their corresponding annualized discount rates for this regime-switching economy. Each cell represents the computed prices and interest rates that correspond to a particular promised transfer value $\bar{H}$ and initial capital stock $k_{2,0}$.

Table 5.17   **Term structure of prices and interest rates in regime-switching economy: 30 percent tax**

	$k_{2,0} = 0.0875$		$k_{2,0} = 0.14$	
s	$p_{t,t+s}$	$r_{t,t+s}$ APR	$p_{t,t+s}$	$r_{t,t+s}$ APR
$\bar{H} = 0.09$				
0	1	0	1	0
1	0.3367	0.0370	0.4453	0.0273
2	6.0523	−0.0296	8.0476	−0.0342
3	2.0412	−0.0079	6.7823	−0.0210
4	8.5075	−0.0177	16.8480	−0.0233
5	15.9863	−0.0183	25.3856	−0.0213
6	7.5427	−0.0112	6.1479	−0.0100
$\bar{H} = 0.11$				
0	1	0	1	0
1	0.2326	0.0498	0.3225	0.0384
2	7.3132	−0.0326	7.1394	−0.0322
3	11.5166	−0.0268	5.8534	−0.0194
4	16.4777	−0.0231	12.1299	−0.0206
5	9.2992	−0.0148	15.5375	−0.0181
6	23.4145	−0.0174	31.7886	−0.0190

Notes: The first column in each cell is the price of the sure-return bond $p_{t,t+s}$ at different maturities s as characterized by equation (16). The second column in each cell is the net interest rate $r_{t,t+s}$ APR implied by the sure-return rate and given in annual percentage rate terms according to equation (17). Full descriptions of the term structure of prices and interest rates for all calibrations and for up to $s = 12$ is provided in the appendix.

Table 5.18 shows our four measures of the fiscal gap as a percent of the net present value of GDP for each of our four combinations of $\bar{H}$ and $k_{2,0}$. Similar to the 80 percent tax regime-switch model, all the measures for the first measure of the fiscal gap (fgap1) are negative. These negative fiscal gaps—and relatively low measures of the fiscal gap for the other measures—occur because the expected H_t after the regime switch is significantly higher than $\bar{H}$. But in all cases, increased $\bar{H}$ increases the fiscal gap.

Finally, we calculate the equity premium and Sharpe ratio for this regime-switching model. The equity premium results in table 5.19 differ little from those in table 5.13. This means that the form of the regime change has little effect on the initial period equity premium. The equity premia here is around 2 percent, with Sharpe ratios around 0.28.

Table 5.20 reports the average equity premium and Sharpe ratio across simulations in the period immediately before the regime switch as compared to their respective values in the first period. Once again, the average equity premium and Sharpe ratio increase significantly from the initial period to the period right before the regime switch in every case. In both the 80 percent and 30 percent wage-redistribution models, the equity premia in the period before the regime switch are close to those observed in the data.

Table 5.18 **Measures of the fiscal gap with regime switching as percent of NPV(GDP): 30 percent tax**

	$k_{2,0} = 0.0875$		$k_{2,0} = 0.14$	
	fgap 1	fgap 2	fgap 1	fgap 2
	fgap 3	fgap 4	fgap 3	fgap 4
$\bar{H} = 0.09$	−0.1241	0.0002	−0.1214	−0.0148
	0.0099	0.0096	0.0079	0.0078
$\bar{H} = 0.11$	−0.1194	0.0064	−0.1190	−0.0108
	0.0172	0.0171	0.0139	0.0138

Notes: Fiscal gap 1 uses the gross sure-return rates $R_{t,t+s}$ from table 5.4 as the discount rates for NPV calculation. Fiscal gap 2 uses the current period gross return on capital R_t from the model as the constant discount rate. Fiscal gap 3 uses the International Monetary Fund (2009) method of an annual discount rate equal to 1 plus the average percent change in GDP plus 0.01 (≈ 2.05). And fiscal gap 4 uses the Gokhale and Smetters (2007) method of an annual discount rate equal to 1 plus 0.0365 (≈ 1.93).

Table 5.19 **Components of the equity premium with regime switching: 30 percent tax**

	$k_{2,0} = 0.0875$		$k_{2,0} = 0.14$	
	30-year	Annual	30-year	Annual
$\bar{H} = 0.09$				
$E[R_{t+1}]$	17.1319	1.0592	12.9708	1.0503
$\sigma(R_{t+1})$	49.4105	n/a	37.2570	n/a
$R_{t,t+1}$	2.9703	1.0370	2.2457	1.0273
Equity premium $E[R_{t+1}] - R_{t,t+1}$	14.1616	0.0223	10.7251	0.0229
Sharpe ratio $\dfrac{E[R_{t+1}] - R_{t,t+1}}{\sigma(R_{t+1})}$	0.2866	n/a	0.2879	n/a
$\bar{H} = 0.11$				
$E[R_{t+1}]$	22.1773	1.0678	16.0801	1.0572
$\sigma(R_{t+1})$	64.1466	n/a	46.3385	n/a
$R_{t,t+1}$	4.2986	1.0498	3.1006	1.0384
Equity premium $E[R_{t+1}] - R_{t,t+1}$	17.8787	0.0180	12.9795	0.0187
Sharpe ratio $\dfrac{E[R_{t+1}] - R_{t,t+1}}{\sigma(R_{t+1})}$	0.2787	n/a	0.2801	n/a

Notes: The gross risky one-period return on capital is $R_{t+1} = 1 + r_{t+1} - \delta$. The annualized gross risky one-period return is $(R_{t+1})^{1/30}$. The expected value and standard deviation of the gross risky one-period return R_{t+1} are calculated as the average and standard deviation, respectively, across simulations. The annual equity premium is the expected value of the annualized risky return in the next period minus the annualized return on the one-period riskless bond.

5.4 Conclusion

Our model is as simple as it gets for examining fiscal sustainability. Yet its findings suggest that maintaining unsustainable policies of the kind currently being conducted in the United States and other developed nations raises an important set of challenges for long-term economic performance.

Table 5.20   Equity premium and Sharpe ratio in period immediately before regime switch: 30 percent tax

	$k_{2,0} = 0.0875$		$k_{2,0} = 0.14$	
	Eq. prem.	Sharpe ratio	Eq. prem.	Sharpe ratio
$\bar{H} = 0.09$				
Period 1	0.0223	0.2866	0.0229	0.2879
Before shutdown	0.0819	0.3266	0.0848	0.3276
Percent bigger	0.6290	0.5367	0.6617	0.5660
Percent smaller	0.0033	0.0957	0.0043	0.1000
$\bar{H} = 0.11$				
Period 1	0.0180	0.2787	0.0187	0.2801
Before shutdown	0.0701	0.3173	0.0739	0.3199
Percent bigger	0.5460	0.4807	0.5913	0.5153
Percent smaller	0.0023	0.0677	0.0027	0.0787

Notes: The "Period 1" row represents the equity premium and Sharpe ratio in the initial period for each specification. The "Before shutdown" row represents the average equity premium and Sharpe ratio across simulations in the period immediately before shutdown for each specification. The "Percent bigger" and "Percent smaller" rows tell how many of the simulated ending values of the equity premium and Sharpe ratio were bigger than or less than, respectively, their initial period values. These percentages do not sum to one because the equity premium and Sharpe ratio do not change in the cases in which the economy shuts down in the second period.

Younger generations have only 100 percent of their earnings to surrender to older generations. As the government enforces ever greater redistribution, the economy saves and invests less and wages either fall or grow at slower rates than would otherwise be true. In the United States, generational policy appears responsible for reducing the rate of national saving from roughly 15 percent in the early 1950s to close to zero percent today. The rate of net domestic investment has plunged as well. And for most American workers, real wage growth has become a distant memory.

Clearly, multiperiod models using the sparse grid techniques developed by Krueger and Kubler (2006) are needed to provide more realistic Monte Carlo simulations of actual or near economic death. Whether such models can be developed in time and in sufficient detail to influence developed-country policymakers to alter their current policies remains to be seen.

Appendix
Description of Calibration

This section details how we arrived at the calibrated parameter values listed in table 5.1. The thirty-year discount factor β is set to match the annual discount factor common in the real business cycle (RBC) literature of 0.96

$$\beta = (0.96)^{30}.$$

We set the coefficient of relative risk aversion at a midrange value of $\gamma = 2$. This value lies in the midrange of values that have been used in the literature.[12] The capital share of income parameter is set to match the US average $\alpha = 0.35$, and the thirty-year depreciation rate δ is set to match an annual depreciation rate of 5 percent:

$$\delta = 1 - (1 - 0.05)^{30}.$$

The equilibrium production process in our two-period model is the following.

$$Y_t = e^{z_t} K_t^{\alpha} \quad \forall t,$$

where labor is supplied inelastically and z_t is the aggregate total factor productivity shock. We assume the shock z_t is an AR(1) process with normally distributed errors.

(5) $\qquad z_t = \rho z_{t-1} + (1 - \rho)\mu + \varepsilon_t$

$$\text{where } \rho \in [0, 1), \mu \geq 0, \quad \text{and} \quad \varepsilon_t \sim N(0, \sigma^2).$$

This implies that the shock process e^{z_t} is lognormally distributed $LN(0, \sigma^2)$. We calibrate the parameters of the shock process (5) to $\rho = 0.95$ and $\sigma = 0.4946$ for annual data, which roughly correspond to standard RBC calibrations although our standard deviation is higher for illustrative purposes.

For data in which one period is thirty years, we have to recalculate the analogous $\tilde{\rho}$ and $\tilde{\sigma}$.

$$z_{t+1} = \rho z_t + (1 - \rho)\mu + \varepsilon_{t+1}$$

$$z_{t+2} = \rho z_{t+1} + (1 - \rho)\mu + \varepsilon_{t+2}$$

$$= \rho^2 z_t + \rho(1 - \rho)\mu + \rho\varepsilon_{t+1} + (1 - \rho)\mu + \varepsilon_{t+2}$$

$$z_{t+3} = \rho z_{t+2} + (1 - \rho)\mu + \varepsilon_{t+3}$$

$$= \rho^3 z_t + \rho^2(1 - \rho)\mu + \rho^2\varepsilon_{t+1} + \rho(1 - \rho)\mu + \rho\varepsilon_{t+2} + (1 - \rho)\mu + \varepsilon_{t+3}$$

$$\vdots$$

$$z_{t+j} = \rho^j z_t + (1 - \rho)\mu \sum_{s=1}^{j} \rho^{j-s} + \sum_{s=1}^{j} \rho^{j-s}\varepsilon_{t+s}.$$

With one period equal to thirty years $j = 30$, the shock process in our chapter should be:

(A1) $\qquad z_{t+30} = \rho^{30} z_t + (1 - \rho)\mu \sum_{s=1}^{30} \rho^{30-s} + \sum_{s=1}^{30} \rho^{30-s}\varepsilon_{t+s}.$

12. Estimates of the coefficient of relative risk aversion γ mostly lie between 1 and 10. See Mankiw and Zeldes (1991); Blake (1996); Campbell (1996); Kocherlakota (1996); Brav, Constantinides, and Geczy (2002); and Mehra and Prescott (1985).

Then the persistence parameters in our one-period-equals-thirty-years model should be $\tilde{\rho} = \rho^{30} = 0.2146$. Define $\tilde{\varepsilon}_{t+30} \equiv \sum_{s=1}^{30} \rho^{30-s} \varepsilon_{t+s}$ as the summation term on the right-hand side of (A1). Then $\tilde{\varepsilon}_{t+30}$ is distributed:

$$\tilde{\varepsilon}_{t+30} \sim N\left(0, \left[\sum_{s=1}^{30} \rho^{2(30-s)}\right]\sigma^2\right).$$

Using this formula, the annual persistence parameter $\rho = 0.95$, and the annual standard deviation parameter $\sigma = 0.4946$, the implied thirty-year standard deviation is $\tilde{\sigma} = 1.5471$. So our shock process should be,

$$z_t = \tilde{\rho} z_{t-1} + (1 - \rho)\tilde{\mu} + \tilde{\varepsilon}_t \quad \forall t \quad \text{where} \quad \tilde{\varepsilon} \sim N(0, \tilde{\sigma}^2),$$

where $\tilde{\rho} = 0.2146$ and $\tilde{\sigma} = 1.5471$. We calibrate μ, and therefore $\tilde{\mu}$, so that the median wage is 50,000.

Lastly, we set the size of the promised transfer $\bar{H}$ to be 32 percent of the median real wage. This level of transfers is meant to approximately match the average per capita real transfers in the United States to the average real wage in recent years. We get the median real wage by simulating a time series of the economy until it hits the shutdown point, and we do this for 3,000 simulated time series. We take the median wage from those simulations. In order to reduce the effect of the initial values on the median, we take the simulation that lasted the longest number of periods before shutting down and remove the first 10 percent of the longest simulation's periods from each simulation for the calculation of the median.

References

Aguiar, M., and G. Gopinath. 2006. "Defaultable Debt, Interest Rates and the Current Account." *Journal of International Economics* 69 (1): 64–83.
Alesina, A., and A. Drazen. 1991. "Why Are Stabilizations Delayed?" *American Economic Review* 81 (5): 1170–88.
Altig, D., A. J. Auerbach, L. J. Kotlikoff, K. A. Smetters, and J. Walliser. 2001. "Simulating Fundamental Tax Reform in the United States." *American Economic Review* 91 (3): 574–95.
Arellano, C. 2008. "Default Risk and Income Fluctuations in Emerging Economies." *American Economic Review* 98 (3): 690–712.
Auerbach, A. J., and K. A. Hassett. 1992. "Tax Policy and Business Fixed Investment in the United States." *Journal of Public Economics* 47 (2): 141–70.
———. 2001. "Uncertainty and the Design of Long-Run Fiscal Policy." In *Demographic Change and Fiscal Policy,* edited by A. J. Auerbach and R. D. Lee, 73–92. Cambridge: Cambridge University Press.
———. 2002. "Fiscal Policy and Uncertainty." *International Finance* 5 (2): 229–49.
———. 2007. "Optimal Long-Run Fiscal Policy: Constraints, Preferences, and the Resolution of Uncertainty." *Journal of Economic Dynamics and Control* 31 (5): 1451–72.

Auerbach, A. J., and L. J. Kotlikoff. 1987. *Dynamic Fiscal Policy.* Cambridge: Cambridge University Press.

Barro, R. J. 2009. "Rare Disasters, Asset Prices, and Welfare Costs." *American Economic Review* 99 (1): 243–64.

Blake, D. 1996. "Effciency, Risk Aversion and Portfolio Insurance: An Analysis of Financial Asset Portfolios Held by Investors in the United Kingdom." *Economic Journal* 106 (438): 1175–92.

Brav, A., G. M. Constantinides, and C. C. Geczy. 2002. "Asset Pricing with Heterogeneous Consumers and Limited Participation: Empirical Evidence." *Journal of Political Economy* 110 (4): 793–824.

Campbell, J. Y. 1996. "Understanding Risk and Return." *Journal of Political Economy* 104 (2): 298–345.

———. 2000. "Asset Pricing at the Millenium." *Journal of Finance* 55 (4): 1515–67.

Cochrane, J. H. 2005. *Asset Pricing,* rev. ed. Princeton, NJ: Princeton University Press.

———. 2011. "Understanding Policy in the Great Recession: Some Unpleasant Fiscal Arithmetic." *European Economic Review* 55 (1): 2–30.

Congressional Budget Office. 2011. *CBO's Long-Term Budget Outlook.* Washington, DC: CBO, June.

Cooley, T. F., and J. Soares. 1999. "A Positive Theory of Social Security Based on Reputation." *Journal of Political Economy* 107 (1): 135–60.

Davig, T., and E. M. Leeper. 2011a. "Monetary-Fiscal Policy Interactions and Fiscal Stimulus." *European Economic Review* 55 (2): 211–27.

———. 2011b. "Temporarily Unstable Government Debt and Inflation." NBER Working Paper no. 16799. Cambridge, MA: National Bureau of Economic Research, February.

Davig, T., E. M. Leeper, and T. B. Walker. 2010. "'Unfunded Liabilities' and Uncertain Fiscal Financing." *Journal of Monetary Economics* 57 (5): 600–619.

———. 2011. "Inflation and the Fiscal Limit." *European Economic Review* 55 (1): 31–47.

De Nardi, M., S. İmrohoroğlu, and T. J. Sargent. 1999. "Projected US Demographics and Social Security." *Review of Economic Dynamics* 2 (3): 575–615.

Gohkhale, J., and K. Smetters. 2007. "Do the Markets Care About the $2.4 Trillion US Deficit?" *Financial Analysts Journal* 63 (2): 37–47.

Hamilton, J. D. 2008. "Regime-Switching Models." In *New Palgrave Dictionary of Economics,* 2nd ed., edited by S. N. Durlauf and L. E. Blume. New York: Palgrave McMillan Ltd.

Hassett, K. A., and G. E. Metcalf. 1999. "Investment with Uncertain Tax Policy: Does Random Tax Policy Discourage Investment?" *The Economic Journal* 109 (457): 372–93.

Huggett, M., and G. Ventura. 1999. "On the Distributional Effects of Social Security Reform." *Review of Economic Dynamics* 2 (3): 498–531.

İmrohoroğlu, A., S. İmrohoroğlu, and D. H. Joines. 1995. "A Life Cycle Analysis of Social Security." *Economic Theory* 6 (1): 83–114.

———. 1999. "Social Security in an Overlapping Generations Model with Land." *Review of Economic Dynamics* 2 (3): 638–65.

International Monetary Fund. 2009. "Fiscal Implications of the Global Economic and Financial Crisis." IMF Staff Position Note SPN/09/13. Washington, DC: IMF.

Kocherlakota, N. R. 1996. "The Equity Premium: It's Still a Puzzle." *Journal of Economic Literature* 34 (1): 42–71.

Kotlikoff, L. J., and J. Green. 2009. "On the General Relativity of Fiscal Language." In *Key Issues in Public Finance: A Conference in Memory of David Bradford,* edited by A. J. Auerbach and D. Shaviro, 241–56. Cambridge, MA: Harvard University Press.

Kotlikoff, L. J., K. Smetters, and J. Walliser. 1998a. "Social Security: Privatization and Progressivity." *American Economic Review* 88 (2): 137–41.

———. 1998b. "The Economic Impact of Transiting to a Privatized Social Security System." In *Redesigning Social Security,* edited by H. Siebert, 327–48. Kiel: Kiel University Press.

———. 2007. "Mitigating America's Demographic Dilemma by Pre-Funding Social Security." *Journal of Monetary Economics* 54 (2): 247–66.

Krueger, D., and F. Kubler. 2006. "Pareto Improving Social Security Reform When Financial Markets Are Incomplete!?" *American Economic Review* 96 (3): 737–55.

Leeper, E. M., and T. B. Walker. 2011. "Fiscal Limits in Advanced Economies." NBER Working Paper no. 16819. Cambridge, MA: National Bureau of Economic Research, February.

Mankiw, N. G., and S. P. Zeldes. 1991. "The Consumption of Stockholders and Nonstockholders." *Journal of Financial Economics* 29 (1): 97–112.

Mehra, R., and E. C. Prescott. 1985. "The Equity Premium: A Puzzle." *Journal of Monetary Economics* 15 (2): 145–61.

Nishiyama, S., and K. Smetters. 2007. "Does Social Security Privatization Produce Efficiency Gains?" *Quarterly Journal of Economics* 122 (4): 1677–719.

Reinhart, C. M., and K. Rogoff. 2009. *This Time Is Different: Eight Centuries of Financial Folly.* Princeton, NJ: Princeton University Press.

Sargent, T. J., and N. Wallace. 1981. "Some Unpleasant Monetarist Arithmetic." *Federal Reserve Bank of Minneapolis Quarterly Review* 5 (3): 1–17.

Shiller, R. J. 1982. "Consumption, Asset Markets, and Macroeconomic Fluctuations." *Carnegie-Rochester Conference Series on Public Policy* 17 (1): 203–38.

Smetters, K., and J. Walliser. 2004. "Opting out of Social Security." *Journal of Public Economics* 88 (7-8): 1295–306.

Trabandt, M., and H. Uhlig. 2009. "How Far Are We from the Slippery Slope? The Laffer Curve Revisited." NBER Working Paper no. 15343. Cambridge, MA: National Bureau of Economic Research, September.

Yue, V. Z. 2010. "Sovereign Default and Debt Renegotiation." *Journal of International Economics* 80 (2): 176–87.

Comment   Douglas W. Elmendorf

This chapter by Rick Evans, Larry Kotlikoff, and Kerk Phillips (henceforth, EKP) is clever and thought-provoking, and I am pleased to have the opportunity to discuss it. The question of how best to quantify fiscal sustainability is one that my colleagues and I at the Congressional Budget Office (CBO) spend a fair amount of time thinking about. Therefore, I attempt two things in my remarks: first, I make some specific comments about the approach to quantification and simulation used in this chapter. Second, I discuss CBO's approach to quantifying the fiscal challenges facing the US federal govern-

Douglas W. Elmendorf is director of the Congressional Budget Office.

For acknowledgments, sources of research support, and disclosure of the author's material financial relationships, if any, please see http://www.nber.org/chapters/c12643.ack.

ment—describing what we do now, some limitations of what we do, and ways we plan to strengthen our analysis.[1]

The Approach to Quantification and Simulation Used in the Chapter

The chapter by EKP examines the probability and timing of insolvency of a government program that transfers resources from young to old, as in the US Social Security program. The key elements of the approach are as follows:

- The program has benefit payments that are fixed and tax collections that vary with the size of the economy. There is uncertainty about the size of the economy and thus about the amount of taxes collected. With fixed benefits and uncertain taxes, there is a possibility of the program going bankrupt.
- When the program goes bankrupt, it can shift to one of two regimes depending on the simulation: one is a complete shutdown of the economy, and the other is a permanent shift to a program in which the benefit payments equal a fixed share of the wages of the young. Naturally, the second regime seems to me a more plausible and interesting one.
- The model incorporates two periods with overlapping generations and rational expectations. The financial system of the economy has both government bonds and claims to risky capital, so the simulation results include an equity premium. The imbalance in the government's intertemporal budget is labeled the "fiscal gap," and the simulation results also include that gap.
- The model is calibrated along some dimensions to the US economy.

This is an interesting setup. It lets the authors explore the interplay of fiscal policy and asset prices in an uncertain world, and the simplicity of the model makes its workings fairly transparent. A number of the qualitative conclusions seem sensible: higher precautionary savings extend the time to bankruptcy, and higher transfers reduce the time to bankruptcy. In cases when the bankruptcy of the program leads to a complete shutdown of the economy, the equity premium is roughly in line with the historical premium. Both the fiscal gap and the equity premium increase as the program approaches bankruptcy; therefore, those indicators provide useful signals that bankruptcy is approaching.

However, there are several problems in trying to link the quantitative results of this modeling to the actual US economy. One is that the modeling shows that a drop in wages reduces taxes paid into the Social Security-like

---

1. The discussion of CBO's analysis refers to the agency's analytic tools and estimates as of December 2011, when a preliminary version of these remarks was presented at an NBER conference.

program but leaves benefits unaffected. The true situation is not as stark as the chapter indicates, however, because aggregate wages affect Social Security benefit payments as well as its tax receipts: when one claims Social Security benefits for the first time, the amount one receives is indexed to average wages. After that initial calculation, however, one's benefits rise with prices rather than wages. So a drop in wages affects the program's tax revenues more than its benefit payments, and indeed hurts the finances of the program, but not as much as suggested by the modeling.

Another problem in linking this model to the US economy is that there are other sources of uncertainty besides aggregate productivity growth. In CBO's stochastic modeling for Social Security, we allow for variation in productivity growth, but also in other economic variables and in demographic outcomes. In a paper we published half a dozen years ago, we estimated that productivity growth was indeed one of the largest sources of uncertainty about Social Security's finances. However, there was also significant uncertainty stemming from fertility, immigration, mortality, and various economic factors.

A third problem is that the US government operates other intergenerational transfer programs besides Social Security. If one cares about the unsustainability of current US fiscal policies, one should care particularly about health care programs for older Americans; outlays for those programs are roughly as large as outlays for Social Security today and are growing faster. One could view those programs as being like Social Security in some respects but with an additional critical source of uncertainty—the growth in health care costs per beneficiary of those programs. All told, uncertainty about productivity is not all or even most of the uncertainty associated with US fiscal outcomes.

A fourth problem is that allowing for only two periods of life limits people's ability to smooth consumption by trading with people from other generations. I am concerned that this limitation might distort the estimated equity premium. For example, since the consumption of the young can be driven to zero, should we not expect that the state prices for consumption would be even higher than they are? Are they held down because the young cannot trade with anybody?

Addressing all of these issues and others would be even more challenging than what the authors have already accomplished, so I am not suggesting that they have overlooked straightforward alternatives. Still, given these considerations, I think the model's value is primarily in suggesting issues and relationships to have in mind rather than in providing a realistic appraisal of the risks facing US fiscal policy.

Indeed, the quantitative estimates may seem surprisingly benign to readers of Kotlikoff's other writings or CBO's projections. The authors estimate that the expected time to bankruptcy of the Social Security-like program is about 100 years, with a 35 percent chance of such bankruptcy occurring in thirty years. The fiscal gap—the difference between the net present value of expected revenues and expected benefits—is less than 4 percent of GDP in most of the scenarios and is actually negative in some scenarios (because of the regime shift).

In contrast, CBO's long-term budget projections imply even more significant risks and even larger fiscal gaps under current US policies.[2] We publish long-term projections of federal debt under two scenarios. The "extended baseline scenario" is an extension of our regular budget projections, which are based on current law. Under current law, the expiration of the tax cuts enacted since 2001, the growing reach of the alternative minimum tax (AMT), the tax provisions of the recent health care legislation, and the way in which the tax system interacts with economic growth would result in steadily higher revenues relative to GDP. Revenues would reach 23 percent of GDP by 2035—much higher than has typically been seen in recent decades—and would grow to larger percentages thereafter. At the same time, under this scenario, spending on everything other than the major health care programs, Social Security, and interest on the debt would decline to the lowest percentage of GDP since before World War II. That significant increase in revenues and decrease in the relative magnitude of other spending would offset much—though not all—of the rise in spending on health care programs and Social Security. As a result, debt held by the public as a share of GDP would increase only slowly from its current high level.

However, CBO estimates that the budget outlook is much bleaker under an "alternative fiscal scenario," which reflects what one might think of as current policies. In particular, this scenario incorporates several changes to law that are widely expected to occur or that would modify some provisions of law that might be difficult to sustain for a long period. In this scenario, the tax cuts are extended; the reach of the AMT is restrained to stay close to its historical extent; over the longer run, tax law evolves further so that revenues remain near their historical average of 18 percent of GDP; and certain spending programs deviate from current law. Under those policies, federal debt would grow very rapidly. Debt held by the public as a share of GDP would exceed its historical peak of 109 percent by 2023 and would approach 190 percent in 2035. The fiscal gap in this scenario is estimated to be nearly 5 percent of GDP over the next twenty-five years (equivalent to about $700 billion this year) and more than 8 percent of GDP over the next seventy-five years as a whole.

Clearly, current policies are unsustainable, and they appear more unsustainable in CBO's projections than in the simulation results of this chapter.

2. See Congressional Budget Office. *CBO's 2011 Long-Term Budget Outlook*. Washington, DC: CBO, June 2011.

The Approach to Quantifying Fiscal Policy Used by CBO

Let me now turn from the chapter by EKP to discuss what we do at CBO to quantify the fiscal challenges facing the US federal government. We currently use four different analytic approaches:

1. First and most important, CBO regularly constructs projections of spending, revenue, deficits, and debt. Three times a year, we publish projections looking ahead ten years; once a year, we publish projections that extend seventy-five years, although we focus on the first twenty-five. As I just mentioned, those projections show that current US fiscal policies would increase federal debt on an unsustainable trajectory.

2. Second, CBO regularly uses its long-term projections to estimate the fiscal gap. We define the gap as the present value of revenues over a given period minus the present value of noninterest outlays over that period, adjusted to keep federal debt at its current percentage of GDP.[3] As I just mentioned, the estimated fiscal gap based on current policies is nearly 5 percent of GDP over the next twenty-five years and more than 8 percent of GDP over the next seventy-five years. Because revenue has averaged 18 percent of GDP and spending 21 percent, a gap of that magnitude requires a large change in policies.

3. Third, CBO regularly quantifies the effects of delay in closing the fiscal gap. For example, we estimated that if policymakers wait about a decade to change policies, the gap rises from nearly 5 percent of GDP to around 8 percent—not even counting the feedback effects on the economy.

4. Fourth, CBO sometimes estimates the distributional impact across generations of waiting to resolve the long-term budget imbalance. In a report in December 2010, we estimated that stabilizing the ratio of debt to output in 2025 instead of 2015 would benefit the average person over age fifty-five today, hurt people not yet born, and have small effects in both directions on people in intermediate cohorts.[4] Of course, in weighing distributional burdens, policymakers also need to take into account the progression of underlying living standards.

These are the analytic approaches that CBO currently uses to quantify fiscal challenges. Let me offer three observations about what I see as the limitations of those approaches and some directions for improvement.

The first observation is that all of the approaches listed involve point estimates and do not explicitly address uncertainty. Indeed, most of CBO's analysis involves point estimates rather than ranges or probabilities.

---

3. CBO's calculations use a discount rate equal to the average interest rate on federal debt held by the public, which is projected to be 2.7 percent on an inflation-adjusted basis in the long term.

4. The estimates depended in part on how the debt was stabilized—by raising marginal tax rates or by reducing federal transfer payments (which go mainly to older people).

There are some good reasons for that predilection: One is that the congressional budget process operates with point estimates. Committees are given allocations of funds, and those are expressed as point values. Another reason for our focus on point estimates is that our methodologies do not readily yield measures of uncertainty. CBO's projections for the economy and the budget do not generally come from formal probability models, so ranges and probabilities do not fall out naturally in the projection process; instead, they would need to be constructed separately. A further reason we focus on point estimates is that communicating uncertainty in an effective way without obscuring the basic results is difficult. When we report ranges for our estimates, it is common for people who would prefer that our estimate be smaller to quote the bottom of our range and for people who would prefer that our estimate be larger to quote the top of our range, which muddies the public discussion of our estimates at least as much as it illuminates it. Thus, the practical gains from our analysis of uncertainty are often smaller than one would hope.

That said, we think it is important that policymakers understand the uncertainty of our methodologies and our estimates, so they can take this uncertainty into account in their decision-making. Therefore, we think and write about uncertainty when we can, and I will say more about that in a moment.

My second observation is that, in constructing point estimates, CBO aims to be in the middle of the distribution of possible outcomes. I have used this phrase repeatedly when talking with members of Congress.

I am not usually explicit, though, about whether the word "middle" refers to the mean or the median of the distribution. In many contexts, the mean and median are probably fairly close to each other, so the distinction is not important. However, for distributions in which the median is noticeably different from the mean—say, distributions with long tails on one side—the best way for CBO to proceed is not clear. One example is our approach to projecting the unemployment rate. Our current approach captures, we think, the normal ebbs and flows of business cycles, but it may not adequately capture the risk of a severe slump like the Great Depression or the current downturn; therefore, we discuss the chance of such a slump as a risk to the long-run budget and economic outlook. Incorporating the possibility of such an event in our numerical projections could make those projections more accurate, on average, over the long run. Yet, the estimates would be too pessimistic almost all of the time and still far too optimistic on the rare occasions when a severe slump occurs. Would such a change in our estimates make the estimates more useful to Congress, or is it more useful to continue with our current approach?

Another concern related to our reporting the middle of the distribution of possible outcomes is whether we are aggregating different sources of uncertainty in the most effective way. For example, when we choose expected values for two variables and then construct a third variable from them, our projection of that third value will not be its expected value if the two underlying variables interact in a nonlinear way. Many of our estimates involve nonlinearities, so we think about how to cope with this challenge, but we do not have a good general way of dealing with it.

My third observation is that CBO is working to be more explicit about the uncertainty in its budget and economic projections. Let me mention several examples:

- One example is to show ranges of effects based on different parameter assumptions. We have been doing this for our estimates of the effects of fiscal policies on the economy, regarding both the near-term impact through changes in aggregate demand and the medium-term and long-term impacts through changes in potential output. Specifically, we have published ranges of estimates for various policies corresponding to different short-term multipliers, different crowding out of investment by government debt, and different elasticities of labor supply with respect to marginal tax rates.
- Another example is our ongoing efforts to extend our stochastic analysis of Social Security to the rest of the budget. For Social Security, we have allowed most of the key demographic and economic factors that underlie the analysis—including fertility and mortality rates, interest rates, and the growth rate of productivity—to vary on the basis of historical patterns of variation, and we sometimes publish 80 percent confidence regions for our projections. In a recent document, for example, we projected that the Social Security trust funds would be exhausted in 2038, but that there was a 10 percent chance of exhaustion in 2030 or earlier and a 10 percent chance of exhaustion in 2059 or later. To extend this approach to the rest of the budget, we are strengthening the health care aspects of the microsimulation model we use in our long-term projections and then will try to quantify the uncertainty about health care spending per beneficiary under current policies.
- A further example is our descriptions of our projections. Our long-term outlook for the budget, which we update each year, now includes a section on the budgetary risks posed by recessions and financial crises, changes in interest rates on federal debt, changes in demographics, changes in health status and health care, long-term changes in productivity, and catastrophic events or major military actions. We also wrote a separate issue brief about the risk of a fiscal crisis, which we defined as investors losing confidence in a government's ability to manage its budget and the government thereby losing its ability to borrow at affordable rates.
- The last example I will mention is analysis of the ways that alternative policies expose the government budget to more or less risk. We are

engaged in a project now with Debbie Lucas and Steve Zeldes about the different amounts of risk in Social Security when benefits are calculated according to different formulas. We are also examining the effects of proposals to transform certain federal health care programs from defined-benefit programs to defined-contribution programs. Of course, policy choices that insulate the federal budget from risk may achieve that insulation by shifting the risk to benefit recipients or taxpayers, and our analyses will make that clear as well.

Conclusion

In sum, this chapter by EKP illuminates some key relationships between fiscal policy and the economy that are important for judging the sustainability of that policy. Their chapter, the projections of CBO, and research by other budget and economic analysts show that the current policies of the US federal government have put federal debt on an unsustainable path and that the adjustments needed to achieve sustainability are very large. Illustrating the consequences of such an unsustainable fiscal policy is critically important work.

How Do Laffer Curves Differ across Countries?

Mathias Trabandt and Harald Uhlig

6.1 Introduction

We seek to understand how Laffer curves differ across countries in the United States and the EU-14. This provides insight into the limits of taxation. As an application, we analyze the consequences of recent increases in government spending and their fiscal consequences as well as the consequences for the permanent sustainability of current debt levels, when interest rates are permanently high, for example, due to default fears.

We build on the analysis in Trabandt and Uhlig (2011). There, we have characterized Laffer curves for labor and capital taxation for the United States, the EU-14, and individual European countries. In the analysis, a neoclassical growth model featuring constant Frisch elasticity (CFE) preferences are introduced and analyzed: we use the same preferences here. The results there suggest that the United States could increase tax revenues considerably more than the EU-14, and that conversely the degree of self-financing of tax cuts is much larger in the EU-14 than in the United States. While we have calculated results for individual European countries, the focus there

Mathias Trabandt is an economist with the Board of Governors of the Federal Reserve System. Harald Uhlig is professor of economics at the University of Chicago and a research associate of the National Bureau of Economic Research.

We are grateful to Roel Beetsma and Jaume Ventura for useful discussions. Further, we are grateful to Alan Auerbach, Alberto Alesina, Axel Boersch-Supan, Francesco Giavazzi, Laurence Kotlikoff, and Valerie Ramey for useful comments and suggestions. The views expressed in this chapter are solely the responsibility of the authors and should not be interpreted as reflecting the views of the Board of Governors of the Federal Reserve System or of any other person associated with the Federal Reserve System. For acknowledgments, sources of research support, and disclosure of the authors' material financial relationships, if any, please see http://www.nber.org/chapters/c12638.ack.

was directed toward a comparison of the United States and the aggregate EU-14 economy.

This chapter provides a more in-depth analysis of the cross-country comparison. Furthermore, we modify the analysis in two important dimensions. The model in Trabandt and Uhlig (2011) overstates total tax revenues to GDP compared to the data: in particular, labor tax revenues to GDP are too high. We introduce monopolistic competition to solve this: capital income now consists of rental rates to capital as well as pure profits, decreasing the share of labor income in the economy. With this change alone, the model now overpredicts the capital income tax revenue. We furthermore assume that only a fraction of pure profit income is actually reported to the tax authorities and therefore taxed. With these two changes, the fit to the data improves compared to the original version (see figure 6.2). In terms of the Laffer curves, this moves countries somewhat closer to the peak of the labor tax Laffer curve and somewhat farther away from the peak of the capital tax Laffer curve. For the cross-country comparison, we assume that all structural parameters for technologies and preferences are the same across countries. The differences between the Laffer curves therefore arise solely due to differences in fiscal policy—that is, the mix of distortionary taxes, government spending, and government debt. We find that labor income and consumption taxes are important for accounting for most of the cross-country differences.

We refine the methodology of Mendoza, Razin, and Tesar (1994) to calculate effective tax rates on labor and capital income. Broadly, we expand the measured labor tax base by including supplements to wages as well as a fraction of entrepreneurial income of households. As a result, the refinements imply a more reasonable labor share in line with the literature. More importantly, the average 1995 to 2010 labor income taxes turn out to be lower while capital income taxes are somewhat higher, as previously calculated in Trabandt and Uhlig (2011).

We update our analysis in Trabandt and Uhlig (2011) by including the additional years 2008 to 2010. This is particularly interesting, as it allows us to examine the implications of the recent substantial tax and revenue shocks. While recent fiscal policy changes were intended to be temporary, we examine the pessimistic scenario that they are permanent. To do so, we calibrate the model to the Laffer curves implied by the strained fiscal situation of 2010, and compare them to the Laffer curves of the average extended sample 1995 to 2010. We find that the 2010 calibration moves almost all countries closer to the peak of the labor tax Laffer curve, with the scope for additional labor tax increases cut by a third for most countries and by up to one-half for some countries. It is important, however, to keep the general equilibrium repercussions of raising taxes in mind: even though tax revenues may be increased by some limited amount, tax bases and thereby output fall when moving to the peak of the Laffer curve due to the negative incentive effects of higher taxes.

We then use these results to examine the scope for long-term sustainability of current debt levels, when interest rates are permanently higher due to, say, default fears. This helps to understand the more complex situation of an extended period with substantially increased interest rates due to, say, default fears. More precisely, we answer the following question: what is the maximum steady state interest rate on outstanding government debt that the government could afford without cutting government spending, based on a calibration to the fiscal situation in 2010? To do so, we calculate the implied peak of the Laffer curve and compute the maximum interest rate on outstanding government debt in 2010 that would still balance the government budget constraint in steady state. The results of our baseline model are in table 6.7: the most interesting column there may be the second one. We find that the United States can afford the highest interest rate if labor taxes are moved to the peak of the Laffer curve: depending on the debt measure used, a real interest rate of 12 to 15.5 percent is sustainable. Interestingly, Ireland can also afford the high rate of 11.2 percent when moving labor taxes only. By contrast, Austria, Belgium, Denmark, Finland, France, Greece, and Italy can only afford permanent real rates in the range of 4.4 to 7.1 percent, when financing the additional interest payments with higher labor tax rates alone, while, say, Germany, Portugal, and Spain can all afford an interest rate somewhere above 9 percent. The picture improves somewhat, but not much, when labor taxes and capital taxes can both be adjusted: notably, Belgium, Denmark, Finland, France, and Italy cannot permanently afford real interest rates above 6.5 percent. In the following we also examine the implications of human capital accumulation and show that the maximum interest rates may be even lower than suggested by our baseline model. It is worth emphasizing that we have not included the possibility of cutting government spending and/or transfers and that our analysis has focused on the most pessimistic scenario of a permanent shift.

In the baseline model, physical capital is the production factor that gets accumulated. It may be important, however, to allow for and consider human capital accumulation when examining the consequences of changing labor taxation. We build on the quantitative endogenous growth models introduced in Trabandt and Uhlig (2011), and provide a more detailed cross-country comparison. We find that the capital tax Laffer curve is affected only rather little across countries when human capital is introduced into the model. By contrast, the introduction of human capital has important effects for the labor income tax Laffer curve. Several countries are pushed on the slippery slope sides of their labor tax Laffer curves once human capital is accounted for. Intuitively, higher labor taxes lead to a faster reduction of the labor tax base since households work less and aquire less human capital, which in turn leads to lower labor income. We recalculate the implied maximum interest rates on government debt in 2010 when human capital accumulation is allowed for in the model. Table 6.9 contains the results: the United States may only afford a real interest rate between 5.8 to 6.6 percent in this case. Most of the European countries cluster between 4 and 4.9 percent except for Denmark, Finland, and Ireland, who can afford real interest rates between 5.9 and 9.5 percent.

We add a cross-country analysis on consumption taxes. In Trabandt and Uhlig (2011), we have shown that the consumption tax Laffer curve has no peak. Essentially, the difference between the labor tax Laffer curve and the consumption tax Laffer curve arises due to "accounting" reasons: the additional revenues are provided as transfers, and are used for consumption purchases to be taxed at the consumption tax rate. In Trabandt and Uhlig (2011), we only provided the analysis for the United States and the aggregate EU-14 economy. Here, we extend the consumption tax analysis to individual countries. The range of maximum additional tax revenues (in percent of GDP) in the baseline model is roughly 40 to 100 percent, while it shrinks to roughly 10 to 30 percent in the model with added human capital. Higher consumption taxes affect equilibrium labor via the labor wedge, similar to labor taxes. As before, human capital amplifies the reduction of the labor tax base triggered by the change in the labor wedge. Overall, maximum possible tax revenues due to consumption taxes are reduced massively, although at fairly high consumption tax rates.

The chapter is organized as follows. Section 6.2 provides the model. The calibration and parameterization of the model can be found in section 6.3. Section 6.4 provides and discusses the results. Section 6.5 discusses the extension of the model with human capital as well as the results for consumption taxation. Finally, section 6.6 concludes.

6.2 Model

We employ the baseline model in Trabandt and Uhlig (2011) and extend it by allowing for intermediate inputs, supplied by monopolistically competitive firms. Time is discrete, $t = 0.1, \ldots, \infty$. Households maximize

$$\max_{c_t, n_t, k_t, x_t, b_t} E_0 \sum_{t=0}^{\infty} \beta^t [u(c_t, n_t) + \upsilon(g_t)]$$

subject to

(1) $(1 + \tau_t^c)c_t + x_t + b_t = (1 - \tau_t^n)w_t n_t + (1 - \tau_t^k)[(d_t - \delta)k_{t-1} + \phi\Pi_t]$

$$+ \delta k_{t-1} + R_t^b b_{t-1} + s_t + (1 - \phi)\Pi_t + m_t$$

$$k_t = (1 - \delta)k_{t-1} + x_t,$$

where $c_t, n_t, k_t, x_t, b_t, m_t$ denote consumption, hours worked, capital, investment, government bonds, and an exogenous stream of payments. The household takes government consumption g_t, which provides utility, as given. Further, the household receives wages w_t, dividends d_t, and profits Π_t, from firms and asset payments m_t. The payments m_t are a stand-in for net imports, modeled here as exogenously given income from a "tree" (see Trabandt and Uhlig 2011 for further discussion). The household obtains interest earnings R_t^b and lump-sum transfers s_t from the government. It has to pay consumption taxes τ_t^c, labor income taxes τ_t^n, and capital income taxes τ_t^k on dividends and on a share ϕ of profits.[1]

As introduced and extensively discussed in Trabandt and Uhlig (2011), but also used in Hall (2009), Shimer (2009), and King and Rebelo (1999), we work with CFE preferences, given by

$$(2) \qquad u(c, n) = \log(c) - \kappa n^{\,1+1/\varphi}$$

if $\eta = 1$, and by

$$(3) \qquad u(c, n) = \frac{1}{1 - \eta}(c^{1-\eta}(1 - \kappa(1 - \eta)n^{1+1/\varphi})^{\eta} - 1)$$

if $\eta > 0$, $\eta \neq 1$, where $\kappa > 0$. These preferences are consistent with balanced growth and feature a constant Frisch elasticity of labor supply, given by φ, without constraining the intertemporal elasticity of substitution.

Competitive final good firms maximize profits

$$(4) \qquad \max_{k_{t-1}, z_t} \quad y_t - d_t k_{t-1} - p_t z_t$$

subject to the Cobb-Douglas production technology, $y_t = \xi^t k_{t-1}^{\theta} z_t^{1-\theta}$, where ξ^t denotes the trend of total factor productivity, and p_t denotes the price of an homogenous input, z_t, which in turn is produced by competitive firms who maximize profits

$$(5) \qquad \max_{z_{t,i}} \quad p_t z_t - \int p_{t,i} z_{t,i} \, di$$

subject to $z_t = (\int z_{t,i}^{1/\omega} di)^{\omega}$ with $\omega > 1$. Intermediate inputs, $z_{t,i}$, are produced by monopolistically competitive firms that maximize profits

$$\max_{p_{t,i}} \quad p_{t,i} z_{t,i} - w_t n_{t,i}$$

subject to their demand functions and production technologies:

$$z_{t,i} = \left(\frac{p_t}{p_{t,i}}\right)^{\omega/(\omega-1)} z_t$$

$$z_{t,i} = n_{t,i}.$$

---

1. We allow for partial profit taxation due to the various deductions and exemptions that are available for firms and households in this regard. Further, note that capital income taxes are levied on dividends net-of-depreciation as in Prescott (2002, 2004) and in line with Mendoza, Razin, and Tesar (1994).

In equilibrium, all firms set the same price, which is a markup over marginal costs. Formally, $p_{t,i} = p_t = \omega w_t$. Aggregate equilibrium profits are given by $\Pi_t = (\omega - 1) w_t n_t$.

The government faces the budget constraint,

$$(6) \qquad g_t + s_t + R_t^b b_{t-1} = b_t + T_t$$

where government tax revenues are given by

$$(7) \qquad T_t = \tau_t^c c_t + \tau_t^n w_t n_t + \tau_t^k [(d_t - \delta) k_{t-1} + \phi \Pi_t].$$

It is the goal to analyze how the equilibrium shifts, as tax rates are shifted. More generally, the tax rates may be interpreted as wedges as in Chari, Kehoe, and McGrattan (2007), and some of the results in this chapter carry over to that more general interpretation. What is special to the tax rate interpretation and crucial to the analysis in this chapter, however, is the link between tax receipts and transfers (or government spending) via the government budget constraint.

The chapter focuses on the comparison of balanced growth paths. We assume that government debt and government spending, as well as net imports, do not deviate from their balanced growth paths; that is, we assume that $b_{t-1} = \psi^t \bar{b}$, $g_t = \psi^t \bar{g}$ as well as $m_t = \psi^t \bar{m}$, where ψ is the growth factor of aggregate output. We consider exogenously imposed shifts in tax rates or in returns on government debt. We assume that government transfers adjust according to the government budget constraint (6), rewritten as $s_t = \psi^t \bar{b} (\psi - R_t^b) + T_t - \psi^t \bar{g}$.

6.2.1   Equilibrium

In equilibrium the household chooses plans to maximize its utility, the firm solves its maximization problem, and the government sets policies that satisfy its budget constraint. In what follows, key balanced growth relationships of the model that are necessary for computing Laffer curves are summarized. Except for hours worked, interest rates, and taxes, all other variables grow at a constant rate $\psi = \xi^{1/(1-\theta)}$. For CFE preferences, the balanced growth after-tax return on any asset is $\bar{R} = \psi^\eta / \beta$. It is assumed throughout that $\xi \geq 1$ and that parameters are such that $\bar{R} > 1$, but β is not necessarily restricted to be less than one. Let $\overline{k/y}$ denote the balanced growth path value of the capital-output ratio k_{t-1}/y_t. In the model, it is given by

$$(8) \qquad \overline{k/y} = \left(\frac{\bar{R} - 1}{\theta(1 - \tau^k)} + \frac{\delta}{\theta} \right)^{-1}.$$

Labor productivity and the before-tax wage level are given by

$$\frac{y_t}{n} = \psi^t \left(\overline{k/y}\right)^{\theta/(1-\theta)} \quad \text{and} \quad w_t = \frac{(1-\theta)}{\omega} \frac{y_t}{n}.$$

The level of equilibrium labor remains to be solved for. Let $\overline{c/y}$ denote the balanced growth path ratio c_t/y_t. With the CFE preference specification and along the balanced growth path, the first-order conditions of the household and the firm imply

$$(9) \qquad (\eta\kappa\bar{n}^{1+1/\varphi})^{-1} + 1 - \frac{1}{\eta} = \alpha\overline{c/y}$$

where $\alpha = \omega(1 + \tau^c)/(1 - \tau^n)(1 + 1/\varphi)/(1 - \theta)$ depends on tax rates, the labor share, the Frisch elasticity of labor supply, and the markup.

In this chapter, we shall concentrate on the case when transfers $\bar{s}$ are varied and government spending $\bar{g}$ is fixed. Then, the feasibility constraint implies

$$(10) \qquad \overline{c/y} = \chi + \gamma\frac{1}{\bar{n}},$$

where $\chi = 1 - (\psi - 1 + \delta)\overline{k/y}$ and $\gamma = (\bar{m} - \bar{g})(\overline{k/y})^{-\theta/(1-\theta)}$. Substituting equation (10) into (9) therefore yields a one-dimensional nonlinear equation in $\bar{n}$, which can be solved numerically, given values for preference parameters, production parameters, tax rates, and the levels of $\bar{b}$, $\bar{g}$, and $\bar{m}$.

After some straightforward algebra, total tax revenues along a balanced growth path can be calculated as

$$(11) \qquad T = \left[\tau^c\overline{c/y} + \tau^n\frac{(1 - \theta)}{\omega} + \tau^k\left(\theta - \delta\overline{k/y} + \phi(1 - \theta)\frac{\omega - 1}{\omega}\right)\right]\bar{y}$$

and equilibrium transfers are given by

$$(12) \qquad \bar{s} = (\psi - R^b)\bar{b} - \bar{g} + \bar{T}.$$

6.3   Data, Calibration, and Parameterization

The model is calibrated to annual postwar data of the United States, the aggregate EU-14 economy, and individual European countries. An overview of the calibration is in tables 6.1 and 6.2.

We refine the methodology of Mendoza, Razin, and Tesar (1994) to calculate effective tax rates on labor and capital income. Broadly, we expand the measured labor tax base by including supplements to wages as well as a fraction of entrepreneurial income of households. As a result, the refinements imply a more reasonable labor share in line with the empirical literature. More importantly, the average 1995 to 2010 labor income taxes turn out to be lower while capital income taxes are higher, as previously calculated in Trabandt and Uhlig (2011). Appendix A provides the new tax rates across countries over time and appendix B contains the details on the calculations with further discussion of the implications for the Laffer curves, among others.

There are two new key parameters compared to Trabandt and Uhlig (2011). The first parameter is ω, the gross markup, due to monopolistic competition. We set $\omega = 1.1$, which appears to be a reasonable number, given the literature.

The second parameter is φ, the share of monopolistic-competition profits that are subject to capital taxes. We set this parameter equal to the capital share, that is, to 0.36. While we could have explored specific evidence to help us pin down this parameter, we have chosen this value rather arbitrarily and with an eye toward the fit of the model to the data instead.

The sample covered in Trabandt and Uhlig (2011) is 1995 to 2007. Here we extend the sample to 2010 using the same data sources. We update all data up to 2010, except for taxes and tax revenues, which we can update only to 2009 due to data availability reasons. For most of the analysis in this chapter, we assume that the 2010 observation for taxes and revenues are the same as in 2009. We also pursue an alternative approach for tax rates for the year 2010 (see subsection 6.3.2 for the details).

We also refine the calculation of transfers in the data compared to Trabandt and Uhlig (2011). In the data, there is a nonneglible difference between government tax revenues and government revenues. This difference is mostly due to "other government revenue" and "government sales." We subtract these two items from the measure of transfers defined in Trabandt and Uhlig (2011).

The US and aggregate EU-14 tax rates, government expenditures, and government debt are set according to the upper part of table 6.1. We also calibrate the model to individual EU-14 country data for tax rates, government spending, and government debt as provided in table 6.2. Although we allow fiscal policy to be different across countries, we restrict the analysis to identical parameters across countries for preferences and technology (see the lower part of table 6.1 for the details).[2]

Finally, the empirical measure of government debt for the United States as well as the EU-14 area provided by the AMECO (annual macroeconomic) database is nominal general government consolidated gross debt (excessive deficit procedure, based on the European System of Accounts [ESA] 1995), which is divided by nominal GDP. For the United States, the gross debt to GDP ratio is 66.2 percent in the sample. For checking purposes, we also examine the implications if we use an alternative measure of US government debt: debt held by the public. See tables 6.1 and 6.2 for the differences. However, given that, to our knowledge, data on "debt held by the public" is not available for European countries, we shall proceed by using gross debt as a benchmark if not otherwise noted. Where appropriate, we shall perform a sensitivity analysis with respect to the measure of US government debt.

6.3.1   Model Fit and Sensitivity

The structual parameters are set such that model-implied steady states are close to the data. In particular, figure 6.1 provides a comparison of the

2. See Trabandt and Uhlig (2011) for the differences with respect to Laffer curves when parameters for technology and preferences are assumed to be identical or country-specific.

Table 6.1　　　　**Baseline calibration and parameterization**

Variable	US	EU-14	Description	Restriction
			Fiscal policy	
τ^n	22.1	34.2	Labor tax rate	Data
τ^k	41.1	36.8	Capital tax rate	Data
τ^c	4.6	16.7	Consumption tax rate	Data
$\overline{g/y}$	18.0	23.1	Gov. consumption + invest. to GDP	Data
			Gross government debt	
$\overline{b/y}$	66.2	67.3	Government gross debt to GDP	Data
$\overline{s/y}$	4.3	11.1	Government transfers to GDP	Implied
		Sensitivity:	*Government debt held by the public*	
$\overline{b/y}$	42.4	—	Government debt held by public to GDP	Data
$\overline{s/y}$	4.9	—	Government transfers to GDP	Implied
			Trade	
$\overline{m/y}$	3.6	–1.2	Net imports to GDP	Data
			Technology	
ψ	1.5	1.5	Annual balanced growth rate	Data
θ	0.36	0.36	Capital share in production	Data
δ	0.07	0.07	Annual depreciation rate of capital	Data
$\overline{R}-1$	4	4	Annual real interest rate	Data
ω	1.1	1.1	Gross markup	Data
ϕ	0.36	0.36	Share of profits subject to capital taxes	Data
			CFE preferences	
η	2	2	Inverse of IES	Data
φ	1	1	Frisch labor supply elasticity	Data
κ	3.30	3.30	Weight of labor	$\overline{n}_{us} = 0.25$

Notes: Baseline calibration and parameterization for the US and EU-14 benchmark model. Numbers expressed in percent where applicable. Sample: 1995–2010. IES denotes intertemporal elasticity of substitution; CFE refers to constant Frisch elasticity preferences; $\overline{n}_{us}$ denotes balanced growth labor in the United States, which is set to 25 percent of total time.

data versus model fit for key great ratios, hours as well as transfers and tax revenues.[3] Overall, the fit is remarkable given the relatively simple model in which country differences are entirely due to fiscal policy.[4]

Most of the structual parameter values in the lower part of table 6.1 are standard and perhaps uncontroversial (see, e.g., Cooley and Prescott 1995; Prescott 2002, 2004, 2006; and Kimball and Shapiro 2008).

3. We assume a mapping of data and model in the literal sense, that is, the one based on the definitions of the national income and product accounts and the revenues statistics. For work that takes an alternative perspective and emphasizes the general relativity of fiscal language, see Green and Kotlikoff (2009).

4. The present chapter, and in particular the comparison of data versus model hours, is closely related to Prescott (2002, 2004) and subsequent contributions by, for example, Blanchard (2004); Alesina, Glaeser, and Sacerdote (2006); Ljungqvist and Sargent (2007); Rogerson (2007); and Pissarides and Ngai (2009).

Table 6.2   Calibration of the model to individual countries

	τ^n			τ^c		τ^k		$\overline{b/y}$		$\overline{m/y}$		$\overline{g/y}$		$\overline{s/y}$	
	∅	2010ᵃ	2010ᵇ	∅	2010	∅	2010	∅	2010	∅	2010	∅	2010	∅	2010
US	22	20	28	5	4	41	38	66	92	4	4	18	20	4	4
USᶜ	22	20	28	5	4	41	38	42	64	4	4	18	20	5	5
EU-14	34	35	40	17	15	37	36	67	83	−1	−1	23	25	11	11
GER	34	35	35	16	17	25	27	64	83	−3	−5	21	21	10	10
FRA	39	39	43	18	16	43	43	63	82	−0	2	27	28	12	12
ITA	36	39	39	14	13	41	45	111	119	−1	2	22	23	13	13
GBR	24	25	36	15	13	52	50	48	80	2	3	22	26	11	11
AUT	43	43	45	20	20	26	24	66	72	−3	−5	21	21	18	18
BEL	39	38	43	17	17	51	50	104	97	−4	−3	24	26	16	16
DNK	43	44	50	34	31	49	56	49	44	−5	−6	28	32	22	22
FIN	44	41	51	26	23	31	30	45	48	−6	−3	25	27	17	17
GRE	29	28	35	15	13	19	17	105	143	10	8	21	21	6	6
IRL	25	24	40	24	19	17	16	48	96	−13	−19	19	23	7	7
NET	36	38	50	19	19	32	23	58	63	−7	−8	27	32	6	6
PRT	22	24	30	19	16	32	34	61	93	9	7	23	24	7	7
ESP	30	30	42	14	10	31	24	54	60	3	2	22	24	8	8
SWE	50	46	43	26	26	40	52	54	40	−7	−6	30	31	16	16

Notes: Individual country calibration of the benchmark model for the average (∅) sample from 1995 to 2010 and for the year 2010. Country codes: Germany (GER), France (FRA), Italy (ITA), United Kingdom (GBR), Austria (AUT), Belgium (BEL), Denmark (DNK), Finland (FIN), Greece (GRE), Ireland (IRL), Netherlands (NET), Portugal (PRT), Spain (ESP), and Sweden (SWE). See table 6.1 for abbreviations of variables. All numbers are expressed in percent.

ᵃDue to data availability reasons, the year 2009 value for tax rates has been assumed to remain in 2010 for most of the analysis in this chapter.

ᵇWe deviate from *a* in subsection 6.3.2 by letting labor taxes in 2010 adjust to balance the 2010 government budget. More precisely, we calculate the 2010 labor tax given government debt and consumption in 2010 as well as average 1995–2010 model implied transfers.

ᶜResults when "debt held by the public" is used for the United States rather than the harmonized cross-country measure of gross government debt provided by the AMECO database.

The new parameters here compared to Trabandt and Uhlig (2011) are the gross markup, $\omega = 1.1$, and the share of monopolistic-competition profits subject to capital taxation, $\phi = \theta = 0.36$. Figure 6.2 contains a sensitivity analysis for ω and ϕ. When $\omega \to 1$, the model overstates labor tax revenues and understates capital tax revenues (see the crosses in figure 6.2).[5] In the adapted model with intermediate inputs, a gross markup $\omega > 1$ reduces the labor tax base. At the same time, profits increase the capital tax base, but too much if profits are fully subject to capital taxation (i.e., $\phi = 1$); see the triangles in figure 6.2. Overall, the fit improves considerably if we set the share of profits subject to capital taxes, $\phi = \theta = 0.36$. The fit is not sensitive

5. Note that in this case, the value of ϕ becomes immaterial since equilibrium profits are zero.

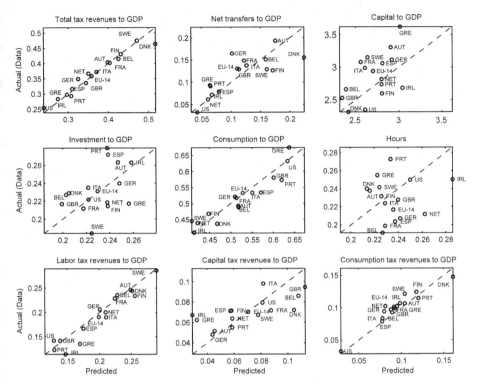

Fig. 6.1   Comparison of "actual" versus "predicted" variables

Notes: "Actual" refers to data sample averages for 1995–2010. "Predicted" refers to model implied steady state (balanced growth path) variables when the model is calibrated as in table 6.2 (gross US debt). Parameters for technology and preferences are set as in table 6.1 (gross debt).

to φ: all values in φ ∈ [0.3, 0.4] work practically just as well in terms of the fit, for example.

6.3.2   The Year 2010

At the end of our sample, government spending and government debt have risen substantially as a fallout of the financial crisis (see table 6.2). We are particularly interested in characterizing Laffer curves for the year 2010. While there is no tax rate data for the year 2010 at the time of this writing, we do have data for government spending and debt in 2010. We wish to consider the pessimistic scenario of a steady state, in which these changes are permanent. We therefore use the government budget constraint of the model to infer the labor tax rate; that is, we calculate the implied labor tax given government debt and government consump-

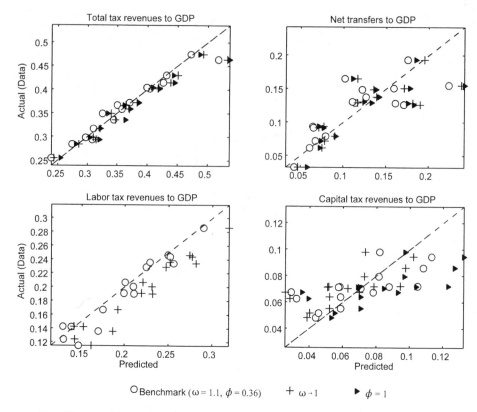

Fig. 6.2   Sensitivity of "actual" versus "predicted" tax revenues and government transfers

Notes: "Actual" refers to data sample averages for 1995–2010. "Predicted" refers to model implied steady state (balanced growth path). Three cases are examined. The benchmark case is the model used in the chapter, and as in figure 6.1. The case $\omega \to 1$ obtains, when there is no market power by intermediate goods producers: this is our previously used model in Trabandt and Uhlig (2011). Finally, there is the intermediate case with monopolistic competition, but where profits are fully subject to capital taxation, $\phi = 1$. Note that all other variables plotted in figure 6.1 are unaffected by the sensitivity analysis, except for hours. However, the impact on hours is small and therefore omitted here. All other parameters and steady states are as in tables 6.1 and 6.2 (gross US debt).

tion in 2010, as well as average 1995 to 2010 model-implied government transfers.

Table 6.2 contains the resulting labor tax rates across countries. According to the model, in the United States and EU-14 labor taxes need to be 5 to 8 percentage points higher to balance the government budget in 2010 compared to the sample average. There is substantial country-specific variation. While, for example, labor taxes in Germany and Italy remain unchanged,

Table 6.3   **Maximum additional tax revenues (in % of baseline GDP)**

	Baseline	τ^n	τ^k	τ^c	$\overline{b/y}$	$\overline{g/y}$	$\overline{m/y}$
			Start with US and impose country calibration for . . .				
US	9.0	9.0	9.0	9.0	9.0	9.0	9.0
US[a]	9.0	9.0	9.0	9.0	9.0	9.0	9.0
EU-14	4.3	4.9	9.3	6.6	9.0	9.6	9.6
GER	5.0	4.8	10.2	6.7	9.0	9.3	9.9
FRA	2.9	3.6	8.8	6.3	9.0	10.2	9.5
ITA	3.6	4.3	9.0	7.0	9.0	9.4	9.6
GBR	6.0	8.4	8.0	6.8	9.0	9.5	9.2
AUT	2.1	2.5	10.1	5.9	9.0	9.3	9.8
BEL	2.4	3.4	8.2	6.4	9.0	9.8	10.0
DNK	0.7	2.4	8.3	3.7	9.0	10.4	10.1
FIN	1.8	2.2	9.7	4.9	9.0	9.9	10.4
GRE	5.6	6.5	10.6	6.9	9.0	9.3	8.3
IRL	9.0	7.9	10.7	5.3	9.0	9.2	11.8
NET	5.2	4.3	9.7	6.1	9.0	10.3	10.4
PRT	6.7	8.9	9.7	6.1	9.0	9.6	8.4
ESP	5.7	6.2	9.7	7.1	9.0	9.5	9.1
SWE	0.9	1.0	9.1	5.0	9.0	10.7	10.5

Notes: Labor tax Laffer curve: sources of differences across countries. The table provides maximal additional tax revenues (in percent of baseline GDP) if labor taxes are varied. "Baseline" refers to the results when the model is calibrated to country-specific averages of 1995–2010 (see table 6.2). Parameters for technology and preferences are set as in table 6.1. All other columns report results if in the US calibration, fiscal instruments are set to country-specific values (each at a time).

[a]Results when "debt held by the public" is used for the United States rather than the harmonized cross-country measure of gross government debt provided by the AMECO database.

those in the United Kingdom, Ireland, Spain, and the Netherlands increase by 10 or more percentage points.

6.4   Results

6.4.1   Sources of Differences of Laffer Curves

What accounts for the differences between the US Laffer curves and (individual) EU-14 Laffer curves? To answer this question, we proceed as follows. As before, we calibrate the model to country-specific averages of 1995 to 2010 (see table 6.2), keeping structural parameters as in table 6.1. Next, we compute Laffer curves.

Results are in the "Baseline" column of tables 6.3 and 6.4. All other columns report results if, in the US calibration, fiscal instruments are set to European country-specific values, one at a time. It appears that labor income

Table 6.4   **Maximum additional tax revenues (in % of baseline GDP)**

		Start with US and impose country calibration for . . .					
	Baseline	τ^n	τ^k	τ^c	$\overline{b/y}$	$\overline{g/y}$	$\overline{m/y}$
US	2.6	2.6	2.6	2.6	2.6	2.6	2.6
US[a]	2.6	2.6	2.6	2.6	2.6	2.6	2.6
EU-14	1.2	1.2	3.1	1.4	2.6	2.8	2.8
GER	2.2	1.2	4.5	1.5	2.6	2.7	3.0
FRA	0.4	0.9	2.3	1.3	2.6	3.1	2.8
ITA	0.8	1.1	2.5	1.6	2.6	2.8	2.8
GBR	0.6	2.4	1.3	1.5	2.6	2.8	2.7
AUT	1.1	0.6	4.4	1.1	2.6	2.7	2.9
BEL	0.1	0.8	1.5	1.4	2.6	2.9	3.0
DNK	0.0	0.6	1.6	0.4	2.6	3.2	3.0
FIN	0.7	0.5	3.7	0.8	2.6	3.0	3.2
GRE	2.7	1.7	5.1	1.5	2.6	2.7	2.3
IRL	4.1	2.2	5.3	0.9	2.6	2.6	3.7
NET	1.9	1.1	3.7	1.2	2.6	3.1	3.2
PRT	2.0	2.6	3.7	1.2	2.6	2.8	2.4
ESP	2.0	1.7	3.7	1.6	2.6	2.8	2.6
SWE	0.2	0.2	2.7	0.8	2.6	3.3	3.2

Notes: Capital tax Laffer curve: sources of differences across countries. The table provides maximal additional tax revenues (in percent of baseline GDP) if capital taxes are varied. "Baseline" refers to the results when the model is calibrated to country-specific averages of 1995–2010 (see table 6.2). Parameters for technology and preferences are set as in table 6.1. All other columns report results if in the US calibration, fiscal instruments are set to country-specific values (each at a time).

[a]Results when "debt held by the public" is used for the United States rather than the harmonized cross-country measure of gross government debt provided by the AMECO database.

and consumption taxes are most important for accounting for cross-country differences.

Imposing country-specific debt-to-GDP ratios has no effect in our calculations, due to Ricardian equivalence: a different debt-to-GDP ratio, holding taxes and government consumption fixed, results in different transfers along the equilibrium path.

Finally, note that compared to Trabandt and Uhlig (2011), intermediate inputs and profit taxation in the present chapter move countries somewhat closer to the peak of the labor tax Laffer curve and somewhat farther away from the peak of the capital tax Laffer curve.

6.4.2   Laffer Curves: Average 1995 to 2010 versus 2010

To compute Laffer curves, we trace out tax revenues across balanced growth paths, as we change either labor tax rates or capital tax rates, and compute the resulting changes in transfers. When changing both tax rates, we obtain a "Laffer hill." We compute Laffer curves and the Laffer hill for a 1995 to 2010 versus 2010 calibration; that is, when the model is calibrated in terms of fiscal policy either to the average of 1995 to 2010 or to the year 2010 (see table 6.2). Structural parameters are set as in table 6.1.

Figure 6.3 shows the resulting Laffer curves for all countries for the average 1995 to 2010 calibration. Figure 6.4 provides a comparison of Laffer curves for the 1995 to 2010 versus 2010 calibration for the US and aggregate EU-14 economy. Further cross-country results in this respect are available in table 6.5 and in figure 6.5. The latter figure shows how far each country is from its peak, given its own tax rate: perhaps not surprisingly, the points line up pretty well. In the figure, we compare it to the benchmark of performing the same calculation for the United States, given by the dash-dotted line: there, we change, say, the labor tax rate, and, for each new labor tax rate, recalculate κ as well as $\bar{g}$, $\bar{m}$, and $\bar{b}$ to obtain the same $\bar{n}$ and $\overline{g/y}$, $\overline{b/y}$, and $\overline{m/y}$ as in table 6.1. We then recalculate $\bar{s}$ and $\overline{s/y}$ to balance the government budget and calculate the distance to the peak of the Laffer curve. One would expect this exercise to result in a line with a slope close to −1, and indeed, this is what the figure shows. The points for the individual countries line up close to this line, though not perfectly: in particular, for the capital tax rate, the distance can be considerable, and is largely explained by the cross-country variation in labor taxes and consumption taxes.

According to the results, the vast majority of countries have moved closer to the peaks of their labor and capital income tax Laffer curves and Laffer hills, respectively. The movements to the peaks are sizable for some countries such as, for example, the United Kingdom, the Netherlands, and Ireland for labor taxes. As before and for the average 1995 to 2010 sample, it does not matter whether "gross US debt" or "US debt held by the public" is used. For the year 2010, however, small differences arise since transfers are kept at the model average for 1995 to 2010.

Finally, table 6.6 provides the output losses associated with moving to the peak of the Laffer curve. According to the model, US and EU-14 output falls by about 27 and 14 percent, respectively, when labor taxes are moved to the peak of the Laffer curve. The magnitudes for the case of capital taxes are similar. There is considerable country-specific variation among European countries: Denmark loses 4 percent while Ireland loses 24 percent of output at the labor tax Laffer curve peak. Clearly, if a country is already close to its Laffer curve peak in terms of tax rates, the output losses associated with increasing taxes a little more to attain the peak are more muted than in a country that has more scope to increase tax revenues. Nevertheless, the table highlights the general equilibrium repercussions of raising taxes: even though tax revenues may be increased by some limited amount, tax bases and thereby output fall when moving to the peak of the Laffer curve due to the negative incentive effects of higher taxes.

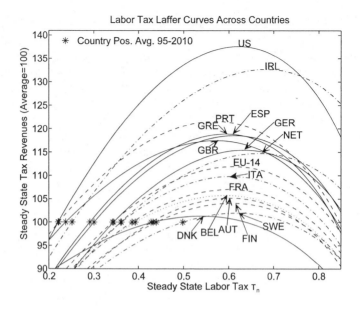

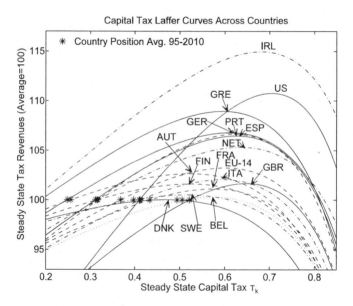

Fig. 6.3 Labor and capital tax Laffer curves across all countries

Notes: The model is calibrated to the average of 1995–2010, see table 6.2 (gross US debt). Parameters for technology and preferences are set as in table 6.1 (gross US debt). Shown are steady state (balanced growth path) total tax revenues when labor taxes (upper panel) or capital taxes (lower panel) are varied between 0 and 100 percent. All other taxes and parameters are held constant. Total tax revenues at the average 1995–2010 tax rates are normalized to 100. Stars indicate positions of respective countries on their Laffer curves. In cases without an arrow, the first letter of each country name indicates the peak of the respective Laffer curve.

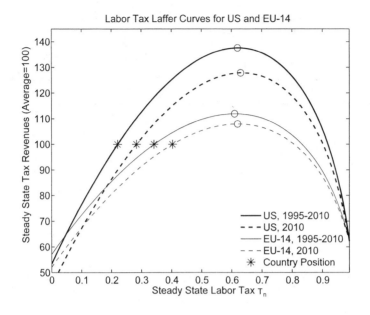

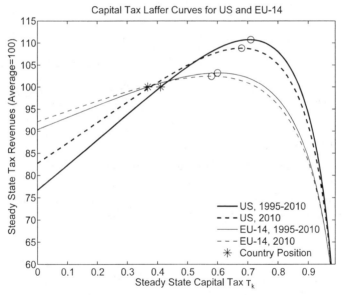

Fig. 6.4 Comparing the US and the EU-14 labor and capital tax Laffer curve

Notes: The model is either calibrated to the average of 1995–2010 or to 2010, see table 6.2 (gross US debt). Parameters for technology and preferences are set as in table 6.1 (gross US debt). Shown are steady state (balanced growth path) total tax revenues when labor taxes (upper panel) or capital taxes (lower panel) are varied between 0 and 100 percent. All other taxes and parameters are held constant. Total tax revenues at the average 1995–2010 or at the year 2010 tax rates are normalized to 100. Stars indicate positions of respective countries on their Laffer curves.

Table 6.5   Maximum additional tax revenues (in %): Average 1995–2010 versus year 2010

	Vary labor taxes, τ^n $\Delta \bar{T}_{\text{Max}}$		Vary capital taxes, τ^k $\Delta \bar{T}_{\text{Max}}$		Vary τ^n and τ^k jointly $\Delta \bar{T}_{\text{Max}}$	
	$\varnothing$	2010	$\varnothing$	2010	$\varnothing$	2010
US	37.6	27.9	10.7	8.8	37.6	28.1
US[a]	37.6	28.2	10.7	8.9	37.6	28.4
EU-14	11.9	7.9	3.2	2.5	12.1	8.2
GER	15.4	14.9	6.8	6.1	16.4	15.7
FRA	7.1	4.6	1.1	0.7	7.1	4.6
ITA	9.8	7.3	2.1	1.1	9.9	7.3
GBR	17.5	8.6	1.7	0.7	17.9	8.8
AUT	5.2	4.7	2.6	2.8	5.8	5.5
BEL	5.7	4.0	0.3	0.1	5.9	4.1
DNK	1.3	0.3	0.0	0.4	1.6	1.0
FIN	4.1	1.6	1.6	1.0	4.4	1.9
GRE	18.9	14.2	8.9	7.8	19.9	15.6
IRL	32.7	21.5	14.9	12.2	35.4	25.9
NET	14.7	6.6	5.3	4.6	15.6	8.6
PRT	21.6	15.4	6.6	4.6	21.8	15.6
ESP	18.5	10.3	6.5	5.4	19.0	11.4
SWE	2.0	3.3	0.5	0.0	2.1	3.5

Notes: Laffer curves and Laffer hill for 1995 to 2010 versus 2010 calibration. The model is either calibrated to the average of 1995–2010 or to 2010 (see table 6.2). Parameters are set as in table 6.1. $\Delta \bar{T}_{\text{Max}}$ denotes the maximum additional tax revenues (in percent) that results from moving to the peak of the Laffer curve.

[a]Results when "debt held by the public" is used for the United States rather than the harmonized cross-country measure of gross government debt provided by the AMECO database.

6.4.3   Laffer Curve and Interest Rates

What is the maximum interest rate on outstanding government debt that the government could afford without cutting government spending? Put differently, how high can interest rates on government debt be due to, say, default fears (and not due to generally higher discounting by households), so that fiscal sustainability is still preserved if countries move to the peak of their Laffer curves?

To answer this question we pursue the following experiment. We calibrate the model in terms of fiscal policy to the year 2010 (see table 6.2). Structural parameters are set as in table 6.1. We calculate Laffer curves for labor and capital taxation as well as the Laffer hill for joint variations of capital and labor taxes. Keeping model-implied government transfers and government consumption to GDP ratios at their 2010 levels, we calcuate the interest rate that balances the government budget at maximal tax revenues.

For the calcuations, we focus on balanced growth relationships ignor-

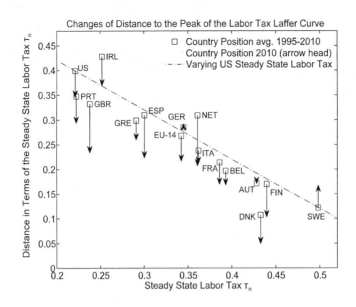

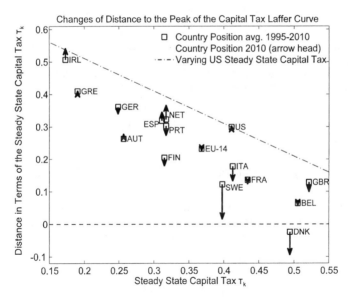

Fig. 6.5   Distance to the peak of Laffer curves for average 1995–2010 versus 2010 calibration

Notes: The model is either calibrated to the average of 1995–2010 or to 2010, see table 6.2 (gross US debt). Parameters for technology and preferences are set as in table 6.1 (gross US debt). Horizontal axis shows calibrated tax rates. Vertical axis shows distance to the peak in terms of tax rates. The dashed-dotted line shows the distance to the peak for the United States when the initial steady state tax is varied and the model is recalibrated for each assumed tax rate.

Table 6.6   Output changes (in %) from moving to the Laffer curve peak

	Vary labor taxes, τ^n $\Delta\bar{y}$ at $\Delta\bar{T}_{\text{Max}}$	Vary capital taxes, τ^k $\Delta\bar{y}$ at $\Delta\bar{T}_{\text{Max}}$	Vary τ^n and τ^k jointly $\Delta\bar{y}$ at $\Delta\bar{T}_{\text{Max}}$
US	−27.2	−21.1	−29.6
US[a]	−27.3	−21.1	−29.7
EU-14	−17.5	−12.8	−20.1
GER	−22.0	−17.7	−26.5
FRA	−14.2	−7.5	−14.3
ITA	−17.6	−8.8	−16.7
GBR	−18.5	−7.3	−15.8
AUT	−14.6	−13.0	−18.9
BEL	−13.6	−3.8	−11.2
DNK	−3.9	6.0	2.2
FIN	−9.0	−8.3	−12.5
GRE	−22.3	−20.3	−27.5
IRL	−23.6	−23.6	−34.6
NET	−15.9	−16.1	−23.7
PRT	−22.6	−16.5	−24.5
ESP	−19.3	−17.7	−24.8
SWE	−12.3	−1.0	−8.5

Notes: Output changes (in %) when moving to the Laffer curve peak. The model is calibrated to the year 2010 (see table 6.2). Parameters are set as in table 6.1. $\Delta\bar{y}$ is the change of balanced growth output in the model from moving from the status quo equilibrium to the peak of the Laffer curve. $\Delta\bar{T}_{\text{Max}}$ denotes the maximum additional tax revenues (in percent) that results from moving to the peak of the Laffer curve.
[a]Results when "debt held by the public" is used for the United States rather than the harmonized cross-country measure of gross government debt provided by the AMECO database.

ing transition issues for simplicity. Consider the scaled government budget constraint along the balanced growth path:

$$(13) \qquad (\overline{s/y})_{2010} + (\overline{g/y})_{2010} = (\overline{b/y})_{2010}(\psi - \bar{R}_{\text{Max}}) + (\overline{T/y})_{\text{Max}},$$

where $(\overline{T/y})_{\text{Max}}$ denotes the maximum additional tax revenues (expressed in percent of baseline GDP) that results from moving from the 2010 status quo to the peak of the Laffer curve. We solve for $\bar{R}_{\text{Max}} = 1 + \bar{r}_{\text{Max}}$ that balances the above government budget constraint.

Table 6.7 contains the baseline model results. For each of the three tax experiments (adjusting only labor taxes, adjusting only capital taxes, and adjusting both), the table lists the maximal additional obtainable revenue as a share of GDP as well as the maximal sustainable interest rate that can be sustained with these revenues. For comparison, the last two columns of the table also contain real long-term interest rates for 2010 downloaded from the European Commission AMECO database. These are nominal ten years government bond interest rates minus inflation—either using the GDP deflator (ILRV, first column) or the consumption deflator (ILRC, second

Table 6.7   **Baseline model: Maximum real interest rates on government debt (in %)**

	Vary labor taxes, τ^n		Vary capital taxes, τ^k		Vary τ^n and τ^k jointly		Data: Long-term interest rates[b]	
	$\Delta T/y_{\text{Max}}$	$\bar{r}_{\text{Max}}$	$\Delta T/y_{\text{Max}}$	$\bar{r}_{\text{Max}}$	$\Delta T/y_{\text{Max}}$	$\bar{r}_{\text{Max}}$		
US	7.3	12.0	2.3	6.5	7.4	12.0	2.0	1.4
US[a]	7.4	15.5	2.3	7.7	7.4	15.6	2.0	1.4
EU-14	3.0	7.6	0.9	5.1	3.1	7.7	2.4	1.5
GER	5.0	10.0	2.0	6.4	5.2	10.3	2.1	0.8
FRA	1.9	6.4	0.3	4.4	1.9	6.4	2.3	1.9
ITA	2.8	6.4	0.4	4.3	2.8	6.4	3.7	2.5
GBR	3.4	8.2	0.3	4.3	3.4	8.3	0.5	−0.4
AUT	1.9	6.6	1.1	5.6	2.2	7.1	1.4	1.1
BEL	1.8	5.8	0.1	4.1	1.8	5.9	1.6	1.6
DNK	0.2	4.4	0.2	4.5	0.6	5.3	−0.5	0.4
FIN	0.7	5.5	0.5	5.0	0.9	5.8	2.6	1.1
GRE	4.4	7.1	2.4	5.7	4.8	7.4	7.3	4.4
IRL	6.9	11.2	3.9	8.1	8.3	12.7	8.4	8.0
NET	2.6	8.2	1.8	6.9	3.4	9.4	1.7	1.5
PRT	5.1	9.5	1.5	5.6	5.2	9.5	4.3	3.7
ESP	3.5	9.8	1.8	7.0	3.9	10.5	3.8	1.8
SWE	1.6	8.0	0.0	4.0	1.7	8.2	1.6	1.6

Notes: Maximum additional tax revenue and interest rates for the labor and capital tax of Laffer curve and Laffer hill, respectively. The model is calibrated to the year 2010 (see table 6.2). Parameters are set as in table 6.1. $\Delta T/y_{\text{Max}}$ denotes the maximum additional tax revenues (expressed in percent of baseline GDP) that results from moving from the 2010 status quo to the peak of the Laffer curve. $\bar{r}_{\text{Max}}$ is the maximum net real interest rate that the government could afford on outstanding debt in the year 2010 if all additional tax revenue is spent on interest rate payments.

[a]Results when "debt held by the public" is used for the United States rather than the harmonized cross-country measure of gross government debt provided by the AMECO database.

[b]Real long-term interest rates for 2010 downloaded from the European Commission AMECO database. These are nominal ten years government bond interest rates minus inflation—either using the GDP deflator (ILRV, first column) or the consumption deflator (ILRC, second column). EU-14 value is the real GDP weighted average of European countries. All numbers in the table in percent.

column). The value for the aggregate EU-14 is the real GDP weighted average of individual European countries.

The most interesting column in table 6.7 may be the second one. We find that the United States can afford the highest interest rate if labor taxes are moved to the peak of the Laffer curve: depending on the debt measure used, a real interest rate of of 12 to 15.5 percent is sustainable. Interestingly, Ireland can also afford the high rate of 11.2 percent when moving labor taxes only. By contrast, Austria, Belgium, Denmark, Finland, France, Greece, and Italy can only afford permanent real rates in the range of 4.4 to 7.1 percent when financing the additional interest payments with higher labor tax rates alone, while, say, Germany, Portugal, and Spain can all afford an interest rate somewhere above 9 percent. The picture improves somewhat, but not much, when labor taxes and capital taxes can both be adjusted: notably, Belgium, Denmark, Finland, France, and Italy cannot permanently afford real interest rates above 6.5 percent.

Note that now, the comparison of "US gross government debt" versus "US debt held by the public" matters for the results since government spending is kept constant. Indeed, the United States could afford higher interest rates if "US debt held by the public" is considered.

Interestingly, in the next section, we also examine the implications of human capital accumulation and show that the maximum interest rates may be even lower than suggested by our baseline model.

For the above analysis, some caveats should be kept in mind. The interest rate on outstanding government debt deviates from the one on private capital but does not crowd out private investment. In other words, it is implicitly assumed that the interest rate payments due to the higher interest rate are paid lump-sum to the households and thereby do not affect household consumption, hours, or investment, and that it does not affect the rate at which firms can borrow privately.[6]

Note that the steady state safe real interest rate is calibrated to equal 4 percent and therefore represents the lower bound for $\bar{r}_{\text{Max}}$: our analysis on sustainable rates may therefore be too optimistic, keeping in mind that the interest rates are real interest rates, not nominal interest rates. It is worth emphasizing that we have not included the possibility of cutting government spending and/or transfers and that our analysis has focused on the most pessimistic scenario of a permanent shift.

6.5   Extensions: Human Capital, Consumption Taxes

6.5.1   Baseline Model versus Human Capital Accumulation

We compare the distance to the peak of Laffer curves for the above baseline model and the above baseline model with added human capital accumulation (see table 6.8). More specifically, we assume that human capital is accumulated following the second-generation case considered in Trabandt and Uhlig (2011).[7]

In particular, we assume that human capital can be accumulated by both learning-by-doing as well as schooling, following Lucas (1998) and Uzawa

---

6. For related work, see, for example, Bi (2011) and Bi, Leeper, and Leith (2010).

7. See Jones (2001), Barro and Sala-i-Martin (2003), or Acemoglu (2008) for textbook treatments of models with endogenous growth and human capital accumulation. While first-generation endogenous growth models have stressed the endogeneity of the overall long-run growth rate, second-generation growth models have stressed potentially large level effects, without affecting the long-run growth rate. We shall focus on the second-generation case here since little evidence has been found that taxation impacts on the long-run growth rate; see, for example, Levine and Renelt (1992).

Table 6.8   **Distance to peak in terms of tax rates (in %)**

	Vary labor taxes, τ^n		Vary capital taxes, τ^k	
	Baseline	Human capital	Baseline	Human capital
US	39.9	20.9	29.9	27.9
US[a]	39.9	20.9	29.9	27.9
EU-14	26.8	7.8	23.2	22.2
GER	28.5	11.5	36.1	36.1
FRA	21.4	1.4	13.6	12.6
ITA	23.8	3.8	17.7	15.7
GBR	33.2	11.2	12.9	9.9
AUT	17.2	−3.8	26.3	22.3
BEL	19.7	−1.3	6.5	4.5
DNK	10.7	−15.3	−2.4	−5.4
FIN	17.0	−4.0	20.5	20.5
GRE	29.9	7.9	41.0	34.0
IRL	42.8	34.8	50.7	56.7
NET	30.9	17.9	32.3	36.3
PRT	34.8	12.8	30.3	26.3
ESP	31.0	12.0	31.9	28.9
SWE	12.2	−8.8	12.2	13.2

Notes: Distance to the peak of Laffer curves for baseline model and baseline model with added human capital accumulation (second generation, see the main text and Trabandt and Uhlig 2011 for details). Distance is measured in terms of tax rates. All numbers are expressed in percent. The model is calibrated to the average of 1995–2010 for fiscal variables. Standard parameters for technology and preferences are set as in table 6.1. Parameters for human capital accumulation are set as in the main text and Trabandt and Uhlig (2011). All numbers in the table in percent.

[a]Results when "debt held by the public" is used for the United States rather than the harmonized cross-country measure of gross government debt provided by the AMECO database.

(1965). The agent splits total nonleisure time n_t, into workplace labor $q_t n_t$, and schooling time $(1 - q_t)n_t$, where $0 \le q_t \le 1$. Agents accumulate human capital according to

$$(14) \qquad h_t = (Aq_t n_t + B(1 - q_t)n_t)^v h_{t-1}^{1-v} + (1 - \delta_h)h_{t-1},$$

where $A \ge 0$ and $B > A$ parameterize the effectiveness of learning-by-doing and schooling, respectively, and where $0 < \delta_h \le 1$ is the depreciation rate of human capital. Wages are paid per unit of labor and human capital so that the after-tax labor income is given by $(1 - \tau_t^n)w_t h_{t-1}q_t n_t$. Given this, the adaptions of the model on the parts of firms is straightforward so that we shall leave them out here.

The model is calibrated to the average of 1995 to 2010 for fiscal variables. Standard parameters for technology and preferences are set as in table 6.1. Parameters for human capital accumulation are set as in Trabandt and Uhlig (2011). More precisely, the same calibration strategy for the initial steady state is applied as in the above baseline model, except assuming now $\bar{q}\bar{n}_{US} = 0.25$.

Further, $v = 0.5$ and $\delta_h = \delta$ are set for simplicity. Parameter A is set such that initial $\bar{q}_{US} = 0.8$. Moreover, B is set to have $h_{US} = 1$ initially.

Figure 6.6 shows the comparison for the United States and the EU-14. Further cross-country results are contained in figure 6.7. Interestingly, the capital tax Laffer curve is affected only very little across countries when human capital is introduced. By contrast, the introduction of human capital has important effects for the labor income tax Laffer curve. Several countries are pushed on the slippery slope sides of their labor tax Laffer curves. This result is due to two effects. First, human capital turns labor into a stock variable rather than a flow variable as in the baseline model. Higher labor taxes induce households to work less and to aquire less human capital which in turn leads to lower labor income. Consequently, the labor tax base shrinks much more quickly when labor taxes are raised. Second, the introduction of intermediate inputs moves countries closer to the peaks of their labor tax Laffer curves already in the baseline model compared to Trabandt and Uhlig (2011). This effect is reinforced when human capital is introduced.

Finally, we recalculate the implied maximum interest rates on government debt in 2010 when human capital accumulation is allowed for in the model. Table 6.9 contains the results: the United States may only afford a real interest rate between 5.8 to 6.6 percent in this case. Most of the European countries cluster between 4 and 4.9 percent except for Denmark, Finland, and Ireland, who can afford real interest rates between 5.9 and 9.5 percent.

6.5.2   Consumption Taxes

We compute maximum additional tax revenues that are possible from increasing consumption taxes (see table 6.10). We do this in the previous baseline model and in the model with added human capital accumulation, as in the previous subsection. The model is calibrated to the average of 1995 to 2010 for fiscal variables. Standard parameters for technology and preferences are set as in table 6.1. Parameters for human capital accumulation are set as in the previous subsection.

The upper panel of figure 6.8 shows the comparison for the United States and EU-14. Further cross-country results are shown in the lower panel of the same figure. As documented and examined in Trabandt and Uhlig (2011), the consumption tax Laffer curve has no peak. However, the introduction of human capital has important quantitative effects across countries. The range of maximum additional tax revenues (in percent of GDP) in the above baseline model is roughly 40 to 100 percent, while it shrinks to roughly 10 to 30 percent in the model with added human capital. Higher consumption taxes affect equilibrium labor via the labor wedge, similar to labor taxes. Human capital amplifies the reduction of the labor tax base triggered by the change in the labor wedge by the same argument as in the previous subsection. Overall, maximum possible tax revenues due to consumption taxes are reduced massively, although at fairly high consumption tax rates.

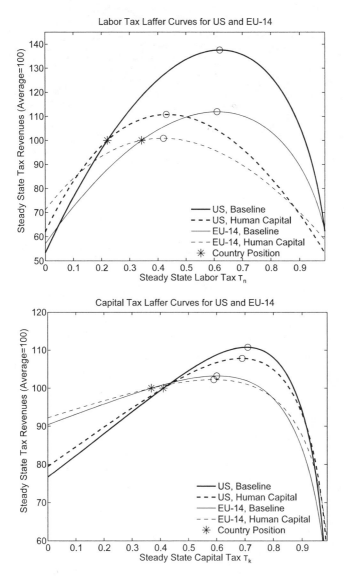

Fig. 6.6   Labor and capital tax Laffer curves: The impact of endogenous human capital accumulation

Notes: Shown are steady state (balanced growth path) total tax revenues when labor taxes are varied between 0 and 100 percent in the United States and EU-14. All other taxes and parameters are held constant. Total tax revenues at the average tax rates are normalized to 100. Two cases are examined. First, the benchmark model with exogenous growth. Second, the benchmark model with a second-generation version of endogenous human capital accumulation (see the main text and Trabandt and Uhlig 2011 for details). The model is calibrated to the average of 1995–2010 for fiscal variables. Standard parameters for technology and preferences are set as in table 6.1 (gross US debt). Parameters for human capital accumulation are set as in the main text and Trabandt and Uhlig (2011).

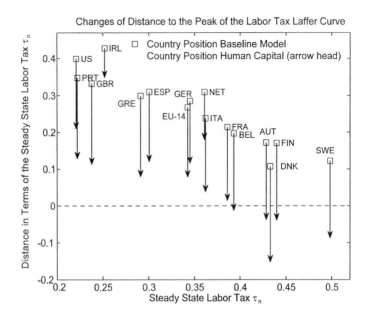

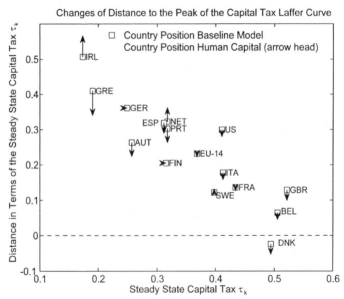

Fig. 6.7 Distance to the peak of Laffer curves for baseline model and baseline model with added human capital accumulation

Notes: Second generation, see the main text and Trabandt and Uhlig (2011) for details. The model is calibrated to the average of 1995–2010 for fiscal variables. Standard parameters for technology and preferences are set as in table 6.1 (gross US debt). Parameters for human capital accumulation are set as in the main text and Trabandt and Uhlig (2011). Horizontal axis shows calibrated tax rates. Vertical axis shows distance to the peak in terms of tax rates.

Table 6.9   **Model with human capital: Maximum real interest rates on government debt (in %)**

	Vary labor taxes, τ^n		Vary capital taxes, τ^k		Data: Long-term interest rates[b]	
	$\Delta \overline{T/y}_{\text{Max}}$	$\overline{r}_{\text{Max}}$	$\Delta \overline{T/y}_{\text{Max}}$	$\overline{r}_{\text{Max}}$		
US	1.7	5.8	1.7	5.8	2.0	1.4
US[a]	1.7	6.6	1.7	6.6	2.0	1.4
EU-14	0.0	4.0	0.6	4.8	2.4	1.5
GER	0.8	4.9	1.7	6.0	2.1	0.8
FRA	0.1	4.1	0.1	4.2	2.3	1.9
ITA	0.0	4.0	0.2	4.1	3.7	2.5
GBR	0.0	4.0	0.1	4.1	0.5	−0.4
AUT	0.1	4.1	0.7	5.0	1.4	1.1
BEL	0.1	4.1	0.0	4.0	1.6	1.6
DNK	2.4	9.5	0.2	4.5	−0.5	0.4
FIN	0.9	5.9	0.3	4.6	2.6	1.1
GRE	0.2	4.1	1.3	4.9	7.3	4.4
IRL	4.0	8.1	4.8	9.0	8.4	8.0
NET	0.3	4.5	2.2	7.5	1.7	1.5
PRT	0.4	4.4	0.9	4.9	4.3	3.7
ESP	0.1	4.2	1.3	6.1	3.8	1.8
SWE	0.1	4.3	0.0	4.0	1.6	1.6

Notes: Model with human capital: maximum additional tax revenue and interest rates for the labor and capital tax Laffer curves. Second-generation model with human capital accumulation, see the main text and Trabandt and Uhlig (2011) for details. The model is calibrated to the year 2010, see table 6.2. Parameters are set as in table 6.1. For human capital accumulation parameters see the main text and Trabandt and Uhlig (2011). $\Delta \overline{T/y}_{\text{Max}}$ denotes the maximum additional tax revenues (expressed in percent of baseline GDP) that results from moving from the 2010 status quo to the peak of the Laffer curve. $\overline{r}_{\text{Max}}$ is the maximum net real interest rate that the government could afford on outstanding debt in the year 2010 if all additional tax revenue is spent on interest rate payments. All numbers in the table in percent.

[a]Results when "debt held by the public" is used for the United States rather than the harmonized cross-country measure of gross government debt provided by the AMECO database.

[b]Real long-term interest rates for 2010 downloaded from the European Commission AMECO database. These are nominal ten years government bond interest rates minus inflation—either using the GDP deflator (ILRV, first column) or the consumption deflator (ILRC, second column). EU-14 value is the real GDP weighted average of European countries. All numbers in the table in percent.

6.6   Conclusion

We have studied how Laffer curves differ across countries in the United States and the EU-14. This provides insight into the limits of taxation. To that end, we extended the analysis in Trabandt and Uhlig (2011) to include monopolistic competition as well as partial taxation of the monopolistic-competition profits: we have shown that this improves the fit to the data considerably. We have also provided refined data for effective labor and capital income taxes across countries. For the cross-country comparison, we assume

Table 6.10   Vary consumption taxes: Distance to peak in terms of tax revenues (in % of GDP)

	Baseline	Human capital
US	90.7	27.2
US[a]	90.7	27.2
EU-14	63.9	19.9
GER	61.7	20.2
FRA	58.7	17.9
ITA	67.8	20.0
GBR	79.7	23.5
AUT	62.6	18.5
BEL	58.2	17.3
DNK	48.9	14.4
FIN	47.0	15.2
GRE	97.8	27.3
IRL	44.2	18.1
NET	42.3	15.8
PRT	91.2	26.8
ESP	76.0	23.2
SWE	37.8	12.5

Notes: Maximum additional tax revenues due to consumption taxes. Baseline model versus baseline model with added human capital accumulation (second-generation human capital accumulation growth model, see the main text and Trabandt and Uhlig 2011 for details). Additional tax revenues are measured in percent of baseline GDP. The model is calibrated to the average of 1995–2010 for fiscal variables. Standard parameters for technology and preferences are set as in table 6.1. Parameters for human capital accumulation are set as in the main text and Trabandt and Uhlig (2011). All numbers in the table in percent.

[a]Results when "debt held by the public" is used for the United States rather than the harmonized cross-country measure of gross government debt provided by the AMECO database.

that all structural parameters for technologies and preferences are the same across countries. The differences between the Laffer curves therefore arise solely due to differences in fiscal policy; that is, the mix of distortionary taxes, government spending, and government debt. We find that labor income and consumption taxes are important for accounting for most of the cross-country differences.

To examine recent developments, we calibrate the steady state of the model to the Laffer curves implied by the strained fiscal situation of 2010, and compare them to the Laffer curves of the average extended sample 1995 to 2010. We find that the 2010 calibration moves all countries considerably closer to the peak of the labor tax Laffer curve, with the scope for additional labor tax increases cut by a third for most countries and by up to one-half for some countries. In this context, we show that it is important to keep the general equilibrium repercussions of raising taxes in mind: even though tax revenues may be increased by some limited amount, tax bases and thereby

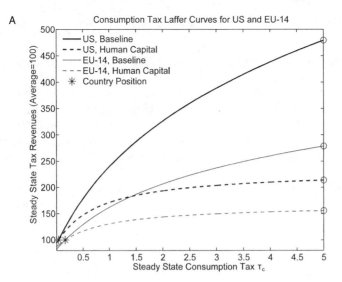

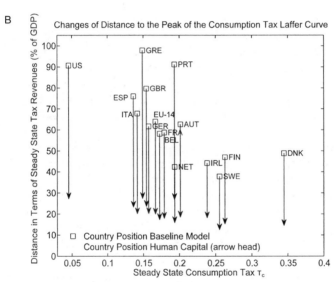

Fig. 6.8   *A*, Consumption tax Laffer curve in the United States and EU-14: The
impact of endogenous human capital accumulation; *B*, Distance to the peak of
Laffer curves for baseline model and baseline model with added human
capital accumulation

Notes: Shown are steady state (balanced growth path) total tax revenues when consumption
taxes are varied between 0 and 500 percent. All other taxes and parameters are held constant.
Total tax revenues at the average consumption tax rate are normalized to 100. Two cases are
examined. First, the benchmark model with exogenous growth. Second, the benchmark
model with a second-generation version of endogenous human capital accumulation (see the
main text and Trabandt and Uhlig 2011 for details). The model is calibrated to the average of
1995–2010 for fiscal variables. Standard parameters for technology and preferences are set as
in table 6.1 (gross US debt). Parameters for human capital accumulation are set as in the main
text and Trabandt and Uhlig (2011). Horizontal axis shows calibrated tax rates. Vertical axis
shows distance to the peak in terms of tax revenues (in percent of GDP).

output fall when moving to the peak of the Laffer curve due to the negative incentive effects of higher taxes.

We calculate the implications for the long-term sustainability of current debt levels by calculating the maximal permanently sustainable interest rate. We calculated that the United States can afford the highest interest rate if only labor taxes are adjusted to service the additional debt burden: depending on the debt measure used, a real interest rate of of 12 to 15.5 percent is sustainable. Interestingly, Ireland can also afford the high rate of 11.2 percent when moving labor taxes only. By contrast, Austria, Belgium, Denmark, Finland, France, Greece, and Italy can only afford permanent real rates in the range of 4.4 to 7.1 percent, when financing the additional interest payments with higher labor tax rates alone, while, say, Germany, Portugal, and Spain can all afford an interest rate somewhere above 9 percent. The picture improves somewhat, but not much, when labor taxes and capital taxes can both be adjusted: notably, Belgium, Denmark, Finland, France, and Italy cannot permanently afford real interest rates above 6.5 percent.

We have shown that the introduction of human capital has important effects for the labor income tax Laffer curve across countries. Several countries are pushed on the slippery slope sides of their labor tax Laffer curves once human capital is accounted for. We recalculated the implied maximum interest rates on government debt in 2010 when human capital accumulation is allowed for in the model. In this case, the United States may only afford a real interest rate between 5.8 to 6.6 percent. Most of the European countries cluster between 4 and 4.9 percent except for Denmark, Finland, and Ireland, who can afford real interest rates between 5.9 and 9.5 percent.

We have performed a cross-country analysis on consumption taxes. We document that the range of maximum additional tax revenues (in percent of GDP) in the baseline model is roughly 40 to 100 percent, while it shrinks to roughly 10 to 30 percent in the model with added human capital, although the underlying consumption taxes are fairly high in both cases.

Appendix A
Tax Rate Tables

Table 6A.1   Labor income taxes in percent across countries and time

	1995	1996	1997	1998	1999	2000	2001	2002	2003	2004	2005	2006	2007	2008	2009	2010[a]
US	22.2	22.8	23.3	23.5	23.8	24.1	23.8	21.7	20.7	20.6	21.6	21.9	22.3	21.4	20.0	20.0
EU-14	34.9	35.0	34.9	34.3	34.7	33.8	33.6	33.2	33.5	33.4	33.7	34.1	34.3	34.8	34.8	34.8
GER	35.2	34.4	34.6	35.0	35.1	34.9	35.2	34.4	34.0	33.5	33.2	33.7	34.1	34.3	35.2	35.2
FRA	38.7	39.2	39.2	38.3	38.9	38.5	37.9	37.7	38.3	38.0	39.1	39.1	38.7	38.7	38.6	38.6
ITA	33.7	36.3	37.6	34.8	35.4	34.9	34.8	35.0	35.5	35.7	35.8	36.0	37.4	38.4	39.0	39.0
GBR	22.7	21.9	21.6	22.6	23.2	23.6	23.6	23.1	23.3	24.2	24.6	25.2	25.7	25.8	24.8	24.8
AUT	40.8	41.8	42.8	43.0	42.9	42.4	43.8	43.8	43.7	43.4	42.6	42.4	42.3	43.0	43.4	43.4
BEL	39.0	39.0	39.6	39.7	39.5	39.2	39.1	40.0	40.3	40.6	39.7	38.8	38.6	38.8	38.5	38.5
DNK	42.0	42.3	43.0	42.2	44.7	44.9	44.2	43.3	43.3	42.4	42.4	42.1	43.4	43.3	44.4	44.4
FIN	47.4	48.2	46.0	45.7	44.7	44.9	44.4	44.0	42.7	41.8	42.7	43.2	42.8	42.3	41.4	41.4
GRE	NaN	NaN	NaN	NaN	NaN	26.8	28.3	29.7	30.5	29.7	29.5	29.2	29.3	30.3	28.5	28.5
IRL	NaN	NaN	NaN	NaN	NaN	NaN	NaN	23.8	24.4	25.8	25.9	27.0	26.7	24.3	24.4	24.4
NET	40.7	38.0	38.3	34.2	35.5	35.6	32.9	33.1	33.2	33.5	34.2	36.9	36.6	38.4	38.1	38.1
PRT	20.9	21.1	21.3	21.2	21.2	21.7	22.4	22.4	22.7	22.0	22.1	22.7	23.4	23.4	23.6	23.6
ESP	NaN	NaN	NaN	NaN	NaN	28.9	29.5	29.7	29.8	29.8	30.2	30.7	31.3	30.6	30.0	30.0
SWE	48.5	50.0	52.0	53.6	55.3	51.5	49.8	48.4	49.8	50.2	50.2	50.2	48.2	47.6	45.9	45.9

Note: Country codes: Germany (GER), France (FRA), Italy (ITA), United Kingdom (GBR), Austria (AUT), Belgium (BEL), Denmark (DNK), Finland (FIN), Greece (GRE), Ireland (IRL), Netherlands (NET), Portugal (PRT), Spain (ESP), and Sweden (SWE). NaN = not available number (no numeric data available).

[a]Due to data availability reasons, 2010 tax rates are assumed to be the same as in 2009. For an alternative, see subsection 6.3.2 in the main text.

Table 6A.2   Capital income taxes in percent across countries and time

	1995	1996	1997	1998	1999	2000	2001	2002	2003	2004	2005	2006	2007	2008	2009	2010[a]
US	44.0	42.6	41.7	42.6	41.9	43.2	39.9	37.4	38.7	38.7	40.9	42.1	45.6	42.6	37.6	37.6
EU-14	33.4	35.6	37.7	38.2	40.3	39.8	37.9	35.3	34.1	34.6	36.7	39.0	38.3	37.1	35.5	35.5
GER	22.9	23.6	23.8	25.1	27.8	29.4	20.9	21.7	23.5	22.9	24.2	25.9	25.7	26.3	27.1	27.1
FRA	34.6	38.5	40.7	42.0	44.8	44.0	45.9	44.1	41.9	44.5	44.4	48.6	46.5	48.4	42.8	42.8
ITA	41.1	43.0	45.8	39.1	41.9	37.0	39.0	38.0	35.8	36.0	37.6	44.1	46.1	46.1	44.8	44.8
GBR	47.3	46.2	50.3	54.7	55.6	61.6	62.7	52.4	48.0	48.0	52.1	54.9	50.1	49.7	50.2	50.2
AUT	22.0	26.0	27.9	27.6	26.2	25.9	32.1	25.3	25.4	25.3	24.5	23.5	24.6	26.4	24.1	24.1
BEL	44.8	48.5	50.0	54.2	54.6	53.2	56.6	52.4	47.9	45.1	49.0	50.5	48.6	52.4	50.4	50.4
DNK	40.0	41.4	41.7	50.9	44.0	42.8	46.7	47.4	48.5	49.4	55.1	58.7	57.1	56.0	55.5	55.5
FIN	26.1	30.8	32.0	33.8	34.1	40.6	32.0	31.7	30.1	30.4	30.8	30.1	30.4	30.7	30.1	30.1
GRE	NaN	NaN	NaN	NaN	NaN	27.3	20.6	20.3	17.9	17.5	19.0	17.2	18.6	17.3	16.8	16.8
IRL	NaN	NaN	NaN	NaN	NaN	NaN	NaN	15.2	16.4	17.7	18.1	20.4	18.8	17.6	15.7	15.7
NET	31.6	35.7	35.9	36.9	37.3	35.4	36.5	33.4	29.8	30.5	33.1	29.1	28.8	27.4	23.3	23.3
PRT	25.0	27.1	27.5	26.9	30.7	33.7	30.1	32.1	31.3	30.2	33.7	34.8	37.0	40.3	33.8	33.8
ESP	NaN	NaN	NaN	NaN	NaN	28.7	27.1	29.0	29.7	32.5	37.3	40.1	41.3	28.1	24.4	24.4
SWE	27.3	34.2	36.4	36.6	38.0	48.3	44.4	37.6	34.8	35.8	40.1	38.0	39.9	40.2	52.5	52.5

Note: Country codes: Germany (GER), France (FRA), Italy (ITA), United Kingdom (GBR), Austria (AUT), Belgium (BEL), Denmark (DNK), Finland (FIN), Greece (GRE), Ireland (IRL), Netherlands (NET), Portugal (PRT), Spain (ESP), and Sweden (SWE). NaN = not available number (no numeric data available).

[a]Due to data availability reasons, 2010 tax rates are assumed to be the same as in 2009.

Table 6A.3   Consumption taxes in percent across countries and time

	1995	1996	1997	1998	1999	2000	2001	2002	2003	2004	2005	2006	2007	2008	2009	2010[a]
US	5.1	5.1	5.0	5.0	4.9	4.7	4.6	4.5	4.4	4.4	4.5	4.5	4.3	4.1	4.0	4.0
EU-14	17.0	17.1	17.1	17.3	17.6	17.4	16.9	16.8	16.7	16.6	16.5	16.6	16.7	16.1	15.2	15.2
GER	15.4	15.3	15.0	15.2	16.0	16.0	15.6	15.5	15.7	15.3	15.1	15.3	16.7	16.6	16.7	16.7
FRA	18.6	19.4	19.6	19.6	19.8	18.8	18.1	18.0	17.5	17.6	17.5	17.4	17.1	16.5	15.6	15.6
ITA	15.4	14.4	14.2	15.1	14.7	15.6	14.9	14.6	14.1	13.7	13.7	14.2	14.0	13.1	12.5	12.5
GBR	16.7	16.9	16.7	16.7	16.7	16.3	15.7	15.5	15.6	15.6	15.0	14.8	14.7	14.1	13.0	13.0
AUT	19.3	20.0	21.0	21.0	21.6	20.5	20.2	20.7	20.2	20.2	20.0	19.2	19.6	19.6	19.5	19.5
BEL	16.5	16.8	17.1	17.0	18.0	17.9	16.8	17.2	17.0	17.8	18.2	18.3	17.8	16.8	16.5	16.5
DNK	32.4	33.9	34.2	35.4	36.4	35.7	35.8	35.7	35.0	34.8	35.6	36.0	35.3	33.1	31.0	31.0
FIN	26.5	26.4	28.9	28.5	28.9	28.1	26.8	26.7	27.2	26.2	26.1	25.8	24.8	23.9	22.9	22.9
GRE	15.7	15.8	16.3	15.6	15.8	15.1	15.7	15.6	14.9	14.5	14.2	14.4	14.8	14.1	12.8	12.8
IRL	24.1	24.4	24.8	26.0	26.5	25.4	22.3	23.5	23.3	25.0	26.0	25.9	24.5	21.1	19.3	19.3
NET	17.9	18.4	18.5	18.7	19.5	19.3	19.9	19.1	19.2	19.8	20.7	20.5	20.5	20.2	18.7	18.7
PRT	19.2	19.8	19.5	20.6	20.6	19.4	19.5	20.2	20.0	19.7	20.5	20.7	19.6	18.4	15.9	15.9
ESP	12.8	13.1	13.5	14.3	15.0	14.7	14.2	14.3	14.7	14.7	14.9	14.9	14.3	12.4	10.2	10.2
SWE	26.8	25.4	25.2	25.5	25.0	24.7	25.1	25.1	25.1	25.3	25.7	25.8	26.1	26.3	25.8	25.8

Note: Country codes: Germany (GER), France (FRA), Italy (ITA), United Kingdom (GBR), Austria (AUT), Belgium (BEL), Denmark (DNK), Finland (FIN), Greece (GRE), Ireland (IRL), Netherlands (NET), Portugal (PRT), Spain (ESP), and Sweden (SWE).

[a]Due to data availability reasons, 2010 tax rates are assumed to be the same as in 2009.

Appendix B
Calculation of Tax Rates

We use the same data sources as in Trabandt and Uhlig (2011); that is, the AMECO database of the European Commission, the Organization for Economic Cooperation and Development (OECD) revenue statistics database and the national income and product accounts (NIPA) database of the Bureau of Economic Analysis (BEA).

In this chapter, we refine the methodology of Mendoza, Razin, and Tesar (1994) to calculate effective tax rates on labor and capital income. Broadly, we expand the measured labor tax base by including supplements to wages as well as a fraction of entrepreneurial income of households. Supplements to wages beyond employers' Social Security contributions account for about 7 percent of US GDP. Also, entrepreneurial income of households is sizable as a fraction of GDP but entirely accounted for as capital income in Mendoza, Razin, and Tesar (1994). We argue that at least a fraction, say α, of this income ought to be attributed to labor income. As a result, the refinements imply a more reasonable labor share in line with the empirical literature. More importantly, the average 1995 to 2010 labor income taxes turn out to be lower while capital income taxes are higher, as previously calculated in Trabandt and Uhlig (2011). Appendix table 6B.1 provides an overview of the refinements.[8] The following list explains the abbreviations used in appendix table 6B.1.

1100: Income, profit, and capital gains taxes of individuals, revenue statistics (OECD).

1200: Income, profit, and capital gains taxes of corporations, revenue statistics (OECD).

2000: Social Security contributions, revenue statistics (OECD).

2200: Social Security contributions of employers, revenue statistics (OECD).

3000: Payroll taxes, revenue statistics (OECD).

4000: Property taxes, revenue statistics (OECD).

4100: Recurrent taxes on immovable property, revenue statistics (OECD).

4400: Taxes on financial and capital transactions, revenue statistics (OECD).

OS: Net operating surplus: total economy (AMECO, NIPA).

W: Gross wages and salaries: households and nonprofit institutions serving households. (NPISH) (AMECO, NIPA).

OSPUE+PEI: Gross operating surplus minus consumption of fixed capital plus mixed income plus net property income: households and NPISH (AMECO).

---

8. Note that we retain the assumption in Mendoza, Razin, and Tesar (1994) that, implicitly, income from capital and labor is taxed at the same rate. In future research, it would be interesting to take differences in the taxation of labor and capital income explicitly into account when calculating tax rates.

Table 6B.1   **Calculations of effective tax rates: Mendoza, Razin, and Tesar (1994) as used in Trabandt and Uhlig (2011) versus this chapter**

Income tax	Mendoza, Razin, and Tesar (1994)	This chapter
Personal:	$\tau^h = \dfrac{1100}{\text{OSPUE} + \text{PEI} + W}$	$\tau^h = \dfrac{1100}{(1 - \alpha + \alpha)(\text{OSPUE} + \text{PEI}) + W + W^{\text{suppl}}}$
Labor:	$\tau^n = \dfrac{\tau^h W + 2000 + 3000}{W + 2200}$	$\tau^n = \dfrac{\tau^h[W + W^{\text{suppl}} + \alpha(\text{OSPUE} + \text{PEI}] + 2000 + 3000}{W + W^{\text{suppl}} + \alpha(\text{OSPUE} + \text{PEI}) + 2200}$
Capital:	$\tau^k = \dfrac{\tau^h(\text{OSPUE} + \text{PEI}) + 1200 + 4100 + 4400}{OS}$	$\tau^k = \dfrac{\tau^h(1 - \alpha)(\text{OSPUE} + \text{PEI}) + 1200 + 4100 + 4400}{OS - \alpha(\text{OSPUE} + \text{PEI})}$

Table 6B.2   **Comparison of effective tax rates**

	Labor taxes, τ^n		Capital taxes, τ^k		Labor share	
	TU (2011)	This chapter	TU (2011)	This chapter	TU (2011)	This chapter
US	0.27	0.22	0.35	0.41	0.50	0.64
EU-14	0.41	0.34	0.32	0.37	0.48	0.58
GER	0.41	0.34	0.22	0.25	0.49	0.60
FRA	0.45	0.39	0.35	0.43	0.50	0.59
ITA	0.47	0.36	0.34	0.41	0.38	0.52
GBR	0.28	0.24	0.44	0.52	0.50	0.60
AUT	0.50	0.43	0.24	0.26	0.48	0.57
BEL	0.48	0.39	0.43	0.51	0.48	0.60
DNK	0.48	0.43	0.50	0.49	0.50	0.56
FIN	0.48	0.44	0.32	0.31	0.48	0.53
GRE	0.41	0.29	0.17	0.19	0.32	0.46
IRL	0.27	0.25	0.17	0.17	0.42	0.45
NET	0.44	0.36	0.28	0.32	0.45	0.55
PRT	0.28	0.22	0.27	0.32	0.44	0.56
ESP	0.35	0.30	0.27	0.31	0.46	0.55
SWE	0.56	0.50	0.39	0.40	0.51	0.57

Notes: "TU (2011)" stands for Trabandt and Uhlig (2011), who use the methodology proposed by Mendoza, Razin, and Tesar (1994). The table shows the implications of the refined calculations of effective tax rates as well as the implied labor share. See appendix B for details.

W^{suppl}: Supplements to wages: households and NPISH. Calculated as the residual of compensation of employees minus wages and salaries minus Social Security contributions of employers.

We select a value for α such that the average 1995 to 2010 labor share, that is, $[W + W^{suppl} + \alpha(\text{OSPUE} + \text{PEI}) + 2200]/\text{GDP}$, equals 64 percent in the United States. It turns out that we need to set $\alpha = 0.35$. We keep the same value for α for all other countries.

Appendix table 6B.2 shows the resulting effective tax rates across countries and compares them to those when the standard Mendoza, Razin, and Tesar (1994) methodology is applied as used, for example, in Trabandt and Uhlig (2011). It turns out, that due to the broader labor tax base, effective labor taxes are somewhat smaller while effective capital taxes are higher.

Finally, appendix table 6B.3 provides maximum additional tax revenues that result from moving from the peak of the Laffer curve when either the standard Mendoza, Razin, and Tesar (1994) tax rates or the refined version proposed in this chapter are used. Further, the table also shows the implications of imperfect versus perfect competition. The introduction of imperfect competition reduces the effective labor tax base and thus less additional tax revenues are attainable when varying labor taxes. By contrast, profits arising from market power increase maximum additional tax revenues when capital

Table 6B.3   Laffer curves for the 1995–2010 calibration

	Vary labor taxes, τ^n $\Delta \bar{T}_{\text{Max}}$			Vary capital taxes, τ^k $\Delta \bar{T}_{\text{Max}}$		
	This chapter		TU (2011)	This chapter		TU (2011)
	$\omega = 1.1$	$\omega \to 1$	$\omega \to 1$	$\omega = 1.1$	$\omega \to 1$	$\omega \to 1$
US	37.6	42.5	33.3	10.7	8.2	7.3
EU-14	11.9	13.9	8.4	3.2	1.6	1.0
GER	15.4	17.3	10.1	6.8	3.9	2.3
FRA	7.1	8.6	4.9	1.1	0.3	0.3
ITA	9.8	11.6	4.2	2.1	0.9	0.3
GBR	17.5	21.0	18.7	1.7	0.9	1.6
AUT	5.2	6.1	2.0	2.6	1.0	0.3
BEL	5.7	7.2	3.0	0.3	0.0	0.0
DNK	1.3	2.1	0.6	0.0	0.4	0.9
FIN	4.1	5.1	2.9	1.6	0.4	0.2
GRE	18.9	21.0	8.2	8.9	5.6	2.1
IRL	32.7	36.3	32.3	14.9	10.7	9.4
NET	14.7	16.9	8.7	5.3	3.0	1.6
PRT	21.6	25.1	18.6	6.6	4.5	3.6
ESP	18.5	21.0	15.0	6.5	4.0	3.1
SWE	2.0	2.7	0.7	0.5	0.0	0.0

Notes: $\Delta \bar{T}_{\text{Max}}$ denotes the maximum additional tax revenues (in percent) that results from moving from to the peak of the Laffer curve. Results are shown for the standard Mendoza, Razin, and Tesar (1994) taxes used in Trabandt and Uhlig (2011), "TU," as well as for the refined tax rate calculations discussed in appendix B. Further, the case of imperfect competition with a gross markup $\omega = 1.1$ is compared to the case of perfect competition (i.e., $\omega \to 1$).

taxes are varied. The third column shows the results when the standard Mendoza tax rates are used in the analysis and are essentially those obtained by Trabandt and Uhlig (2011). In this case, higher effective labor taxes at the status quo eqilibrium reduce the scope for more tax revenues when labor and capital taxes are varied.

References

Acemoglu, D. 2008. *Introduction to Modern Economic Growth,* 1st ed. Princeton, NJ: Princeton University Press.
Alesina, A., E. Glaeser, and B. Sacerdote. 2006. "Work and Leisure in the US and Europe: Why So Different?" In *NBER Macroeconomics Annual 2005,* vol. 20, edited by Mark Gertler and Kenneth Rogoff, 1–100. Cambridge, MA: MIT Press.
Barro, R. J., and X. Sala-i-Martin. 2003. *Economic Growth,* 2nd ed. Cambridge, MA: MIT Press.
Bi, H. 2011. "Sovereign Default Risk Premia, Fiscal Limits, and Fiscal Policy." Bank of Canada Working Paper 2011-10, March.

Bi, H., E. M. Leeper, and C. Leith. 2010. "Stabilization versus Sustainability: Macroeconomic Policy Tradeoffs.." Prepared for the European Central Bank's Conference on Monetary and Fiscal Policy Challenges in Times of Financial Stress. December 2–3.

Blanchard, O. 2004. "The Economic Future of Europe." *Journal of Economic Perspectives* 18 (4): 3–26.

Chari, V. V., P. J. Kehoe, and E. R. McGrattan. 2007. "Business Cycle Accounting." *Econometrica* 75 (3): 781–836.

Cooley, T. F., and E. Prescott. 1995. "Economic Growth and Business Cycles." In *Frontiers of Business Cycle Research,* edited by T. F. Cooley, 1–38. Princeton, NJ: Princeton University Press.

Green, J., and L. J. Kotlikoff. 2009. "On the General Relativity of Fiscal Language." *Key Issues in Public Finance—A Conference in Memory of David Bradford,* edited by Alan J. Auerbach and Daniel Shaviro, 241–56. Cambridge, MA: Harvard University Press.

Hall, R. E. 2009. "Reconciling Cyclical Movements in the Marginal Value of Time and the Marginal Product of Labor." *Journal of Political Economy* 117 (2): 281–323.

Jones, C. I. 2001. *Introduction to Economic Growth,* 2nd ed. New York: Norton.

Kimball, M. S., and M. D. Shapiro. 2008. "Labor Supply: Are the Income and Substitution Effects Both Large or Both Small?" NBER Working Paper no. 14208. Cambridge, MA: National Bureau of Economic Research.

King, R. G., and S. T. Rebelo. 1999. "Resuscitating Real Business Cycles." In *Handbook of Macroeconomics,* edited by J. B. Taylor and M. Woodford, 927–1007. Amsterdam: Elsevier.

Levine, R., and D. Renelt. 1992. "A Sensitivity Analysis of Cross-Country Growth Regressions." *American Economic Review* 82 (4): 942–63.

Ljungqvist, L., and T. J. Sargent. 2007. "Do Taxes Explain European Employment? Indivisible Labor, Human Capital, Lotteries, and Savings." In *NBER Macroeconomics Annual 2006,* vol. 21, edited by D. Acemoglu, K. Rogoff, and M. Woodford, 181–224. Cambridge, MA: MIT Press.

Lucas, R. E. 1988. "On the Mechanics of Economic Development." *Journal of Monetary Economics* 22:3–42.

Mendoza, E. G., A. Razin, and L. L. Tesar. 1994. "Effective Tax Rates in Macroeconomics: Cross-Country Estimates of Tax Rates on Factor Incomes and Consumption." *Journal of Monetary Economics* 34:297–323.

Pissarides, C., and L. R. Ngai. 2009. "Welfare Policy and the Sectoral Distribution of Employment." Center for Structual Econometrics Discussion Paper no. 09/04. London: London School of Economics.

Prescott, E. C. 2002. "Prosperity and Depression." *American Economic Review* 92:1–15.

———. 2004. "Why Do Americans Work So Much More Than Europeans?" *Quarterly Review, Federal Reserve Bank of Minneapolis* 28:2–13.

———. 2006. "Nobel Lecture: The Transformation of Macroeconomic Policy and Research." *Journal of Political Economy* 114 (2): 203–35.

Rogerson, R. 2007. "Taxation and Market Work: Is Scandinavia an Outlier?" *Economic Theory* 32 (1): 59–85.

Shimer, R. 2009. "Convergence in Macroeconomics: The Labor Wedge." *American Economic Journal: Macroeconomics* 1 (1): 280–97.

Trabandt, M., and H. Uhlig. 2011. "The Laffer Curve Revisited." *Journal of Monetary Economics* 58 (4): 305–27.

Uzawa, H. 1965. "Optimum Technical Change in an Aggregative Model of Economic Growth." *International Economic Review* 6:18–31.

Comment   Jaume Ventura

In their chapter, Trabandt and Uhlig compute Laffer curves for the United States and fourteen European countries. Their goal is to assess the limits of taxation in these countries and its implications for government deficit and the sustainability of current debt levels. Overall, I think this is a very interesting research project and a most welcome contribution to the current debate on fiscal policy in Europe and elsewhere. Undoubtedly, the estimates provided by the authors are subject to a number of important critiques, some of which I detail following. Despite this, we desperately need quantitative estimates of the effects of fiscal policy and the methodology developed by the authors can help us obtain those.

In this short comment, I first review the authors' methodology and highlight its basic strengths and weaknesses. This takes up the majority of these comments. After doing this, I briefly describe the main results and add some general remarks on them.

The methodology used by the authors can be summarized in five steps or assumptions. I describe next these steps or assumptions using a simplified version of the model that does not take into account monopolistic competition or human capital accumulation. These extensions are important from a quantitative perspective, but are not central when it comes to explaining and commenting on Trabandt and Uhlig's methodology.

The first step is to assume that aggregate production in the United States and the fourteen European countries can be well described by a Cobb-Douglas technology of the following sort:

$$(1) \qquad y_t = \xi^t \cdot k_t^\theta \cdot n_t^{1-\theta} = \xi^{t/(1/\theta)} \cdot \left(\frac{k_t}{y_t} \right)^{\theta/(1-\theta)} \cdot n_t,$$

where I use the same notation as the authors. In particular, y_t is output; k_t and n_t are the stocks of capital and labor; ξ^t denotes the trend in total factor productivity; and θ is a parameter such that $\theta \in (0, 1)$. This is routinely assumed in macroeconomics. But still I cannot resist mentioning here again that this might be a poor assumption when one goes beyond building theo-

Jaume Ventura is professor of economics at Universitat Pompeu Fabra, a senior researcher at Centre de Recerca en Economia Internacional (CREI), and a research associate of the National Bureau of Economic Research.

For acknowledgments, sources of research support, and disclosure of the author's material financial relationships, if any, please see http://www.nber.org/chapters/c12639.ack.

retical examples and tries instead to use the models to make quantitative assessments. In open economies, international trade affects the aggregate production function. Comparative advantage and increasing returns lead countries to specialize their production in different sets of industries. Even if all the countries in the sample had the same industry production functions, their aggregate production functions might differ substantially as the latter also depend on these countries' industry mix.[1] This might be important for the calculations. As taxes are changed, patterns of specialization are altered and so is the shape of the production function. It is hard to assess here the biases that this misspecification of the model induces in the results, however. But it certainly induces additional uncertainty regarding the estimates.

The second step is to assume that factors markets are competitive and, as a result, factors are paid their marginal product:[2]

$$(2) \quad w_t \cdot n_t = (1 - \theta) \cdot \xi^t \cdot k_t^\theta \cdot n_t^{1-\theta} = (1 - \theta) \cdot \xi^{t/(1-\theta)} \cdot \left(\frac{k_t}{y_t}\right)^{\theta/(1-\theta)} \cdot n_t$$

$$(3) \quad (r_t - \delta) \cdot k_t = \theta \cdot \xi^t \cdot k_t^\theta \cdot n_t^{1-\theta} - \delta \cdot k_t = \left(\theta - \delta \cdot \frac{k_t}{y_t}\right) \cdot \xi^{t/(1-\theta)} \cdot \left(\frac{k_t}{y_t}\right)^{\theta/(1-\theta)} \cdot n_t$$

where w_t is the wage and $r_t - \delta$ is the rental minus the depreciation rate. This assumption is also standard in quantitative, but widely acknowledged to be unrealistic. Collective bargaining, regulations of various sorts, and many other frictions ensure that labor markets in many European countries are anything but competitive. Adverse selection, agency costs, oligopolistic behavior by banks, and other frictions create a wedge between the rates of return to investment and those that are perceived by savers. This might also be important for the calculations. As taxes are changed, factor rewards might change more or less than proportionally, depending on the nature of these frictions. Once again, it is hard to assess the biases that this misspecification of the model induces in the results, however. This depends on the specific frictions that are more prevalent in labor markets, but a good dose of healthy skepticism should be used after assuming that the United States and Spain have the same competitive labor and financial markets.

The first couple of steps that allow us to write tax revenues are as follows:

$$(4) \quad T^k = \tau^k \cdot \left(\theta \cdot \frac{y_t}{k_t} - \delta\right) \cdot k_t = \tau^k \cdot \left(\theta - \delta \cdot \frac{k_t}{y_t}\right) \cdot \xi^{t/(1-\theta)} \cdot \left(\frac{k_t}{y_t}\right)^{\theta/(1-\theta)} \cdot n_t$$

$$(5) \quad T^n \equiv \tau^n \cdot w_t \cdot n_t = \tau^n \cdot (1 - \theta) \cdot \xi^{t/(1-\theta)} \cdot \left(\frac{k_t}{y_t}\right)^{\theta/(1-\theta)} \cdot n_t$$

1. See Ventura (2005) for a detailed discussion of this point, and Fadinger (2011) for an attempt to quantify its importance when estimating cross-country productivity differences.
2. With monopolistic competition, the wage becomes lower than the marginal product of labor, but it is still proportional to it.

(6)
$$T^c \equiv \tau^c \cdot c_t = \tau^c \cdot \frac{c_t}{y_t} \cdot \xi^{t/(1-\theta)} \cdot \left(\frac{k_t}{y_t}\right)^{\theta/(1-\theta)} \cdot n_t,$$

where τ^k, τ^n, and τ^c are the applicable tax rates on capital income, labor income, and consumption, respectively; while T^k, T^n, and T^c are the respective tax collections. Computing Laffer curves consists of plotting tax revenues as the applicable tax rates increase. To be able to do this, we need a theory of the capital-income ratio; employment and the propensity to consume out of income vary with these tax rates. That is, we need a theory of how k_t/y_t, n_t and c_t/y_t react to changes in τ^k, τ^n, and τ^c. And this is what the next couple of steps provide.

Before doing this, it is useful to highlight a very positive feature of this methodology in that it recognizes that sometimes, the main effects on tax revenues of a change in a given tax work through other taxes! For instance, an increase in capital income taxes might have a larger negative effect on labor tax revenues than on capital income taxes. By studying all these taxes together, this methodology allows us to consider these general equilibrium effects.

The third step in Trabandt and Uhlig's methodology is to assume that the behavior of savings and employment are well approximated by the steady state of an infinite-horizon neoclassical growth model. In such a model, the first-order conditions on savings and labor choice imply that:

(7)
$$1 + \left(\theta \cdot \left(\frac{k_t}{y_t}\right)^{-1} - \delta\right) \cdot (1 - \tau^k) = \xi^{\eta/(1-\theta)} \cdot \beta^{-1}$$

(8)
$$(\eta \cdot \kappa \cdot n_t^{1+(1/\varphi)})^{-1} + 1 - \frac{1}{\eta} = \frac{1+\tau^c}{1-\tau^n} \cdot \frac{1+(1/\varphi)}{1-\theta} \cdot \frac{c_t}{y_t},$$

where β is the rate of time preference and φ is the constant Frisch elasticity of the labor supply. These equations are standard, and equate the growth in the marginal utility of consumption with the interest rate and the marginal utility of consumption times the wage with the disutility of labor. As is typical in macroeconomics, the authors use a description of aggregate choice that abstracts from demographic structure. Surely changes in taxes have different effects on the young and the old, and therefore demographic structure might be an important factor. Moreover, this demographic structure might be quite different across countries.

The fourth step consists of assuming that the government adjusts transfers as tax revenues change. Then, the resource constraint implies that:

(9)
$$\frac{c_t}{y_t} = 1 - (\xi^{1/(1-\theta)} - 1 + \delta) \cdot \frac{k_t}{y_t} - \overline{g} \cdot \left(\frac{k_t}{y_t}\right)^{-\theta/(1-\theta)} \cdot n_t^{-1}.$$

This step highlights another positive feature of this methodology in that it forces us to make assumptions on what the government does (or stops doing) when tax revenues change. An assumption of this sort is needed, since the impact of a reduction of tax rates depends crucially on what the government does with the additional revenue. But I wonder whether it would have been more realistic to assume that tax revenues are used to reduce debt levels. This would certainly complicate some of the technical details of the calibration. But it might be quite different to assume that the government pays creditors rather than transfers back the taxes to those that have been taxed. If, as it is the case in many countries, creditors are foreigners, debt reduction has a negative wealth effect that is not taken care of in the current set of results. This negative wealth effect is likely to reduce tax collections substantially.

Despite these caveats, the methodology is clear and sound. We can now solve equations (7), (8), and (9) for k_t/y_t, n_t, and c_t/y_t as a function of τ^k, τ^n, and τ^c; and then plug the results into equations (4), (5), and (6). Once this is done, we can compute Laffer curves. For instance, the capital-tax Laffer curve for τ^k traces how total revenue $T \equiv T^k + T^n + T^c$ changes with τ^k keeping other taxes constant. Analogous procedures yield the labor-tax and consumption-tax Laffer curves. Also, it is possible to construct Laffer hills by combining two taxes. Only one thing is missing to be able to perform this quantitative exercise, and this is to choose parameter values.

The fifth and final step of this methodology is to choose these values. Here Trabandt and Uhlig assume that all countries have the same parameter values, except for their fiscal policy variables; that is, tax rates, government spending, and public debt. Then, they choose parameter values in the usual RBC style. This is perhaps where there is more room to make improvements at a low cost. Surely one can choose parameter values differently for each country, drawing from the large literature on quantitative macroeconomic models that has been developed in the last couple of decades.

The methodology described before (with some refinements that include monopolistic competition and human capital accumulation) generates an interesting result: assuming all changes in revenue went into paying interest on the debt, what is the highest interest that countries could pay? If only labor taxes are used, the United States could afford real interest rates rates between 12 and 15 percent, Ireland could afford rates of 11 percent, Germany, Portugal, and Spain close to around 9 percent, while Austria, Belgium, Denmark, Finland, France, Greece, and Italy cannot afford interest rates above 6 percent. These interest rates grow a bit when capital income taxes can be used, but not too much. On the one hand, these are the kind of quantitative results that we need to produce as a profession. On the other hand, the crudeness of the assumptions discussed earlier makes us wonder about how seriously we should take these numbers. To what extent is the model reliable and/or stable across countries? To what extent do frictions in labor and financial markets affect the reaction of the tax base to changes in taxes? To what extent are the assumptions of a stable fiscal policy without sovereign defaults; for instance, a reasonable characterization of the current situation? To what extent is the long-run analysis performed here a good guide for policy in the current depression? It would be unfair to ask Trabandt and Uhlig to answer all these questions in a single piece of research.

References

Fadinger, H. 2011. "Productivity Differences in an Interdependent World." *Journal of International Economics* 84 (2): 221–32.
Ventura, J. 2005. "A Global View of Economic Growth." In *Handbook of Economic Growth,* edited by P. Aghion and S. Durlauf, 1419–97. Amsterdam: Elsevier.

Perceptions and Misperceptions of Fiscal Inflation

Eric M. Leeper and Todd B. Walker

7.1 Introduction

Not so long ago, macroeconomists interested in understanding inflation and its determinants were comfortable sweeping fiscal policy under the carpet, implicitly assuming that the fiscal adjustments required to allow monetary policy to control inflation would always be forthcoming. This sanguine view is reflected in recent graduate textbooks, which make scant mention of fiscal policy, and in the economic models at central banks, which all but ignore fiscal phenomena. It is also reflected in the widespread adoption of inflation targeting by central banks, but the nearly complete absence of the adoption of compatible fiscal frameworks.

The Great Recession and accompanying worldwide financial crisis have brought an abrupt halt to researchers' benign neglect of fiscal policy. Figure 7.1 underlies the sudden shift in attitude among economists and policymakers alike. Fiscal deficits worldwide, but particularly in advanced economies, shot up and public debt as a share of GDP ballooned to nearly 100 percent in advanced economies. As central banks lowered nominal interest rates toward their zero bound, they moved to quantitative actions that dramatically expanded the size and riskiness of their balance sheets. Europe's

Eric M. Leeper is professor of economics at Indiana University, Distinguished Visiting Professor of Business and Economics at Monash University, and a research associate of the National Bureau of Economic Research. Todd B. Walker is assistant professor of economics at Indiana University.

Walker acknowledges support from NSF grant SES-0962221. We would like to thank seminar participants at the NBER Summer Institute, and Alberto Alesina, Michael Bordo, George von Furstenberg, Jordi Galí, Francesco Giavazzi, Jürgen von Hagen, Chris Sims, and Harald Uhlig for helpful comments. For acknowledgments, sources of research support, and disclosure of the authors' material financial relationships, if any, please see http://www.nber.org/chapters /c12644.ack.

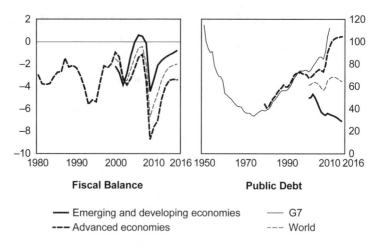

Fiscal Balance   **Public Debt**

—— Emerging and developing economies   —— G7
--- Advanced economies   --- World

Data from 2011-2016 are projected fiscal balance and public debt

Fig. 7.1   In percent of GDP
Source: International Monetary Fund (2011).

monetary union has been stressed, perhaps to the breaking point, by member nations' fiscal woes. With both fiscal *and monetary* authorities taking fiscal actions, professional and policy focuses have now shifted to fiscal matters and the interactions of monetary and fiscal policies.

With the shift in focus has come enhanced interest in the potential channels through which fiscal policy can affect aggregate demand and inflation. And, in light of the facts in figure 7.1, a pressing question is, "Do profligate fiscal policies threaten the progress many countries have made toward achieving low and stable inflation?" In the conventional monetary paradigm that underlies central bank models and, we conjecture, the thinking of central bankers, the answer is, "No, so long as the central bank steadfastly refuses to print new currency to finance deficits."

This paradigm maintains that there is no mechanism by which fiscal policy can be inflationary that is independent of monetary policy and money creation. Sargent and Wallace (1981) model this conventional view and dub it "unpleasant monetarist arithmetic." In their setup, fiscal policy runs a chronic primary deficit—spending exclusive of debt service less tax revenues—that is independent of inflation and government debt and a simple quantity theory demand for money holds, so the price level adjusts to establish money market equilibrium. The economy faces a fiscal limit because the private sector's demand for bonds imposes an upper bound on the debt-GDP ratio. Sargent and Wallace's government bonds are real: claims to payoffs denominated in units of goods.

If primary deficits are exogenous—one notion of "profligate" fiscal policy—and the exogeneity is immutable, then monetary policy loses its ability to control inflation. Standard reasoning underlies the result. If monetary policy initially aims to control inflation by setting money growth independently of fiscal policy, then eventually the exogenous deficit will drive debt to the fiscal limit. At the limit, if government is to remain solvent, monetary policy has no alternative but to print money to generate the seigniorage revenues needed to meet interest payments in the debt.[1] Eventually, money growth must rise and, by the quantity theory, so must inflation. Long-run monetary policy is driven by the need to stabilize debt and the inflation rate is determined by the size of the total fiscal deficit, including interest payments.

This conventional paradigm reflects common perceptions of fiscal inflations. But it is a *mis*perception to believe that fiscal policy can affect inflation only if monetary policy monetizes deficits in the manner that Sargent and Wallace envision.

The tight connection between seigniorage financing and inflation in Sargent and Wallace's model stems from the assumption that bonds are real, or perfectly indexed to the price level. Higher real debt requires the government to raise more *real* resources—like seigniorage—to fully back the debt. But in practice only a small fraction of government debt issued by advanced economies is indexed. Even in the United Kingdom, which has a thick market for indexed government bonds, about 80 percent of outstanding debt is nominal. Ninety percent of US treasuries are nominal and fractions are still higher elsewhere.

Recognizing that bonds are denominated in nominal terms introduces a direct channel from fiscal policy to inflation. Called the *fiscal theory of the price level,* this channel does not rely on "monetizing deficits" or on insufficient inflation-fighting resolve by the central bank.[2] Instead, it springs from the fact that a nominal bond is a claim to a *nominal* payoff—dollars, euros, or shekels—and that the *real* value of the payoff depends on the price level.

Higher nominal debt may be fully backed by real resources—real primary surpluses and seigniorage—or it may be backed only by *nominal* cash flows. When real resources fully back the debt, the conventional paradigm prevails and fiscal policy is inflationary only if the central bank monetizes deficits. But when the government cannot or will not raise the necessary real backing, the fiscal theory creates a direct link between current and expected deficits and inflation.[3]

Even though the data in figure 7.1 have sent some policymakers and finan-

1. We are assuming that in the long run the economy's growth rate is below the real interest rate on debt.
2. Leeper (1991), Sims (1994), Woodford (1995), and Cochrane (1998) describe the fiscal theory and its implications.
3. The terms "fiscal theory" and "quantity theory" are unfortunate because they suggest that these are distinct models of price-level determination. As we show, the price level and inflation *always* depend on both monetary and fiscal policy behavior. The fiscal and quantity "theories" emerge under alternative monetary-fiscal regimes, as Gordon and Leeper (2006) show.

Table 7.1   Net present value of impact on fiscal deficit of aging-related spending, in percent of GDP

Country	Aging-related spending
Australia	482
Canada	726
France	276
Germany	280
Italy	169
Japan	158
Korea	683
Spain	652
United Kingdom	335
United States	495
Advanced G-20 countries	409

Source: International Monetary Fund (2009).

cial markets into apoplexy, they are but the tip of the fiscal stress iceberg. Table 7.1 describes the real problem. Aging populations and promised government old-age benefits that far outstrip revenue provisions imply massive "unfunded liabilities." Plans to bring current deficits under control do little to address the coming fiscal stress. We have no special insights into the political solutions to this unprecedented fiscal problem, but we can shed light on the economic consequences—particularly for inflation—of alternative private-sector beliefs about how the fiscal stress will be resolved.

We work from the premise that central bankers have learned the unpleasant monetarist arithmetic lesson, so explicit monetization of deficits is off the table in advanced economies, though this is not a universally held view (Cochrane 2011b). For the most part, we also exclude outright default on the government liabilities of those countries. Ongoing developments in the euro area vividly illustrate the lengths to which policymakers will go to avoid default, and policymakers in the United Kingdom, the United States, and elsewhere hold similar views.

There remain two possible resolutions to fiscal stress. First, government could successfully persuade the public that future revenue and spending adjustments will occur. With fiscal policy taking care of itself, we return to the sanguine world in which central banks retain control of inflation. Numbers in table 7.1 underscore how large those adjustments must be. Economic theory tells us that those policies must also be credible to firmly anchor expectations on the necessary fiscal adjustments, which is what is required for monetary policy to retain control of inflation as in the conventional paradigm.

Because the first resolution is well understood, this chapter focuses on a variety of alternative policy scenarios in which aspects of the second resolution—price-level changes induced by the fiscal theory—come into play.

We focus on the fiscal theory because it seems to be poorly understood and quickly discarded by central bankers. For example, in their discussion of the implications of fiscal stress for central banks, Cecchetti, Mohanty, and Zampolli (2010, footnote 23) acknowledge the fiscal theory, but immediately dismiss it as "untested and controversial." As we point out later, the fiscal theory is no more or less testable than the quantity theory or its recent offspring, the new Keynesian/Taylor rule model of inflation. And it is controversial, we believe, because it is relatively new, its implications are unsettling, and its economic mechanisms have not yet been fully absorbed by monetary economists and policymakers.

7.1.1   What We Do

Section 7.2 uses a simple model to illustrate how the price level is determined in the conventional paradigm and in the fiscal theory. The conventional policy mix (Regime M) has monetary policy target inflation and fiscal policy stabilize the value of debt. An alternative mix (Regime F) is available when governments issue nominal bonds. That mix assigns monetary policy to stabilize debt and fiscal policy to control the price level, giving rise to the fiscal theory equilibrium.

In Regime M, deficit-financed tax cuts or spending increases do not affect aggregate demand because the private sector expects the resulting increase in government debt to be exactly matched by future tax increases or spending reductions. Expansions in government debt do not raise wealth. This fiscal behavior relieves monetary policy of debt stabilization, freeing the central bank to target inflation.

Regime F posits different policies that align closely to actual behavior in many countries recently. Suppose that higher deficits do not create higher expected surpluses and that central banks either peg short-term nominal interest rates or raise them only weakly with inflation. Because a tax cut today does not portend future tax hikes, individuals initially perceive the increase in nominal debt to be an increase in their real wealth. They try to convert higher wealth into consumption goods, raising aggregate demand. Rising demand brings with it rising prices, which continue to rise until real wealth falls back to its pre-tax-cut level and individuals are content with their original consumption plans. By preventing nominal interest rates from rising sharply with inflation, monetary policy prevents debt service from growing too rapidly, which stabilizes the value of government bonds. In this stylized version of the fiscal theory, monetary policy can anchor expected inflation on the inflation target, but fiscal policy determines actual inflation.

The section goes on to describe how the maturity structure of nominal government bonds can alter the time series properties of inflation and it lays out the precise role that monetary policy plays in a fiscal equilibrium. A fiscal theory equilibrium is consistent with a wide range of patterns of correlation in data, including a positive correlation between inflation and money growth, a negative correlation between inflation and the debt-GDP ratio, and any correlation between inflation and nominal debt growth and deficits.

Having established that under Regime F policies monetary policy does not control inflation, section 7.3 turns to plausible scenarios in which the central bank does not control inflation even in Regime M. One example arises when the public believes the economy may hit its fiscal limit, the point at which taxes and spending can no longer adjust to stabilize debt, at some point in the future. Even if monetary policy aggressively targets inflation in the years before the limit, it cannot determine the inflation rate and it cannot even anchor expected inflation. A second type of fiscal limit stems from the risk of sovereign default. When the central bank sets the interest rate on short-term government bonds, a higher probability of default feeds directly into current inflation. Finally, in a monetary union, the member nation whose fiscal policies are profligate will determine the union-wide price level, even if other member countries run fiscal policies that consistently target real debt.

In section 7.4 we consider the empirical implications of monetary-fiscal policy interactions. This section lays out some observational equivalence results that arise in models of section 7.2 Restrictions on policy behavior and/or exogenous driving processes are crucial in discerning whether observed time series on inflation, debt, and deficits are generated by a Regime M or a Regime F equilibrium.

Central bankers who aim to hit an inflation target need to know whether the economy resides in Regime M or in Regime F. Observational equivalence informs us that existing research may not be able to address this fundamental issue without first confronting the observational equivalence problem. Until we tackle this formidable empirical challenge, we cannot use data to distinguish perceptions from misperceptions about fiscal inflation.

This chapter leaves many important topics unexplored. For analytical clarity, we consider only endowment economies with flexible prices. Kim (2003), Woodford (1998b), Cochrane (2011a), and Sims (2011) study the fiscal theory in sticky-price models. We also do not explore the differences among debt devaluations arising from price-level changes, outright default, and debt dilution—all issues that are particularly timely now. Untouched by our chapter are the game-theoretic aspects of monetary-fiscal interactions that Dixit and Lambertini (2001, 2003a, 2003b) and Bassetto (2002) study.

7.2   Simple Model of Monetary-Fiscal Interactions

We present a simple analytical model of price-level and inflation determination that is designed to illustrate the role that the interactions between monetary and fiscal policies play in the inflation process. Throughout the analysis we restrict attention to rational expectations equilibria, so the results can be readily contrasted to prevailing views, which also are based on rational expectations.

The model draws from Leeper (1991), Sims (1994), and Woodford (2001) to lay the groundwork for how monetary and fiscal policies *jointly* determine equilibrium. These results are well known, but the broader implications of thinking about macro policies jointly are not fully appreciated.

An infinitely lived representative household is endowed each period with a constant quantity of nonstorable goods, y. To keep the focus away from seigniorage considerations, we initially examine a cashless economy, which can be obtained by making the role of fiat currency infinitesimally small. (The next section brings money back into the picture.) Government issues nominal one-period bonds, allowing us to define the price level, P, as the rate at which bonds exchange for goods.

The household chooses sequences of consumption and bonds, $\{c_t, B_t\}$, to maximize

$$(1) \qquad E_0 \sum_{t=0}^{\infty} \beta^t u(c_t), \quad 0 < \beta < 1,$$

subject to the budget constraint

$$(2) \qquad c_t + \frac{B_t}{P_t} + \tau_t = y + z_t + \frac{R_{t-1} B_{t-1}}{P_t},$$

taking prices and $R_{-1} B_{-1} > 0$ as given. The household pays taxes, τ_t, and receives transfers, z_t, each period, both of which are lump sum.

Government spending is zero each period, so the government chooses sequences of taxes, transfers, and debt to satisfy its flow constraint

$$(3) \qquad \frac{B_t}{P_t} + \tau_t = z_t + \frac{R_{t-1} B_{t-1}}{P_t},$$

given $R_{-1} B_{-1} > 0$, while the monetary authority chooses a sequence for the nominal interest rate.

After imposing goods market clearing, $c_t = y$ for $t \geq 0$, the household's consumption Euler equation reduces to the simple Fisher relation

$$(4) \qquad \frac{1}{R_t} = \beta E_t \left(\frac{P_t}{P_{t+1}} \right).$$

The exogenous (fixed) gross real interest rate, $1/\beta$, makes the analysis easier but is not without some lose of generality, as Davig, Leeper, and Walker (2010) show in the context of fiscal financing in a model with nominal rigidities. This is less the case in a small open economy, so one interpretation of this model is that it is a small open economy in which government debt is denominated in terms of the home nominal bonds ("currency") and all debt is held by domestic agents.

The focus on price-level determination is entirely for analytical convenience; it is not a statement that inflation is the only thing that macro policy authorities do or should care about. Because price-level determination is the first step toward understanding how macro policies affect the aggregate economy, the key insights derived from this model extend to more complex environments.

Price-level determination depends on monetary-fiscal policy behavior. At a general level, macroeconomic policies have two tasks to perform: control inflation and stabilize government debt. Monetary and fiscal policy are perfectly symmetric with regard to the two tasks and two different policy mixes can accomplish the tasks. The conventional assignment of tasks (Regime M) instructs monetary policy to target inflation and fiscal policy to target real debt (or the debt-GDP ratio). But an alternative assignment (Regime F) also works: monetary policy is tasked with maintaining the value of debt and fiscal policy is assigned to control inflation. We now describe these two regimes in detail.

7.2.1   Regime M: Active Monetary/Passive Tax Policy

This policy regime reproduces well-known results about how inflation is determined in the canonical model of monetary policy, as presented in textbooks by Woodford (2003) and Galí (2008), for example. This regime— denoted active monetary and passive fiscal policy—combines an interest rate rule in which the central bank aggressively adjusts the nominal rate in response to current inflation with a tax rule in which the tax authority adjusts taxes in response to government debt sufficiently to stabilize debt.[4] In this textbook world, monetary policy can consistently hit its inflation target and fiscal policy can achieve its target for the real value of debt.

To derive the equilibrium price level for the model laid out previously, we need to specify rules for monetary, tax, and transfers policies. Monetary policy follows a conventional interest rate rule, which for analytical convenience, is written somewhat unconventionally in terms of the inverse of the nominal interest and inflation rates

$$(5) \qquad R_t^{-1} = R^{*-1} + \alpha\left(\frac{P_{t-1}}{P_t} - \frac{1}{\pi^*}\right), \quad \alpha > \frac{1}{\beta},$$

where π^* is the inflation target and $R^* = \pi^*/\beta$ is the steady state nominal interest rate. The condition on the policy parameter α ensures that monetary policy is sufficiently hawkish in response to fluctuations in inflation that it can stabilize inflation around π^*.

Fiscal policy adjusts taxes in response to the state of government debt

$$(6) \qquad \tau_t = \tau^* + \gamma\left(\frac{B_{t-1}}{P_{t-1}} - b^*\right), \quad \gamma > r = \frac{1}{\beta} - 1$$

---

4. Applying Leeper's (1991) definitions, "active" monetary policy targets inflation, while "passive" monetary policy weakly adjusts the nominal interest rate in response to inflation; "active" tax policy sets taxes independently of government debt and "passive" tax policy changes rates strongly enough when debt rises to stabilize the debt-GDP ratio (or fiscal policy could be associated with setting transfers instead of taxes).

where b^* is the real debt (or debt-GDP) target, τ^* is the steady state level of taxes, and $r = 1/\beta - 1$ is the net real interest rate. Imposing that γ exceeds the net real interest rate guarantees that any increase in government debt creates an expectation that future taxes will rise by enough to both service the higher debt and retire it back to b^*.

Government transfers evolve exogenously according to the stochastic process

$$(7) \qquad z_t = (1 - \rho)z^* + \rho z_{t-1} + \varepsilon_t, \quad 0 < \rho < 1,$$

where z^* is steady-state transfers and ε_t is a serially uncorrelated shock with $E_t \varepsilon_{t+1} = 0$.

Equilibrium inflation is obtained by combining (4) and (5) to yield the difference equation

$$(8) \qquad \frac{\beta}{\alpha} E_t \left(\frac{P_t}{P_{t+1}} - \frac{1}{\pi^*} \right) = \frac{P_{t-1}}{P_t} - \frac{1}{\pi^*}.$$

Aggressive reactions of monetary policy to inflation imply that $\beta/\alpha < 1$ and the unique bounded solution for inflation is

$$(9) \qquad \pi_t = \pi^*,$$

so equilibrium inflation is always on target, as is expected inflation.[5]

If monetary policy determines inflation, how must fiscal policy respond to disturbances in transfers to ensure that policy is sustainable? This is where passive tax adjustments step in. Substituting the tax rule, (6), into the government's budget constraint, (3), taking expectations conditional on information at $t - 1$, and employing the Fisher relation, (4), yields the expected evolution of real debt

$$(10) \qquad E_{t-1}\left(\frac{B_t}{P_t} - b^* \right) = E_{t-1}(z_t - z^*) + (\beta^{-1} - \gamma)\left(\frac{B_{t-1}}{P_{t-1}} - b^* \right).$$

Because $\beta^{-1} - \gamma < 1$, debt that is above target brings forth the expectation of higher taxes, so (10) describes how debt is expected to return to steady state following a shock to z_t. In a steady state in which $\varepsilon_t \equiv 0$, debt is $b^* = (\tau^* - z^*)/(\beta^{-1} - 1)$, equal to the present value of primary surpluses.

---

5. As Sims (1999) and Cochrane (2011a) emphasize, echoing Obstfeld and Rogoff (1983), there is a continuum of *explosive* solutions to (8), each one associated with the central bank threatening to drive inflation to infinity if the private sector's expectations are not anchored on π^*. Cochrane uses this logic to argue that fundamentally, only fiscal policy can uniquely determine inflation and the price level. Sims argues, in a monetary model that supports a barter equilibrium, that only a fiscal commitment to a floor value of real money balances can deliver a unique equilibrium. Determinacy comes from the fiscal authority committing to switch from a passive stance if the price level gets too high to adopt a policy that redeems government liabilities at a fixed floor real value. If the fiscal commitment is believed, in equilibrium, this fiscal "backstop" will never need to be used and only stable price-level paths will be realized. Both Cochrane and Sims argue that there is nothing monetary policy alone can do to eliminate the explosive price-level paths. Although there is a unique bounded *inflation* process, this regime does not pin down the *price-level* process.

Another perspective on the fiscal financing requirements when monetary policy is targeting inflation emerges from a ubiquitous equilibrium condition. In any dynamic model with rational agents, government debt derives its value from its anticipated backing. In this model, that anticipated backing comes from tax revenues net of transfer payments, $\tau_t - z_t$. The value of government debt can be obtained by imposing equilibrium on the government's flow constraint, taking conditional expectations, and "solving forward" to arrive at

$$(11) \qquad \frac{B_t}{P_t} = E_t \sum_{j=1}^{\infty} \beta^j (\tau_{t+j} - z_{t+j}).$$

This intertemporal equilibrium condition provides a new perspective on passive tax policy. Because P_t is nailed down by monetary policy and $\{z_{t+j}\}_{j=1}^{\infty}$ is being set independently of both monetary and tax policies, any increase in transfers at t, which is financed by new sales of nominal B_t, *must* generate an expectation that taxes will rise in the future by exactly enough to support the higher value of real B_t/P_t.

In this model, the only potential source of an expansion in debt is disturbances to transfers. But passive tax policy implies that this pattern of fiscal adjustment must occur regardless of the reason that B_t increases: economic downturns that automatically reduce taxes and raise transfers, changes in household portfolio behavior, changes in government spending, or central bank open-market operations. To expand on the last example, we could modify this model to include money to allow us to imagine that the central bank decides to tighten monetary policy exogenously at t by conducting an open-market sale of bonds. If monetary policy is active, then the monetary contraction both raises B_t (bonds held by households) and it lowers P_t; real debt rises from both effects. This can be an equilibrium *only if* fiscal policy is expected to support it by passively raising future real tax revenues. That is, given active monetary policy, (11) imposes restrictions on the class of tax policies that is consistent with equilibrium; those policies are labeled "passive" because the tax authority has limited discretion in choosing policy. Refusal by tax policy to adjust appropriately undermines the ability of open-market operations to affect inflation in the conventional manner, just as Wallace (1981) illustrates.

A policy regime in which monetary policy is active and tax policy is passive produces the conventional outcome that inflation is always and everywhere a monetary phenomenon and a hawkish central bank can successfully anchor actual and expected inflation at the inflation target. Tax policy must support the active monetary behavior by passively adjusting taxes to finance disturbances to government debt—from whatever source, including monetary policy—and ensure policy is sustainable.

Although conventional, this regime is not the only mechanism by which monetary and fiscal policy can jointly deliver a unique bounded equilibrium. We turn now to the other polar case.

7.2.2   Regime F: Passive Monetary/Active Tax Policy

Passive tax behavior is a stringent requirement: the tax authority must be willing and able to raise taxes in the face of rising government debt. For a variety of reasons, this does not always happen, and it certainly does not happen in the automated way prescribed by the tax rule in (6). Political factors may prevent taxes from rising as needed to stabilize debt, as in the United States today.[6] Some countries simply do not have the fiscal infrastructure in place to generate the necessary tax revenues. Others might be at or near the peak of their Laffer curves, suggesting they are close to the fiscal limit.[7] In this case, tax policy is active and $0 \leq \gamma < 1/\beta - 1$.

Analogously, there are also periods when the concerns of monetary policy move away from inflation stabilization and toward other matters, such as output stabilization or financial crises. These are periods in which monetary policy is no longer active, instead adjusting the nominal interest rate only weakly in response to inflation. Woodford (2001) cites the Federal Reserve's bond-price pegging policy during and immediately after World War II as an example of passive monetary policy. Bordo and Hautcoeur (2007) point out that the Banque de France pegged nominal bond prices in the 1920s at the same time that political gridlock prevented the fiscal adjustments necessary to stabilize debt. Inflation rose and the franc depreciated during this mix of passive monetary and active fiscal policies. The recent global recession and financial crisis is a striking case where central banks' concerns shifted away from inflation. In some countries the policy rate was reduced to its zero lower bound. Then monetary policy is passive and, in terms of policy rule (5), $0 \leq \alpha < 1/\beta$.

We focus on a particular policy mix that yields clean economic interpretations: the nominal interest rate is set independently of inflation, $\alpha = 0$ and $R_t^1 = R^{*-1} \geq 1$, and taxes are set independently of debt, $\gamma = 0$ and $\tau_t = \tau^* > 0$. These policy specifications might seem extreme and special, but the qualitative points that emerge generalize to other specifications of passive monetary/active tax policies.

One result pops out immediately. Applying the pegged nominal interest rate policy to the Fisher relation, (4), yields

$$(12) \qquad E_t\left(\frac{P_t}{P_{t+1}}\right) = \frac{1}{\beta R^*} = \frac{1}{\pi^*}$$

---

6. Davig and Leeper (2006, 2011) generalize (6) to estimate Markov switching rules for the United States and find that tax policy has switched between periods when taxes rise with debt and periods when they do not.

7. Trabandt and Uhlig (2011) characterize Laffer curves for capital and labor taxes in 14 EU countries and the United States to find that some countries—Denmark and Sweden—are on the wrong side of the curve, suggesting that those countries must lower tax rates to raise revenues.

so expected inflation is anchored on the inflation target, an outcome that is perfectly consistent with one aim of inflation-targeting central banks. It turns out, however, that another aim of inflation targeters—stabilization of actual inflation—that can be achieved by active monetary/passive fiscal policy, is no longer attainable.

Impose the active tax rule on the intertemporal equilibrium condition, (11),

$$(13) \qquad \frac{B_t}{P_t} = \left(\frac{\beta}{1-\beta}\right)\tau^* - E_t\sum_{j=1}^{\infty}\beta^j z_{t+j},$$

and use the government's flow constraint, (3), to solve for the price level

$$(14) \qquad P_t = \frac{R^* B_{t-1}}{[1/(1-\beta)]\tau^* - E_t\sum_{j=0}^{\infty}\beta^j z_{t+j}}.$$

At time t, the numerator of this expression is predetermined, representing the nominal value of household wealth carried into period t. The denominator is the expected present value of primary fiscal surpluses from date t on, which is exogenous. So long as $R^*B_{t-1} > 0$ and the present value of revenues exceeds the present value of transfers, a condition that must hold if government debt has positive value, expression (14) delivers a unique $P_t > 0$. In contrast to the active monetary/passive fiscal regime, this policy mix uniquely determines both inflation and the price level.

We have done nothing mystical here, despite what some critics claim (for example, Buiter 2002, or McCallum 2001). In particular, the government is not assumed to behave in a manner that violates its budget constraint. Unlike competitive households, the government is not required to choose sequences of control variables that are consistent with its budget constraint for all possible price sequences. Indeed, for a central bank to target inflation, it *cannot* be choosing its policy instrument to be consistent with any sequence of the price level; doing so would produce an indeterminate equilibrium. Identical reasoning applies to the fiscal authority: the value of a dollar of debt $(1/P_t)$ depends on expectations about fiscal decisions in the future; expectations, in turn, are determined by the tax rule the fiscal authority announces. The fiscal authority credibly commits to its tax rule and, given the process for transfers, this determines the backing of government debt and, therefore, its market value.

Using the solution for the price level in (14) to compute expected inflation, it is straightforward to show that $\beta E_t(P_t/P_{t+1}) = 1/R^*$, as required by the Fisher relation and monetary policy behavior.[8] This observation leads to a

---

8. To see this, compute

$$E_{t-1}\frac{1}{P_t} = \frac{[1/(1-\beta)]\tau^* - E_{t-1}\sum_{j=0}^{\infty}\beta^j z_{t+j}}{R^* B_{t-1}}.$$

To find expected inflation, simply use the date $t-1$ version of (14) for P_{t-1} and simplify to obtain $\beta E_{t-1}(P_{t-1}/P_t) = 1/R_{t-1} = 1/R^*$.

sharp dichotomy between the roles of monetary and fiscal policy in price-level determination: monetary policy alone appears to determine *expected* inflation by choosing the level at which to peg the nominal interest rate, R^*, while conditional on that choice, fiscal variables appear to determine *realized* inflation. Monetary policy's ability to target expected inflation holds in this simple model with a fixed policy regime; as we show in section 7.3, when regime change is possible, monetary policy may not be able to control even expected inflation.

To understand the nature of this equilibrium, we need to delve into the underlying economic behavior. This is an environment in which changes in debt do *not* elicit any changes in expected taxes, unlike in section 7.2.1. First consider a one-off increase in current transfer payments, z_t, financed by new nominal debt issuance, B_t. With no offsetting increase in current or expected tax obligations, at initial prices households feel wealthier and they try to shift up their consumption paths. Higher demand for goods drives up the price level and continues to do so until the wealth effect dissipates and households are content with their initial consumption plan. This is why in expression (13) the value of debt at t changes with expected, but not current, transfers. Now imagine that at time t households receive news of higher transfers in the future. In the first instance, there is no change in nominal debt at t, but there is still an increase in household wealth. Through the same mechanism, P_t must rise to revalue current debt to be consistent with the new expected path of transfers: the value of debt falls in line with the lower expected present value of surpluses.

Cochrane (2009, 5) offers another interpretation of the equilibrium in which "'aggregate demand' is really just the mirror image of demand for government debt." An expectation that transfers will rise in the future reduces the household's assessment of the value of government debt. Households can shed debt only by converting it into demand for consumption goods, hence the increase in aggregate demand that translates into a higher price level.

Expression (14) highlights that in this policy regime the impacts of monetary policy change dramatically. When the central bank chooses a higher rate at which to peg the nominal interest rate, the effect is to *raise* the inflation rate next period. This echoes Sargent and Wallace (1981), but the economic mechanism is different. In the current policy mix, a higher nominal interest rate raises the interest payments the household receives on the government bonds it holds. Higher $R^* B_{t-1}$, with no higher anticipated taxes, raises household nominal wealth at the beginning of t, triggering the same adjustments as before. In this sense, as in Sargent and Wallace, monetary policy has lost control of inflation.

This section has reviewed existing results on price-level determination under alternative monetary-fiscal policy regimes. In each regime a bounded inflation rate is uniquely determined, but the impacts of changes in policy differ markedly across the two regimes. We now turn to elaborate on a key difference between the fiscal theory and unpleasant arithmetic.

7.2.3   Why the Fiscal Theory Is Not Unpleasant Arithmetic

It is not uncommon for policymakers to equate fiscal inflations to the mechanism that Sargent and Wallace (1981) highlighted and then to dismiss its relevance. As King (1995, 171–72) wrote about unpleasant arithmetic:

> I have never found this proposition very convincing. . . . [A]s an empirical matter, the proposition is of little current relevance to the major industrial countries. This is for two reasons. First, seigniorage—financing the deficit by issuing currency rather than bonds—is very small relative to other sources of revenues. Second, over the past decade or so, governments have become increasingly committed to price stability. . . . This sea change in the conventional wisdom about price stability leaves no room for inflation to bail out fiscal policy.

Later in the same commentary, King (173) acknowledges that "periodic episodes of *unexpected* inflation . . . have reduced debt-to-GDP ratios." This observation is consistent with the fiscal theory, though King does not attribute the inflation to fiscal news.

A fiscal theory equilibrium can be consistent with *any* average rate of inflation and money creation. This point emerges clearly in Leeper's (1991) local analysis around a given deterministic steady state: on average, inflation could be zero, yet monetary and fiscal shocks generate all the results shown in section 7.2.2. In the previous model, the unconditional mean of inflation is π^*, the inflation target, and in a monetary version of the model, π^* is determined by average money growth (or seigniorage revenues).

A key difference between the fiscal theory and unpleasant arithmetic is that the former operates only in an economy with nominal government debt, whereas the latter is typically discussed under the assumption of real debt. Without a fully fleshed-out model, the distinction between nominal and real debt can be understood by examining the corresponding intertemporal equilibrium conditions—the analogs to (13). We add fiat currency to make a point about the role of seigniorage revenues. For nominal debt the equilibrium condition is

$$(15) \qquad B_{t-1} = P_t \sum_{j=0}^{\infty} \beta^j E_t \left[\tau_{t+j} - z_{t+j} + \frac{M_{t+j} - M_{t+j-1}}{P_{t+j}} \right],$$

while for real debt, v_t, it is

$$(16) \qquad v_{t-1} = \sum_{j=0}^{\infty} \beta^j E_t \left[\tau_{t+j} - z_{t+j} + \frac{M_{t+j} - M_{t+j-1}}{P_{t+j}} \right].$$

Both conditions involve the expected present value of primary surpluses plus seigniorage. The fiscal theory is about how changes in this expected present value lead to changes in P_t. Unpleasant arithmetic is about how increases in v_{t-1} induce increases in expected future seigniorage, $(M_{t+j} - M_{t+j-1})/P_t$.

To understand the differences, consider a hypothetical increase in P_t, holding all else fixed. In (15), higher P_t raises the nominal backing to debt, so it implies higher cash flows in the form of nominal primary surpluses: more nominal debt can be supported with no change in real surpluses or seigniorage. In (16), higher P_t lowers the real backing to debt because it reduces seigniorage revenues and *real* cash flows.

This makes clear why the fiscal theory is *not* about seigniorage: even if real balances are arbitrarily small or the economy is on the wrong side of the seigniorage Laffer curve, under the fiscal theory, higher P_t increases the backing of debt by raising the nominal cash flows associated with primary surpluses. In this case, as (16) shows, higher P_t does nothing to affect the backing of real debt.

7.2.4   Regime F: Two-Period Government Debt

Restricting attention to one-period debt makes it seem that fiscal news must generate jumps in the current price level. This need not happen. To get a richer sense of inflation dynamics in the passive monetary/active fiscal regime, suppose that the government issues nominal bonds with a maximum maturity of two periods. Let $B_t(j)$ denote the face value of zero-coupon nominal bonds outstanding at the end of period t, which mature in period j, and let $Q_t(j)$ be the corresponding nominal price for those bonds. At the beginning of period t, the nominal returns, $R_t(t+1)$ and $R_t(t+2)$, are known with certainty and are risk free. Clearly, $R_t(t+1)^{-1} = Q_t(t+1)$, $R_t(t+2)^{-1} = Q_t(t+2)$, $Q_t(t) = 1$, and $B_t(j) = 0$ for $j \leq t$. To economize on notation, we assume that each period the government retires outstanding debt and issues new one- and two-period bonds.

The government's flow budget constraint is

$$(17) \quad \frac{Q_t(t+1)B_t(t+1)}{P_t} + \frac{Q_t(t+2)B_t(t+2)}{P_t} + x_t = \frac{B_{t-1}(t)}{P_t} + \frac{Q_t(t+1)B_{t-1}(t+1)}{P_t},$$

where x_t is the primary surplus inclusive of seigniorage revenues, defined as

$$(18) \quad x_t \equiv \tau_t - z_t + \frac{M_t - M_{t-1}}{P_t},$$

where M_t is the nominal quantity of fiat money outstanding.

We bring money in by positing a simple, interest inelastic, demand for money[9]

$$(19) \quad \frac{M_t}{P_t} = f(c_t)$$

that, in equilibrium, implies that real money balances are constant

---

9. This specification may be obtained from a cash-in-advance model or from money-in-utility/transactions-cost models in which the interest elasticity is driven to the zero limit.

(20)
$$\frac{M_t}{P_t} = k.$$

In a frictionless economy with a constant real interest rate, the household's Euler equation delivers the one- and two-period nominal bond prices

(21)
$$Q_t(t+1) = \beta E_t \left(\frac{P_t}{P_{t+1}} \right)$$

(22)
$$Q_t(t+2) = \beta E_t Q_{t+1}(1+2) \left(\frac{P_t}{P_{t+1}} \right).$$

Using (21) in (22) yields

(23)
$$Q_t(t+2) = \beta^2 E_t \left(\frac{P_t}{P_{t+2}} \right).$$

Take expectations of the government budget constraint, impose the asset-pricing relations and the transversality condition, which requires the expected present value of the market value of debt to be zero, to obtain the intertemporal equilibrium condition

(24)
$$\frac{Q_t(t+1)B_t(t+1) + Q_t(t+2)B_t(t+2)}{P_t} = \sum_{i=1}^{\infty} \beta^i E_t x_{t+i}.$$

Combining (24) with the government's flow constraint, (17), yields

(25)
$$\frac{B_{t-1}(t) + Q_t(t+1)B_{t-1}(t+1)}{P_t} = \sum_{i=0}^{\infty} \beta^i E_t x_{t+i}.$$

The left side of (25) is the market value of debt outstanding at the beginning of period t. Two terms in this value—the face value of outstanding nominal bonds $B_{t-1}(t)$ and $B_{t-1}(t+1)$—are carried into period t from period $t-1$, so they are predetermined at t. But two other terms—the price of two-period bonds issued at $t-1$ and sold at t, $Q_t(t+1)$, and the price level, P_t—are determined at period t and respond to shocks and news that arrive at t.

Using equilibrium relationship (21) in (25) makes clear the trade-offs that monetary policy faces when primary surpluses are fixed

(26)
$$\frac{B_{t-1}(t)}{P_t} + \beta B_{t-1}(t+1)E_t \frac{1}{P_{t+1}} = \sum_{i=0}^{\infty} \beta^i E_t x_{t+i}.$$

Monetary policy faces two limiting cases. It can lean strongly against current inflation to fix P_t, but then it must permit future inflation, $E_t(1/P_{t+1})$; to adjust. Alternatively, it can stabilize expected inflation at $t+1$, but then it must allow P_t to adjust. The trade-off between current and future inflation depends on the ratio $B_{t-1}(t+1)/B_{t-1}(t)$, the ratio between the outstanding quantities of two-period to one-period bonds, a role for the maturity structure of government debt that Cochrane (2001) emphasizes. As debt becomes of increasingly short maturity, this ratio falls and a larger change in expected inflation is required to compensate for a given change in current inflation.

Fiscal Expansions and Inflation

We employ the two equilibrium conditions, (20) and (26), to derive the implications for inflation of alternative policy environments. Monetary policy controls the one-period nominal bond price, $Q_t(t+1)$, which is equivalent to controlling the short-term nominal interest rate, $R_t = 1/Q_t(t+1)$.

For this exposition, we make the simplifying assumption that the primary surplus, $\{\tau_t - z_t\}$, is exogenous or at least independent of the price level and the value of outstanding government debt. This may seem like an extreme and implausible assumption in light of Hall and Sargent's (2011) accounting that since World War II, adjustments in primary surpluses have been an important determinant of US debt-GDP dynamics. Of course, Hall and Sargent's is an accounting exercise that does not aim to establish that fluctuations in government debt *caused* subsequent surplus adjustments that were designed to stabilize debt.[10] But even if we make the bold assumption of causality, Hall and Sargent do not find that surpluses *always* adjust to rationalize the value of debt. Other evidence, whose causal interpretation is also in question, suggests that US fiscal policy has fluctuated between regimes in which policies systematically raise future surpluses in response to high debt and regimes in which surpluses evolve largely independently of debt (Davig and Leeper 2006).

The fiscal stress that advanced economies face is extreme relative to experiences of those economies since World War II. Given the political economy forces at play, simple extrapolations of past policy behavior into coming decades are tenuous at best. Assuming that fiscal policy will go through periods in which surpluses are set independently of debt or that private decision makers *believe* such periods are possible—even likely—is a reasonable working assumption. Exogenous surpluses are a tractable way to examine the qualitative nature of equilibria in which debt is not systematically stabilized by primary surpluses.

We take the primary fiscal surplus sequence, $\{\tau_t - z_t\}$, as exogenous and imagine that information arrives at t that causes agents to revise downward their views about current or expected surpluses.

The first term on the right side of (26) may be written as $x_t = \tau_t + s_t - z_t$. In equilibrium—imposing equilibrium condition (20)—seigniorage is

$$(27) \qquad s_t = \frac{M_t - M_{t-1}}{P_t} = k - \frac{M_{t-1}}{P_t}.$$

---

10. Bohn (1998) is often cited as evidence that establishes this causality, but his methods cannot distinguish between estimates of a behavioral relation for fiscal policy and an equilibrium relation between surpluses and debt (Li 2011).

Then the second equilibrium condition, (26), becomes

$$(28) \qquad \frac{B_{t-1}(t) + M_{t-1}}{P_t} + \beta B_{t-1}(t+1)E_t \frac{1}{P_{t+1}} = k + \tau_t - z_t + \sum_{i=1}^{\infty} \beta^i E_t x_{t+i}.$$

For a given debt maturity structure, summarized by the ratio $B_t(t+2)/B_t$ $(t+1)$, monetary policy behavior determines the mix of current and expected inflation that arises from lower current or anticipated surpluses.

Current Inflation. Suppose initially that the central bank pegs the short-bond price at $Q_t(t+1) = Q^*$ for all t, effectively pegging expected inflation through the Euler equation, (21). Then (28) becomes

$$(29) \qquad \frac{W_{t-1}}{P_t} = \widehat{\mathrm{EPV}}_t(x),$$

where $W_{t-1} \equiv B_{t-1}(t) + M_{t-1} + Q^* B_{t-1}(t+1)$ and $\widehat{\mathrm{EPV}}_t(x) \equiv k + \tau_t - z_t + \sum_{i=1}^{\infty} \beta^i E_t x_{t+i}$. By pegging the bond price, the central bank forces the full adjustment to news about lower surpluses to occur through increases in the current price level, which revalue the outstanding nominal government liabilities. For an incremental change in surpluses, $d\widehat{\mathrm{EPV}}_t(x)$, the change in the price level is

$$(30) \qquad dP_t = -\frac{W_{t-1}}{[\widehat{\mathrm{EPV}}_t(x)]^2} d\widehat{\mathrm{EPV}}_t(x),$$

so the rise in the price level is increasing in total nominal government liabilities outstanding and decreasing in the initial market value of those liabilities.

A higher price level raises nominal money demand. To maintain the pegged bond price at Q^*, the central bank must expand the nominal money stock by $dM_t = kdP_t$, which ensures that the money market clears at t. It does this by buying outstanding bonds with newly issued M_t. With Q^* pegged, this open-market purchase can occur in either one- or two-period bonds, to the same effect. As ever, characterizing monetary policy as controlling the nominal interest rate entails a supporting open-market policy.

Expressed in proportional changes, the equilibrium is

$$(31) \qquad \frac{dP_t}{P_t} = \frac{dM_t}{M_t} = -\frac{d\widehat{\mathrm{EPV}}_t(x)}{\widehat{\mathrm{EPV}}_t(x)}.$$

The supporting open-market policy is not the textbook case of $\Delta M_t = -\Delta B_t$, in which new money is swapped for bonds, dollar-for-dollar. Instead, given the new equilibrium price level from (30) and the associated new equilibrium level of money balances, $dM_t = kdP_t$, the new level of nominal bonds outstanding must be consistent with the government's flow budget constraint. Denote the face value of government bonds outstanding at t by $\mathcal{B}_t \equiv B_t(t+1) + Q^* B_t(t+2)$. In equilibrium, the change in $\mathcal{B}_t$ consistent with the government's budget constraint and the equilibrium in (31) may be expressed as

(32)
$$\frac{dB_t}{B_t} = \left(\frac{k + \tau_t - z_t}{Q^*(B_t/P_t)}\right)\frac{d\widehat{\mathrm{EPV}}_t(x)}{\widehat{\mathrm{EPV}}_t(x)}.$$

News at t that primary surpluses will be lower in the future raises P_t. To maintain equilibrium in the money market and allow the short-term bond price to be pegged at Q^*, the central bank passively expands M_t in proportion to the rise in prices. In general, this is not the end of the policy adjustments because the higher price level that arises from news about *future* surpluses leaves the government's budget out of balance by revaluing outstanding debt obligations. As (32) makes clear, in equilibrium the face value of government bonds may rise or fall—more or fewer bonds will be in the hands of the public in period t—as a consequence of the news of lower future surpluses. If the current (modified) primary surplus $(k + \tau_t - z_t)$ is positive, the face value of bonds declines; if it is negative, the face value rises.

The empirical implications of this equilibrium underscore the difficulties associated with drawing causal inferences from the patterns of correlation that a fiscal inflation produces. To summarize, news of lower future surpluses creates the following correlations:

- Negative correlation between inflation and market value of initial government liabilities, W_{t-1}/P_t
- Positive correlation between inflation and money growth
- *Any* correlation between nominal debt growth and inflation (or money growth)
- Higher inflation and money growth predicts *future* fiscal deficits, contradicting the Granger-causality results of King and Plosser (1985)

Evidently, monetary policy behavior—the pegging of short bond prices—plays a central role in this equilibrium. But that role is not the traditional one of monetizing debt and there will be no evidence in time series data that inflation is being produced by high current budget deficits or open-market purchases of government bonds, although there will be strong evidence that inflation is proportional to money growth.

Future Inflation. By pegging the short-term nominal rate in *every* period, the central bank also pegs the long-term (two-period) interest rate. This forces all adjustments to fiscal news into the current price level and leaves expected price levels unchanged. A different monetary policy can force all adjustments into future prices, leaving the current price level unchanged. Rewrite equilibrium condition (28) as

(33)
$$\frac{B_{t-1}(t) + M_{t-1}}{P_t} + \beta[B_{t-1}(t+1) + M_t]E_t\frac{1}{P_{t+1}} = \widehat{EPV}_t(x),$$

where $\widehat{EPV}_t(x) \equiv (1+\beta)k + \tau_t - z_t + \tau_{t+1} - z_{t+1} + \sum_{i=2}^{\infty}\beta iE_t x_{t+1}.$[11]

---

11. To obtain (33) we used $\beta E_t s_{t+1} = E_t[(M_{t+1} - M_t)/P_{t+1}] = \beta[k - M_t E_t(1/P_{t+1})].$

We seek an equilibrium in which $dP_t = 0$, implying that $dM_t = 0$ also. In such an equilibrium, news that revises down the expected present value, $\widehat{EPV}_t$ (x), affects expected inflation according to

(34)
$$d\left(E_t \frac{P_t}{P_{t+1}} \right) = \frac{1}{\beta[(B_{t-1}(t+1) + M_t)/P_t]} d\widehat{EPV}_t(x).$$

Lower expected primary surpluses produce higher expected inflation.

The central bank implements the equilibrium in which lower expected surpluses raise future, but not current, prices by adjusting the one-period nominal interest rate appropriately. First write the equilibrium change in expected prices in (34) in terms of $E_t(P_t/P_{t+1})$ and note that the Euler equation implies that $Q_t(t+1) = \beta E_t(P_t/P_{t+1})$. Monetary policy pushes into the future the inflationary consequences of anticipated fiscal expansions by setting policy as

(35)
$$dQ_t(t+1) = \frac{1}{[B_{t-1}(t+1) + M_t]/P_t} d\widehat{EPV}_t(x).$$

If the expected present value of surpluses falls, the central bank reduces the price of one-period bonds, raising the one-period nominal interest rate. That is, monetary policy leans against expected fiscal expansion.

At $t + 1$, when the higher price level is realized, M_{t+1} must rise proportionately. The equilibrium displays patterns of correlation analogous to those above and conventional empirical approaches to fiscal policy and inflation will have a difficult time finding evidence that fiscal expansions are inflationary. Inflation occurs at $t + 1$, but surpluses can change at any $t + k$, $k \geq 0$, so there is no simple Granger-causal ordering between inflation and fiscal variables. Data will contain overwhelming support, however, for positive money growth/inflation correlation.

7.2.5   Regime F: Long-Term Government Debt

Inflation dynamics become still richer when we posit that the government issues only consols, a perpetuity that never matures.[12] The government's flow budget constraint is

(36)
$$\frac{Q_t B_t}{P_t} + x_t = \frac{(1 + Q_t)B_{t-1}}{P_t}.$$

We also have the Euler equation for consols

(37)
$$Q_t = \beta E_t \frac{P_t}{P_{t+1}}(1 + Q_{t+1}).$$

Again, the economy has a constant endowment.

Iterate on the flow constraint, (36), impose (37) and the transversality

---

12. This exposition draws on Cochrane (2001, 2011c).

condition, and combine the result with the flow budget constraint to yield the intertemporal equilibrium condition

$$(38) \qquad \frac{(1+Q_t)B_{t-1}}{P_t} = \sum_{j=0}^{\infty} \beta^j E_t x_{t+j} = \mathrm{EPV}_t(x).$$

The intertemporal equilibrium condition implies a convenient expression linking, *in equilibrium,* the bond price, the current price level, and the expected present value of surpluses

$$(39) \qquad \frac{d(1+Q_t)}{1+Q_t} - \frac{dP_t}{P_t} = \frac{d\mathrm{EPV}_t(x)}{\mathrm{EPV}_t(x)}.$$

From (37), the price of the consol can be expressed in terms of the entire expected future path of inflation rates

$$(40) \qquad Q_t = \sum_{j=1}^{\infty} \beta^j E_t \frac{P_t}{P_{t-j}}$$

$$(41) \qquad = \sum_{j=0}^{\infty} E_t \left(\prod_{i=0}^{j} \frac{1}{R_{t+j}} \right),$$

where R_t is the one-period nominal interest rate controlled by the central bank. The associated short-term nominal bond is priced as $1/R_t = \beta E_t(P_t/P_{t+1})$.

Using (39), (40), and (41), a given percentage decrease in the expected present value of surpluses can be apportioned into any mix of current and expected inflation rates consistent with (38) and (40). Substituting (40) into (38) and denoting the inflation rate as $\pi_t \equiv P_t/P_{t-1}$ reveals that the expected present value of surpluses determines "total inflation," defined as the expected present value of inflation rates

$$(42) \qquad \frac{B_{t-1}}{P_{t-1}} \sum_{j=0}^{\infty} \beta^j E_t \left(\frac{1}{\prod_{k=0}^{j} \pi_{t+k}} \right) = \mathrm{EPV}_t(x).$$

Monetary policy behavior determines the precise pattern of expected inflation rates through its setting of current and expected short-term nominal interest rates.[13]

Consols, though not a realistic maturity structure for government bonds, help to make clear the range of possible inflation processes that a fiscal theory equilibrium can produce. First, inflation effects are larger when they are concentrated in only a few periods and smaller when they are spread over many periods. Second, because only the present value of inflation is pinned down by (38) and (40), news of lower future surpluses can generate *any* path of expected inflation: it can rise or fall in various periods, so long as the pres-

---

13. Because in this policy regime the equilibrium price level is uniquely determined by (38), together with equilibrium $\{Q_t\}$, monetary policy may be treated as setting the sequence of short rates, $\{R_t\}$, exogenously in any pattern desired, without fear of generating indeterminacy of equilibrium.

ent value of expected inflation adjusts to satisfy (42). Third, because many paths of the surplus are consistent with a given expected present value, the expected surplus can also rise or fall over various horizons, as long as they deliver the expected present value.

7.3   How Fiscal Policy Can Undermine Monetary Control of Inflation

This section examines situations in which fiscal policy can undermine monetary control of inflation. We provide three scenarios in which monetary policy may not be able to target inflation. These scenarios are by no means exhaustive, but serve to illustrate the extent to which monetary and fiscal policy must coordinate in order to effectively control the price level. One example draws on Davig, Leeper, and Walker (2010), Leeper (2011), and Leeper and Walker (2011), and assumes Regime M is operative until a fiscal limit is hit at date T. A fiscal limit is the point at which tax rates, either through political or economic constraints, can no longer adjust to passively raise future tax revenues. A second example introduces risky sovereign debt to show that a higher probability of default feeds directly into higher current inflation. The third scenario is a two-country monetary union in which one country follows Regime F with the central bank pegging the nominal interest rate. We demonstrate in this case that even if the other country implements Regime M, then inflation in the monetary union is determined by the Regime F country, *regardless of the country's size*. This analysis draws on work by Sims (1997), Bergin (2000), Dupor (2000), Daniel (2001), and Daniel and Shiamptanis (2011).

7.3.1   Fiscal Limit

This section modifies the cashless model in section 7.2 by assuming the economy at some known future date T reaches a fiscal limit. We starkly model the reluctance to increase taxes to stabilize debt in the face of growing transfer payments by assuming that at date T, taxes reach their maximum, $\tau^{\max}$.[14]

Leading up to T, policy is in the active monetary/passive fiscal regime described before, but from date T on, tax policy has no option but to become active, with $\tau_t = \tau^{\max}$ for $t \geq T$. If monetary policy remained active, neither authority would stabilize debt and debt would explode. Existence of a bounded equilibrium requires that monetary policy switch to being passive, which stabilizes debt. Table 7.2 summarizes the assumptions about policy behavior.

---

14. In this model with lump-sum taxes there is no upper bound for taxes or debt, so long as debt does not grow faster than the real interest rate. But in a more plausible production economy, in which taxes distort behavior, there would be a natural fiscal limit—the peak of the Laffer curve. See Davig, Leeper, and Walker (2010, 2011) for further discussion and Bi (2011) for an application of an endogenous fiscal limit to the issue of sovereign debt default.

Table 7.2	Monetary-fiscal policy regimes before and after the fiscal limit at date T	
	Regime M $t = 0, 1, \ldots, T-1$	Regime F $t = T, T+1, \ldots$
Monetary policy	$R_t^{-1} = R^{*-1} + \alpha\left(\dfrac{P_{t-1}}{P_t} - \dfrac{1}{\pi^*}\right)$	$R_t^{-1} = R^{*-1}$
Tax policy	$\tau_t = \tau^* + \gamma\left(\dfrac{B_{t-1}}{P_{t-1}} - b^*\right)$	$\tau_t = \tau^{\max}$

We assume that government transfers evolve exogenously according to the stochastic process

$$(43) \qquad z_t = (1 - \rho)z^* + \rho z_{t-1} + \varepsilon_t, \quad 0 < \rho < 1$$

where z^* is steady-state transfers and ε_t is a serially uncorrelated shock with $E_t \varepsilon_{t+1} = 0$.

The intertemporal equilibrium condition now is the sum of two distinct parts

$$(44) \qquad \frac{B_0}{P_0} = E_0 \sum_{j=1}^{T-1} \beta^j s_j + E_0 \sum_{j=T}^{\infty} \beta^j s_j,$$

where the function for the primary surplus, s_t, changes at the fiscal limit according to

$$(45) \qquad s_t = \begin{cases} \pi^* - \gamma\left(\dfrac{B_{t-1}}{P_{t-1}} - b^*\right) - z_t, & t = 0, 1, \ldots, T-1 \\ \tau^{\max} - z_t, & t = T, \ldots, \infty \end{cases}$$

Expression (44) decomposes the value of government debt at the initial date into the expected present value of surpluses leading up to the fiscal limit and the expected present value of surpluses after the limit has been hit. Date T is assumed to be known.[15]

Evaluating the second part of (44) and letting $\tau^{\max} = \tau^*$, after the limit is hit at T

$$(46) \qquad E_0 \sum_{j=T}^{\infty} \beta^j s_j = E_0\left(\frac{B_{T-1}}{P_{T-1}}\right)$$

$$= \frac{\beta^T}{1-\beta}(\tau^* - z^*) - \frac{(\beta\rho)^T}{1-\beta\rho}(z_0 - z^*).$$

15. Davig, Leeper, and Walker (2010, 2011) and Leeper and Walker (2011) relax this assumption by modeling T as a random variable. In this case, there are expectational spillover effects that further strengthen the arguments made in this section.

The first part of (44) is given by

$$(47) \quad E_0 \sum_{j=1}^{T-1} \beta^j s_j = \sum_{j=1}^{T-1} \left(\frac{\beta}{1 - \gamma\beta} \right)^j [(\tau^* - \gamma b^*) - E_0 z_j]$$

$$= (\tau^* - \gamma b^* - z^*) \sum_{j=1}^{T-1} \left(\frac{\beta}{1 - \gamma\beta} \right)^j - (z_0 - z^*) \sum_{j=1}^{T-1} \left(\frac{\beta\rho}{1 - \gamma\beta} \right)^j.$$

Pulling together (46) and (47) yields equilibrium real debt at date $t = 0$ as a function of fiscal parameters and the date 0 realization of transfers

$$(48) \quad \frac{B_0}{P_0} = (\tau^* - \gamma b^* - z^*) \sum_{i=1}^{T-1} \left(\frac{\beta}{1 - \gamma\beta} \right)^i - (z_0 - z^*) \sum_{i=1}^{T-1} \left(\frac{\beta\rho}{1 - \gamma\beta} \right)^i$$

$$+ \left(\frac{\beta}{1 - \gamma\beta} \right)^{T-1} \left[\frac{\beta^T}{1 - \beta} (\tau^{\max} - z^*) - \frac{(\beta\rho)^T}{1 - \beta\rho} (z_0 - z^*) \right].$$

This expression determines the equilibrium value of debt at $t = 0$ and, by extension, at each date in the future. We make three observations. First, this economy will *not* exhibit Ricardian equivalence for $\tau^{\max}$ sufficiently small and sufficiently large increases in transfers. In the previous derivations, we set $\tau^{\max} = \tau^*$, but a sufficient condition for our results to go through is given by $\tau^{\max} < \tau^* + \gamma(B_{t-1}/P_{t-1} - b^*)$ for all realizations of z_t. The fiscal rule after T implies that positive innovations to transfers will not be entirely offset by future changes in tax rates. Only in the absence of the fiscal limit or if $\tau^{\max}$ is sufficiently large will Ricardian equivalence hold. This occurs despite the fact that in the absence of a fiscal limit such a tax rule delivers Ricardian equivalence, as it did in section 7.2.1. Second, higher transfers at time 0, z_0, which portend a higher future path of transfers because of their positive serial correlation, reduce the value of debt. This occurs for the reasons that section 7.2.2 lays out: higher expected government expenditures reduce the backing and, therefore, the value of government liabilities. Finally, how aggressively tax policy responds to debt before hitting the fiscal limit, γ, matters for the value of debt. The Ricardian equivalence that exists in the permanent active monetary/passive tax regime implies that the *timing* of taxation is irrelevant: how rapidly taxes stabilize debt has no bearing on the value of debt so long as debt is sustainable.

To calculate the price level at $t = 0$, use the government's flow budget constraint and the fact that $s_0 = \tau_0 - z_0$, with taxes following the rule shown in table 7.2 to solve for P_0:

$$P_0 = \frac{R_{-1} B_{-1}}{b_0 + \tau_0 - z_0}.$$

Given $R_{-1} B_{-1} > 0$, (49) yields a unique $P_0 > 0$. Entire sequences of equilibrium $\{P_t, R_t^{-1}\}_{t=0}^{-1}$ are solved recursively: having solved for B_0/P_0 and P_0, obtain R_0 from the monetary policy rule in table 7.2, and derive the nomimal value of debt. Then use (48) redated at $t = 1$ to obtain equilibrium B_1/P_1 and the government budget constraint at $t = 1$ to solve for P_1 using (49) redated at $t = 1$, and so forth.

The equilibrium price level has the same features as it does under the passive monetary/active tax regime in section 7.2.2. This is because forward-looking agents know that higher current or expected transfers are not backed in present-value terms by expected taxes. This, in turn, raises household wealth, which increases the demand for goods and drives up the price level (reducing the value of debt to an equilibrium value). Similarities between this equilibrium and that in section 7.2.2 stem from the fact that price-level determination is driven by beliefs about policy *in the long run*. From T on, this economy is identical to the fixed-regime passive monetary/active fiscal policies economy, and it is beliefs about long-run policies that determine the price level. Alternatively, one may think of price level determination in this economy as coming from agents learning about (44), along the lines of Eusepi and Preston (2011). In such an economy, agents coordinate beliefs on long-run policies and the equilibrium would be one in which fiscal policy is active and monetary policy is passive. Of course, before the fiscal limit the two economies are quite different and the behavior of the price level will also be different.

In this environment, monetary policy continues to determine expected inflation while fiscal policy determines realizations. Combining (4) with the monetary policy rule in table 7.2, we obtain an expression in expected inflation

$$(50) \qquad E_t\left(\frac{P_t}{P_{t+1}} - \frac{1}{\pi^*}\right) = \frac{\alpha}{\beta}\left(\frac{P_{t-1}}{P_t} - \frac{1}{\pi^*}\right)$$

for $t \geq 0$. As argued earlier, the equilibrium price level sequence, $\{P_t\}_{t=0}^{\infty}$, is determined by versions of (48) and (49) for each date t, so (50) describes the evolution of expected inflation. Given equilibrium P_0 from (49) and an arbitrary P_{-1} (arbitrary because the economy starts at $t = 0$ and cannot possibly determine P_{-1}, regardless of policy behavior) (50) shows that $E_0(P_0/P_1)$ grows relative to the initial inflation rate. In fact, throughout the active monetary policy/passive fiscal policy phase, for $t = 0, 1, \ldots, T - 1$, expected inflation grows at the rate $\alpha\beta^{-1} > 1$. In periods $t \geq T$ monetary policy pegs the nominal interest rate at R^*, and expected inflation is constant: $E_t(P_t/P_{t+1}) = (R^*\beta)^{-1} = 1/\pi^*$.

The implications of the equilibrium laid out in equations (48), (49), and (50) for government debt, inflation, and the anchoring of expectations on the target values (b^*, π^*) are most clearly seen in a simulation of the equilibrium. Figure 7.2 contrasts the paths of the debt-GDP ratio from two models: the fixed (permanent) passive monetary/active tax regime in section 7.2.2—dashed line—and the present model in which an active monetary/passive tax regime is in place until the economy hits the fiscal limit at date T, when

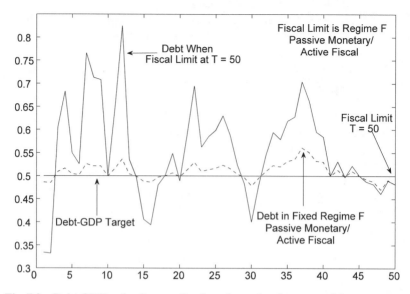

Fig. 7.2   Debt-GDP ratios for a realization of transfers for two models

Notes: The two models are a fixed passive monetary/active tax regime in section 7.2.2 (dashed line) and an active monetary/passive tax regime in place until the economy hits the fiscal limit at date *T*, when policies switch permanently to passive monetary/active tax (solid line).

policies switch permanently to a passive monetary/active tax combination—solid line.[16] The fixed regime displays stable fluctuations of real debt around the 50 percent steady state debt-GDP, which, of course, the other model also produces once it hits the fiscal limit. Leading up to the fiscal limit, however, it is clear that the active monetary/passive tax policy combination does not keep debt as close to target.

Expected inflation evolves according to (50). Since leading up the fiscal limit monetary policy is active, with $\alpha > 1/\beta$, there is no tendency for expected inflation to be anchored on the inflation target. Figure 7.3 plots the inflation rate from the fixed-regime model in section 7.2.2 (dashed line) and from the present model (solid line) along with expected inflation from the present model (dotted dashed line). Inflation in the fixed regime fluctuates around π^* and, of course, with the pegged nominal interest rate, expected inflation is anchored on target. But in the period leading up to the fiscal limit, the price level is being determined primarily by fluctuations in the real value of debt which, as figure 7.2 shows, deviates wildly from b^*. Expected

16. Figures 7.2 through 7.5 use the following calibration. Leading up to the fiscal limit, $\alpha = 1.50$ and $\gamma = 0.10$, and at the limit and in the fixed-regime model, $\alpha = \gamma = 0.0$. We assume steady-state values $\tau^* = 0.19$, $z^* = 0.17$, $\pi^* = 1.02$ (gross inflation rate) and we assume $1/\beta = 1.04$ so that $b^* = 0.50$. The transfers process has $\rho = 0.90$ and $\sigma = 0.003$. Identical realizations of transfers were used in all the figures.

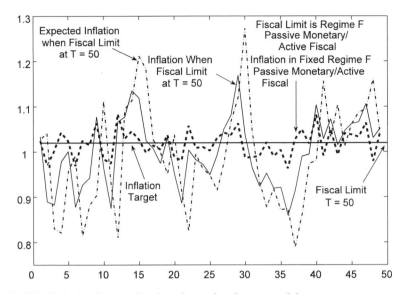

Fig. 7.3   Inflation for a realization of transfers for two models

Notes: The two models are a fixed passive monetary/active tax regime in section 7.2.2 (dashed line) and an active monetary/passive tax regime in place until the economy hits the fiscal limit at date *T*, when policies switch permanently to passive monetary/active tax (solid line); expectation of inflation from present model (dotted dashed line).

inflation in that period, though not *independent* of the inflation target, is certainly not anchored by the target. Instead, under active monetary policy, the deviation of expected inflation from target grows with the deviation of actual inflation from target in the previous period. The figure shows how equation (50) makes expected inflation *follow* actual inflation, with active monetary policy amplifying movements in expected inflation.

To underscore the extent to which inflation is unhinged from monetary policy, even in the active monetary/passive tax regime before the fiscal limit, suppose that tax policy reacts more aggressively to debt. Normally, this would return debt to target more rapidly. But in the presence of a fiscal limit, a higher value of γ can have unexpected consequences. Expression (48) makes clear that raising γ *amplifies* the effects of transfers shocks on debt. A more volatile value of debt, in turn, translates into more volatile actual and expected inflation. Figures 7.4 and 7.5 show this result by repeating the previous figures, but with a passive tax policy that responds more strongly to debt (γ is raised from 0.10 to 0.15).

Figures 7.4 and 7.5 also illustrate a general phenomenon: as the economy approaches the fiscal limit at time T, the equilibrium with different tax policies converge. As we also see in figures 7.2 and 7.3, of course, as time approaches T, the equilibrium also converges to the fixed-regime economy.

An analogous exercise for monetary policy illustrates its impotence when

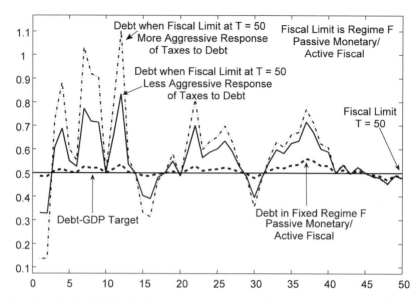

Fig. 7.4   Debt-GDP ratios for two settings of tax policy

Notes: The two settings are the fixed passive monetary/active fiscal regime in section 7.2.2 (dashed lines) the active monetary/passive fiscal regime before the fiscal limit at date T with weaker response of taxes to debt ($\gamma = 0.10$) (solid line), and the active monetary/passive fiscal regime before the fiscal limit at date T with stronger response of taxes to debt ($\gamma = 0.15$) (dotted dashed line).

there is a fiscal limit. A more hawkish monetary policy stance, higher α, has no effect whatsoever on the value of debt and inflation: α does not appear in expression (48) for real debt or expression (49) for the price level. More hawkish monetary policy does, however, *amplify* the volatility of expected inflation, as the evolution of expected inflation, equation (50), shows.

Because monetary policy loses control of inflation after the fiscal limit is reached, forward-looking behavior implies it also loses control of inflation before the fiscal limit is hit. By extension, changes in fiscal behavior in the period leading up to the limit affect both the equilibrium inflation process and the process for expected inflation.

7.3.2   Risky Sovereign Debt and Inflation

Bi, Leeper, and Leith (2010) explore how the possibility of sovereign debt default can further complicate the central bank's efforts to control inflation. Here we show this basic result in a simple example.

Consider a constant endowment, cashless economy in which the equilibrium real interest rate, $1/\beta$, is also constant. Government default is the sole source of uncertainty and, for the current purposes, the decision to default by the fraction $\delta_t \in 0, 1]$ on outstanding debt is exogenous and follows a known stochastic process. Let R_t be the gross risky rate of return on nominal

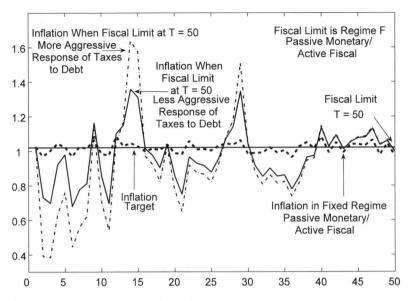

Fig. 7.5   Inflation for two settings of tax policy

Notes: Actual inflation in fixed passive monetary/active fiscal regime in section 7.2.2 (dashed lines) expected inflation in the active monetary/passive fiscal regime before the fiscal limit at date T with weaker response of taxes to debt ($\gamma = 0.10$) (solid line), and expected inflation in the active monetary/passive fiscal regime before the fiscal limit at date T with stronger response of taxes to debt ($\gamma = 0.15$) (dotted dashed line).

government debt and $\pi_t = P_t/P_{t-1}$ be the inflation rate. Household optimization yields the Fisher relation

(51)
$$\frac{1}{R_t} = \beta E_t \left[\frac{1 - \delta_{t+1}}{\pi_{t-1}} \right]$$

while trade in risk-free bonds (assumed to be in zero net supply) gives an analogous relation for the risk-free interest rate, R_t^f,

(52)
$$\frac{1}{R_t^f} = \beta E_t \left[\frac{1}{\pi_{t+1}} \right].$$

The government's budget constraint is

(53)
$$\frac{B_t}{P_t} + s_t = \frac{(1 - \delta_t)}{\pi_t} R_{t-1} \frac{B_{t-1}}{P_{t-1}}$$

where s_t is the primary surplus. Write this constraint at $t + 1$, take expectations conditional on information at t, impose the Euler equation $\beta^{-1} = E_t(1 - \delta_{t+1})R_t/\pi_{t+1}$, and solve for B_t/P_t to yield

(54)
$$\frac{B_t}{P_t} = \beta E_t \frac{B_{t+1}}{P_{t+1}} + \beta E_t s_{t+1}.$$

When the real interest rate is fixed, both the nominal rate and the inflation rate reflect default, so that the expected default rate drops out once expectations are taken. This implies that only surprises in default directly affect the evolution of real government debt in this flexible-price endowment economy. In light of this, we obtain, by iterating on (54) and imposing the household's transversality condition

$$(55) \qquad \frac{B_t}{P_t} = \sum_{j=1}^{\infty} \beta^j E_t s_{t+j}.$$

Expression (55) is the usual intertemporal equilibrium condition that equates the value of government debt to the expected present value of "cash flows," which are primary surpluses.

Fiscal policy sets the surplus in order to stabilize the post-default value of government debt

$$(56) \qquad s_t - s^* = \gamma \left[(1 - \delta_t) \frac{B_{t-1}}{P_{t-1}} - b^* \right]$$

where s^* and b^* are target and steady-state values for the surplus and real debt and $b_{t-1} = B_{t-1}/P_{t-1}$.

Substituting (56) into (53) and taking expectations at time t yields the evolution of expected debt

$$(57) \qquad E_t b_{t+1} + (s^* - \gamma b^*) = [\beta^{-1} - \gamma(1 - E_t \delta_{t+1})] b_t.$$

One result that emerges immediately from (57) is that stability of the debt process in the face of debt default requires that

$$(58) \qquad \gamma > \frac{\beta^{-1} - 1}{1 - E_t \delta_{t+1}},$$

a condition that potentially is far more demanding than the usual one that $\gamma > \beta^{-1} - 1$, particularly when substantial default rates are possible. Here stability also has the unusual property of being time varying, changing with the conditional expectation of default. Provided this condition is fulfilled, however, fiscal policy remains passive and capable of stabilizing the real value of government debt.

Following Uribe (2006) and Schabert (2010), we assume that monetary policy sets the rate on short-term government debt, the risky nominal interest rate, R_t, according to a simple Taylor rule

$$(59) \qquad \frac{1}{R_t} = \frac{1}{R^*} + \alpha \left(\frac{1}{\pi_t} - \frac{1}{\pi^*} \right).$$

Monetary policy targets inflation by setting $\alpha/\beta > 1$. Aside from being the dominant rule in the literature, in the context of our cashless model it is natural for monetary policy to be implemented by varying the contractual interest rate on government debt, rather than the risk-free interest rate on private debt, over which the government has no direct control and which is in zero net supply in equilibrium. More generally, in the transmission from the very short-term rates targeted through open-market operations to the wider economy and, ultimately inflation, the central bank would expect to see a significant degree of pass through to the contractual interest rates employed throughout the economy.[17] Indeed, since government bonds typically form the collateral for the repo contracts undertaken by central banks, it is inevitable that without an offsetting policy adjustment, the policy rates pick up some of the default risk.[18]

When monetary policy controls the risky interest rate, R_t, default influences the ability of the monetary authority to target inflation, even if fiscal policy remains passive and monetary policy is active. To see this, combine the monetary policy rule in (59) with the Fisher relation to yield the dynamic equation for inflation

$$(60) \qquad \frac{1}{\pi_t} - \frac{1}{\pi^*} = \frac{\beta}{\alpha} E_t \left(\frac{1 - \delta_{t+1}}{\pi_{t+1}} - \frac{1}{\pi^*} \right),$$

which now depends on the expected default rate.

Active monetary policy implies that the unique locally bounded solution for inflation is

$$(61) \qquad \frac{1}{\pi_t} = \frac{1}{\pi^*} \left(1 - \frac{\beta}{\alpha} \right) \left\{ 1 + E_t \sum_{i=1}^{\infty} \left(\frac{\beta}{\alpha} \right)^i \prod_{j=1}^{i} (1 - \delta_{t+j}) \right\}.$$

In the absence of default, $\delta_t \equiv 0$, monetary policy achieves its inflation target exactly, $\pi_t = \pi^*$. Higher expected default rates in the future raise current inflation. The farther into the future default is expected, the more it is discounted by $\beta/\alpha < 1$, and the smaller is its impact on inflation at time t. Notice also that if the default rate is constant, $\delta_t = \delta \equiv 0,1]$, then more aggressive monetary policy enhances the central bank's control of inflation. A constant default rate yields the solution for inflation

$$(62) \qquad \pi_t = \pi^* \left[\frac{1 - (1 - \delta)(\beta/\alpha)}{1 - (\beta/\alpha)} \right],$$

so that $\pi_t \to \pi^*$ as $\alpha \to \infty$. A more aggressive monetary policy response to inflation reduces the inflationary consequences of default. Importantly, the

---

17. Empirical evidence suggests that the rate at which policy interest rates pass through to bank interest rates is quite high—about 90 percent within a quarter (Gambacorta 2008). We are implicitly assuming similarly high rates of pass through to government bond yields.

18. Sims (2008) emphasizes that the unconventional operations of many central banks—particularly the Fed and the European Central Bank (ECB)—in recent years have made the central banks' balance sheets riskier. If foreign reserves are an important component of the bank's assets, as for the ECB, then surprise appreciation of the euro devalues its assets relative to its liabilities. The Fed's increased holdings of long-term Treasuries expose its balance sheet to more interest-rate risk than normal. Riskiness is exacerbated if the central bank is not assured that the fiscal authority will back it in times of large declines in asset values.

effectiveness of monetary policy is conditional on fiscal policy behaving passively.

Finally, consider a stylized experiment. At time t news arrives that raises the expected default rate at $t + 1$, $E_t\delta_{t+1} > 0$, but all subsequent expected default rates are zero, $E_t\delta_{t+1}.1 = 0$ for $j > 1$. Then (61) reduces to

$$(63) \qquad \pi_t = \pi^* \left[\frac{1}{1 - (\beta/\alpha)E_t(\delta_{t+1})} \right] > \pi^*.$$

and again we see that higher expected default raises inflation, but the extent to which it does so is mitigated by a more aggressive monetary response to inflation in the form of a higher α.

The source of this inflationary response to default can be seen in contrasting the interest rate rules when defined in terms of risky and risk-free interest rates. A risk-free rule, coupled with a passive fiscal policy, can successfully target inflation. To see why the rule defined in terms of the risky-rate cannot, it is helpful to return to the simple case where the default rate is constant, $\delta_t \equiv \delta \in 0,1]$, so that $1/R_t = (1 - \delta)/R_t^f$. Rewrite (59) in terms of the risk-free rate as

$$(64) \qquad \frac{1}{R_t^f} = \frac{1}{R^*} + \frac{\alpha}{1 - \delta} \left[\frac{1}{\pi_t} - \left(\frac{1}{\pi^*} - \frac{\delta}{\alpha R^*} \right) \right].$$

The monetary policy rule defined in terms of the risky rate of interest can be transformed into a rule of the same form as that defined in terms of the risk-free rate, but with two important differences. First, default does not make monetary policy less active; in fact, it raises the coefficient on excess inflation, $\alpha/(1 - \delta) > \alpha$. Second, default raises the effective inflation target from π^* to $\pi^*/(1 - \delta\beta/\alpha)$. Intuitively, a higher rate of default creates partial monetary policy accommodation: in the presence of default, the monetary authority must allow the risky rate of interest to rise to induce bondholders to continue holding the stock of government bonds. Given the monetary policy rule, the monetary authority will not raise interest rates without a rise in inflation. Bondholders attempt to sell bonds, increasing aggregate demand as they try to increase their consumption paths. This behavior pushes up the price level until bondholders are being compensated for their default risk and inflation and interest rates are consistent with the monetary rule. Stronger responsiveness of policy to inflation, higher α, reduces the effective rise in the inflation target needed to achieve the rise in interest rates desired by bondholders.[19]

As a general proposition, the possibility of default can undermine the central bank's control of inflation: there is a tight connection between expected default rates and inflation, as in Uribe (2006), but the mechanism differs

---

19. As Bi, Leeper, and Leith (2010) note, monetary policy can regain its control of inflation through a policy rule that allows the central bank to react directly to the possibility of default, but such a rule is anathema to many central bankers.

from Uribe's. Uribe obtains his result through a standard fiscal theory of the price level mechanism by coupling an active monetary policy rule like (59) with an active fiscal rule akin to setting $\gamma = 0$ in (56), just as in Loyo (1999) and, more recently, Sims (2011). Such analyses echo the logic of Sargent and Wallace's (1981) unpleasant arithmetic, where the fiscal consequences of a tight monetary policy can ultimately generate higher inflation because fiscal policy does not adjust to stabilize government debt. In contrast, the present result stems from the monetary policy response to default, but where the policy rule remains active and fiscal policy passive. Although there is a positive link between default and inflation, that link differs from existing results in crucial ways. For example, in Uribe (2006), delaying default supports unstable inflation dynamics for longer, making it more difficult for the monetary authority to hit its inflation target. In this active monetary/passive fiscal regime, however, the impact of future default on prices is discounted so that delaying default reduces the immediate inflationary consequences of default. In Uribe's setup, raising α further destabilizes inflation dynamics and moves the economy farther from its inflation target. More active monetary policy in Bi, Leeper, and Leith's (2010) environment reduces deviations from the inflation target due to default.

7.3.3   Monetary Union

The example in section 7.3.1 shows that the inability of policymakers to commit to a particular policy stance in the future has repercussions today. We now provide an example of an economy in which fiscal authorities in two countries in a monetary union are unable (or unwilling) to commit to passive fiscal behavior. It turns out that it takes only one country to deviate in order for the fiscal theory of the price level to emerge in the monetary union. The exposition simplifies the setup in Bergin (2000).

Consider two symmetric countries in a monetary union. One simplification of Bergin is to consider a cashless economy and another is to assume a constant world endowment of goods, $y_t = y_{1,t} + y_{2,t} = y$ for all t. A representative household in country j maximizes

$$E_0 \sum_{t-0}^{\infty} \beta^t u(c_{j,t})$$

subject to

(65) $$c_{j,t} + \frac{B_{j,t}}{P_t} + \tau_{j,t} = y_{j,t} + z_{j,t} + \frac{R_{t-1} B_{j,t-1}}{P_t}.$$

Countries retain fiscal sovereignty in the sense that they set taxes, $\tau_{j,t}$, and transfers, $z_{j,t}$, independently. But there is a common price level, P_t, and a common one-period nominal interest rate, R_t, across the economies. A common price level implicitly assumes that all goods are traded and purchasing power parity holds. Following, we describe how the single central bank sets R_t each period.

Country j's government chooses policies to satisfy the flow budget constraint

$$(66) \qquad \frac{D_{j,t}}{P_t} + \tau_{j,t} + v_{j,t} = z_{j,t} + \frac{R_{t-1}D_{j,t-1}}{P_t},$$

where $v_{j,t}$ is lump-sum transfers received from the common central bank.

The central bank buys and sells bonds, $B_{m,t}$, to implement its interest rate policies. The bank does not levy taxes or issue debt. Interest earnings from its portfolio holdings, $v_{1,t}$ and $v_{2,t}$, are rebated to the countries' national governments. The central bank's budget constraint is

$$(67) \qquad \frac{B_{m,t}}{P_t} + v_{1,t} + v_{2,t} = \frac{R_{t-1}B_{m,t-1}}{P_t}.$$

The Euler equation from household j's optimization is

$$(68) \qquad u'(c_{j,t}) = \beta R_t E_t \frac{P_t}{P_{t+1}} u'(c_{j,t+1}).$$

Households also have the transversality condition

$$(69) \qquad \lim_{T \to \infty} \beta^T E_t u'(c_{j,t+T}) \frac{B_{j,t+T}}{P_{t+T}} = 0.$$

Goods and bond market clearing conditions are

$$c_{1,t} + c_{2,t} = y_{1,t} + y_{2,t} = y$$

$$B_{1,t} + B_{2,t} + B_{m,t} = D_{1,t} + D_{2,t}.$$

Although not strictly necessary for an equilibrium, we follow Sims (1997) and Bergin (2000) in imposing that each individual government must choose policies that are consistent with individual solvency.[20]

Assume that preferences are quadratic, as in Bergin (2000): $u(c_{j,t}) = c_{j,t} - (a/2)c_{j,t}^2$ for each $j = 1,2$. Then with a constant worldwide endowment of goods, adding the Euler equations in (68) for $j = 1,2$ implies the simple Fisher relation

$$(70) \qquad \frac{1}{R_t} = \beta E_t \frac{P_t}{P_{t+1}},$$

and applying (68) to each j, country-specific consumptions are random walks

$$c_{1,t} = E_t c_{1,t+1}$$

$$c_{2,t} = E_t c_{2,t+1}.$$

20. Woodford (1998b) observes that private optimizing behavior imposes only that the sum $D_{1,t} + D_{2,t}$ would satisfy transversality. In this case, debt issued by one country can grow exponentially as long as the other country is willing to buy that debt without limit and without any expectation of being repaid. Sims (1997) points out that any effort to rationalize government policies would lead immediately to transversality conditions for $D_{j,t}$ individually: it would not be politically optimal for a country to extend unlimited loans to another member country. An analogous argument applies to rule out overaccumulation of debt by the central bank.

Imposing equilibrium, the Fisher relation, and government flow budget constraints on iterated versions of (66), yields two country-specific intertemporal equilibrium conditions

(71)
$$\frac{R_{t-1}D_{1,t-1}}{P_t} = \sum_{j=0}^{\infty} \beta^j E_t [\tau_{1,t+j} + \nu_{1,t+j} - z_{1,t+j}]$$

(72)
$$\frac{R_{t-1}D_{2,t-1}}{P_t} = \sum_{j=0}^{\infty} \beta^j E_t [\tau_{2,t+j} + \nu_{2,t+j} - z_{2,t+j}],$$

and an analogous intertemporal equilibrium condition that stems from private and central bank behavior

(73)
$$\frac{R_{t-1}B_{m,t-1}}{P_t} = \sum_{j=0}^{\infty} \beta^j E_t [\nu_{1,t+j} + \nu_{2,t+j}].$$

Consider a mix of monetary and fiscal policies in which the central bank pegs the nominal interest rate at $R_t = R^*$ for all t, while country 1 sets the primary surplus, $x_{1,t} = \{\tau_{1,t} - z_{1,t}\}$, exogenously and country 2 makes its primary surplus, $x_{2,t}$, strongly responsive to the state of its government debt

(74)
$$x_{2,t} - x_2^* = \gamma \left(\frac{D_{2,t-1}}{P_{t-1}} - b_2^* \right),$$

where x_2^* is the steady-state primary surplus and b_2^* is the steady-state value of government debt in country 2. By setting $\gamma > 1/\beta - 1$, the government in country 2 adjusts future surpluses in response to deviations of debt from b_2^* by enough to retire debt back to steady state.

Two results immediately emerge. First, if $\{x_{1,t}\}$ is exogenous and rebates from the central bank to the government, $\{\nu_{1,t}\}$, are independent of the state of government debt in country 1, then the worldwide price level, P_t, is determined by equilibrium condition (71). At time t, $R_{t-1}D_{1,t-1}$ is predetermined and the expected present value of primary surpluses plus rebates are independent of P_t, so the price level must adjust to ensure that (71) holds. News of lower taxes or rebates or of higher transfers payments, reduces the value of country 1's debt, inducing agents in country 1 to substitute out of bonds and into consumption goods. This higher demand for goods raises the price level until agents are content to buy their initial consumption baskets.

In turn, a higher price level reduces the value of country 2's debt and, via the surplus rule in (74), reduces expected surpluses in that country. Thus, fiscal disturbances in country 1 spill over to country 2 through general equilibrium effects on the price level. The quantitative importance of these spillover effects depend upon the size of the tax cut or transfer payment in country 1.[21]

Second, if the central bank determines rebates to member countries as a

---

21. In this setting, where all goods are traded, the size of country 1 does not matter: Greece can determine euro-wide price levels. Incorporating nontraded goods and distinguishing among country-specific and euro-wide price levels attenuates this stark and implausible result.

function of each country's fiscal stance—the value of outstanding debt—
then (71) no longer imposes any restrictions on the equilibrium price level,
even if country 1 continues to maintain exogenous primary surpluses. To
uniquely determine the price level, the central bank must shift from pegging
the nominal interest rate to targeting the inflation rate. It can do this by setting the nominal rate according to

$$(75) \qquad \frac{1}{R_t} = \frac{1}{R^*} + \alpha \left(\frac{P_{t-1}}{P_t} - \frac{1}{\pi^*} \right),$$

where π^* is the inflation target and $\alpha > 1/\beta$ to ensure a unique, stable inflation process.

Although this policy mix delivers a unique bounded equilibrium, it carries
an important distributional message. Efforts by the central bank to reduce
inflation will translate into higher values of debt in each country—conditions (71) and (72). Country 2, which is following the surplus rule in (74),
will need to raise future surpluses. Country 1, which continues to set primary
surpluses exogenously, now requires a relatively larger rebate from the central bank. As condition (73) makes clear, a higher rebate to country 1 may
require a *lower* rebate to country 2, forcing country 2 to raise taxes or cut
transfer payments still further.[22]

7.4 Empirical Aspects of Policy Interactions

Given the differences in the equilibria described earlier, it might seem
straightforward to distinguish an equilibrium time series generated by active
monetary/passive fiscal policies from a time series generated by passive
monetary/active fiscal policy. Unfortunately, subtle observational equivalence results may make it difficult to identify which regime is "active" and
which regime is "passive." In this section we highlight two identification
challenges—one in which observational equivalence exists between determinant and indeterminant equilibrium, which follows Cochrane (2011a),
and another that demonstrates the challenges in distinguishing between
regimes M and F from empirical observation. We view these results as provocative but only suggestive—further study is needed to determine whether
the results generalize to more sophisticated setups. One implication flows
even from the simple experiments conducted here: empirically testing for the
interactions between monetary and fiscal policy by examining simple correlations in the data will lead to spurious results and potentially false conclusions. This suggests that existing efforts to "test" for the fiscal theory may be
more challenging than originally believed (Bohn 1998; Canzoneri, Cumby,

---

22. Implicit in the equilibrium condition pertaining to the central bank's liabilities, (73), is the
notion that if transfers to country 2 are unbounded above, then transfers (taxes) to country 1
must be unbounded below. This underscores that there may be limits to the ability of the central
bank to retain control of inflation if one member of the union pursues an active fiscal policy.

and Diba 2001; Cochrane 1998, 2005; Woodford 1998a, 2001; Leeper 1991; Sims 2011).

7.4.1   Indeterminacy and Observational Equivalence

There is a straightforward observational equivalence due to Cochrane (2010, 2011a) in which indeterminant equilibria can generate time series that are indistinguishable (same covariance generating process) from determinant ones.

To show this result, consider the simple model consisting of a Fisher relation and monetary policy rule

$$R_t = r + E_t\pi_{t+1}$$

$$R_t = r + \alpha\pi_t + x_t$$

$$x_t = b(L)\varepsilon_{x,t},$$

where R_t is the nominal interest rate, π_t is inflation, and r is the constant real rate. The only restriction we impose on the stochastic process for the monetary policy disturbance, x_t, is square summability, $\Sigma_j b_j^2 < \infty$. The following proposition shows that there exists a stochastic process for the monetary policy rule that generates an observational equivalence between the determinant and indeterminant equilibria.

PROPOSITION 1 (COCHRANE). *For any stationary time series process for $\{R_t, \pi_t\}$ that solves*

(76) $$E_t\pi_{t+1} = \alpha\pi_t + x_t$$

and for any α, one can construct an x_t process that generates the same process for the observables $\{R_t, \pi_t\}$ as a solution to (76) using the alternative α. If $\alpha > 1$, the observables are generated as the unique bounded forward-looking solution. Given an assumed α and the process $\pi_t = a(L)\varepsilon_{x,t}$, where $a(L)$ is a polynomial in the lag operator L, we can construct $x_t = b(L)\varepsilon_{x,t}$ with

$$b_j = a_{j+1} - \alpha a_j$$

or

(77) $$b(L) = (L^{-1} - \alpha)a(L) - a(0)L^{-1}.$$

PROOF. To prove the proposition, note that for $\alpha > 1$ and $x_t = b(L)\varepsilon_{x,t}$, the unique π_t is given by

(78) $$\pi_t = \left(\frac{Lb(L) - \alpha^{-1}b(\alpha^{-1})}{1 - \alpha L}\right)\varepsilon_{x,t} = a(L)\varepsilon_{x,t}.$$

For $\alpha < 1$, the equilibrium will not be uniquely determined and one may construct a π_t solved "backward" to obtain $\pi_t = x_t/(1 - \alpha L)$. Specifying $b(L)$ as (77) and substituting into (78) gives $\pi_t = x_t/(1 - \alpha L)$. Under this restriction, the inflation process generated by $\alpha < 1$ will be identical to the inflation process generated by $\alpha > 1$. Proving the converse (starting with $\alpha < 1$ and showing that there exists an $\alpha > 1$ that generates the observational equivalence) is straightforward since one can always write the solution as $\pi_{t+1} = \alpha\pi_t + x_t + \delta_{t+1}$, where δ_{t+1} is an arbitrary shock. In this case, setting $\delta_{t+1} = a_0\varepsilon_{t+1}$ delivers the result. Note that because $R_t = r + E_t\varepsilon_{t+1}$, matching the inflation process also delivers an equivalence in the nominal interest rate.

The proposition illustrates that important identifying restrictions are imposed on the model through the specification of the exogenous processes. The cross-equation restrictions of (78) make clear the tight relationship between exogenous and endogenous variables. As Cochrane (2011a) emphasizes, for an exogenous process given by (77), it is impossible to tell if observed time series are generated by a determinant or an indeterminate equilibrium.

Proposition 1 relies on the indeterminant equilibria taking a very particular form. But by definition, there are an infinite number of indeterminant equilibria. We now show that a type of observational equivalence, similar in spirit to proposition 1, applies for *unique* equilibria that emerge from models with decoupled determinacy regions. The two regimes described in section 7.2, for example, arise from decoupled determinacy regions, as do many of the linear rational expectation models that researchers and policy institutions use to study monetary-fiscal interactions. Examining the dynamic properties of the two equilibria for general exogenous processes delivers an equivalence between the two unique rational expectations equilibria, which we believe is a more provocative finding than proposition 1.

This section establishes that observational equivalence results *can* emerge when examining fiscal and monetary interactions. Our example is a trivial one and we do not provide a rigorous treatment of the issues here; a careful treatment would require more than a few pages and is beyond the scope of the current chapter. But even this simple demonstration is sufficient to signal a note of caution when examining the empirical aspects of monetary-fiscal interactions.

To the model in section 7.2, add monetary and fiscal policy rules that are deterministic and obey

$$(79) \qquad\qquad R_t = R^*\pi_t^\alpha$$

$$(80) \qquad\qquad s_t = s^*b_{t-1}^\gamma$$

for $t \geq 0$, where $\pi_t \equiv P_t/P_{t-1}$ and $b_t \equiv B_t/P_t$. As in section 7.2, we examine the two policy regimes (Regime M and Regime F), defined in terms of the monetary and fiscal parameters (α, γ).

The log-linearized equilibrium equations are given by

$$(81) \qquad\qquad \hat{R}_t = \hat{\pi}_{t+1}$$

(82) $$\hat{b}_t + (\beta^{-1} - 1)\hat{s}_t = \beta^{-1}\hat{b}_{t-1} + \beta^{-1}(\hat{R}_{t-1} - \hat{\pi}_t),$$

where $\hat{x}_t \equiv \ln(x_t) - (x^*)$ and we have used that in steady state, $s/b = \beta^{-1} - 1$. These equations hold for $t \geq 0$, given $R_{-1}b_{-1} > 0$.

Substituting the linearized policy rules, (79) and (80), into (81) and (82) reduces the system to

(83) $$\hat{\pi}_{t+1} = \alpha\hat{\pi}_t, t \geq 0$$

(84) $$\hat{b}_t + \beta^{-1}\hat{\pi}_t = \gamma^*\hat{b}_{t-1} + \alpha\beta^{-1}\hat{\pi}_{t-1}, t \geq 1$$

(85) $$\hat{b}_0 + (\beta^{-1} - 1)\hat{s}_0 = \beta^{-1}(\hat{b}_{-1} + \hat{R}_{-1})$$

where $\gamma^* \equiv \beta^{-1} - \gamma(\beta^{-1} - 1)$.

For ease of exposition, we consider the special case in which $R_{-1}B_{-1}$ is at its steady-state value, so $\hat{b}_{-1} = \hat{R}_{-1} = 0$.[23]

Consider Regime M, in which $\alpha > 1$ and $\gamma > 1$ (implying that $0 < \gamma^* < 1$). There is a unique bounded equilibrium of a trivial form

(86) $$\hat{\pi}_t = 0, \hat{R}_t = 0, \hat{b}_t = 0, \hat{s}_t = 0, \quad \text{for all } t \geq 0.$$

We can implement the equilibrium in (86) by adopting the passive monetary and active fiscal policy rules

(87) $$\hat{R}_t = 0$$

(88) $$\hat{s}_t = 0$$

for $t \geq 0$. These rules emerge when $\alpha = \gamma = 0$.

These policy rules can deliver the remaining aspects of the Regime M equilibrium in (86). Equation $\hat{R}_t = 0, t \geq 0$ and a constant real interest rate imply that $\hat{\pi}_{t-j} = 0$ for $j \geq 1$; $\hat{R}_t = 0$ and $\hat{s}_t = 0, t \geq 0$, imply that (because $\gamma = 0, \gamma^* = \beta^{-1}$) in equilibrium the law of motion for debt is

(89) $$\hat{b}_t = \beta^{-1}\hat{b}_{t-1} - \beta^{-1}\hat{\pi}_t.$$

Iterating forward on this law of motion and taking expectations yields

(90) $$\hat{b}_t = \sum_{j=1}^{\infty} \beta^j\hat{\pi}_{t+j} = 0.$$

But if $\hat{b}_t = 0$, then (89) implies that $\hat{\pi}_t = 0$, delivering precisely the equilibrium in (86). Constant primary surpluses and pegged nominal interest rates imply that future financing of debt is constant, which fixes the value of debt.

---

23. If instead $R_{-1}B_{-1} > 0$, the results that follow continue to hold, but in modified form. Regime M and Regime F equilibria can still be observationally equivalent—delivering identical equilibrium paths for $\{\hat{R}_t, \hat{\pi}_t, \hat{b}_t, \hat{s}_t\}$ for $t \geq 0$ but under different fiscal rules from the ones considered here. Differences come from the fact that, although $\hat{R}_t = \hat{\pi}_t = 0, t \geq 0$ continues to hold, the present value of surpluses must equal initial debt, $\hat{b}_{-1} + \hat{R}_{-1}$. Regime M implements this by setting $\gamma > 1$, while Regime F implements this with an exogenous process for $\{\hat{s}_t\}$. Given time paths for equilibrium $\{\hat{R}_t, \hat{\pi}_t, \hat{s}_t\}$, the equilibrium debt sequence comes from (82).

This derivation shows that when the equilibrium real interest rate is constant, the unique bounded equilibrium produced by Regime M can be exactly reproduced by Regime F.

These results are merely suggestive of problems that lurk in the endeavor to identify whether observed time series are produced by Regime M or Regime F. One can easily construct monetary models in which determinacy regions are not decoupled (and ignoring fiscal policy altogether is not a viable way of achieving decoupling, in our view). For example, a Blanchard (1985)–Yaari (1965) model with a probability of death can generate wealth effects that modify the determinacy regions sufficiently that it is no longer tenable to maintain the distinctions between monetary and fiscal policy (Richter 2011). Yun (2011) develops a number of mechanisms—learning, sovereign risk, financial frictions, and alternative roles for government debt—that break the decoupling by introducing debt directly into the consumption Euler equation. It is also not clear if these identification problems extend to more general setups. The more sophisticated the model and policy rule, the greater the likelihood that the identification problems discussed here become less severe.

Scant attention has been paid to these identification issues in the literature (but see Cochrane 2011a and Sims 2011 for exceptions). Many authors have attempted to discern whether equilibrium data were generated by Regime M or Regime F. Many of these attempts use reduced-form models in which policy behavior is not identified, relying instead on the restrictions imposed by the government's intertemporal financing constraint to identify policy regimes. These efforts cannot work: the government's budget constraint and the associated intertemporal equilibrium condition *must* be satisfied in *any* equilibrium, regardless of the underlying policy regimes.

7.5   Concluding Remarks

An argument that holds substantial currency among economists and policymakers is that central bankers learned the lessons of past periods of high inflation that, for example, Fischer, Sahay, and Végh (2002) document. First, too-rapid money growth generates inflation. Second, operationally separating the central bank from the fiscal authority ensures that the finance ministry cannot require the central bank to provide any specific cash flows or seigniorage revenues. The understanding of the connection between money growth and inflation, coupled with the operational independence of the central bank, the argument goes, permits the monetary authorities today to achieve their policy objectives.

This argument builds on Friedman's (1970) aphorism that "inflation is always and everywhere a monetary phenomenon" and it makes an implicit and essential assumption: fiscal policy will always behave in the "appropriate" manner. Sims (1999, 424) defines "appropriate" fiscal behavior in his description of central bank independence: "A truly independent central bank is one that can act, even under inflationary or deflationary stress, without any worry about whether the necessary fiscal backing for its actions will be forthcoming." That is, if in pursuit of its objectives a central bank were to encounter balance sheet difficulties, an independent bank would be automatically recapitalized by the fiscal authority.

Sims's point connects to Wallace's (1981) Modigliani-Miller theorem for open-market operations: the impacts of central bank asset swaps depend on fiscal policy behavior. In Wallace's paper, open-market sales of bonds have no effects on equilibrium allocations and prices. Under alternative assumptions on fiscal behavior, such monetary contractions may reduce inflation, while under Sargent and Wallace's (1981) assumptions, the contractions raise inflation.

The aforementioned theory introduces an additional dimension to the monetary-fiscal interactions that Wallace considers: the channel for price-level determination that operates through nominally denominated outstanding government debt and expected future primary fiscal surpluses. Because this channel is more subtle than Sargent and Wallace's monetization mechanism, fiscal policy can affect inflation even if an operationally independent central bank dutifully avoids printing new fiat money to cover fiscal budget shortfalls.

Policymakers need a broad understanding of the factors that determine inflation. The conventional view, what we call Regime M, proposes that monetary policy can control inflation. A requirement of this view is that fiscal policy must reliably adjust surpluses to ensure that government debt is stable. When governments issue nominal debt, an alternative mix of policies (Regime F) reverses the roles of the two macro policies, with fiscal policy determining inflation and monetary policy stabilizing debt.

If current and projected fiscal stress in advanced economies continues unresolved, economic agents will grow more uncertain that the fiscal adjustments that Regime M requires will occur. And central bank behavior in recent years has shown people that monetary policy does not always aggressively lean against inflation—at times, other concerns are paramount. As beliefs become increasingly centered on Regime F, monetary policy loses its ability to control inflation and influence economic activity in the usual ways. Because these developments are driven primarily by fiscal behavior, there is little that independent central bankers can do to anchor expectations on Regime M policies.

Regimes M and F produce equilibria in which monetary and fiscal disturbances have very different effects on macroeconomic time series. Despite these differences, we have shown that it can be difficult to determine which regime generated observed data.

This conclusion may seem iconoclastic or even depressing. But if observational equivalence extends to more general classes of models, such as those that policy institutions employ, then it points toward two constructive conclusions for policy modeling. First, policy modelers could adopt more general driving processes and be aware that they achieve identification through arbitrary assumptions about unobservables. Second, to the extent that simple ad hoc specifications of policy rules are integral to interpretations of data, these specifications can be varied to admit more general interpretations.

There is also a message in these results for policymakers themselves. Because two very different understandings of the inflation process can be equally consistent with observed data, it is prudent to broaden the perspective on inflation determination beyond the single, conventional view that dominates policy thinking.

References

Bassetto, M. 2002. "A Game-Theoretic View of the Fiscal Theory of the Price Level." *Econometrica* 70 (6): 2167–95.

Bergin, P. R. 2000. "Fiscal Solvency and Price Level Determination in a Monetary Union." *Journal of Monetary Economics* 45 (1): 37–53.

Bi, H. 2011. "Sovereign Risk Premia, Fiscal Limits and Fiscal Policy." Forthcoming, *European Economic Review.*

Bi, H., E. M. Leeper, and C. Leith. 2010. "Stabilization versus Sustainability: Macroeconomic Policy Tradeoffs." Unpublished Manuscript. Indiana University, November.

Blanchard, O. J. 1985. "Debts, Deficits, and Finite Horizons." *Journal of Political Economy* 93 (2): 223–47.

Bohn, H. 1998. "The Behavior of US Public Debt and Deficits." *Quarterly Journal of Economics* 113 (3): 949–63.

Bordo, M. D., and P.-C. Hautcoeur. 2007. "Why Didn't France Follow the British Stabilisation After World War I?" *European Review of Economic History* 11 (1): 3–37.

Buiter, W. H. 2002. "The Fiscal Theory of the Price Level: A Critique." *Economic Journal* 112 (481): 459–80.

Canzoneri, M. B., R. E. Cumby, and B. T. Diba. 2001. "Is the Price Level Determined by the Needs of Fiscal Solvency?" *American Economic Review* 91 (5): 1221–38.

Cecchetti, S. G., M. S. Mohanty, and F. Zampolli. 2010. "The Future of Public Debt: Prospects and Implications." BIS Working Papers no. 300, Monetary and Economic Department, March.

Cochrane, J. H. 1998. "A Frictionless View of US Inflation." In *NBER Macroeconomics Annual 1998*, vol. 14, edited by B. S. Bernanke and J. J. Rotemberg, 323–84. Cambridge, MA: MIT Press.

———. 2001. "Long Term Debt and Optimal Policy in the Fiscal Theory of the Price Level." *Econometrica* 69 (1): 69–116.

———. 2005. "Money As Stock." *Journal of Monetary Economics* 52 (3): 501–28.

———. 2010. "Online Appendix to 'Determinacy and Identification with Taylor Rules.'" Manuscript. University of Chicago, September. http://faculty.chicago

booth.edu/john.cochrane/research/papers/cochrane_taylor_rule_online
_appendix_B.pdf.

———. 2011a. "Determinacy and Identification with Taylor Rules." *Journal of Political Economy* 119 (3): 565–615.

———. 2011b. "Inflation and Debt." *National Affairs* Fall (9): 56–78.

———. 2011c. "Understanding Policy in the Great Recession: Some Unpleasant Fiscal Arithmetic." *European Economic Review* 55 (1): 2–30.

Daniel, B. C. 2001. "The Fiscal Theory of the Price Level in an Open Economy." *Journal of Monetary Economics* 48 (2): 293–308.

Daniel, B. C., and C. Shiamptanis. 2011. "Fiscal Risk in a Monetary Union.'" Unpublished Manuscript. University at Albany–SUNY, January.

Davig, T., and E. M. Leeper. 2006. "Fluctuating Macro Policies and the Fiscal Theory." In *NBER Macroeconomics Annual 2006*, vol. 21, edited by D. Acemoglu, K. Rogoff, and M. Woodford, 247–98. Cambridge, MA: MIT Press.

———. 2011. "Monetary-Fiscal Policy Interactions and Fiscal Stimulus." *European Economic Review* 55 (2): 211–27.

Davig, T., E. M. Leeper, and T. B. Walker. 2010. "'Unfunded Liabilities' and Uncertain Fiscal Financing." *Journal of Monetary Economics* 57 (5): 600–19.

———. 2011. "Inflation and the Fiscal Limit." *European Economic Review* 55 (1): 31–47.

Dixit, A., and L. Lambertini. 2001. "Monetary-Fiscal Policy Interactions and Commitment versus Discretion in a Monetary Union." *European Economic Review* 45 (4-6): 977–87.

———. 2003a. "Interactions of Commitment and Discretion in Monetary and Fiscal Policies.'" *American Economic Review* 93 (5): 1522–42.

———. 2003b. "Symbiosis of Monetary and Fiscal Policies in a Monetary Union." *Journal of International Economics* 60 (2): 235–47.

Dupor, B. 2000. "Exchange Rates and the Fiscal Theory of the Price Level." *Journal of Monetary Economics* 45 (3): 613–30.

Eusepi, S., and B. Preston. 2011. "Learning the Fiscal Theory of the Price Level: Some Consequences of Debt-Management Policy." *Journal of the Japanese and International Economies* 25 (4): 358–79.

Fischer, S., R. Sahay, and C. A. Végh. 2002. "Modern Hyper- and High Inflations." *Journal of Economic Literature* 40 (3): 837–80.

Friedman, M. 1970. *The Counter-Revolution in Monetary Theory.* London: Institute of Economic Affairs.

Galí, J. 2008. *Monetary Policy, Inflation, and the Business Cycle.* Princeton, NJ: Princeton University Press.

Gambacorta, L. 2008. "How Do Banks Set Interest Rates?" *European Economic Review* 52:792–819.

Gordon, D. B., and E. M. Leeper. 2006. "The Price Level, The Quantity Theory of Money, and the Fiscal Theory of the Price Level." *Scottish Journal of Political Economy* 53 (1): 4–27.

Hall, G. J., and T. J. Sargent. 2011. "Interest Rate Risk and Other Determinants of Post-WWII US Government Debt/GDP Dynamics." *American Economic Journal: Macroeconomics* 3 (3): 1–27.

International Monetary Fund. 2009. "Fiscal Implications of the Global Economic and Financial Crisis." IMF Staff Position Note SPN/09/13. Washington, DC: IMF.

———. 2011. *World Economic Outlook.* Washington, DC: IMF, April.

Kim, S. 2003. "Structural Shocks and the Fiscal Theory of the Price Level in the Sticky Price Model." *Macroeconomic Dynamics* 7 (5): 759–82.

King, M. 1995. "Commentary: Monetary Policy Implications of Greater Fiscal Discipline." In *Budget Deficits and Debt: Issues and Options,* 171–83. Federal Reserve Bank of Kansas City, Jackson Hole Symposium. Jackson Hole, WY, August 31–September 2.

King, R. G., and C. I. Plosser. 1985. "Money, Deficits, and Inflation." *Carnegie-Rochester Conference Series on Public Policy* 22:147–96.

Leeper, E. M. 1991. "Equilibria Under 'Active' and 'Passive' Monetary and Fiscal Policies." *Journal of Monetary Economics* 27 (1): 129–47.

———. 2011. "Anchors Aweigh: How Fiscal Policy Can Undermine 'Good' Monetary Policy." In *Monetary Policy Under Financial Turbulence,* edited by L. F. Céspedes, R. Chang, and D. Saravia, 411–53. Santiago: Banco Central de Chile.

Leeper, E. M., and T. B. Walker. 2011. "Fiscal Limits in Advanced Economies." *Economic Papers: A Journal of Applied Economics and Policy* 30 (1): 33–47.

Li, B. 2011. "On the Identification of Fiscal Policy Behavior." Unpublished Manuscript. Tsinghua University, May.

Loyo, E. 1999. "Tight Money Paradox on the Loose: A Fiscalist Hyperinflation." Unpublished Manuscript. Harvard University.

McCallum, B. T. 2001. "Indeterminacy, Bubbles, and the Fiscal Theory of Price Level Determination." *Journal of Monetary Economics* 47 (1): 19–30.

Obstfeld, M., and K. Rogoff. 1983. "Speculative Hyperinflations in Maximizing Models: Can We Rule Them Out?" *Journal of Political Economy* 91 (4): 675–87.

Richter, A. W. 2011. "The Fiscal Limit and Non-Ricardian Consumers." Unpublished Manuscript. Indiana University, November.

Sargent, T. J., and N. Wallace. 1981. "Some Unpleasant Monetarist Arithmetic." *Federal Reserve Bank of Minneapolis Quarterly Review* 5 (Fall): 1–17.

Schabert, A. 2010. "Monetary Policy under a Fiscal Theory of Sovereign Default." *Journal of Economic Theory* 145 (2): 860–68.

Sims, C. A. 1994. "A Simple Model for Study of the Determination of the Price Level and the Interaction of Monetary and Fiscal Policy." *Economic Theory* 4 (3): 381–99.

———. 1997. "Fiscal Foundations of Price Stability in Open Economies." Unpublished Manuscript. Yale University.

———. 1999. "The Precarious Fiscal Foundations of EMU." *De Economist* 147 (4): 415–36.

———. 2008. "Government and Central Bank Balance Sheets, Inflation and Monetary Policy." Slides, Princeton University, November 3.

———. 2011. "Stepping on a Rake: The Role of Fiscal Policy in the Inflation of the 1970s." *European Economic Review* 55 (1): 48–56.

Trabandt, M., and H. Uhlig. 2011. "The Laffer Curve Revisited." *Journal of Monetary Economics* 58 (4): 305–27.

Uribe, M. 2006. "A Fiscal Theory of Sovereign Risk." *Journal of Monetary Economics* 53 (8): 1857–75.

Wallace, N. 1981. "A Modigliani-Miller Theorem for Open-Market Operations." *American Economic Review* 71 (3): 267–74.

Woodford, M. 1995. "Price-Level Determinacy Without Control of a Monetary Aggregate." *Carnegie-Rochester Conference Series on Public Policy* 43:1–46.

———. 1998a. "Comment on Cochrane's 'A Frictionless View of US Inflation'." In *NBER Macroeconomics Annual 1998,* edited by B. S. Bernanke and J. J. Rotemberg, 390–419. Cambridge, MA: MIT Press.

———. 1998b. "Control of the Public Debt: A Requirement for Price Stability?" In *The Debt Burden and Its Consequences for Monetary Policy,* edited by G. Calvo and M. King, 117–54. New York: St. Martin's Press.

———. 2001. "Fiscal Requirements for Price Stability." *Journal of Money, Credit, and Banking* 33 (3): 669–728.

———. 2003. *Interest and Prices: Foundations of a Theory of Monetary Policy.* Princeton, NJ: Princeton University Press.

Yaari, M. E. 1965. "Uncertain Lifetime, Life Insurance, and the Theory of the Consumer." *The Review of Economic Studies* 32 (2): 137–50.

Yun, T. 2011. "Transmission Mechanisms of the Public Debt." Unpublished Manuscript. Seoul National University, October.

Comment   Jordi Galí

Anchoring Inflation: Three Views

How is inflation determined? What can policymakers do to guarantee price stability? These questions are central to macroeconomics, current and past. The traditional monetarist view, synthesized by Milton Friedman's famous dictum that "inflation is always and everywhere a monetary phenomenon," has been overshadowed in recent years by the New Keynesian approach to monetary policy analysis, which has downplayed the role of monetary aggregates and emphasized instead the importance of *good* interest rate rules as a way of anchoring inflation. A third way, often referred to as the *fiscal theory of the price level,* has also been the focus of considerable attention (and controversy) among macroeconomists. The *fiscalist* approach, as originally developed by Leeper (1991), Sims (1994), and Woodford (1995), has pointed to the possibility of an independent role for fiscal policy in determining inflation. The chapter by Leeper and Walker provides a useful primer on the fiscalist view, as well as an insightful discussion of some implications of that view that may be seen as particularly relevant to the current environment, characterized by large fiscal deficits and growing debt/GDP ratios in most advanced economies.

The Basic Dichotomy

Consider an infinite horizon economy where the government's intertemporal budget contraint is given by

$$(1) \qquad \frac{R_{t-1}B_{t-1}}{P_t} = \sum_{k=0}^{\infty} \beta^k E_t \{\tau_{t+k} - z_{t+k}\},$$

Jordi Galí is director and senior researcher at the Centre de Recerca en Economia Internacional (CREI), professor of economics at the Universitat Pompeu Fabra, research professor at the Barcelona Graduate School of Economics, and a research associate of the National Bureau of Economic Research.

For acknowledgments, sources of research support, and disclosure of the author's material financial relationships, if any, please see http://www.nber.org/chapters/c12645.ack.

where B_{t-1} is the amount of one-period nominally riskless government debt issued in period $t-1$ and yielding a gross nominal rate of R_{t-1}, and where τ_t and z_t denote government taxes and transfers, respectively. Variable P_t is the price level, and β is the representative consumer's discount factor. Under risk neutrality or, as assumed by Leeper and Walker, in a constant endowment economy, the ex ante gross real interest rate $R_t E_t \{P_t / P_{t+1}\}$ is equal to β^{-1}.

Note that equation (1) can be derived by combining an infinite sequence of period budget constraints

$$\frac{B_{t+k}}{P_{t+k}} + \tau_{t+k} = z_{t+k} + \frac{R_{t+k-1} B_{t+k-1}}{P_{t+k}}$$

for $k = 0,1,2,\ldots$, together with two maintained assumptions: (a) no default and (b) a transversality condition of the form $\lim_{T \to \infty} \beta^T E_t \{B_T / P_T\} = 0$.

Intertemporal budget constraint (1) is usefuly for conveying the basic policy regime dichotomy described in the Leeper-Walker chapter. Under regime M (for "monetary," and using the Leeper-Walker terminology) fiscal policy is *passive,* meaning that taxes and/or transfers are endogenously adjusted so that (1) is satisfied for *any* price level path. In that environment (1) does not constrain the evolution of the price level. Instead, the latter— and, hence, inflation—will be uniquely determined by a suitable choice of an *active* monetary policy rule (e.g., an interest rate rule satisfying the Taylor principle). Alternatively, under regime F, fiscal authorities adopt an *active* fiscal policy by choosing an exogenous path for transfers and taxes. Any shock to current or anticipated values of those variables that changes the right-hand side of (1) will have an immediate impact on the price level, since $R_{t-1} B_{t-1}$ is predetermined. In that context, a unique nonexplosive equilibrium arises, as long as the monetary authority accommodates such price changes through the adoption of a *passive* rule; that is, one that adjusts the nominal interest rate weakly in response to inflation.

Having described that basic regime dichotomy, Leeper and Walker (a) clarify the relation between Regime F and Sargent and Wallace's (1981) unpleasant monetarist arithmetic, and (b) discuss how its implications for the determination of inflation carry over to an economy with multiple debt maturities. Later on, Leeper and Walker push the fiscalist view somewhat further, by describing two environments in which monetary policy may not be able to control inflation despite the fact that the economy is under a Regime M (at least apparently). Those environments include (a) the case in which a possible future switch to Regime F is anticipated (as when the economy reaches its "fiscal limit"), and (b) when government debt is subject to the risk of default *and* the interest rate on short-term debt is set by the central bank according to a Taylor-type rule. In addition, they show how an (arbitrarily) small economy that is part of a monetary union may determine the latter's aggregate price level if its fiscal authority follows an active rule. Finally, Leeper and Walker discuss, by means of a simple example, some of the difficulties in establishing empirically the nature of the policy regime in place.

Questions to Ask a Fiscalist

In this section I raise a number of questions provoked by my reading of the Leeper and Walker chapter. These questions are relevant to the fiscalist literature more generally. Questions more specific to their chapter are raised in subsequent sections.

Where Is Inflation?

A stark consequence of the financial and economic crisis of 2008 and 2009 has been the large increase in budget deficits and debt/GDP ratios in a large number of advanced economies, as Leeper and Walker themselves report in their introductory section. The deterioration of public finances has been a natural consequence of the operation of automatic stabilizers during the crisis, though many countries have also made use of countercyclical discretionary fiscal measures. Yet, despite the huge fiscal imbalances observed in recent years, and independently of their ultimate nature, a rise in inflation is nowhere to be found. Thus, average annual inflation among advanced economies over the period 2009 to 2011 has remained at the subdued level of 1.4 percent, and it is only projected to rise to 1.8 percent by 2016.[1] Furthermore, monetary policy has remained extremely accommodative, with policy rates in many countries behaving as if pegged, due to the zero lower bound. All in all, one would think the recent fiscal episode would constitute the ultimate natural experiment for the fiscal theory of the price level. Viewed under that lens it is hard to avoid the conclusion that the recent episode offers no evidence in support of some of the basic predictions of the fiscal theory.

On the (Im)Possibility of Default

One of the maintained assumptions underlying the derivation of the government's intertemporal constraint (1) is the absence of sovereign default. Default events, however, are not just a theoretical curiosity; in fact, as documented by Reinhart and Rogoff (2009), episodes of sovereign default are far from rare, even after World War II. At the time of writing these lines Greece is negotiating with its creditors a bond swap that reduces significantly the former's liabilities and thus amounts to a partial default.

In the real world, when a government comes close or reaches its fiscal limit (as defined by Leeper and Walker), default becomes a likely outcome, and one that would render unnecessary any price level adjustment in order to satisfy (1).

1. IMF (2011).

Multiple Equilibria?

In much of the literature, the passive or active nature of fiscal policy is given exogenously. Once we allow for an endogenous regime decision the possibility of multiple equilibria may emerge. That possibility would seem worth exploring. Thus, if agents expect the government to switch endogenously to a passive fiscal policy in the face of large primary deficits, there will not be a need for a large price adjustment in order to meet the intertemporal budget constraint. As a result public liabilities will remain large, and the government will feel pressure to switch to a policy that stabilizes those liabilities. On the other hand, if agents expect the government to remain stubbornly commited to an active fiscal policy, the price level will rise in response to current or future primary deficits, wiping out the real value of outstanding liabilities and releasing the pressure for a regime change.

The Role of the Transversality Condition

In addition to the no default assumption, a transversality condition of the form $\lim_{T\to\infty}\beta^T E_t\{B_T/P_T\}=0$ is needed in order to derive intertemporal budget constraint (1). That transversality condition is justified—as an implication of utility maximization—in models with an infinite-lived representative agent, but not more generally. Thus, as shown in Diamond (1965), in a neoclassical economy with overlapping generations equilibria may arise that are characterized by a permanent rollover of government debt, with the latter's discounted asymptotic value remaining positive. In such an environment, an increase in current or future primary deficits does not necessarily have to be offset by a reduction in the real value of current debt. Instead it may just lead to permanently higher debt in the future. The possible role of fiscal policy as an anchor for inflation in such an environment would seem more limited.

Normative Issues

Which policy regime is more desirable, Regime M or Regime F? Leeper and Walker, and the fiscalist literature in general, tend to eschew normative aspects of policy design. Strictly speaking, normative considerations are irrelevant in the context of the simple endowment economy used as a reference framework throughout the Leeper-Walker chapter, but they will not be in the context of a richer, more realistic model with embedded monetary nonneutralities and explicit welfare costs of inflation.[2] Can one make a case for Regime F based on its implications for welfare? An issue of particular interest in that analysis is the seeming robustness of global indeterminacy in the equilibrium that arises under Regime M when the central bank follows a Taylor-type rule, but which seems absent under Regime F.

2. See, for example, Woodford (1996).

Next I focus on the analysis of two specific issues dealt with by Leeper and Walker; namely, the role played in the determination of the price level by (a) the risk of default and (b) country-specific fiscal policies in the context of a monetary union.

Default Risk and Inflation

Leeper and Walker provide an example of an economy where one-period nominal government debt is subject to some default risk. They show that, even though the central bank follows an active monetary policy, it cannot fully control inflation, which is shown to fluctuate with the risk of default.

Here I present a simplified version of their model to make clear that their result is unrelated to the fiscal theory of the price level, and can be viewed instead as a particular case of a well-known aspect of the design of interest rate rules in a conventional (Regime M) environment.

The risk of default is assumed to be reflected in the yield on government debt, i_t, which is given by

$$(2) \qquad i_t = r + E_t\{\delta_{t+1}\} + E_t\{\pi_{t+1}\},$$

where δ_{t+1} is the exogenous stochastic haircut at maturity, π_{t+1} is the rate of inflation between t and $t+1$, and r is the required expected real return (which is assumed to be constant for simplicity). The central bank follows an *active* monetary policy, in the form of the simple interest rate rule

$$(3) \qquad i_t = r + \alpha \pi_t,$$

where $\alpha > 1$. Fiscal policy is passive.

Combining (2) and (3) we can derive the following closed-form expression for inflation

$$\pi_t = \sum_{k=1}^{\infty} \left(\frac{1}{\alpha}\right)^k E_t\{\delta_{t+k}\},$$

which makes clear that fluctuations in sovereign default risk lead to fluctuations in inflation.

But the latter conclusion is unrelated to the fiscal theory of the price level. Instead it is an illustration of the limitations of overly simplistic Taylor-type rules to stabilize inflation, in the presence of a time-varying real rate. It is straightforward to show how the assumed Taylor rule can be modified in order to guarantee full price stability, even in the presence of stochastic variations in the risk of default. To see this, assume that the central bank follows instead the interest rule

$$(4) \qquad i_t = r + E_t\{\delta_{t+1}\} + \alpha \pi_t.$$

Combining (2) and (4) yields the locally unique solution:

$$\pi_t = 0$$

for all t. Thus, the presence of time-varying debt default risk does not prevent the central bank from fully stabilizing inflation, and from insulating that variable from the impact of fiscal policy.

Monetary Union and Inflation: A Reductio ad Absurdum?

Leeper and Walker consider a model of a monetary union with fiscal policy decentralized at the country level. The (common) central bank follows a passive monetary policy while the fiscal authorities in all but one country adopt a passive fiscal policy. There is a single homogenous good, traded at price P_t. Leeper and Walker show that the union-wide price level is determined by the intertemporal budget constraint of the government that has adopted an active fiscal policy (and whose variables are denoted by an asterisk):

$$\frac{R_{t-1}B_{t-1}^*}{P_t} = \sum_{k=0}^{\infty} \beta^k E_t \{\tau_{t+k}^* - z_{t+k}^*\}.$$

Thus, in the Leeper-Walker example the (active) fiscal policy of a single country determines the union-wide price level independently of the size of that country and its weight in the union![3]

The implications of the fiscalist view uncovered by the previous example seem clearly unrealistic. In fact, one is tempted to carry them to an extreme by applying the same logic to individuals as opposed to governments. Consider, thus, an infinite-lived household whose intertemporal budget constraint is given by

(5) $$\frac{R_{t-1}A_{t-1}}{P_t} = \sum_{k=0}^{\infty} \beta^k E_t \{c_{t+k} - y_{t+k}\},$$

where A_{t-1} is the amount of one-period nominal bonds purchased in period $t-1$ and yielding a gross nominal rate of R_{t-1}, and where c_t and y_t denote, respectively, consumption and labor income (where the latter is taken to be exogenous, for simplicity). Again, P_t is the price level and β is the constant discount factor.

Note that the derivation of that constraint makes use of the same ingredients as its government counterpart; namely, it combines an infinite sequence of period budget constraints with the maintained assumptions of no default and a transversality condition.

---

3. The same will be true if instead each country is specialized in the production of a differentiated good and one of the country's primary surplus is exogenous in terms of its domestic good. In that case, the country's domestic price level will be pinned down by its government's intertemporal budget constraint. When combined with the equilibrium relative price (determined separately by fundamentals), that will determine the union aggregate price level.

The standard analysis of the household's problem involves the utility maximizing choice of consumption subject to an income path $\{y_{t+k}\}$ and the earlier intertemporal budget constraint. Alternatively, however, the household may be assumed to choose an exogenous consumption path. In that case, and by analogy with the case of an exogenous primary deficit under an active fiscal policy, the price level *will have to adjust* in response to a consumption shocks, and in order to satisfy (5), which can now be interpreted as an equilibrium condition rather than a constraint facing the consumer. Few economists, even among those who advocate the fiscalist approach to price determination, are likely to sponsor such a view of aggregate price level determination. Its logic, however, seems to correspond to that underlying the fiscal theory.

Concluding Remarks

The Leeper-Walker chapter provides a useful primer on the fiscalist approach to inflation determination, focusing on examples that appear to be relevant to the current economic environment. I have raised a number of concerns, some about the fiscalist approach and its implications in general, others about specific details of the Leeper-Walker chapter. Those critical remarks notwithstanding, I think this is an excellent chapter, and one that clearly belongs to any reading list on the fiscal theory of the price level.

References

Diamond, Peter A. 1965. "National Debt in a Neoclassical Growth Model." *The American Economic Review* 55 (5): 1126–50.
International Monetary Fund. 2011. *World Economic Outlook,* October. Washington, DC: IMF.
Leeper, Eric. 1991. "Equilibria under Active and Passive Monetary Policies." *Journal of Monetary Economics* 27:129–47.
Reinhart, Carmen M., and Kenneth S. Rogoff. 2009. *This Time Is Different: Eight Centuries of Financial Folly.* Princeton, NJ: Princeton University Press.
Sargent, Thomas J., and Neil Wallace. 1981. "Some Unpleasant Monetarist Arithmetic." *Federal Reserve Bank of Minneapolis Quarterly Review* 5:1–17.
Sims, Christopher A. 1994. "A Simple Model for the Determination of the Price Level and the Interaction of Monetary and Fiscal Policy." *Economic Theory* 4:381–99.
Woodford, Michael. 1995. "Price-Level Determinacy without Control of a Monetary Aggregate." *Carnegie-Rochester Conference Series on Public Policy* 43:1–46.
———. 1996. "Control of the Public Debt: A Requirement for Price Stability." NBER Working Paper no. 5684. Cambridge, MA: National Bureau of Economic Research, July.

8

The "Austerity Myth"
Gain without Pain?

Roberto Perotti

8.1 Introduction

Budget deficits have come back with a vengeance. In the last three years, they have risen in virtually all countries due to the recession and, in some cases, to bank support measures. What to do next is a matter of bitter controversy. For some, governments should start reining in deficits now, even though most countries have not fully recovered yet; if done properly—namely, by reducing spending rather than by increasing taxes—budget consolidations are not harmful, and might indeed result in a boost to GDP. This is one interpretation of Alesina and Perotti (1995) and Alesina and Ardagna (2010) (AAP hereafter), who study all the episodes of large deficit reductions in Organization for Economic Cooperation and Development (OECD) countries, defined as country—years where the cyclically adjusted deficit falls by more than, say, 1.5 percent of GDP. They compare the averages of macroeconomic variables before, during, and after these episodes,

Roberto Perotti is professor of economics at IGIER-Bocconi University and a research associate of the National Bureau of Economic Research.

I thank Alberto Alesina, John FitzGerald, Patrick Honohan, and Philip Lane for comments, and Marko Oja of the Finnish Ministry of Finance and Sylvie Toly of the OECD for help with the data. I also thank participants at the "10th BIS Annual Conference on Fiscal Policy and Its Implications for Monetary and Financial Stability," Lucern, June 23–24, 2011, and my discussants, Carlo Cottarelli and Harald Uhlig. Elia Boè and Jacopo Perego provided outstanding research assistance. This chapter was written for the IGIER-NBER conference "Fiscal Policy after the Financial Crisis," Milan, December 2011. It was produced as part of the project Growth and Sustainability Policies for Europe (GRASP), a Collaborative Project funded by the European Commission's Seventh Research Framework Programme, contract number 244725. Financial support by the European Research Council (Grant No. 230088) is also gratefully acknowledged. For acknowledgments, sources of research support, and disclosure of the author's material financial relationships, if any, please see http://www.nber.org/chapters/c12652.ack.

and find that consolidations based mainly on spending cuts are typically associated with above average increases in output and private consumption, while consolidations based mainly on revenue increases are associated with recessions.

For others, this evidence on expansionary government spending cuts is flawed, and the aftermaths of a recession are the worst time to start a fiscal consolidation. This is the message of International Monetary Fund (2010) (IMF hereafter). The heart of the matter is that the methodology used to estimate a cyclically adjusted change in the deficit—that part of the change in the deficit that is due to the discretionary action of the policymaker—as opposed to the automatic effects of the cycle on government spending and revenues. The IMF argues that the cyclical adjustment by AAP (in turn a variant of the methodology adopted by the OECD in the *Economic Outlook* and by the IMF in the *World Economic Outlook*) fails to remove important cyclical components, and that this failure can explain a spurious finding of expansionary budget consolidations. The IMF instead estimates "action-based" or "narrative" measures of fiscal consolidations, in the spirit of Romer and Romer (2010), and uses them to estimate a vector autoregression (VAR) and compute impulse responses of GDP and its components to a discretionary shock to the government surplus. They conclude that all fiscal consolidations are contractionary in the short run. Although not based on a formal statistical analysis, Krugman (2010) argues that many cases of "expansionary fiscal consolidation" were driven by a net export boom, hence the mechanism—whatever it is—is not replicable in the world as a whole.

In this chapter, I argue that the IMF criticism of the AAP approach is correct in principle and represents an important potential advance; however, the implementation of the approach has problems of its own, both in the way it computes action-based measures of fiscal consolidations and in the way it estimates impulse responses to fiscal consolidations. On the other hand, large consolidations are typically multiyear affairs, and the means-comparison methodology of AAP is ill suited to deal with these cases. Both approaches are also subject to the reverse causality problems that are almost inevitable with yearly data, and both lump together countries and episodes with possibly very different characteristics.[1]

For all these reasons, I argue that one can learn much from detailed case studies. I present four, covering the largest, multiyear fiscal consolidations that are commonly regarded as spending based. Two of these episodes—Denmark 1982 to 1986 and Ireland 1987 to 1990—were exchange rate based consolidations, while the other two—Finland 1992 to 1998 and Sweden 1993 to 1998—were undertaken in the opposite circumstances, after abandoning a peg. For each episode, I do two things. First, I compute action-based measures of budget consolidations, often using the original documents,

---

1. Favero, Giavazzi, and Perego (2011) study various dimensions of country heterogeneity and how this affects the IMF estimates of the effects of consolidations.

and taking into consideration also fiscal action outside the official budgets, something that was often overlooked by IMF. As I will show, this typically results in smaller discretionary consolidations than estimated by the IMF or the OECD, and in a much smaller share of spending cuts. The reason is that often governments used supplementary budgets during the year to undo some of the spending cuts of the January budgets, and also because the IMF often only considers spending cuts or tax increases.

Second, I study in detail the timeline of budget consolidations, the behavior of interest rates, wages, and the exchange rate, and of GDP and its components, in order to try and learn something about the possible channels at work. I use contemporary sources, like the OECD yearly *Economic Surveys* (ES from now on) of each country, and country-specific studies.

In doing this, I focus on two very specific and narrow questions. First, is there evidence that large budget consolidations, particularly those that are based mainly on spending cuts, have expansionary effects *in the short run*? I will have nothing to say regarding the medium- to long-run effects of fiscal consolidations. As a consequence, I will have nothing to say about their social desirability: it might well be that reducing government spending is socially desirable even if it has contractionary effects in the short run.

Second, if the answer to the first question is in the affirmative, *how useful is the experience of the past as a guide to the present*? For instance, if fiscal consolidations were expansionary in the past because they caused a steep decline in interest rates or inflation, it is unlikely that the same mechanism can be relied on in the present circumstances, with low inflation and interest rates close to zero. Or, if consolidations were expansionary mainly because they were associated with large increases in net exports, this mechanism is obviously not available to a large group of countries highly integrated between them.

That private consumption should boom when government spending falls would come as no surprise to believers in a standard neoclassical model with forward-looking agents. Although in that model alternative time paths of government spending and distortionary taxation can create virtually any response of private consumption, from negative to positive, the basic idea is straightforward; lower government spending means lower taxes and higher household wealth, hence higher consumption. This is sometimes dubbed the "confidence channel" of fiscal consolidations.[2] Lower taxes also mean fewer distortions, hence they *can* lead to higher output and investment. More generally, a large fiscal consolidation may signal a change in regime in a country that is in the midst of a recession, and may boost investment through this channel.

In open economies alternative effects may be at play. A fiscal consolidation might reinforce and make credible a process of wage moderation, either implicitly or by trading explicitly less labor taxes for wage moderation; this in

---

2. Or "confidence fairy," in the less-charitable interpretation of Krugman (2011).

turn feeds into a real effective depreciation and boosts exports. Or, it might reinforce the decline in interest rates by reducing the risk premium or by making a peg more credible. These alternative channels were highlighted, for instance, in Alesina and Perotti (1995, 1997) and Alesina and Ardagna (1998).

The main conclusions of the case studies I present here are as follows:

1. Discretionary fiscal consolidations are often smaller than estimated in the past, and spending cuts are less important than is commonly believed. Only in Ireland were spending cuts larger than revenue increases; in Finland, spending cuts were a negligible component of the consolidation.

2. All stabilizations were associated with expansions in GDP. Except in Denmark (one of the two exchange rate based stabilizations), the expansion of GDP was initially driven by exports. Private consumption typically increased six to eight quarters after the start of the consolidation. And as national source data (as opposed to OECD data that turned out to be incorrect) show, the expansion in what was probably the most famous consolidation of all—Ireland—turned out to be much less remarkable than previously thought.

3. In Denmark the stabilization relied most closely on the exchange rate as a nominal anchor, and as such is of particular interest for small EMU (Economic and Monetary Union of the European Union) members today. Denmark relied on an internal devaluation via wage restraint and incomes policies as a substitute for a devaluation. It exhibited all the typical features of an exchange rate based stabilization: inflation and interest rates fell fast, domestic demand initially boomed; but as competitiveness slowly worsened, the current account started worsening, and eventually growth ground to a halt and consumption declined for three years. The slump lasted for several years.

4. In the second exchange rate based stabilization, Ireland, the government depreciated the currency before starting the consolidation and fixing the exchange rate within the European Exchange Rate Mechanism (ERM). Again, wage restraint and incomes policies played a major role, but a key feature was the concomitant depreciation of the sterling and the expansion in the United Kingdom, which boosted Irish exports and contributed to reducing the nominal interest rate.

5. The two countries that instead floated the exchange rate while consolidating (Finland and Sweden) experienced large real depreciations and an export boom. Also, in both countries inflation targeting was adopted at the same time as the consolidations were started.

6. The budget consolidations were accompanied by large decline in nominal interest rates, from very high levels.

7. Wage moderation was essential to maintain the benefits of the depreciations and to make possible the decline of the long nominal rates. In turn, wage moderation probably had a powerful effect as a signal of regime change.

8. Incomes policies were in turn instrumental in achieving wage moderation, and in signaling a regime shift from the past. Often these policies took the form of an explicit exchange between lower taxes on labor and lower contractual wage inflation. However, the international experience suggests that incomes policies are effective for a few years at best. The experience of Denmark in this study is consistent with this.

These results are useful to understand what are the typical mechanisms and initial conditions that are associated with expansionary fiscal consolidations. Some of the conditions that made these consolidations expansionary (a decline in interest rates from very high levels, wage moderation relative to other countries, perhaps supported by incomes policies) seem not to be applicable in the present circumstances of low interest rates and low wage inflation. The experience of the exchange rate based stabilization—Ireland and Denmark—is particularly interesting, as it is conceivably more relevant for the Eurozone countries that are experiencing budget problems. Both countries managed to depreciate the exchange rate prior to pegging and to the consolidation, an option that is not available to members of the EMU except vis-à-vis the non-Euro countries as a whole. Ireland also benefitted from the appreciation of the currency of its main trading partner, the United Kingdom. In contrast, the Danish expansion was short lived, as it quickly ran into a loss of competitiveness that hampered growth for several years.

The timing and role of exports growth also casts doubt on the "confidence explanation" of expansionary fiscal consolidations; an expansion that is based on a real depreciation and a net export boom is also obviously not available to the world as a whole.

However, even in the short run budget consolidations were probably a necessary condition for output expansion for at least three reasons: first, they were instrumental in reducing the nominal interest rate; second, they made wage moderation possible by signaling a regime change that reduced inflation expectations; third, for the same reason they were instrumental in preserving the benefits of nominal depreciation and thus in generating an export boom.

In my analysis, I do not use formal tools; I do not estimate consumption or investment functions, to test, for instance, whether there are positive residuals during fiscal consolidations. Many consumption and investment functions have been estimated for these countries before with a specific focus on these consolidation episodes,[3] and I do not have anything to add to the existing estimates.

I do not consider political factors, such as whether fiscal consolidations are more frequently observed under majority or minority governments, or

---

3. See, for example, Giavazzi and Pagano (1990) for Ireland and Denmark, Giavazzi and Pagano (1996) for Sweden, Bradley and Whelan (1997) for Ireland, Honkapohja and Koskela (1999) for Finland, Bergman and Hutchsion (2010) for Denmark.

under coalition or single-party governments. Similarly, I do not address the role of budget institutions, such as whether some institutions or processes are more conducive to effective consolidations, or the role of expenditure ceilings. These are all important issues that have been dealt with elsewhere (see, e.g., Alesina, Perotti, and Tavares 1998 and Lessen 2000 on the former issue, and Guichard et al. 2007; Hauptmeier, Heipertz, and Schuknecht 2007; Hardy, Kamener, and Karotie 2011; and Borg 2010 on the latter).

I also have little to say about the composition of spending cuts and revenue increases; again, this is an extremely important question, and the original focus of Alesina and Perotti (1995), but one that is difficult to address in the context of the narrative approach that I use here.

This chapter has obviously numerous antecedents. The closest antecedent is Alesina and Ardagna (1998), who also look at case studies and emphasize the role of wage dynamics and incomes policies. I defer a discussion of this and other papers to section 8.5.

The outline of the chapter is as follows. Section 8.2 presents a simple statistical model that allows a unified treatment of the methodologies of the IMF and of AAP, and discusses the biases associated with each. Section 8.3 focuses on the IMF approach, and section 8.4 on the AAP approach. Section 8.5 discusses the relation with the literature. Section 8.6 presents the case studies. Section 8.7 concludes.

8.2   A Simple Static Model

The intuition for the AAP approach and for the IMF criticism of that approach can be gathered from a simple static model. The equation for the budget surplus is

(1) $\Delta s = \alpha_y \Delta y + \alpha_p \Delta p + \beta_y \Delta_y + \varepsilon_s$ $\alpha_y > 0;$ $\alpha_p > 0;$ $\beta_y > 0,$

where s is the budget surplus as a share of GDP, y is the log of real GDP, and p is the log of asset prices. Due to the operation of automatic stabilizers, the surplus increases automatically (i.e., for given policy parameters like tax rates and eligibility rules for unemployment benefits) when GDP increases ($\alpha_y > 0$). The surplus also increases automatically when asset prices increase, because of their effects on tax revenues ($\alpha_p > 0$).[4] In addition, when GDP increases, a policymaker might implement systematic, countercyclical changes to policy parameters (e.g., increase tax rates) to cool down the economy, and vice versa in recessions: this is captured by $\beta_y > 0$. Finally, the random component ε_s captures discretionary actions by the policymaker, which are not motivated by the response to cyclical developments: for instance, actions motivated by ideology or long-run growth considerations.

---

4. See, for example, Morris and Schuknecht (2007) and Benetrix and Lane (2011).

I allow GDP to depend on the pure discretionary component ε_s, but also on the systematic discretionary component $\beta_y \Delta y$, possibly with different coefficients:

(2) $$\Delta y = \gamma_1 \varepsilon_s + \gamma_2 \beta_y \Delta_y + \varepsilon_y.$$

In a Keynesian world, presumably $\gamma_1 < 0$ and $\gamma_2 < 0$.[5]

Finally, I assume that Δp is white noise: $\Delta p = \varepsilon_p$, and it is positively correlated with Δy: $\mathrm{cov}(\Delta y, \varepsilon_p) > 0$; ε_s instead is a pure policy shock, uncorrelated with ε_p or ε_y.

The issue of estimating the fiscal policy multiplier can be interpreted as finding a consistent estimate of γ_1 in equation (2) (of course, in general this will be done in a dynamic context, such a vector autoregression, but this simple static model is enough for the key intuition). The econometrician, however, in general does not observe ε_s, but only Δs. There are basically two ways to proceed next, which correspond to the two approaches by AAP and IMF.

Authors AAP apply a standard cyclical adjustment method, such as that by the OECD (see, e.g., Fedalino, Ivanova, and Horton 2009): they use existing estimates of the automatic output elasticity α_y to subtract $\alpha_y \Delta y$ from the observed change in the surplus.[6] Hence, one ends up with the AAP measure of the cyclically adjusted surplus:

(3) $$\Delta s^{AAP} = \beta_y \Delta_y + \alpha_p \varepsilon_p + \varepsilon_s.$$

There are clearly two potential problems with using this measure of the surplus, as emphasized by IMF. The first arises because Δs^{AAP} includes a countercyclical response by policymakers to output shocks, $\beta_y \Delta y$, which is positively correlated with output changes since $\beta_y > 0$. I call this the *countercyclical response* problem.[7] The second problem arises because Δs^{AAP} contains a component, $\alpha_p \varepsilon_p$, which is positively correlated with output since

5. I am simplifying considerably here. While a textbook Keynesian model like the IS/LM (Investment–Saving/Liquidity preference–Money supply) model usually does imply $\gamma_1 < 0$, virtually any contemporaneous or dynamic relation between the surplus and GDP can occur in a neoclassical model, with or without price rigidity. Only for simplicity I will sometimes refer to the case of $\gamma_1 > 0$ as "neoclassical effects" of fiscal policy, or "expansionary effects of fiscal consolidations."

6. The OECD constructs the cyclically adjusted change in the surplus using external estimates of the elasticity to output of each type of tax revenues. The actual implementation of this approach by AAP is different: they first regress budget variables on the unemployment rate, and then take the residuals of these regressions.

7. The cyclical adjustment method "omits years during which actions aimed at fiscal consolidation were followed by an adverse shock and an offsetting discretionary stimulus. For example, imagine that two countries adopt identical consolidation policies, but then one is hit by an adverse shock and so adopts discretionary stimulus, while the other is hit with a favorable shock. . . . The standard approach would therefore tend to miss cases of consolidation followed by adverse shocks, because there may be little or no rise in the [cyclically adjusted primary balance] despite the consolidation measures" (IMF, 4).

standard cyclical adjustments do not correct for asset price changes and $\alpha_p > 0$. I call this the *imperfect cyclical adjustment* problem.[8]

The action-based, or narrative, measure of fiscal policy stance constructed by IMF is an attempt to solve both problems by constructing a series for ε_s directly, using the original official estimates of the effects on spending and revenues of each specific measure in a budget or in a spending or tax bill. Hence

(4) $\Delta s^{IMF} = \varepsilon_s$.

Now consider using these two measures of the discretionary fiscal stance to estimate γ_1. The reduced form for output is

(5) $\Delta y = k\gamma_1\varepsilon_s + k\varepsilon_y; \quad k = \dfrac{1}{1 - \gamma_2\beta_y}$.

An OLS regression of Δy on Δs^{IMF} therefore gives:

(6) $\gamma^{IMF} = k\gamma_1 = \dfrac{\gamma_1}{1 - \gamma_2\beta_y}$.

Hence, if the world is Keynesian ($\gamma_1 < 0$) the IMF estimate of γ_1 is biased toward 0 because of the countercyclical response problem. Following a unitary realization of ε_s, GDP falls by γ_1; then the policymaker reacts, on average, by increasing the surplus by β_y, which leads to a decline in output by $|\gamma_2\beta_y|$, and so on. If one is interested in studying how much GDP reacts to a unit exogenous change in the surplus, and not in these indirect effects via the policymaker response, the estimated coefficient from the IMF approach is biased toward 0: one estimates a less powerful Keynesian effect of fiscal policy than in the true model. However, it is likely that this particular bias of the IMF approach is relatively small.

Note that the problem stems from the use of annual data. With quarterly data, it would be plausible to assume $\beta_y = 0$, since the policymaker would not be able to learn about an output shock and react to it within three months. This was indeed the key identifying assumption in Blanchard and Perotti (2002). Note the parallel with changes in the Federal Fund rate (FFR) target. Virtually all policy changes to the FFR are driven by countercyclical considerations. But, by assuming that changes in the FFR did not affect GDP within a month, with monthly data one can identify the component of the FFR forecast error that is orthogonal to GDP forecast errors.

---

8. "The first problem is that cyclical adjustment methods suffer from measurement errors that are likely to be correlated with economic developments. For example, standard cyclical-adjustment methods fail to remove swings in government tax revenue associated with asset price or commodity price movements from the fiscal data, resulting in changes in the [cyclically-adjusted primary balance] that are not necessarily linked to actual policy changes. Thus, including episodes associated with asset price booms—which tend to coincide with economic expansions—and excluding episodes associated with asset price busts from the sample introduces an expansionary bias" (IMF, 4).

Now consider the AAP approach. The estimated OLS effect of a regression of Δy on Δs^{AAP} is

(7) $$\gamma^{AAP} = \frac{\text{cov}(\Delta s^{AAP}, \Delta y)}{\text{var}(\Delta s^{AAP})} > \gamma_1.$$

It is easy to show that the bias generated by the AAP approach is bigger than the IMF bias, essentially because the AAP approach is affected both by the imperfect adjustment problem and by the countercyclical response problem.[9] An incomplete cyclical adjustment biases the coefficient toward zero because it generates a positive correlation between the change in the AAP surplus and the error term in the estimated GDP equation; hence, it biases the results again toward a less powerful Keynesian effect of fiscal policy.

Thus, methodologically the IMF approach is potentially an important step forward. However, contrary to what it is claimed, it does not explain the key finding of AAP, namely the expansionary effects of spending-based consolidations. In addition, its implementation suffers from other problems of its own that complicate its interpretation. I now turn to these issues.

8.3   The IMF Approach

In the simplest version of the IMF approach, one computes impulse responses from single equations regressions like

(8) $\Delta y_t = \rho_1 \Delta y_{t-1} + \ldots + \rho_k \Delta y_{t-k} + \lambda_0 \varepsilon_{s,t} + \lambda_1 \varepsilon_{s,t-1} + \ldots + \lambda_h \varepsilon_{s,t-h} + \eta_t.$

In the more general case, one computes a VAR, in which lags 0 to h of $\varepsilon_{s,t}$ appear as exogenous variables in each equation.

Panel data VARs are always dangerous objects: they impose the same dynamics on potentially very different groups of countries (see Favero, Giavazzi, and Perego 2011 on this), and they introduce a bias from the presence of lagged endogenous variables. Besides these well-known problems, I will focus here on three others that are more specific to the particular application.

8.3.1   Why the IMF Approach Does Not Explain the Expansionary Fiscal Stabilization Results

The key methodological point of IMF is that the bias generated by the imperfect cyclical adjustment problem and by the countercyclical response problem can explain the expansionary fiscal consolidation results of AAP. This is incorrect.

To understand why, note that IMF and AAP agree that, on average, fiscal consolidations are associated with a recession in the short run. Where they

---

9. Note in particular that the IMF approach is unbiased if $\beta_y = 0$, while the AAP approach continues to be biased.

differ is in the effects of spending-based consolidations: still contractionary according to IMF, expansionary according to AAP.

However, contrary to the claim by IMF, the *imperfect cyclical adjustment bias* cannot explain this difference—in fact, it goes in the opposite direction. In other words, removing this bias would *reinforce* the main finding of AAP—that revenue-based consolidations are contractionary while spending-based ones are expansionary. In fact, if the IMF is correct, in periods of high growth, cyclically adjusted revenues are overestimated, hence the AAP approach imparts a spurious *positive* bias to the correlation between increases in the surplus that are due to increases in revenues and GDP growth; but the AAP method finds a *negative* correlation.

The *countercyclical response bias* also is unlikely to explain the expansionary consolidations result. For discretionary fiscal policy to react to GDP developments within the current fiscal year, discretionary fiscal action has to be quick. Changing taxes is typically easier, and works faster, than changing spending; thus, as a first response policymakers will usually cut taxes in response to negative shocks, and will increase taxes in response to positive shocks. Again, this would impart a *positive* bias to the correlation between revenue-based increases in the surplus and GDP growth, while the AAP method finds a *negative* correlation.

8.3.2   The Censoring Bias of the IMF Approach

The IMF records only positive values of ε_s, and sets all negative values to 0. It is easy to show that censoring of the independent variable generates a bias away from 0 of the coefficient of interest: figure 8.1, adapted from Rigobon and Stoker (2003), provides the intuition. Rigobon and Stoker also show that the bias can be substantial if a large share of the observations are censored; in the IMF study, these are about 60 percent of the whole sample. Hence, if fiscal policy has Keynesian effects, censoring of the independent variable will show even stronger Keynesian effects; symmetrically, if fiscal policy has neoclassical effects, censoring will show even stronger neoclassical effects.

8.3.3   The Standard Error of the Impulse Responses

The IMF reports impulse responses with one standard error bands. While this is somewhat typical of the fiscal policy literature, I now agree with Ramey (2011) that there is no reason why only this particular literature should deviate from the norm in macroeconomics.[10] The problem is almost certainly more serious in a panel VAR, because of the correlation of errors across countries, which is bound to be an issue in this context; in the micro literature, this correlation has been shown to lead to a downward bias in the estimated standard errors by a factor that can easily reach ten or more (see,

10. With apologies, having used one standard error bands in my own work.

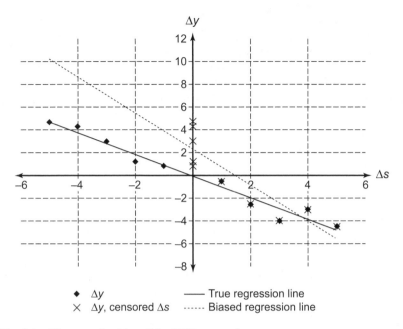

Fig. 8.1   The censoring bias of the IMF approach

e.g., Angrist and Pischke 2008 or Bertrand, Duflo, and Mullainathan 2004). Failure to correct for this can therefore lead to a vast underestimation of the uncertainty surrounding the estimated impulse response. If one considers that the reported impulse responses would already not be significant if two standard error bands were used, it is doubtful how much confidence we should put in these estimates—a point to which I will return in the following.

8.3.4   Omitting the Countercyclical Response in the IMF Approach

In computing its action-based measure of consolidations, IMF includes only those actions that can be ascribed to the goal of enhancing long-run growth or reducing the deficit, thus excluding actions undertaken with the goal of stabilizing short-run fluctuations. While omitting the countercyclical response of fiscal policy has an obvious motivation for the purposes of estimating the multiplier of fiscal policy actions (as in Romer and Romer 2010), it can provide the wrong picture of the actual fiscal policy stance when trying to gather the size of a fiscal consolidation. It is also not easy to implement on a large set of countries, often without the help of primary sources like the original budget documents.

Perhaps most importantly, it is very difficult to identify motives behind a certain policy action, and it must have been even more difficult to contemporaries. It is conceivable that most policy actions are justified at some point by the desire to achieve such worthy goals as growth or fiscal discipline; finding the "true" motivation is likely to be nearly impossible. It is unlikely, however, that the public at the time would weigh differently the different measures, depending on their alleged motivation.

For all these reasons, omitting these actions gives a distorted picture of the fiscal stance: for instance, as I show later, IMF concludes that there was a large budget consolidation in Finland between 1992 and 1995, but in fact there was hardly any, because spending cuts in the main budgets were often interspersed with spending increases in supplementary budgets that are largely ignored by IMF. Some of these supplementary measures might have had a countercyclical motivation (if so, it was rarely stated explicitly); more likely, these measures were taken in response to a political opposition to the earlier budget cuts—perhaps within the government itself.

In other cases, the difference in motivations was extremely (perhaps too) subtle even with hindsight. For instance, in September 1982 the new Danish government introduced a package of budget austerity in order to curb the current account deficit. In 1986 it increased taxes to achieve the same goal. True, the former occurred in a context of a much larger budget deficit, but the main motivation appears to have been the same. The IMF counts the former, but not the latter.

8.4   Comparing Averages in the AAP Approach

The AAP approach consists of comparing average values of several macro variables before, during, and after large fiscal consolidations. First, AAP define a country-year as a fiscal consolidation if in that year the cyclically-adjusted primary balance improves by, say, at least 1.5 percent of GDP. Then they compute average values across episodes of the change in the primary surplus—of GDP, of consumption growth, and a number of other variables—"during" the year of the consolidation and in the two years "before" and "after" the consolidation. They repeat the exercise separately for "expansionary" consolidations (those that were accompanied by an increase in growth) and for "contractionary" ones.

Finding the effects of fiscal consolidations is not different from estimating (possibly nonlinear) fiscal policy multipliers, an issue that has been the object of a heated methodological debate recently. What is the justification, then, for comparing averages of large consolidations? Three possible reasons come to mind: (a) there are large measurement errors, which are minimized by focusing on large consolidations; (b) the effects of fiscal policy can be nonlinear, so that it makes sense to isolate large consolidations; (c) consolidations are random events that are independent of initial conditions and other variables.

However, even if assumptions (a) to (c) are correct, it is not clear what are the advantages of comparing means relative to running a VAR (the method adopted by the IMF, although subject to the censoring bias illustrated before). But there are two more potential problems with the implementation of the mean-comparison method. Both have to do with the fact that large consolidations are seldom one-year events. I illustrate them using the most recent incarnation of the AAP approach, Alesina and Ardagna (2010).

8.4.1   Identifying Multiyear Fiscal Consolidations

If, say, year t and $t + 2$ are both consolidations years according to the previous definition, year $t + 2$ appears both in the "after" average of the year t consolidation and in the "during" average of the year $t + 2$ consolidation. The issue becomes trickier because, if there are three consecutive years of consolidation, t, $t + 1$, and $t + 2$, Alesina and Ardagna (2010) consider only year t as during and years $t + 1$ and $t + 2$ as after; in other words, now year $t + 2$ is no longer considered the during year of a different consolidation.

8.4.2   Endogeneity and Preexisting Trends

Conceptually, the means-comparison method is not different from a difference-in-difference (DD) estimator, in which one compares, say, the difference in the rates of growth of GDP after and before an expansionary consolidation with the same difference in contractionary consolidations. In DD estimation, a key problem is that of preexisting trends: perhaps the finding that the rate of growth increases more in expansionary consolidations is just a result of a preexisting stronger trend in the countries that we then assign to the expansionary group.

This problem is related to that of endogeneity of fiscal policy. We have seen that the imperfections in the cyclical adjustment of revenues, of the type emphasized by IMF, cannot explain the expansionary fiscal adjustment result of AAP. But there are other possible problems with the cyclical adjustment that may pollute the interpretation of the evidence. There is anecdotal evidence that the cyclical adjustment may be particularly problematic in large recessions or expansions. For instance, during the recessions of the late 1980s and early 1990s, Finland and Sweden experienced dramatic automatic increases in welfare-related spending, of several percentage points of GDP in just one year. If this is true, there is an alternative reading of the means-comparison evidence on expansionary adjustments. Suppose there is an exogenous, persistent positive shock to growth: government spending as a share of GDP will fall as GDP growth accelerates, giving the impression of an expansionary, spending-based consolidation, while in reality fiscal policy was completely passive. This frequently heard criticism of the expansionary fiscal consolidation view is difficult to address, but at a minimum it seems to require a more satisfactory treatment of the dynamics of consolidations than just looking at the one year of the consolidation.

8.5   Relation with the Literature

The literature on fiscal consolidations is large, and it has been surveyed in part in Alesina and Ardagna (2010). Here, I will focus specifically on recent work that is more closely related to this chapter.

The closest antecedents of this chapter are Alesina and Ardagna (1998) and Broadbent and Daly (2010). Alesina and Ardagna (1998) apply the means-comparison method, followed by ten case studies. Most of the cases are one- or two-year episodes; only Ireland and Denmark last three years. The treatment of each case is necessarily more concise than in the present chapter. Like this chapter, the papers emphasize the role of wage developments, although they do not study in detail the evolution of wage negotiations and the relation with GDP and its components. Also, their conclusions are sometimes difficult to reconcile with the evidence they present: as Jordi Galí points out in his discussion, relative unit labor costs actually *increase* immediately after the start of the expansionary consolidations, while the trade balance *improves* significantly during the recessionary consolidations. There is also no discussion of the role of interest rates, which play a critical role in my analysis.

Broadbent and Daly (2010) also apply the means-comparison method and present three short case studies, which display the salient features of each episode. The basic message is similar to Alesina and Ardagna (1998), with an additional emphasis on the role of the fall in interest rates. They point out correctly that interest rates declined in revenue-based consolidations as well.

Baker (2010) and Jajadev and Konczal (2010) study the samples of fiscal consolidations of Alesina and Ardagna (2010) and Broadbent and Daly (2010) with a view to their applicability to current circumstances. They both point out that a key feature of the consolidations of the past is the scope for reducing interest rates, which is not available now. Jajadev and Konczal (2010) also argue that growth in the year preceding the adjustment was already strong, on average, in the sample of Alesina and Ardagna's (2010) expansionary consolidations.

Lilico, Holmes, and Sameen (2009) also present six case studies, although they focus more on the budget and political processes of the consolidations.

8.6   Case Studies

I now present four case studies. All four cover small, open European countries. The first two, Denmark 1983 to 1986 and Ireland 1987 to 1989, are typically regarded as the classic examples of expansionary fiscal consolidations. They are also examples of exchange rate based stabilizations, in which a country pegs the exchange rate to obtain a rapid decline in inflation (although, as we will see, things are not so clear-cut in the case of Ireland). The next two cases are Finland 1992 to 1998 and Sweden 1993 to 1998. These were also associated with an economic expansion, but undertaken under opposite circumstances in one important respect; that is, after abandoning a peg and letting the currency float.

For each country, I display four tables, displaying my reconstruction of a narrative measure of yearly discretionary changes in spending and revenues, various types of interest rates and spreads, various measures of exchange rates, unit labor costs, inflation, and GDP and its components.

8.6.1   Denmark

In 1980 and 1981 Denmark entered a recession. The deficit worsened quickly, from 1.5 percent of GDP in 1979 to 11 percent in 1982; interest payments rose, but the government also increased spending under pressure from rising unemployment; as a consequence, the primary deficit increased by 7.5 percent of GDP. The recession was relatively mild, in part because the government devalued or realigned the Krone several times during 1979 to 1982.[11] In fact, in those three years the nominal effective exchange rate depreciated by about 15 percent and exports increased by about 25 percent cumulatively.

In 1982 GDP expanded strongly, at 4 percent, spurred mostly by investment: private consumption was subdued, and so were exports. Wage dynamics accelerated, the current account deficit rose to 4 percent of GDP, and the Krone came under strong pressure; to preempt a further worsening of the macroeconomic picture, the new government that took office in September 1982 embarked in a medium-run stabilization program.

The program adopted a two-pronged approach to achieve its goals of enhancing competitiveness and reducing the budget deficit: it explicitly ruled out devaluations, relying instead on the exchange rate as a nominal anchor, and emphasized incomes policies to achieve wage restraint. As we will see, the Danish episode exhibits all the hallmarks of a typical exchange rate based stabilization (see, e.g., Ades, Kiguel, and Liviatan 1993 and Detragiache and Hamann 1999): an initial rapid decline in inflation and nominal interest rates, a boom in domestic demand led by private consumption (especially durables) and, to a lesser extent, by private investment; a gradual appreciation of the real exchange and a deterioration of the current account, which eventually led to the undoing of the program.

Budget Timetable

Overall, I calculate that between 1983 and 1987 discretionary measures improved the primary balance by 8.9 percent of GDP, 55 percent of which were tax increases (see table 8.1). The IMF estimates instead a smaller consolida-

---

11. The krone was devalued unilaterally in November 1979, adjusted downward on the occasion of general ERM realignments in September 1979 and February 1982, while it stood firm when other currencies realigned in October 1981 and June 1982.

Table 8.1   **Denmark: Discretionary budget measures**

	Spending	Revenues	Surplus	Spending IMF	Revenues IMF	Surplus IMF
1983 total	−1.8	0.9	2.8	−1.8	0.9	2.8
Cumulative	−1.8	0.9	2.8	−1.8	0.9	2.8
1984 total	−1.2	1.5	2.7	−1.7	0.7	2.4
Cumulative	−3.1	2.4	5.5	−3.6	1.6	5.1
1985 total	−0.9	0.3	1.1	−0.8	0.8	1.5
Cumulative	−4.0	2.7	6.6	−4.3	2.4	6.7
1986 total	0.0	2.1	2.1	0.0	0.0	0.0
Cumulative	−4.0	4.7	8.7	−4.3	2.4	6.7
1987 total	0.0	0.2	0.2	0.0	0.0	0.0
Cumulative	−4.0	4.9	8.9	−4.3	2.4	6.7

Source: For columns (2) to (4), OECD *Economic Survey of Denmark*, various issues.

tion, 6.7 percent of GDP, 35 percent of which tax increases.[12] The IMF and I agree almost exactly on the size and timing of spending cuts, but IMF records much smaller tax increases because it omits the austerity measures of December 1985 and March 1986, totaling about 2 percent of GDP, on the grounds that they were undertaken for countercyclical reasons. However, this underscores the difficulties of attributing a sharp motive to fiscal policy actions: officially, these measures were undertaken for the same reasons as the initial 1982 consolidation, namely to tackle the current account deficit.

The fiscal consolidation itself was in two parts. The package introduced in September 1982 abolished the automatic indexation of tax schedules, froze unemployment benefits, imposed a tax on pension schemes (to be replaced from 1984 by a tax on their interests and dividends earnings), and increased employers' social security contributions. The result was almost 2 percent of GDP in spending cuts and 1 percent of GDP in revenue increases in 1983.[13]

After the draft 1984 budget was rejected in December 1983, elections were held and the government was confirmed in office. The April 1984 budget and various measures taken during the year cut spending by 1.2 percent of GDP and increased taxes by 1.5 percent of GDP.

In December of 1985, following continuing worsening of the trade balance in the second half of the year, the government decided on a new austerity package, which was followed by two more in March and October 1986. All three relied mostly on tax increases. The third one in particular (the "potato diet") was worth 1.5 percent of GDP and introduced a 20 percent tax on interests (exceptions included mortgages, loans to businesses, and to students) and further restrictions on consumer credit.

12. These numbers and the IMF numbers that follow are based on Devries et al. (2011).
13. Local taxes also increased markedly (see 1982/83 ES, 26); 1983/84 ES (9) also reports considerable reductions in local governments' public investment (recall that "ES" stands for "OECD Economic Survey"). These effects have not been quantified.

Table 8.2   **Denmark: Interest rates**

	1980	1981	1982	1983	1984	1985	1986	1987	1988	1989	1990
Nom. long	19.9	20.0	21.2	15.0	14.4	11.6	10.1	11.3	9.9	9.7	10.6
Nom. short	17.6	15.2	16.8	12.7	11.7	10.3	9.1	10.1	8.5	9.6	10.9
Real long	7.6	8.3	11.1	8.1	8.1	6.9	6.4	7.3	5.3	4.9	8.0
Real short	5.3	3.5	6.7	5.8	5.4	5.6	5.5	6.1	3.9	4.8	8.3
Long–short	2.3	4.8	4.5	2.3	2.7	1.3	0.9	1.2	1.4	0.1	−0.3
Long–long DEU	11.3	9.8	12.2	6.8	6.3	4.4	3.8	4.9	3.3	2.6	1.9

Sources: OECD *Economic Outlook*, No. 88; long-term interest rate for Germany until 1990: OECD *Economic Outlook*, No. 72.

Inflation, Wage Dynamics, Competitiveness, and Interest Rates

Between 1980 and 1982 relative unit labor costs in manufacturing fell by more than 15 percent, thanks to the depreciation of the krone and a good productivity performance. Thus, Denmark entered the consolidation phase after accumulating a large depreciation. However, the price of this policy of devaluations and realignments was high interest rates and a large differential vis à vis Germany: in September 1982, long-term interest rates reached a peak of 23 percent (see tables 8.2 and 8.3).

As we have seen, an important component of the September 1982 stabilization package was the use of the exchange rate as a nominal anchor. This policy gained credibility in March 1983 when the krone (kr) followed the DM (drogerie markt) in appreciating in an ERM realignment; the interest differential with Germany came down quickly. A second precondition for the credibility of the policy was wage restraint. The government planned to achieve this through active intervention in the wage negotiation process.

The incomes policies adopted were in several steps. As part of the comprehensive package of September 1982, the new government suspended all indexation of wages, salaries, and transfer incomes until 1985; it limited the increases in public sector wages to 4 percent, with the explicit intent of making this a guideline for the wage negotiation between the trade unions and the employers' organization, coming up in March 1983.[14] The subsequent wage agreement indeed followed closely these guidelines, implying a strong deceleration of the wage dynamics. The package also froze the maximum amount of unemployment and sickness benefits until April 1986. After the election of spring 1984, the government approved new incomes policy measures, mainly an extension of the suspension of wage and transfer indexation until March 1987.

By April 1983 long-term interest rates were down to 14 percent. Contemporary sources[15] attributed the decline to the strict budget policies, to

14. The government announced a tax cut of krone 2.5bn (about .5 percent of GDP) to support wage and salary freeze, but the tax cut was later rejected by Parliament.
15. See, for example, 1982/83 ES (35), 1983/84 ES (12), and 1985/86 ES (17).

Table 8.3   Denmark: Competitiveness indicators

	1980	1981	1982	1983	1984	1985	1986	1987	1988	1989	1990
Hourly earn., manuf.[a]		9.4	9.9	6.6	4.7	4.8	5.1	9.0	6.6	4.5	4.8
ULC, all economy[b]	11.0	9.2	9.2	6.6	3.9	4.1	2.8	8.9	5.3	3.5	2.7
ULC, manuf.[b]	7.1	9.2	8.6	2.7	5.8	6.0	7.8	10.8	3.2	0.9	4.0
Nom. eff. exch. rate[b]	-7.3	-5.5	-3.4	0.9	-2.3	2.2	5.7	3.6	-1.1	-1.6	8.1
Relative ULC, manuf.[b]	-10.0	-4.9	-1.2	1.6	0.9	4.1	8.8	11.5	-0.2	-4.7	
Relative nom. wages, manuf.[c]	-8.6	-6.6	-1.9	2.1	-3.0	1.2	6.6	9.5	-0.2	-3.2	3.9
Relative ULC, all economy[c]	-12.2	-6.8	-2.6	0.3	2.1	3.8	10.1	11.9	0.4	-4.3	8.9
Labor prod. per person, all economy[a]	1.3	1.2	3.5	2.3	2.7	1.3	1.0	0.6	1.8	1.6	2.5
Labor prod. per person, manuf.[a]	4.6	1.4	3.8	8.3	-0.1	-1.6	-0.7	-2.2	1.8	4.4	-2.1
Labor prod. per hour, all economy[a]	0.0	3.0	2.9	2.6	3.0	2.2	0.8	2.8	3.0	2.7	3.0
Labor prod. per hour, manuf.[a]	4.3	2.9	2.6	7.5	0.1	0.7	-2.0	0.3	2.2	6.0	-1.5
CPI[c]	12.3	11.8	10.1	6.9	6.3	4.7	3.7	4.0	4.5	4.8	2.6

Note: An increase in measures of the nominal exchange rate or relative ULC (unlimited liability corporation) or wages is an appreciation.

[a]OECD *Main Economic Indicators*

[b]OECD *Economic Outlook*, No. 88

[c]EUROSTAT

the increased credibility of the hard currency policy when the Krone followed the DM in the revaluation of March 1983, and to the moderate wage settlements. The large capital outflows of late 1982 also turned into inflows. Interest rates kept falling following the April 1984 budget, which included further incomes policy measures (1983/84 ES, 14). The liberalization of capital movements also contributed to reducing interest rates.

After the failure of decentralized wage negotiations in early 1985 and a pessimistic Public Finance Report, in March 1985 the government tried to have tripartite negotiations but was not successful. However, it decided further incomes policy measures, including a ceiling on public and private sector salary increases at 2 percent in 1985/86 and 1.5 percent in 1986/87. It supported this proposal by a cut in employers' social security contributions, financed by higher taxes on profits.[16] By the beginning of 1986 long interest rates were down to 10 percent, and the differential with Germany to 3 percentage points.

Thus, the years 1983 to 1985 were years of wage moderation, helped by government intervention. The year 1986 displayed the first signs of wage pressure. The government was no longer willing to provide wage targets for the 1987 wage negotiations; these resulted in wage growth of 9 and 7 percent in 1987 and 1988. Two explanations have been offered (see Andersen and Risager 1990, 173): first, public sector workers' discontent; second, the upcoming 1987 elections. Also, in 1986 the nominal effective exchange rate started appreciating; as a result of these developments, relative unit labor costs increased, by about 10 percent in 1986 and 1987.

Thus, the benefits of incomes policies, to the extent that they were behind the wage restraint of 1983 to 1985, were short-lived: wage negotiations in 1987 to 1989 largely undid the benefits of the earlier wage restraint.[17] As I show later, growth halted from 1987 to 1989, and thereafter remained slow until 1994.

GDP and Its Components

Contrary to the case of the other countries that we will study, growth was already high (at 4 percent) when the September 1982 package started the consolidation, and it stayed there until 1986. The recovery was broadly based. Investment was the most dynamic component, increasing at more than 10 percent per annum from 1982 to 1986, after falling by almost 30 percent in 1980 and 1981. Consumption grew roughly at the same rate as GDP until 1985, and then at a remarkable 7.5 percent in 1986. During this period average export growth was less than 4 percent, far below that of the other countries of this study (see table 8.4).

---

16. In 1985 a radical reform of the budget process also took place.
17. As argued by Andersen and Risager (1990, 171), this is a common pattern with incomes policies.

Table 8.4   Denmark: GDP and its components

	1980	1981	1982	1983	1984	1985	1986	1987	1988	1989
GDP	−0.4	−0.9	3.7	2.7	4.2	4.0	4.9	0.3	−0.1	0.6
Priv. consumption	−2.8	−1.7	1.4	2.0	3.8	4.3	7.5	−1.9	−1.7	0.0
Exports	5.7	8.5	3.2	4.6	3.5	6.0	1.3	4.9	8.8	4.7
Gr. dom. cap. form.	−11.1	−17.6	10.3	4.3	11.2	15.3	19.3	2.3	−6.4	1.6

Source: Statistics Denmark.

The increase in consumption in 1983 came as a surprise to contemporaries, against the expectations that the March wage agreement would produce a decline in consumption; but because inflation also declined fast, real salaries remained constant. Initially the consumption acceleration was due largely to durables: car registration increased by 36 percent; this contributed to about half of the increase in private consumption (see 1983/84 ES, 20).

Obviously, also the decline in nominal interest rates generated a wealth effect that stimulated consumption. House prices increased by 60 percent in nominal terms (35 percent in real terms) between 1982 and 1986. The 1986/87 ES (32) calculates that this implied an increase by kr 200bn at current prices, or kr 100bn at 1982 prices, or about half of total private consumption in 1982. Before the 1986 potato diet, tax treatment of consumer credit was also extremely favorable: interest was totally deductible.[18] The stock market also boomed: real share prices almost doubled between 1982 and 1983.

However, most accounts of the Danish consolidation stop at 1986. What happened next is equally interesting. As we have seen, after a few years the attempt at internal devaluation failed, as the incomes policy managed to contain wage growth only until 1986. In the meantime, the exchange rate appreciation and the lackluster productivity performance meant that relative unit labor costs slowly worsened. Eventually, the trade balance worsened so much that the government was compelled to sharply increase interest rates and introduce other measures to cool demand. Between 1987 and 1989 GDP growth halted, thereafter it was about 1 percent per year until 1993; consumption declined by a cumulative 4 percent between 1987 and 1989.

Thus, Denmark displayed the standard pattern of exchange rate stabilizations, with a sudden but short lived boom driven by domestic demand[19] and a gradual worsening of competitiveness that eventually led to a prolonged slump. Ades, Kiguel, and Liviatan (1993) attribute the boom in domestic demand also to overconfidence: GDP and consumption forecasts consis-

18. See table 14 in 1986/87 ES (33).
19. Interestingly, not all contemporaries had the same perception: some viewed the recovery of those years as driven mostly by investment and exports: "The current recovery is more 'healthy' [than that of 1976 to 1979] because it is based on exports and investment" (1985/86 ES, 23).

tently exceeded realizations during those years, boosting consumption and especially investment. Inflation was also expected to decline faster than it did in reality, thus leading to a fast decline in nominal interest rates and in nominal and real wages.

8.6.2   Ireland

The story of the two Irish stabilizations has been told many times.[20] Between 1982 and 1984 the government attempted to cut the deficit by raising personal income and consumption taxes. The primary budget deficit did fall by 3.7 percent of GDP between 1982 and 1986; this however was less than the discretionary increase in taxes (as estimated by IMF), due to a lackluster growth performance and significant increases in social transfers and public wages.[21] As a consequence, in 1986 public debt was 110 percent of GDP, 30 percentage points of GDP higher than in 1982; the overall deficit had declined by only 2.5 percent of GDP, the primary deficit by little more than 3 percent of GDP.[22] Thus, what is regarded as the prototypical revenue-based consolidation was not a success story. By all accounts, in 1987 the mood in the country was gloomy, with a palpable sense of an impending crisis. In this chapter, I focus on the second consolidation, which started in 1987 and is widely associated with an impressive economic turnaround.

Budget Timeline

In March 1987 a new minority government was formed by the former opposition party Fianna Fail. While Fianna Fail had campaigned on a populist platform, once in office it changed its mind and started a drastic fiscal consolidation that lasted until 1989. In that year, the deficit was 2.6 percent of GDP, against 10.6 in 1986. In the same period, the primary balance switched from a deficit of 2 percent of GDP in 1986 to a surplus of 4.6 percent in 1989. For the first time since the beginning of the 1970s, public debt had stopped growing as a share of GDP, and actually declined by 10 percentage points. The GDP growth went from .4 percent in 1986 to 5.6 percent in 1989 and 7.7 percent in 1990 (see table 8.5).

Estimating a narrative measure of fiscal policy changes is particularly challenging in Ireland. The Irish budget process at the time was extremely complicated. Some decisions for year t (except, crucially, most decisions on social transfers and government wages and employment) were taken in the fall of year $t - 1$ in a document called the "Estimates," while decisions

---

20. See, for example, Dornbusch (1989) for the first stabilization, and Giavazzi and Pagano (1990), McAleese (1990), and Honohan and Walsh (2002) for the second.

21. In 1985 and 1986 in particular, public sector wage increases, in part awarded by an arbitrator, caused a sizable overshoot of public spending. For instance, in 1985 the arbitrator awarded a 10 percent increase to all school teachers in excess of the increase for all public sector workers.

22. Here and in the remainder of the chapter the cyclically unadjusted budget figures refer to the general government and are usually taken from the OECD *Economic Outlook*.

Table 8.5   Ireland: Discretionary budget measures

	Spending	Revenues	Surplus	Spending IMF	Revenues IMF	Surplus IMF
1997 total	−1.48	0.34	1.82	−1.14	0.53	1.67
Cumulative	−1.48	0.34	1.82	−1.14	0.53	1.67
1988 total	−1.79	2.20	3.99	−1.99	0.00	1.99
Cumulative	−3.27	2.54	5.81	−3.13	0.53	3.66
1989 total	−0.49	−2.69	−2.20	0.00	0.00	0.00
Cumulative	−3.76	−0.15	3.61	−3.13	0.53	3.66

Sources: For columns (2) to (4), Estimates and Financial Statements, various years.

on transfers and on taxes were taken in the January Budget of year *t*. To complicate things further, it is never exactly clear what is the reference value for a change in, say, government spending in these documents: whether the previous year outcome, or some notion of "constant legislation" spending, or the Estimates of the previous period, and so forth.

Because of this complexity, it appears that IMF sometimes misses one of the two documents. A case in point is 1989: IMF—which, to repeat, only considers discretionary *improvements* in the primary balance—reports a value of zero, because the 1989 Budget "introduced a number of tax cuts and spending increases" (IMF, fn 54, 46). However, the 1989 Estimates also introduced substantial spending cuts, almost double the spending increases of the Budget: as a result, 1989 was the third year of the fiscal consolidation.

More importantly, IMF does not count the contribution of a tax amnesty that netted 2.1 percent of GDP in 1988, nor the introduction of self assessment that netted .3 percent of GDP on a permanent basis. With these two measures, the consolidation of the years 1987 and 1988 would be equally divided between spending cuts and tax increases. This interpretation is consistent with at least one account by an insider:

> Briefly, there was no significant reduction in the real volume of current spending as a result of Bord Snip I [the expenditure review set up by the new government in 1987]. There was a further squeeze on capital spending, a mistake in retrospect, but most of the adjustment came on the revenue side. The "slash and burn" stories about 1987, references to the finance minister as "Mac the Knife," decimation of public services and so forth are just journalistic invention. It never happened. (McCarthy 2010, 45)

Overall, if one compares the last year of the consolidation, 1989, and the year preceding the consolidation, 1986, I estimate a discretionary change in the primary balance of 3.6 percent of GDP, all from spending cuts: almost half of these cuts fell on capital spending.[23] If one, like IMF, stops at 1988,

23. Ireland is the only country where I was able to estimate the breakdown between capital and current spending cuts.

Table 8.6	Ireland: Interest rates								
	1982	1983	1984	1985	1986	1987	1988	1989	1990
Nom. long	17.1	13.9	14.6	12.8	11.2	11.3	9.4	9.2	10.3
Nom. short	16.3	13.2	13.2	11.9	12.5	10.8	8.0	10.0	11.3
Real long	−0.1	3.4	6.0	7.3	7.5	8.1	7.2	5.1	6.9
Real short	−0.8	2.7	4.6	6.5	8.8	7.7	5.9	5.9	8.0
Long–short	0.7	0.8	1.4	0.9	−1.3	0.4	1.3	−0.9	−1.0
Long–long DEU	8.0	5.7	6.5	5.6	4.9	4.9	2.8	2.0	1.6

Sources: OECD *Economic Outlook*, No. 88; long-term interest rate for Germany until 1990 and short-term interest rate for Ireland until 1983: OECD *Economic Outlook*, No. 72.

then I estimate an improvement of 5.8 percent of GDP, almost equally divided between spending cuts and revenue increases. As mentioned, this is due to the large amnesty of 1988. As a comparison, over the period 1987 to 1988 IMF calculates cumulative spending cuts by 3.1 percent of GDP and tax increases by .5 percent of GDP (IMF does not count 1989 as a consolidation year).[24]

These figures, however, ignore temporary measures like the tax amnesty. When temporary measures are important, a more appropriate measure of fiscal consolidation is one that answers the question, on average, how much were discretionary expenditures (taxes) lower (higher) in each year of the consolidation, relative to the year preceding the start of the consolidation? This is equivalent to including all discretionary measures, weighted by the time they were in effect. The figures in this case are about 2.7 percent of GDP of spending cuts and .85 percent of tax increases.

Thus, the consolidation was significant, although perhaps not so large as it is often believed, and the contribution of tax increases was larger than usually assumed.

Inflation, Wage Dynamics, Competitiveness, and Interest Rates

In 1979—three years before the first fiscal consolidation—Ireland had stopped pegging to the sterling and joined the European Exchange Rate Mechanism (ERM). Like in many exchange rate based stabilizations, this soon led to a large decline in Consumer Price Index (CPI) inflation, which came down from a peak of 20.4 percent in 1981 to 3.8 percent in 1986 (see tables 8.6 and 8.7).

The nominal and real interest rates declined until 1983, as the punt managed to avoid an appreciation by keeping the central parity during two realignments when the DM revalued, and by devaluing in 1983. But interest rate stopped falling afterwards, despite a further decline in inflation, as

24. The actual figures calculated by the IMF are 3.1 percentage points of GDP of spending cuts and .5 of tax increases. However, IMF uses a figure for GDP at the denominator that turns out to be incorrect; using the correct CSO figures gives the numbers I cite in the text.

Table 8.7   Ireland: Competitiveness indicators

	1982	1983	1984	1985	1986	1987	1988	1989	1990
Hourly earnings in manuf.[a]	14.5	11.6	10.5	8.7	7.5	5.8	5.3	4.8	5.4
ULC, all economy[b]	11.6	9.6	4.0	4.0	7.3	0.5	−0.9	0.9	−0.3
ULC, manuf.[b]	11.6	9.6	4.0	4.9	5.9	−3.6	−4.1	−2.7	−2.1
Nom. eff. exch. rate[b]	−.4	−2.6	−3.6	1.6	8.0	−.4	−1.9	−.7	8.6
Relative ULC, manuf.[b]	5.0	4.9	−0.7	1.5	9.3	−6.2	−7.3	−6.8	0.3
Relative nominal wages, manuf.[c]	4.5	3.2	−3.1	0.4	8.5	−4.3	−2.6	−5.4	0.8
Relative ULC, all economy[c]	4.6	−6.7	−7.4	−3.2	2.6	−10.5	−7.0	−5.4	2.2
Labor prod. per person, manuf.[a]	1.2	14.2	14.8	1.6	0.4	9.4	7.1	5.1	6.7
CPI[b]	17.1	10.5	8.6	5.5	3.8	3.2	2.1	4.1	3.3

Notes: An increase in measures of the nominal exchange rate or relative ULC or wages is an appreciation.
[a]OECD Main Economic Indicators
[b]OECD *Economic Outlook*, No. 88
[c]EUROSTAT

the punt started appreciating. Thus, until 1986 real interest rates remained extremely high and the long-term interest rate differential with Germany fluctuated between 6 and 5 percentage points. As Walsh (1993) shows, during all of the 1990s the long-term interest rate differential with Germany tracked closely the sterling exchange rate: it increased when the sterling appreciated, and fell when the sterling depreciated.

In summer of 1986, the Irish pound had appreciated by 20 percent vis-à-vis the sterling pound. In August 1986 the government devalued the Irish pound by 8 percent within the ERM. The 1986 devaluation, however, was the last one until January 1993: ERM participation was regarded as a nominal anchor policy (see Dornbusch 1989 and Giavazzi and Pagano 1990), and "the year 1986 was a watershed in Irish exchange rate policy" (Walsh 1993, 2). Initially, long-term interest rates kept rising because of fears of budget slippages and further devaluations: in October 1986 they reached 13 percent. Pressure on the Irish punt and on long-term interest rates abated only when the sterling stopped depreciating in early 1987. Happily, this coincided with the second fiscal consolidation, and turned out to be a key difference relative to the first, failed consolidation.

The years of the failed stabilization of 1982 to 1986 saw also the abandonment of centralized wage setting and the move to decentralized wage setting (see Durkan 1992). The government, having embarked in a process of tax increases, realized that it had nothing to offer at the negotiating tables and withdrew from the process. However, this did not prevent a strong deceleration of wage inflation: average manufacturing earnings increased at a rate of 14.5 percent in 1982 and 7.5 percent in 1986, less than in the United Kingdom.

As part of the new stabilization package, in 1987 the government returned to a tripartite wage bargaining process; in October it published the *Program for National Recovery,* which had been agreed upon with the trade unions and the employers. It included two wage agreements, one for the public sector and the other between trade unions and employers in the private sector. It set a maximum increase in wages by 2.5 percent in 1988, 1989, and 1990. Table 8.7 shows that wage inflation came further down, from 7.5 percent in 1986 to 5.4 percent in 1990; real effective exchange rates based on unit labor costs and on wages in manufacturing, both of which had been worsening until 1986, improved dramatically.[25] As Honohan and Walsh (2002) put it, "wage restraint has been the hallmark of the recovery" (28). "How much of this [improvement in competitiveness] should be attributed to the new pay negotiation environment? Despite the inconclusive econometric results, most observers regard the coincidence of timing of the reversal of the deteriorating trend in competitiveness with the new approach to pay bargaining as suggestive that the latter did pay dividends" (33). Labor relations also changed radically: the number of strikes fell dramatically relative to the previous period, and relative to the United Kingdom;[26] this contributed to an impression of regime change that probably had important effects on private investment.

As Lane (2000) writes, low inflation was a precondition for wage restraint: the unions would probably not have accepted the latter without being sure of the former. In this respect, the second stabilization benefitted from the disinflation process of the first failed stabilization. In turn, the spending cuts were also probably a precondition for wage restraint, as they made possible a credible promise by the government to lower taxes in 1988 and 1989, by about .6 percent of GDP, in exchange for wage moderation.[27]

As wage moderation set in the market learned that the exchange rate policy was credible, nominal interest rates fell precipitously to 8 percent in 1988. The spread with the long German rate fell from 5 percentage points in 1986 to 2 in 1989, then it went further down. In this, Ireland was helped by the appreciation of the sterling, which instead had been depreciating during much of the first stabilization. Thus, because the largest decline in inflation had occurred before 1987, the declines in nominal interest rates afterwards were also largely declines in the real rate, contrary to the experience during the first stabilization, when real interest rates increased.[28]

---

25. Measures of competitiveness based on unit labor costs in Ireland are somewhat misleading, because of the very large weight in manufacturing of a few multinationals that, because of transfer pricing and highly valued patented products, exhibit enormous profits per employee and a very small share of labor costs: see Honohan and Walsh (2002, 22).

26. See Hohanan and Walsh (2002, 32).

27. Both tax cuts are missed by IMF; they do not show explicitly in table 8.5, where the 1988 tax cut is summed algebraically with the effects of the tax amnesty.

28. The steep decline in nominal interest rates is likely to have prompted a large increase in the value of government debt held by households; the exact effect is difficult to quantify since we do not have measures of government debt at market values.

Table 8.8   Ireland: GDP and its components, CSO data

	1982	1983	1984	1985	1986	1987	1988	1989	1990
GDP	1.49	−0.73	3.21	1.95	0.43	3.64	3.00	5.61	7.71
Priv. consumption	−4.30	−1.79	0.86	2.74	2.80	2.06	3.60	3.35	3.23
Exports	4.47	10.53	16.25	6.60	2.71	13.88	8.15	11.42	9.17
Gr. dom. cap. form.	−4.51	−8.61	−2.65	−7.90	−0.49	−2.34	−0.17	13.52	13.86
Mach. and equipm.	−9.37	−2.61	−2.09	−7.65	1.64	1.52	1.75	16.57	10.72

Source: Central Statistical Office.

GDP and Its Components

The GDP growth was 0 in 1986. In the first year of the second stabilization (1987) it rose to 3.5; it then reached almost 8 percent in 1990. By all measures, the second stabilization was a spectacular success.

For a long time growth was driven by exports that rose at an average rate above 10 percent between 1987 and 1990. This strong performance of exports started in the second half of 1986, hence before the fiscal consolidation, and can be attributed to two factors: the growth of export markets, on average 8.8 percent between 1985 and 1988, in particular in the United Kingdom; and the improvement in competitiveness following the August 1986 devaluation, coupled with the wage restraint of 1987 and 1988.

Domestic demand was subdued for a long time. The average growth rate of consumption in 1987 and 1988 was 2.8 percent, the same as in 1985 and 1986—two recession years. Data on sales are consistent with the notion that consumption growth was modest: sales started to pick up only in 1988:Q3, but until then they remained below the 1985 and 1986 levels.[29]

The pattern exhibited by gross fixed capital formation is even starker: it was negative in 1987 and 1988, and turned positive only in 1989 after seven consecutive years of negative numbers. Figures for the aggregate can be misleading, because of the large cuts to public sector investment, and the Central Statistical Office (CSO) data do not have a breakdown between government and private gross fixed capital formation. But investment in machinery and equipment tells a similar story: it increases by less than 2 percent in 1986 and 1987, well below the rate of growth of GDP, and starts growing at 17 percent only in 1989.

Why this difference with the standard story of the Irish miracle? The

---

29. Contemporary sources had the same impression: in October 1987, about three quarters after the budget plans had been announced, the 1987/88 ES states: "Trade statistics for the first three quarters of the year show a major expansion of exports due to renewed growth of the exports of foreign companies and to the strong rise in United Kingdom imports. . . . At constant prices, the external balance improvement is the major factor behind the projected 2 percent expansion in GNP this year. By contrast, most of the component of domestic demand remain rather depressed. Retail sales have been weak for most of the year" (30).

Table 8.9   Ireland: GDP and its components, OECD data

	1982	1983	1984	1985	1986	1987	1988	1989	1990
GDP	2.28	-0.24	4.35	3.09	-0.43	4.66	5.22	5.81	8.47
Priv. consumption	-7.06	0.85	2.01	4.59	2.01	3.32	4.49	6.52	1.41
Exports	5.54	10.45	16.59	6.58	2.89	13.72	9.02	10.31	8.73
Gr. dom. cap. form.	-3.41	-9.29	-2.52	-7.71	-2.79	-1.14	5.24	10.13	13.40
Mach. and equipm.	-8.42	-3.79	-3.30	-8.51	-1.44	5.24	10.06	14.23	8.49

Source: OECD Economic Outlook database.

OECD data typically used in international comparisons are very different (see table 8.9): for instance, relative to CSO data the rate of growth of GDP in 1988 is more than 2 percentage points higher in OECD data, the rate of growth of consumption in 1989 is more than double, and gross fixed capital formation turns positive (and large, at 5 percent) already in 1988.

As it turns out, following an inquiry of mine the OECD Statistical Directorate realized that it had not received the revised Irish national accounts for 1970 to 1995, hence these were not available for incorporation in the Economic Outlook database. The OECD has communicated to me that the Irish CSO data are more appropriate for historical analysis.[30]

Thus, there was no explosion of domestic demand in Ireland following the second Irish consolidation: for almost two years after the start of the consolidation, GDP growth was driven largely by exports. At the same time, the budget consolidation of 1987 to 1989 was substantial but not "brutal," and tax increases (particularly from the tax amnesty) were significant.

But what can account for the difference between the two consolidations, 1982 to 1986 and 1987 to 1989? After all, as Giavazzi and Pagano (1990) correctly point out, exports were strong even during the first stabilization (see table 8.8). The most often cited difference is in the composition of the budget consolidation, which was tax-based during the first and spending-based during the second. It is easy to see why it could matter: spending cuts made room for tax cuts on labor income, which in turn enhanced competitiveness; wage reductions in the public sector that were announced repeatedly during the first stabilization but implemented only during the second, enhanced the confidence in the ability of the government to carry out its program and set the stage for more wage moderation in the private sector (see Honohan 1989, 205).

Table 8.7 shows that a second important difference was the behavior of wages and relative unit labor costs in manufacturing. They were growing, although at declining rates, in the first stabilization, and declining during the second. As we have seen, the change in labor relations was the key to

30. Historical data for Ireland have been temporarily suspended in the new issue of the *Economic Outlook,* pending a complete integration of the new series.

this development. All indicators of competitiveness worsened dramatically in 1986, the year growth came to a halt after two years that averaged growth above 2.5 percent, only slightly below the figure for 1987 to 1988.

A third difference that is rarely mentioned[31] is the behavior of real long-term interest rates.[32] Table 8.6 shows that these were high and rising during the first stabilization, and declined at the beginning of the second stabilization. The decline of the spread with the German long rate was particularly pronounced. The reason is that during the first stabilization inflation and inflation expectations were coming down fast because of the depreciation of the sterling, but precisely for the same reason the Irish rates remained high. As mentioned before, in this sense the second stabilization could afford low real rates because inflation had come down already and the sterling was now appreciating for the first two years. Thus, although both stabilizations were exchange rate based, the second benefitted from the appreciation of the sterling, which improved competitiveness and allowed the nominal and real interest rate to decline.[33]

It is also important to understand the similarities and differences between the second stabilization and the experience of Denmark. Like Ireland, Denmark pursued an exchange rate based stabilization, and achieved a remarkable decline in nominal and real interest rates. In both countries the exchange based stabilization was initially sustained by wage moderation and the involvement of the government in the wage formation process. On the other hand, Denmark's consolidation occurred in a boom, rather than in a recession as in Ireland; and it was not spending based, but it was equally divided between revenue increases and spending cuts.

But perhaps the key difference is that in Denmark the expansion that occurred at the time of the consolidation was driven by domestic demand; for a long time in Ireland it was driven mostly by exports. Three possible explanations stand out. First, during the consolidation Denmark suffered from a deterioration of relative unit labor costs, while Ireland experienced an improvement (because of the appreciation of the sterling) of a few realignments in which it did not follow the DM, and a much better productivity performance. Second, Denmark experienced a house price and a stock market boom at the time of the consolidation, both much stronger than in Ireland, partly because of the steeper decline in interest rates. Third, the term structure remained steeper in Denmark, providing an incentive for higher consumption.[34]

31. Dornbusch (1989) emphasizes the role of high real interest rates during the first stabilization, but was writing just at the beginning of the second stabilization.

32. Because I do not have data on expected inflation over this period, I compute the real long-term interest rate as the difference between the nominal rate and inflation over the last year.

33. Also, during the first stabilization, the primary deficit came down as fast as during the second, but started from a higher level: high real interest rates combined with still high primary deficits meant growing debt.

34. Giavazzi and Pagano (1990) offer another explanation: the more advanced credit markets for consumers in Denmark. However, as observed by Drazen (1990) in his comments to the

It is useful to summarize the main conclusions: (a) the Irish budget consolidation of 1987 to 1989 was smaller and more tax based than previously thought; (b) for several quarters the GDP expansion was mostly export-driven—consumption and private investment recovered six to eight quarters after the start of the consolidation, and their recovery was more subdued than previously thought; (c) in 1987 to 1989 Ireland pursued an exchange rate based stabilization, after a substantial devaluation and a large decline in inflation, but crucially, it did manage to depreciate the punt during a few realignments, and relative to the sterling; (d) this second stabilization saw a decline of long rates and an even more pronounced decline of the differential with Germany. This was helped by the appreciation of the sterling, which statistically is associated with a reduction in the Irish rates. The decline in the long rate was not large, but it was in marked difference to the first stabilization, which had suffered from high and increasing real rates; (e) the decline in inflation made possible a substantial wage moderation that was also instrumental in enhancing competitiveness and in signaling a change in regime, and incomes policies by the government were instrumental in consolidating the process of wage moderation; (f) the budget consolidation probably played an important role in ensuring the credibility of a regime shift to low inflation, wage moderation, and lower interest rates.

8.6.3   Finland

The next two case studies, Finland and Sweden, differ from the first two because they pursued a budget consolidation after abandoning a peg. During the 1980s in Finland, financial deregulation and tax incentives for housing investment fueled a boom characterized by huge capital inflows, large private sector indebtedness, and asset price inflation. In the early 1990s Finland suffered the worst recession of all OECD countries. Real GDP fell by 14 percentage points between the 1990 peak and the 1993 trough. The recession was exacerbated by four factors: a banking crisis when asset prices collapsed, the demise of the Soviet Union, a deterioration of the terms of trade, and the decision to defend the peg to the ECU (European Currency Unit) against speculative attacks. By late 1991 the central bank had raised the overnight lending rate to 50 percent, while the one month interbank Helibor rate stood at 27 percent. Because inflation was low, real interest rates were extremely high throughout the recession. The government finally agreed to devalue in November 1991 by 12 percent vis-à-vis the ECU; the

---

paper the numbers on the *change* in consumer credit in the two countries do not seem to be large enough to explain the difference in the behavior of consumption. Three more factors are often mentioned as explanations of the Irish boom of 1987 to 1990 (see, e.g., Whelan 2010): the inflow of EU structural funds, investment by multinationals, and emigration, which eased unemployment. The first two, however, started in earnest after 1989 (see, e.g., Barry 2000); the role of the latter is difficult to assess, and deserves more scrutiny. Obviously, it can still be the case that the large investment by multinationals in the 1990s was made possible by the change in regime signaled by the budget cuts of 1987 to 1989.

decision to float the markka in September 1992 was followed by a further depreciation by 15 percent.

Meanwhile, the budget balance moved from a surplus of 7 percent of GDP in 1989 to a deficit of 8 percent in 1993. Contrary to other countries, interest payments did not play a role: the change in the primary balance was virtually identical. During the same years, government debt as a share of GDP quadrupled, from 14 percent to 56 percent.

By the end of 1992 Finland was widely considered the basket case of Europe. Then, like in many other countries, GDP growth turned positive in late 1993; in 1994 it was 4 percent, the highest in Europe, and it stayed there for several years.

Budget Timeline

The IMF reports a discretionary improvement in the budgetary position in each of the years 1992 to 1997, with cumulative spending cuts of 12.1 percent of GDP and a cumulative consolidation of 11.4 percent of GDP. It is easy to see why this is probably a considerable overestimate of the discretionary consolidation. Over the same years, the cyclically unadjusted primary balance improved by about 7 percent of GDP; thus, cyclical conditions would have caused a *worsening* of the balance by 4 percent of GDP—yet except for 1992, these were years of very high growth.

This can be seen even more clearly for the years 1994 and 1995, which saw a cumulative GDP growth of about 8 percent. The cyclically unadjusted primary balance improved by 3.4 percent of GDP; IMF reports a cumulative discretionary improvement by 5.1 percent of GDP, once again implying that in those two years cyclical factors caused an increase in the deficit by almost 2 percent of GDP despite the exceptionally high growth.

My reconstruction of the discretionary improvement in the budget balance over the 1992 to 1998 period is less than half of the IMF estimate: 4.9 percent of GDP against 11.4 (see table 8.10). Spending cuts amount to only 1 percent of GDP; the remaining 4 percent are tax increases. Thus, this was a much smaller fiscal consolidation than in IMF data, and it was revenue based. In contrast, in the IMF data it was all spending based.

What explains this discrepancy between the IMF estimates and mine? Often several supplementary budgets undid the budget cuts decided in the January budgets; in some cases IMF misses these supplementary budgets, in others it mentions them but does not consider their effects on the grounds that they had a countercyclical motivation.[35] As I discuss earlier, I am skeptical that motivations can be detected so sharply, and in many cases the spending increases were probably motivated not by countercyclical considerations, but by political pressure to ease the effects of the January budget cuts. In fact, many of these spending increases were financed by tax increases, which

35. See IMF footnotes 30, 31, and 32, pp. 29–31.

Table 8.10   **Finland: Discretionary budget measures**

	Spending	Revenues	Surplus	Spending IMF	Revenues IMF	Surplus IMF
1992 total	0.91	0.00	–0.91	–0.91	0.00	0.91
Cumulative	0.91	0.00	–0.91	–0.91	0.00	0.91
1993 total	–2.17	0.00	2.17	–3.71	0.00	3.71
Cumulative	–1.25	0.00	1.25	–4.62	0.00	4.62
1994 total	–0.86	2.27	3.12	–2.76	0.69	3.45
Cumulative	–2.11	2.27	4.38	–7.38	0.69	8.07
1995 total	2.61	–0.09	–2.70	–2.28	–0.63	1.65
Cumulative	0.50	2.18	1.68	–9.66	0.05	9.71
1996 total	–1.44	1.75	3.19	–1.48	0.00	1.48
Cumulative	–0.94	3.93	4.87	–11.14	0.05	11.19
1997 total	0.38	–0.14	–0.52	–0.94	–0.71	0.24
Cumulative	–0.57	3.79	4.35	–12.08	–0.65	11.43
1998 total	–0.29	0.26	0.55	0.00	0.00	0.00
Cumulative	–0.85	4.05	4.90	–12.08	–0.65	11.43
1999 total	0.48	–0.55	–1.03	0.00	0.00	0.00
Cumulative	–0.37	3.49	3.87	–12.08	–0.65	11.43

Sources: For columns (2) to (4), *Economic Survey of Finland*, Ministry of Finance, various issues; OECD *Economic Survey of Finland*, various issues.

is also the reason why IMF reports virtually no tax increases: for example, in 1996 supplementary budgets increased revenues by 1.75 percent of GDP, but this does not appear in the IMF estimates. In the end, omitting these discretionary changes offers a highly distorted picture of discretionary fiscal policy during these years.

In addition, my data (and, a fortiori, the IMF data) almost certainly underestimate the extent of tax increases during the consolidation, because the effects of changes in tax rates are not always quantified in the budget documents. Thus, between 1992 and 1994 several measures to increase taxes were adopted (see, e.g., the list in 1993 ES, 81 and 84 and 1995 ES, 104) but their effects did not appear in any document.

Note also that during these years the central government increased spending on several measures to support the banking system by about 10 percent of GDP between 1991 and 1995;[36] if these were included, cumulatively spending would *increase,* instead of decreasing, over these years. Banking support operations were indeed widely perceived as government spending, much as the support of the banking system in the United States and the United Kingdom has been a major item of contention in the debate on fiscal policy during the recent financial crisis. As it is well known, however,

36. This figure includes loans, preferred capital, and ordinary shares acquired by the Government Guarantee Fund; I do not consider guarantees, which would add another 6.5 percent of GDP. See 1996 ES (48) for details on bank support measures by type and year.

exactly how to treat bank support measures is not obvious: for instance, a capital injection is a financial investment to be counted below the line, but a capital injection in a bank that is essentially bankrupt is a capital, or even a current, transfer. Furthermore, some loans are repaid, but repayment might escape measurement as they are seldom given the same prominence as the original loan.

Turning to actual developments, the fiscal consolidation process of 1992 to 1998 can be divided into two phases, which coincide with two different governments. In 1992, the government elected in March 1991 announced a fiscal consolidation program based on a new medium-term framework. I estimate that by the end of its mandate in 1994 this resulted in a cumulative improvement in the discretionary balance by 4.4 percent of GDP, equally divided between spending cuts and tax increases. During this period, the only year with a substantial spending cut was 1993;[37] this was followed in 1994 by a large tax increase of 2.3 percent of GDP, from two supplementary budgets.[38] The discretionary improvement in the primary balance estimated by IMF over the same period is double my estimate, all of it from spending cuts.

Contemporaries could be forgiven if they did not realize that a brutal spending-based consolidation was under way. Headline numbers did not help: the general government deficit was still 6.1 percent of GDP in 1995, above the 1992 level; similarly, government debt as a share of GDP was larger in 1995 than in 1992.

In April 1995 a new government took office, and immediately introduced an austerity package. However, my data and IMF present two radically different pictures of what happened next. Overall, between 1995 and 1998 I estimate a further improvement in the discretionary primary balance of only .8 percent of GDP; during this period, discretionary spending actually *increased* by .5 percent of GDP. The IMF instead estimates spending cuts by 4.7 percent of GDP and tax *cuts* by 1.3 percent of GDP.

The difference on the spending side is due to two years, 1995 and 1997. In 1995 the new government did make good on the promise to cut spending by 2 percent of GDP: this is the number reported by IMF. However, the January budget of the outgoing government had already included an increase in government spending by 2.4 percent of GDP, due to the costs of EU accession (spending increased mainly because the government compensated farmers for the abolition of tariffs). Two supplementary budgets, one in late 1994 and the second in early 1995, further increased 1995 spending

37. Here and in what follows it is sometimes hard to attribute spending cuts to a given year. The third supplementary budget increased spending by 1.7 percent of GDP; because it was approved in October 1992, I attribute it to 1993. If instead it were to be attributed to 1992, it would imply a spending cut in 1992 and an increase in spending in 1993.

38. There was a further increase in taxes because of the decision to postpone tax refunds to 1995; of course this also shows up in 1995 as a tax cut.

Table 8.11	Finland: Interest rates									
	1990	1991	1992	1993	1994	1995	1996	1997	1998	1999
Nom. long	13.2	11.7	12.0	8.8	9.0	8.8	7.1	6.0	4.8	4.7
Nom. short	14.0	13.1	13.3	7.8	5.4	5.8	3.6	3.2	3.6	3.0
Real long	7.8	8.8	10.3	5.6	4.3	5.0	3.0	2.0	2.2	1.8
Real short	7.8	8.8	10.3	5.6	4.3	5.0	3.0	2.0	2.2	1.8
Long–short	–0.8	–1.4	–1.3	1.1	3.7	3.0	3.5	2.7	1.2	1.8
Long–long DEU	4.5	3.3	4.1	2.3	2.2	1.9	0.9	0.3	0.2	0.2

Sources: OECD *Economic Outlook*, No. 88; long-term interest rate for Germany until 1990: OECD *Economic Outlook*, No. 72.

by almost 1 percent of GDP.[39] As a result, in 1995 discretionary spending actually *increased,* instead of falling as reported by IMF.

In 1997 a spending cut of 1 percent of GDP was offset by a cut in employers' contributions, largely due to the Incomes Policy Agreement of late 1995 that traded wage moderation for tax cuts. However, once supplementary budgets are included, spending actually increased, and other tax increases nearly offset the tax cuts.

On the tax side, the difference between my data and IMF is mostly due to 1996, when a supplementary budget introduced a tax hike by 1.5 percent of GDP that was ignored by IMF.

Inflation, Wage Dynamics, Competitiveness, and Interest Rates

Thanks to the November 1991 devaluation and the subsequent floating of the markka in November 1992, the nominal effective exchange rate depreciated by 25 percent between 1991 and 1993 (see tables 8.11 and 8.12).[40]

At the beginning of the consolidation phase interest rates were very high, due to the attempted defense of the markka. They fell fast after the devaluation and subsequent floating: the three months' Helibor (interbank) interest rate fell from 17 percent in September 1992 to 7.5 percent in June 1993. The spread with the German interest rate had disappeared by that date. The long-term interest rates also came down considerably, but because the short-term interest rate had been pushed up by the defense of the markka against very strong speculation, the yield curve from negatively sloped became positively sloped at the beginning of 1994, with the differential between the ten year and the three months' interest rate at about 2 percent (this is about the time when durable consumption—but not yet nondurable consumption—

39. Another supplementary budget in November 1995, which I attribute to 1996, further increased spending by .6 percent of GDP in connection with the employment measures of the *Employment Programme* of fall 1995.

40. In October 1996, Finland joined the European Monetary System, thus ending the period of floating.

Table 8.12   **Finland: Competitiveness indicators**

	1990	1991	1992	1993	1994	1995	1996	1997	1998	1999
Hourly earnings in manuf.[a]	9.76	6.14	2.08	1.55	4.48	7.06	3.83	2.81	3.65	3.17
ULC, all economy[b]	9.21	5.96	-1.48	-4.26	-1.93	2.84	0.75	-0.88	2.21	0.96
ULC, manuf.[b]	7.32	7.76	-5.66	-7.15	-3.16	5.39	0.88	-4.24	-2.23	-2.82
Nom. eff. exch. rate[b]	3.93	-2.87	-12.18	-10.01	13.39	15.00	-2.44	-2.09	3.21	2.67
Relative ULC, manuf.[b]	5.31	-0.95	-20.74	-24.22	5.23	15.96	-5.47	-5.93	-0.28	0.30
Relative nominal wages, manuf.[c]	4.53	-2.35	-16.97	-19.03	6.11	11.61	-3.61	-5.28	-0.64	-2.64
Relative ULC, all economy[c]	4.19	-2.60	-21.23	-18.65	6.58	15.96	-3.70	-6.05	-1.75	-5.38
Labor prod. per person, all econ.[a]	1.84	-0.57	4.11	6.13	5.69	2.14	2.22	2.55	2.89	1.58
Labor prod. per person, manuf.[a]	1.82	-4.28	11.41	11.60	11.26	2.27	2.37	6.21	6.43	5.89
Labor prod. per hour, all econ.[a]	3.74	0.67	3.79	5.97	4.53	2.07	2.28	2.80	3.47	1.37
Labor prod. per hour, manuf.[a]	4.32	-0.57	11.64	10.53	8.93	2.13	2.72	5.39	5.79	7.10
CPI[b]	6.15	4.31	2.92	2.19	1.09	0.79	0.63	1.19	1.40	1.16

Notes: An increase in measures of nominal or real exchange rate is an appreciation.

[a]OECD *Main Economic Indicators*

[b]OECD *Economic Outlook*, No. 88

[c]EUROSTAT

started to grow: a steep yield curve with very low short interest rates is the right time to buy durable goods).

What made possible this decline in nominal interest rates? As in the case of Ireland, there are three plausible candidates. First, the budget consolidation, although as we have seen smaller than commonly thought, signaled a change of direction. Second, an often overlooked event that took place at the same time was the formal adoption in February of 1993 of inflation targeting, signaling another change in regime. Third, the nominal depreciation translated into a real depreciation thanks to wage moderation.[41] During 1992 and 1993 manufacturing unit labor costs fell by almost 15 percent, and relative unit labor costs fell by an impressive 45 percent. Two successive centralized wage agreements[42] in 1992 and 1993 froze contractual wage increase. This contributed to the enormous gains in competitiveness in those two years. In fact, in June 1993 the 1993 ES wrote, "[w]hen market confidence improved by the announcement of a government package aiming at fiscal consolidation, and by a pay settlement implying no wage increase for a second consecutive year, short term interest rates were allowed to ease gradually" (33).[43]

In 1995, however, these gains in competitiveness were threatened by a combination of nominal appreciation and wage slippages. At the end of 1993, the government had disengaged itself from the tripartite negotiations for 1994, and negotiations became entirely decentralized. After a moderate round of wage settlements for 1994, negotiations in late 1994 set contractual wage increases for 1995 at 4 percent, partly as a consequence of the tightening labor market. That year, hourly earnings in manufacturing increased by 7 percent, unit labor costs by 5 percent, and relative unit labor costs in manufacturing by 15 percent, thanks also to the appreciation of the nominal exchange rate.

As inflation expectations rose and doubts about the stabilization emerged, interest rates moved back up in 1994 and especially in 1995. To counteract the inflation threat posed by the decentralized wage settlements of late 1994, between December 1994 and February 1995 the Central Bank increased its tender rate by 1 percentage point.

At this point, the government, concerned that high wage settlements could undo the effects of its austerity package, returned to the table and promoted a new round of tripartite negotiations. These ended with an Incomes Policy Agreement in October 1995 that set an increase in wages of 1.8 percent in

---

41. Honkapohja and Koskela (1999, 36) put forth an interesting reason for wage moderation in Finland during these years: they argue that the costs of job loss are increasing in the level of household indebtedness.

42. In Finland wage negotiations occur first at a centralized level; although not binding, they set the tone for the more decentralized negotiations that follow.

43. Obviously interest rates came down in the rest of Europe too, but the descent was particularly fast in Finland. Because expected inflation also declined fast, thanks to the moderate wage agreements, real interest rates stayed fairly high. However, if government debt is net wealth and it is in nominal terms, a decline in the nominal interest rate pushes up its real value.

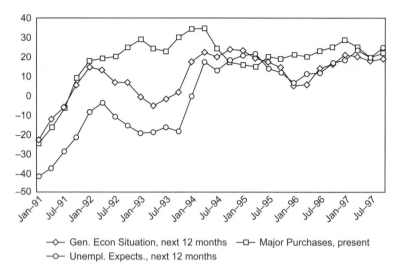

Fig. 8.2   Finland, consumer confidence

1996 and 1.3 percent in 1997. The government contributed by enacting a tax cut for 1997. Unit labor costs stopped growing in 1996 and then declined in 1997; relative unit labor costs declined by more than 5 percent in each of those two years. At the same time, consumer confidence picked up again. Between October 1995 and March 1996, after the October 1995 Incomes Policy Agreement and the Employment Programme, the Central Bank cut the tender rate by 3.5 percentage points (see 1996 ES, 38).

Thus, the 1995 Incomes Policy Agreement explicitly traded wage moderation for lower income taxes and social insurance contributions; this agreement was instrumental in gaining back competitiveness after the slippages of 1994 and 1995. It is here that the modest budget cuts of those years might have had the most important effect: by enabling the government to enact tax cuts in support of the incomes policies that started in late 1995. As Jonung, Kiander, and Vartia (2008) write: "perhaps the biggest change in the 1990s in Finland was the adoption and wide acceptance of a policy of long term wage moderation" (35).

Indices of consumer confidence shed further light on this by allowing tracking changes in consumer sentiment at a higher frequency. Three questions were asked in Finland before 1995: unemployment prospects of the country, the intention to make major purchases, and general economic conditions in the next twelve months (see figure 8.2).[44] Confidence had started

---

44. I multiply the balance of the responses to the unemployment question by –1, so that an increase in the index means higher confidence that unemployment will decline.

Table 8.13   **Finland: GDP and its components**

	1990	1991	1992	1993	1994	1995	1996	1997	1998	1999
GDP	0.5	−6.0	−3.5	−0.8	3.6	4.0	3.6	6.2	5.0	3.9
Priv. consumption	−1.1	−3.7	−3.8	−3.5	2.4	4.5	3.8	3.3	4.6	2.8
Exports	1.7	−7.2	10.0	16.3	13.5	8.5	5.9	13.9	9.2	11.1
Priv. gr. dom. cap. form.	−5.7	−20.6	−17.9	−13	−1.6	18.5	9.3	9.2	13.3	4.0

Source: Statistics Finland.

improving before the fiscal consolidation. It fell in the second half of 1994 when tripartite wage negotiations broke down, and recovered at the beginning of 1996, when the Income Policy Agreement was reached, but also one year after the austerity program by the new government was announced. Thus, the timing of the measure of consumer confidence also points to the importance of wage agreements and incomes policies as a signal of regime change.

GDP and Its Components

As the large depreciation set in, exports began to pick up in 1992, and grew at an average rate above 10 percent per year until 2000 (see table 8.13). However, all components of private domestic demand initially tanked. The GDP growth was very negative in 1992, still negative in 1993, and turned positive only in 1993:Q3. After that it posted an average growth of about 4.5 percent until the end of the decade.

Total private consumption started increasing only in 1994, after which it grew at above 3 percent until the rest of the decade, and private investment only in 1995, after which it kept growing at a very fast pace, between 8 and 19 percent.

Thus, the recovery was initially driven by exports; in fact, still in July 1996 the 1996 ES could write: "The divergence between exports and domestic demand has become very pronounced indeed, with the former at 150 percent and the latter at 75 percent of their 1990 levels by 1995" (3). It was not until 1999 that domestic demand recovered the level of 1990.

In addition, as we have seen, 1994 was a year of large tax increases; 1995 was a year of spending increases, preceded and followed by even larger tax increases. Thus, it is hard to relate the consumption recovery to the crowding in effects of a spending-based consolidation that did not actually take place in those years. It is tempting instead to relate it to the export boom and lower interest rates. As consumption of durables turned around in late 1993, the Ministry of Finance's 1994 *Economic Survey* wrote that "although . . . *the tightening of taxation* [emphasis added] continued to reduce disposable income, [at the beginning of 1994] brighter economic prospects and a fall in interest rates raised consumers' propensity to consume" (48).

Although the Finnish consolidation was implemented under a float and the Irish one under a peg, the two episodes have several features in common. On close inspection, they are both smaller and more revenue based than previously thought—in fact, in the case of Finland spending cuts were minimal, at around 1 percent of GDP cumulatively. Both entered the consolidation phase with a substantial depreciation, which was truly large in the case of Finland. In both countries the initial GDP expansion was driven by exports, and started before the consolidation; the growth of consumption started six to eight quarters after the start of the consolidation; in both wage moderation played a key role; in both incomes policies by the government were instrumental in consolidating the process of wage moderation after a temporary slippage that threatened to derail the stabilization. In Finland, it was only after the new round of wage negotiations signaled a regime change that consumption and investment picked up. In addition, in Finland inflation targeting further contributed to a signal of regime change, and the nominal interest rate displayed a large decline.

Why, then, did the appreciation and loss of competitiveness of 1994 and 1995 not lead to a prolonged slowdown like in Denmark almost ten years before? One can only speculate, but one plausible reason is that the government intervened to restore wage moderation, thus enhancing the credibility of the stabilization program; second, because of booming demand abroad exports kept growing at a remarkable rate even during the temporary slowdown, except for 1996.

8.6.4   Sweden

The Swedish boom of the 1980s and bust of the early 1990s had several features in common with Finland. Financial liberalization with tax incentives for borrowing fueled a consumption and housing boom, followed by a recession that started in 1990. Inflation fell, and the real interest rate rose drastically, causing a housing bust and a banking crisis. By 1993 unemployment was at 7.5 percent, and the budget deficit had increased to 11.2 percent of GDP from a surplus of 3.2 percent in 1989. As in Finland, this dramatic worsening of the budget balance was not due to interest payments: the primary budget showed exactly the same deterioration.

Throughout the recession the government, like in Finland, tried to defend the exchange rate to anchor inflation expectations, causing a steep loss of competitiveness and a drastic hike in interest rates. Eventually, like in Finland, the krona had to abandon the peg and began floating in November 1992. The GDP kept declining in 1993, then it turned around in 1994, when it grew at 4 percent, a pace that it maintained to the end of the decade except for a brief respite in 1995 and 1996, when growth slowed to about 2 percent. By 1998 the budget was in surplus, reaching 3 percent of GDP in 2000.

Table 8.14   **Sweden: Discretionary budget measures**

	Spending	Revenues	Surplus	Spending IMF	Revenues IMF	Surplus IMF
1993 total	−1.25	0.67	1.92	−1.39	0.42	1.81
Cumulative	−1.25	0.67	1.92	−1.39	0.42	1.81
1994 total	−0.52	0.95	1.47	−0.59	0.19	0.78
Cumulative	−1.76	1.62	3.39	−1.98	0.61	2.59
1995 total	−1.11	1.69	2.80	−2.10	1.40	3.50
Cumulative	−2.88	3.32	6.19	−4.08	2.01	6.09
1996 total	0.43	2.20	1.77	−1.20	0.80	2.00
Cumulative	−2.44	5.51	7.96	−5.28	2.81	8.09
1997 total	−1.76	−0.87	0.89	−0.90	0.60	1.50
Cumulative	−4.21	4.64	8.85	−6.18	3.41	9.59
1998 total	0.60	0.20	−0.40	−0.60	0.40	1.00
Cumulative	−3.61	4.84	8.44	−6.78	3.81	10.59

Sources: For columns (2) to (4), OECD *Economic Survey of Sweden*, various issues.

Budget Timeline

The consolidation started in 1993, and was over by 1998.[45] During this period, I estimate a discretionary change in the primary balance by 8.4 percent of GDP, 40 percent of which were from spending cuts (see table 8.14). The IMF estimates a total improvement in the primary balance by 10.5 percent of GDP, more than 60 percent of which were from spending cuts. Most of the difference between my estimate and IMF's estimates can be explained by the same factors that were at play in Finland: IMF does not count the higher spending due to EU accession, and it does not count some spending increases in supplementary budgets.

As a caveat, it should be noted that it is extremely difficult to reconstruct discretionary changes in spending and revenues in Sweden. For 1993 and 1994, IMF is based on two documents: the fiscal consolidation program of September 1992, and the 1993 Budget. For the crucial years 1995 to 1998, it is based entirely on the reconstruction of consolidation measures by the Ministry of Finance, with its breakdown by calendar year, made ex post in 1998. However, this source is not entirely reliable, because it is partly a political document; in fact, it includes only measures that cut spending or increased taxes, and reproduces as-is the original deficit reduction plan of September 1994, later published as the Convergence Program for EU membership.

As an example, that document includes as part of the consolidation kr 20bn (1 percent of GDP) of extra revenues needed to finance the costs of EU accession, but it does not record on the spending side the kr 20bn of new

45. On the Swedish consolidation, see Henriksson (2007).

spending due to EU accession. In addition, like in the case of Finland, IMF does not consider several supplementary budgets and other measures not in the main budgets or in fiscal consolidation programs; and, for example, it only counts spending cuts in the 1995/96 budget, but not spending increases.

Unfortunately, hard data on the items not included in the Finance Ministry document of 1998 are hard to get, partly because—again, as in the case of Finland—the effects of some tax or spending changes have not been quantified.

And again like in Finland, the result is that IMF most likely overestimates the size of the consolidation, and the share of spending cuts in it. For instance, IMF shows a fiscal consolidation in 1993 of 1.8 percent of GDP. However, the primary surplus declined by more than 3 percent of GDP; it seems unlikely that the recession by itself would have been responsible for a deterioration of the primary balance by about 5 percent of GDP (the OECD cyclically adjusted primary surplus falls by a 1 percent of GDP). As it turns out, if one includes the effects of a June 1993 supplementary budget and of extra spending decided in the fiscal consolidation package of September 1992, there was hardly any decline in spending.

Another example is 1998, when IMF reports a discretionary consolidation of 1 percent of GDP. This exceeds the increase in the unadjusted primary surplus, implying that, without discretionary action the primary balance would have worsened, despite growth at 4 percent, the highest in the decade. The explanation is that IMF does not include extra spending for 1.1 percent of GDP, due to the five-point program to enhance job creation, which does not appear in the official Finance Ministry rendition of fiscal consolidation.

Turning to the main policy developments, similar to Finland one can distinguish two phases in the Swedish consolidation. The first one runs from 1993 to 1994, and corresponds to the center-right coalition government. The second phase corresponds to the social democratic government that took office after the elections of September 1994.

During the first phase the discretionary improvement in the balance amounted to 3.4 percent of GDP, almost equally divided between spending cuts and tax increases. The second phase started with the November 1994 consolidation package, which together with the 1995/96 Budget of January 1995 and a supplementary budget in April envisaged a cumulative consolidation by about 4.5 percent of GDP by 1998. With subsequent modifications, this became about 5 percent of GDP, about two-thirds of which were tax increases. In particular, note that in 1995 and 1996 the primary budget improved by 4.5 percent of GDP, but spending cuts amounted to only about .7 percent of GDP.

Inflation, Wage Dynamics, Competitiveness, and Interest Rates

Like Finland and (to a lesser extent) Ireland, Sweden entered the budget consolidation phase with a large depreciation following the decision to float

Table 8.15   **Sweden: Interest rates**

	1990	1991	1992	1993	1994	1995	1996	1997	1998	1999
Nom. long	13.2	10.7	10.0	8.6	9.7	10.3	8.1	6.7	5.0	5.0
Nom. short	13.7	11.6	13.1	8.4	7.4	8.8	5.8	4.1	4.2	3.1
Real long	2.8	1.3	7.6	3.8	7.6	7.8	7.5	6.0	5.3	4.5
Real short	3.4	2.2	10.7	3.7	5.3	6.3	5.3	3.5	4.5	2.7
Long–short	–0.5	–0.9	–3.1	0.2	2.3	1.5	2.2	2.5	0.8	1.9
Long–long DEU	4.5	2.3	2.2	2.1	2.8	3.4	1.8	1.0	0.4	0.5

Sources: OECD *Economic Outlook*, No. 88; long-term interest rate for Germany until 1990: OECD *Economic Outlook*, No. 72.

Table 8.16   **Sweden: Competitiveness indicators**

	1990	1991	1992	1993	1994	1995	1996	1997	1998	1999
Hourly earnings in manuf.[a]	8.5	5.5	4.6	3.3	4.1	5.4	6.6	4.4	3.6	1.8
ULC, total economy[b]	11.4	6.3	–0.1	0.3	0.9	0.1	4.7	0.5	0.3	–0.9
ULC, manuf.[b]	7.8	7.7	–0.5	–7.6	–7.2	–2.5	4.5	–4.4	–4.7	–6.8
Nom. eff. exch. rate, chain-linked[b]	0.4	0.9	2.4	–17.7	1.2	0.4	10.1	–3.3	–0.2	–0.3
Relative ULC, manuf.[b]	2.5	2.9	–2.7	–26.8	–6.4	–4.1	12.8	–7.2	–6.4	–7.0
Real eff. exch. rate, nom. wages[c]	2.8	1.2	–1.4	–18.8	0.2	–1.1	13.6	–4.4	–3.4	–4.5
Real eff. exch. rate, ULC[c]	1.2	2.6	–1.5	–25.1	–6.7	–4.1	12.6	–7.5	–6.6	–9.5
Labor prod. per person, all econ.[a]	1.1	0.4	2.1	5.4	5.3	3.1	2.6	4.4	2.4	2.5
Labor prod. per person, manuf.[a]	2.0	0.5	5.2	10.1	15.5	7.0	3.7	9.3	6.6	9.7
Labor prod. per hour, all econ.[a]	1.4	1.3	1.0	4.3	2.8	2.8	1.8	4.1	2.5	2.0
Labor prod. per hour, manuf.[a]	1.2	0.8	4.3	7.1	10.4	6.4	3.5	9.6	6.5	9.0
CPI[b]	10.4	9.4	2.4	4.7	2.2	2.5	0.5	0.7	–0.3	0.5

Note: An increase in measures of nominal or real exchange rate is an appreciation.

[a]OECD *Main Economic Indicators*

[b]OECD *Economic Outlook*, No. 88

[c]EUROSTAT

the krona in November 1992—by almost 20 percent in 1993 in nominal terms on a multilateral basis. As in Ireland and Finland, long interest rates came down quickly, from 10 percent to 7 percent by the end of 1993; the differential with Germany also declined sharply to 1.5 percent (see tables 8.15 and 8.16).

The candidate explanations for the decline in interest rates are the same as in Finland and, except for the inception of inflation targeting, as in Ireland. First, budget austerity. Second, in January 1993—hence, at the same time as the start of the fiscal consolidation—Sweden adopted inflation targeting. Although it was decided that it would become fully operational in 1995, the Riksbank announced that it would pursue a target of 2 percent as of 1993. Inflation remained subdued in 1993, less than 4 percent, and there was no upward pressure on inflation expectations after the float. Third, the consolidation years were characterized by a surprising degree of wage moderation, with a short-lived slippage in 1995 and 1996—again like in Finland. Apart from the slack in the labor market and the sense of national crisis, one important reason for wage moderation was probably the move to inflation targeting in January 1993, which "had a profound impact on the behavior of labor market participants" (Jonung, Kiander, and Vartia 2008, 37). As a sign of confidence in the Riksbank, a non-indexed two-year collective agreement was signed in 1993 for 1994 and 1995, and three-year agreements were signed thereafter.

Sweden did not have a formal incomes policy agreement like Finland. But the "internal devaluation" package of September 1992 added to the exchange rate depreciation by reducing employers' social security contributions, financed by an increase in value added tax (VAT). Thus, in early 1991 a two-year centralized bargaining kept contractual wage increases at a low 2 percent for 1993, which including wage drift, would have caused hourly wages to increase at about 4 percent; the reduction in social security contributions decreased it back to 2 percent (see 1993 ES, 7). Also, unlike Finland, in 1993 Sweden had a tax reform that reduced the marginal tax rate on labor.

Together with improvements in productivity and the depreciation of the nominal exchange rate, this implied large declines in multilateral unit labor costs, by almost 40 percent between 1992 and 1995!

But then, again like in Finland, from late 1994 wage settlements drifted up;[46] also, the krona appreciated from the second half of 1995. As a result, unilateral and multilateral unit labor costs increased sharply in 1996. The results of the wage negotiations and higher inflation expectations prompted the Riksbank to increase the repo rate sharply;[47] the long interest rate rose as well. Then the appreciation of the krona reined in inflation,[48] and wage settlements showed signs of moderation; this allowed the Riksbank to decrease the repo rate by a cumulative 4 percent between January and December 1996. The differential with Germany was back to 1.25 percent in September 1996 and to .75 percent in December 1997. At the end of 1996, inflation was down to 0.[49]

GDP and Its Components

The first year of the consolidation, 1993, saw GDP fall by 2 percent (see table 8.17). Domestic demand collapsed: private consumption fell by almost

---

46. The increase in 1996 was partly due to technical reasons, as "[T]he finalisation [of the 1995 agreements] was spread out through the year, so that recorded wage growth was artificially low in 1995 with a corresponding increase in early 1996" (1998 ES, 31).

47. See Ministry of Finance (2000), Annex 5, for a detailed discussion of monetary policy in those years.

48. "The reduction in headline inflation during 1996 and into 1997 owed much to lower interest rates and the preceding appreciation of the krona" (1998 ES, 39).

49. The yield curve became very steep: this did not reflect inflation expectation, but probably a risk premium against European currencies, reflecting uncertainty on EMU participation (1997 ES, 51).

Table 8.17   **Sweden: GDP and its components**

	1990	1991	1992	1993	1994	1995	1996	1997	1998	1999	2000
GDP	1.0	−1.1	−1.2	−2.1	4.0	3.9	1.6	2.7	4.2	4.7	4.5
Priv. consumption	−0.5	0.9	−1.3	−3.6	2.1	1.1	1.8	2.8	3.3	4.0	5.3
Exports	2.1	−1.9	2.0	8.3	13.5	11.3	4.4	13.8	9.0	7.2	11.7
Gr. dom. cap. form.	0.2	−8.5	−11.3	−14.6	7.0	9.9	4.7	0.6	8.8	8.7	5.7
Mach. and equipm.	−0.2	−12.0	−13.8	−14.4	25.1	23.7	7.5	3.5	9.7	6.3	1.7
Dwellings	7.2	−2.4	−11.6	−33.5	−33.6	−23.5	8.9	−8.1	5.4	13.3	14.8
Other construction	−2.0	−5.9	−6.4	−2.1	13.9	11.4	−1.9	−6.2	2.6	−2.6	2.9

Source: Statistics Sweden.

4 percent, as the reduction in house prices increased the savings rate while the reduction in the deductibility of interest payments increased the net-of-tax interest payments on mortgages. Investment declined by 15 percent. Thanks to the large depreciation, exports grew by 8 percent, and more in the following years. This was also helped by the recovery abroad, which concentrated on investment goods and consumer durables that have a large share in Swedish exports. The year 1994 saw the beginning of a recovery, with GDP increasing by 4 percent, again led by exports, and, in the second part, by investment and consumer durables. But consumer surveys show a continuing deterioration of consumer confidence, which 1994 ES (9) attributes to "higher interest rates and the announcement of tax increases and other budget consolidation measures." In fact, private consumption grew in 1994 at the fairly modest rate of 2 percent. Investment was stronger: machinery and equipment grew by 25 percent, although dwelling fell further by 33 percent (until 1994 the official Swedish statistics do not distinguish between government and private investment).

As we have seen, the first two years of the new government's consolidation program, 1995 and 1996, saw an improvement in the primary balance by 4.5 percent of GDP, which was almost entirely financed by taxes. The GDP growth remained high in 1995 at around 4 percent. It was still driven by exports and by investment; private consumption remained subdued, at 1 percent. Most of the modest recovery in consumption was led by durables and car registration: "Other indicators, such as retail sales, convey an impression of continued retrenchment in consumer spending" (1997 ES, 19).

Then in the second half of 1995 and first half of 1996, growth slowed markedly, in parallel with the hike in interest rates, the appreciation of the krona, and the relapse in wage moderation. Export growth declined sharply, and in the first half of 1996 GDP growth fell to 0; only housing investment was strong. Private consumption and exports started recovering in the second half of 1996. By 1997 exports had recovered their high rate of growth of above 10 percent.

Thus, except for 1996, during the consolidation period exports always exhibited a growth rate near or well above 10 percent. In contrast, private consumption grew slowly after the rapid declines of 1990 to 1993, and it really started picking up only in 1998, toward the end of the five-year consolidation. Still, in 1998 the perception was that growth was driven by exports and investment: "The economy is now in the fifth year of an expansion which has relied on exports and business fixed investment for most of its momentum" (1998 ES, 17).

In many respects, the Swedish consolidation of the 1990s is similar to the Finnish consolidation that occurred at the same time, and to the Irish consolidation of the previous decade. Like them, its discretionary component is smaller and more revenue-based than previously thought. Particularly, like in Finland, the budget consolidation was preceded by a large depreciation. The expansion was driven initially by export and by investment; the growth of consumption was muted for a long time after the start of the consolidation. Wage moderation was an important factor that reinforced the decline in interest rates; in turn, tax reductions made possible by spending cuts were important in consolidating the process of wage moderation after a temporary slippage. Like in Finland, the budget consolidation was contemporaneous with the introduction of inflation targeting.

8.7   Conclusions

In this chapter, I have looked more closely at four episodes of large fiscal consolidations. Two of these episodes occurred immediately after pegging the exchange rate, while two occurred in the opposite circumstances, immediately after floating. I have argued that typically these consolidations relied on tax increases to a much larger extent than previously thought.

All four were associated with an expansion. But only in the Danish exchange rate based stabilization was domestic demand the initial driver of growth; and, as the effects of incomes policies faded, after four years the gradual loss of competitiveness led to a slump that lasted six years. This is consistent with the experience of several exchange rate based consolidations. In the second exchange rate based stabilization, Ireland, exports were the engine of growth for several quarters, as relative unit labor costs fell because of wage moderation and a concomitant appreciation of the main trading partner's currency, the sterling.

In the two consolidations under a float, Finland and Sweden, the initial boom was also driven by exports, following extremely large depreciations after the abandonment of the fixed exchange rate. The adoption of inflation targeting, which occurred at the same time as the consolidation in both countries, also helped maintain competitiveness by reducing inflation and inflation expectations.

In all episodes, interest rate declined quickly, also helped by wage moderation and by the nominal anchor (the exchange rate in the exchange rate based stabilizations, and inflation targeting in the two episodes under a float). Wage moderation was essential to maintain the benefits of the depreciations and to make possible the decline of the long nominal rates. Incomes policies were in turn instrumental in achieving wage moderation, and in signaling a regime shift from the past. Often these policies took the form of an explicit exchange between lower taxes on labor and lower contractual wage inflation; however, international experience shows that incomes policies can rarely be sustained for long periods, and the experience of Denmark is consistent with this pattern.

These results cast doubt on some versions of the "expansionary fiscal consolidations" hypothesis, and on its applicability to many countries in the present circumstances. A depreciation is not available to EMU members, except possibly vis-à-vis non-Euro members. An expansion based on net exports is not available to the world as a whole. A further decline in interest rates is unlikely in the current situation. Incomes policies are not currently popular, and in any case, are probably ineffective for more than a few years.

However, even in the short run budget consolidations were probably a necessary condition for output expansion for at least three reasons: first, they were instrumental in reducing the nominal interest rate; second, they made wage moderation possible by signaling a regime change that reduced inflation expectations; third, for the same reason they were instrumental in preserving the benefits of nominal depreciation and thus in generating an export boom.

References

Ades, A., M. Kiguel, and N. Liviatan. 1993. "Exchange-Rate-Based Stabilization: Tales from Europe and Latin America." World Bank Policy Research Working Paper WPS 1087. Washington, DC: World Bank.

Alesina, A., and S. Ardagna. 1998. "Tales of Fiscal Adjustment." *Economic Policy* 13 (27): 487–545.

———. 2010. "Large Changes in Fiscal Policy: Taxes versus Spending." In *Tax Policy and the Economy,* vol. 24, edited by Jeffrey R. Brown. Chicago: University of Chicago Press.

Alesina, A., and R. Perotti. 1995. "Fiscal Expansions and Adjustments in OECD Economies." *Economic Policy* 10 (21): 207–47.

———. 1997 "Fiscal Adjustments in OECD Countries: Composition and Macroeconomic Effects." *International Monetary Fund Staff Papers* 44 (2): 210–48.

Alesina, A., R. Perotti, and J. Tavares. 1998. "The Political Economy of Fiscal Adjustments." *Brookings Papers on Economic Activity,* Spring. Washington, DC: Brookings Institution.

Andersen, T., and O. Risager. 1990. "Wage Formation in Denmark." In *Wage Formation and Macroeconomic Policies in Nordic Countries,* edited by L. Calmfors. New York: Oxford University Press.

Angrist, J., and J. S. Pischke. 2008. *Mostly Harmless Econometrics: An Empiricist's Companion.* Princeton, NJ: Princeton University Press.

Baker, D. 2010. "The Myth of Expansionary Fiscal Austerity." Washington, DC: Center for Economic and Policy Research.

Benetrix, A. S., and P. R. Lane. 2011. "Financial Cycles and Fiscal Cycles." Prepared for the EUI-IMF conference, Fiscal Policy, Stabilization and Sustainability. Florence, Italy, June 6–7.

Bergman, U. M., and M. M. Hutchinson. 2010. "Expansionary Fiscal Contractions: Re-evaluating the Danish Case." *International Economic Journal* 24 (1): 71–93.

Bertrand, M., E. Duflo, and S. Mullainathan. 2004. "How Much Should We Trust Differences-in-Differences Estimates?" *The Quarterly Journal of Economics* 119 (1): 249–75.

Blanchard, O. J., and R. Perotti. 2002. "An Empirical Characterization of the Dynamic Effects of Changes in Government Spending and Taxes on Output." *The Quarterly Journal of Economics* 117 (4): 1329–68.

Borg, A. 2010. "Getting Fiscal Consolidation Right: Lesson from Sweden." Speech at the London School of Economics, January 14, 2010, available at http://sweden.gov.se/sb/d/9698/a/138026.

Bradley, J., and K. Whelan. 1997. "The Irish Expansionary Fiscal Contraction: A Tale from One Small European Economy." *Economic Modelling* 14:175–201.

Broadbent, Ben, and Kevin Daly. 2010. "Limiting the Fall-out from Fiscal Adjustment." Goldman Sachs Global Economics Paper no. 195. New York: Goldman Sachs.

Detragiache, E., and A. J. Hamann. 1999. "Exchange Rate-Based Stabilization in Western Europe: Greece, Ireland, Italy, and Portugal." *Contemporary Economic Policy* 17 (3): 358–69.

Devries, P., J. Guajardo, D. Leigh, and A. Pescatori. 2011. "A New Action-Based Dataset of Fiscal Consolidations." IMF WP/11/128. Washington, DC: International Monetary Fund. http://www.imf.org/external/pubs/cat/longres.aspx?sk=24892.0

Dornbusch, R. 1989. "Ireland's Disinflation." *Economic Policy* April:173–201.

Drazen, A. 1990. "Comment on 'Can Severe Fiscal Contractions Be Expansionary? Tales of Two Small European Countries,' by Francesco Giavazzi and Marco Pagano." In *NBER Macroeconomics Annual 1990,* edited by O. Blanchard and S. Fischer, 111–15. Cambridge, MA: MIT Press.

Durkan, J. 1992. "Social Consensus and Incomes Policy." *The Economic and Social Review* 23 (3): 347–63.

Favero, C., F. Giavazzi, and J. Perego. 2011. "Country Heterogeneity and the International Evidence on Fiscal Policy." *IMF Economic Review* 59:652–82.

Fedalino, A., A. Ivanova, and M. Horton. 2009. *Computing Cyclically Adjusted Balances and Automatic Stabilizers.* International Monetary Fund Technical Notes and Manuals, Fiscal Affairs Department. Washington, DC: IMF.

Giavazzi, F., and M. Pagano. 1990. "Can Severe Fiscal Contractions Be Expansionary? Tales of Two Small European Countries." In *NBER Macroeconomics Annual 1990,* edited by O. Blanchard and S. Fischer, 75–111. Cambridge, MA: MIT Press.

———. 1996. "Non-Keynesian Effects of Fiscal Policy Changes: International Evidence and the Swedish Experience." *Swedish Economic Policy Review* 3 (1): 67–103.

Guichard, S., M. Kennedy, E. Wurzel, and C. André. 2007. "What Promotes Fiscal Consolidation: OECD Country Experiences." OECD Economic Department Working Paper ECO/WKP(2007)13. Paris: Organization for Economic Cooperation and Development.

Hardy, P., L. Kamener, and L. Karotie. 2011. *European Fiscal Consolidations: Four Factors That Will Support Success.* The Boston Consulting Group.

Hauptmeier, S., M. Heipertz, and L. Schuknecht. 2007. "Expenditure Reform in Industrialized Countries: A Case Study Approach." *Fiscal Studies* 28 (3): 293–342.

Henriksson, J. 2007. "Ten Lessons about Budget Consolidations." The Bruegel Essay and Lecture Series.

Honkapohja, S., and E. Koskela. 1999. "The Economic Crisis in the 1990s in Finland." The Research Institute of the Finnish Economy, Discussion Paper no. 683.

Honohan, P. 1989. "Comments to Dornbusch." *Economic Policy* April:202–05.

Honohan, P., and B. Walsh. 2002. "Catching Up with the Leaders: The Irish Hare." *Brookings Panel on Economic Activity* I:1–57.

International Monetary Fund. 2010. "Will It Hurt? Macroeconomic Effects of Fiscal Consolidations." *The World Economic Outlook,* chapter 3, October. Washington, DC: IMF.

Jayadev, A., and M. Konczal. 2010. *The Boom Not the Slump: The Right Time for Fiscal Austerity.* The Roosevelt Institute.

Jonung, L., J. Kiander, and P. Vartia. 2008. "The Great Financial Crisis in Finland and Sweden." Economic Paper, DG ECFIN.

Krugman, P. 2010. "Myths of Austerity." *New York Times,* July 1. http://www.nytimes.com/2010/07/02/opinion/02krugman.html?ref=paulkrugman.

———. 2011. "When Austerity Fails." *New York Times,* May 22. http://www.nytimes.com/2011/05/23/opinion/23krugman.html?ref=paulkrugman.

Lane, P. R. 2000. "Disinflation, Switching Nominal Anchors and Twin Crises: The Irish Experience." *Policy Reform* 3:301–26.

Lilico, A., E. Holmes, and H. Sameen. 2009. *Controlling Spending and Government Deficits: Lessons from History and International Experience.* Policy Exchange Report. www.policyexchange.org.uk.

Ljungman, G. 2008. "Expenditure Ceilings—A Survey." International Monetary Fund Working Paper WP/08/282. Washington, DC: IMF.

McAleese, D. 1990. "Ireland's Economic Recovery." *Irish Banking Review* Summer:18–32.

McCarthy, C. 2010. "Ireland's Second Round of Cuts: A Comparison with the Last Time." In *Dealing with Debt: Lessons from Abroad,* edited by J. Springford, 41–54. CentreForum Canada, Ernst & Young.

Ministry of Finance. 2000. "An Account of Fiscal and Monetary Policy in the 1990s." In Government Bill 2000:01, Annex 5. Swedish Ministry of Finance, Stockholm.

Morris, R., and L. Schuknecht. 2007. "Structural Balances and Revenue Windfalls: The Role of Asset Prices Revisited." European Central Bank Working Paper Series no. 737. Frankfurt: ECB.

OECD. Various years. *Economic Survey.* In print and online (since approx. 2002, www.oecd.org).

Ramey, V. A. 2011. "Identifying Government Spending Shocks: It's All in the Timing." *The Quarterly Journal of Economics* 126 (1): 1–50.

Rigobon, R., and T. Stoker. 2003. "Censored Regressors and Expansion Bias." MIT Sloan Working Paper no. 4451-03.

Romer, C., and D. Romer. 2010. "The Macroeconomic Effects of Tax Changes: Estimates Based on a New Measure of Fiscal Shocks." *American Economic Review* 100 (3): 763–801.

Walsh, B. 1993. "Credibility, Interest Rates and the ERM: The Irish Experience." *Oxford Bulletin of Economics and Statistics* 55 (4): 439–52.

Whelan, K. 2010. "The Enduring Influence of Ireland's 1987 Adjustment." *Irish Economy* blog. http://www.irisheconomy.ie/index.php/2010/08/20/the-enduring -influence-of-irelands-1987-adjustment/.

Comment   Philip R. Lane

This excellent chapter revisits the influential "expansionary fiscal contraction" (EFC) hypothesis. The EFC hypothesis highlights that there are nonlinearities in fiscal dynamics, with the impact of fiscal austerity sharply differing between fiscally-stable and fiscally-unstable economies. If fiscal austerity signals to investors that the debt level will stabilize or even decline over time, it may be associated with a decline in sovereign default risk and a reduction in interest rates. For countries with a flexible exchange rate, it may also signal a reduction in inflation and the expected rate of devaluation, so that it further reduces nominal interest rates through this channel. If fiscal austerity reduces the expected future tax burden on workers/households and investors, it can also boost the real economy by raising the expected post-tax return to working and investing.

It is notoriously difficult to test the EFC hypothesis. The number of cases of sustained fiscal austerity is relatively small and many factors influence macroeconomic outcomes, so there is a limited value to econometric studies. Rather, Perotti's chapter provides a careful treatment of a number of important case studies and this approach is highly informative.

The author provides a useful feedback rule for the fiscal surplus

$$(1) \qquad \Delta s = \alpha_y \Delta y + \alpha_p \Delta p + \beta_y \Delta y + \varepsilon_s,$$

where $\alpha_y > 0$ captures the operation of automatic stabilizers, $\alpha_p > 0$ allows for revenue windfalls from asset price booms, $\beta_y > 0$ reflects activist countercyclical policy interventions, and ε_s measures acyclical shifts in the fiscal position. In fact, the set of financial factors that can influence fiscal outcomes extends beyond asset prices (Benetrix and Lane 2011). Large current account deficits mean that spending levels are ahead of income levels, which boosts revenues from indirect tax sources. In related fashion, rapid credit growth can reorientate the economy from tax-poor export activity to tax-rich nontradables production (since VAT is not levied on exports) and also boost revenue from transaction taxes (stamp duties on housing purchases).

Furthermore, it should be recognized that governments follow procyclical policies in many countries. Revenue windfalls from a financial boom may prompt additional spending or tax cuts, such that $\alpha_p <= 0$ is possible. In a

Philip R. Lane is the Whately Professor of Political Economy at Trinity College, Dublin.
For acknowledgments, sources of research support, and disclosure of the author's material financial relationships, if any, please see http://www.nber.org/chapters/c12653.ack.

similar vein, political economy factors or cognitive problems (a failure to differentiate between cyclical upturns and improvements in trend growth) mean that output expansions may induce discretionary fiscal expansions so that $\beta_y <= 0$. Given the cross-country and cross-time heterogeneity in these coefficients, panel-type estimation will limited value in understanding the specific experiences of individual countries, which reinforces the desirability of the case-study approach developed in this chapter.

The careful treatment of the fiscal data for each country in this chapter is a salutary lesson for empirical fiscal research. It underlines the importance of differentiating between announced fiscal plans and the actual implementation, with the role of midyear fiscal adjustments especially important in understanding fiscal outcomes. Another lesson is that the multiyear nature of fiscal adjustment episodes means that it is important that the "event window" is selected appropriately, in order to fully capture the full impact of fiscal adjustment programs. Again, this provides a warning against "one size fits all" empirical approaches, since the appropriate event window may vary across different episodes. An important substantial finding from Perotti's forensic data investigation is that the contribution of revenue growth in these fiscal adjustment episodes has been understated in previous research.

In terms of the economics of fiscal austerity, Perotti points to several key issues. First, fiscal austerity was accompanied by exchange rate devaluation in several cases, which may have been an important support to output growth during these episodes (in addition, the export channel was affected by the general state of demand in trading partners). Second, there were sizable declines in nominal and real interest rates, which can be largely attributed to a decline in expected inflation. In turn, there was a virtuous cycle by which lower inflation was reinforced by wage moderation, with this process faciliated by incomes policies in various countries.

It is important to assess the lessons from these case studies from the 1980s and 1990s for the current wave of fiscal austerity programs. The author highlights that competitiveness gains are hard to achieve in the absence of nominal exchange rate flexibility, especially when wage inflation is also low in partner countries. With the exception of imposed nominal wage cuts in the public sectors of crisis-hit countries, the evidence so far points to considerable downward wage rigidities: export-led output growth is hard to engineer under these conditions, especially when growth is also anaemic in major trading partners.

Perotti points to incomes policies as a factor in wage moderation during these episodes. It would be good to know about the conditions required for incomes policies to be effective. In particular, incomes policies may be more feasible under crisis conditions than in periods of robust labor demand, if inflation is low but still substantially positive, and in environments in which a combination of fiscal austerity and wage moderation can plausibly provide direct (if partial) payoffs to the real incomes of workers through lower interest rates (lower mortgage rates) and a stronger level for the exchange rate (lower cost of imported consumer goods).

For the euro area, a common central bank means that policy interest rates do not respond to country-specific fiscal actions. That said, the very high country spreads that have emerged during the euro crisis means that fiscal dynamics can be improved by austerity programs that successfully reduce perceived default risks. In turn, in relation to the wider economy, the sovereign risk premium influences the cost of funding for the domestic banking system, even if some larger corporates might be able to obtain international funding at a lower cost.

The analysis in this chapter also indicates that there is plenty of room for new research on several dimensions of fiscal adjustment. In relation to revenue growth, the relative contribution of tax rate increases versus the broadening of the tax base is an important topic. In terms of spending cuts, the balance across transfer programs, public consumption, and public investment should be further assessed in relation to their relative impact on short-term and long-term economic performance.

A major issue concerns the impact of banking crises on the design and execution of fiscal adjustment programs. While Perotti classifies Finland and Sweden in the 1990s as representing adjustment under flexible-rate (inflation-targeting) regimes, the banking crises suffered by these countries are central to fiscal and macroeconomic dynamics during these episodes.

While there is much to learn from previous episodes, it is important to bear in mind some key structural shifts. In particular, the levels of domestic and international financial development are far greater now than twenty years ago. The ratios of domestic credit to GDP have grown sharply (especially in the euro periphery), while the ratios of cross-border financial assets and liabilities to GDP have expanded even more rapidly. This means that balance sheet mechanisms are more powerful now than in the past, which can change the design of optimal fiscal policy. For instance, the interaction of credit constraints and high sectoral debt levels (households, firms) mean that declines in current disposable income have a disproportionate impact on private-sector default rates. In turn, if taxpayers are the ultimate underwriters of the banks, this can offset the fiscal impact of austerity measures. Especially for countries that cannot devalue, an important implication is that the realistic and optimal speed of fiscal adjustment is slower than in previous episodes.

In addition, the very large increase in cross-border financial positions means that the spillover impact of financial market stress has grown considerably. This consideration, reinforced by the synchronized timing of fiscal austerity in many countries in the current crisis, means that it is vital that a global perspective on fiscal adjustment is maintained by policymakers. Accordingly, country-by-country fiscal analysis should be supplemented by broader research that fully incorporates the various macroeconomic and financial interdependencies across countries.

Reference

Benetrix, A. S., and P. R. Lane. 2011. "Financial Cycles and Fiscal Cycles." Prepared for the EUI-IMF conference, Fiscal Policy, Stabilization and Sustainability. Florence, Italy, June 6–7.

Can Public Sector Wage Bills Be Reduced?

Pierre Cahuc and Stéphane Carcillo

9.1 Introduction

In most countries, public wage bills represent a large share of public expenditure (about 55 percent on average in 2009). For this reason, governments that make fiscal adjustments ought to have a hold on the level of their public wage bills (Alesina and Perotti 1995). In this chapter, we analyze the adjustment of public wage bills and public deficits over business and political cycles. We examine how the transparency of governments,[1] the freedom

Pierre Cahuc is professor of economics at the École Polytechnique, and a research fellow at the Centre for Research in Economics and Statistics (CREST-ENSAE), the Institute for the Study of Labor (IZA), and the Centre for Economic Policy Research (CEPR). Stéphane Carcillo is senior economist at the Organization for Economic Cooperation and Development (OECD), a fellow in the Department of Economics, Sciences Po (Paris), and a research fellow of the Institute for the Study of Labor (IZA).

This chapter was commissioned for the NBER conference, "Fiscal Policy after the Financial Crisis," at IGIER-Bocconi University in Milan, Italy, in December 2011. This version was revised following the preconference held at the NBER 2011 Summer Institute on July 14–15. We thank Ariane Salem for excellent research assistance. We also thank Andrea Bassanini as well as all the participants in the preconference for their useful remarks. The opinions expressed and arguments employed here are our responsibility and do not necessarily reflect those of our corresponding institutions. For acknowledgments, sources of research support, and disclosure of the authors' material financial relationships, if any, please see http://www.nber.org/chapters /c12648.ack.

1. Recent papers have connected economic policy with the transparency of governments. Alt and Lassen (2006) and Shi and Svensson (2006) show that electoral cycles in fiscal balances are more pronounced in countries with lower transparency. Gavazza and Lizzeri (2009) show that imperfect observability generates an incentive for politicians to offer excessive transfers partly financed through public deficits. Alesina, Campante, and Tabellini (2008) and Lane (2003) analyze the cyclical behavior of fiscal policy in OECD countries. Lane stresses that political economy factors play an important role in determining the degree of cyclicality in government spending across OECD countries, especially for wage government consumption. Alesina, Campante, and Tabellini (2008) argue that more corrupt countries display more procyclical fiscal

of the press, the union coverage, the political regime (parliamentary versus presidential),[2] and the electoral rule (majoritarian versus proportional) influence the ability to adjust public wage bills.[3]

Our main results are well illustrated by two countries. In Greece, the share of public wage bill in GDP increased from 9.6 percent in 1996 to 12.2 percent in 2008. During the same period, public deficit averaged 4.9 percent of GDP. Strikingly, increases in the share of public wage bill in GDP occurred when the output gap was positive rather than negative. In Denmark, the share of public wage bill in GDP averaged 17.4 percent over the same period. It is much higher than in Greece! However, Denmark managed to control not only the evolution of the public wage bill, which remained stable, but also the public budget, which exhibited an average positive surplus of 1.7 percent of GDP. According to our findings, Greece is a typical example of a country where the weak transparency of the government and the lack of freedom of the press induce drifts of public wage bills during booms and election years that governments have no incentive to counteract when economic difficulties arise. At the opposite, in Denmark, transparency of public institutions and freedom of the press put pressure on governments to avoid unsustainable increases in public wage bills. All in all, our chapter stresses that the transparency of the government and the freedom of the press contribute to prevent unsustainable increases in public wage bills.

We start out by describing the relations between public deficits and public wage bills. It turns out that there is no systematic *cross-country* relation between the share of public wage bills in GDP and the level of public deficits. There are very large cross-country differences in the share of public wage bills in terms of GDP, which ranges from 6.3 percent of GDP (Japan) to 17.5 percent of GDP (Denmark) over the 1990 to 2009 period. But countries with larger wage bills do not necessarily have larger public deficits. However, there is a strong positive within-country correlation between public wage bills and public deficits, even when these two variables are averaged over five-year periods. This indicates that public deficits tend to increase in countries where public wage bills increase faster than GDP.

In order to describe more precisely the situations where there is lack of control of public wage bills, we define episodes of what we call "fiscal drift,"

policies because when more resources are available (i.e., in booms), the common-pool problem is more severe, and the fight over common resources intensifies, leading to budget deficits, this effect being stronger in more corrupt countries.

2. Persson (2002) finds that, empirically, presidential regimes are associated with smaller and less persistent responses of spending to income shocks, a stronger post-election cycle in aggregate spending and revenue, but a weaker cycle in social transfers.

3. Persson and Tabellini (2000, ch. 9) argue that electoral cycles, showing up in spending or taxes, should be weaker under proportional representation compared to majority rules, because the incumbents' career concerns are stronger with individual accountability stemming from majority rules and because these concerns are at their strongest just before elections.

where there are simultaneous *increases* in the share of public wage bills in GDP and in public deficits. We interpret the occurrence of such episodes as the sign of a lack of control of public wage bills and public expenditure. We also look at episodes of "fiscal tightening," where there are simultaneous *decreases* in the share of public wage bills in GDP and in public deficits. Such episodes occur when the control of public expenditure is sustained, at least partially, by a strong control of public wage bills.

With these definitions in mind, we analyze in turn the probability that fiscal drift and fiscal tightening episodes appear. In doing so, we identify when these episodes occur around economic or political cycles, conditional to the degree of transparency of the government, the freedom of the press, the union coverage, the political regime, and the electoral rule.

Strikingly, we find that fiscal drift episodes do not come out more frequently during slumps, as could be expected, but during booms. This suggests that fiscal drift episodes are mostly induced by a perverse functioning of institutions. The fact that fiscal drift episodes are more frequent during election years reinforces the relevance of this interpretation. Consistently, we find that booms and election years significantly decrease the probability that fiscal tightening episodes come out.

The analysis of the interactions between cycles and institutions allows us to shed more light on this phenomenon. We find that fiscal drift associated with booms is less frequent when governments are more transparent, when there is more freedom of the press, and when the political regime is presidential, while larger union coverage tends to increase the probability of fiscal drift and decrease the probability of fiscal tightening.

The chapter is organized as follows. Section 9.2 presents the relation between public deficits and public wage bills in Organization for Economic Cooperation and Development (OECD) countries over the last fifteen years. Section 9.3 is devoted to the description of fiscal drift and fiscal tightening episodes. In section 9.4, we analyze the relations between the occurrence of fiscal drift and fiscal tightening episodes and the economic cycles, the election years, the transparency of governments, the freedom of the press, the union coverage, the political regime, and the electoral rules.

9.2   Public Wage Bills and Public Deficits

9.2.1   Data

Public Wage Bills

The definition of public wage bills hinges on the definition of the scope of the public sector. The public sector can comprise only general government employment, or general government and public corporations employment (legal entities that are owned or controlled by the government and produce most of their goods and services for sale in the market at economically significant prices).

There are multiple national sources of data collection, and very few cross-country comparable data on public employment and public wage bills. Unfortunately, there is very limited cross-country information on public employment.[4] There is more information on public wage bills, thanks to the rules of accountability of general government expenditures. Public wage bills include the total compensation of employees of the general government sector, which comprises all levels of government (central, state, local, and social security) and includes ministries, agencies, and nonprofit institutions controlled by government.[5] According to this definition, public wage bills do not include the compensation of employees in public corporations.

Measures of public payroll as a share of GDP come from annual national accounts. The UN system of national accounts (SNA) is a set of internationally agreed-upon recommendations to collect data with the latest operational revision dating from 1993. On this basis, homogeneous data for OECD countries are available for the period 1995 to 2009.[6]

Unfortunately, the quality of data on public employment does not allow us to decompose changes in public wage bills into changes in employment and in remunerations. Data on wages and on employment do not overlap exactly. Moreover, even if it were the case, data on hours worked, or at least the share of part-time jobs, would be needed to address this issue.

Public Deficit

General government national accounts usually report net-lending/ net-borrowing, which represents the amount the government has available to lend or must borrow to finance its nonfinancial operations. This figure comprises the interest payable for the service of the debt. Net lending data comes from the OECD annual SNA database. Data are available for most countries since 1980.

9.2.2   Cross-Country Correlations between Public Wage Bills and Public Deficits

Figure 9.1 shows that there are large cross-country differences in the share of public wage bill in GDP over the period 1995 to 2009. The average share

4. The OECD has recently released homogenous data on public employment now available for 1995, 2000, 2005, and 2008 (Government at a Glance) based on questionnaires that improve the comparability across country. The International Labor Organization (ILO) also provides, in coordination with the OECD, such information extracted from a combination of different sources (administrative data or surveys) for a varying number of years depending on the country.

5. Public wage bills do not include public pensions.

6. There are homogeneous data for all countries since 1995 for most OECD countries, and some data from 1970 to 1995 (few countries with observations as old as 1970, half of the countries with observations as old as 1980).

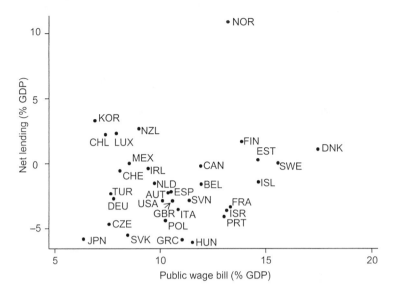

Fig. 9.1   **Average public wage bill and net lending in OECD countries over the period 1995–2009**

Source: OECD data.

of public wage bill in GDP goes from 6.4 percent in Japan to 17.4 in Denmark. Public deficits are also very different across countries. Hungary is in the worst situation, with an average deficit equal to 6 percent of GDP. Over the same period, Norway had a positive net lending, equal to 11 percent of GDP.

Figure 9.1 shows that there is no cross-country correlation between the share of public wage bill in GDP and public deficits, even though public wage bill represents a large share of public expenditure. Scandinavian countries have the largest public wage bills associated with the largest positive net lending. At the opposite, Japan, the Czech Republic, and the Slovak Republic have the smallest public wage bills but the largest public deficits. Overall, figure 9.1 indicates that it is possible to have very large public sectors and sustainable public finances, but also very small public sectors and unsustainable public finances.

9.2.3   Within-Country Correlations between Public Wage Bills and Public Deficits

Figure 9.2 shows that OECD countries have experienced very different changes over time in public wage bills and public deficits since the mid-1990s. There is no common general tendency across OECD countries. There is a negative trend in Austria, France, Germany, Israel, Luxembourg, Slovak Republic, and Sweden. The trend is positive in Belgium, Greece, Ireland,

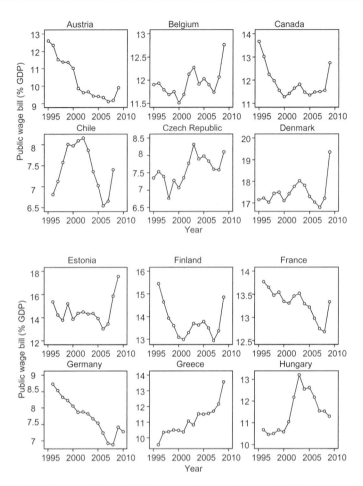

Fig. 9.2   Public wage bills in OECD countries over the period 1995–2009
Source: OECD data.

United Kingdom, and United States. Public wage bills fluctuate without showing any trend in other countries. There is also a strong increase in the share of wage bill in GDP in 2009 in most countries because the recession induced large drops in GDP in most countries.

Although there is no cross-country correlation between public wage bills and public deficits, it turns out that there is a strong correlation between these two variables over time within countries. Table 9.1 shows the within-country correlation between net public lending and public wage bills when these two variables are averaged over five-year periods (i.e., 1995 to 1999, 2000 to 2004, 2005 to 2009). It turns out that there is a significant and sizable correlation between these two variables, even when one controls for GDP growth, the share of population over sixty-five year old, and below 15 years

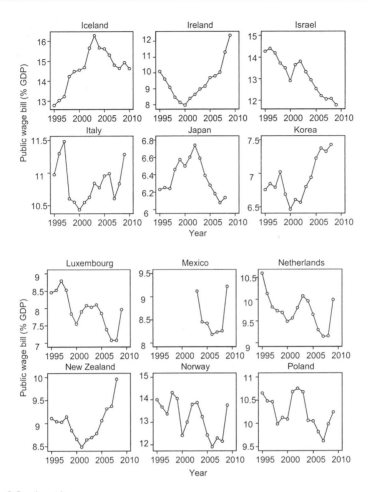

Fig. 9.2   (cont.)

old. One percentage point increase in the share of public wage bill in GDP is associated with a 1.5 percentage point decrease in net public lending.

This correlation suggests that countries where the share of public wage bill in GDP has been increasing since the mid-1990s have also experienced worsening public deficits. In the next section, we identify the features of the countries that experience worsening public deficits associated with increases in public wage bills. We also shed light on the features that enable countries to reduce their public deficits thanks to public wage bill compressions.

9.3   Episodes of Fiscal Drift and Fiscal Tightening

Even though larger public wage bills tend to be associated with lower net lending positions within countries, the fact that some countries with high

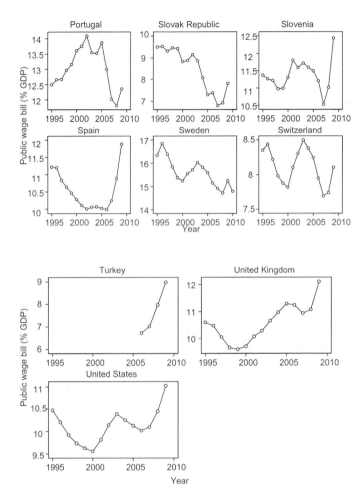

Fig. 9.2   (cont.)

levels of public employment do not experience large and recurrent deficits (e.g., Denmark or Sweden) raises the question about the ability to *adjust* the size of public administration when it becomes necessary. To study this type of adjustment we look at "bad" episodes, where both deficits and wage spending increase, but also at "good" episodes, where both deficits and wage spending decrease.

9.3.1   Definition of Fiscal Drift and Fiscal Tightening Episodes

Fiscal Drift Episodes

A fiscal drift episode induced by public wage bill drift is a situation where there are simultaneous increases in the GDP share of public wage bill and

Table 9.1   **Within-country correlation between public net lending and public wage bill**

	Net lending		
Public wage bill	−1.581***	−1.598**	−1.494**
	(0.546)	(0.589)	(0.655)
GDP growth		−0.053	0.057
		(0.222)	(0.278)
Pop. over 65			0.398
			(0.320)
Pop. below 15			0.041
			(0.237)
Constant	28.731***	29.117***	12.106
	(9.549)	(10.486)	(9.973)
Country effects (5-year avg.)	Yes	Yes	Yes
R^2	0.900	0.900	0.907
Adj. R^2	0.846	0.843	0.848
Obs.	84	84	84

Notes: Robust standard errors in parentheses. OLS with country fixed effects. Period 1995–2009. Variables are averaged over five-year periods: 1995–1999, 2000–2004, 2005–2009.
***Significant at the 1 percent level.
**Significant at the 5 percent level.
*Significant at the 10 percent level.

in the GDP share of public deficit. Obviously, by definition, there is necessarily a public deficit during such fiscal drift episodes (i.e., a negative public net lending during and at the end of the episode, but not necessarily at the beginning). We consider two different definitions of fiscal drift.

There is a short fiscal drift episode if there are simultaneous increases in the GDP shares of public wage bill and public deficit during at least one year. There are 105 fiscal drift episodes over 308 country/year observations with public deficits available for the OECD countries over the period 1995 to 2009.

The second definition is more restrictive: "long fiscal drift episodes" occur if there are simultaneous increases in the GDP shares of public wage bill and public deficit during at least two years. Such fiscal drift episodes occur for sixty country/year observations.

Fiscal Tightening Episodes

A fiscal tightening episode induced by public wage bill policy is a situation where there are simultaneous decreases in the GDP share of public wage bill and in the GDP share of public deficit. By definition, there is a public deficit at the beginning of fiscal tightening episodes (i.e., in the year preceding the episode). As for fiscal drifts, there are two different definitions of fiscal tightening.

There is a short fiscal tightening episode if there are simultaneous decreases in the GDP shares of public wage bill and public deficit during at least one year. There are 129 fiscal tightening episodes over 305 country/year observations with public deficits available for the OECD countries over the period 1995 to 2009.

The second definition is more restrictive: long fiscal tightening episodes occur if there are simultaneous increases in the GDP shares of public wage bill and public deficit during at least two years. Such fiscal tightening episodes occur for ninety-six country/year observations.

9.3.2   Description of Fiscal Drift Episodes

Table 9.2 displays the short fiscal drift episodes for every country. It turns out that short fiscal drift episodes occurred in almost all countries. There are only two exceptions: Korea and Norway, where net lending is always positive over the period. Most countries experienced more than one short fiscal drift episode. The highest number of short fiscal drift episodes, equal to six, is observed in Slovenia and in the United States, where all fiscal drift episodes appeared in the 2000s. Following these countries are Belgium, Greece, Italy, Portugal, and Slovak Republic, where five short fiscal drift episodes are observed.

Deficits are significantly higher during short fiscal drift episodes. On average, public net lending amounts to –4.5 percent of GDP during short fiscal drift episodes, while it averages to –0.5 percent of GDP excluding these episodes.[7] Not surprisingly, the GDP share of public wage bill also increases much more during fiscal drift episodes (0.46 percentage point of GDP) than outside these episodes where this share actually decreases (–0.12 percentage point of GDP).

Long fiscal drift episodes are observed more scarcely. Only fifteen countries among the thirty-two OECD countries for which data are available experienced long fiscal drift episodes. On average, public deficits and changes in public wage bills are not statistically different during long and short fiscal drift episodes.

9.3.3   Description of Fiscal Tightening Episodes

Table 9.3 displays the short fiscal tightening episodes for every country. As for fiscal drift episodes, there are no fiscal tightening episodes in Korea and Norway, because their net lending is never negative over the period. Most countries have several fiscal tightening episodes. Countries that reduce almost continuously their public wage bills over the period, like Austria, France, Germany, and Israel, have a relatively large number of fiscal tightening episodes, comprised between six and eight. But some other countries, which alternate periods of reductions and periods of increases in public wage bills, also have several fiscal tightening episodes. This is the case

---

7. These figures are equal to –3.5 percent and –0.45 percent, respectively, if 2009 is excluded.

Table 9.2   Fiscal drift episodes

	AUT	BEL	CAN	CHL	CZE	DNK	EST	FIN	FRA	DEU	GRC	HUN	ISL	IRL	ISR	ITA	JPN	KOR	LUX	MEX	NLD	NZL	NOR	POL	PRT	SVK	SVN	ESP	SWE	CHE	GBR	USA
1995	•			n/a	n/a				•		n/a	n/a	n/a		n/a		•			n/a			n/a	n/a	n/a	n/a	n/a					
1996				n/a	n/a							n/a	n/a		•		•			n/a					n/a	•	n/a					
1997																				n/a												
1998												•	•				•			n/a					•							
1999				•			•													n/a							•					
2000																				n/a							•					
2001	•	•	•	•	•				•	•	•	•	•	•	•	•	•			n/a	•				•		•			•		•
2002		•			•				•		•	•	•		•	•				n/a	•			•	•	•			•	•	•	•
2003						•							•							n/a	•						•			•	•	•
2004		•														•			•									•				
2005					•							•													•							
2006																										•						
2007											•									•												
2008		•	•				•				•			•	•	•	n/a	n/a	•	•		n/a		•		•	•	•			•	•
2009	•	•	•		•	•		•	•	•	•			•		•	n/a	n/a	•		•			•	•	•	•	•	•		•	•

Source: OECD data.

Notes: There is a fiscal drift episode if there are simultaneous increases in the GDP shares of public budget deficits and public wage bills. "n/a" stands for not available.

Table 9.3   Fiscal tightening episodes

	AUT	BEL	CAN	CHL	CZE	DNK	EST	FIN	FRA	DEU	GRC	HUN	ISL	IRL	ISR	ITA	JPN	KOR	LUX	MEX	NLD	NZL	NOR	POL	PRT	SVK	SVN	ESP	SWE	CHE	GBR	USA
1995	•	•	•	n/a	n/a	•		•	•	•	n/a	n/a	n/a	•	n/a	•				n/a	•		n/a		n/a	n/a	n/a	•	•	•	•	•
1996		•	•	n/a						•	•	n/a		•	•		•			n/a	•				n/a	n/a	n/a	•			•	•
1997	•	•	•			•	•	•	•	•		•			•					n/a	•			•		•	•	•		•	•	•
1998								•	•	•					•	•				n/a	•			•				•	•	•	•	•
1999	•						•			•					•	•				n/a								•		•	•	
2000	•	•		•					•			•								n/a								•		•		
2001	•																			n/a												
2002																				n/a								•				
2003			•	•	•	•					•						•			n/a		•										
2004	•								•	•		•	•		•		•				•					•		•	•			
2005	•	•			•				•	•					•						•			•			•					•
2006				•	•				•	•		•			•		•		•		•			•	•		•	•		•		•
2007	•	•								•		•			•	•					•			•	•	•	•	•		•	•	•
2008												•					n/a	n/a				n/a		•			•					
2009																	n/a	n/a														

Source: OECD data.

Notes: There is a fiscal tightening episode if there are simultaneous decreases in the GDP shares of public budget deficits and public wage bills. "n/a" stands for not available.

for Poland, Spain, the Netherlands, the United Kingdom, and the United States. At the opposite, Greece, Ireland, and Portugal have no more than two short fiscal tightening episodes because their public wage bills increased over almost all the period.

9.4   Determinants of Fiscal Drift and Fiscal Tightening Episodes

We are now looking at the determinants of fiscal drift and fiscal tightening episodes. We begin to describe how the interactions between business cycles, political cycles, and some institutions may influence the occurrence of these episodes. Then, we present the econometric method and the empirical results.

9.4.1   Cycles and Institutions

The impact of booms on the occurrence of fiscal drift and fiscal tightening episodes is a priori ambiguous. On the one hand, increases in GDP mechanically reduce the GDP shares of public wage bills and budget deficits. But on the other hand, as stressed by Alesina, Campante, and Tabellini (2008), in weakly transparent and strongly corrupt countries, GDP increases can intensify the fight over common resources, leading to larger budget deficits and larger public wage bills. Accordingly, the probability to observe fiscal drift (respectively tightening) episodes should be higher (respectively lower) during booms when governments are more opaque and more corrupt. This probability should also be lower in presidential regimes, where there is overall less possibility of discretionary increases in public expenditure and less fragmentation of power than in parliamentary regimes.

At first sight, fiscal drift episodes are more likely to come out during slumps, since reductions in the growth rate of GDP mechanically increases public deficits and the share of public wage bills in GDP. The opposite holds true for fiscal tightening episodes.

The impact of slumps on fiscal drift and fiscal tightening episodes may depend on the quality of the government for at least two reasons. In the first place, in recessions, more transparent governments should have more incentives to adjust public wage bills in order to avoid soaring public deficits: when the actions of the government are transparent, voters are well-informed about the use of public money, the effectiveness of spending, and the long-term consequences of deficits. In the second place, more transparent governments should also be able to react more quickly: it is easier to cut spending when it is used in a transparent way than to cut rents that are distributed to secure future votes. Political institutions might also play a role, as suggested by Persson and Tabellini (2000). For instance, countries with parliamentary regimes and proportional electoral systems tend to experience countercyclical changes in public spending and deficits, with a sort of ratchet effect (spending and deficits increase during slumps but do not decrease in the same proportion during booms). Unions in the public sector[8], usually supported by other unions, could also influence the ability to adjust (Alesina 1999). Because they often defend insiders first, unions are typically opposed to a wage or hiring freeze, and even more so to public employment cuts in situations of negative GDP shock, thus delaying the adjustment. They would also tend to ask for more public employment or higher wages during booms, which would tend to foster fiscal drift.

The occurrence of fiscal drift and fiscal tightening episodes can also be influenced by elections. During election years, candidates have incentives to increase public wage bills, possibly at the expense of worsening budget deficits. This type of behavior is likely to be amplified by corruption and lack of transparency (Shi and Svensson 2006; Alesina, Campante, and Tabellini 2008). Election cycles could also be institution-dependent. For instance, majoritarian countries should in theory experience larger election cycles because of the individual accountability of incumbents and incentives to spend more just before elections. One would expect countries with presidential regimes to spend less than countries with parliamentary regimes during election years since checks and balances are stricter in presidential regimes. Finally, in countries where unions are strong, election cycles could be even stronger, with higher wages or hiring during the years of elections.

9.4.2   Econometric Method

In what follows, we evaluate to what extent the emergence of fiscal drift episodes is influenced by the features of public institutions, booms, slumps, and elections. To answer this question, we estimate the following linear probability model:[9]

$$(1) \quad y_{i,t} = a_1 y_{i,t-1} + a_2 \text{shock}_{i,t} + a_3 \text{shock}_{i,t} * \text{instit}_i + a_4 x_{i,t} + a_5 D_{2009} + \mu_i + \varepsilon_{i,t},$$

where $y_{i,t}$ is equal to 1 if there is a fiscal drift (or tightening) episode in country i at date t, and zero otherwise. What we call $\text{shock}_{i,t}$ for simplicity stands for a vector of events in country i at date t influencing the fiscal stance, which includes positive output gaps, negative output gaps, and election years. The output gap is computed using the Hodrick-Prescott filter.[10] We distinguish two different variables for the output gap to the extent that positive and nega-

---

8. Union coverage rates (i.e., the share of employees covered by collective wage agreements) can summarize the blocking power of unions better than union density. In some countries, such as France, union density can be very low (about 8 percent), but union coverage quite high (about 90 percent), which gives unions a lot of influence in the political debates.

9. It is well known that the linear probability model for a binary dependent variable yields an unbiased estimator but necessarily has a heteroskedastic error term. We deal with this problem by computing heteroskedasticity-robust statistics (see, e.g., Wooldridge 2002). The estimation of dynamic panel data discrete choice nonlinear models with fixed effects and instrumental variables, which is still an area of research for econometricians, is beyond the scope of this chapter.

10. With this specification we regress the outcome of a difference (the probability of drifts or tightening is the result of a changes in surpluses and public wage bills) on the output gap, which is also a difference between the output and its long-term trend.

tive output gaps may have different effects on the occurrence of fiscal drift and fiscal-tightening episodes. The variable "positive output gap" is equal to the output gap when it is positive and to zero otherwise. The variable "negative output gap" is defined similarly (in absolute terms); $instit_i$ stands for a vector of institutional characteristics of country i, which includes the degree of transparency, the political regime (presidential versus parliamentary), the election rule (proportional versus majoritarian),[11] and the union coverage rate.[12] Variable $x_{i,t}$ is a vector of control variables that comprises the share of the population over sixty-five and the share of population below fifteen. Variable D_{2009} is a dummy for the recession year 2009. Variable μ_i is a country fixed effect and $\varepsilon_{i,t}$ is a residual term.

We consider different versions of equation (1) including alternative measures of the features of public institutions and definitions of the fiscal drift and fiscal tightening episodes. This equation raises several issues that call for specific treatments:

- First, the presence of the lagged independent variable $y_{i,t-1}$ is justified by the fact that fiscal stances are typically persistent over time. In this dynamic setting the ordinary least squares (OLS) estimated are systematically biased (the residuals are auto-correlated) and do not converge unless we use a large number of time observations, which is not our case. Some techniques, such as the Arellano-Bond method, allow us to account for this autocorrelation issue.
- Second, the $shock_{i,t}$ variable might be endogenous; in the case of the output gap, it is clear that the intensity of the shock on public finance can be reduced in the short-run by large deficits and higher public employment compensation spending. Thus, this variable needs to be instrumented with variables that are not influenced by the fiscal stance or by the change in public employment spending. We consider two different instruments for the output gap for country i at date t. First, the past values of output gaps of country i. Second, the contemporaneous output gaps of all countries except country i.
- Third, the vector of institutional characteristics $instit_i$ is assumed to be constant over time. Actually, electoral rules and political systems do not change over time in most countries. The measures of transparency display some changes over time. However, transparency might be

11. We use the Quality of Government database (http://www.qog.pol.gu.se/) for the type of political regime and the election rule.
12. We use the Database on Institutional Characteristics of Trade Unions, Wage Setting, State Intervention and Social Pacts, 1960–2010 (ICTWSS) from the Amsterdam Institute for Advanced Labour Studies (AIAS), University of Amsterdam. Union coverage rates in the public sector are only available for one-fourth of observations in our panel, while the general union coverage rates are available for the full panel. We consider the latter. However, the two types of rates appear to be strongly correlated (the coefficient of correlation is 0.92), and the general union coverage rate (like the coverage rate in the private sector) strongly predicts the coverage rate in the public sector.

potentially endogenous; for instance, if transparency is measured as the perception of corruption of public officers by voters, this perception might be influenced over time by the economic situation, which in turn can be influenced by the fiscal stance; also, acts of corruption might be more frequently observed at some times than others, such as general elections. For that reason, we interact the shock with the *average* value of the measure of transparency and other institutional variables over the period. This is also justified by the fact that there is little change over time in the measures the institutional variables over the relatively short period of time covered by our data.

Our benchmark specification considers the first definition of fiscal drift episodes, which corresponds to years where there are simultaneously an increase in general government payroll and a decrease in public net lending in a situation of public deficit. The transparency of the government is measured with the corruption perception index of Transparency International, which takes on values from 0 to 10, a higher score corresponding to more transparent governments. In what follows, we use this variable centered on its average value over all the period 1995 to 2009 for all countries.

9.4.3 Empirical Results

The Impact of Output Gap and Elections

This section analyzes the relation between business and political cycles and fiscal episodes. We begin by neglecting the role of institutions by estimating equation (1) without interaction terms between cycles and institutions (i.e., assuming that coefficient a_3 is equal to zero).

Table 9.4 shows that the occurrence of *short* fiscal drift episodes is more likely when there are election years and during economic booms. Strikingly, fiscal drift episodes are not more frequent when there are recessions, setting aside the effect of the year 2009. This result shows up for different specifications of equation (1), which account for the autocorrelation of residuals and for the endogeneity of GDP shocks. Table 9.5 shows that the same result holds true for *long* fiscal drift episodes regarding positive output gaps, but not for elections. This clearly stems from the fact that general elections are rarely held two years in a row. Table 9.6 shows that this pattern is specific to wage spending compared to non-wage spending. Indeed, when we analyze similar episodes of fiscal drift, but this time featuring a simultaneous increase of *non-wage* spending and deficits, fiscal drifts seem to be also associated with economic downturns, not only economic booms. This can be explained by the fact that most non-wage spending is made of transfers that are often countercyclical (e.g., income replacement benefits).

Tables 9.4 to 9.6 indicate that periods of simultaneous increases in public wage bills and in public budget deficits are not induced by adverse economic

Table 9.4   Correlation between short fiscal drifts and shocks

	(1)	(2)	(3)	(4)
Lagged fiscal drift	0.099	0.112*	0.080	−0.067
	(0.060)	(0.060)	(0.053)	(0.292)
Neg. output gap	0.029	0.031	0.034*	0.093
	(0.019)	(0.020)	(0.018)	(0.061)
Pos. output gap	0.031*	0.038**	0.034**	0.070*
	(0.015)	(0.016)	(0.015)	(0.041)
Election	0.103**	0.087**	0.097**	0.117***
	(0.046)	(0.041)	(0.042)	(0.042)
Pop. below 15	−0.039	−0.048	−0.044	−0.022
	(0.032)	(0.036)	(0.031)	(0.038)
Pop. over 65	−0.045	−0.053	−0.054	−0.054
	(0.043)	(0.049)	(0.047)	(0.038)
$d\,2009$	0.540***	0.529***	0.527***	0.479***
	(0.095)	(0.100)	(0.091)	(0.143)
Constant	1.451	1.733	1.673	1.208
	(1.150)	(1.293)	(1.177)	(1.153)
R^2	0.172			
Adj. R^2	0.157			
Obs.	387	375	375	362

Notes: Robust standard errors in parentheses. Period 1995–2009.
(1) OLS with country fixed effects; (2) Arellano-Bond method; (3) Arellano-Bond method where the output gap is instrumented by its lagged values; (4) Arellano-Bond method where the output gap of country i is instrumented by the average output gap of all OECD countries but country i.
***Significant at the 1 percent level.
**Significant at the 5 percent level.
*Significant at the 10 percent level.

events. It seems that it is rather loose management of governments during economic booms as well as during periods of elections that fosters fiscal drifts.

Tables 9.7 and 9.8 show that fiscal tightening episodes come out less often during booms than during slumps. The sign of the coefficient associated with election year is also negative, but not significant at 10 percent level of confidence. These results are consistent with those obtained for fiscal drift episodes. All in all, they show that fiscal problems are not resolved during booms. On the contrary, during booms, governments provide less effort to control public wage bills and public deficits.

As shown by figures 9.3 and 9.4, this phenomenon is well illustrated by Greece, where all fiscal drift episodes show up during booms (except in 2009, where the large drop in GDP induced a simultaneous increase in public deficit and in the share of public wage bill in GDP). There has been an increase in the public wage bill by 2.6 points of GDP (from 9.56 to 12.15 percent of GDP) between 1995 and 2008. Most of this increase (2 points) occurred

Table 9.5 **Correlation between long fiscal drifts and shocks**

	(1)	(2)	(3)	(4)
Lagged long fiscal drift	0.591***	0.556***	0.559***	0.297***
	(0.032)	(0.042)	(0.040)	(0.111)
Neg. output gap	−0.004	−0.001	−0.005	0.043
	(0.008)	(0.012)	(0.009)	(0.038)
Pos. output gap	0.037***	0.029**	0.032**	0.103***
	(0.013)	(0.015)	(0.012)	(0.030)
Election	0.003	0.010	0.004	0.020
	(0.034)	(0.036)	(0.033)	(0.031)
Pop. below 15	−0.031	−0.070***	−0.031	−0.010
	(0.019)	(0.021)	(0.022)	(0.026)
Pop. over 65	−0.023	−0.058***	−0.030	−0.044*
	(0.021)	(0.016)	(0.023)	(0.026)
d 2009	0.126***	0.007	0.108***	0.192*
	(0.040)	(0.054)	(0.039)	(0.104)
Constant	0.927	2.148***	1.038	0.788
	(0.618)	(0.582)	(0.691)	(0.760)
R^2	0.350			
Adj. R^2	0.338			
Obs.	387	375	375	362

Note: See notes for table 9.4.
***Significant at the 1 percent level.
**Significant at the 5 percent level.
*Significant at the 10 percent level.

Table 9.6 **Correlation between short fiscal drifts (using nonwage spending) and shocks**

	(1)	(2)	(3)	(4)
Lagged fiscal drift (non-wage)	0.049	0.036	0.036	0.395
	(0.059)	(0.058)	(0.051)	(0.288)
Neg. output gap	0.046**	0.044**	0.051**	0.129*
	(0.021)	(0.020)	(0.020)	(0.070)
Pos. output gap	0.034*	0.037**	0.037**	0.153***
	(0.018)	(0.019)	(0.018)	(0.045)
Election	0.100*	0.092*	0.088*	0.111**
	(0.055)	(0.049)	(0.051)	(0.047)
Pop. below 15	−0.037	−0.062**	−0.037	0.016
	(0.027)	(0.030)	(0.026)	(0.040)
Pop. over 65	−0.044	−0.071*	−0.042	−0.038
	(0.039)	(0.041)	(0.042)	(0.040)
d 2009	0.526***	0.566***	0.526***	0.355**
	(0.105)	(0.102)	(0.101)	(0.157)
Constant	1.423	2.283**	1.402	0.162
	(0.998)	(1.100)	(1.035)	(1.183)
R^2	0.154			
Adj. R^2	0.139			
Obs.	384	373	373	361

Note: See notes for table 9.4.
***Significant at the 1 percent level.
**Significant at the 5 percent level.
*Significant at the 10 percent level.

Table 9.7   **Correlation between short fiscal tightenings and shocks**

	(1)	(2)	(3)	(4)
Lagged fiscal tight.	0.203***	0.213***	0.211***	0.074
	(0.045)	(0.046)	(0.045)	(0.201)
Neg. output gap	-0.007	-0.001	-0.007	-0.083
	(0.019)	(0.022)	(0.020)	(0.057)
Pos. output gap	-0.051***	-0.050***	-0.051***	-0.118***
	(0.018)	(0.018)	(0.018)	(0.043)
Election	-0.062	-0.063	-0.054	-0.070
	(0.043)	(0.040)	(0.039)	(0.045)
Pop. below 15	0.023	0.063	0.037	-0.003
	(0.024)	(0.041)	(0.030)	(0.038)
Pop. over 65	0.022	0.033	0.024	0.023
	(0.018)	(0.030)	(0.024)	(0.038)
d 2009	-0.271***	-0.291***	-0.266***	-0.206
	(0.071)	(0.075)	(0.069)	(0.149)
Constant	-0.430	-1.333	-0.719	0.166
	(0.638)	(1.119)	(0.834)	(1.100)
R^2	0.102			
Adj. R^2	0.086			
Obs.	387	375	375	362

Note: See notes for table 9.4.
***Significant at the 1 percent level.
**Significant at the 5 percent level.
*Significant at the 10 percent level.

Table 9.8   **Correlation between long fiscal tightenings and shocks**

	(1)	(2)	(3)	(4)
Lagged long fiscal tight.	0.461***	0.491***	0.481***	0.191**
	(0.038)	(0.032)	(0.033)	(0.092)
Neg. output gap	-0.004	-0.005	-0.006	-0.077
	(0.014)	(0.018)	(0.014)	(0.047)
Pos. output gap	-0.043***	-0.052***	-0.045***	-0.101***
	(0.014)	(0.018)	(0.013)	(0.037)
Election	-0.009	-0.009	-0.002	-0.022
	(0.033)	(0.029)	(0.030)	(0.038)
Pop. below 15	0.020	0.042	0.019	0.009
	(0.020)	(0.032)	(0.018)	(0.032)
Pop. over 65	0.005	0.014	0.006	0.019
	(0.016)	(0.022)	(0.016)	(0.032)
d 2009	-0.160**	-0.167**	-0.160***	-0.109
	(0.061)	(0.077)	(0.059)	(0.126)
Constant	-0.272	-0.812	-0.277	-0.112
	(0.545)	(0.832)	(0.512)	(0.921)
R^2	0.276			
Adj. R^2	0.262			
Obs.	387	375	375	362

Note: See notes for table 9.4.
***Significant at the 1 percent level.
**Significant at the 5 percent level.
*Significant at the 10 percent level.

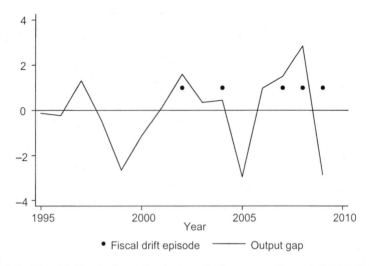

Fig. 9.3   Fiscal drift episodes and output gap in Greece over the period 1995–2009
Source: OECD data.

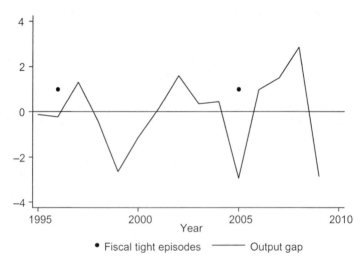

Fig. 9.4   Fiscal tightening episodes and output gap in Greece over the period 1995–2009
Source: OECD data.

during fiscal drift episodes corresponding to periods of positive output gap. This clearly indicates that the unsustainable raise in the public wage bill occurred for the most part during booms in Greece, but not during slumps.

The Role of Institutions

The procyclicality of fiscal drift episodes suggests that misgovernance may influence the emergence of fiscal drift episodes. In order to shed some

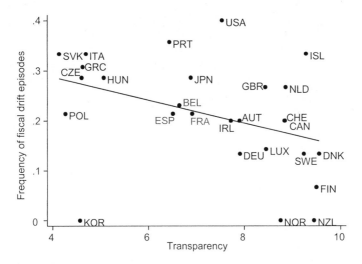

Fig. 9.5   Frequency of fiscal drift episodes and transparency of governments over the period 1995–2009
Source: OECD and Transparency International data.

light on this issue, we estimate the impact of the transparency of the government and that of the freedom of the press on the occurrence of fiscal episodes, along with other institutional factors such as the political regime, the type of election rules, and the power of unions.

Transparency of Government and Other Factors. The analysis of cross-country correlations shows that there is a negative relationship between the transparency of governments and the frequency of fiscal drift episodes, as shown by figure 9.5. Countries with transparent governments experienced less fiscal drift episodes than countries where the government was weakly transparent over the period 1995 to 2009. The gap is sizable, equal to 30 percentage points between the most and the least transparent countries. There is a similar relation between the frequency of fiscal drifts and freedom of the press, as shown by figure 9.6. Except for these two relations, cross-country correlations do not allow us to exhibit any other significant relation between our measures of institutions and the emergence of fiscal drift or fiscal tightening episodes. However, within-country correlations enable us to shed some light on the influence of institutions on the ability of governments to adjust public wage bills during business and political cycles. Formally, we estimate the coefficient associated with the interaction term between institutions and business and electoral cycles in equation (1).

Table 9.9 presents the results when equation (1) is estimated using *short* fiscal drift episodes as dependent variable, and table 9.10 using *long* fiscal drift episodes, using the Transparency International index as a measure of transparency. Column (1) in both tables estimates this equation using coun-

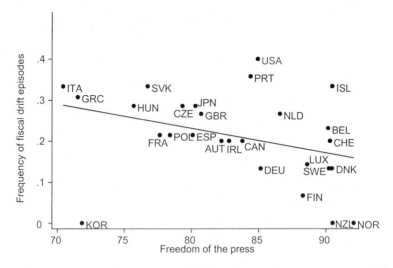

Fig. 9.6   Frequency of fiscal drift episodes and freedom of the press over the period 1995–2009

Source: OECD and Freedom House data.

try fixed effects. This column shows, again, that there is an overall positive and significant (at the 5 percent level) correlation between the contemporaneous positive output gap (for a country of average transparency)[13] and the occurrence of fiscal drift episodes. The correlation with slumps is weaker. The relationship with booms is stronger for long episodes (at the 1 percent level). The occurrence of long fiscal drift episodes is not correlated with negative output gaps.

The crossed effect between booms and transparency is negative and significant at the 5 percent level for short and long episodes only. This means that the emergence of fiscal drift episodes of at least two years is less sensitive to booms in countries where governments are more transparent. In other words, more transparent governments are on average less prone to increase public deficits and public wage bills when the economy grows faster. In countries with the lowest degree of transparency, the relationship between booms and fiscal drift episodes becomes even positive.[14] The effect of transparency is sizable due to large observed differences in this variable across countries: Mexico, which features the lowest average level of transparency, gets a low score of 3.4, whereas Denmark gets a top score equal to 9.3. This means that booms have a significant and negative impact on the probability of

13. The institutional variables are centered on their means, so that the coefficients of the output gap hold for an "average" country in terms of institutional features.

14. For this country, the value of the transparency index is negative and the sign of the estimated coefficient of the crossed effect is also negative, while the sign of the estimated coefficient of the positive output gap variable is positive.

Table 9.9   Correlation between short fiscal drifts and shocks interacted with institutions (using the Transparency International index for transparency)

	(1)	(2)	(3)	(4)
Lagged fiscal drift	0.092	0.107	0.092	0.022
	(0.072)	(0.071)	(0.069)	(0.163)
Neg. output gap	0.029	0.024	0.028	0.080
	(0.019)	(0.019)	(0.018)	(0.065)
Pos. output gap	0.032**	0.033**	0.031**	0.106*
	(0.015)	(0.015)	(0.014)	(0.064)
Neg. output gap * transparency	−0.007	−0.009	−0.007	−0.032
	(0.011)	(0.012)	(0.011)	(0.024)
Pos. output gap * transparency	−0.022**	−0.027***	−0.022**	−0.029
	(0.010)	(0.010)	(0.009)	(0.023)
Neg. output gap * presidential	0.004	0.008	0.005	0.133
	(0.076)	(0.076)	(0.072)	(0.276)
Pos. output gap * presidential	0.035	0.026	0.036	0.333
	(0.077)	(0.087)	(0.074)	(0.300)
Neg. output gap * majoritarian	0.161**	0.144**	0.162**	0.321**
	(0.069)	(0.069)	(0.067)	(0.147)
Pos. output gap * majoritarian	0.068	0.061	0.069	0.197
	(0.059)	(0.060)	(0.057)	(0.139)
Neg. output gap * union coverage	0.003***	0.003***	0.003***	0.004**
	(0.001)	(0.001)	(0.001)	(0.002)
Pos. output gap * union coverage	0.002*	0.002*	0.002**	0.001
	(0.001)	(0.001)	(0.001)	(0.002)
Election	0.136***	0.127***	0.135***	0.145***
	(0.040)	(0.038)	(0.038)	(0.054)
Election * presidential	−0.277**	−0.256**	−0.277***	−0.398**
	(0.105)	(0.105)	(0.101)	(0.171)
Election * transparency	−0.058***	−0.059***	−0.058***	−0.075**
	(0.019)	(0.019)	(0.019)	(0.030)
Election * majoritarian	−0.067	−0.058	−0.066	−0.130
	(0.088)	(0.082)	(0.084)	(0.128)
Election * union coverage	0.001	0.001	0.001	−0.000
	(0.002)	(0.002)	(0.002)	(0.003)
Pop. below 15	−0.058	−0.064	−0.059*	−0.034
	(0.037)	(0.042)	(0.036)	(0.050)
Pop. over 65	−0.065	−0.079**	−0.066*	−0.016
	(0.040)	(0.035)	(0.038)	(0.050)
d 2009	0.542***	0.543***	0.543***	0.519***
	(0.098)	(0.099)	(0.094)	(0.150)
Constant	2.077*	2.366**	2.087*	0.850
	(1.176)	(1.187)	(1.126)	(1.409)
R^2	0.241			
Adj. R^2	0.201			
Obs.	382	353	353	325

Note: See notes for table 9.4.
***Significant at the 1 percent level.
**Significant at the 5 percent level.
*Significant at the 10 percent level.

Table 9.10   **Correlation between long fiscal drifts and shocks interacted with institutions (using the Transparency International index for transparency)**

	(1)	(2)	(3)	(4)
Lagged long fiscal drift	0.598***	0.568***	0.598***	0.316**
	(0.038)	(0.038)	(0.037)	(0.124)
Neg. output gap	−0.001	−0.005	−0.002	0.006
	(0.010)	(0.012)	(0.009)	(0.051)
Pos. output gap	0.038***	0.033**	0.038***	0.084*
	(0.013)	(0.014)	(0.012)	(0.050)
Neg. output gap * transparency	−0.007	0.005	−0.007	−0.032*
	(0.006)	(0.007)	(0.006)	(0.019)
Pos. output gap * transparency	−0.021**	−0.011	−0.021***	−0.038**
	(0.008)	(0.009)	(0.007)	(0.018)
Neg. output gap * presidential	0.012	0.081*	0.012	0.144
	(0.038)	(0.043)	(0.037)	(0.220)
Pos. output gap * presidential	0.061	0.155**	0.061	0.298
	(0.072)	(0.072)	(0.069)	(0.241)
Neg. output gap * majoritarian	0.037	0.039	0.037	0.238**
	(0.028)	(0.029)	(0.027)	(0.116)
Pos. output gap * majoritarian	0.017	0.029	0.017	0.143
	(0.036)	(0.039)	(0.034)	(0.109)
Neg. output gap * union coverage	0.000	0.001	0.000	0.002
	(0.000)	(0.000)	(0.000)	(0.002)
Pos. output gap * union coverage	0.001*	0.001*	0.001*	0.001
	(0.000)	(0.001)	(0.000)	(0.002)
Election	0.008	0.010	0.008	0.013
	(0.021)	(0.023)	(0.020)	(0.042)
Election * presidential	−0.209***	−0.202***	−0.208***	−0.252*
	(0.053)	(0.054)	(0.051)	(0.135)
Election * transparency	−0.025***	−0.023***	−0.025***	−0.029
	(0.009)	(0.008)	(0.008)	(0.024)
Election * majoritarian	0.092**	0.080*	0.093***	0.053
	(0.035)	(0.042)	(0.033)	(0.100)
Election * union coverage	0.002***	0.002**	0.002***	0.002
	(0.001)	(0.001)	(0.001)	(0.002)
Pop. below 15	−0.039*	−0.069***	−0.039**	−0.034
	(0.020)	(0.018)	(0.019)	(0.038)
Pop. over 65	−0.023	−0.045***	−0.023	0.004
	(0.018)	(0.016)	(0.017)	(0.039)
d 2009	0.118***	0.026	0.118***	0.268**
	(0.041)	(0.050)	(0.040)	(0.120)
Constant	1.071*	1.945***	1.074**	0.550
	(0.563)	(0.484)	(0.543)	(1.075)
R^2	0.400			
Adj. R^2	0.369			
Obs.	382	353	353	325

Note: See notes for table 9.4.
***Significant at the 1 percent level.
**Significant at the 5 percent level.
*Significant at the 10 percent level.

experiencing a fiscal drift in very transparent countries, while they have a significant positive impact of experiencing a fiscal drift in nontransparent countries. Interestingly, the impact of output gaps—negative or positive—is not influenced by the political regime or by election rules. However, fiscal drift episodes are more likely to occur during periods of negative output gap in countries where union coverage is higher. The resistance of strong trade unions to wage and employment compressions during recessions may explain this relationship.

Election years are positively correlated with the occurrence of short fiscal drifts: the coefficient is large and significant at the 1 percent level. Interestingly, this relationship does not seem to prevail for presidential regimes: the crossed-effects between elections and the corresponding dummy is large, negative, and significant. This supports the intuition that the checks and balances typical of presidential regimes prevent fiscal drift in election years. There is no significant relationship with the type of election rule (majoritarian countries). Also, in more transparent countries, election years are less often associated with long and short fiscal drifts (but the size of the crossed effect is much smaller than that of the political regime).

Column (2) in tables 9.9 and 9.10 presents the results when equation (1) is estimated with the Arellano and Bond method to account for autocorrelation of residuals due to the presence of the lagged dependent variable. The results turn out to be close to those obtained with the fixed effect method for short episodes: the interaction term between the positive output gap and transparency is now significant at the 5 percent level (for short episodes this time), while the positive output gap alone still has a significant effect. The positive relation with elections and the negative crossed effect relation with presidential regimes and transparency are still significant, for short and long episodes. In column (3), we use the same method, but we take into account that the output gap might be endogenous (and so is instrumented by its lagged values and lagged differences accordingly). Results turn out to be similar. Column (4) shows the results using the same instruments as in the Arellano-Bond method for the lagged fiscal drift but where we instrument the output gap of each country using the average output gap of all other countries. The direct effect of output gaps does not come up. However, short fiscal drift episodes are still correlated with election years and their interaction with transparency and the type of political regime. Long fiscal drifts are still negatively correlated with the crossed effect of positive output gaps and transparency, as well as with the interaction of elections and presidential regimes. All in all, tables 9.7 and 9.8 show that fiscal drift episodes are more likely to emerge during booms in countries where there is a parliamentary regime and where the transparency of the government is low.

Tables 9.11 and 9.12 are devoted to short fiscal tightening and long fiscal

Table 9.11 **Correlation between short fiscal tightenings and shocks interacted with institutions (using the Transparency International index for transparency)**

	(1)	(2)	(3)	(4)
Lagged fiscal tight.	0.193***	0.189***	0.192***	−0.291
	(0.051)	(0.051)	(0.049)	(0.215)
Neg. output gap	−0.005	−0.003	−0.005	−0.125
	(0.017)	(0.020)	(0.016)	(0.079)
Pos. output gap	−0.051***	−0.052***	−0.052***	−0.155**
	(0.018)	(0.017)	(0.017)	(0.076)
Neg. output gap * transparency	0.000	0.000	0.000	−0.003
	(0.011)	(0.012)	(0.011)	(0.030)
Pos. output gap * transparency	−0.011	−0.010	−0.011	−0.039
	(0.011)	(0.010)	(0.010)	(0.030)
Neg. output gap * presidential	−0.038	−0.043	−0.037	−0.170
	(0.057)	(0.057)	(0.054)	(0.335)
Pos. output gap * presidential	−0.069	−0.089	−0.068	−0.345
	(0.072)	(0.072)	(0.069)	(0.361)
Neg. output gap * majoritarian	−0.083***	−0.060*	−0.082***	−0.311*
	(0.029)	(0.034)	(0.028)	(0.168)
Pos. output gap * majoritarian	−0.062	−0.031	−0.061	−0.333**
	(0.050)	(0.053)	(0.047)	(0.169)
Neg. output gap * union coverage	−0.002***	−0.002**	−0.002***	−0.004
	(0.001)	(0.001)	(0.001)	(0.003)
Pos. output gap * union coverage	−0.001	−0.001	−0.001	−0.002
	(0.001)	(0.001)	(0.001)	(0.003)
Election	−0.056	−0.063*	−0.056	−0.043
	(0.038)	(0.036)	(0.037)	(0.065)
Election * presidential	0.144	0.147	0.145	0.173
	(0.102)	(0.091)	(0.098)	(0.205)
Election * transparency	0.034	0.027	0.033	0.003
	(0.022)	(0.022)	(0.021)	(0.036)
Election * majoritarian	−0.099	−0.084	−0.098	−0.030
	(0.108)	(0.099)	(0.103)	(0.154)
Election * union coverage	−0.004*	−0.004*	−0.004*	−0.002
	(0.002)	(0.002)	(0.002)	(0.003)
Pop. below 15	0.023	0.034	0.022	0.010
	(0.032)	(0.038)	(0.030)	(0.057)
Pop. over 65	0.029	0.013	0.029	0.008
	(0.021)	(0.027)	(0.020)	(0.061)
d 2009	−0.274***	−0.284***	−0.273***	−0.216
	(0.074)	(0.074)	(0.071)	(0.182)
Constant	−0.529	−0.497	−0.520	0.342
	(0.812)	(1.012)	(0.780)	(1.637)
R^2	0.144			
Adj. R^2	0.099			
Obs.	382	353	353	325

Note: See notes for table 9.4.
***Significant at the 1 percent level.
**Significant at the 5 percent level.
*Significant at the 10 percent level.

Table 9.12   **Correlation between long fiscal tightening episodes and shocks interacted with institutions (using the Transparency International index for transparency)**

	(1)	(2)	(3)	(4)
Lagged long fiscal tight.	0.460***	0.475***	0.460***	−0.035
	(0.040)	(0.043)	(0.038)	(0.154)
Neg. output gap	−0.000	−0.006	−0.000	−0.056
	(0.014)	(0.019)	(0.014)	(0.065)
Pos. output gap	−0.043***	−0.062***	−0.043***	−0.085
	(0.012)	(0.019)	(0.012)	(0.062)
Neg. output gap * transparency	0.012	0.017*	0.012	0.005
	(0.009)	(0.009)	(0.009)	(0.023)
Pos. output gap * transparency	0.002	0.008	0.002	−0.012
	(0.007)	(0.008)	(0.007)	(0.022)
Neg. output gap * presidential	−0.036	−0.064	−0.036	−0.150
	(0.057)	(0.064)	(0.054)	(0.262)
Pos. output gap * presidential	−0.072	−0.135	−0.072	−0.230
	(0.066)	(0.085)	(0.063)	(0.286)
Neg. output gap * majoritarian	0.001	0.015	0.001	−0.172
	(0.037)	(0.046)	(0.036)	(0.137)
Pos. output gap * majoritarian	−0.057***	−0.018	−0.057***	−0.295**
	(0.018)	(0.029)	(0.017)	(0.146)
Neg. output gap * union coverage	−0.001	−0.001	−0.001	−0.004*
	(0.001)	(0.001)	(0.001)	(0.002)
Pos. output gap * union coverage	−0.001**	−0.001*	−0.001***	−0.004*
	(0.001)	(0.001)	(0.001)	(0.002)
Election	−0.006	−0.011	−0.006	0.037
	(0.026)	(0.023)	(0.025)	(0.051)
Election * presidential	0.134*	0.166***	0.134**	0.034
	(0.066)	(0.054)	(0.063)	(0.163)
Election * transparency	0.019	0.024*	0.019	−0.015
	(0.015)	(0.014)	(0.014)	(0.029)
Election * majoritarian	−0.058	−0.037	−0.058	0.015
	(0.070)	(0.059)	(0.067)	(0.121)
Election * union coverage	−0.003*	−0.002*	−0.003**	−0.002
	(0.001)	(0.001)	(0.001)	(0.002)
Pop. below 15	0.032	0.038	0.032	0.040
	(0.022)	(0.032)	(0.022)	(0.046)
Pop. over 65	0.016	0.019	0.016	0.025
	(0.017)	(0.016)	(0.016)	(0.049)
d 2009	−0.152**	−0.195***	−0.152***	−0.145
	(0.057)	(0.075)	(0.055)	(0.142)
Constant	−0.640	−0.769	−0.639	−0.719
	(0.609)	(0.768)	(0.590)	(1.311)
R^2	0.307			
Adj. R^2	0.271			
Obs.	382	353	353	325

Note: See notes for table 9.4.
***Significant at the 1 percent level.
**Significant at the 5 percent level.
*Significant at the 10 percent level.

tightening episodes, respectively. We use the same empirical strategy as for the study of fiscal drift episodes. Overall, fiscal tightening episodes appear less frequently during booms. But the interaction terms between the output gap and the institutional variables such as the transparency of the government, the political regime, and the electoral rule are not correlated with the emergence of fiscal tightening episodes. Election years appear to decrease the occurrence of fiscal tightening episodes. However, this effect is reversed in countries with presidential regimes, where election years are more often associated with fiscal tightening episodes. This result is consistent with those of Brender and Drazen (2008) who find that leaders who reduce the deficit during an election year, relative to the previous year, have a higher probability of being reelected.

Freedom of the Press. The analysis of cross-country correlations shows that there is a negative relationship between the freedom of the press and the frequency of fiscal drift episodes, as shown by figure 9.6. As for transparency, countries with strong freedom of the press experienced less fiscal drift episodes than countries where the freedom of the press was weak over the period 1995 to 2009.

In tables 9.13 to 9.16, we estimate equation (1) where transparency is proxied by the freedom of press (from Freedom House[15]) instead of perceptions of the exercise of public power for private gain (i.e., the typical definition used to build corruption indexes). Here, like for the two previous measures, a higher index means higher transparency so the results can be interpreted in the same way. Tables 9.13 and 9.14 show that the probability that a fiscal drift episode occurs is lower in countries with stronger freedom of the press. In particular, fiscal drift episodes are less frequent during booms and election years in countries where there is more freedom of the press. Tables 9.15 and 9.16 show that fiscal tightening episodes are not correlated with the interaction terms between the freedom of press and the output gap or the election years, as is the case with the other measures of transparency.

Robustness

Transparency. Our results about the relation between the occurrence of fiscal episodes and transparency of governments may rely on a specific measure of transparency. In order to deal with this issue, we use an alternative measure of transparency. Table 9.17 for long fiscal drift episodes[16] (and 9.18 for long fiscal tightening episodes) is similar to table 9.10 (respectively, 9.12) except that it uses the World Bank measure of corruption instead of that of

15. Freedom House is a nongovernmental organization that supports the expansion of freedom around the world, notably the freedom of press (http://www.freedomhouse.org).
16. In this section we show results for long episodes only for the sake of simplicity. However, results are comparable using short episodes instead.

Table 9.13   Correlation between short fiscal drifts and shocks interacted with institutions (using the Freedom of Press index as a proxy for transparency)

	(1)	(2)	(3)	(4)
Lagged fiscal drift	0.092	0.103	0.092	0.051
	(0.071)	(0.070)	(0.068)	(0.171)
Neg. output gap	0.027	0.021	0.026	0.071
	(0.019)	(0.020)	(0.018)	(0.061)
Pos. output gap	0.033**	0.033**	0.032**	0.096
	(0.015)	(0.016)	(0.015)	(0.061)
Neg. output gap * press	−0.008*	−0.006	−0.008*	−0.020*
	(0.005)	(0.006)	(0.004)	(0.012)
Pos. output gap * press	−0.006**	−0.005*	−0.006**	−0.011*
	(0.003)	(0.003)	(0.003)	(0.006)
Neg. output gap * presidential	0.007	0.026	0.008	0.051
	(0.074)	(0.072)	(0.071)	(0.264)
Pos. output gap * presidential	0.035	0.032	0.035	0.237
	(0.076)	(0.083)	(0.073)	(0.281)
Neg. output gap * majoritarian	0.150**	0.141**	0.151**	0.275*
	(0.064)	(0.064)	(0.062)	(0.144)
Pos. output gap * majoritarian	0.042	0.037	0.043	0.156
	(0.057)	(0.058)	(0.055)	(0.132)
Neg. output gap * union coverage	0.003***	0.003***	0.003***	0.004**
	(0.001)	(0.001)	(0.001)	(0.002)
Pos. output gap * union coverage	0.002*	0.002	0.002**	0.001
	(0.001)	(0.001)	(0.001)	(0.002)
Election	0.136***	0.125***	0.136***	0.149***
	(0.041)	(0.040)	(0.040)	(0.053)
Election * presidential	−0.225**	−0.195**	−0.224**	−0.312*
	(0.096)	(0.094)	(0.092)	(0.160)
Election * press	−0.011*	−0.011**	−0.011**	−0.019**
	(0.006)	(0.005)	(0.006)	(0.008)
Election * majoritarian	−0.138	−0.122	−0.137	−0.241**
	(0.092)	(0.087)	(0.088)	(0.121)
Election * union coverage	0.000	0.001	0.000	−0.001
	(0.002)	(0.002)	(0.002)	(0.002)
Pop. below 15	−0.053	−0.057	−0.053	−0.033
	(0.037)	(0.043)	(0.035)	(0.049)
Pop. over 65	−0.064	−0.074**	−0.064*	−0.023
	(0.040)	(0.037)	(0.038)	(0.049)
d 2009	0.546***	0.555***	0.547***	0.507***
	(0.101)	(0.100)	(0.097)	(0.146)
Constant	1.959	2.189*	1.969*	0.948
	(1.169)	(1.230)	(1.121)	(1.378)
R^2	0.237			
Adj. R^2	0.197			
Obs.	382	353	353	325

Note: See notes for table 9.4.

***Significant at the 1 percent level.

**Significant at the 5 percent level.

*Significant at the 10 percent level.

Table 9.14 **Correlation between long fiscal drifts and shocks interacted with institutions (using Freedom of Press index as a proxy for transparency)**

	(1)	(2)	(3)	(4)
Lagged long fiscal drift	0.596***	0.572***	0.596***	0.346***
	(0.037)	(0.037)	(0.036)	(0.121)
Neg. output gap	−0.002	−0.007	−0.002	−0.021
	(0.010)	(0.012)	(0.010)	(0.048)
Pos. output gap	0.039***	0.032**	0.039***	0.060
	(0.013)	(0.015)	(0.013)	(0.046)
Neg. output gap * press	−0.007**	0.001	−0.007***	−0.026***
	(0.003)	(0.003)	(0.003)	(0.009)
Pos. output gap * press	−0.005**	−0.001	−0.005***	−0.014***
	(0.002)	(0.002)	(0.002)	(0.005)
Neg. output gap * presidential	0.011	0.082**	0.011	0.076
	(0.038)	(0.042)	(0.036)	(0.209)
Pos. output gap * presidential	0.061	0.158**	0.061	0.219
	(0.076)	(0.073)	(0.073)	(0.222)
Neg. output gap * majoritarian	0.026	0.051	0.027	0.182
	(0.029)	(0.032)	(0.028)	(0.112)
Pos. output gap * majoritarian	−0.007	0.027	−0.007	0.083
	(0.041)	(0.043)	(0.039)	(0.103)
Neg. output gap * union coverage	0.000	0.001*	0.000	0.002
	(0.000)	(0.000)	(0.000)	(0.002)
Pos. output gap * union coverage	0.001	0.001	0.001	0.001
	(0.001)	(0.001)	(0.000)	(0.001)
Election	0.007	0.009	0.007	0.006
	(0.022)	(0.023)	(0.021)	(0.042)
Election * presidential	−0.181***	−0.184***	−0.181***	−0.198
	(0.059)	(0.058)	(0.056)	(0.127)
Election * press	−0.005**	−0.005***	−0.005***	−0.008
	(0.002)	(0.001)	(0.002)	(0.006)
Election * majoritarian	0.068	0.058	0.068	0.018
	(0.044)	(0.045)	(0.042)	(0.095)
Election * union coverage	0.002***	0.002**	0.002***	0.002
	(0.001)	(0.001)	(0.001)	(0.002)
Pop. below 15	−0.035*	−0.068***	−0.035*	−0.040
	(0.020)	(0.017)	(0.019)	(0.038)
Pop. over 65	−0.022	−0.045***	−0.022	−0.004
	(0.017)	(0.016)	(0.017)	(0.038)
d 2009	0.119***	0.027	0.119***	0.286**
	(0.040)	(0.053)	(0.039)	(0.119)
Constant	0.979*	1.916***	0.981*	0.821
	(0.551)	(0.458)	(0.531)	(1.052)
R^2	0.396			
Adj. R^2	0.365			
Obs.	382	353	353	325

Note: See notes for table 9.4.
***Significant at the 1 percent level.
**Significant at the 5 percent level.
*Significant at the 10 percent level.

Table 9.15 **Correlation between short fiscal tightenings and shocks interacted with institutions (using the Freedom of Press index as a proxy for transparency)**

	(1)	(2)	(3)	(4)
Lagged fiscal tight.	0.195***	0.188***	0.195**	−0.174
	(0.051)	(0.051)	(0.049)	(0.189)
Neg. output gap	−0.003	−0.002	−0.004	−0.095
	(0.018)	(0.021)	(0.017)	(0.070)
Pos. output gap	−0.050***	−0.051***	−0.051***	−0.130**
	(0.018)	(0.017)	(0.017)	(0.065)
Neg. output gap * press	−0.005	−0.007	−0.005	−0.012
	(0.005)	(0.004)	(0.005)	(0.014)
Pos. output gap * press	−0.003	−0.004	−0.003	0.009
	(0.003)	(0.002)	(0.003)	(0.007)
Neg. output gap * presidential	−0.054	−0.064	−0.053	−0.018
	(0.054)	(0.053)	(0.051)	(0.301)
Pos. output gap * presidential	−0.078	−0.099	−0.077	−0.168
	(0.072)	(0.068)	(0.068)	(0.318)
Neg. output gap * majoritarian	−0.088**	−0.068	−0.087**	−0.327**
	(0.037)	(0.043)	(0.035)	(0.158)
Pos. output gap * majoritarian	−0.082*	−0.053	−0.082**	−0.397**
	(0.043)	(0.048)	(0.041)	(0.157)
Neg. output gap * union coverage	−0.002**	−0.001	−0.002***	−0.003
	(0.001)	(0.001)	(0.001)	(0.002)
Pos. output gap * union coverage	−0.002*	−0.001	−0.002*	−0.003
	(0.001)	(0.001)	(0.001)	(0.002)
Election	−0.057	−0.064*	−0.058	−0.045
	(0.039)	(0.037)	(0.037)	(0.061)
Election * presidential	0.119	0.125	0.120	0.152
	(0.097)	(0.089)	(0.093)	(0.181)
Election * press	0.005	0.004	0.005	−0.004
	(0.004)	(0.003)	(0.003)	(0.009)
Election * majoritarian	−0.049	−0.047	−0.048	−0.003
	(0.095)	(0.089)	(0.091)	(0.139)
Election * union coverage	−0.003*	−0.003*	−0.003*	−0.002
	(0.002)	(0.002)	(0.002)	(0.003)
Pop. below 15	0.024	0.036	0.023	0.003
	(0.032)	(0.039)	(0.031)	(0.054)
Pop. over 65	0.028	0.011	0.028	0.013
	(0.021)	(0.028)	(0.020)	(0.057)
d 2009	−0.275***	−0.285***	−0.274***	−0.229
	(0.076)	(0.076)	(0.072)	(0.169)
Constant	−0.533	−0.490	−0.524	0.320
	(0.830)	(1.037)	(0.797)	(1.520)
R^2	0.142			
Adj. R^2	0.096			
Obs.	382	353	353	325

Note: See notes for table 9.4.
***Significant at the 1 percent level.
**Significant at the 5 percent level.
*Significant at the 10 percent level.

Table 9.16   **Correlation between long fiscal tightenings and shocks interacted with institutions (using the Freedom of Press index as a proxy for transparency)**

	(1)	(2)	(3)	(4)
Lagged long fiscal tight.	0.457***	0.473***	0.457***	0.192*
	(0.040)	(0.044)	(0.038)	(0.115)
Neg. output gap	−0.001	−0.007	−0.001	−0.005
	(0.015)	(0.020)	(0.014)	(0.054)
Pos. output gap	−0.042***	−0.062***	−0.043***	−0.047
	(0.012)	(0.019)	(0.012)	(0.050)
Neg. output gap * press	0.001	0.003	0.001	−0.004
	(0.004)	(0.004)	(0.004)	(0.010)
Pos. output gap * press	−0.001	0.000	−0.001	−0.005
	(0.002)	(0.002)	(0.002)	(0.006)
Neg. output gap * presidential	−0.045	−0.078	−0.045	−0.028
	(0.053)	(0.062)	(0.051)	(0.230)
Pos. output gap * presidential	−0.085	−0.157**	−0.085	−0.136
	(0.064)	(0.079)	(0.061)	(0.246)
Neg. output gap * majoritarian	0.015	0.036	0.015	−0.118
	(0.039)	(0.053)	(0.037)	(0.123)
Pos. output gap * majoritarian	−0.062***	−0.020	−0.062***	−0.746*
	(0.019)	(0.030)	(0.018)	(0.127)
Neg. output gap * union coverage	−0.001	−0.001	−0.001	−0.003*
	(0.001)	(0.001)	(0.001)	(0.002)
Pos. output gap * union coverage	−0.001**	−0.001	−0.001**	−0.003*
	(0.001)	(0.001)	(0.001)	(0.002)
Election	−0.006	−0.011	−0.006	0.034
	(0.026)	(0.023)	(0.025)	(0.046)
Election * presidential	0.126**	0.153***	0.126**	0.055
	(0.058)	(0.051)	(0.056)	(0.138)
Election * press	0.005*	0.005*	0.005*	−0.003
	(0.002)	(0.003)	(0.002)	(0.007)
Election * majoritarian	−0.028	−0.004	−0.028	−0.007
	(0.062)	(0.050)	(0.059)	(0.105)
Election * union coverage	−0.003*	−0.002*	−0.003**	−0.003
	(0.001)	(0.001)	(0.001)	(0.002)
Pop. below 15	0.032	0.034	0.032	0.025
	(0.022)	(0.032)	(0.021)	(0.041)
Pop. over 65	0.015	0.015	0.015	0.016
	(0.017)	(0.017)	(0.016)	(0.043)
d 2009	−0.141**	−0.179**	−0.141***	−0.184
	(0.057)	(0.073)	(0.055)	(0.126)
Constant	−0.625	−0.0642	−0.624	−0.443
	(0.605)	(0.767)	(0.584)	(1.166)
R^2	0.307			
Adj. R^2	0.270			
Obs.	382	353	353	325

Note: See notes for table 9.4.

***Significant at the 1 percent level.

**Significant at the 5 percent level.

*Significant at the 10 percent level.

Table 9.17   Correlation between long fiscal drifts and shocks interacted with institutions (using the World Bank corruption index for transparency)

	(1)	(2)	(3)	(4)
Lagged long fiscal drift	0.598***	0.566***	0.598***	0.320**
	(0.038)	(0.038)	(0.037)	(0.124)
Neg. output gap	−0.001	−0.005	−0.001	0.004
	(0.010)	(0.012)	(0.010)	(0.051)
Pos. output gap	0.038***	0.032**	0.038***	0.083*
	(0.013)	(0.014)	(0.012)	(0.049)
Neg. output gap * WBTransparency	−0.019	0.015	−0.019	−0.094*
	(0.016)	(0.018)	(0.015)	(0.048)
Pos. output gap * WBTransparency	−0.051**	−0.025	−0.051***	−0.107**
	(0.020)	(0.025)	(0.020)	(0.047)
Neg. output gap * presidential	0.012	0.081*	0.012	0.147
	(0.038)	(0.042)	(0.036)	(0.221)
Pos. output gap * presidential	0.063	0.156**	0.063	0.307
	(0.072)	(0.072)	(0.069)	(0.240)
Neg. output gap * majoritarian	0.037	0.039	0.037	0.236**
	(0.028)	(0.028)	(0.027)	(0.116)
Pos. output gap * majoritarian	0.014	0.028	0.014	0.141
	(0.037)	(0.039)	(0.035)	(0.109)
Neg. output gap * union coverage	0.000	0.001	0.001	0.002
	(0.000)	(0.000)	(0.000)	(0.002)
Pos. output gap * union coverage	0.001*	0.001	0.001*	0.001
	(0.000)	(0.001)	(0.000)	(0.002)
Election	0.009	0.011	0.009	0.016
	(0.021)	(0.023)	(0.020)	(0.042)
Election * presidential	−0.205***	−0.198***	−0.205***	−0.250*
	(0.052)	(0.052)	(0.049)	(0.134)
Election * WBTransparency	−0.067***	−0.062***	−0.067***	−0.076
	(0.022)	(0.020)	(0.021)	(0.061)
Election * majoritarian	0.093**	0.081*	0.093***	0.049
	(0.034)	(0.041)	(0.033)	(0.099)
Election * union coverage	0.002***	0.002**	0.002***	0.002
	(0.001)	(0.001)	(0.001)	(0.002)
Pop. below 15	−0.039*	−0.069***	−0.039**	−0.036
	(0.020)	(0.018)	(0.019)	(0.038)
Pop. over 65	−0.023	−0.045***	−0.023	0.005
	(0.017)	(0.016)	(0.017)	(0.040)
d 2009	0.117***	0.025	0.118***	0.270**
	(0.042)	(0.050)	(0.040)	(0.121)
Constant	1.058*	1.935***	1.061**	0.584
	(0.560)	(0.484)	(0.540)	(1.078)
R^2	0.400			
Adj. R^2	0.368			
Obs.	382	353	353	325

Note: See notes for table 9.4.
***Significant at the 1 percent level.
**Significant at the 5 percent level.
*Significant at the 10 percent level.

Table 9.18   **Correlation between long fiscal tightenings and shocks interacted with institutions (using the World Bank corruption index for transparency)**

	(1)	(2)	(3)	(4)
Lagged long fiscal tight.	0.460***	0.474***	0.460***	0.186
	(0.040)	(0.043)	(0.038)	(0.118)
Neg. output gap	−0.001	−0.007	−0.001	−0.011
	(0.015)	(0.019)	(0.014)	(0.056)
Pos. output gap	−0.043***	−0.062***	−0.043***	−0.055
	(0.012)	(0.019)	(0.012)	(0.054)
Neg. output gap * WBTransparency	0.028	0.043*	0.028	−0.001
	(0.022)	(0.023)	(0.021)	(0.054)
Pos. output gap * WBTransparency	−0.001	0.015	−0.001	−0.047
	(0.019)	(0.020)	(0.018)	(0.052)
Neg. output gap * presidential	−0.038	−0.067	−0.038	−0.061
	(0.057)	(0.065)	(0.054)	(0.236)
Pos. output gap * presidential	−0.075	−0.141*	−0.075	−0.160
	(0.065)	(0.084)	(0.062)	(0.258)
Neg. output gap * majoritarian	0.002	0.017	0.003	−0.132
	(0.037)	(0.047)	(0.036)	(0.122)
Pos. output gap * majoritarian	−0.057***	−0.018	−0.057***	−0.227*
	(0.018)	(0.028)	(0.017)	(0.128)
Neg. output gap * union coverage	−0.001	−0.001	−0.001	−0.003
	(0.001)	(0.001)	(0.001)	(0.002)
Pos. output gap * union coverage	−0.001**	−0.001*	−0.001***	−0.003
	(0.001)	(0.001)	(0.001)	(0.002)
Election	−0.006	−0.012	−0.006	0.036
	(0.026)	(0.023)	(0.025)	(0.046)
Election * presidential	0.129*	0.161***	0.129**	0.034
	(0.065)	(0.054)	(0.062)	(0.145)
Election * WBTransparency	0.043	0.053	0.043	−0.030
	(0.037)	(0.037)	(0.036)	(0.067)
Election * majoritarian	−0.056	−0.033	−0.056	−0.003
	(0.069)	(0.058)	(0.066)	(0.108)
Election * union coverage	−0.003*	−0.002*	−0.003**	−0.003
	(0.001)	(0.001)	(0.001)	(0.002)
Pop. below 15	0.031	0.037	0.031	0.024
	(0.022)	(0.033)	(0.021)	(0.041)
Pop. over 65	0.015	0.018	0.015	0.014
	(0.017)	(0.017)	(0.016)	(0.044)
d 2009	−0.151**	−0.193**	−0.151***	−0.190
	(0.057)	(0.075)	(0.055)	(0.127)
Constant	−0.620	−0.747	−0.619	−0.387
	(0.607)	(0.775)	(0.588)	(1.170)
R^2	0.307			
Adj. R^2	0.270			
Obs.	382	353	353	325

Note: See notes for table 9.4.

***Significant at the 1 percent level.

**Significant at the 5 percent level.

*Significant at the 10 percent level.

Transparency International.[17] Again, the crossed effect between the output gap and corruption is significantly positive for long fiscal drift episodes (but still not significant for fiscal tightening episodes) and even larger in size than with the previous measure with all methods of estimation. Positive output gap alone is still, on average, positively correlated with the occurrence of fiscal drift, and negatively correlated with the occurrence of fiscal tightening. The correlations with election years crossed with the type of political regime and with transparency remain unchanged.

Political Cycle. The variable "election year" accounts for the impact of elections on fiscal episodes in a very crude way. For instance, when an election is held in the first quarter of a given year it might be more relevant to focus on the year just before the election rather than on the year of the election. Moreover, an index for preelection years and another for post-election years could help better identify the presence of budget cycles. We tested these alternative definitions and none changed significantly the overall impact previously identified of elections on fiscal drifts and the absence of fiscal drift in presidential regimes the year of elections or the year just before (tables are available upon request).

Business Cycle. Our finding that fiscal drift episodes occur more frequently during booms than during recessions might be driven by our measure of booms and slumps, which are merely defined as periods of either positive or negative output gap. To show that this is not the case, we define booms and slumps in a more restrictive way. Tables 9.19 to 9.22 reproduce tables 9.5, 9.8, 9.10, and 9.12, but considering this time output gap variations of at least 1 percent in absolute value (which make up approximately one-third of all observed changes in output gaps). Table 9.19 (respectively, 9.20) shows that the results are very stable: long fiscal drift episodes (respectively, long fiscal tightening episodes) are still positively (respectively, negatively) and significantly correlated with positive output gaps (and not negative ones). Table 9.21 (respectively, 9.22) shows that the crossed-effect of transparency with positive output gaps on the occurrence of fiscal drift episodes (respectively tightening episodes) is still negative and significant (respectively not significant), even when the economy experiences large shocks. Results regarding

---

17. The World Bank measure of corruption, as well as the Freedom of Press index used later, are not available for 2009 (the last available year in our data set), but these indexes are very stable over time and we have considered that their average values over 1995 to 2008 apply to 2009 as well in order to have comparable results with the main tables that use the Transparency International index (tables 9.6 and 9.7). The exclusion of the year 2009 in the regressions in tables 9.6 and 9.7 slightly reinforces the correlation of short fiscal drifts with positive output gaps, but has only a marginal impact on the relationship with long fiscal drifts (which are mechanically less often observed at the end of the considered period). The exclusion of the same year from the regressions in tables 9.8 to 9.11 has a very small impact on the results overall.

Table 9.19   Correlation between long fiscal drifts and shocks (considering output gaps of ±1 percent and over)

	(1)	(2)	(3)	(4)
Lagged long fiscal drift	0.589***	0.552***	0.517***	0.291**
	(0.032)	(0.042)	(0.041)	(0.113)
Neg. output gap	−0.003	0.003	0.002	0.027
	(0.008)	(0.011)	(0.010)	(0.038)
Pos. output gap	0.038***	0.031**	0.037***	0.077***
	(0.012)	(0.014)	(0.013)	(0.028)
Election	0.003	0.011	0.005	0.019
	(0.034)	(0.036)	(0.033)	(0.031)
Pop. below 15	−0.032	−0.069***	−0.030	−0.017
	(0.019)	(0.021)	(0.025)	(0.025)
Pop. over 65	−0.023	−0.058***	−0.042*	−0.044*
	(0.021)	(0.016)	(0.025)	(0.026)
d 2009	0.120***	−0.002	0.094**	0.195*
	(0.040)	(0.052)	(0.044)	(0.104)
Constant	0.936	2.134***	1.180	0.950
	(0.622)	(0.576)	(0.775)	(0.747)
R^2	0.351			
Adj. R^2	0.339			
Obs.	387	375	375	362

Note: See notes for table 9.4.
***Significant at the 1 percent level.
**Significant at the 5 percent level.
*Significant at the 10 percent level.

election years and crossed-effects with the type of regime, transparency, or union coverage are broadly unchanged.

Panel Composition. Finally, we check that our results are not driven by outliers by removing countries one by one from the panel to check to what extent results could rely solely on one country. Tables 9.23 and 9.24 present the estimated coefficients as in tables 9.10 and 9.12, column (3)—that is, correlations of long episodes of fiscal drifts and fiscal tightening with shocks and institutions—using the transparency international index and the Arellano-Bond method with endogenous output gaps. Results turn out very stable.

9.5   Conclusion

This chapter shows that there is a strong relation between worsening public finances and increases in public wage bills. However, this relation does not mean that large public wage bills are systematically conducive to worsening public finances. Actually, countries with the highest GDP shares

Table 9.20   Correlation between long fiscal tightenings and shocks (considering output gaps of ±1 percent and over)

	(1)	(2)	(3)	(4)
Lagged long fiscal tight.	0.461***	0.491***	0.479***	0.189**
	(0.038)	(0.032)	(0.033)	(0.093)
Neg. output gap	−0.003	−0.004	−0.008	−0.048
	(0.013)	(0.017)	(0.014)	(0.046)
Pos. output gap	−0.039***	−0.046***	−0.042***	−0.065*
	(0.013)	(0.017)	(0.014)	(0.035)
Election	−0.009	−0.009	−0.006	−0.020
	(0.032)	(0.029)	(0.031)	(0.038)
Pop. below 15	0.021	0.043	0.030	0.018
	(0.020)	(0.033)	(0.022)	(0.032)
Pop. over 65	0.005	0.013	0.016	0.017
	(0.016)	(0.022)	(0.022)	(0.032)
$d\,2009$	−0.154**	−0.155**	−0.146**	−0.131
	(0.059)	(0.077)	(0.066)	(0.129)
Constant	−0.294	−0.829	−0.615	−0.311
	(0.551)	(0.843)	(0.646)	(0.911)
R^2	0.273			
Adj. R^2	0.260			
Obs.	387	375	375	362

Note: See notes for table 9.4.
***Significant at the 1 percent level.
**Significant at the 5 percent level.
*Significant at the 10 percent level.

of public wage bill also have the highest public net lending. This means that large public sectors have been compatible with sustainable public budgets in the OECD countries over the last fifteen years. Our chapter clearly shows that countries unable to adjust their public wage bills to make them compatible with sustainable public budgets are not those that are especially hit by negative economic shocks. Their main handicap is a lack of transparency and a lack of checks and balances on the political power of elected politicians. And in these countries, in the absence of institutional reform, the fiscal stance might deteriorate even further in upcoming economic booms because of public employment.

Table 9.21

Table 9.21   Correlation between long fiscal drifts and shocks (considering output gaps of ±1 percent and over) interacted with institutions (using the Transparency International index for transparency)

	(1)	(2)	(3)	(4)
Lagged long fiscal drift	0.597***	0.564***	0.597***	0.270*
	(0.038)	(0.037)	(0.037)	(0.161)
Neg. output gap	−0.001	−0.004	−0.001	0.046
	(0.009)	(0.012)	(0.009)	(0.067)
Pos. output gap	0.038***	0.034**	0.038***	0.116*
	(0.013)	(0.014)	(0.012)	(0.065)
Neg. output gap * transparency	−0.002	0.009	−0.002	−0.035
	(0.006)	(0.006)	(0.005)	(0.023)
Pos. output gap * transparency	−0.018**	−0.010	−0.018**	−0.044**
	(0.008)	(0.009)	(0.007)	(0.022)
Neg. output gap * presidential	0.023	0.089**	0.023	0.428
	(0.037)	(0.039)	(0.036)	(0.308)
Pos. output gap * presidential	0.065	0.148**	0.065	0.548*
	(0.072)	(0.073)	(0.069)	(0.313)
Neg. output gap * majoritarian	0.029	0.029	0.029	0.195
	(0.024)	(0.023)	(0.023)	(0.131)
Pos. output gap * majoritarian	0.019	0.029	0.019	0.159
	(0.033)	(0.036)	(0.032)	(0.131)
Neg. output gap * union coverage	0.000	0.000	0.000	0.002
	(0.000)	(0.000)	(0.000)	(0.002)
Pos. output gap * union coverage	0.001*	0.001	0.001*	0.001
	(0.000)	(0.001)	(0.000)	(0.002)
Election	0.007	0.008	0.007	0.011
	(0.020)	(0.022)	(0.019)	(0.053)
Election * presidential	−0.206***	−0.194***	−0.206***	−0.287*
	(0.053)	(0.055)	(0.051)	(0.174)
Election * transparency	−0.024***	−0.021**	−0.024***	−0.024
	(0.009)	(0.009)	(0.008)	(0.030)
Election * majoritarian	0.088**	0.075*	0.088***	0.042
	(0.035)	(0.042)	(0.034)	(0.129)
Election * union coverage	0.002**	0.002**	0.002***	0.001
	(0.001)	(0.001)	(0.001)	(0.003)
Pop. below 15	−0.040*	−0.068***	−0.040**	−0.055
	(0.020)	(0.018)	(0.019)	(0.049)
Pop. over 65	−0.021	−0.044***	−0.021	−0.027
	(0.018)	(0.016)	(0.017)	(0.051)
d 2009	0.112**	0.023	0.112***	0.191
	(0.042)	(0.049)	(0.041)	(0.157)
Constant	1.059*	1.909***	1.061*	0.566
	(0.565)	(0.477)	(0.543)	(1.328)
R^2	0.401			
Adj. R^2	0.369			
Obs.	382	353	353	325

Note: See notes for table 9.4.

***Significant at the 1 percent level.

**Significant at the 5 percent level.

*Significant at the 10 percent level.

| | Table 9.22 | Correlation between long fiscal tightenings and shocks (considering output gaps of ±1 percent and over) interacted with institutions (using the Transparency International index for transparency) |

Table 9.22 Correlation between long fiscal tightenings and shocks (considering output gaps of ±1 percent and over) interacted with institutions (using the Transparency International index for transparency)

	(1)	(2)	(3)	(4)
Lagged long fiscal tight.	0.461***	0.477***	0.461***	−0.031
	(0.040)	(0.043)	(0.039)	(0.170)
Neg. output gap	0.003	−0.001	0.003	−0.077
	(0.013)	(0.018)	(0.013)	(0.072)
Pos. output gap	−0.036***	−0.054***	−0.036***	−0.105
	(0.011)	(0.017)	(0.011)	(0.068)
Neg. output gap * transparency	0.008	0.012	0.008	0.007
	(0.008)	(0.008)	(0.008)	(0.024)
Pos. output gap * transparency	0.001	0.006	0.001	−0.004
	(0.006)	(0.006)	(0.006)	(0.022)
Neg. output gap * presidential	−0.058	−0.085	−0.058	−0.275
	(0.051)	(0.059)	(0.049)	(0.304)
Pos. output gap * presidential	−0.075	−0.131*	−0.075	−0.351
	(0.060)	(0.075)	(0.057)	(0.310)
Neg. output gap * majoritarian	0.005	0.019	0.005	−0.125
	(0.030)	(0.043)	(0.029)	(0.129)
Pos. output gap * majoritarian	−0.052**	−0.017	−0.052***	−0.278*
	(0.019)	(0.026)	(0.018)	(0.149)
Neg. output gap * union coverage	−0.001	−0.001	−0.001	−0.003*
	(0.001)	(0.001)	(0.001)	(0.002)
Pos. output gap * union coverage	−0.001***	−0.001*	−0.001***	−0.004*
	(0.000)	(0.001)	(0.000)	(0.002)
Election	−0.004	−0.009	−0.004	0.037
	(0.026)	(0.023)	(0.025)	(0.054)
Election * presidential	0.134*	0.169***	0.134**	0.070
	(0.069)	(0.058)	(0.066)	(0.178)
Election * transparency	0.018	0.022	0.018	−0.013
	(0.015)	(0.014)	(0.014)	(0.031)
Election * majoritarian	−0.060	−0.038	−0.060	0.028
	(0.070)	(0.060)	(0.067)	(0.133)
Election * union coverage	−0.003*	−0.002*	−0.003**	−0.002
	(0.001)	(0.001)	(0.001)	(0.003)
Pop. below 15	0.034	0.038	0.034	0.046
	(0.023)	(0.034)	(0.022)	(0.049)
Pop. over 65	0.014	0.015	0.014	0.016
	(0.018)	(0.018)	(0.017)	(0.054)
d 2009	−0.150**	−0.191**	−0.150***	−0.094
	(0.057)	(0.075)	(0.054)	(0.161)
Constant	−0.670	−0.747	−0.669	−0.686
	(0.629)	(0.811)	(0.609)	(1.378)
R^2	0.303			
Adj. R^2	0.267			
Obs.	382	353	353	325

Note: See notes for table 9.4.

***Significant at the 1 percent level.

**Significant at the 5 percent level.

*Significant at the 10 percent level.

Table 9.23 Correlation between long fiscal drifts and shocks interacted with institutions (using the Transparency International index for transparency)

Country removed from panel	Neg. output gap	Pos. output gap	Pos. output gap * transparency	Pos. output gap * union coverage	Election * presidential	Election * transparency	Election * union coverage
AUS	-0.002	0.038***	-0.021***	0.001*	-0.208***	-0.025***	0.002***
AUT	-0.001	0.039***	-0.021***	0.001**	-0.201***	-0.025***	0.002***
BEL	-0.001	0.037***	-0.019***	0.001	-0.209***	-0.027***	0.002***
CAN	-0.001	0.038***	-0.022***	0.001**	-0.180***	-0.028***	0.002***
CHE	0.001	0.039***	-0.020***	0.001*	-0.203***	-0.027***	0.002***
CHL	-0.002	0.038***	-0.021***	0.001*	-0.208***	-0.025***	0.002***
CZE	-0.000	0.038***	-0.024***	0.001*	-0.198***	-0.023***	0.002***
DEU	-0.001	0.039***	-0.020***	0.001*	-0.209***	-0.025***	0.002***
DNK	-0.001	0.040***	-0.021***	0.001*	-0.209***	-0.025***	0.002***
ESP	-0.000	0.038***	-0.020***	0.001*	-0.210***	-0.023***	0.002***
EST	-0.002	0.038***	-0.021***	0.001*	-0.208***	-0.025***	0.002***
FIN	-0.001	0.041***	-0.020***	0.001*	-0.206***	-0.024***	0.002***
FRA	-0.001	0.037***	-0.021***	0.001*	-0.208***	-0.024***	0.002*
GBR	-0.005	0.034***	-0.022***	0.001**	-0.234***	-0.024***	0.002***
GRC	-0.002	0.036***	-0.019**	0.001**	-0.191***	-0.020***	0.002***
HUN	-0.002	0.036***	-0.021***	0.001*	-0.207***	-0.025***	0.002***
IRL	-0.000	0.041***	-0.020***	0.001	-0.219***	-0.025***	0.002***
ISL	-0.006	0.037***	-0.022***	0.001*	-0.207***	-0.025***	0.002***

ISR	-0.002	0.038***	-0.021***	0.001*	-0.208***	-0.025***
ITA	-0.001	0.038***	-0.023***	0.001**	-0.214***	-0.028***
JPN	0.000	0.043***	-0.019**	0.001	-0.185***	-0.024***
KOR	0.007	0.048***	-0.022***	0.001*	-0.217***	-0.026***
LUX	-0.003	0.040***	-0.020***	0.001*	-0.208***	-0.025***
MEX	-0.003	0.035***	-0.020***	0.001*	-0.205***	-0.025***
NLD	0.000	0.038***	-0.021***	0.001*	-0.215***	-0.028***
NOR	-0.004	0.042***	-0.020***	0.001*	-0.207***	-0.025***
NZL	-0.002	0.039***	-0.021***	0.001*	-0.208***	-0.025***
POL	0.000	0.037***	-0.020***	0.001*	-0.232***	-0.023***
PRT	-0.002	0.036***	-0.020***	0.001*	-0.227***	-0.028***
SVK	-0.005	0.032***	-0.014*	0.001**	-0.229***	-0.030***
SVN	-0.002	0.038***	-0.021***	0.001*	-0.208***	-0.025***
SWE	-0.001	0.041***	-0.020***	0.001**	-0.207***	-0.025***
TUR	-0.002	0.037***	-0.021***	0.001*	-0.208***	-0.025***
USA	-0.003	0.033***	-0.024***	0.001**	-0.188***	-0.024**

Notes: Excluding countries are removed one by one. Robust standard errors in parentheses. Period 1995–2009. Arellano-Bond method where the output gap is instrumented by its lagged values.

***Significant at the 1 percent level.

**Significant at the 5 percent level.

*Significant at the 10 percent level.

Table 9.24 Correlation between long fiscal tightening and shocks interacted with institutions (using the Transparency International index for transparency)

Country removed from panel	Neg. output gap	Pos. output gap	Pos. output gap * transparency	Pos. output gap * union coverage	Election * presidential	Election * transparency	Election * union coverage
AUS	-0.000	-0.043***	0.002	-0.001***	0.134**	0.019	-0.003**
AUT	-0.004	-0.045***	0.003	-0.002***	0.148**	0.020	-0.002*
BEL	0.002	-0.043***	0.000	-0.001***	0.137**	0.016	-0.002*
CAN	0.001	-0.042***	0.002	-0.001***	0.143**	0.017	-0.002*
CHE	-0.007	-0.042***	0.003	-0.002***	0.115*	0.024*	-0.003**
CHL	-0.000	-0.043***	0.002	-0.001***	0.134**	0.019	-0.003**
CZE	0.004	-0.040***	0.000	-0.002***	0.172***	0.027**	-0.002*
DEU	-0.001	-0.042***	0.002	-0.001***	0.132**	0.019	-0.003**
DNK	-0.001	-0.044***	0.001	-0.001***	0.133**	0.019	-0.003**
ESP	0.003	-0.042***	-0.001	-0.001**	0.128**	0.018	-0.003**
EST	-0.000	-0.043***	0.002	-0.001***	0.134**	0.019	-0.003**
FIN	0.002	-0.045***	0.001	-0.002***	0.139**	0.020	-0.002*
FRA	-0.003	-0.040***	0.001	-0.001**	0.140**	0.029**	-0.004***
GBR	-0.002	-0.042***	0.001	-0.001***	0.135**	0.018	-0.003**
GRC	-0.001	-0.044***	0.002	-0.001***	0.141**	0.021	-0.003**
HUN	0.006	-0.043***	0.002	-0.001***	0.105*	0.015	-0.003**
IRL	-0.002	-0.045***	0.002	-0.001***	0.144**	0.018	-0.002*
ISL	-0.002	-0.045***	0.001	-0.002***	0.125**	0.016	-0.003**

ISR	-0.000	-0.043***	0.002	-0.001***	0.134**	0.019	-0.003**
ITA	0.001	-0.042***	0.002	-0.002**	0.118*	0.010	-0.002***
JPN	-0.008	-0.043***	0.001	-0.001**	0.149**	0.020	-0.002*
KOR	-0.001	-0.046***	0.002	-0.001***	0.138***	0.020	-0.003**
LUX	0.000	-0.046***	0.001	-0.001***	0.134*	0.019	-0.003**
MEX	0.001	-0.044***	0.003	-0.001***	0.153***	0.013	-0.003**
NLD	-0.003	-0.038***	0.004	-0.001***	0.136**	0.020	-0.003**
NOR	0.001	-0.051***	-0.001	-0.001***	0.132**	0.018	-0.003**
NZL	0.001	-0.040***	0.003	-0.002***	0.135*	0.020	-0.003**
POL	0.003	-0.040***	0.002	-0.001***	0.071	0.023*	-0.003**
PRT	0.002	-0.042***	0.001	-0.001***	0.127**	0.018	-0.003**
SVK	-0.004	-0.042***	0.000	-0.002***	0.139*	0.020	-0.003**
SVN	-0.000	-0.043***	0.002	-0.001***	0.134**	0.019	-0.003**
SWE	-0.003	-0.046***	0.001	-0.002***	0.126**	0.017	-0.003**
TUR	-0.000	-0.043***	0.002	-0.001***	0.134**	0.019	-0.003**
USA	0.001	-0.035***	0.007	-0.002***	0.144	0.022	-0.003**

Notes: Excluding countries are removed one by one. Robust standard errors in parentheses. Period 1995–2009. Arellano-Bond method where the output gap is instrumented by its lagged values.

***Significant at the 1 percent level.

**Significant at the 5 percent level.

*Significant at the 10 percent level.

References

Alesina, A. 1999. "Too Large and Too Small Governments." In *Economic Policy and Equity,* edited by V. Tanzi, K. Chu, and S. Gupta, 216–34. Washington, DC: International Monetary Fund.

Alesina, A., F. Campante, and G. Tabellini. 2008. "Why is Fiscal Policy So Often Procyclical?" *Journal of the European Economic Association* 6 (5): 1006–36.

Alesina A., and R. Perotti. 1995. "Fiscal Expansions and Fiscal Adjustments in OECD Countries." *Economic Policy* 10 (21): 205–48.

Alt, James E., and David Dreyer Lassen. 2006. "Transparency, Political Polarization, and Political Budget Cycles in OECD Countries." American Journal of Political Science 50 (3): 530–50.

Brender, A., and A. Drazen. 2008. "How Do Budget Deficits and Economic Growth Affect Reelection Prospects? Evidence from a Large Panel of Countries." *American Economic Review* 98 (5): 2203–20.

Gavazza, A., and A. Lizzeri. 2009. "Transparency and Economic Policy." *Review of Economic Studies* 76 (3): 1023–48.

Lane, P. 2003. "The Cyclical Behavior of Fiscal Policy: Evidence from the OECD." *Journal of Public Economics* 87:1661–75.

Persson, T., and G. Tabellini. 2000. *Political Economics: Explaining Economic Policy.* Cambridge, MA: MIT Press.

Persson, T. 2002. "Do Political Institutions Shape Economic Policy?" *Econometrica* 70 (3): 883–905.

Shi, M., and J. Svensson. 2006. "Political Budget Cycles: Do They Differ across Countries and Why?" *Journal of Public Economics* 90 (8–9): 1367–89.

Wooldridge, J. 2002. *The Econometric Analysis of Cross Section and Panel Data.* Cambridge, MA: MIT Press.

Comment   Paolo Pinotti

While the impact of fiscal policy on growth is a recurrent theme in the economics literature, the analysis of the opposite direction of causality, from growth to taxes, is much less developed. The chapter by Cahuc and Carcillo addresses exactly this issue, investigating the effect of output gaps on fiscal outcomes, as mediated by political and labor market institutions. To deal with the obvious reverse causality issues raised by such analysis, the authors exploit time variation in common business cycle components across countries.

The empirical findings suggest that positive output gaps increase the probability of fiscal drifts (simultaneous increases in the share of public wage bill and the public deficit over GDP) and reduce the probability of fiscal

Paolo Pinotti is assistant professor of economics at Bocconi University.

For acknowledgments, sources of research support, and disclosure of the author's material financial relationships, if any, please see http://www.nber.org/chapters/c12649.ack.

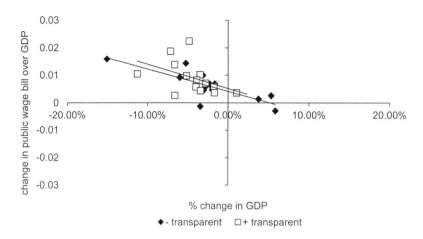

Fig. 9C.1   Change in the share of public wages over GDP, year 2009

Notes: This figure shows the change, between year 2008 and 2009, in the share of public wages over GDP in more and less transparent countries, defined as those above and below the median in terms of the ranking of Transparency International.

tightening episodes (the simultaneous decrease in public wages and deficits), both effects being greater in countries with less transparent government and more powerful labor unions. This result is extremely interesting, because higher welfare spending during economic downturns, as well as the existence of labor and fiscal rigidities, would in principle lead to countercyclical fiscal drifts. Their procyclicality may point thus at the importance of political economy drivers of public expenditure, as expansionary periods may relax the constraints of politicians and raise their incentives to engage in electoral spending.

As to negative output gaps, the authors claim that they do not find a significant effect on the probability of either drift or tightening episodes. However, the empirical evidence is not conclusive in this respect. In many tables, the effect of negative output gaps on (short) fiscal drifts is actually very similar to that of positive output gaps and close to being statistically significant (see, e.g., tables 9.4, 9.9, and 9.21). Moreover, the estimating equation is absorbing the effect of the last crisis in a dummy for the year 2009, which is associated with large fiscal drifts in almost all countries. Therefore, excluding such a dummy would increase the magnitude and statistical significance of the average effect of negative output gaps even more.

More generally, the coefficient for the year 2009 dummy is large and strongly statistically significant in most specifications. While the last crisis was indeed exceptional in many respects, this does not seem an adequate motive for partialing out its effect when estimating the coefficient of negative output gaps; for the very same reason, the year 2009 could be the single

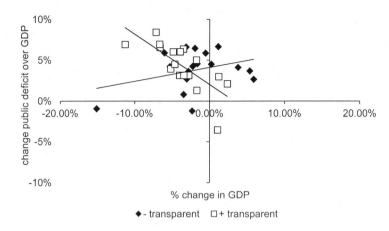

Fig. 9C.2   Change in the share of public deficits over GDP, year 2009

Notes: This figure shows the change, between year 2008 and 2009, in the share of public deficits over GDP in more and less transparent countries, defined as those above and below the median in terms of the ranking of Transparency International.

most important data point when estimating such a coefficient. This is even more true in light of the fact that the last crisis was essentially an exogenous shock for many countries.

Another issue concerns the construction of the dependent variables. Lumping together the dynamics of public wages and budgets provides an intuitive measure of "drift" and "tightening" episodes, yet it may hide differences in the dynamics of the two variables over the business cycle. Considering again the case of the last crisis, there appear to be significant differences in the change of wages and budgets across countries. In particular, the weight of public wages over GDP increased markedly both in more and less transparent countries (figure 9C.1), while public deficits were strongly countercyclical only in the latter group (figure 9C.2). Incidentally, these last findings point again at the informative power of the last crisis for understanding the impact of economic shocks on fiscal policy.

Entitlement Reforms in Europe
Policy Mixes in the Current Pension Reform Process

Axel H. Börsch-Supan

10.1 Introduction

Europe is proud of its entitlement programs. They include, in approximate order of size: (a) public pensions, (b) public health care and health insurance, (c) unemployment insurance and active labor market policies, and (d) others, which are primarily child care, maternity benefits, family cash benefits, and means-tested social assistance, plus sickness benefits, long-term care insurance, and many smaller programs. Together, these entitlement programs represent between 20 and 30 percent of GDP in most European countries—with considerable variation, especially in Eastern Europe (figure 10.1)—while entitlement programs are about 18.5 percent of GDP in the United States.

The generosity of the European entitlement programs is considered a great social achievement because it has historically provided social stability over the life cycle and across business and political cycles. Population aging, negative incentive effects, and other design flaws, however, threaten the very core of these public support systems. As the current debt crisis in Europe shows, they may themselves become a source for fiscal instability due to their large costs.

Axel H. Börsch-Supan is director of the Munich Center for the Economics of Aging (MEA) at the Max Planck Institute for Social Law and Social Policy, Munich, Germany, and a research associate of the National Bureau of Economic Research.

I am grateful for helpful comments by the editors, my discussant David Wise, and many conference participants. This review rests on projects with funding provided by the German Science Foundation (DFG), the State of Baden-Württemberg, the German Insurance Association (GDV), and the US National Institute on Aging (NIA). For acknowledgments, sources of research support, and disclosure of the author's material financial relationships, if any, please see http://www.nber.org/chapters/c12650.ack.

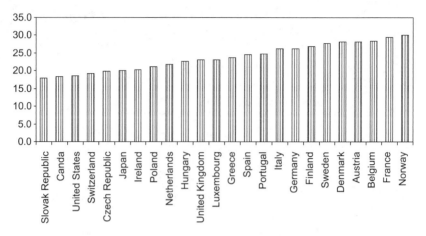

Fig. 10.1   Entitlement programs in Europe and other selected countries (percentage of GDP, 2011)

Source: OECD Social Expenditure database (SOCX, www.oecd.org/els/social/expenditure, November 2011).

Not only the size but also the structure of entitlements by the four above-mentioned program groups is quite different across countries (see table 10.1).

Pension expenditures account for more than half of entitlements in Italy and Greece, while they are less than 20 percent in Ireland and Denmark. Health care, in turn, accounts for the largest share of entitlements in the United States and Canada with more than 40 percent, while it is only about 22 percent in Estonia and Finland. The Mediterranean countries have large pensions systems, but small unemployment insurance and social assistance systems, a structure of public expenditures that has regained prominence in the current debt crisis because it worsens both long-term prospects for debt reduction (due to the implicit debt created by pensions entitlements) and the ability to sustain austerity programs (due to the lack of sufficient unemployment insurance and social assistance).

Since public pension expenditures are the single largest item in the social budget in almost all European countries, this chapter largely focuses on public pension systems. They alone represent a substantial share of GDP. In 2011, Italy and France are frontrunners with some 14 percent of GDP, and in Greece, Portugal, and Austria, this share is about 12 percent—roughly twice the share of GDP compared to the United States (6.7 percent of GDP). In terms of fiscal stability in the current debt crisis, pension systems are a scary example of how current program design, the size of future entitlements, and political credibility interact as either virtuous or vicious spirals. This chapter argues that it is not a coincidence that the countries that spend the highest share of GDP in pension entitlements are also the countries that are currently most pressured to offer very high yields to sell government bonds.

Table 10.1   **Structure of entitlement programs, 2011 (percent of total entitlement programs)**

2011	Pensions (%)	Health (%)	Working age (%)	Children/other (%)
Austria	43.0	24.5	20.5	12.1
Belgium	31.8	25.7	27.5	15.1
Canada	23.9	*44.1*	14.5	17.5
Czech Republic	32.7	29.2	23.1	15.1
Denmark	**19.6**	22.3	26.8	*31.3*
Estonia	31.7	**22.1**	*30.4*	15.8
Finland	31.6	**22.0**	25.1	21.3
France	42.5	25.0	16.6	15.9
Germany	39.4	30.6	15.6	14.4
Greece	*51.1*	25.8	**10.0**	13.1
Hungary	40.8	22.8	23.6	12.8
Ireland	**16.8**	27.0	*36.8*	19.3
Italy	*51.9*	24.7	11.5	11.8
Japan	46.5	33.5	**8.5**	11.5
Luxembourg	27.8	27.7	28.1	16.4
Netherlands	21.3	27.5	27.3	23.9
Norway	22.6	25.4	26.4	25.6
Poland	45.2	22.0	17.2	15.5
Portugal	44.8	26.9	18.7	**9.7**
Slovak Republic	31.9	30.7	23.7	13.7
Slovenia	41.5	24.3	19.2	15.0
Spain	33.0	23.8	25.5	17.8
Sweden	26.4	24.4	20.8	*28.5*
Switzerland	33.2	28.2	24.7	13.9
United Kingdom	23.0	29.3	23.2	24.6
United States	32.9	*44.7*	15.1	**7.3**

Source: OECD Social Expenditure database (SOCX, www.oecd.org/els/social/expenditure, November 2011).

Note: The countries with the two highest and two lowest values are marked in bold and italics.

Through this mechanism, high pension costs imply high costs of debt service, thereby worsening the fiscal balance and crowding out other spending.

Ironically, in spite of their size, some of the expensive pension programs nevertheless fail to provide adequate support for certain population groups since they are targeted heavily to the middle-class median voter. Greeks aged sixty-five and over, for example, face a poverty rate of 22.7 percent, almost twice as large as the Organization for Economic Cooperation and Development (OECD) average.

This chapter links the causes for current problems to the cures required to make the typically pay-as-you-go financed entitlement programs in Continental Europe sustainable above and beyond the financial crisis. It discusses examples that appear, from a current point of view, to be the most viable and effective options to bring the entitlement system closer to fiscal balance and still achieve their key aims (e.g., preventing old-age poverty). It stresses that there is nothing like "the optimal pension reform" since the initial state (in particular the current institutional setup) varies as much as the causes for problems in the future. In any case, solutions to the demographic challenges ahead require a mix of reform elements, as no single element is likely to suffice quantitatively in the face of the dimensions of population aging.

The first part of the chapter sets the stage with a brief overview of the current landscape of entitlement programs in Europe (section 10.2).

The main body of the chapter focuses on the pension reform process in Europe. Section 10.3 is devoted to the causes for reform, while section 10.4 outlines possible cures and presents concrete examples. Specifically, section 10.3 describes (a) the lack of sustainability due to population aging, (b) the negative incentive effects that threaten not only the stability of pension systems but economic growth at large, and (c) examples of where pension adequacy fails.

Section 10.4 is then devoted to the respective cures: (a) setting limits to contribution rates and increasing retirement age will lower the weight of pay-as-you-go financed public pensions; (b) private saving and longer working lives will have to fill the emerging gaps, obtaining a larger weight in retirement income; and (c) since the reform steps have large redistributive consequences, they may require additional targeting.

Section 10.5 provides some estimates of the fiscal effects of these reforms, and section 10.6 concludes.

10.2   The Current Design of Pension Systems in Europe

Figure 10.1 and table 10.1 have shown how different the European entitlement programs are, both in overall size (as percent of GDP) and structure (pensions vs. health care vs. working age vs. children).

Similarly, pension systems are very different across Europe. We focus on four dimensions that characterize the pension systems in Europe: prefunding versus pay-as-you-go financing; earnings-related versus flat benefits; generosity in terms of replacement rate; and eligibility age for pension benefits. The point is not to provide an exhaustive description of European pension systems (for that purpose, see, e.g., OECD 2011), but to give an idea how diverse the initial positions are for potential pension reform in Europe.

The first characterizing dimension is the share of retirement income provided by public pay-as-you-go pension pillars vis-à-vis occupational and private pillars that are, in general, fully funded (see figure 10.2).[1] This dimension is important because pay-as-you-go pensions have to be financed by the next generation through contributions while prefunded pensions are financed by the same generation through savings, which also enjoys the con-

1. Some occupational pensions in France are also at least partly pay-as-you-go.

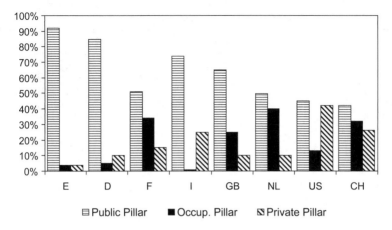

Fig. 10.2   Public, occupational, and private pension income in selected countries (percentage of total retirement income)
Source: Updated from Börsch-Supan and Miegel (2001).

sumption value of pensions. The share of the public pay-as-you-go pillars in total retirement income varies greatly between 92 percent in Spain and 42 percent in Switzerland.

The second characterizing dimension is the linkage between pension benefits and contributions, which are usually a fixed percentage of earnings. Its importance stems from the underlying negative incentive effects on labor supply. It has two extremes: flat pensions without any link to earnings, usually associated with the name of Lord Beveridge, and pensions that are strictly proportional to contributions, usually associated with the name of Chancellor Bismarck. In a Beveridgian system, contributions tend to be interpreted as taxes with resulting labor supply disincentives, while in a Bismarckian system, contributions are closer to insurance premiums.[2] There are many refinements: some pension systems define pension benefits ex ante, while in others benefits emerge ex post as the outcome of lifetime contributions. Often, the public pension systems consists of two parts: a flat-benefit part to prevent poverty ("pillar 0" in the language of the World Bank; Holzmann and Hinz 2005), and an earnings-related part that is usually capped at a maximum benefit level ("pillar 1").

Table 10.2 is adapted from OECD (2011) and characterizes European pension systems along these lines. The Denmark and the Netherlands, for example, have a basic pension that is essentially independent from the contributions paid and/or the income earned during working life (Beveridge type). France and Germany, on the other hand, have earnings-related pensions based on a point system that defines the benefits (Bismarck type).

---

2. See Börsch-Supan and Reil-Held (2001).

Table 10.2 **Structure of pension programs, 2010**

	Poverty prevention part ("pillar 0")			Earnings-related part ("pillar 1") Type
	Resource tested	Basic	Minimum	
Austria				DB
Belgium	x		x	DB
Czech Rep.		x	x	DB
Denmark	x	x		
Estonia		x		Points
Finland			x	DB
France			x	DB+points
Germany	x			Points
Greece			x	DB
Hungary				DB
Ireland		x		
Italy	x			NDC
Japan		x		DB
Luxembourg	x	x	x	DB
Netherlands		x		
Norway			x	NDC
Poland			x	NDC
Portugal			x	DB
Slovak Republic			x	Points
Slovenia			x	DB
Spain			x	DB
Sweden			x	NDC
Switzerland	x		x	DB
United Kingdom	x	x	x	DB
United States				DB

Source: Adapted from OECD, *Pensions at a Glance,* 2011.

Notes: Resource-tested plans pay a higher benefit to poorer pensioners. The value of benefits depends on income from other sources and, in some countries, on assets. Basic schemes pay flat benefits (in some countries, their value depends on years of work but not on past earnings. Additional retirement income does not change the entitlement. Minimum pensions are resource-tested plans in which the value of entitlements takes account only of pension income but it is not affected by income from savings, etc. In some countries, benefits for workers with very low earnings are calculated as if the worker had earned at a higher level. Defined-benefit (DB) plans are those in which retirement income depends on the number of years of contributions and individual earnings. Point schemes are those in which workers earn pension points based on their earnings each year. At retirement, the sum of pension points is multiplied by a pension-point value to convert them into a regular pension payment. Defined-contribution (DC) plans are those in which contributions flow into an individual account. The accumulation of contributions and investment returns is converted into a pension-income stream at retirement. Notional defined countribution (NDC) plans record contributions in an individual account and apply a rate of return to the balances. The accounts are "notional" in that the balances exist only on the books of the managing institution. At retirement, the accumulated notional capital is converted into a stream of pension payments using a formula based on life expectancy.

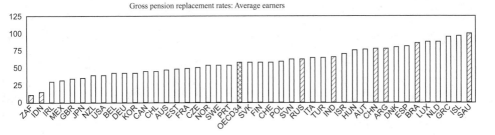

Fig. 10.3   Gross relative pension level (average pension in percent of average earnings)

Sources: OECD pension models; StatLink (http://dx.doi.org/10.1787/8888932370835); OECD, *Pensions at a Glance* (2011).

Sweden and Italy introduced notional defined contribution systems (NDC). These are pay-as-you-go pension systems mimicking funded systems insofar as they accrue interest on the contributions into personal accounts that are, upon retirement, converted into annuities. They feature the closest link between contributions and benefits, followed by the point systems (e.g., in France and Germany).

Third, pension replacement rates are a measure for the generosity (and thus costs) of pension systems. Figure 10.3 shows the average pension in percentage of average earnings before taxes, with a very large variation from just over 25 percent to almost 100 percent. Ireland has the lowest and Greece the highest replacement rate in Europe. The OECD average is slightly above 50 percent.

Finally, the fourth characterizing dimension is the eligibility (commonly, retirement) age because of its strong influence on labor supply and system costs. Figure 10.4 shows the statutory and effective retirement ages. Already the statutory retirement ages display an enormous variation and even more so the effective retirement ages.

The figures in this section show clearly how different the current pension systems in Europe are. They vary in all policy-relevant dimensions: financial mechanism, structure, generosity, and labor market influence. Much of this is due to historical country-specific political and cultural preferences. As a first consequence, pension expenditures are only loosely related to the demographic structure of a country (see next section). Secondly, there is no single optimal design strategy for pension reform in Europe; rather, pension reform has to focus on different design dimensions in each country to account for the country-specific initial states.

10.3   Causes for Reform

Population aging is one important reason to align current entitlements with future fiscal capacity. As a consequence, pension and entitlement reform

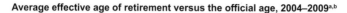

Average effective age of retirement versus the official age, 2004–2009[a,b]

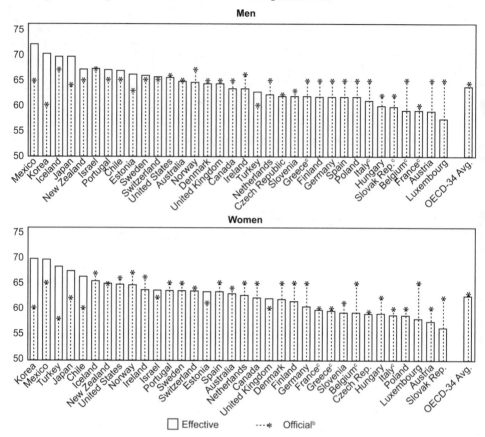

Fig. 10.4   Statutory and effective retirement age
Source: OECD, *Pensions at a Glance* (2011).

is an ongoing process in virtually all European countries. It therefore may come as a surprise how weakly the current demographic structure is linked to the current relative size of the European public pension programs (see figure 10.5).

This is mainly due to the many design differences between European pension systems described in the previous section. Some of these designs are self-stabilizing and thus prevent high cost increases. This is the case, for example, for Estonia, Poland, and Sweden, and is described in section 10.4. Other designs create strong negative incentive effects on labor supply and generate early retirement, which decreases economic capacity and thus threatens fiscal capacity and economic growth at large. This in turn increases the force of population aging on pension expenditures. Figure 10.6 shows,

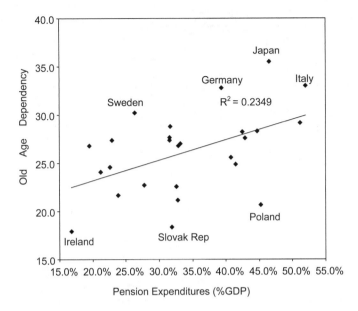

Fig. 10.5   Pension expenditures (percent of GDP, 2011) by old-age dependency (percent)

Source: OECD Social Expenditure database (SOCX, www.oecd.org/els/social/expenditure, November 2011).

that, while almost all European countries face increasing pension costs as percent of GDP, there are very large differences across countries. On average across the European Union, the cost share will increase by 16 percent until 2030 and by 37 percent until 2050. In Greece and Luxembourg, however, pension expenditures will more than double until 2050, while they are projected to decline in Estonia, Poland, and Sweden.

The weak correlation between aging and projected pension costs, and the huge variation in cost increases, are a symptom of many other reasons for reform. Subsection 10.3.1 describes the link between demography and sustainability as a reason to reform the pension systems. Subsection 10.3.2 analyses the link between expected cost increases and incentive effects that reduce labor supply. Finally, subsection 10.3.3 is concerned with the redistributive features of European pension systems and the alleviation of old-age poverty.

10.3.1   Population Aging and Lack of Sustainability

While all European countries are aging, there are remarkable differences. Italy, Austria, and Germany will experience a particularly dramatic change in the age structure of the population. Such change is much less incisive in France, Great Britain, and Scandinavia. The severity of the demographic

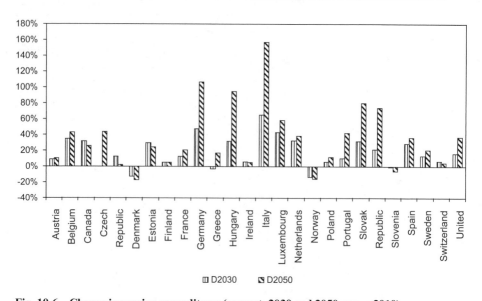

Fig. 10.6   Change in pension expenditures (percent, 2030 and 2050 versus 2010)
Sources: EPC projections in EU, OECD elsewhere; OECD Social Expenditure database (SOCX, www
.oecd.org/els/social/expenditure, November 2011).

transition in most of Europe has two causes: a quicker increase in life expectancy than elsewhere, partly due to a relatively low level until the 1970s, and
a more incisive baby boom/baby bust transition (e.g., relative to the United
States) to a very low fertility rate in some countries (1.2 children per lifetime
in Italy, Spain, and Greece, 1.3 in Austria and Germany).

Both demographic developments have a similar consequence: the ratio
of elderly to working-age persons—the old-age dependency ratio—will
increase steeply (see figure 10.7). According to the latest projections of the
European Union, the share of elderly (aged sixty-five and above) will exceed
a quarter of the population in 2030. The old-age dependency ratio will more
than double during the next fifty years. In Italy, Spain, Austria, and Germany, there will be one person aged sixty-five and over for every two other
persons. Moreover, population aging is not a transitory phenomenon but
will persist even after the baby boom generation will be deceased: the dependency ratio plateaus after 2040 for most European countries and will not
return to preaging levels for the foreseeable future.

While both demographic developments—decreasing fertility and increasing longevity—have similar consequences, it is important to distinguish the
two causes because they imply different policy responses, which is often
confused in the public debate. We take Germany as an example, but similar
features exist in its neighboring countries: Austria, the Netherlands, and
Switzerland (see figure 10.8). The sharpness of the change is generated

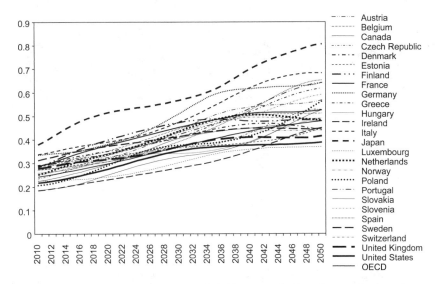

Fig. 10.7   The old-age dependency ratio in Europe and selected countries (population 65+/population 20–64: 2010–2050)

Sources: EPC projections in EU, OECD elsewhere; OECD Social Expenditure database (SOCX, www.oecd.org/els/social/expenditure, November 2011).

by the first cause, the sudden decline in birth rates during the baby boom to baby bust transition in the 1970s. The number of children born during the baby boom in the 1960s was about 2.4 children per woman and led to the bulge in the age pyramids of figure 10.8. In 1997, these children were about thirty-five years old. The baby bust started with a sudden decline to 1.3 children per woman, visible in the much smaller number of persons aged below thirty-five. Thirty years from now, the numerous baby boomers will be pensioners, and the much smaller baby bust generation will have to finance them. Compensating this by changes in the retirement age is virtually impossible and other policy responses are needed.

The second cause for the demographic transition is the secular change in life expectancy. This is a more steady development, and it is likely to persist after 2035. Figure 10.9 shows that since 1970, the remaining life expectancy of German men and women at age sixty-five has increased by four years. It is projected to increase another three years until 2030. This implies that a pension in 2030 will be paid seven more years than in 1970. Since the average length of pension receipt was about fifteen years in 1970, the increase in life expectancy represents an expansion of pension benefits by almost 50 percent. An increase in the actual retirement age is a feasible and effective cure for this cause of financial strain.

Public health insurance (and in particular long-term care insurance, LTC) face similar sustainability problems because they are financed pay-as-you-go

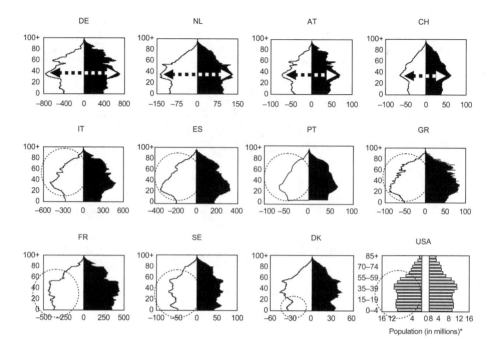

Fig. 10.8 Baby boom to baby bust transition in Europe
Sources: Own depiction based on Eurostat and US Census IDB data.
*US Census Bureau International Database.

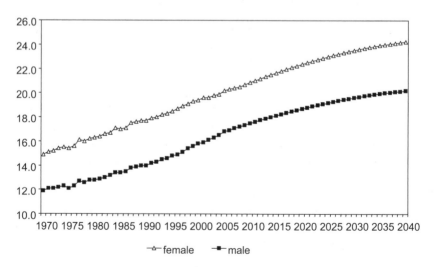

Fig. 10.9 Life expectancy at age 65, German men and women, 1970–2040
Sources: For 1970–2008, Statistisches Bundesamt; for 2009–2040, MEA-Projection.

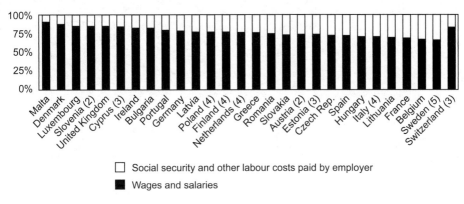

Fig. 10.10   Composition of total hourly labor compensation in Europe (percent, Eurostat)
Source: Eurostat (online data codes: lc_an_struc and lc_an_struc_r2).

by the younger generation and give the bulk of benefits (all in LTC) to the older generation.

10.3.2   Design Flaws and Negative Incentive Effects

The well-known demographically-induced problems are not the only challenges for the European entitlement programs. Another challenge are the distortions created through financing mechanisms and design flaws.

Some entitlement programs may be considered a fair insurance because the expected benefits of the program equals the expected contributions over the life-course. Therefore, at least according to traditional economies, one would not expect very large labor supply disincentive effects.[3] Examples are most defined contribution pensions (including NDC systems) and most private health insurance. Most programs, however, have strong transfer components (see section 10.2), for example, payroll-tax financed pension programs with flat benefits (in Great Britain, Netherlands, and Switzerland). Such payroll taxes are known to distort labor supply of the younger generation (Blundell, Duncan, and Meghir 1998). Since contributions to social insurance are a large part of total labor compensation (see figure 10.10), and increase total labor costs, demand for labor declines, with consequent higher unemployment and lower economic growth. Reducing the contribution burden is therefore not only important for the long-run stability and sustainability of the pension system itself, but for fiscal stability and economic performance at large. It is important to keep both in mind, since economic growth is an important source to finance future pensions.

There are two additional tax components in pension contributions. Since

---

3. See the implicit tax argument in pay-as-you-go systems.

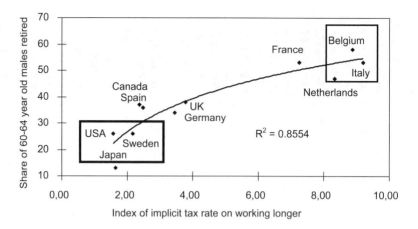

Fig. 10.11   Tax force and early retirement
Source: Börsch-Supan (2000) adapted from Gruber and Wise (1999).

the implicit return from a mandatory pay-as-you-go system tends to be lower than the explicit return on the voluntary investment in a funded pension, there is an implicit tax in all pay-as-you-go systems (see Börsch-Supan and Reil-Held 2001). Moreover, most public pension systems are not actuarially neutral because they distort labor supply of the older generation through early retirement incentives. This creates an implicit tax on working longer, measured, for example, by the Gruber-Wise group and the OECD.[4] Figure 10.11 links an index of this implicit tax to the share of those men who are already retired at age sixty to sixty-four. In countries with a large implicit tax on working longer (e.g., Belgium, France, Italy, and the Netherlands), the share of retirees is much larger than in countries with a low implicit tax (e.g., Sweden, the United States, and Japan).

The aggregate correlation in figure 10.11 permits no causal interpretation. Supplemental analyses, however, have produced convincing evidence for causality. First, figure 10.12 shows that especially in Belgium, France, the Netherlands, and Italy, very few workers aged sixty to sixty-four are still in the labor force. This is quite different from what it was in the 1960s, in spite of a lower life expectancy and a higher prevalence of illness at that time.

Second, this decline is not a "natural trend" tied to secular income growth. It did not occur, for example, in Japan and Sweden. Rather, the decline happened exactly when the tax force on working longer increased; the decline has been largely "engineered" by the incentive effects that are intrinsic in some of the public pension systems, in particular by an incomplete adjustment of benefits to retirement age. A particularly striking historical example for the exogenous policy change that can be exploited for formal micro-

---

4. Gruber and Wise (1999); Blondal and Scarpetta (1998).

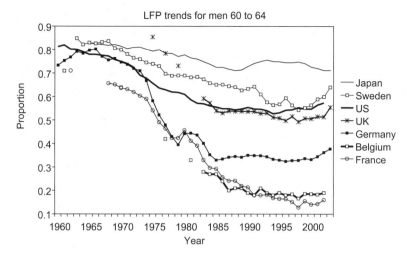

Fig. 10.12   Labor force participation among men aged 60–64, 1960–2008 (proportion of male population 60 to 64)
Source: Gruber and Wise (2010).

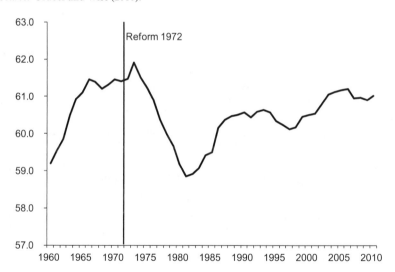

Fig. 10.13   Average retirement age in Germany, 1960–2008
Source: Updated from Börsch-Supan and Schnabel (2010).

econometric evidence with a causal interpretation is the German pension reform in 1972 (see figure 10.13).[5]

The German public pension system with its "flexible retirement" introduced in 1972 tilted the retirement decision heavily toward the earliest retire-

5. Börsch-Supan and Schnabel (1998); Börsch-Supan (2000); Gruber and Wise (2003).

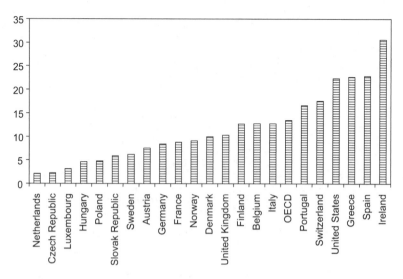

Fig. 10.14   Old-age poverty rates, 2010 (OECD, 2008)
Source: OECD, *Pensions at a Glance* (2011).

ment age applicable because the annual benefit was essentially independent of the retirement age. Hence, retiring earlier gave a worker essentially the same pension for a longer time. At the then prevailing generous replacement rates, this was a pretty good deal. The 1992 reform, in force after 1997, has diminished this incentive effect, but pension benefits are still not actuarially neutral at conventional interest rates.

The retirement behavior of entrants into the German public retirement insurance system reflects these incentive effects quite clearly in figure 10.13. Immediately after the introduction of "flexible retirement" in 1972, the average retirement age declined dramatically by more than three years. We interpret this as a clear sign of a policy reaction. The most popular retirement age switched by five years, from age sixty-five to age sixty. As a striking example of effective reform, a large part of this decline has been reversed since 1997.

10.3.3   Lack of Adequacy and Perverse Redistribution

Many countries have a minimum pension, either as statutory basic or minimum pension or effective through social assistance mechanisms.[6] As figure 10.14 shows, this has kept poverty rates low in most European countries, at least relative to the OECD average and certainly vis-à-vis the United States.

There are, however, three striking exceptions where the old-age poverty rate exceeds 20 percent of individuals aged sixty-five and over: Greece, Spain,

6. For example, in Germany: the tax-financed "Grundsicherung im Alter," which is not part of the German public pension system.

Table 10.3   **Synopsis of pension reform elements in Europe, 1980–2010**

	Retirement age	Link of benefits to contributions	Indexation
Austria	women → 65	+	
Germany	all → 67	(universal point sys)	Sustainability
France	all → 62	Basis of point system	
Italy		NDC	NDC
Spain			
Greece		Partially	
Denmark	all → 67 rev		
Sweden	DI	NDC	NDC
Norway		point	life expectancy
Finland	UI tunnel	scale factors	
Netherlands	EEA, DI		
UK	all → 68		price → wage
US	all → 67		

and Ireland. Ireland spends very little on pensions, as we saw in table 10.1. Greece and Spain, however, have both above-average pension replacement rates (see figure 10.3) but nevertheless very high old-age poverty rates. While in most countries, pension systems and/or their associated social assistance systems distribute from rich to poor, this suggests some extent of perverse redistribution in Greece and Spain.

10.4   Curing the Problems

Reform processes are under way in almost all European countries. Some countries reformed early in the 1980s (e.g., Sweden), most countries much later, and some not at all (e.g., Greece). Typically, we have experienced "reforms in installments." These reforms have combined parametric elements (introducing actuarial adjustments, changing the benefits indexation formula, increasing the retirement age) with fundamental elements (changing the financial mechanism by moving substantial parts of retirement income from public pensions to private savings). Table 10.3 presents a synopsis.

The multitude of reform elements in Europe is partly a result of initially different and different political preferences. It also reflects the fact that there is no single reform measure that can lead to a stable and sustainable system of old-age provision; rather, a mix of several reform elements is needed. If the goal is to restore fiscal sustainability, then reform will require an overhaul of the existing pay-as-you-go systems as well as the reintroduction of private saving as a major source of future retirement income. Extreme policies are unlikely to work: the public pension systems alone cannot provide a sufficient retirement income at reasonable tax and contribution rates, and private savings cannot fully substitute for pay-as-you-go pensions.

Relying on public pay-as-you-go financed pensions alone is not possible because the resulting tax and contribution rates from maintaining the current generosity (and thus costs, see figure 10.6) will damage economic growth through the negative labor supply incentive effects described earlier. Further increases of the tax and contribution rates are particularly damaging in those EU countries that already have high total labor costs—in particular Germany, Austria, Denmark, and Sweden (see figure 10.10).

In turn, transiting pensions entirely to private saving is also not a policy option. One fatal reason against such an option is simply that it is too late. Saving requires time, and there will not be sufficient time until 2030 for the baby boomers to accumulate funds in the order of magnitude required to finance a full pension. Time and history is of the essence in pension reform. The baby boom/baby bust transition dictates the time schedule and makes reforms impossible that were possible twenty-five years ago, such as a complete transition to a fully funded system.

There are other reasons to advocate a more subtle but also more complex multipillar system rather than a pure pay-as-you-go or a pure fully funded system. An important reason is diversification. Pay-as-you-go systems carry large demographic and political risks, while fully funded systems carry large capital market risks. Since these risks are not perfectly correlated, diversification provides lower risk of poor outcomes than monolithity.

Hence, in order to achieve long-run fiscal balance, reforms typically need to include two components: adapting the public system to demographic change under the restriction that taxes and contributions cannot increase much further, and strengthening private savings under the restriction that not much time is left until 2035. Subsection 10.4.1 addresses the first, and subsection 10.4.2 the second element. Subsection 10.4.3 discusses issues of targeting and poverty alleviation.

10.4.1   Adapting Pay-as-You-Go Public Pension Systems

Stabilizing tax and contribution rates implies expenditure cuts if and when at the same time demographic change reduces the number of contributors to, and increases the number of beneficiaries from, the pay-as-you-go pension systems. Pension expenditures have two dimensions: the level of benefits (via the replacement rate) and the duration of benefits (via the retirement age). Expenditure cuts are easier to shoulder if they involve both dimensions.

Both dimensions are politically difficult. Fortunately, the demographic change, while dramatic, is of a magnitude that is far from absorbing all available resources. Figure 10.15 shows a rough approximation of the force of aging on economic growth, represented by the loss of productive capacity due to a decline of the number of workers relative to the number of consumers. It is measured as the percentage change of the old-age dependency ratio (from figure 10.7). The dependency ratio deteriorates at a rate of about

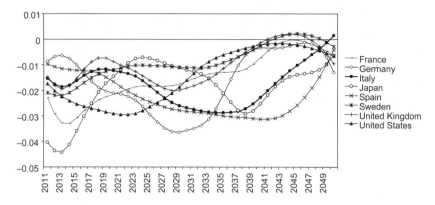

Fig. 10.15   The force of aging in terms of the rate of economic growth
Source: Own calculations based on OECD Social Expenditure database (SOCX, www.oecd
.org/els/social/expenditure, November 2011).

0.2 to 0.5 percent p.a. (per annum), with a large variation in timing across
the selected countries. This is much less than the long-run averages of productivity growth, which is about 1.5 to 2.5 percent p.a. for most European
countries. Hence, population aging absorbs between a seventh and a third of
future productivity growth, leaving the bulk for real income growth. Pension
benefits can therefore rise in real terms in spite of population aging, and all
that is required is a growth rate of benefits that remains below the growth
rate of wages.

Adapting the Level of Benefits: Reducing the Replacement Rate

How much benefit increases have to be dampened depends on the speed
and the extent of demographic change in each country relative to its productivity growth. France and Sweden, for example, will need less adaptation
than Italy and Germany. Some countries have formalized this link between
demographics and benefit level. Sweden and Italy have introduced notional
defined contribution (NDC) systems, which compute benefits on the basis of
the accumulated contributions plus some fictitious interest, which depends
on demographic essentials such as life expectancy and dependency ratio
and wage growth. In macroeconomic abstraction, this interest rate should
be the labor force growth rate plus productivity growth. Since the labor
force growth rate is declining as a population ages, an NDC system features
a declining replacement rate in the course of population aging. Moreover,
longevity decreases the value of the annuity emanating from the accumulated notional wealth.

Germany has taken an apparently very different approach, preserving
the defined benefit structure that has so much political acceptance in many
countries. It augmented the conventional benefit indexation formula, which

increases benefits at the rate of wage (in other countries: price) increases by a new factor, the so-called "sustainability factor."[7] This factor reflects the development of the relative number of contributors to pensioners, the system dependency ratio, which is the most important long-term determinant of pension financing. The annual benefit changes are then proportional to two factors: changes in gross earnings minus contributions to the pension system (positively related), and changes in the system dependency ratio (inversely related), weighted harmonically:[8]

$$PV_t = PV_{t-1} \left(\frac{AGE_t}{AGE_{t-1}} \frac{(1 - \tau_t)}{(1 - \tau_{t-1})} \right) a \cdot \left(\frac{SDR_{t-1}}{SDR_t} \right)^{1-a},$$

where PV is pension value per earnings point, AGE is average gross earnings, τ is contribution rate to public and private pensions, and SDR is system dependency ratio: pensioners/contributors.

The weight has been set achieve a politically determined contribution rate target. This new pension formula will lead to decreases in pension benefit levels vis-à-vis the path of wages. Currently, gross benefits are about 48 percent of gross earnings. This corresponds to a net pension level of about 70 percent of net earnings. In 2035, when the plafond of population aging is reached, the gross pension level will be about 40 percent.

The Swedish and the German reform approaches look very different. However, as Börsch-Supan and Wilke (2005) point out, the sustainability factor can almost perfectly mimic a national defined contribution system; it can thus be interpreted as a notional defined contribution system "wrapped" as a defined benefit system. The different selling approaches responded to the political economy differences between Sweden and Germany.

Adapting the Duration of Benefits: Increasing the Retirement Age

The other crucial dimension of pension expenditures is the duration of pension benefits, determined by the difference between the age at which pension benefits are taken up and life expectancy. As pointed out earlier, life expectancy is projected to increase by about three years between now and 2030. This increase is expected to be about the same for all European countries. Figure 10.4 has shown the international differences in both normal retirement age (the statutory age to take up old-age pensions) and actual retirement age (the age in which workers leave the labor force) which in most European countries is equal to the age in which some kind of public pension is taken up. The two main policy instruments to reduce the duration of benefits are increasing the statutory retirement age and reducing early retirement benefits. Both instruments are extremely unpopular throughout Europe.

---

7. Börsch-Supan and Wilke (2005); Börsch-Supan (2007).
8. The actual formula avoids exponentiation and features various lags due to data availability.

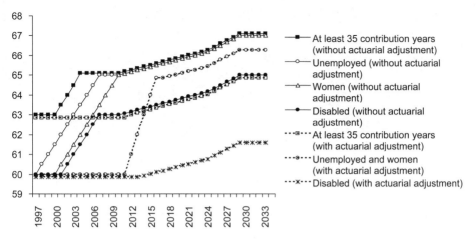

Fig. 10.16   Projected retirement age, Germany, 1997–2035
Source: Updated from Berkel and Börsch-Supan (2004).

In Germany, the 1992 reform has succeeded in abolishing most early retirement pathways without actuarial adjustments. This law became effective in 1997, but it has a transition period until 2017 (see figure 10.16).

In addition, Denmark, Germany, France, and the United Kingdom have enacted increases of the statutory normal retirement age (e.g., Denmark and Germany from sixty-five to sixty-seven years, United Kingdom even to sixty-eight years, while in France only from sixty to sixty-two years). Most increases are slow and gradual. In Germany, it started in 2011 with monthly steps such that the retirement age of sixty-seven will be reached in 2029. This increase corresponds to two-thirds of the projected change in life expectancy. This approximately keeps the ratio of time spent in working life to time spent in retirement constant and thus neutralizes, from an expenditure point of view, the effect of longevity increases on pension expenditures.

In some countries, the statutory retirement age is not the primary determinant of actual retirement age but the number of years worked. In Germany, forty-five years of contributions will generate a full pension even if these service years are reached before age sixty-five. In some countries, the number of required contribution years is much lower, notably in France, Greece, and Italy, and vary by profession (see the quite colorful Greek case described by Börsch-Supan and Tinios 2002). With increasing life expectancy, such mechanisms create a very long and thus costly duration of pension benefit recipiency. If one follows the previous logic, the required number of service years should also be adapted to the longer life span. This has been particularly controversial in France and Italy.

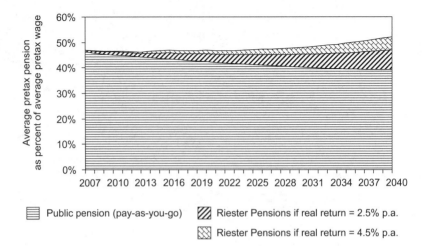

Fig. 10.17   **Projected retirement income components, Germany, 2002–2040**
Source: Börsch-Supan et al. (2008).

10.4.2   Private Saving and Prefunding

Reducing the first pillar of pay-as-you-go financed public pensions creates a gap in retirement income relative to what workers have become accustomed to. There are only two mechanisms to fill the gap: working longer and saving more.[9] A reasonable approach is of course to exploit both mechanisms, in spite of the unpopularity (particularly of the first mechanism described in the preceding subsection).

Figure 10.17 shows how this can work, again using the recent German reform proposals as an example. Taking account of the increase in the normal retirement age to sixty-seven, which increases pension benefits according to the German benefit formula, and adding income from private retirement savings, the reform proposal manages to deliver an income level for retirees that is comparable to today's income level, in spite of the reduction of public pillar pensions according to the sustainability formula. This projection assumes a private retirement saving rate of four percent of gross income from 2009 on. These 4 percent are the current limit of tax-subsidization, if either occupational pensions ("second pillar") or private savings ("third pillar") are used to finance additional retirement income. Under many circumstances, both subsidies can be combined such that 8 percent of gross income can be tax-privileged.

9. Higher fertility is only a long-run solution and does not help to offset the fiscal strains generated by the baby-boom generation. Higher migration would help but net immigration numbers need to be unrealistically large to offset the domestic aging process (see United Nations Population Division 2001).

This is important for the early baby boomers. Figure 10.17 shows the crux of all transition schemes to more funded pensions via private saving: the transition generation will have to pay extra in order to maintain their total retirement income when the income from pay-as-you-go pensions is reduced. For the younger generation, born after about 1980 and retiring after about 2040, 4 percent is sufficient to maintain or even to obtain higher retirement income levels than today, but a saving rate of 8 percent is required for the cohort with the highest transition burden, the early baby boomers born in the 1950s and early 1960s.

Such high saving rates are feasible, but they of course hurt consumption. They are the price for reforming too late. Figure 10.2 shows the weight of the three pillars in selected European countries. Those countries, which have reformed their pension systems in the 1980s by transiting to multi-pillar systems (Switzerland, the Netherlands, and Great Britain), have succeeded in lower contribution rates; they also need lower private saving rates because they have saved for a longer time, accumulating more capital and enjoying higher compound interest. The latecomers in this process (Spain, Germany, France, and Italy) still have dominant first pillars and need to save much more and much quicker, if they want to alleviate the tax and contribution burden and at the same time maintain their accustomed retirement income levels. Given the short time period until the baby boomers retire, this may only be an option for later generations but not feasible for them.

10.4.3   Targeting and Redistribution

Cutting pay-as-you-go pensions to a sustainable share of GDP will particularly hurt those who have earned very little and whose saving capacity is also low. The reform-driven reduction of replacement rates will drive workers who have earned incomes only slightly above the poverty line into old-age poverty after retirement.

This dilemma between sustainability and old-age poverty can only be solved by targeting policies for those who are in danger of old-age poverty. One instrument is basic and/or minimum pensions (see table 10.2). Another instrument is a nonlinear (concave from above) schedule linking benefits to contributions (e.g., via the PIA/AIME [primary insurance amount/average indexed monthly earnings] conversion in the US Social Security system).

Some countries have basic or minimum pensions that prevent old-age poverty virtually by definition, as they set the minimum level of pension income just above the poverty level (e.g., Denmark and Germany). In other countries, such basic or minimum pensions are nonexistent or provide income below the poverty line (e.g., Greece and Ireland). Such countries need to redistribute more from rich to poor pensioners if they want to prevent old-age poverty.

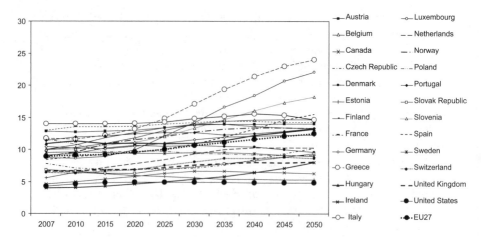

Fig. 10.18   Projected public pension expenditures (percent of GDP), 2007–2050
Sources: EPC projections in EU, OECD elsewhere; OECD Social Expenditure database
(SOCX, www.oecd.org/els/social/expenditure, November 2011).

10.5   Implications for Fiscal Stability

Because pensions are a large part of entitlements, which in turn take up
a large share of public expenditures, fiscal stability is closely linked to the
path of future pension expenditures. The Economic Policy Committee of the
EU, together with the OECD, provide projections on future public pension
expenditures, see figure 10.18.

Two countries stand out: Italy, because it has currently the highest public
pension expenditures, and Greece, because it features the most dramatic
increase. While both countries have very high pension expenditures today,
their dynamics could not be more different: expenditures in Italy are stable
until 2030, rise only weakly until 2040 and then decline, while they rise in
proportion to the dependency rate in Greece.

The reason for this tale of two countries is quickly told. As section 10.2
described, Greece has a defined benefit system with a high replacement rate
and very early retirement. So far, there is no feedback of demography to this
generosity. Italy features two pension systems. The old system is similar to
the current Greek system, while the new system is modeled after the Swedish NDC system. Workers who started after 1993 are completely in the new
NDC system, while those who had more than eighteen years contribution
before 1996 are completely in the old system. Those in between are under a
"pro rata" system: benefits corresponding to contributions before 1993 are
paid according to the old system and the ones after 1993 according to the
NDC.[10] Hence, the Italian system has not yet deeply cut benefits. The new

10. I am grateful to Agar Brugiavini for this description.

Table 10.4   **Decomposition of projected changes in pension expenditure, 2005–2050 (gross public pension expenditures as percent of GDP)**

	Level 2005	Percent change 2005–2050	Dependency ratio	Employment rate	Take-up ratio	Benefit ratio	Residual (interaction)
Austria	13.2	–1.0	11.3	–1.3	–5.8	–4.3	–0.8
Belgium	10.4	5.1	7.7	–1.5	–0.4	–0.6	–0.1
Denmark	9.5	3.2	7.2	–0.4	–2.8	–0.5	–0.3
Finland	10.4	3.3	8.8	–0.9	–3.1	–0.9	–0.6
France	12.9	2.0	9.7	–0.9	–1.9	–3.5	–0.5
Germany	11.1	1.9	7.5	–1.1	–0.6	–3.5	–0.4
Ireland	4.6	6.5	7.9	–0.5	–1.4	0.8	–0.2
Italy	14.3	0.4	11.5	–2.0	–3.2	–5.3	–0.7
Luxembourg	10.0	7.4	7.2	–4.4	2.5	2.1	0.0
Netherlands	7.4	3.8	6.3	–0.2	–1.6	–0.4	–0.3
Portugal	11.5	9.3	13.7	–0.2	–3.9	–3.0	–0.4
Spain	8.7	7.0	12.4	–1.8	–2.3	–0.8	–0.4
Sweden	10.4	0.9	4.8	–0.6	0.2	–2.8	–0.2
United Kingdom	6.7	1.9	4.7	–0.1	0.0	0.0	–2.6

Source: Carone et al. (2008).

system, however, has a strongly stabilizing influence on pension expenditures (see section 10.4) if it is actually implemented. Some crucial parameters, such as the fictitious interest rate of the NDC system and the conversion factor of the notional wealth into the pension annuity, however, are politically much more vulnerable in the Italian copy than in the Swedish original; the pension costs expected by financial markets may thus be higher than suggested by figure 10.18. It is therefore no coincidence that Greece and Italy are currently most under pressure from financial markets.

In order to understand how the projections in figure 10.18 depend on demographic trends and future policy actions, it is helpful to decompose the projected expenditure increases into four potential causes (old-age dependency, employment rate, take-up ratio, and benefit ratio) according to the following equation (see Carone et al. 2008):

$$\frac{\text{PensExp}}{\text{GDP}} = \frac{\text{Pop} > 65}{\text{Pop}(15-64)} \times \frac{\text{Pop}(15-64)}{\text{EmplNo}} \times \frac{\text{PensNo}}{\text{Pop} > 65} \times \frac{\text{PensExp/PensNo}}{\text{GDP/EmplNo}}.$$

Results are displayed in table 10.4.

The demographic pressure, measured as the dependency ratio effect, is positive in all countries, especially the Mediterranean countries. Some countries have strong counterbalancing forces, for example, Sweden and Italy. This is the effect of the automatic stabilizers in the NDC systems, which are somewhat weaker in Germany with its sustainability factor and the gradual increase of its retirement age. These mechanisms reduce the benefit and

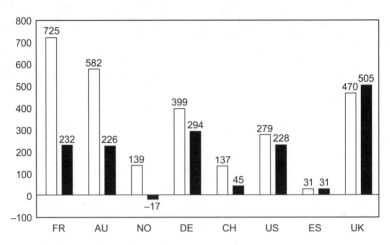

Fig. 10.19   **Projected implicit pension debt before and after recent reforms (percent of GDP)**
Source: Moog, Müller, and Raffelhüschen (2010).

take-up ratios and increase the employment, mainly through later retirement. In other countries, such as Spain (Greece did not provide figures for this EU exercise), demographic factors were not or only very little dampened by countervailing policy measures. Table 10.4 shows that the demographic pressures can effectively be counteracted by the policy mixes described in section 10.4.

Moog, Müller, and Raffelhüschen (2010) have provided estimates of the implicit pension debt and its reduction through pension reform. He computes the present discounted value of future pension entitlements and subtracts the present discounted value of future contributions. In virtually all countries, entitlements exceed contributions in present discounted value, leaving an implicit debt. Figure 10.19 shows the effect of selected recent reforms on this implicit pension debt, expressed as percent of GDP. While these figures rest on many assumptions and are very sensitive to the choice of a discount rate, the overall message is robust: the implicit pension debt exceeds the explicit government debt in most European countries by several multiples. Pension reform has improved this fiscal imbalance dramatically in some countries (e.g., France and Austria), and significantly in others (e.g., Germany). There is, however, little change in the United States and even an increase in the United Kingdom.

Werding (2007) provides a similar calculation for the effects of the various German reform steps (see figure 10.20). The gap between unfunded pension liabilities and future contributions corresponds to the implicit pension debt of figure 10.19. His estimate of the reform effects are larger. The 1992, 2001, and 2004 acts reduced the benefit ratio in several steps, while the last reform step increased the statutory eligibility age from sixty-five to sixty-seven. The

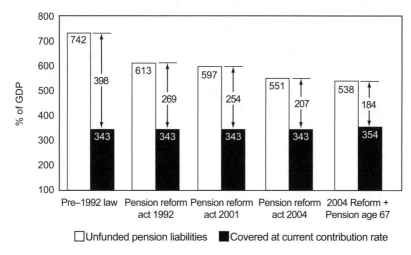

Fig. 10.20   Projected implicit pension debt before and after recent reforms (percent of GDP)
Source: Werding (2007).

largest effect was the change from gross to net wage indexation in 1992, and the introduction of the sustainability factor in 2004. Figure 10.20 reiterates our earlier message: the fiscal pressure of entitlement programs can and have been reduced substantially by relatively mild parametric reforms.

An indicator of long-term fiscal balance that is less sensitive to assumptions about the discount rate and thus timing of events is the sustainability gap. It departs from a projection of pension expenditures, a projection of pension contributions, and a final level of debt (e.g., the 60 percent of GDP defined in the Maastricht treaty) to be achieved after a target date. The sustainability gap then measures the additional income (primary balance as percent of GDP) necessary to avoid ending up with a higher final level of debt at the target date. In figure 10.21, based on the latest report by the European Commission, S1 takes the year 2060 as the target date, while S2 assumes an infinite horizon.

The commission report shows that only Denmark features a fiscally sustainable pension system according to these calculations. Denmark is closely followed by Finland and Sweden, plus Bulgaria and Estonia. In all other European countries, achieving fiscal sustainability requires further reforms. Figure 10.21 shows the particularly precarious situation of Greece, but also the unsustainability of the pension systems in Ireland and the United Kingdom. The results by the commission depicted in figure 10.21 only partly include the costs of the financial crisis. Since the calculations were made, the debt taken on through stimulus and bank rescue packages have worsened the debt situation considerably.

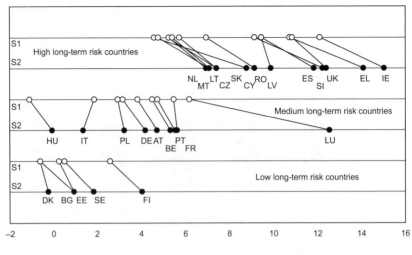

Fig. 10.21   Sustainability gap in Europe (percent GDP)
Source: European Commission (2010).

10.6   Conclusions

The major European pension systems (France, Germany, Italy, and Spain) still have some ways to go in order to become financially sustainable. This chapter has shown that this goal is achievable with a combination of reasonable policy steps. Italy, for example, has introduced a new entrants system that will stabilize pension expenditures if it is implemented consistently also in the future. Sweden, with its NDC system, has no sustainability gap. Germany has substantially reduced its implicit pension debt through a set of politically accepted gradual steps: increasing retirement age, indexing benefits to the system dependency ratio, and introducing individual-accounts-type private pensions to fill the emerging pension gap.

The recent crisis makes pension reform even more urgent. It is no coincidence that Greece and Italy are currently most under pressure. These countries have the highest pension expenditures as share of GDP in Europe. In Italy, these high pension expenditures are at least stable; but they will remain a fiscal challenge as they will not get lower for the foreseeable future and its parameters face political risks. Pension expenditures are still dramatically increasing in Greece. Without pension reform, which cuts the high share of pension expenditures in GDP, no fiscal consolidation appears possible.

There is no single "optimal pension policy" since the initial state (general welfare state design emerged through culture, history, and political preferences) and problems (pressure through demography, design flaws) differ so much among countries. Rather, the policy mix between reducing pay-as-you-go benefit levels, increasing retirement age, introducing actuarial adjustments, and establishing occupational and individual funded pensions has to be different across countries.

Moreover, restrictions differ across countries. Building up funded pensions takes time. The feasibility of a transition strategy depends on the time left until the "baby-boom bulge" will enter retirement. This differs across countries. Moreover, it depends on the current size of the pay-as-you-go pillars. The higher the pay-as-you-go share is currently, the harder is a transition during the remaining years.

What has emerged as the most effective reform? The introduction of NDC systems have reduced fiscal strain when it was done early and consistently, like in Sweden. In Italy, not only is the demographic pressure much higher, but the introduction was also effectively postponed until after the baby boom generation will have retired, and there are many loopholes in the actual implementation, for example, in the definition of the conversion rate to an annuity that leaves room for political maneuvering. The "dressing" of the reform as a new NDC system did help in the political economy situation in Sweden, and to some extent also in Italy. It failed, however, in Germany, where the taste of a funded system seems unpalatable. "Dressing" a similar reform in terms of a complex defined benefit formula was politically much easier.

Automatic stabilizers, such as the NDC systems in Sweden, Italy, and Poland, and the indexation of pension benefits to the system dependency ratio in Germany, may help to put pension systems on a long-run fiscally sustainable path since they are sheltered from day-to-day political opportunism. One may want to introduce similar automatic rules for the retirement age, such as a proportionality rule that keeps the ratio of time spent in retirement to time spent working constant. The sheltering effect, of course, goes only so far. In Germany, for example, the sustainability factor in the benefit formula has been set out of force through a "pension benefit guarantee" that rules out any nominal benefit reduction, and parts of the dynamic increase in the retirement age have been offset by the introduction of new duration-of-service rules. By and large, however, pension reforms introducing automatic stabilizers have been more successful in achieving long-term fiscal balance than those without such mechanisms.

References

Berkel, B., and A. Börsch-Supan. 2004. "Pension Reform in Germany: The Impact on Retirement Decisions." *Finanzarchiv* 60 (3): 393–421.

Blondal, S., and S. Scarpetta. 1998. "The Retirement Decision in OECD Countries." Working Papers, OECD Economics Dept., no. 202.

Blundell, R., A. Duncan, and C. Meghir. 1998. "Estimating Labor Supply Responses Using Tax Reforms." *Econometrica* 66 (4): 827–62.

Börsch-Supan, A. 2000. "Incentive Effects of Social Security on Labor Force Participation: Evidence in Germany and across Europe." *Journal of Public Economics* 78:25–49.

Börsch-Supan, A. 2005. "Suomen vuoden 2005 eläkeuudistus." ["2005 Pension Reform in Finland"]. *Kansantaloudellinen aikakauskirja* [*The Finnish Economic Journal*] 1/2005 (101): 52–71.

Börsch-Supan, A. 2007. "Rational Pension Reform." *Geneva Papers on Risk and Insurance: Issues and Practice* 4:430–46.

Börsch-Supan, A., T. Bucher-Koenen, A. Reil-Held, and C. Wilke. 2008. "Zum künftigen Stellenwert der ersten Säule im Gesamtsystem der Alterssicherung." *DRV-Schriften* Band 80:13–31.

Börsch-Supan, A., and M. Miegel, eds. 2001. *Pension Reform in Six Countries*. Heidelberg: Springer.

Börsch-Supan, A., and A. Reil-Held. 2001. "How Much is Transfer and How Much Insurance in a Pay-As-You-Go System? The German Case." *Scandinavian Journal of Economics* 130 (3): 505–24.

Börsch-Supan, A., and R. Schnabel. 1998. "Social Security and Declining Labor-Force Participation in Germany." *American Economic Review* 88:173–78.

———. 2010. "Early Retirement and Employment of the Young in Germany." In *Social Security Programs and Retirement around the World: The Relationship to Youth Employment*, edited by J. Gruber and D. A. Wise, 147–66. Chicago: University of Chicago Press.

Börsch-Supan, A., and P. Tinios. 2002. "The Greek Pension System: Strategic Framework for Reform." In *Greece's Economic Performance and Prospects,* edited by R. C. Bryant, N. C. Garganas, and G. S. Tavlas, 361–451. Bank of Greece.

Börsch-Supan, A., and C. B. Wilke. 2005. "The German Public Pension System: How It Will Become an NDC System Look-Alike." In *Pension Reform—Issues and Prospects for Non-Financial Defined Contribution (NDC) Schemes,* edited by Robert Holzmann and Edward Palmer, 573–610. Washington, DC: World Bank.

Carone, Giuseppe, Declan Costello, Nuria Diez Guardia, Per Eckefeldt, and Gilles Mourre. 2008. "Economic Growth and Fiscal Sustainability in the EU: The Impact of an Ageing Population." In *Fiscal Sustainability: Analytical Developments and Emerging Policy Issues,* edited by Daniele Franco, 169–216. Rome: Banca d'Italia [Bank of Italy].

European Commission. 2010. "Joint Report by the Economic Policy Committee (Ageing Working Group), the Social Protection Committee (Indicators Sub-Group), and the Commission services (DG for Economic and Financial Affairs and DG Employment, Social Affairs, and Equal Opportunities) on Pensions." Progress and Key Challenges in the Delivery of Adequate and Sustainable Pensions in Europe. European Economy Occasional Papers 71.

Gruber, J., and D. A. Wise, eds. 1999. *Social Security and Retirement around the World.* Chicago: University of Chicago Press.

———. 2003. *Incentive Effects of Public Pension Systems.* Chicago: University of Chicago Press.

———. 2010. *Social Security Programs and Retirement around the World: The Relationship to Youth Employment.* Chicago: University of Chicago Press.

Holzmann, Robert, and Richard Hinz. 2005. "Old-Age Income Support in the 21st Century: The World Bank's Perspective on Pension Systems and Reform." Washington, DC: World Bank.

Moog, Stefan, Christoph Müller, and Bernd Raffelhüschen. 2010. "Ehrbare Staaten? Die deutsche Generationenbilanz im internationalen Vergleich: Wie gut ist

Deutschland auf die demografische Herausforderung vorbereitet?" ["Germany's Generational Accounts in International Comparison: How Well Is Germany Prepared for Demographic Change?"] Diskussionspapier Forschungszentrum Generationenverträge, Albert-Ludwigs-Universität Freiburg.

OECD. 2011. *Pensions at a Glance.* Paris: OECD.

OECD Social Expenditure Database. 2011. SOCX, www.oecd.org/els/social /expenditure, November.

United Nations Population Division. 2001. "Replacement Migration: Is It a Solution to Declining and Ageing Populations?" New York: UN.

Werding, M. 2007. "Implicit Pension Debt and Fiscal Sustainability: An Assessment for Germany." In *Money, Finance and Demography: The Consequences of Ageing,* edited by Morten Balling, Ernest Gnan, und Frank Lierman, 147–74. Vienna: SUERF.

Comment   David A. Wise

Axel Börsch-Supan has presented a very careful summary of the pension reforms in Europe. He brings out the substantial complexity of getting from here to there. And he emphasizes two critical dimensions of pension expenditures—the level of benefits and the duration of benefits. I cannot offer important areas of improvement in his discussion. Instead I will try to add additional framing and context to his analysis. In particular, I emphasize, and hope to contribute to, an understanding of the core of the problem that has led to the need for reform. In doing this, I will focus on working lives and years in retirement, the part that lies behind what Börsch-Supan terms the duration of benefits.

The core of the problem is promises that cannot be met—social security plan provisions that promise benefits that are often unsustainable. Why? Countries did not adjust to the demographic changes that occurred over the past four decades. They did not accommodate declining mortality and increasing life expectancy. And countries did not adjust to changing health. Expansions in "work capacity" were not matched by more work. It is now too late to address the problem only by saving more. Social and economic customs must adapt to demographic trends. I will expand on three points:

1. Living longer and working less without regard to demographic trends.
2. The relationship between employment of older workers and mortality (taken as one important indicator of health).

David A. Wise is the John F. Stambaugh Professor of Political Economy at the Kennedy School of Government, Harvard University, and area director, health and retirement programs, at the National Bureau of Economic Research.

Most of the figures used in this discussion were adapted from Gruber and Wise (1999, 2007) or Milligan and Wise (2012). Figure 10C.2 was adapted from a 2007 talk at the US State Department. For acknowledgments, sources of research support, and disclosure of the author's material financial relationships, if any, please see http://www.nber.org/chapters/c12651.ack.

3. The change in employment by mortality over time and the implications for employment.

I will not discuss it further, but I emphasize that working longer not only helps to pay for all costs associated with living longer—social security and health care, for example—but also other needs, such as education of the young for which expenditure may be driven out by increasing resources allocated to older persons.

The Change in Work over Three or Four Decades

First I will return to a figure that Börsch-Supan used in his chapter. The figure shows the labor force participation (LFP) trends for men aged sixty to sixty-four from the 1960s to the early 2000s—the data are shown for twelve countries in two parts in figure 10C.1. These figures are an adaptation of those presented in Gruber and Wise (2007). I emphasize three features of the data. First, in the early 1960s the differences in labor force participation rates across countries were relatively small, most between 70 and 85 percent. This feature is marked by circles in each of the figures. Second, by the mid-1990s, however, the difference had widened greatly, ranging from about 13 percent in France to about 75 percent in Japan. Third, the labor force participation rate started to increase in each of the countries in the mid-1990s, marked by vertical lines on each of the figures. Six of the twelve countries are marked with arrows and in these countries the increase can be associated with pension reforms, changes in the provisions of the plans. But the increase in labor force participation is common to all countries, suggesting that some of the increase may be due to other forces.

The decline in work was unrelated to, and in spite of, demographic trends. Figure 10C.2 (adapted from a talk at the US State Department 2007) shows the percent increase in life expectancy of men at sixty-five, paired with the decline in the labor force participation of men age sixty to sixty-four between the 1960s and early 2000s. For example, in the United States, life expectancy increased about 30 percent over this time period and labor force participation decreased by about 28 percent. In France, life expectancy increased by 37 percent and labor force participation decreased by 77 percent.

Thus, as life expectancy increased labor force participation was declining in all countries, but the change in labor force participation across countries was unrelated to demographic trends. Figure 10C.3 shows the relationship between the percent decline in labor force participation and the percent increase in life expectancy. Excluding Japan there is essentially no relationship between the two; even including Japan the relationship is not statistically meaningful.

However, the relationship is strongly related to social security plan provisions. Figure 10C.4 (Milligan and Wise 2012) shows the relationship between

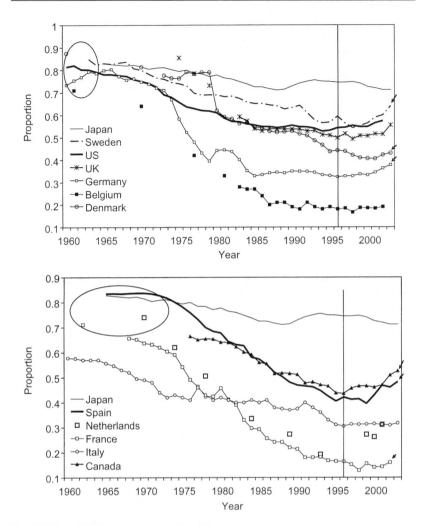

Fig. 10C.1   LFP trends for men 60 to 64

the percent decline in labor force participation and the "tax force to retire." To understand this measure it is useful to think of wage compensation for working an additional year in two components. The first is wage earnings. The second component is the increase in the expected present discounted value of promised future social security benefits. It is natural to think of this difference as positive, or at least not negative. That is, if a person works for an additional year and thus forgoes one year of benefits, it might be expected that benefits begun one year later would be increased enough to offset the fact that they are received for one fewer years. In most countries, however, the accrual is significantly negative. This is a consequence in large part of

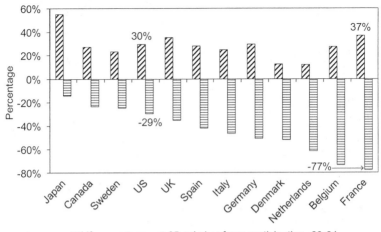

Fig. 10C.2   Increase in life expectancy and decline in labor force participation of men, 1960s to early 2000s

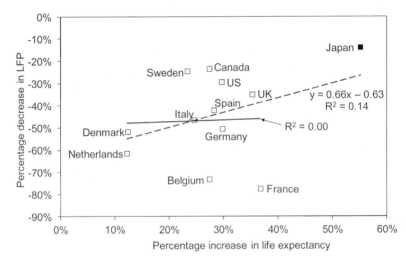

Fig. 10C.3   Change in LFP versus increase in life expectancy at 65 for men in 12 countries

not increasing benefits enough if the age of benefit receipt is delayed; that is, benefits are not actuarially fair. Thus the gain in wage earnings is partially, or even largely, offset by a loss in future social security benefits. The ratio of this loss to wage earnings (after tax) is called the social security implicit tax on earnings (Gruber and Wise 1999). In many countries this tax can be 80

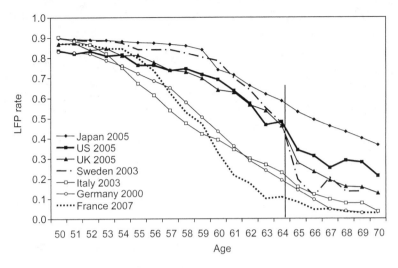

Fig. 10C.4   Employment by age for seven countries, men

percent or more at certain ages. To provide a simple summary of the country-specific incentives for early retirement, the implicit tax rates on continued work are summed from age fifty-five or at the early retirement age—when a person is first eligible for social security benefits—and running through age sixty-nine. This measure is called the "tax force" to retire (Gruber and Wise 1999). Figure 10C.4 shows that this measure—based on plan provisions in the mid-1990s—is strongly related to the decline in labor force participation over the prior three or four decades. That is, the decline in labor force participation was induced in large part by social security plan provisions.

Employment by Age versus Employment by Mortality ("Health")

I explain that the cross-country variation in both employment by age and employment by mortality are similarly related to social security plan provisions—the inducement to retire early inherent in social security plan provisions. Figure 10C.4 (adapted from Milligan and Wise 2012) shows the relationship between age and employment in seven countries. Two features of the figure stand out. First, at ages in the early fifties there was little difference across countries in the employment rate. But by age sixty-four the difference had widened greatly, ranging from about 10 percent in France to almost 60 percent in Japan.

Now consider employment by mortality. Figure 10C.5 (adapted from Milligan and Wise 2012) shows this relationship for the same seven countries. Again two features of the figures stand out. First, at the ages at which the

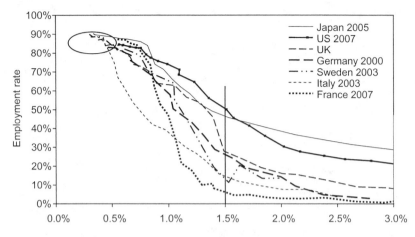

Fig. 10C.5   Employment versus mortality, selected countries, by one-year intervals

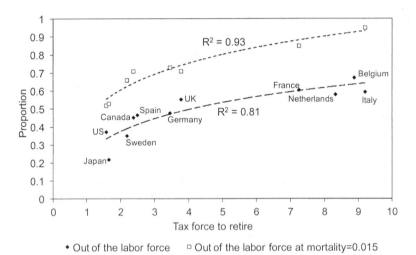

Fig. 10C.6   The tax force to retire versus: (1) men 55 to 65 not in the labor force, and (2) men not in the labor force when the mortality rate is 1.5 percent

mortality rate was about 0.5 percent, employment was very similar in all of the countries, approximately between 85 and 90 percent in each of the countries. But at the ages at which the mortality rate was 1.5 percent, the spread in the employment rate had become very large, from a low of 5 percent in France to about 50 percent in the United States.

Now consider these two relationships: (1) the relationship between the tax force to retire and the proportion of men fifty-five to sixty-five *not* in the labor force, and (2) the relationship between the tax force to retire and the proportion of men not in the labor force when the mortality rate is 1.5

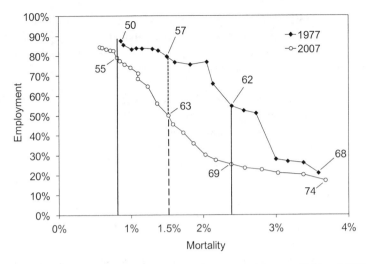

Fig. 10C.7   Employment by mortality, men in the United States, 1977 and 2007

percent. Both are shown in figure 10C.6 (adapted from Milligan and Wise 2012). The first relationship—the lower line in the figure—is as reported in Gruber and Wise (1999). The second relationship follows essentially the same pattern. That is, the incentive effects inherent in social security pension plans are a strong determinant of work by age and a strong determinant of work by health (mortality) and the one relationship essentially mimics the other. I conclude from these two relationships that mortality as a measure of health means the same thing in France and Italy as it does in the United States. If the tax force to retire were the same in France and Italy as in the United States the relationship suggests that work at older ages would be about the same in France and Italy as in the United States and work when health was the same (1.5 percent mortality) would be about the same in France and Italy as in the United States. Or put another way, if plan provisions were similar, work by mortality ("health") would be about the same in Italy and France as in the United States, Canada, and Sweden.

Change in Employment by Mortality

Figure 10C.7 (adapted from Milligan and Wise 2012) shows the employment rate by mortality in 1977 and 2007 in the United States, together with selected ages corresponding to the mortality rate in each year (adapted from Milligan and Wise 2012). For example, consider the employment rate when the mortality rate was 1.5 percent. In 1977, the employment rate was 80 percent—corresponding to age fifty-seven. In 2007, the employment rate was only 50 percent when the mortality rate was 1.5 percent—corresponding to age sixty-three. That is, the probability of being employed when the mortality rate was 1.5 percent was 0.8 in 1977 and 0.5 in 2007.[1] Thus, on average, at age sixty-three men worked 0.3 fewer years in 2007 than they did in 1977. If we add up such differences from age fifty-five to age sixty-nine, men in this age group worked on average 3.7 fewer years in 2007 than in 1977 (8.3 versus 12.0 years, a decline of 31 percent). In other words, if at each "health" level (measured by mortality) men had worked as much in 2007 as they did in 1977, average employment in the fifty-five to sixty-nine age range would have been 3.7 years greater in 2007 than it was.

Recall from figure 10C.2 that life expectancy of men at age sixty-five increased 30 percent between 1977 and 2007. Many analysts have suggested that official retirement ages—early social security and normal retirement ages—might be indexed in some way to life expectancy. If the average retirement age were in fact indexed to mortality, beginning in 1977, employment of men aged fifty-five to sixty-nine in 2007 would have been greater than employment in 1977.

The differences in employment by "health" between countries are also very large. For example, if employment by mortality level in 2007 had been the same in France as in the United States, employment in France in the fifty-five to sixty-nine age range would have been 4.62 years larger than it was.

In summary, the need for reform of social security systems now has developed over time because countries failed to adapt to the demographic tidal wave that rolled over most countries in the past four or five decades. Countries did not adjust institutional and economic policies to accommodate the demographic imperative, declining mortality and increasing life expectancy. Instead, living longer was accompanied by working less. Better health and expansions in "work capacity" were not matched by more work. Now, working longer will likely be a component of reform in virtually all countries, consistent with Axel H. Börsch-Supan's excellent summary and discussion.

References

Gruber, J., and D. A. Wise. 1999. "Introduction and Summary." In *Social Security and Retirement around the World,* edited by J. Gruber and D. A. Wise, 1–35. Chicago: University of Chicago Press.

Gruber, J., and D. A. Wise. 2007. "Introduction and Summary." In *Social Security Programs and Retirement around the World: Fiscal Implications,* edited by J. Gruber and D. A. Wise, 1–42. Chicago: University of Chicago Press.

Milligan, Kevin, and David A. Wise. 2012. "Health and Work at Older Ages: Using Mortality to Assess Employment Capacity across Countries." NBER Working Paper no. 18229. Cambridge, MA: National Bureau of Economic Research, July.

1. Looking at the data another way, consider the age at which 50 percent of men were employed. In 2007, the mortality rate at the age when 50 percent of men were employed was 2.7 percent; thirty years later in 2007, the mortality rate was only 1.5 percent. That is to say, for the employment rate to be 50 percent in 2007, men "had to be" much healthier (by the mortality measure) than they were in 1977.

"Fiscal Devaluation" and Fiscal Consolidation
The VAT in Troubled Times

Ruud de Mooij and Michael Keen

11.1   Introduction

In the aftermath of the financial crisis and in the midst of sovereign debt tensions—amounting to full-blown crisis for some Eurozone members—fiscal policy in many advanced economies is a high-stakes game played under severe constraints. In order to achieve long-term fiscal sustainability, there is a need for substantial fiscal consolidation, to both reduce levels of public debt and provide space to address looming pension and (especially) health expenditure needs associated with aging.[1] Figure 11.1, setting out an illustrative adjustment path for the average advanced economy, illustrates the scope of the former challenge. At the same time, fostering growth is a key to both reducing hardship and improving debt dynamics.

For the shorter term, several countries face immediate and severe unemployment problems: above-average fiscal deficits are found along with above-average unemployment rates in the United States, France, Portugal, Greece, Ireland, Slovak Republic, and Spain (figure 11.2). For these countries, rapid

Ruud de Mooij is deputy division chief in the Tax Policy Division of the Fiscal Affairs Department at the International Monetary Fund. Michael Keen is deputy director of the Fiscal Affairs Department, International Monetary Fund.

We are grateful to Leon Bettendorf, Carlo Cottarelli, Julio Escolano, Alexander Klemm, Daniel Leigh, Jim Poterba, Mick Thackray, Florian Wöhlbier, and participants in the NBER conference, "Fiscal Policy after the Financial Crisis," for useful comments and suggestions, and to Oana Luca for excellent research assistance. Views expressed here are those of the authors and should not be attributed to the IMF, its executive board, or its management. For acknowledgments, sources of research support, and disclosure of the authors' material financial relationships, if any, please see http://www.nber.org/chapters/c12646.ack.

1. Public health care spending in advanced countries is projected to increase, on average, by about 3 percent of GDP over the next twenty years and by 6.5 percent over the next forty years (IMF 2010c). Public pension costs are expected to rise by 2.4 percent of GDP during the next fifty years in Europe (European Commission 2009).

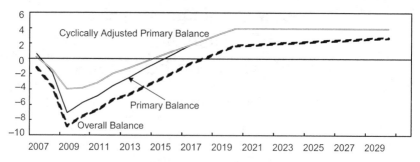

Fig. 11.1   Fiscal consolidation in advanced economies

Source: IMF (2011b).

Note: Figure shows a path of average balances that would reduce gross public debt to the lower of 60 percent or the precrisis level (and net debt to 80 percent of GDP in Japan).

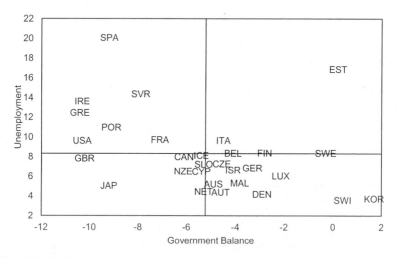

Fig. 11.2   Deficits and unemployment in advanced economies

Source: IMF World Economic Outlook database.

Notes: Data refer to 2010, except for Ireland where the projected deficit in 2011 is taken.

fiscal consolidation risks impeding economic recovery and raising unemployment, while slow adjustment risks losing market confidence, triggering higher spreads, and inducing a nasty circle of higher spending and worsening deficits. Over the medium and longer terms, growth is critical to improving the debt dynamics, reducing the relative scale of adjustment needed. And underlying poor growth performance in many countries are structural problems that are especially pronounced in some of the troubled Eurozone countries, and made evident in their sustained trade deficits: Greece and Portugal, for instance, ran trade deficits prior to their crises in the order of 11 percent of GDP.

All this poses substantial challenges for the detailed design of a wide range of tax and expenditure policies. For the latter, the core challenges are to reparameterize public pension schemes and, conceptually much harder, limit rising health costs. On the tax side—the focus of this chapter—the need is to identify reforms that strengthen the fiscal position while being, if not growth-promoting, at least minimally distortionary and growth-retarding, while respecting equity concerns.

The purpose here is not to review the full range of tax options to support fiscal sustainability: this is done, for instance, in IMF (2010b) and Cottarelli and Keen (2011). Instead the focus is on two key issues surrounding some of the core instruments that, ultimately, will have to bear the brunt of adjustment, and in the redesign of which can be seen real prospects for meeting the consolidation, growth, and structural challenges.

The first issue is the potential value and effectiveness of revenue-neutral tax shifts in addressing competitiveness and employment problems. Certainly there is strong evidence that labor taxation is harmful for employment (see, for instance, Nickell and Layard 1999; Bassanini and Duval 2006; and OECD 2011)—although there are several subtleties in this relationship and interactions with labor-market institutions are important—which has led to increased interest in reducing labor taxation in general and social contributions in particular. So too has the perception that high labor costs are a key structural problem in several of the troubled Eurozone countries, with their reduction seen as a way to ease and accelerate the needed adjustment. Measures of this sort have featured in stimulus programs and indeed in 2010 eight OECD countries reduced the social contribution rate (SCR) for employers. The difficulty, of course, is that cutting social contributions runs counter to consolidation objectives, and is quite simply not affordable in many of the countries in the upper left corner of figure 11.2. The question, then, is whether there exist "tax shifts" combining such a cut with increases in revenue from other sources that do not offset the beneficial labor market and competitiveness effects. In Europe, this has led to prominent proposals for "fiscal devaluations"—sometimes also referred to as "internal devaluations" or, in France, a "social VAT"—in the form of a revenue-neutral (or revenue-enhancing) shift from social contributions to the VAT (value added tax). This was a major element, for instance, of Portugal's initial arrangement with the IMF (International Monetary Fund). Section 11.2 explores the theoretical case for tax shifts of this kind, provides what appears to be the first empirical analysis of whether and how these and other tax shifts might affect trade performance, and discusses some of the detailed design issues that arise in practice.[2]

The second set of issues concern the VAT itself. This has already emerged as a focus of consolidation efforts in the EU, and its greater use or introduction are widely viewed as leading options (indispensible, in the views of

---

2. A brief account and an assessment can also be found in ECB (2011).

some) for fiscal sustainability in both Japan and the United States, respectively. In Europe, a strengthening of the VAT would be required for countries that aim at a substantial tax shift along the lines of a fiscal devaluation. The aim in section 11.3 is therefore to assess the merits of the VAT in achieving consolidation, growth, and fairness objectives and, more particularly, to develop and begin to apply a methodology for diagnosing weaknesses in VAT design and implementation so as to find ways to these ends that are likely to be less distortionary and fairer than raising the standard rate from levels that are in many cases already very high. Conclusions on these two issues are set out briefly in section 11.4.

11.2   Fiscal Devaluation: Tax Shifts to Promote Employment and Competitiveness

The rise in unemployment rates during the crisis has led many countries to implement job strategies to reverse these developments. These often include reductions in the social contributions paid by employers (SCR rates) as well as wage subsidy schemes. For instance, the OECD *Employment Outlook 2010* reports that twelve countries expanded their job subsidy programs in 2010, while, as noted earlier, another eight reduced their SCR rates. The underlying hope, of course, is that lower labor costs will raise labor demand, reduce unemployment, and (for Eurozone countries facing deep structural problems) improve international competitiveness. But, in direct terms at least, cutting SCR rates is revenue-losing. This raises the question of whether, without negating the hoped-for beneficial effects of an SCR cut, revenue could be preserved, or even increased, by at the same time increasing the VAT (or perhaps some other suitable revenue source). The potential effectiveness and design of such a fiscal devaluation has become an urgent issue: it has been presented as one of the few options left for Eurozone countries faced with dire fiscal, unemployment, and competitiveness problems.

11.2.1   Fiscal Devaluation—in Principle

The Basic Argument

The idea that tax changes can, to some degree, mimic the effect of a devaluation is not new. In 1931, Keynes noted that the combination of an import tariff and an export subsidy has much the same effect, raising the domestic price of importables and reducing the foreign price of exportables.[3] But explicit taxes on trade—tariffs in any event clearly ruled out for most countries by trade commitments—are not needed to have this effect: discussion of the appropriate regime for commodity taxation in the European Union

---

3. Laker (1981) provides an early review of the literature on fiscal measures to replicate a nominal devaluation.

prompted a recognition that moving from the taxation of final goods, at a uniform rate, on an origin basis—that is, according to where they are produced—to their taxation on a destination basis—according to where they are consumed—is essentially equivalent to an exchange rate devaluation: such a shift brings imports into tax, and takes exports out.[4] With such changes in commodity taxation ruled out by adoption of the destination base as the international norm for commodity taxation, the next device that suggests itself is to shift away from production-based taxes effectively levied on an origin basis, offsetting the revenue loss as need be by increasing broad-based destination-based taxes, the most obvious (but not only) candidate for the latter role being the VAT. This is the essence of a fiscal devaluation.

The classic form of fiscal devaluation as it has been discussed in Europe combines a reduction in the SCR with an increase in the VAT sufficient to at least preserve government revenue. The focus on the employers' social contribution—rather than the employee's, or even personal taxes on labor income—reflects a view that the relevant rigidity comes from contracts specified in terms of payment *net* of the SCR.[5] The reduction in the SCR is assumed to be fully passed on as a reduction in gross labor costs, and then into output prices, so that, with the exchange rate fixed, the foreign currency price of exports falls correspondingly; the increased VAT does not dampen this effect, since—as a destination-based tax—it simply does not apply to exports. The reduced SCR also reduces the producer price of domestically produced goods sold in the home market, while leaving the producer price of competing imports unaffected; and since the increased VAT applies equally to both imports and domestically produced goods, the combined effect is an increase in the relative consumer price of imported goods. Thus exports become cheaper abroad and imports more expensive at home. The effect is not precisely equivalent to an exchange rate depreciation:[6] there is no change, for instance, in the foreign currency value of assets denominated in the domestic currency, and the fiscal devaluation is likely to affect relative producer prices (reflecting differing labor intensities) in a way that a nominal devaluation would not. Nonetheless, the direct impact on the trade balance could be expected to be much the same.

The effectiveness of this strategy, it should be stressed, requires rigidity in *both* the exchange rate and the nominal wage. With a flexible exchange rate, the increased demand for exports and reduced demand for imports prompted by this tax shift would cause an appreciation of the nominal exchange rate that undoes its competitiveness impact. And even if the exchange rate is

4. Calmfors (1998) recognized long ago the potential for countries adopting the euro to engineer effective devaluations in this way.

5. If instead the net wage received by the worker were supposed fixed, a cut in the employee's contribution (SCE) or personal income tax (PIT) would do just as well.

6. Fahri, Gopinath, and Itskhoki (2011) establish conditions under which tax shifts of this kind can precisely replicate a nominal devaluation; with foreign holding of domestically-denominated assets of this kind, these include a partial default.

fixed, a fiscal devaluation will have no real effect if—or when—domestic wages adjust, as one would expect them to do: as workers find their real wage reduced by the increased VAT rate, they (or their unions) will aim to increase their nominal wages, moving the real producer wage back toward the pre-reform equilibrium (a process that any wage indexation, of course, would accelerate). In the meantime, a fiscal devaluation would be expected to reduce unemployment and improve the trade balance; but, because of this wage adjustment, to have little long-run impact on product or labor market outcomes.[7]

That the effects of a fiscal devaluation are likely to be largely temporary does not mean they must be unimportant. Temporary effects could last some time. Moreover, the case for fiscal devaluation may be especially strong when the economy, owing to downward rigidities in nominal wages, is initially in marked disequilibrium, with a highly overvalued real exchange rate and extensive involuntary unemployment. A fiscal devaluation could then accelerate needed adjustments. The end result—the point to which the real exchange rate and the unemployment rate converge in the long run—may not be much affected by the fiscal devaluation, but the convergence could be much faster. Quick improvement and adjustment is critical in countries where doubts may otherwise arise on the sustainability of the adjustment process under a pegged exchange rate.

A Closer Look

To explore further the analytics of a fiscal devaluation and guide the later empirics, this section considers the impact of a tax shift away from the SCR toward the VAT in the setting of a small, two-period open economy with a representative consumer, with features key to the previous argument. Production in period t is characterized by a revenue function $R(P_t, L_t)$ defined on and homogeneous of degree one in the N-vector[8] of world prices P_t (exogenous and fixed throughout) and labor use L; the fixed exchange rate is normalized at unity. For simplicity, the discount rate is assumed to be zero, so that the $2N$-vector of present value producer prices over the two periods is $P \equiv (P_1', P_2')'$. Labor supply in each period is inelastic in amount $\bar{L}$. In period 2 there is (for simplicity) no taxation of labor, and the labor market clears. In period 1, however, there is a fixed nominal wage W and a tax T^r (thought of as the SCR) levied on top of this, with the two leaving the price of labor above the market-clearing rate $R_L(P, \bar{L})$. Employment $L_1(T^r)$ is then determined from

(2.1) $R_L(P_1, L_1) = W + T^r,$

7. To the extent that a VAT increase acts as a lump sum tax on accumulated assets at the time of the increase, there could be a permanent effect from a reduced need to use distorting taxes.
8. Vectors are column vectors, a prime indicating transposition. Derivatives are indicated by subscripts for functions of many variables, by a prime for functions of just one.

so that (suppressing P here and elsewhere)

$$(2.2) \qquad L_1'(T^r) = \frac{1}{R_{LL}} < 0,$$

meaning that a cut in the SCR increases employment in the first period. Though in practice levied in ad valorem form, it is convenient to characterize the VAT as a vector of specific taxes, $T^v \equiv (T_1^v, T_2^v)'$. Consumer prices,[9] assumed fully flexible to changes in VAT rates, are then $Q = P + T^v$. Preferences are characterized by an expenditure function $E(Q, U)$, U denoting utility; compensated demands are thus $E_Q(Q, U)$.

Revenue from the SCR and VAT is assumed to be returned to the consumer as a lump sum.[10] Since these are not the only taxes levied in practice, for structuring the empirics it is useful to allow for another tax instrument, the simplest way being to suppose that a lump sum tax in amount $(1 + \gamma)A_t$ is levied in period t but returned to the consumer only in amount A_t, with $\gamma \geq 0$ being an ad hoc characterization of some associated inefficiency. With perfect capital markets, the consumer's budget constraint thus implies

$$(2.3) \qquad E(P + T^v, U) = R(\bar{L}) + R(L_1(T^r)) + T^{v'} E_Q(P + T^v, U) - \gamma A,$$

where $A \equiv A_1 + A_2$. The value at world prices of net exports in period 1[11] is thus (recalling that outputs are given by the price derivatives of the revenue function)

$$(2.4) \qquad N_1 = P_1'(R_p(L_1(T^r) - E_{Q_1}(Q, U)).$$

The question of interest is how N_1 is affected by reducing T^r and increasing T^v.

For this, it is shown in appendix A that, for arbitrary small changes in the available tax instruments,

$$(2.5) \qquad dN = \beta_r dT^r + \beta_v' dT^v + \beta_A dA$$

where

$$(2.6) \qquad \beta_r \equiv -\Omega\left(1 - \frac{P_1' E_{QU}}{P' E_{QU}}\right)L_1$$

$$(2.7) \qquad \beta_v' \equiv -P_1' E_{Q_1 Q} + (P_2' E_{Q_2 Q} + P_1' E_{Q_1 Q})\left(\frac{P_1' E_{QU}}{P' E_{QU}}\right)$$

---

9. With the fixed nominal wage, there is no need for an additional normalization of consumer prices.

10. Having revenues instead finance the provision of some good that enters preferences adds only complexities.

11. No assumption is made on the sign of net exports in period 1. Used in (2.3), linear homogeneity of the expenditure and revenue functions implies that trade is balanced over the two periods (aside from the γ term, since this is pure waste).

(2.8)
$$\beta_A \equiv \gamma \left(\frac{P_1' E_{Q_1 U}}{P' E_{QU}} \right) > 0,$$

and $\Omega \equiv -R_L/(LR_{LL}) > 0$ denotes the elasticity of labor demand.

To interpret the effects in equations (2.6) through (2.8), it is helpful to begin with that of an increase in the unmodeled "other" tax A. The distortionary impact of this lowers lifetime consumer welfare by γ, leading to reduced demand and so tending to increase net exports; how much of this reduced demand occurs in period 1, however—and thus increases the value of net exports then—depends on the proportion of that reduced expenditure that occurs in period 1, given by $P_1' E_{Q_1 U}/P' E_{QU}$; loosely, the improvement in period 1 net exports is greater the larger is the marginal propensity to consume in that period.

Turning to β_r, an increase in the employers' contribution tends to reduce period 1 net exports, and, as one would expect, by a larger amount the more elastic is the demand for labor. The effect is smaller, however, the greater is the marginal propensity to consume in period 1; this is because the distortionary effect of such an increase leads to a reduction in welfare that triggers demand effects of the kind just described, which tend to increase net exports. Under the very weak assumption that the marginal propensity to consume in period 2 is strictly positive, however, the direct effect through the demand for labor dominates, so that $\beta_r < 0$: a higher SCR unambiguously reduces net exports in period 1.

Equation (2.7) shows that an arbitrary change in the $2N$-vector of VAT rates T^v affects net exports in two ways. The first is the direct impact on period 1 demand, which, through the $(N \times 2N)$-matrix $E_{Q_1 Q}$, reflects not only within-period effects from changes in period 1 prices (through $E_{Q_1 Q_1}$) but also substitution effects from the change in period 2 prices (through $E_{Q_1 Q_2}$). The second channel is the impact on first period demand, again reflecting relative marginal propensities to consume, of the welfare loss from the distortions induced by the change in T^v. Unsurprisingly, the impact of a change dT^v in the VAT structure thus depends on the details of that change and on the structure of demand responses. Raising the tax on items with highly elastic compensated demand, for instance, will do more to reduce net exports than doing so on those in inelastic demand; and intertemporal substitution effects will come into play when consumer prices are raised by differing proportionate amounts in the two periods.

There is, however, one special case in which the effect of a VAT reform is unambiguous—that in which $dT^v = \mu Q$, for some scalar μ; that is, in which the effect is to increase all consumer prices by the same proportion. Since linear homogeneity of the expenditure function implies that $E_{Q_1 Q} Q = 0$, in this case $\beta_y' dT^v = 0$; there is then no effect on net exports, the reason being that such a tax change is equivalent to a lump sum tax. And the most obvious case in which a VAT reform cause an equiproportionate increase in all consumer prices is when it is levied at a uniform (tax-exclusive) rate, τ, in both periods, so that $dT^v = Q(d\tau/(1 + \tau))$. This result—that increasing the rate of a VAT applied to all commodities has no impact on net exports—is elegant, but its practical relevance is open to doubt: most VATs are from being levied at a uniform rate.

What, then, is the effect of a fiscal devaluation, in the sense of a reduction in T^r combined with a change in T^v that maintains revenue unchanged? No general results appear to be available, in that while the cut in the employers' contribution increases net exports, simply imposing on dT^v the further requirement of maintaining overall revenue does not remove the dependence on the complexities of design and demand responses just discussed. In the special case of a uniform VAT (or, more generally, a reform that raises all consumer prices by the same proportion), however, the ambiguity vanishes, since then $dN = \beta_r dT_r > 0$: only the effect of the cut in the employer's contribution remains, and a fiscal devaluation—indeed, any shift toward the VAT, even if not revenue-neutral—increases period 1 net exports. It is also, as shown in appendix A, welfare-improving.[12]

Other Considerations

There are other important features of reality ignored in the model. Some affect the purposive design of tax shifts, and these are taken up in subsection 11.2.3, others impact the positive analysis of tax changes that may be reflected in the empirics.

Prominent among the latter is the neglect of nontradables. Feldstein and Krugman (1990) argue, for instance, that tradables are generally taxed more heavily under the VAT than are nontradables; and indeed nine EU Member States currently make use of special provisions enabling the application of reduced rates to specified nontradable labor-intensive services. In these circumstances, a higher standard VAT rate will reduce the relative consumer price of nontradables, encouraging substitution out of tradables. This is not the only possibility, however. In some cases, reduced VAT rates apply to tradables, such as zero-rated food in the United Kingdom. The net direction of the impact of an increase in the standard rate of VAT on net exports is then unclear. The presence of nontradables also complicates the impact of the SCR cut. If, as could plausibly be the case, the production of these is relatively labor-intensive, then the reduction in the SCR will differentially

---

12. This analysis is greatly simplified, it should be noted, by the assumption of inelastic labor supply: this means that labor supply effects have no impact on employment not only in period 1, when this is demand-determined, but in period 2 as well. Suppose, for instance, that labor supply is instead assumed sensitive (only) to the period 2 wage and consumer prices. Introducing a small, uniform rate VAT in the presence of a preexisting labor tax $T^r > 0$ will then tend to reduce both labor supply in period 2 and, because of the increased efficiency cost of the labor tax, lifetime welfare. Net exports in period 2 would then be expected to fall, with a corresponding increase in period 1 net exports that reflects the income effect on commodity demands.

promote their production. This, then, limits the tendency for an improved trade balance.

More generally, just as the VAT is far more complex than a tax applied at a single rate to all consumption (a point explored in more detail in section 11.3), so the structure of the employer's social contribution is often more complex than can be described, as the earlier theory presumes, by a single parameter. There may be an upper limit on contributions, for instance, and, still more fundamentally, to the extent that payment is requited by the expectation of future benefits, the incentive effects of social contributions may be quite different from those of a tax on labor (Disney 2004).

Issues of timing and compliance are also critical. For instance, a permanent VAT increase that is announced in advance may induce households to bring their consumption forward in anticipation of the higher consumer prices. This could have temporary adverse effects on net exports (experiences of this sort being recounted in section 11.3.3). On the other hand, a VAT increase that is implemented instantaneously and announced as being a temporary measure may lead consumers to postpone their consumption, so that the improvement in the current account will be reinforced. Tax compliance is generally negatively correlated with tax rates. Hence, increases in the standard VAT rate may exacerbate tax evasion and avoidance, while lower SCR rates may improve compliance. The net impact is not a priori clear, and is likely to vary with countries' circumstances and administrative capacity: greater noncompliance in the VAT may be especially problematic, for instance, where the standard VAT rate is already high and the capacity to collect taxes other than by withholding is weak.

It should be stressed also that the VAT, although it has been the focus of debate, is not the only way in which the revenue lost by a cut in SCR can be recouped without necessarily offsetting the impact on net exports. Broadly, any tax that does not directly affect labor costs would have the same effect, such as excises on the consumption of some particular commodity or taxes on residential property.[13] The wider issue raised by the fiscal devaluation debate—on which the empirical results will also be reported following—is that of how the full range of tax instruments may affect trade performance.

11.2.2   Tax Effects on Net Exports—Empirics

There is substantial evidence that reductions in labor taxation can increase employment. But there is almost no empirical evidence bearing on the likely trade impact of a fiscal devaluation, or on trade impacts of tax reforms more generally.

Several papers do, however, bear on some aspects of the issue. Poterba, Rotemberg, and Summers (1986) explore how the mix between taxes on

---

13. Keen and Syed (2006), for example, find a complex pattern of effects on net exports associated with changes in corporate taxation.

producers and consumers affects prices and wages, as a way of testing for the presence of nominal rigidities. They find such rigidities to be important, suggesting that assumptions underlying the case for a fiscal devaluation may indeed—or at least did—hold reasonably good in practice. Alesina and Perotti (1997) find that labor tax variables increase unit labor costs in a panel of OECD (Organization for Economic Cooperation and Development) countries, thus also supporting the presence of real wage rigidities. The effect, however, is only found to be significant in countries with an intermediate level of wage bargaining, as opposed to centralized or decentralized bargaining. Neither paper looks at the trade effects of the tax mix. Lane and Perotti (1998 and 2003) estimate net export equations using cross-country panels, but look only at total labor taxes and not at all at consumption taxes. Keen and Syed (2006) explore the impact of corporate taxes and the VAT on net exports, finding that the mix between the two matters significantly for the trade balance in the short run. But they do not include social contributions in their analysis. Franco (2011) estimates a number of VAR (vector autoregression) equations with Portuguese data and then simulates the impact of an SCR reduction and an offsetting increase in the VAT on both exports and imports. The analysis here is similar, but focuses on the full set of OECD countries, differences between exchange rate regimes, and a wider range of tax instruments.

Methodology

The aim in what follows is to look to the data for signs of whether tax changes appear to affect net exports in ways consistent with the rationale offered for fiscal devaluations, as set out earlier.

Allowing for the potentially complex dynamics, the previous analysis suggests regressions of the single equation error correction form:

$$(2.9) \quad \Delta N_{it} = \lambda N_{i,t-1} + \beta_{Dr}\Delta SCR_{it} + \beta_{Dv}\Delta VAT_{it} + \beta_{Lr}SCR_{it-1} + \beta_{Lv}VAT_{it-1}$$
$$+ \beta'_{DX}\Delta X_{i,t} + \beta'_{LX}X_{i,t-1} + \alpha_i + \varepsilon_t + u_{it},$$

where i and t index, respectively, countries and time, N again denotes net exports, SCR indicates the employer's social contribution, and VAT the value added tax (both variously measured, as described later), and α_i and ε_t are country and time fixed effects. Among the controls in X are the revenue from other taxes, denoted A, and the government balance (positive for a surplus) BAL.[14] This structure allows for a rich dynamic pattern of responses to tax changes.[15] The contemporaneous impact of an increase in some tax variable k is given by the coefficient on the differenced tax variable, β_{Dk}, and

14. The real exchange rate is not included in the regressions, since this is the route through which tax changes are expected, at least in part, to take effect.

15. Tax changes may also have indirect effects on net exports by affecting future values of (endogenous but predetermined) variables in X: they might induce a reduction in growth, for instance, that leads, indirectly, to a future effect on net exports. These are not captured here.

the long-run impact is given by the coefficient on the lagged tax variable relative to that on the lagged dependent variable, $\beta_{Lk}/-\lambda$ (unless $\lambda = 0$, in which case the short- and long-run effects are the same).

The arguments in subsection 11.2.1 give reason to expect both SCR-related coefficients β_{Dr} and β_{Lr} to be negative; the immediate impact of a VAT increase β_{Dv}, might be expected to be small or zero, while the longer-term impact β_{Lv}, reflecting the unwinding of effects in the labor market, might be negative. The earlier arguments also imply that β_A be positive but perhaps small. While the previous model allows no role for BAL, it is included in the empirics to allow for non-Ricardian effects: empirical studies generally report a positive effect of the government balance on the current account (see, for example, chapter 4 of IMF 2011b). Including the government balance means that the coefficients on the tax terms are to be interpreted as identifying effects conditional on other measures to maintain the government balance unchanged. Also included among the controls X are variables that have become fairly standard in the international trade literature,[16] such as the dependency ratio (DEP, the population over sixty-five relative to that between fifteen and sixty-five), the growth rate of GDP (GROWTH), and, in some regressions, unemployment (UNEMPL).

Following Lane and Perotti (1998 and 2003), we allow responses in (2.9) to differ according to the exchange rate regime. Given the particular interest in fiscal devaluation in Eurozone countries, we distinguish between country-years of Eurozone membership and its complement. Coefficients related to the SCR and VAT, and on the lagged dependent variable, are estimated separately for euro and non-euro observations by interacting them with respective dummies.[17] To check the importance of the restriction imposed by this approach, of identical coefficients for euro and non-euro observations for all other variables (including other taxes and the fiscal balance), appendix B reports results where the sample is split into Eurozone and non-Eurozone countries, allowing all coefficients to vary between the two sets: the results are somewhat less robust than those in the following text.

The data set, described in appendix C, is an unbalanced panel of thirty OECD countries between 1965 and 2009. For the net export series, the Im-Pesaran-Shin statistic suggests that not all countries have a unit root. Looking at the individual time series, a unit root cannot be rejected for eighteen countries, including many of those currently in the Eurozone; for non-euro countries, however, the unit root is typically rejected. This is as one might expect—shocks to net exports are more persistent when the nomi-

16. See, for example, Chinn and Prasad (2003), Gruber and Kamin (2007), and Lee et al. (2008).

17. We also ran regressions for an alternative classification of exchange rate regimes, based on Ilzetzki, Reinhart, and Rogoff (2008). The results are partially consistent with larger effects in fixed exchange rate regimes, but not for all regimes. However, the sample size for some categories is rather small, so that results might be less reliable.

nal exchange rate cannot move—and allowing the coefficient on the lagged dependent variable to differ across the two regimes provides room for this effect. These time series properties also suggest that wages are not flexible enough to offset the effect of a rigid exchange rate, providing tentative indication of scope for a fiscal devaluation to have some effect.

In estimating (2.9), two alternative measures of the tax variables of central interest, SCR and VAT, are used. First, we use data on the shares of their respective revenues in GDP, based on either actual or cyclically adjusted data. This has two significant advantages. The first is that the revenue raised by some tax instrument is a summary indicator of the whole range of complex features of its rate and base. The second is that the impact on net exports of a shift between revenue sources that leaves total revenue unchanged can be seen easily by combining coefficients. The short-run impact of reducing the employers' social contribution by 1 percent of GDP and recovering the revenue from increasing the VAT, for instance, is simply the difference in the coefficients on the changes in tax revenues from these sources:

(2.10) $$\theta_S = \beta_{D,\text{VAT}} - \beta_{D,\text{SCR}},$$

while the long-run effect, from the lagged terms, is:

(2.11) $$\theta_L = -\left(\frac{\beta_{L,\text{SCR}} - \beta_{L,\text{VAT}}}{\lambda} \right).$$

The second approach is to use the main statutory rates of SCR and VAT. These do not capture changes in the base of either the VAT or the SCR, or in changes other than the standard rates at which they are charged, that might be expected to have effects similar to those set out in the previous model. Moreover, the impact of a shift between revenue sources on net exports cannot be read directly from the regressions; instead, assumptions must be made on the expected revenue from changes in tax rates and impacts inferred from combinations of rate changes that would be expected to be revenue-neutral. This approach may, however, have merit in addressing endogeneity issues.

Endogeneity is a pervasive and well-known problem in macro regressions of the kind explored here, calling for great caution in interpreting causality. The ratio of actual tax revenue to GDP, in particular, may well be correlated with the error term u, leading to biased and inconsistent estimators: shocks that cause export demand to fall, for instance, might also result in lower social contributions as employment falls. We cannot claim to have resolved the problem, but do seek to mitigate the endogeneity bias in several ways. First, the inclusion of GDP growth as a control should to some degree reduce biases from this source. Second, so should estimation by the system GMM (generalized method of moments) method of Arellano and Bover (1995) and Blundell and Bond (1998), which uses a system comprising both the first-differenced equation and the model in levels to estimate (2.9); this also addresses potential inconsistency arising from correlation of the lagged dependent variable with the fixed effects. The standard rate of VAT and the marginal SCR rate are used as external instruments in these regressions. Third, we use in our preferred regressions cyclically adjusted revenue data, reported in the OECD *Economic Outlook,* as an alternative to actual revenue data. By filtering revenues for cyclical effects, this corrects for one important source of endogeneity in the independent variable. It does not entirely remove the possibility of endogeneity, however, since policy responses that affect the cyclically adjusted balance may be made in light of expected developments in net exports. For this reason, as well as for comparability with the results using actual revenue data,[18] we again report results using the system GMM estimator. However, in this case we also report fixed effects regressions in which tax variables are not instrumented (but in which GDP growth is instrumented with its lagged value). Finally, using tax rates, rather than revenues, may be the best way to avoid endogeneity since it eliminates effects working directly though common shocks affecting tax bases (though the issue of endogenous policy responses remains). This potential advantage of using tax rates must be weighed, however, against their potential inadequacy in summarizing policy or administrative measures affecting these instruments.

Results

Table 11.1 reports estimates of (2.9). Regressions using raw revenue data are presented in column (1), those using cyclically adjusted revenue data in columns (2), (3), and (4), and those using statutory rates in (5).[19] The Sargan test for overidentification and Arellano-Bond statistic for second-order serial correlation are encouraging, except for the raw data in column (1) where the Sargan test cannot reject overidentification. In all cases, and despite efforts to minimize the number of instruments, the very high Hansen statistic points to weak instruments and potential finite sample bias (toward the least squares results), although the Hansen falls noticeably below 1 in column (5). This is likely a lesser concern in columns (2) to (5), insofar as these alternative revenue measures seem inherently less prone to endogeneity issues.

Control variables contribute little to the regressions in table 11.1. One might expect a higher dependency ratio to be associated with lower net exports as a result of net dissaving by the elderly. The coefficient is indeed negative, but insignificant. Perhaps more surprising is that GDP growth is insignificant. Revenue from sources other than the SCR and VAT is insignifi-

18. This, however, may not be too great a concern given the fairly long time dimension.
19. Time effects are not included in the results reported here. Their inclusion does not greatly change the results, as GDP growth picks up common trends. The coefficient on SCR becomes slightly larger, suggesting that part of the trade effect associated with tax changes operates through changed GDP growth, but there is a sizable reduction in degrees of freedom and the diagnostics for second-order serial correlation and overidentification become poorer.

Table 11.1 Fiscal devaluation and net exports

	Tax-GDP ratios		Cyclically adjusted series		Tax rates
	(1)	(2)	(3)	(4)	(5)
L.N × Euro	-0.18*** (0.07)	-0.10** (0.05)	-0.09*** (0.03)	-0.15*** (0.03)	-0.24 (0.28)
L.N × Non-E	-0.27* (0.15)	-0.21* (0.12)	-0.13 (0.09)	-0.22*** (0.05)	-0.25 (0.21)
ΔSCR × Euro	-2.97* (1.59)	-3.42*** (1.26)	-2.66*** (0.78)	-0.75* (0.44)	-0.11 (0.12)
L.SCR × Euro	-0.22** (0.10)	-0.13 (0.10)	-0.23 (0.19)	-0.16 (0.13)	-0.08 (0.10)
ΔVAT × Euro	0.47 (0.92)	0.56 (1.00)	-0.04 (0.49)	-0.39 (0.27)	0.23** (0.11)
L.VAT × Euro	0.10 (0.14)	0.05 (0.17)	0.09 (0.10)	0.07 (0.13)	0.10 (0.16)
ΔSCR × Non-E	-2.49 (1.56)	-2.84** (1.30)	-2.11*** (0.81)	-0.65** (0.27)	0.03 (0.12)
L.SCR × Non-E	0.03 (0.14)	-0.06 (0.11)	-0.17 (0.23)	-0.06 (0.08)	-0.02 (0.03)
ΔVAT × Non-E	-0.01 (0.92)	-0.05 (0.94)	-0.62 (0.54)	-0.49*** (0.13)	0.01 (0.09)
L.VAT × Non-E	-0.11 (0.23)	-0.03 (0.17)	0.05 (0.14)	-0.01 (0.06)	0.01 (0.08)
ΔUNEMPL			0.79 (0.72)		
L.UNEMPL			-0.10 (0.20)		
ΔSCR × UNEMPL			-0.02 (0.08)		
L.SCR × UNEMPL			0.01 (0.02)		
ΔDEP	-26.2 (53.4)	-31.9 (52.8)	-12.6 (40.5)	-21.1 (30.3)	-5.7 (43.6)
L.DEP	-6.06 (7.63)	-11.63 (8.11)	-5.03 (4.40)	1.60 (6.10)	-15.5 (13.5)
ΔBAL	0.11 (0.17)	-0.09 (0.23)	0.24 (0.16)	0.11 (0.10)	-0.37 (0.35)
L.BAL	0.12 (0.11)	-0.13 (0.09)	0.00 (0.05)	-0.00 (0.05)	-0.15 (0.16)
ΔA	0.22 (0.24)	0.16 (0.39)	-0.00 (0.44)	-0.18 (0.12)	0.83 (0.95)
L.A	0.18** (0.08)	0.18 (0.12)	0.11 (0.09)	0.07 (0.06)	0.30 (0.21)
ΔGROWTH	-0.18 (0.16)	-0.16 (0.11)	0.02 (0.16)	0.06 (0.26)	-0.15 (0.32)
L.GROWTH	-0.07 (0.13)	-0.09 (0.11)	0.09 (0.14)	-0.07 (0.17)	-0.14 (0.25)

(continued)

Table 11.1   (continued)

	Tax-GDP ratios		Cyclically adjusted series		Tax rates
	(1)	(2)	(3)	(4)	(5)
Number of obs.	337	369	349	638	3.69
AB AR (1)	0.00	0.02	0.02		0.04
AB AR (2)	0.06	0.22	0.31		0.35
Sargan	0.02	0.18	0.21		0.19
Hansen	0.99	0.99	1.00		0.84
F-test Euro	0.13	0.02	0.00	0.00	
F-test Non-Euro	0.27	0.09	0.02	0.00	
			Fiscal devaluation		
θ_S Euro	3.44** (1.72)	3.98*** (1.55)		0.35 (0.66)	0.90* (0.52)
θ_L Euro	1.80* (0.92)	1.92 (2.05)		1.54 (1.43)	3.81 (5.87)
θ_S Non-Euro	2.48 (1.66)	2.80* (1.58)		0.15 (0.26)	-0.05 (0.48)
θ_L Non-Euro	-0.52 (1.23)	0.18 (1.11)		0.21 (0.43)	-0.22 (1.91)
F-test E = Non-E	0.01	0.00	0.00	0.71	0.00

Notes: Single equation error correction model, controlled for country fixed effects. Estimation is by one step robust system GMM (except in column (4) where it is by fixed effects with only growth instrumented by its own lagged values), treating lagged and tax-rate variables as predetermined and with rates for VAT and SCR as external instruments in (1) to (3). Laglimits (2, 3) and instruments collapsed. Heteroskedasticity robust standard errors in brackets. The F-tests report the p-value for F-statistic on the null hypotheses that the coefficients on both ΔSCR and ΔVAT are zero (F-test Euro and F-test Non-Euro) and the null that the short-term effect of a fiscal devaluation in the euro sample is equal to that in the non-Euro (F-test E–Non-E). Calculation of θ's in column (5) based on point estimates multiplied by a factor to translate into a change of 1 percent of GDP.

***Significant at the 1 percent level.

**Significant at the 5 percent level.

*Significant at the 10 percent level.

cant in changes, but in column (1) enters positively in lag—broadly consistent with the earlier prediction of a lasting positive effect to the extent that these other sources are distortionary. Perhaps surprisingly, but consistent with the simple model from before, the government balance has no significant impact in any of the regressions.

Interest centers, of course, on the coefficients related to VAT and SCR. On this, the results in column (1) are strikingly different for Eurozone and non-Eurozone countries.[20] For the non-Eurozone, no significant effects emerge, either in change or lagged; and the F-test does not reject the null that both coefficients on the tax changes are zero. For the euro countries, in contrast, both the change in and the lags of the SCR variable show a significant negative effect on net exports, consistent with the theory. And the effects are quite large: a reduction in the share of GDP taken in the employers' social contribution—offset by other (non-VAT) measures to keep the government balance unchanged—increases net exports, in the short term, by almost 3 percent of GDP. The differenced VAT variable has a positive impact for the euro observations, but this effect is far from significant. Indeed, the VAT is rarely significant in any of the results in table 11.1, reminiscent of the theoretical implication of no short-run impact of an increase in the VAT if applied uniformly to all commodities—strikingly so, indeed, given how nonuniform VATs are in practice.

The difference in coefficients for ΔSCR and ΔVAT suggests that a fiscal devaluation in euro countries would indeed increase net exports. As reported at the bottom of the table, the point estimate of θ_S implies that a shift of 1 percent of GDP from SCR to VAT would increase net exports by 3.44 percent of GDP, and the effect is statistically significant at 5 percent. For non-euro observations, the point estimates suggest an effect that is not only smaller but also statistically insignificant. The long-run impact of a fiscal devaluation, θ_L, is positive for euro countries (contrasting with the theoretical presumption of no permanent effect) but this is significant only at 10 percent. For non-euro countries, it is insignificant. The F-test firmly rejects the null that θ_S is the same for Eurozone and non-Eurozone countries.

The results point to a fairly complex time profile of effects, which differs between the Eurozone and non-Eurozone countries. In particular, the smaller coefficient for lagged net exports in Eurozone countries suggests that the adjustment toward the new equilibrium is more sluggish—any impact from the fiscal devaluation lasts longer—than in non-Eurozone countries. For instance, the coefficients imply a half life for euro countries of 3.5 years, while for non-euro countries it is 2.2 years: so, for instance, 3.5 years after a fiscal devaluation in a Eurozone country, net exports still remain higher than they would otherwise have been by around 1 3/4 percent of GDP.

---

20. For brevity we speak here and later as if the sample were partitioned by country; current Eurozone members, however, are of course in the "non-euro" subsample prior to their entry.

The second column of table 11.1 reports results using the cyclically adjusted revenue data. The diagnostics are more reassuring than when using raw revenue data. For the euro countries, the coefficient on the change in SCR is somewhat larger and noticeably more precise, being significant at 1 percent, while that on the lag becomes insignificant. Now, the coefficient for the change in the SCR variable is also significantly negative for non-euro countries. For the VAT, there is again no significant effect, for either change or the lag, in either group. The F-test rejects that both tax coefficients are zero for Eurozone countries, but cannot reject this for non-Eurozone observations at 5 percent (but can do so at the 10 percent level).

Point estimates of the short-run impact of a pure fiscal devaluation suggest an increase in net exports of 4 percent of GDP in Eurozone countries, significant at 1 percent. For non-Eurozone observation the effect is smaller at 2.8 percent of GDP and significant only at 10 percent. The implication is that while a fiscal devaluation might also have an impact outside the Eurozone, the effect seems smaller and more uncertain. Also, adjustment is again more sluggish for the Eurozone, with a lagged net export coefficient of –0.10, compared to –0.21 for non-euro countries (implying half lives of 6.6 years in the Eurozone and 2.9 years in the non-euro countries). The estimates of θ_L indicate that a fiscal devaluation has no long-run effect in either euro or non-euro countries.

Column (3) in table 11.1 adds to the regression in column (2) unemployment as a control variable, as well as the interaction of the SCR variables with unemployment. The latter is intended to capture the possibility, raised earlier, that changes in the SCR may have a bigger effect on trade if unemployment is high, perhaps because wages adjust less rapidly. There is, however, little support for this: the interaction term is insignificant. Other results are qualitatively unaffected.[21]

Column (4) is the same as column (2), but adopts a standard fixed-effects regression in which only growth is instrumented with its lagged value. The regression thus differs primarily in the instruments used: it neither uses tax rates as external instruments nor the lagged internal variables used in system GMM. The results indicate that the instruments matter greatly. The coefficient for the differenced SCR variable is much smaller and only significant at 10 percent for Eurozone countries. For non-euro countries, the coefficient is small too, but significant at 5 percent. There is now also a significant negative coefficient on the lagged VAT variable, but only in non-Eurozone countries. The effects of a fiscal devaluation are now all insignificant, both in the short run and in the long run, and the F-test cannot reject the null that the effects of a fiscal devaluation are the same for euro and non-euro countries. This

---

21. Note that the SCR variables for Eurozone and non-Eurozone countries should be interpreted differently, since the total impact of changes in the SCR also depend on the coefficient of the interaction between unemployment and the change in SCR. We therefore do not report effects of a fiscal devaluation in column (3).

qualitative pattern of results is hard to explain, and, with the diagnostics, one (perhaps charitable) interpretation is that endogeneity is indeed a real issue, and system GMM goes a good way toward addressing it.

The last column of table 11.1 shows results using statutory tax rates, rather than revenue ratios.[22] The diagnostics provide support for the choice of instruments and the Hansen statistic is no longer close to 1. All tax effects are in this case insignificant, however, except for a positive impact of the differenced VAT in the Eurozone. It is of some interest, nonetheless, to combine the coefficient point estimates with information on tax bases to gauge the implied impact of a revenue-neutral fiscal devaluation of 1 percent of GDP. The implied VAT base[23] in non-euro countries is 38 percent of GDP, and the implied SCR base is 35 percent. A shift from SCR to VAT by 1 percent of GDP would therefore require raising the VAT rate by 2.5 percentage points and reducing the SCR rate by 2.9 percentage points. For euro observations, a VAT increase of 2.7 percentage points and an SCR reduction of 2.6 percentage points would be needed. The point estimates then imply that a fiscal devaluation in the Eurozone would generate a short-run increase in net exports of about 0.9 percent of GDP, and this effect is significant at 10 percent. The estimated long-run effect is larger, but statistically insignificant. The effects for non-Eurozone countries are of opposite sign but very small and insignificant. The F-test rejects the null of equal effects between Eurozone and non-Eurozone countries, largely consistent with the result in column (2), except that now the effects are smaller and fiscal devaluation has no effect outside the Eurozone.

As stressed earlier, the VAT is not the only way in which an SCR reduction might be financed, so that a range of alternative forms of fiscal devaluation could be envisaged. Table 11.2 addresses this, and the wider issue of how a variety of tax instruments appear to affect net exports. It reports the results of estimating a specification along the lines of column (2) in table 11.1, using cyclically adjusted data, but including, in addition to SCR and VAT, the personal income tax (PIT), employee's social contribution (SCE), and corporate income tax (CIT). For brevity, only the coefficients for the differenced tax variables are reported, capturing the short-term impact of a tax change. The regression reported also makes no distinction between Eurozone and non-Eurozone countries.

A relatively strong negative effect from the SCR term again emerges, but it now lacks significance. The effect from the VAT is positive, but also insignifi-

22. We have also explored using the average tax wedge (including SCR and employee social contributions as well as personal income tax, evaluated at 67 percent of the average wage) instead of the SCR rate. This variable consistently shows a significant positive coefficient, contrary to the theory. However, the inclusion of employee contributions and PIT makes this variable less suitable for regressions on fiscal devaluation.

23. Meaning VAT revenue in percent of GDP divided by the standard rate; and for the SCR, revenue divided by the SCR rate.

Table 11.2   Short-term effects of a wider range of taxes

	ΔTax-coefficient		Impact on net exports of SCR-cut financed by	
SCR	−1.74	(1.14)		
PIT	−0.52	(0.57)	1.22	(1.21)
CIT	1.44	(0.86)	3.18**	(1.64)
SCE	0.89	(1.69)	2.64	(1.82)
VAT	0.81	(1.69)	2.56*	(1.57)

Note: Specification and estimation as in column (2) of table 11.1, but with no distinction between coefficients for Eurozone and non-Eurozone coefficients.

cant. Increases in PIT have an adverse effect on net exports, but less marked than those for SCR. For both the SCE and the CIT, the coefficient is positive but insignificant The final column of table 11.2 shows the impact of cutting the SCR rate and preserving revenue by increasing one of the other four taxes: the analogue, that is, of θ_S. Financing the SCR reduction by either a higher SCE or a higher PIT does not significantly increase net exports. Doing so by a higher VAT, however, increases net exports by 2.56 percent of GDP, with statistical significance of 10 percent. A conventional form of fiscal devaluation thus appears both to have a marked effect and, in terms of net exports, does so more than some alternatives. But even better for short-term net exports, the results in table 11.2 imply, is financing the SCR cut by increased reliance on corporate taxation. This is consistent with Keen and Syed (2006), who also find positive short-term effects of such a tax shift on the trade balance. Intuitively, increases in the CIT are likely to induce a net outflow of capital abroad in the short run, which comes along with short-run increases in net exports. However, these effects can be expected to reverse as the income from investments abroad subsequently increases.

What, then, is one to conclude from these results? Although in some respects problematic, the empirics do tend to confirm that, at least for countries in the Eurozone, domestic tax reforms can have significant effects, of broadly the kind that the theory set out previously predicts, on trade performance. Some of the results imply a quite sizable effect, with the short-run increase in net exports from a shift of 1 percent of GDP ranging between 1 and 4 percent of GDP. There is also good reason to suppose, however, that any effects of a fiscal devaluation will be temporary.

11.2.3   Policy Implications

Both analytics and empirics thus suggest that judicious tax shifts can have a noticeable impact on trade performance. In building on this to derive policy prescriptions, however, several issues arise that are not captured in the analytical framework above.

First, the assumption of a representative consumer masks important distributional impacts from such tax shifts and the likely need for accompanying measures. The increased VAT component of the fiscal devaluation reduces the value to consumers of their non-labor income, whether from transfers or capital income. To the extent that out-of-work benefits to the unemployed are not updated to reflect the increased VAT, most labor market models suggest a long-term fall in structural unemployment. This suggests still stronger effects on employment and output. But there will also be a reduction in the real value, for instance, of pensions. And increasing the VAT may also give rise to other equity concerns, perhaps especially so if—as the analysis in the next section suggests would be the best approach in many countries—it took the form of an increase in reduced rates, since these are often (albeit unwisely) motivated by distributional concerns. This means that there is likely to be pressure to increase some social benefits to address equity concerns, diluting the net revenue raised by the VAT increase and so allowing only a smaller reduction in the SCR and hence also a smaller gain in employment and labor supply. The distributional impact of the reform will also depend on the precise way in which the SCR is cut: on whether or not, for instance, the upper limit on contributions that some countries impose is also reduced.

Second, across-the-board cuts in SCRs are expensive, and more targeted measures may give a larger bang-for-buck in output and employment effects. In the job plans proposed or implemented in OECD countries, SCR relief is often targeted to specific categories of job or worker. Reduced labor costs for low wage earners may be particularly attractive to relax constraints induced by minimum wage legislation or by sectoral minimum wages agreed-upon by trade unions and employers. Moreover, employment of this group tends to be relatively sensitive to tax considerations. Targeting SCR relief to low-wage earners may thus reinforce the impact of a fiscal devaluation on employment, output, and the trade balance. Two other common forms of targeting SCR cuts (or equivalent financial incentives to employers)—on new employment, and on small firms—are more problematic (see appendix E).

Third, the payment of social contributions is generally linked—albeit in many cases very weakly—with entitlement to benefits. If the value of the latter is to be maintained while the SCR is cut, two options arise. One is to decouple the two, and move toward tax-based finance of social benefits: this risks worsening labor supply distortions, if contributions are indeed seen as a form of forced savings (but has been advocated for the United Kingdom, for instance, in the recent Mirrlees review[24]). The alternative—feasible if cumbersome—is to maintain the link and make transfers from general revenue to provide workers with explicit credits for the SCR not directly paid (as done, for instance, with the social security holiday in the United States).

Fourth, it is important to remember that other taxes can also have a role

---

24. Mirrlees et al. (2011).

in recouping revenue lost from cutting the SCR. One particular possibility beyond those noted earlier—not included in the empirical exercise of table 11.1 given the absence of cyclically adjusted revenue data—is residential property taxation, the appeal of which in this context is that this has little direct impact on production costs. There is indeed some evidence that this is a relatively growth-friendly source of finance (Arnold 2008), with untapped revenue potential in many countries, often non-Anglophone.

Finally, the analysis may suggest a coordination problem. A fiscal devaluation could indeed appeal simultaneously to many countries; but if all or many undertake it, the impact on the net exports of each is diminished. Thus, there may seem to be a risk of competitive fiscal devaluations as a form of international tax competition. One important reason for adoption of the euro was to eliminate the opportunity for countries to pursue such competitive devaluations. There is an important difference, however, from standard results on the harm suffered, for instance, from tax competition to attract mobile capital. There, damage arises from the undertaxation of a base that is much less mobile from the collective perspective than from the national: the outcome of the consequent game between countries, in which all ultimately set lower tax rates on capital than is collectively optimal, leaves them all worse off.[25] For a fiscal devaluation, however, the endpoint is an increase in the rate of consumption taxation and a reduction in the taxation of labor. Empirically, there is some evidence that, at least in the OECD, heavier reliance on consumption rather than income taxation is associated with faster growth (Kneller, Bleaney, and Gemmell 1999). In this respect, the downside of fiscal devaluation is limited: even a fiscal devaluation that has no effect on net exports, perhaps because of the adoption of similar reforms elsewhere, may ultimately lead to a more efficient tax structure.

This somewhat optimistic view of fiscal devaluation does not mean, of course, that tax policy is the best or only way to address the structural problems underlying wage rigidities. The point is, rather, that it can perhaps provide some temporary mitigation, while more fundamental reforms are considered.

11.3 The Role of the Value Added Tax in Fiscal Consolidation

The VAT has already played a prominent part in fiscal consolidation efforts in Europe. Between 2009 and 2011, thirteen of the twenty-seven EU member states raised their standard rate of VAT; in the two years to 2008, in contrast, only one did so.[26] And the increases are in several cases substantial:

25. This oversimplifies: some countries, particularly small ones, may benefit from tax competition of this kind.
26. As a stimulus measure, the United Kingdom preannounced a temporary reduction in the standard rate from 17.5 to 15 percent in 2009; it was subsequently raised to 20 percent. The exception noted is Germany, which increased the standard rate by 3 points in 2006.

Greece and Portugal, for instance, raised their standard rates by 4 and 3 percentage points, respectively, to 23 percent. Further increases in standard VAT rates now look problematic for many European countries, including in terms of increased risk of noncompliance, and there is a general agreement between EU Member States (though not a legally binding one) not to exceed a maximum of 25 percent.[27]

In other prominent fiscally challenged countries, however, the situation is the converse. The possibility of substantially increasing revenue from the VAT is technically clear in both Japan and the United States: at 5 percent, the former has almost the lowest VAT rate in the world,[28] and the latter remains the only OECD country without a VAT. But attempting to realize this potential has proved close to politically suicidal.

This section considers the place of the VAT in fiscal consolidation, and how the very different obstacles in Europe and the no/low VAT countries could be overcome.[29]

11.3.1   The Case for the VAT

There is a large literature on the comparison between consumption and income-based taxation, which need not be reviewed here.[30] To some extent, it is for present purposes beside the point: almost all countries have both, and—even leaving aside standard optimal tax theoretic considerations— do so for good practical reasons: to diversify compliance risks and exploit economies of scope in application.[31]

But the case for the VAT over alternative forms of consumption taxation—notably the retail sales tax (RST)—is still sometimes questioned, at least in the United States. When each functions perfectly, they are equivalent in taxing only final consumption; and both then have the appeal of excluding intermediate transactions from tax, consistent with the Diamond-Mirrlees (1971) result that production efficiency is a necessary condition for Pareto-efficiency.[32] The difference arises when enforcement is imperfect. Suppose,

27. Some have found evidence of Laffer-type effects for the VAT: Matthews (2003), for instance, reports an estimated revenue-maximizing VAT rate in the EU of around 19 percent.

28. Iran has the lowest, at 3 percent.

29. More issues of design and implementation arise than can be discussed here. For a sense of these, see the following: on general design issues arising under EU VAT rules, Crawford, Keen, and Smith (2010) and Cnossen (2003); on Japan, Keen et al. (2011); on the United States the papers in *Tax Law Review* (2010), vol. 28.

30. See, for instance, Auerbach (2006) and Banks and Diamond (2010).

31. Boadway, Marchand, and Pestieau (1994) show that with imperfect compliance it is generally optimal to deploy both a sales tax and a wage tax even under circumstances under which, with full compliance, they would be equivalent. A further practical consideration is that information obtained from one tax can be used to help enforce the other: opposition against the VAT in many countries often comes from small traders whose primary fear is that it improves the effectiveness of the income tax.

32. The conditions for the Diamond-Mirrlees theorem are strong—including perfect competition and the ability to tax rents at any rate—but few simple rules emerge when they fail, leaving it as the practicable first guide to policy design.

for instance, that some retailer fails to remit tax. Under an RST, no tax is collected at all; under a VAT, however—the essence of which is that tax is payable on the entirety of every firm's sales, but with a credit or refund of tax it has itself been charged on its inputs—the tax collected on purchases by the retailer remains. In this sense revenue is more secure under the VAT. This comes at some potential cost to production efficiency, of course, but with a presumption that the consequent input-taxation is not too bad a substitute for the missing taxation on value-added at the final stage.[33]

The structure of the VAT also introduces an element of self-enforcement into the system: if firm A's supplier is VAT-compliant, that reduces A's gain from not being VAT compliant itself (because registering for the VAT enables it to reclaim that tax); and if A's customer is VAT-compliant, A has an incentive to register and charge tax (because that customer will be able to reclaim the tax A charges them, and along the way A can reclaim the tax it has been charged on its own inputs). The point should not, however, be overstated: if A's customer is not VAT-compliant, then A has an incentive not to comply either.[34] Nonetheless, given also other haphazard features of RSTs in practice—including particular difficulty in taxing services (largely excluded from most state VATs in the United States) and a tendency to levy substantial charges on business inputs[35]—the technical superiority of the VAT, at least when substantial revenue must be raised,[36] seems clear. A rule of thumb has been that noncompliance difficulties make RSTs at rates of more than 10 percent seriously problematic.[37]

There are signs that these theoretical merits of the VAT have to some extent been realized in practice. If the VAT is indeed a particularly efficient form of taxation, as these and other considerations suggest, one would expect countries with a VAT—since they have a lower marginal social cost of raising revenue—to collect more total tax revenue, all else equal, than those without. The evidence is that, for high income countries, this is indeed the case (Keen and Lockwood 2010).

11.3.2   Diagnosing the VAT

In practice, VATs differ widely in their design and implementation, as can be seen from table 11.3, which summarizes key features of those in the OECD in 2008—the latest year for which comparable data are available (and

33. Newbery (1986) shows that it may be optimal to tax intermediate goods when not all final goods can be taxed.
34. The possibility of "bad" VAT chains forming is analyzed by de Paula and Scheinkman (2007), who find evidence of such an effect in Brazil.
35. Ring (1989) found that around 40 percent of revenue from state sales taxes in the United States was collected from sales to businesses.
36. A fuller account of the comparison between the VAT and RST is in Cnossen (1987).
37. While figures cited for a federal VAT in the United States are often lower than this (6.5 percent for the Domenici-Rivlin plan [Bipartisan Policy Center 2010], for instance), state and local sales taxes (ranging from around 4 to 12 percent where present) need to be added in order to arrive at effective RST rates.

Table 11.3   **Key features of OECD VATs, 2008**

Country	Standard rate	Reduced rates	Revenue (percent of GDP)	C-efficiency
Australia	10.0	0.0	3.4	49
Austria	20.0	10.0/12.0	7.8	61
Belgium	21.0	0.0/6.0/12.0	7.0	49
Canada[a]	5.0	0.0	2.7	74
Chile	19.0	—	8.9	75
Czech Republic	20.0	10.0	7.1	59
Denmark	25.0	0.0	10.1	62
Finland	22.0	0.0/8.0/13.0	8.4	58
France	19.6	2.1/5.5	7.0	49
Germany	19.0	7.0	7.1	55
Greece	19.0	4.9/9.0	7.2	46
Hungary	25.0	5.0/18.0	7.7	57
Iceland	25.5	0.0/7.0	9.1	54
Ireland	21.0	0.0/4.8/13.5	7.1	55
Israel	16.0	—	7.8	68
Italy	20.0	4.0/10.0	6.0	41
Japan	5.0	—	2.5	67
Korea	10.0	0.0	4.3	65
Luxembourg	15.0	3.0/6.0/12.0	5.8	93
Mexico	16.0	0.0	3.8	35
Netherlands	19.0	6.0	7.2	60
New Zealand	12.5	0.0	8.6	98
Norway	25.0	0.0/8.0/14.0	7.3	57
Poland	22.0	0.0/7.0	7.9	49
Portugal	20.0	5.0/12.0	8.4	51
Slovak Republic	19.0	10.0	6.9	54
Slovenia	20.0	8.0/8.5	8.5	68
Spain	16.0	4.0/7.0	5.3	46
Sweden	25.0	0.0/6.0/12.0	9.3	58
Switzerland	7.6	0.0/2.4/3.6	3.7	77
Turkey	18.0	1.0/8.0	4.9	35
United Kingdom[b]	17.5	0.0/5.0	6.4	46

Source: OECD (2011).

Notes: Rates applicable on January 1, 2008. Special rates applying to regions are not shown. "Revenue" and "C-efficiency" refer to 2008.

[a]Newfoundland and Labrador, New Brunswick, and Nova Scotia have harmonized their provincial sales taxes with the federal Goods and Services Tax and levy a rate of GST/HST of 13 percent. Other Canadian provinces, with the exception of Alberta, apply a provincial tax to certain goods and services. These provincial taxes apply in addition to GST. (HST stands for harmonized sales tax.)

[b]The standard rate of VAT was temporarily reduced from 17.5 percent to 15.0 percent for the period December 1, 2008–December 31, 2009 inclusive and reverted to 17.5 percent with effect from January 2010.

predating many of the recent standard rate increases noted above). The final column reports a handy indicator for assessing the performance of a VAT. This is its C-efficiency, E^C, defined as the ratio of the revenue it yields to the product of consumption and the standard rate of VAT, τ_S:

$$(3.1) \qquad E^C \equiv \frac{\text{VAT revenue}}{\tau_S \times \text{Consumption}}.$$

For a perfectly enforced VAT levied at a single rate on all consumption, C-efficiency would be 100 percent. But this is no more than a convenient benchmark. A VAT, for instance, that did not refund exporters the tax charged on their inputs could score a very high E^C even though it consequently acts in part as a tax on exports rather than on consumption.

Despite this and other conceptual limitations,[38] the C-efficiency ratios reported in table 11.3 are suggestive. Two observations stand out. First, C-efficiency in many European countries is very low, with the example of New Zealand—held in the highest esteem by VAT specialists—showing scope for a significant increase. This means that considerably more revenue could be raised from the VAT even without increasing the standard rate. If Italy, for instance, were to increase its C-efficiency to the level found in France, it would increase its VAT revenue by about 1.2 percent of GDP. Second, C-efficiency is, in contrast, rather high in Japan: so a significant increase in revenue is likely to require increasing the standard rate.

But low C-efficiency can arise from either poor implementation, poor policy design, or both. While, as in the case of Italy, it can quickly indicate scope for improvement (in the sense of increasing revenue without raising the standard rate), a low C-efficiency ratio gives little clue as to how to do it. For this, more is needed. To this end, it is shown in appendix D that C-efficiency can be decomposed as

$$(3.2) \qquad E^C = (1 - \text{policy gap}) \times (1 - \text{compliance gap}),$$

where (formal characterization of these terms being in the appendix) the compliance gap reflects the difference between actual VAT collected and that theoretically due, while the policy gap relates to aspects of design, and can be further decomposed as

$$(3.3) \quad (1 - \text{policy gap}) = (1 - \text{rate differentiation}) \times (1 - \text{exemptions}),$$

where the first term on the right reflects departures from a uniform rate structure and the second the impact of exemptions.[39]

---

38. These are discussed in Ebrill et al. (2001) and OECD (2011).

39. Some VAT terminology is needed here. Under both "exemption" and "zero-rating," no VAT is charged on sales; the difference is that input tax can be recovered under zero-rating but not under exemption (sometimes referred to for this reason as "input taxation"). Exemptions levied other than at final sale tend to increase tax revenue, since the unrecovered tax cascades into the tax paid on the further sales, so that the exemption effect in (3.3) may in principle be negative.

Table 11.4   **Decomposing C-efficiency**

Country	C-efficiency	Compliance gap	Policy gap	Decomposing the policy gap	
				Rate differentiation	Exemptions
Austria	61	13	30	14	19
Belgium	50	12	43	19	30
Denmark	63	7	33	0	33
Finland	60	5	36	10	29
France	51	7	45	22	30
Germany	54	14	37	8	31
Greece	44	29	38	21	22
Ireland	67	4	30	28	3
Italy	41	27	44	25	26
Luxembourg	89	2	9	26	−23
Netherlands	58	6	38	17	26
Portugal	52	8	43	22	27
Spain	57	8	38	32	10
Sweden	55	4	43	14	34
United Kingdom	48	15	44	22	28

Sources: "C-efficiency" (for 2004) from table 5.14 of European Commission (2011); "Compliance gap" (for 2006) from Reckon (2009); "Rate differentiation" (for 2003) from table 5 of Mathis (2004). Incompleteness of coverage reflects gaps in the last of these. See appendix D for a full account of the decomposition.

Equations (3.2) and (3.3) in principle provide an elegant decomposition of C-efficiency that could be a powerful tool for diagnosing VAT performance. They also have the convenient feature that independent estimates of all gaps are not needed: in principle, any one can be estimated as a residual given information on all the others. In practice, however, and perhaps surprisingly, the information required to decompose C-efficiency in this way is rarely available. By way of illustration, table 11.4 assembles information from disparate sources on the situation in several European countries in around 2005 that at least provides an illustration of the method.[40]

What emerges is that the primary issue in most of these countries is (or at least was) in design, rather than implementation—which to some extent runs counter, for instance, to the emphasis often placed on issues of carousel[41] and other forms of fraud and evasion in the EU. There are some cases, most notably Greece and Italy, in which noncompliance seems far

40. Note that the C-efficiency figures in table 11.4 differ from those in table 11.3: they are for an earlier year (so as to be roughly synchronous with such information on other items needed for the decomposition as is available).

41. Frauds of this kind are explained and discussed, along with VAT noncompliance issues more generally, in Keen and Smith (2006b), one aspect being that the revenue loss is, in some cases, in principle unbounded. The publicity such schemes have attracted is, in part, an aspect of administration's compliance strategies.

higher than in peer groups, and so naturally attracts attention as an area for improvement. Mostly, however, it is the scope for improving the uniformity and coverage of the VAT that stands out.

As between the two elements of the policy gap, the significance of exemptions suggested in table 11.4 is both striking and surprising. Being calculated as a residual, it seems in part to reflect estimated noncompliance that in many countries seems almost implausibly low. The calculations of the rate differentiation effect also require closer evaluation. Other estimates for the United Kingdom, for example, suggest that the statutory rate dispersion effect is 48 percent and the exemption effect is 8 percent. It is thus the rate structure—and above all the zero-rating of food and other items, which takes almost half of consumer spending out of the VAT base—that should be the focus of attention in considering any further increase in revenue from the VAT. What is perhaps most shocking, however, is that—with few exceptions, among which the United Kingdom is prominent—the information needed for this kind of exercise is generally not available, even, it seems, within governments.

11.3.3   Obstacles

There is, then, clearly a case for many advanced economies to look at the VAT for a substantial part of their consolidation needs. While significant changes have been made in Europe, these have focused largely on raising the standard rate, tending to reduce C-efficiency rather than increase it.[42] And in Japan, no changes have yet been made.[43] This section considers some of the key obstacles to the kind of reforms discussed before.

Distributional Issues and Rate Differentiation

One obstacle common to both European circumstances and those of Japan and the United States is the perception that the VAT is a particularly regressive tax. This is much less true, of course, if regressivity is assessed relative not to current income but to current expenditure, the latter being a better indicator of lifetime welfare to the extent that it reflects permanent income (see, for instance, Metcalf 1994). More fundamentally, however, it is the distributional effect of the tax-spending system as a whole, not of any individual component, that ultimately matters. And advanced economies generally have much better instruments with which to pursue their distributional objectives than differential rates of commodity taxation. The best way to help the poor and vulnerable is not by setting a low tax rate on, say, food—the largest monetary benefit from that goes to the rich, since they

---

42. Items have also in some cases been moved from standard to reduced rates, amplifying the departure from uniformity.

43. Japan did, however, announce in January 2012 its intention to raise the VAT rate to 8 percent in 2014, and to 10 percent in 2015.

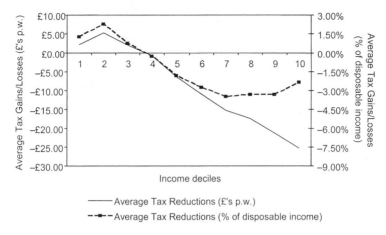

Fig. 11.3   Distributional impact of a VAT reform package in the United Kingdom
Source: Crawford, Keen, and Smith (2010).

spend a larger absolute amount on food than the poor even though it is a smaller share of their budget—but by supporting them through targeted transfers.

Take, for example, the United Kingdom. Figure 11.3 shows the distributional impact of eliminating zero- and reduced rates (unifying them at 17.5 percent), but at the same time increasing a range of social benefits. The three lowest income deciles are winners from the package. Moreover, revenue—net of the increased social support costs—is increased by about 11 billion pounds, which is around 14 percent of initial VAT revenue.

As in this example, dealing with the distributional implications of VAT reform may well reduce the net revenue finally available for consolidation or other purposes. In Japan too, for instance, the revenue gain from increasing the VAT rate would be reduced by automatic indexation of pension benefits. The key point, however, is that hesitation in raising or eliminating reduced VAT rates for fear of the distributional consequences—and, by the same token any inclination to include such reduced rates in a new VAT—is essentially misplaced for most advanced economies.

While the reform shown in figure 11.3 addresses the distributional concerns associated with a VAT reform of this kind, it does raise marginal effective tax rates on earned income—reflecting the impact of the full tax-benefit system—in the lowest deciles: tighter targeting of social support has a cost. And it does alter relative consumer prices and hence demand patterns. The question, then, is whether rate differentiation might have served a useful efficiency role in reconciling revenue needs with work incentives.

Broadly, a reduced rate of taxation on some commodity or activity can be justified on efficiency grounds if it is a substitute for untaxed work effort, whether in the home or marketplace.[44] Existing empirical knowledge gives little reason, however, for confident differentiation on these grounds. Food itself (eaten at home), for example, seems from results in Crawford, Keen, and Smith (2010) to be, if anything, a candidate for higher rather than lower taxation. An argument can be made for some reduced rates on these grounds: for child care, for instance, due to its complementarity with working and (an argument that has led the European Commission to allow reduced rates for a few such items) labor-intensive services. But these are minor concerns, and experience in the EU is that the reduced rates have done little to increase compliance or employment.[45] The presumption for uniformity under the VAT seems strong on efficiency grounds as well as distributional ones.

Aggregate Demand Effects

Especially when countries are experiencing unemployment at the levels many show in figure 11.2, a natural concern in raising the VAT, whether by widening the base or increasing the standard rate, is that there will be an adverse impact on the level of activity through aggregate demand effects. This worry may, however, be overstated—even leaving aside any beneficial confidence effects through an improved fiscal position.

First, a preannouncement of future VAT increases would be to expected stimulate current consumption, with the expectation of a jump in the price level, leading consumers to bring forward their consumption, especially of large durables. In effect, the expected increase in the price level tends to reduce the real return on saving, and so, through an intertemporal substitution effect, to increase current consumption. There is indeed now substantial evidence of such frontloading of consumption in advance of moderately sizable VAT increases. Ito and Mishkin (2006), for instance, find that before Japan increased its VAT rate in 1997 from 3 to 5 percent, consumers accelerated their spending in the preceding quarter by about 1.5 percent. In 2009, the United Kingdom reduced its VAT rate from 17.5 to 15 percent as an explicitly temporary one-year measure.[46] Though there has as yet been no ex post study of this event, Crossley, Low, and Wakefield (2009) estimated a likely boost in consumer spending in 2009 of 1.25 percent. Also, German consumers who were anticipating a 3 percentage point VAT increase in 2007 brought forward their consumption by one year. To some extent this effect may be mitigated as firms adapt their pricing policies: Carare and Danninger (2008) show that the rise in demand in 2006 allowed German firms to increase their prices well before the actual VAT increase took place. The impression, nonetheless, is that intertemporal shifting of consumption can be significant, albeit largely confined to particular durable sectors.

44. Crawford, Keen, and Smith (2010) provide a summary of the theory on commodity tax differentiation and an analysis of the efficiency arguments for rate differentiation.
45. Copenhagen Economics (2007).
46. The standard rate was subsequently (January 2011) raised to 20 percent.

Indeed, some have suggested deliberately using a phased VAT increase to stimulate consumption. Feldstein (2002) in particular argues that a phased increase in the VAT accompanied by a gradual cut in the income tax—to render the increase revenue neutral—could raise demand through this intertemporal substitution effect, advocating this for Japan in particular. However, simulations suggest that these effects are likely small and would not substantially accelerate an exit from deflation (Auerbach and Obstfeld 2004).

Second, the evidence suggests that any lasting impact on aggregate demand—beyond reversal of the bringing forward of some consumption noted earlier—is likely to be small. In Japan, for instance, resistance to a further increase in the rate of the consumption tax largely reflects a perception that the increase in the rate from 3 to 5 percent in 1997 contributed to its falling back into recession later. But consumption picked up only one quarter after the tax increase. Looking at the household level data, moreover, Cashin and Unayama (2011) find only a very modest impact on spending levels beyond the shifting noted before. Other factors, notably the onset of the Asian financial crisis, seem to have played a much bigger role.

And measures can, of course, be taken to limit aggregate demand effects. Indeed, accompanying VAT reform with targeted protection of the poorest consumers, of the type discussed in figure 11.4, will automatically limit the impact on those likely to have the highest marginal propensity to consume.

Political Economy

Despite the strong counterarguments sketched before, the popular perception of the VAT as inherently regressive persists, impeding both base-broadening in Europe and rate-raising or introduction in Japan and the United States, and fostering a willingness to deploy reduced rates. It would be comforting to believe that resistance of this kind will be overcome by good analysis communicated effectively. But these points have been well-known (to key policymakers at least) for many years and yet no real progress has been made.

Why resistance is so deep remains somewhat mysterious. Perhaps it is the very costliness of supporting the poor through reduced rates that makes doing so a means by which politicians can signal the depth of their concern for the vulnerable. In any event, something more than enlightenment seems needed if VAT policies are to be improved.

Part of the difficulty may be that of credibly presenting reform as a package: in the United Kingdom example, for instance, consumers may doubt whether support through the tax-benefit system to offset the impact of eliminating zero-rating really would be forthcoming or sustained. One recurrent suggestion for addressing such doubts is to earmark the proceeds of a reformed VAT for some valued purpose. Burman (2009), for instance, proposes earmarking the proceeds of a VAT in the United States for health-

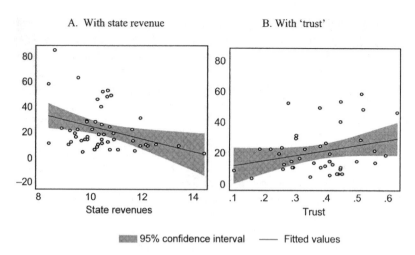

Fig. 11.4   Correlates of earmarking in the US states

Notes: Percentage of state revenues earmarked, for 1997, from Pérez (2008); state revenues (in percent of personal income), for 1997, from Tax Policy Center, http://www.taxpolicycenter .org/taxfacts/; trust indicator from Uslaner (2006).

care costs. In Japan it has been suggested to earmark the proceeds from an increased rate to social security spending. Earmarking is, however, unattractive in standard public financial management terms: either it genuinely constrains spending on the favored item, in which case it impedes efficient resource allocation, or it does not, in which case it risks being an exercise in "misleading taxpayers rather than expanding democracy" (IFS 1993, 65). These disadvantages may in principle be outweighed if earmarking does indeed secure approval for some tax measure that would otherwise be blocked by voters distrustful of government.[47] Empirically, however, little is known about the causes or consequences of earmarking. Simple correlations for the US states—the only case, it seems, in which good data on the extent of earmarking are available—raise more questions than they answer: panel A of figure 11.4, for instance, shows that revenue is lower in states that earmark more (so that earmarking does not seem to be used to squeeze out an increase in already high revenues). And panel B shows—contrary to the idea that "[t]he prevalence of earmarking indicates a lack of confidence in the governmental system and the budgetary process"[48]—that earmarking is actually more extensive where trust in the state government is higher.

These are clearly issues on which understanding remains very limited. There are certainly examples of tax systems that have become harmfully fragmented through excessive earmarking, as in Korea for instance. At a

47. Brett and Keen (2000).
48. Goode (1984, 12).

minimum, labeling may be important, as with the Domenici-Rivlin Commission naming their proposed VAT a 'Debt Reduction Sales Tax.' If, however, earmarking is ultimately the only way in which fundamental resistance to inherently sensible tax measures can be overcome, it may be a pragmatic price worth paying.

The most powerful force overcoming resistance to deep VAT reform, however, is likely to be dire fiscal need. In this setting, the (informal) EU agreement on a maximum VAT rate—which may have seemed misplaced some years back, when the more evident concern was the risk of downward tax competition—has come to seem a useful commitment device for ensuring that, beyond some point, increased revenue needs will be met not by raising the standard rate but by base-broadening and improving implementation.

In the particular context of the United States, there is, it should be noted, a particular technical and political challenge that would need to be faced in introducing a federal VAT: that of determining its interaction with existing state- and local-level sales taxes.[49] It might seem natural to convert those taxes into VATs too, but the VAT is not well-suited to implementation at lower levels in federal systems. This is because the zero-rating of exports (and bringing into tax of imports) commonly relies on border controls not desired within federations.[50] It is no coincidence that the other prominent latecomers to the VAT—Australia and India—are both federal states. Technical solutions can be found, for instance in the form of a VIVAT (viable integrated VAT), under which all sales between registered businesses are taxed at a common, federation-wide rate, while lower levels add on an additional charge for sales to final consumers.[51] The massive variation in the bases and structures of current state and local sales taxes in the United States, however, make this much more easily said than done.

But the United States also has an advantage to exploit. This is the possibility of learning from the experiences of other countries and from the intellectual advances made. The most prominent example may be in the area of financial services, where it is now clear that there are alternatives to the increasingly problematic exemption[52] approach adopted by the EU. Perhaps

49. Another striking feature of the political debate on VAT adoption in the United States is the concern that it would prove to be a "money machine." This is explored in Keen and Lockwood (2006), who find some evidence that the VAT has indeed looked like an innovation leading to government growth, rather than a consequence of an increase in desired government size. Fiscal rules, however, seem a better way to impose aggregate constraints than foregoing the use of efficient tax instruments.

50. These difficulties have come to the fore in the EU since the removal of internal fiscal frontiers, a prominent example being the "carousel fraud" mentioned before; which—a thought developed furthest in Aujean (2011)—the VIVAT described later could also go a long way to resolve.

51. Keen (2001) proposes such a scheme operating across all states and McLure (2010) proposes one operating across localities within states.

52. Exemption results in overtaxation of business use of financial services (from unrecovered VAT on purchases by financial institutions) and undertaxation of use by final consumers (because of the exclusion of the value added by financial institutions). It is now understood how, at least in principle, to bring financial services more fully into the VAT: Crawford, Keen,

the most important lesson to learn, however, is again political: initial decisions about VAT design, for instance, in providing reduced rates on equity grounds, are extraordinarily hard to change.

11.4   Conclusion

The deep fiscal challenges that many advanced economies face will require adjusting a wide range of tax and spending instruments, and the appropriate mix will vary widely across them. This chapter has focused on just two broad issues within this much wider set. But they are ones that are already to the fore in almost all of these economies, and are likely to be of continuing importance.

The first is a very immediate focus of concern in many Eurozone countries: the possibility of adjusting to an overvalued real exchange rate not by a nominal depreciation or painful and sluggish price adjustment but, at least in part, by a fiscal devaluation. The empirical evidence presented here, though by no means entirely robust and subject to lingering endogeneity concerns, suggests that revenue-neutral shifts from the employers' social contribution toward the VAT in Eurozone countries could indeed improve the trade balance, with quite sizable short-run effects. As expected, the effects seem to disappear in the long run, so that the case for such shifts rest largely on their potential to accelerate adjustment to deeper underlying problems. What is important, however, is that the data do seem to show evidence of the effects that theory predicts.

The second issue addressed here is the scope for more effective deployment of the VAT as an instrument for fiscal consolidation, not least where (as in many EU members) the standard rate is now so high that further increases are problematic. A simple diagnostic tool has been set out that could help identify where the scope for improvement is most likely to lie, but surprisingly and depressingly, the information needed to apply this, while very basic, is generally unavailable. Clearly there is potential for substantially improving understanding of where the weaknesses of VAT design and implementation lie. Reviewing such evidence as is available, however, the VAT in many countries—and not just those that currently have low rates, or no VAT at all—still appears to have considerable untapped potential. Indeed this (and not least the particularly strong case in advanced economies for a single-rate VAT on a broad base) is widely recognized, including by many policymakers. The difficulty is overcoming the political resistance to such reforms that nonetheless persists. For that, something more than technically compelling arguments are needed.

---

and Smith (2010) outline the issues and possible solutions, and IMF (2010a) proposes a Financial Activities Tax (on the sum of wages and profits of financial institutions) that could go some way to mitigate the problems created by exemption.

Appendix A
Derivation of (2.5) to (2.8)

Perturbing (2.3), normalizing $E_U = 1$ gives

(A1) $\qquad dU = R_L L_1' dT^r + T^{v'} E_{QQ} dT^v + T^{v'} E_{QU} dU - \lambda dA.$

Recalling (2.3) and noting that (since $Q' E_{QU} = E_U$ by linear homogeneity of the expenditure function) $T^{v'} E_{QU} = (Q - P)' E_{QU} = 1 - P' E_{QU}$, this implies that

(A2) $\qquad (P' E_{QU}) dU = \left(\dfrac{R_L}{RLL} \right) dT^r + T^{v'} E_{QQ} T^v - \lambda dA.$

Perturbing net exports in (2.4):

(A3) $\qquad dN_1 = P_1' (P_{PL} dL_1 - E_{Q_1Q} dT^v - E_{Q_1U} dU).$

Substituting dU from (A2) into (A3), the result follows on using (2.3), the implication of linear homogeneity of the revenue function that $P' R_P = R_{LL}$ (because $P' R_p = R$) and noting that

(A4) $\qquad T^{v'} E_{QQ} = (Q - P)' E_{QQ} = -P' E_{QQ} = -(P_1' E_{Q_1Q} + P_2' E_{Q_2Q}).$

That a reform combining in a cut in T^r with an increased uniform VAT rate is welfare-improving follows from (A2), since then $E_{QQ} dT^v = E_{QQ} d\tau/(1 + \tau) = 0.$

Appendix B
Separate Regressions for Eurozone and Non-Eurozone Countries

Table 11B.1   **Taxation and net exports**

	Cyclically adjusted data		Tax rate data	
	Non-Euro	Euro	Non-Euro	Euro
L. Net exports	−0.21** (0.106)	−0.03 (0.05)	−0.30* (0.16)	−0.23 (0.24)
ΔSCR	−2.52 (1.62)	−2.81* (1.64)	−0.08 (0.14)	−0.11 (0.67)
L.SCR	−0.07 (0.11)	−0.06 (0.07)	0.00 (0.05)	−0.09 (0.07)
ΔVAT	0.10 (0.96)	−0.78 (0.88)	−0.09 (0.09)	0.28 (0.17)
L.VAT	0.02 (0.21)	−0.45*** (0.09)	0.03 (0.12)	−0.14 (0.12)
ΔDEP	−0.38 (0.69)	0.23 (0.45)	−51.63 (66.56)	5.78 (47.55)
L.DEP	−0.12 (0.09)	−.07 (0.07)	28.20 (42.08)	−11.1 (15.53)
ΔA	0.49 (0.77)	−0.49 (0.36)	1.21 (1.08)	−0.25 (0.81)
L.A	0.21 (0.16)	0.11*** (0.03)	−0.22 (0.40)	0.31 (0.29)
ΔGROWTH	−0.13 (0.13)	−0.06 (0.12)		
L. GROWTH	−0.11 (0.14)	−0.03 (0.06)		

(*continued*)

Table 11B.1   (continued)

	Cyclically adjusted data		Tax rate data	
	Non-Euro	Euro	Non-Euro	Euro
ΔBAL	0.00 (0.35)	0.11 (0.28)	0.31 (0.47)	−0.14 (0.20)
L.BAL	−0.08 (0.10)	−0.25*** (0.10)	0.28 (0.21)	−0.07 (0.19)
No. of obs.	265	94	232	94
AB AR(1)	0.03	0.01	0.04	0.04
AB AR(2)	0.33	0.97	0.54	0.31
Sargan	0.44	0.16	0.13	0.65
Hansen	0.91	1.00	0.25	0.99
Short-run	2.62 (1.83)	2.03 (2.34)	0.01	1.04
Long-run	1.39 (1.21)	−11.26 (16.67)		
F-test	0.29	0.00		

Notes: Single equation error correction model, controlled for country fixed effects. Estimation is by one step robust system GMM, including fixed effects, treating lagged and tax-rate variables as predetermined and with tax rates as external instruments. Laglimits (2, 3) and instruments collapsed. The F-test reports the p-value for the F-statistic on the null hypothesis that the coefficients on both ΔSCR and ΔVAT are zero.

***Significant at the 1 percent level.
**Significant at the 5 percent level.
*Significant at the 10 percent level.

Appendix C
Data

The data on net exports are from the world development indicators of the World Bank. Data on tax revenues in percent of GDP are from the OECD *Revenue Statistics.* The key variables of interest are the series for "employer social security contributions" (number 2200 in the OECD classification) and "value added taxes" (5111 in the OECD classification). The data on total tax revenue, GDP growth, and the government balance are also from the OECD, as are the population data used to compute old-age dependency ratio. Data on the standard VAT rate and the employer social contributions are from various sources.

The cyclically adjusted revenue data, however, are not available on as disaggregated a basis as the raw revenue data. For instance, there is only one cyclically adjusted series for social contributions and one for indirect taxes. Under the assumption that the same adjustment applies to subcomponents of these series, we create cyclically adjusted series for the SCR and VAT by dividing the cyclically adjusted by the nonadjusted series for total social contributions and total indirect taxes (respectively, OECD classification 2000 and 5000) and using the result to scale the raw revenue data for the SCR and VAT (respectively, OECD classification 2200 and 5111). Although the adjusted and nonadjusted series try to capture the same set of taxes, the cyclically adjusted series contains a slightly broader set than the non-cyclically adjusted series, implying that the ratio between them is somewhat larger than 1. This explains why there are somewhat higher numbers for the tax-to-GDP ratios of the cyclically adjusted series in table 11B.1, as compared to the nonadjusted series. The variation in the cyclically adjusted series, however, should properly reflect the variation in the underlying data.

Table 11B.1 shows some descriptive statistics. Net exports are zero on average across country-year observations, ranging from –34 percent of GDP to 33 percent of GDP positive. The government balance is –2 percent of GDP on average, with a standard deviation of 4.2 percent. Substantially fewer observations are available, however, for the government balance than for total tax and net exports. The tax-to-GDP ratio lies between 9 and 52 percent, with an average of 32. Excluding revenue from VAT and SCR, the average declines to slightly less than 23 percent of GDP. The statutory SCR rate varies between 0.9 percent and 51 percent, with an average of 22.38. Standard VAT rates vary from 3 to 30 percent, while the average is 17.2 percent.

The PIT on average raises most revenue, at more than 9 percent of GDP. The VAT raises almost 5 percent of GDP, while SCR on average raises 4.6 percent of GDP. The corresponding averages for the cyclically adjusted series are somewhat higher, for reasons explained earlier.

Table 11C.1   **Summary statistics of data**

Variable	No. obs	Mean	Std. dev.	Minimum	Maximum
In percent of GDP					
Net exports	1,241	–.00	6.635	–34.681	33.240
Gross exports	1,241	35.99	22.84	5.206	179.77
Gov. balance	754	–1.99	4.166	–15.593	19.087
Total tax	1,248	32.44	8.898	9.278	52.246
Tax ex VAT/SCR	1,126	23.89	5.715	7.964	40.767
VAT base	865	37.84	8.591	0	70.541
SCR base	521	35.83	32.43	10.957	50.700
Revenue in percent of GDP					
PIT	1,177	9.370	4.848	0	26.545
CIT	1,080	2.518	1.672	–.463	12.954
ESC	1,192	2.629	1.977	0	11.445
SCR	1,192	4.600	3.347	0	14.005
VAT	1,181	4.856	3.239	0	11.282
Cyclically adjusted series					
Government balance	779	–.107	2.963	–15.298	7.4704
PIT	732	11.24	5.127	2.384	29.181
CIT	668	2.607	1.340	–.497	6.5574
ESC	715	3.380	2.125	0	11.878

(continued)

Table 11C.1   (continued)

Variable	No. obs	Mean	Std. dev.	Minimum	Maximum
SCR	715	6.195	3.526	.0003	14.219
VAT	734	6.636	3.167	0	13.445
Statutory tax rates					
SCR rate	583	22.38	12.270	.87	51
VAT rate	914	17.20	5.148	3	30
Average tax	330	32.39	11.246	7	51.37
Marginal tax	330	40.97	13.560	7	71.311
Other					
GDP growth	1,197	3.13	3.083	−11.615	14.787
Dependency ratio	1,340	18.68	5.050	5.596	35.592

Appendix D
Decomposing C-Efficiency

Denote by C_i and C_i^*, respectively, the values of the true consumption of commodity i and the part that is brought into tax, (possibly at a zero rate), the difference between the two reflecting imperfect implementation; and by T_i and T_i^* the statutory and effective rates of tax on final consumption of i, the latter reflecting not only of tax levied directly on i but also of indirect effects through exemptions on intermediate inputs (mediated by the input-output structure, as described, for instance, in Ebrill et al. (2001). Total revenue, for instance, is thus $\sum_i T_i^* C_i^*$. Equations (3.2) and (3.3) then follow on writing

$$(D1) \qquad E^C \equiv \frac{\sum_i T_i^* C_i^*}{\tau_S \sum_i C_i} = \left(\frac{\sum_i T_i^* C_i^*}{\sum_i T_i C_i^*} \right) \left(\frac{\sum_i T_i C_i^*}{\sum_i T_i C_i} \right) \left(\frac{\sum_i T_i C_i}{\tau_S \sum_i C_i} \right),$$

which bears the interpretation in the text with:

$$(D2) \qquad \text{Exemptions} \equiv \frac{\sum_i (T_i - T_i^*) C_i^*}{\sum_i T_i C_i^*}$$

$$(D3) \qquad \text{Compliance gap} \equiv \frac{\sum_i T_i (C_i - C_i^*)}{\sum_i T_i C_i}$$

$$(D4) \qquad \text{Rate Differentiation} \equiv 1 - \frac{\sum_i T_i C_i}{\tau_S \sum_i C_i} = \frac{\tau_S - \sum_i T_i \omega_i}{\tau_S}$$

where

$$\omega_i \equiv \frac{c_i}{\sum c_j^*}.$$

The impact of exemptions is thus measured by the loss of revenue from taxing at effective rather than statutory rates—which may be negative, given the cascading effect of exempting intermediate transactions (an instance of poor design that leads to higher C-efficiency). The compliance gap is measured simply as the revenue loss (at nominal tax rates) from failing to bring some final consumption into tax. And the rate differentiation effect reflects the extent to which the weighted average VAT rate is lower than the standard rate—which could also in principle be negative, though (since $\tau_s - \Sigma_i T_i \omega_i = (\tau_s - E[T]) + \text{cov}(T, \omega)$) is sure to be positive if reduced rates are prevalent (so that nonstandard rates are on average lower than standard) and positively correlated with budget shares.

Appendix E
Should Social Contribution Cuts Be Targeted on New Employment and Small Firms?

A number of schemes—including the Obama jobs plan—limit SCR cuts (or provide analogous financial incentives to employers) to "new" employment. This has the intuitive appeal of avoiding a revenue loss on inframarginal employees, and maintains the impact on producer prices to the extent that these are driven by marginal rather than average cost. But such schemes are not without difficulty. Deadweight loss still arises to the extent that new employment would also have emerged without the relief. Moreover, targeting to new employment may have displacement effects: newly hired employees may replace existing employees. Some studies report that these effects can be as large as 65 percent (Dahlberg and Forslund 2005). These schemes can also create perverse incentives (for instance, in laying off workers in any period between announcement and reference date relative to which increased employment is measured). They can also have high transaction costs, and are inevitably somewhat complex, provision being needed to ensure that enterprises do not relabel themselves so as to count all employment as new. Experience has been that take-up rates can be low, especially among smaller firms: Chirinko and Wilson (2010) provide an extensive analysis of the impact of such schemes operated by the US states, where they have been quite common, and conclude that the net employment effects are positive, but very small.

Some countries target SCR relief to small firms. There is widespread belief among policymakers that small companies are the main source of job growth. Early writers indeed report evidence supporting this claim for the United States (see, for example, Birch 1987). This has led governments to introduce special tax relief measures for small companies. However, more recent evidence casts doubt on these claims. Davis, Haltiwanger, and Schuh (1996) discuss statistical and measurement problems and stress the need to distinguish between gross and net job creation. Accounting for such pitfalls, Neumark, Wall, and Zhang (2011) find that small firms actually contribute less to net job growth than do large firms. Haltiwanger, Jarmin, and Miranda (2011) find that, when one controls for firm age, there is no systematic relationship between firm size and employment growth in the United States. Instead, job growth comes more than proportionally from young firms and start-ups.

References

Alesina, Alberto, and Roberto Perotti. 1997. "The Welfare State and Competitiveness." *American Economic Review* 87:921–39.

Arellano, Manuel, and Olympia Bover. 1995. "Another Look at the Instrumental Variable Estimation of Error-Component Models." *Journal of Econometrics* 68 (1): 29–51.

Arnold, Jens. 2008. "Do Tax Structures Affect Aggregate Economic Growth? Empirical Evidence from a Panel of OECD Countries." OECD Working Paper no. 643. Paris: Organization for Economic Cooperation and Development.

Auerbach, Alan J. 2006. "The Choice between Income and Consumption Taxes: A Primer." NBER Working Paper no. 12307. Cambridge, MA: National Bureau of Economic Research.

Auerbach, Alan J., and Maurice Obstfeld. 2004. "Monetary and Fiscal Remedies for Deflation." *American Economic Review* 94 (2): 71–75.

Aujean, Michel. 2011. "Towards a Modern EU VAT system: Associating VIVAT and Electronic Invoicing." *EC Tax Review* 2011/5:211–16.

Banks, James, and Peter Diamond. 2010. "The Base for Direct Taxation." In *Dimensions of Tax Design: The Mirrlees Review,* edited by James Mirrlees et al., 548–648. Oxford: Oxford University Press, Institute for Fiscal Studies.

Bassanini, Andrea, and Romain Duval. 2006. "Employment Patterns in OECD Countries: Reassessing the Role of Policies and Institutions." OECD Social, Employment and Migration Working Paper no. 35. Paris: OECD.

Bipartisan Policy Center. 2010. *Restoring America's Future.* Report of the Debt Reduction Task Force, Co-Chairs Pete Domenici and Alice Rivlin. Washington, DC.

Birch, David L. 1987. *Job Creation in America: How Our Smallest Companies Put the Most People to Work.* New York: The Free Press.

Blundell, Richard, and Stephen Bond. 1998. "Initial Conditions and Moment Restrictions in Dynamic Panel Data Models." *Journal of Econometrics* 87:115–43.

Boadway, Robin, Maurice Marchand, and Pierre Pestieau. 1994. "Toward a Theory of the Direct-Indirect Tax Mix." *Journal of Public Economics* 55:71–88.

Brett, Craig, and Michael Keen. 2000. "Political Uncertainty and the Earmarking of Environmental Taxes." *Journal of Public Economics* 75:315–40.

Burman, Leonard E. 2009. "Blueprint for Tax Reform and Health Reform." *Virginia Tax Review* 28:287–323.

Cashin, David, and Takashi Unayama. 2011. "The Intertemporal Substitution and

Income Effects of a VAT Rate Increase: Evidence from Japan." Discussion Paper 11045, Research Institute of Economy, Trade and Industry (RIETI).

Calmfors, Lars. 1998. "Macroeconomic Policy, Wage Setting, and Employment— What Difference Does the EMU Make?" *Oxford Review of Economic Policy* 14:125–51.

Carare, Alina, and Stephan Danninger. 2008. "Inflation Smoothing and the Modest Effect of VAT in Germany." IMF Working Paper no. 08/175. Washington, DC: International Monetary Fund.

Chinn, Menzie D., and Eswar S. Prasad. 2003. "Medium-Term Determinants of Current Accounts in Industrial and Developing Countries: An Empirical Exploration." *Journal of International Economics* 59:47–76.

Chirinko, Robert S., and Daniel J. Wilson. 2010. "Job Creation Tax Credits and Job Growth: Whether, When, and Where?" Working Paper Series 2010-25, Federal Reserve Bank of San Francisco.

Cnossen, Sijbren. 1987. "VAT and RST: A Comparison." *Canadian Tax Journal* 35 (3): 559–615.

———. 2003. "Is the VAT's Sixth Directive Becoming an Anachronism?" *European Taxation* 43 (12): 434–42.

Copenhagen Economics. 2007. *Study on Reduced VAT Applied to Goods and Services in the Member States of the European Union.* Prepared for DG Taxud, European Commission.

Cottarelli, Carlo, and Michael Keen. 2011. "Fiscal Policy and Growth: Overcoming the Constraints." In *Ascent after Decline: Regrowing Global Economies after the Great Recession,* edited by Oliviano Canuto and Danny Leipziger, 87–133. Washington, DC: World Bank.

Crawford, Ian, Michael Keen, and Stephen Smith. 2010. "VAT and Excises." In *Dimensions of Tax Design: The Mirrlees Review,* edited by James Mirrlees et al., 275–362. Oxford: Oxford University Press, Institute for Fiscal Studies.

Crossley, Thomas, Hamish Low, and Matthew Wakefield. 2009. "The Economics of a Temporary VAT Cut." *Fiscal Studies* 30 (1): 3–16.

Dahlberg, Matz, and Anders Forslund. 2005. "Direct Displacement Effects of Labor Market Programs." *Scandinavian Journal of Economics* 107:475–94.

Davis, Steven J., John Haltiwanger, and Scott Schuh. 1996. "Small Business and Job Creation: Dissecting the Myth and Reassessing the Facts." *Small Business Economics* 8:297–315.

de Paula, Áureo, and José A. Scheinkman. 2007. "The Informal Sector." PIER Working Paper 07-033, Penn Institute for Economic Research, Department of Economics, University of Pennsylvania.

Diamond, Peter, and James A. Mirrlees. 1971. "Optimal Taxation and Public Production I: Production Efficiency, II: Tax Rules." *American Economic Review* 61:8–27, 261–78.

Disney, Richard. 2004. "Are Contributions to Public Pension Programs a Tax on Employment?" *Economic Policy* 19:267–311.

Ebrill, Liam, Jean-Paul Bodin, Michael Keen, and Victoria Summers. 2001. *The Modern VAT.* Washington, DC: International Monetary Fund.

European Central Bank. 2011. *Monthly Bulletin,* box 12, p. 101. December.

European Commission. 2009. "The 2009 Ageing Report: Economic and Budgetary Projections for the EU-27 Member States (2008–60)." *European Economy* 2, April.

———. 2011. "Tax Reforms in EU Member States." Taxation Papers, Working Paper no. 28.

Farhi, Emmanuel, Gita Gopinath, and Oleg Itskhoki. 2011. "Fiscal Devaluations." CEPR Discussion Paper no. 8721, Harvard and Princeton.

Feldstein, Martin. 2002. "The Role for Discretionary Fiscal Policy in a Low Interest Rate Environment." NBER Working Paper no. 9203. Cambridge, MA: National Bureau of Economic Research.

Feldstein, Martin, and Paul Krugman. 1990. "International Trade Effects of Value-Added Taxation." In *Taxation in the Global Economy,* edited by A. Razin and J. Slemrod, 263–82. Chicago: University of Chicago Press.

Franco, Francesco. 2011. "Adjustment to External Imbalances within the EMU, the Case of Portugal." Unpublished Manuscript. University of Lisbon.

Goode, Richard. 1984. *Government Finance in Developing Countries.* Washington, DC: Brookings Institution.

Gruber, Joseph, and Steven Kamin. 2007. "Explaining the Global Pattern of Current Account Imbalances." *Journal of International Money and Finance* 26:500–22.

Haltiwanger, John, Ron S. Jarmin, and Javier Miranda. 2011. "Who Creates Jobs? Small vs. Large vs. Young." NBER Working Paper no. 16300. Cambridge, MA: National Bureau of Economic Research, August.

Ilzetzki, Ethan O., Carmen M. Reinhart, and Kenneth S. Rogoff. 2008. "Exchange Rate Arrangements into the 21st Century: Will the Anchor Currency Hold?" http://www.carmenreinhart.com/research/publications-by-topic/exchange-rates -and-dollarization.

Institute for Fiscal Studies (IFS). 1993. "Options for 1994: The Green Budget." *Commentary 40.* London: IFS. http://www.ifs.org.uk/publications/5613.

International Monetary Fund (IMF). 2010a. "A Fair and Substantial Contribution by the Financial Sector: Final Report to the G20." http://www.imf.org/external /np/g20/pdf/062710b.pdf.

———. 2010b. "From Stimulus to Consolidation: Revenue and Expenditure Policies in Advanced and Emerging Economies." IMF Policy Paper, April 20.

———. 2010c. "Macro-Fiscal Implications of Health Care Reform in Advanced and Emerging Economies." IMF Policy Paper, December 28.

———. 2011a. *Fiscal Monitor.* September.

———. 2011b. *World Economic Outlook.* September.

Ito, Takatoshi, and Fredric S. Mishkin. 2006. "Two Decades of Japanese Monetary Policy and the Deflation Problem." In *Monetary Policy with Very Low Inflation in the Pacific Rim,* edited by Takatoshi Ito and Andrew Rose, 131–93. Chicago: University of Chicago Press.

Keen, Michael. 2001. "States' Rights and the Value-Added Tax: How a VIVAT Would Work in the US." *Proceedings of the National Tax Association* 2001: 195–200.

Keen, Michael, and Ben Lockwood. 2006. "Is the VAT a Money Machine?" *National Tax Journal* 59:905–28.

———. 2010. "The Value-Added Tax: Its Causes and Consequences." *Journal of Development Economics* 92:138–51.

Keen, Michael, Mahmoud Pradhan, Kenneth Kang, and Ruud de Mooij. 2011. "Raising the Consumption Tax in Japan: Why, When and How?" Staff Discussion Note 11/13. Washington, DC: International Monetary Fund.

Keen, Michael, and Stephen Smith. 2006a. "The Future of Value-Added Tax in the European Union." *Economic Policy* 23:373–411, 419–20.

———. 2006b. "VAT Fraud and Evasion: What Do We Know and What Can Be Done?" *National Tax Journal* 59:861–87.

Keen, Michael, and Murtaza Syed. 2006. "Domestic Taxes and International Trade: Some Evidence." IMF Working Paper 06/47. Washington, DC: International Monetary Fund.

Kneller, Richard, Michael F. Bleaney, and Norman Gemmell. 1999. "Fiscal Policy and Growth: Evidence from OECD Countries." *Journal of Public Economics* 74:171–90.

Laker, John F. 1981. "Fiscal Proxies for Devaluation: A General Review." *Staff Papers, International Monetary Fund* 28:118–43.

Lane, Philip, and Roberto Perotti. 1998. "The Trade Balance and Fiscal Policy in the OECD." *European Economic Review* 42:887–95.

———. 2003. "The Importance of Composition of Fiscal Policy: Evidence from Different Exchange Rate Regimes." *Journal of Public Economics* 87:2253–79.

Lee, Jaewoo, Gian Maria Milesi-Ferretti, Jonathan D. Ostry, Alessandro Prati, and Lucca Ricci. 2008. "Exchange Rate Assessments: CGER Methodologies." IMF Occasional Paper no. 261. Washington, DC: International Monetary Fund.

Mathis, Alexandre. 2004. "VAT Indicators." Taxation Papers, Working Paper no. 2.

Matthews, Kent. 2003. "VAT Evasion and VAT Avoidance: Is There a European Laffer Curve for VAT?" *International Review of Applied Economics* 17:105–14.

McLure, Charles. 2010. "How to Coordinate State and Local Sales Taxes with a Federal Value Added Tax." *Tax Law Review* 60:639–704.

Metcalf, Gilbert. 1994. "Lifecycle vs. Annual Perspectives on the Incidence of a Value-Added Tax." In *Tax Policy and the Economy,* vol. 8, edited by James M. Poterba, 45–64. Cambridge, MA: MIT Press.

Mirrlees, James, Stuart Adam, Timothy Besley, Richard Blundell, Stephen Bond, Robert Chote, Malcolm Gammie, Paul Johnson, Gareth Myles, and James Poterba. 2011. *Tax by Design: The Mirrlees Review.* Oxford: Oxford University Press, Institute for Fiscal Studies.

Nickell, Stephen, and Richard Layard. 1999. "Labor Market Institutions and Economic Performance." In *Handbook of Labor Economics,* vol. 3C, edited by Orley Ashenfelter and David Card, 800. Amsterdam: North-Holland.

Neumark, David, Brandon Wall, and Jurfu Zhang. 2011. "Do Small Businesses Create More Jobs? New Evidence for the United States from the National Establishment Time Series." *Review of Economics and Statistics* 93 (1): 16–29.

Newbery, David M. 1986. "On the Desirability of Input Taxes." *Economics Letters* 20:267–70.

Organization for Economic Cooperation and Development. 2010. *Consumption Tax Trends.* Paris: OECD.

———. 2011. *Taxation and Employment.* OECD Tax Policy Studies no. 21. Paris: OECD.

Pérez, Arturo. 2008. *Earmarking State Taxes.* Washington, DC: National Conference of State Legislatures.

Poterba, James M., Julio Rotemberg, and Lawrence H. Summers. 1986. "A Tax-Based Test for Nominal Rigidities." *American Economic Review* 76 (4): 659–75.

Reckon LLP. 2009. *Study to Quantify and Analyze the VAT Gap in the EU-25 Member States.* London: Reckon LLP.

Ring, Raymond J., Jr. 1989. "Proportion of Consumers' and Producers' Goods in the General Sales Tax." *National Tax Journal* 42:167–79.

Uslaner, Eric M. 2006. "The Civil State: Trust, Polarization, and the Quality of State Government." In *Public Opinion in State Politics*, edited by Jeffrey E. Cohen, 142–62. Stanford, CA: Stanford University Press.

Comment   James M. Poterba

This chapter by de Mooij and Keen presents new evidence on two important and topical issues. The first is whether there is empirical support for the claim that "fiscal devaluations"—increases in value added tax (VAT) accompanied by reductions in employer contributions for social insurance—can generate a short-run increase in exports. For countries that operate under a fixed exchange rate regime with many of their trading partners, such as those in the Eurozone, this possibility—the use of tax instruments to achieve an outcome similar to an exchange rate devaluation—has attracted significant policy attention. The authors note that a number of European nations have adopted such policies in recent years. This chapter offers both a careful theoretical analysis of the effect of a fiscal devaluation, as well as new empirical evidence on how VATs and social insurance taxes affect net exports.

The second part of the chapter investigates the structure and revenue yield of current VATs, to assess the potential for generating additional revenue from these taxes without raising rates. The chapter focuses primarily on potential changes in the structure of the VAT. The authors present a very informative decomposition of the revenue collected by current VATs relative to the hypothetical revenue that could be collected if a tax at the statutory VAT rate were levied on all consumption. This provides a rough estimate of the revenue yield of base-broadening VAT reforms. Such reforms would be associated with only modest increases in the distortionary cost of the tax system, and in some cases might even yield efficiency gains. Both components of the chapter are well-executed and offer important new information on both the structure and the effects of VATs in OECD nations. My comments will focus on each component of the chapter in turn.

The analysis of fiscal devaluations begins by examining the theoretical basis for a link between fiscal devaluations and net exports. One of the key findings is that the effects of such policies are likely to depend substantially on the nature of the VAT increase that is used to offset the revenue loss associated with the drop in social insurance contributions. To summarize the key findings, recall that labor supply depends on the real after-tax product wage, $(1 - \tau)w/(1 + \theta)p$, where w is the nominal wage and p the nominal product price for output, while labor demand depends on the real wage facing the firm, inclusive of required social insurance contributions, $w(1 + \sigma)/p$. The tax parameters are τ, the income tax rate (which is included for completeness but is assumed to remain fixed), θ, the rate of VAT, and σ, the employer payroll tax rate. A revenue neutral fiscal devaluation reduces σ and raises θ.

The effect of a fiscal devaluation depends critically on the flexibility of

James M. Poterba is the Mitsui Professor of Economics at the Massachusetts Institute of Technology and president of the National Bureau of Economic Research.

For acknowledgments, sources of research support, and disclosure of the author's material financial relationships, if any, please see http://www.nber.org/chapters/c12647.ack.

nominal wages. If nominal wages instantly adjust to the tax change, then the fiscal devaluation may not have any real effects. If nominal wages rise to offset the effect of higher consumer prices associated with the increase in θ, then $w(1 + \sigma)$ will remain roughly unchanged and there will be little effect on labor demand. There will be no effect if the VAT covers all goods in the economy, and if all goods are produced domestically using labor inputs that are affected by the change in social insurance taxes. After the rise in nominal wages, both the real after-tax product wage and the real cost of labor to the firm would be the same as before the fiscal devaluation.

The analysis becomes more complicated when there are imported goods, when nominal wages are sticky, and when labor in some sectors is not covered by the social insurance tax or output from some sectors is not covered by the VAT. The first part of the chapter carefully explores these issues. When nominal wages do not adjust immediately to the rise in consumer prices induced by the increase in VAT, the firm's real cost of labor declines when σ is reduced. Facing lower labor costs, the firm can reduce prices, increase output, and hire more workers. Foreign firms that compete with domestic firms will *not* benefit from the reduction in social insurance tax rates, but their goods will be affected by the increase in VAT, just as the domestic firm's goods will be. The net effect is an increase in the relative competitiveness of domestic producers vis-à-vis the foreign firms that produce imported goods. A parallel effect improves the competitive posture of domestic firms competing in markets abroad: reduced net-of-tax labor costs can be passed along in the form of lower product prices, thereby improving competitiveness. Because domestic firms are now more competitive both at home and abroad, one might expect an increase in aggregate net exports. The empirical work in this chapter is designed to quantify this.

One of the chapter's most important theoretical contributions is its demonstration that the scope of a nation's VAT is an important determinant of the effects of a fiscal devaluation. Most VATs only cover a fraction of consumption spending. They often exempt substantial sectors such as banking, education, and health. In such settings, an increase in the VAT rate exacerbates the efficiency costs associated with intersectoral distortions. In contrast to VATs, which usually have limited coverage, social insurance taxes generally cover a very high fraction of employees in most sectors, so a fiscal devaluation may be moving from a broader based to a narrower based tax. The importance of VAT structure in determining the effects of a fiscal devaluation parallels Feldstein and Krugman's (1990) emphasis on the limited coverage of the VAT in their discussion of how a shift from an income tax to a VAT would affect the tradable goods sector. Farhi, Gopinath, and Itskhoki (2011) explore related issues in the context of a VAT-replacing-social insurance tax reform. The current chapter shows that one of the few settings in which it is possible to make unqualified statements about the effect of fiscal devaluation is when the VAT applies to all goods at a fixed rate.

While the chapter focuses on the limited coverage of the VAT, in practice, one could also envision fiscal devaluations that involve a reduction in social insurance taxes for a limited set of firms. For example, policymakers might target the social insurance taxes on firms that are engaged in international trade, perhaps proxied by "manufacturing" or a similar set of broad categorical identifiers. Such policies would involve additional distortions across sectors because of the induced differences in social insurance tax burdens on labor, but they would permit a smaller increase in VAT to achieve revenue neutrality. There are many tax policies that target particular industries, such as reduced corporate income tax rates for firms in the manufacturing sector in the United States. It would be interesting to know more about the structure of reductions in social insurance contribution rates that have been associated with fiscal devaluations.

After presenting a careful theoretical analysis of fiscal devaluations, the authors develop new empirical findings on how net exports respond to changes in employer social insurance contributions and VAT. This analysis can be viewed as part of a broader agenda, which links macroeconomics and public economics, directed at understanding how tax policies affect the components of aggregate demand as well as overall economic growth. The authors focus on just one component of aggregate demand, and they recognize that there are a number of empirical challenges to the interpretation of aggregate time series regressions linking net exports to tax variables such as the change in the VAT rate and the change in the payroll tax rate.

One of the chapter's strengths is the use of a range of different strategies to assess the most important empirical problems. Throughout their analysis, the authors include in their estimating equations a standard list of explanatory variables that have been used in previous studies of the determinants of net exports. Even with this approach, however, and with the use of instrumental variables (statutory tax rates) for some of the aggregate measures of tax receipts, there remain some empirical issues that should be noted.

First, the problem of policy endogeneity could affect the empirical analysis in many ways. For example, a country that is trying to encourage exports might adopt a fiscal devaluation and at the same time adopt other policies designed to increase net exports. If the other policy measures are not reflected in set of explanatory variables that are included in the modeling, and if those measures matter, then the results may overstate the actual effects of the tax variables because these variables may be correlated with omitted variables that describe other policy actions. It is also possible for policy endogeneity to lead to understatement of the actual effects of fiscal devaluation. If countries that experience adverse shocks to their net exports are more inclined to adopt a fiscal devaluation, then the effect of the policy may be confounded by the coincidence of its adoption with the arrival of the adverse shock.

Policy endogeneity is difficult to address in a fully satisfactory fashion, because there is little consensus on how best to measure the external shocks facing a nation or the full set of factors that may lead to the enactment of specific tax policies. The authors follow the standard strategy of using various instrumental variables, and as is often the case, the results are somewhat dependent on the specification. One strategy that future researchers might explore, to complement the approach taken in this chapter, is to identify episodes when social insurance tax rates or VAT rates were changed for reasons that were not related to concerns about the current account or macroeconomic performance more generally, and to study those episodes in detail. This strategy has been applied to the study of how income tax rates affect revenue and economic growth by Romer and Romer (2010).

A related endogeneity concern involves the measurement of tax variables. The authors devote substantial attention to this issue, and they present a range of empirical findings using different tax variables. The underlying problem arises because there is no single summary variable that can describe most modern complex tax systems. Even the simplest VATs have some exemptions and special rules for some goods and industries, and social insurance contributions often apply to only a subset of the employees in an economy. This means that a single statutory rate variable may not capture the full detail of the tax code. A standard alternative approach, which is to use the ratio of tax revenue from a particular source to GDP as the tax variable, suffers from another problem. Consider the use of the ratio (VAT Revenue – Social Insurance Tax Revenue)/GDP as a litmus test for fiscal devaluation; when this ratio rises, a country is pursuing that policy. The difficulty is that this variable may be affected by the overall level of economic activity. If the elasticity of wage income with respect to GDP differs from the elasticity of consumer spending in sectors that are covered by the VAT, then this ratio could also exhibit cyclical variability. If net exports also vary over the cycle, a measured correlation between the indicator for fiscal devaluation and net exports could be a manifestation of the underlying correlations between the tax shares, net exports, and GDP, and not the result of a causal link from fiscal devaluation to net exports.

The authors attack this problem in three ways: they include measures of aggregate economic activity in their list of control variables, they use cycle-adjusted measures of revenue as a share of GDP, and they present robustness results using tax rates rather than total revenue scaled by economic output as the indicator of tax policy stance. The results, presented in table 11.1, show that the estimated link between tax variables and net exports is sensitive to the tax measurement issue. In particular, the standard errors of the estimated coefficients are substantially smaller when the cycle-adjusted variables are used in place of the simple tax-to-GDP ratios, and the coefficient estimates when the tax rate variables are used are quite different from those with either revenue share of GDP.

Which estimates should be viewed as the benchmark results? My preferred specifications are those using the cyclically adjusted tax-to-GDP ratios to capture tax policy. These variables reflect the breadth of the tax base as well as the rate structure, and they allow relatively flexible control for the differential elasticity of the tax bases for different tax instruments. The results using these variables suggest that reductions in the social insurance contribution rate have a statistically significant and positive effect on net exports, with a larger effect in countries that are part of the Euro area. These findings are consistent with the theoretical framework that is developed at the start of the chapter. The effects of increases in the VAT on net exports are less well determined, and in most specifications the point estimates are insignificantly different from zero. This means that when these findings are used to evaluate the policy experiment of raising the VAT and lowering the social insurance contribution, most of the impact is flowing through the estimated effect of social insurance contributions.

The empirical findings are generally supportive of the potential for fiscal devaluations to raise net exports. Because the estimating equations include lagged values of net exports, they also generate adjustment paths that offer some insights on the decay rate of the real effects of these tax policy changes. Here, the findings are a bit surprising: a half-life of over six years in countries that use the euro, and about three years in other nations. It would be interesting to compare the implicit speed of nominal adjustment in wages that these estimates imply with results from the literature that focuses on wage determination. Because tax policy shifts are relatively discrete events, one might expect that nominal wages would adjust more rapidly to these shocks than to other shocks. Moreover, there is little role for learning in response to tax changes, while if one is trying to examine how other macroeconomic shocks might affect nominal wages, it may take some time for labor market participants to disentangle the underlying shock that they need to respond to from the background noise in economic activity.

One issue that the chapter notes only in passing is the role of policy coordination across nations in affecting the impact of a shift from social insurance taxes to a VAT. A fiscal devaluation is likely to have a larger effect when one country adopts this policy in isolation than when there are a number of countries pursuing similar fiscal devaluations in tandem. While the chapter does not attempt to assess the extent to which coordinated action reduces the impact of this policy, the coincidence of policy actions in a number of European nations during the last few years suggests that it might be possible to investigate this issue. A first pass would include measures of the policy actions in a country's major trading partners in the empirical analysis, although given the difficulties in teasing out the effect of domestic policy actions, identifying the effect of actions in other nations is probably a tall order.

The second part of the chapter examines the efficiency cost of current VATs and the potential to raise more revenue, at lower incremental efficiency cost, by reforming the VAT base. The authors bring together data from a range of different sources and develop a simple and revealing measure of the operation of the VAT: the C-efficiency ratio. This is the ratio of the revenue that is currently collected using the VAT and the revenue that would be collected if the VAT rate was applied to all consumption spending. For most countries, this ratio is around 0.50, which suggests substantial opportunities to raise additional revenue by broadening the VAT base. There is also substantial disparity across countries in the C-efficiency ratio, with Italy and Greece below 45 percent, Luxembourg at 89 percent, and Ireland, Austria, and Denmark all above 60 percent.

The authors emphasize the insight that raising the VAT rate on the existing base increases distortions between goods, while expanding the VAT base reduces these distortions. While these distortions are likely to be difficult to estimate because they depend on many parameters in consumer demand systems, in some cases the distortions may be quite substantial. The insight that there may exist ways to expand VAT revenues with a modest efficiency cost could have important implications for policy design. The chapter not only provides statistics on the C-efficiency ratio, but it also decomposes this ratio into a factor that is the result of tax evasion, and a factor that is the result of a narrow tax base. This decomposition, which again shows significant variation in the contributions of these two factors across nations, provides a road map for potential policy reform.

The discussion of expanding the VAT base also addresses the important question of whether a broad-based VAT would fall more heavily on lower-income households than a narrower VAT that excludes necessities such as food, medical care, and housing from the tax base. The authors suggest that the VAT should not be considered as a fiscal instrument *in isolation,* but rather should be recognized as one component of a broader fiscal matrix. This implies that distributional effects associated with a change in the VAT base may be offset by changes in other policies, particularly income taxes. This is a point of great importance for practical tax analysis, and it also connects with a long theoretical literature on optimal tax design. When the VAT is part of a tax system that also includes an income tax, policymakers have multiple instruments that can be used to achieve their redistributive objectives. Atkinson and Stiglitz (1976) and Kaplow (2010) are two examples of analyses that demonstrate theoretically that in a broad set of economic environments, attempting to achieve distributive goals by modifying a VAT is less efficient than levying a flat-rate consumption tax along with an income tax that addresses distributional objectives.

The authors note, however, that the economic analysis of the choice between an income tax and a narrow consumption tax may not capture the full set of political economy considerations that arise in practical policy design. In particular, if it is easier for politicians to change income tax rates than to alter the base of the VAT, then those who are concerned about regressive taxes may oppose VAT base broadening, even when accompanied by income tax reform, because they fear that the income tax policy will be reversed in the future. This alone is an interesting topic for future work: the degree of commitment that is associated with different types of tax policies, and whether this affects popular support for different policy actions.

In conclusion, this chapter offers a very insightful analysis of the role of tax policy instruments in achieving macroeconomic policy objectives. While the authors focus on how fiscal devaluations affect net exports, the analysis could be expanded in at least two directions. One is to consider the impact of tax policy more generally on economic growth. Daveri and Tabellini (2000) is one example of a study that explores the link between labor income taxes, particularly social insurance contribution rates, and long-term economic growth and real per capita GDP. It concludes that high and rising labor income tax rates, including social insurance contribution rates, slowed economic growth in Europe during the latter part of the twentieth century. At a time when stronger economic growth can make an important contribution in reducing the burden of fiscal consolidation, there is likely to be growing attention to tax policy and growth. As the analysis in this chapter illustrates, however, there are substantial empirical challenges in developing convincing evidence about these linkages.

A second direction for future work is to move beyond the analysis of fiscal devaluations and to consider a broader range of tax policies that might achieve macroeconomic policy objectives. There are many settings in which taxes can alter relative prices, either across sectors or over time, and thereby induce various behaviors that matter for aggregate economic activity. Feldstein (2002) and Hall (2011), for example, discuss the potential for a preannounced set of VAT increases to encourage current consumption by operating as an alternative to a monetary policy that supports inflation. Just as this chapter focuses on how tax policies may substitute for exchange rate policy, there may also be ways for tax policy to augment or replace monetary policy in some dimensions.

References

Atkinson, Anthony B., and Joseph E. Stiglitz. 1976. "The Design of Tax Structure: Direct versus Indirect Taxation." *Journal of Public Economics* 6:55–75.

Daveri, Francesco, and Guido Tabellini. 2000. "Unemployment, Growth, and Taxation in Industrial Countries." *Economic Policy* 15:47–104.

Farhi, Emmanuel, Gita Gopinath, and Oleg Itskhoki. 2011. "Fiscal Devaluations." NBER Working Paper no. 17662. Cambridge, MA: National Bureau of Economic Research, December.

Feldstein, Martin S. 2002. "Commentary: Is There a Role for Discretionary Fiscal Policy?" *Proceedings, Economic Policy Symposium* (Federal Reserve Bank of Kansas City): 151–62.

Feldstein, Martin S., and Paul R. Krugman. 1990. "International Trade Effects of

Value Added Taxation." In *Taxation in the Global Economy,* edited by Assaf Razin and Joel Slemrod, 263–78. Chicago: University of Chicago Press.

Hall, Robert. 2011. "The Long Slump." *American Economic Review* 101:431–69.

Kaplow, Louis. 2010. *The Theory of Taxation and Public Economics.* Princeton, NJ: Princeton University Press.

Romer, Christina D., and David H. Romer. 2010. "The Macroeconomic Effects of Tax Changes: Estimates Based on a New Measure of Fiscal Shocks." *American Economic Review* 100:763–801.

Fiscal Rules
Theoretical Issues and Historical Experiences

Charles Wyplosz

12.1 Introduction

The European sovereign debt crisis is an unwelcome reminder that no country can ignore the requirement of fiscal discipline. It should also clarify many issues on the nature of fiscal discipline and on the ways to achieve it. We knew it all, but a few aspects have been made more concrete.

The crisis illustrates how slowly fiscal discipline can assert itself. Governments can run budget deficits for years, even decades, before first facing the wrath of financial markets and next facing their emergency lenders. This is illustrated for the Organization for Economic Cooperation and Development (OECD) countries by table 12.1, which shows the percent of years when a country has run a budget deficit since 1960. This should happen about half of the time in a disciplined-government country, and indeed this is what is found for Denmark, New Zealand, and Sweden (Norway being a clear outlier because of its intergenerational saving into the Petroleum Fund). For all other countries except Finland, deficits have occurred in four years out of five (or more), with two countries (Italy and Portugal) achieving a perfect 100 percent. The table also shows that the last time when Austria, Greece, and France achieved a surplus was before the first oil shock. Thus

Charles Wyplosz is professor of international economics at the Graduate Institute of International and Development Studies in Geneva, where he is director of the International Centre of Money and Banking Studies (ICMB).

Without implicating them, I am grateful to Alberto Alesina, Frits Bos, Xavier Debrun, Francesco Giavazzi, and Lucio Pench for their comments on earlier versions. I also benefited from comments from participants at the NBER conference in Cambridge in July 2011 and at the NBER-Bocconi conference in Milan in December 2011. I acknowledge with gratitude financial support from the European Commission under the PEGGED program. For acknowledgments, sources of research support, and disclosure of the author's material financial relationships, if any, please see http://www.nber.org/chapters/c12656.ack.

Table 12.1   Percent years of deficit over 1960–2011

	Australia	Austria	Belgium	Canada	Germany
Percent (%)	80	82	96	76	78
Last surplus	2008	1974	2006	2007	2008
	Denmark	Spain	Finland	France	UK
Percent (%)	48	78	20	90	84
Last surplus	2008	2007	2008	1974	2001
	Greece	Ireland	Italy	Japan	Netherlands
Percent (%)	80	80	100	68	88
Last surplus	1972	2007		1992	2008
	Norway	New Zealand	Portugal	Sweden	US
Percent (%)	4	46	100	42	92
Last surplus	2011	2008		2008	2000

Sources: Economic Outlook, OECD; and Eichengreen and Wyplosz (1998) for older data.
Note: Sample starts later for Australia (1962), Canada (1961), Spain (1962), and Portugal (1977).

deficits can be the rule, with few exceptions, for fifty years or more while these countries record AAA or close ratings.[1]

The euro area countries currently under International Monetary Fund–European Union (IMF–EU) programs (Greece, Ireland, and Portugal) have all expressed shock at finding themselves under market pressure. This may reflect a misleading conviction that debt crises only occur in developing or emerging market countries. It also reflects that years and decades of lenient appraisal by the financial markets and rating agencies can come to a surprisingly abrupt end. Sudden stops have long been seen as a very serious threat, quite possibly reflecting self-fulfilling phenomena. Debts can grow unnoticed until they get noticed. They represent the kind of vulnerability that gives rise to self-fulfilling crises.

Three unmistakable implications follow. First, fiscal discipline is not a year-by-year concept, in sharp contrast with the prescription of the Stability and Growth Pact. It is a medium- to long-term characteristic, which may allow for significant temporary slippages along with eventual offsetting surpluses. Second, a good track record is not sufficient to rule bad equilibria.[2]

1. It can be argued that primary budget balances offer a more accurate description of government behavior. Time series are shorter (going back to 1970 at best). They provide a similar picture, although highly indebted governments do much better, and are available from the author upon request. It remains that the budget laws, voted by parliaments, highlight the overall balance, which represents what policymakers explicitly decide upon.
2. Both Spain and Ireland achieved large debt reductions in the years leading to the financial crisis. Yet, they had to deal with the consequences of their housing price bubbles—they were not able to reassure the financial markets that they had the ability to eventually close their deficits.

A solid budgetary framework is a necessary, but not sufficient, condition because private debts can become public debts in crisis situations. Finally, the policy dominance issue is a concern that no central bank can escape, no matter how independent it may be.

Von Hagen and Harden (1994) take a wide view of what constitutes a budget process, including arrangements within the government. The thrust of their analysis is that, year in and year out, fiscal discipline is achieved either when the Finance Minister is given enough authority to control the process, or when the political forces that support the government agree to adequate contracts. Hallerberg, Strauch, and von Hagen (2009) provides some supporting empirical evidence in the case of European countries. This chapter takes a different, but related approach. It directly looks at two types of processes: fiscal numerical rules and fiscal institutions. This is in line with the recent literature (see, e.g., Kopits and Symanski 2001; Wyplosz 2005; and Debrun, Hauner, and Kumar 2009).

Fiscal rules come in a large variety of forms but they share the characteristic of imposing numeral norms. These norms can concern the budget balance, public spending, or government revenues. The limitations of rules are well known (Kydland and Prescott 1977): because they are fundamentally arbitrary and noncontingent, rules must sometimes be suboptimal, which creates a serious time-consistency problem. This argues in favor of institutions, meaning formal arrangements that are designed to prescribe actions optimally designed to respond to unforeseen contingencies. Unfortunately, the conditions required for fiscal institutions to be effective are rarely met in practice.

The next section examines the theoretical foundations for fiscal rules and their empirical relevance. Section 12.3 presents the theory behind the need to adopt restraints on the budgetary process. Section 12.4 then describes the various forms of rules. Section 12.5 considers a number of arrangements and draws policy implications. The last section concludes.

In this chapter I define restrictively fiscal rules as numerical rules (Kopits and Symanski 2001). This definition excludes institutions; that is, formal procedures that do not rely on quantitative restraints but that shape the budgetary process. Both rules and institutions have a role to play because it can be valuable to constrain policymakers. Indeed, policymakers display a deficit bias for fundamental reasons, which are examined in section 12.3.

12.2   The Deficit Bias: Theory and Evidence

In the absence of any deficit bias, we would observe budgets to be alternatively in deficit and in surplus depending on economic and/or political conditions. These fluctuations would be mainly driven by business cycles when fiscal policy is run countercyclically, as should be. The frequency of balance fluctuation could also be longer when governments borrow to invest

Fig. 12.1   Debt/GDP ratios for Greece and Ireland: 1961–2009
Source: Historical public debt database, IMF (2010).

during a catch-up phase, or because of war efforts, or else in the aftermath of
a financial crisis that has led the government to bail some of its banks out.
Fiscal discipline is present when, over the long run, the debt-to-GDP ratio
is stationary.[3] The point is illustrated in figure 12.1, which compares Greece
and Ireland and provides two main messages. First, after a period of quick
accumulation, Ireland rolled its debt back in the 1990s, a strong signal of discipline. The Greek debt, on the other hand, has enormously increased over
the whole period, yet it has been stationary over the two decades preceding
the crisis. Second, why did disciplined Ireland loose control of its debt after
2007 and run afoul of markets at about the same time as Greece? The answer
is that the authorities allowed for a build-up of private debts (public sector
salaries were also raised in an era of plenty). When the housing price bubble
blew up, the banking system collapsed and the government was compelled
to rescue its banks. This illustrates an important point: fiscal discipline may
be threatened in a myriad of ways that have apparently nothing to do with
the regular budget. Fiscal discipline is hard to assess because unexpected
spending needs may arise.

Why should governments ever be fiscally undisciplined? After all, the

3. Formally, fiscal discipline requires that the government be solvent, that is, that the transversality condition be upheld. This condition can never be tested because it refers to the future
evolution of the public debt. Debt stationarity is one way to make the transversality condition
operational.

budget constraint cannot be avoided. If it is ignored, it reestablishes itself through inflation or defaults. A large literature identifies a number of reasons that explain the widespread deficit bias phenomenon.[4] Although many reasons have been advanced (Wren-Lewis [2011b] offers an exhaustive list), two of them seem to dominate. The first one is the tendency to push out the discipline burden to future governments or even to future generations. The second reason is the interplay of democratic processes and interest group politics. Politicians enhance their (re)election probabilities by catering to interest groups and providing public largesse, at the expense of future taxpayers. Even when there is an understanding that the process is unstable, finding political support to rein in deficits may be impossible or take too long to achieve, along the lines of attrition games (Alesina and Drazen 1991).

Shifting the debt burden to future governments and spending above taxing level can both be seen as a manifestation of the common pool problem, which arises when the beneficiaries of public spending (or tax advantages) ignore the externality that they impose on all other taxpayers. "Money grab" by pressure groups is an intratemporal externality, while pushing out taxes on future generations is an intertemporal externality.

The common pool problem is inherent to democratic systems unless the voters are perfectly homogeneous and care about their descendants exactly as they care about themselves. It should not come as a surprise, therefore, that the deficit bias, the tendency of governments to run far too frequent deficits, is such an ubiquitous phenomenon, as evidenced in table 12.1. In fact, the surprise is that some countries could be free of the bias; finding out how they do so is a main objective of the present chapter.

A weakness of table 12.1 is that it does not take into account the relative sizes of deficits and surpluses, nor does it take into account the growth rate. For example, Japan only had deficits over 68 percent of the years, but its 2011 debt, at 204 percent of GDP according to the OECD, is vastly larger than that of the Netherlands, where it stands at 78 percent of GDP while deficits have occurred in 88 percent of the same years. A theoretically better gauge is the evolution of the debt as ratio to GDP. A country can be said to have been fiscally disciplined if this ratio has been stationary over a sustained period.[5] Unfortunately, the powers of stationarity tests are famously weak. This is why table 12.2 presents the results of two opposite tests: the standard ADF test (Augmented Dickey Fuller), which asks whether a series is nonstationary, and the KPSS test (Kwiatkowski, Phillips, Schmidt, and Shin), which asks the opposite question—namely, whether a series is stationary. Being

4. A synthetic treatment is offered by Persson and Tabellini (2000).
5. The proper concept is the transversality condition, but it cannot be observed. Requiring that the debt be stationary is a sufficient but not necessary condition. An alternative is to look at fiscal policy reaction functions as in Bohn (1998), Galí and Perotti (2003), and Wyplosz (2006), and check whether a dynamic stability condition is satisfied.

Table 12.2   Stationarity tests: 1960–2006

Test	Null	Australia	Austria	Belgium	Canada
ADF	Nonstationary			Reject*	
KPSS	Stationary	Reject**	Reject***	Reject**	Reject**
Conclusion		Nonstationary	Nonstationary	Ambiguous	Nonstationary

Test	Null	Finland	France	Germany	Greece	Ireland
ADF	Nonstationary					
KPSS	Stationary	Reject**	Reject***	Reject***	Reject***	
Conclusion		Nonstationary	Nonstationary	Nonstationary	Nonstationary	

Test	Null	Italy	Japan	Netherlands	New Zealand	Norway
ADF	Nonstationary					
KPSS	Stationary	Reject***	Reject***			
Conclusion		Nonstationary	Nonstationary	Ambiguous		Ambiguous

Test	Null	Portugal	Spain	Turkey	UK	US
ADF	Nonstationary				Reject*	
KPSS	Stationary	Reject**	Reject**		Reject**	Reject**
Conclusion		Nonstationary	Nonstationary	Ambiguous	Ambiguous	Nonstationary

Source: Abbas et al. (2010).

Notes: The sample includes all countries for which the data cover the period 1960 to 2006, after filling in some missing observations with linear interpolation. The ADF test looks for a unit root while the KPSS test computes an LM (Lagrange multiplier) statistic concerning the variance of a random walk component in the decomposition of the original series into a constant and a random walk.

***Significant at the 1 percent level.
**Significant at the 5 percent level.
*Significant at the 10 percent level.

weak, both tests tend to not reject the hypothesis being tested. This is indeed what is often found when looking at countries for which comparable data on the debt-to-GDP ratios exist going back to 1960. The sample stops in 2006, in order to avoid the exceptional increases associated with the financial crisis.

Table 12.2 indicates whether any of these two hypotheses is rejected by the corresponding test. Because of low test power, nonrejection of the null hypothesis is probably often misleading. More interesting, therefore, is when the test is rejected, but even so the combination of both tests can yield ambiguous results. Of the nineteen countries included in the sample, nonstationarity is only rejected twice by the ADF test (for Belgium and the United Kingdom), but in both instances, stationarity is also rejected by the KPSS test. The opposite case, when neither stationarity nor nonstationarity is rejected occurs twice, in the cases of Ireland and the Netherlands. For the remaining fifteen countries, nonstationarity is not rejected while stationarity is rejected, suggesting that fiscal indiscipline is indeed the rule, with no clear exception. Interestingly, the debt crisis has (so far) only affected two of these fifteen countries, as well as Ireland, which is classified as ambiguous.

12.3   An Analysis of Policy Rules

The previous section has shown that the deficit bias is widespread among developed countries. It has also argued that the intra and intertemporal common pool phenomena are likely to be key reasons for the deficit bias. This bias is often cited as an argument for intervention in the political process that drives the preparation, adoption, and execution of the budget. The precise form of this intervention must be carefully tailored to achieve a second-best outcome.

In particular, if the goal is to reduce the deficit bias via a reformed budget process, then the policy intervention needs to target the political failure that gives rise to deficit bias, in effect internalizing the common pool externality as shaped by the political process. Von Hagen (2002) concludes that the solution depends on the electoral process and the form of government. In particular rules, which are time-inconsistent by construction, are likely to be dominated by institutions, as argued in Wyplosz (2005). On the other hand, political acceptability of fiscal policy institutions seems highly limited, if one judges from the small number of countries that have adopted some, as described in section 12.5. Numerical rules, on the other hand, are widespread and they often have been successful, so far at least. For this reason it is worthwhile to examine fiscal rules with an open mind. This section starts with theoretical considerations, asking how fiscal rules fare on four key dimensions: the time inconsistency problem, burden sharing across generations in aging societies, capture by special interests, and government hierarchies.

12.3.1   Time Inconsistency

As a commitment device, a rule is vulnerable to time inconsistency. Indeed, there will always be instances when it is suboptimal to abide by previous commitments. Much as a rule that can be easily evaded is useless, a rule that is strictly set stands not to be respected in some situations.[6] Two main implications follow. First, it must be recognized that there exist unforeseeable events likely to break the rule. The usual solution is to write escape clauses into the rule. Escape clauses, however, cannot be fully contingent, because too many relevant events are unforeseeable. This opens up a major risk of circumvention. Second, some foreseeable events may warrant foreseeable adjustments to the rule without affecting its disciplinary effect. This is clearly the case for cyclical fluctuations. While each business cycle is sui generis, in principle it is possible for countercyclical fiscal policies to be compatible with debt stability. It is also desirable because procyclical policies are particularly subject to time inconsistency.

12.3.2   Aging and Burden Shifting to Future Generations

The common pool temptation is nearly irresistible in the face of an aging population. Aging has two origins: increases in life duration and reduced fertility. The first one is slow and, presumably, permanent. The second one probably is a one-off event (i.e., fertility will remain low) that will create a new steady state with a permanently smaller population. As is well known, the resulting demographic transition between two steady states creates a situation whereby the next generation, the first one to be less numerous, faces a larger burden than the previous and the following ones. Part of the increase comes from higher health costs, which each generation should finance for itself.

But another part of the impact of the demographic transition, probably the bulk, comes from the need to pay for retirement benefits. In a pay-as-you-go system, each generation cares for the previous one and will be taken care of by the next one; clearly the demographic transition breaks the fairness of this arrangement at the expense of the generation in between. The common pool problem implies that the first generation, the baby boomers, will endeavor to shift the burden to the next one. Indeed, estimates by the European Commission (2009) indicate that, given current policies, twenty of the twenty-seven EU countries will raise the annual costs of pension by more than 2 percent of GDP by 2060. The average additional cost for these countries is estimated to represent 5.8 percent of GDP.

Reducing this considerable burden shift requires that current voters approve paying more taxes, receiving less pension benefits, or working lon-

6. The financial crisis is a good example. Many governments sincerely committed to fiscal discipline ended up reluctantly opening up large deficits.

ger. Several countries have started to move in this direction. These moves can be seen as numerical rules that affect some specific elements of the budget. Even though not all countries have enacted such rules, or not sufficiently so, the fact that voters are willing to support such decisions illustrates one important advantage of rules when they are transparent: they make the externality clear and its internalization acceptable.

An alternative and intriguing interpretation is that the current generation expects the next one to shift the burden as well to the following one, which would do the same, and so forth. This could be optimal intergenerational burden smoothing. Yet another possibility is that the externality could be entirely internalized within families if baby boomers leave adequate bequests. This would be a way of reducing wealth redistribution—and perpetuating inequalities.

12.3.3   Capture

The standard common pool effect describes interest groups vying for financial favors from the government, under the assumption that the corresponding taxes will be paid for mostly by others. In equilibrium, each interest group pays for all the favors, an externality that is the source of a deficit bias. Obviously, the solution to the common pool problem is that the government rejects all favors, carrying out spending and transfers purely on the basis of welfare principles exactly as the mythical benevolent dictator would do. The deficit bias arises because there is no benevolent dictator, only governments that court the support of voters and that are captured to varying degrees by interest groups. A number of empirical studies provide indirect support to this interpretation, showing that any source of heterogeneity (income inequality, political fragmentation, ethnic diversity) that enhances externalities ceteris paribus leads to larger deficits.[7]

The response to the common pool problem is to centralize the budget process in order to centralize the externalities. A large number of solutions have been proposed and many of them have been implemented. They all aimed at improving the governance of the budget process, reflecting the fact that the deficit bias can be seen as a political failure, a weakness of democratic systems.[8] The following sections examine and evaluate these solutions.

12.3.4   Central and Local Governments and International Aspects

Of particular interest is the relationship between central and subcentral governments. This situation opens up an additional common pool problem when local governments may reasonably expect to receive transfers from the

---

7. The classics are Roubini and Sachs (1989) and Alesina and Perotti (1995). For a recent contribution, see Larch (2010).
8. A survey of recent changes is IMF (2009).

central (or higher-up) governments.[9] As a result, subcentral governments are subject to two mutually reinforcing sources of a deficit bias.

A similar situation arises at the international level when a national government receives external financing, either as part of regular transfers or as bailouts. This is why the IMF only provides loans and requires that these loans be senior and fully serviced. The same applies to World Bank lending, with the exception of Individual Development Account (IDA) grants to the poorest countries.

The European monetary union can be seen as an intermediate case between a federal arrangement and a purely international agreement. There exist regular transfers, under the structural funds program and the common agricultural policy, which together absorb the bulk of a small budget (about 40 percent of a budget that represents about 1 percent of European GDP). Yet, for some countries, these transfers amount to several percentage points of GDP.[10] The crucial question is whether a government can be bailed out in case of budgetary difficulties. Within the monetary union, the no-bailout clause (art. 125) was intended to be the solution to the international common pool problem. As is well known, the clause has been ignored and bailouts have been handed out to three member countries (at the time of writing). In order to compensate for the corresponding deficit bias incentive, a strengthened Stability and Growth Pact is currently under adoption.

12.4   Arrangements for Fiscal Policy Discipline

Arrangements to limit the deficit bias must offset the incentives generated by the common pool problem. Whatever form they take, they must act as a constraint on the budgetary process and therefore on those who decide on the budget. The challenge is that those who have incentives to allow for a deficit bias are asked to adopt arrangements that will eliminate or reduce these incentives. There are basically three possibilities: (1) delegation to an agent; (2) binding numerical rules; (3) a better budgetary process.

12.4.1   The Democratic Requirement

All democracies share the property that budgets are set jointly by the executive and the legislative branches. Budgets require approval by elected bodies, essentially because fiscal policy is redistributive. Taking from some to give to others is only legitimate if it is the outcome of an uncontroversial

9. See, for example, Alesina, Angeloni, and Etro (2001) and Krogstrup and Wyplosz (2010). Pisauro (2003) notes that, on top of the common pool problem, there exists a moral hazard problem created by the possibility of a bailout of local governments by the central government. While the mechanics of bailouts are indeed different from those of transfers, a bailout can be seen as part of the more general common pool problem.
10. Schuknecht, von Hagen, and Wolswijk (2008) find that EU countries that are net beneficiaries of transfers face a lower risk premium ceteris paribus, and that the same applies to Canadian provinces.

democratic process ("no taxation without representation"). Any constraining arrangement must be democratically legitimate. How do potential solutions to the deficit bias measure up to this requirement?

A first solution is to delegate some aspects of fiscal policy to an unelected agent. This may well be the first-best solution. Indeed, the deficit bias can be reduced or eliminated through delegation to an agent who is not exposed to pressure by interest groups. Taking power out of the hands of elected officials in favor of bureaucrats may seem excessive, but that is exactly what is achieved with central bank independence.[11] Monetary policy, however, has limited redistribution effects, mostly between borrowers and lenders as the result of interest rate changes. In the absence of inflation, these effects are likely to be reversed along the cycle. For this reason, delegation of monetary policy is different from delegation of budgetary responsibilities. Even though delegation could be limited to just setting the budget balance, which has limited redistributive effects, it is not observed in practice. Delegation to nonelected officials appears to be difficult, if not impossible.[12]

Numerical rules are more acceptable because they are self-imposed by the very elected officials that they are designed to bind. In fact, rules are like laws that restrict freedom for the common good. Governments and parliaments routinely operate under such laws, many of which are inscribed in constitutions. Naturally, elected officials wish to avoid limits on their own freedom of action. Since laws can be amended or even repudiated, the challenge is not just to have such limits adopted, but that they remain in place when they become binding. There are several instances of potentially useful rules that were rescinded when they were needed most. This is the case of Europe's Stability and Growth Pact or of former Chancellor of the Exchequer Gordon Brown's self-imposed fiscal responsibility principle. Another example is the US Gramm-Rudman-Hollings deficit reduction law of 1985; the annual deficit target was raised in 1987 when it proved politically difficult to meet.

The last solution avoids any formal straitjacket. Instead, it aims at encouraging policymakers to internalize among themselves the externalities that give rise to the deficit bias. Various solutions have been suggested. Hallerberg, Strauch, and von Hagen (2009) distinguish between two categories: delegation and contract. Under delegation, some power is vested with a player, for example the finance minister, whose role is to achieve fiscal discipline. Under contract, the political parties that join in a governing coalition agree upon fiscal discipline. Hallerberg and colleagues note that the success of any arrangement depends on whether it is compatible with the political backstage. For example, coalition governments are unlikely to devolve strong power to a finance minister who necessarily represents one party

11. In noneconomic matters, other references include a Supreme Court of Justice and Constitutional Courts.
12. Wren-Lewis (2011a) makes a similar point.

and its supporting interest groups. Another type of attempt at improving the budget process is to empower somewhat the administration, seen as less likely to bend to pressure groups. In this case the bureaucrats do not make decisions, but sort out and shape the options that are presented to policymakers.

12.4.2   Types of Rules

Existing numerical rules vary from one country to another. They frequently stipulate upper limits on the budget balance, the debt, spending, or they set lower limits on tax revenues. Quite often, several of these limits are combined. Some rules apply year by year, others define limits over several years, sometimes over the entire business cycle or over the duration of a government. Some are national, with subcentral government components. The European Monetary Union's Stability and Growth Pact is a supranational rule.[13] According to IMF (2009), eighty countries have adopted some rule or another.

In theory, if they are well-designed and implemented, fiscal rules can eliminate the deficit bias. In practice, however, rules are often disappointing. A first difficulty harks back to the old debate on rules versus discretion, and the time inconsistency problem. Because rules can never be fully contingent, situations may arise that would make any rule very costly to respect. The financial crisis, which has led to cumulated debt increases of some 30 percent of GDP in many developed economies, is a case in point.

For this reason, any rule must be flexible enough to accommodate unforeseeable contingencies. As a consequence, the precise design of rules becomes of the utmost importance. The presumption is that rules should be simple enough to be understood by policymakers and citizens alike, but flexibility is bound to come at the expense of simplicity. Consider, for example, strict balanced budget rules, which imply procyclical fiscal policies. In order to avoid procyclicality, and possibly to encourage countercyclicality, the rule must target the budget over a whole cycle or be stated in terms of a cyclically adjusted measure. Since business cycles cannot be predicted, an over-the-cycle rule can lose much of its meaning, although solutions have been proposed, as discussed later. Cyclical correction is more art than science and is not easily comprehended by the public at large, which opens the door to manipulations and, quite possibly, to an eventual repeal.

More generally, rules can always be manipulated. Crucially, since they are forward-looking, budgets are constructed on the basis of assumptions about economic and financial conditions over the next fiscal year. This gives much leeway to the government, often enough to loosen the rule. Independent ex

13. Both African monetary unions and the East Caribbean monetary union also operate supranational fiscal rules.

post evaluations of outcomes is a solution, but it involves judgment and, anyway, evaluations will always come too late.[14]

Furthermore, the democratic requirement articulated in the previous section implies that the politics of fiscal rules is not encouraging. A government subject to the deficit bias can fairly easily convince its public opinion that today's circumstances are special and that technocratic arrangements should not stand in the way of serving people's interests. In addition, rules only work if noncompliance is sanctioned with a high degree of certainty. In democracies, however, voters seldom sanction governments that fail to deliver on their promises, unless they violate the law. Fiscal discipline rarely defines election outcomes—otherwise we would not observe the frequent lapses documented in table 12.1. Legal sanctions require that the law be written in precise enough terms to face powerful challenges, which runs against the simplicity principle. Worse, laws can always be changed at the worst time if they are time-inconsistent. Debrun (2011) provides an example where a rule is time-inconsistent for the currently elected government but not for the public at large.

This all implies that fiscal rules are unlikely to be a panacea. This is indeed what the evidence suggests (see, e.g., Kopits 2001; Guichard et al. 2007; and IMF 2009). On the other hand, Debrun and Kumar (2007) provide panel-data estimates of the impact of fiscal rules on the primary budget balance and find that rules can be effective. Yet, the evidence is not overwhelming. This may be because rules differ too widely in their details for valid cross-section comparisons. It may also reflect that the unobserved political and institutional context matters. Another interpretation, suggested by Debrun and Kumar (2007), is that the evidence may suffer from reverse causality, namely that disciplined governments may wish to adopt rules as a way of cementing and signaling their determination.

12.4.3   Rules versus Institutions

The limits of rules may be seen as making fiscal institutions an attractive alternative. Defined broadly to include nonnumerical rules, fiscal institutions encompass a wide variety of arrangements. Examples include the (possibly partial) delegation of the budget process to an independent body, intragovernmental agreements, multiyear programming, and codes of good behavior. The advantage of institutions is that they are less likely to be time-inconsistent, if only because they do not require specifying all contingencies that may arise and what to do when they arise. Institutions instead can have a mandate (to establish fiscal discipline in the long run) and they may involve people who can think. If these people are sufficiently independent and competent, mandates should do better than rules.

---

14. A solution is to require that outruns be compensated (see the Swiss Debt Brake). Even so, massive crises like the current one cannot be dealt with easily.

This means that institutions can work but only if they are well-designed. What are the conditions for an effective design? Hallerberg, Strauch, and von Hagen (2009) convincingly argue that there is no single answer to that question. In order to work well, institutions must be adapted to the political institutions, including electoral systems, types of governments, and degree of ideological differences in society. They provide evidence that well-adapted institutions work.

Fiscal policy councils are a particular case of fiscal institutions. Their remits can vary all the way from just "telling the truth" to actually deciding on the budget balance. In the earlier case, the council is intended to be an official watchdog, one that benefits from official recognition and provides unbiased views. For example, the council may be formally consulted to evaluate the government forecasts of spending and income, which are based on forecasts of variables such as GDP growth, inflation, the interest and exchange rates, and so forth. Its own forecasts may be for mandatory use in budget planning or simply produced for advisory purposes.

Up to now, there does not exist any fiscal policy council with the power to decide on the budget balance, probably because it would clash with the democratic requirement. On the other hand, councils with formal advisory roles have become frequent in recent years. Calmfors and Wren-Lewis (2011) list eleven independent councils with advisory or nonbinding control roles in developed countries.[15] Debrun, Hauner, and Kumar (2009) report that similar councils have been set up in other developed or emerging-market countries (Japan, Chile, Indonesia, Jordan, Korea, and Mexico). Several international institutions, including the IMF, the OECD, and the European Commission, have recommended the establishment of such councils.

A growing empirical literature has begun to evaluate the design and effectiveness of fiscal policy councils. Country studies (e.g., Calmfors 2010; IMF 2005; and Debrun, Hauner, and Kumar 2009) suggest that, in order to have a detectable disciplinary impact, fiscal councils must be allowed to make normative, quantified statements. Yet it also appears that the political costs for a government not to heed such advice are very limited.[16]

A fair conclusion is that advisory fiscal policy councils have made a tangible contribution to fiscal discipline in countries where policymakers have shown a willingness to listen to them, which is why they created them in the first place—a case of reverse causality. Elsewhere, the councils provide

15. These committees are in Austria (Government Debt Committee established in 1997); Belgium (High Council of Finance, 1989); Canada (Parliamentary Budget Office, 2008); Denmark (Economic Council, 1962); Germany (Council of Economic Experts, 1962); Hungary (Fiscal Council, 2008); Netherlands (Central Planning Bureau, 1947); Slovenia (Fiscal Council, 2010); Sweden (Fiscal Policy Council, 2007); the United Kingdom (Office for Budget Responsibility, 2010); and the United States (Congressional Budget Office, 1975).

16. A good example is Hungary. A fiscal policy committee was set up in 2008 but was effectively dismantled a couple of years later when a new government came to power.

useful analyses and viewpoints but their recommendations are frequently ignored. Like fiscal rules, advisory fiscal policy councils are not a panacea.

12.4.4 Rules and Institutions

There is a tendency to consider rules and institutions as substitutes. Yet, the limitations of each approach suggest that combining them may help. Because they can never be adequately contingent, rules are too rigid and therefore time-inconsistent; they simply cannot be respected in some situations. Fiscal institutions may be seen as too open-ended and therefore time-inconsistent in the sense that they may be too flexible in the face of unforeseen events. But fiscal institutions that apply and interpret not fully contingent rules are promising. Like a supreme court that applies and interprets laws voted by the parliament, or like a central bank that follows a flexible inflation-targeting rule, fiscal institutions can appeal to a rule to guide and justify their actions. Rules can be deviated from when needed without losing their credibility if an independent and competent institution authorizes such deviations. The examples that follow illustrate the benefits from combining rules and institutions.

12.5 Historical Experiences

This section presents a few examples of fiscal arrangements from developed and emerging market countries. While most arrangements have been introduced rather recently, other countries have long sought to buttress fiscal discipline.

12.5.1 Central Government Rules and Institutions

The Netherlands

Following years of deficits, the Netherlands started to build original arrangements in the early 1980s. These arrangements have been gradually refined. As figure 12.2 shows, the Netherlands has performed better than the other European countries. Its public debt has been reduced from 1993 onward, until the onset of the financial and economic crisis. Even though part of the measured (gross) debt reduction is related to asset sales and to natural gas revenues, the prima facie evidence—based on both timing and the fact that these actions have not been squandered—is that the Netherlands has become fiscally disciplined following the adoption of its new fiscal policy regime.

The Dutch arrangement combines rules and institutions.[17] The key rule is a path for the budget ceiling, determined in constant euro and set for the duration of each parliament. The institutional setup is quite elaborate and

17. For a detailed presentation, see Bos (2007).

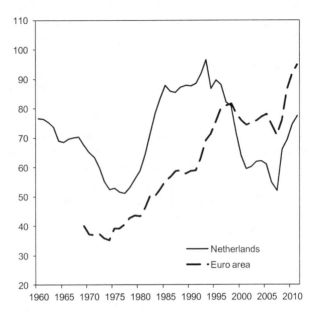

Fig. 12.2   Gross public debt in the Netherlands and the Eurozone (percent of GDP)
Source: AMECO, European Commission.

rests on an explicit agreement among coalition parties before they take office and is valid until the next election. Two bodies are involved: the CPB (Netherlands Bureau for Economic Analysis) and the SER (Social and Economic Council of the Netherlands).

The CPB is a technical agency that makes economic and budget forecasts. The originality of the Dutch approach is that it evaluates the budgetary implications of political party programs *before* elections. After the election, the parties that form a coalition work out a binding medium-term program for the duration of the legislature. This program is evaluated by the CPB, taking into account its own macroeconomic projections. Then, as annual budgets are being prepared (preparations start two years ahead), the ministry of finance relies exclusively on CPB forecasts and medium-term projections. As a highly respected neutral agency, the CPB thus takes the responsibility for macroeconomic and budget forecasts out of political hands.

The SER is a tripartite advisory body composed of one-third employers, one-third trade unions, and one-third experts, including the CPB. It deals with the social security system and with pensions (and wage negotiations). Its recommendations are not binding on the government but influential when it can reach an agreement.

A key element is the required adoption of medium-term spending ceilings (for each ministry) at the beginning of the legislature. These ceilings are based on a detailed list of policy measures agreed upon in the coalition agreement. The agreement itself is built around explicit deficit and debt targets for the end of the legislature. There is no standard—and arbitrary—mandatory target numbers but, given that governments always involve several parties, the practice has a clear moderating impact.[18] There is a little bit of flexibility (1 percent) for shifting spending from one year to the next but "growth bonuses" are not usable later. The result is a tendency for procyclical policies. This aspect may be of limited importance for a small and very open economy. Taxes become the main macroeconomic instrument, under the scrutiny of the CPB, which evaluates debt sustainability.

The effectiveness of the Dutch arrangement can be traced to three elements. First, the combination of rules and institutions. Second, the fact that the numerical rule is not tied to a particular, arbitrary number but left to publicly visible negotiations among coalition partners. Third, they are well-adapted to the Dutch political system. As argued by Hallerberg, Strauch, and von Hagen (2009), legislative contracts work well in multiparty government coalitions.

Switzerland and Germany

The constitutional rule adopted by Germany in 2009 is due to be fully implemented in 2016.[19] It is closely patterned after the Swiss "debt brake" that was adopted and written into the constitution in 2000 and came into force in 2003. Figure 12.3 shows that the rule has reversed the familiar trend of debt build-up, a reversal particularly spectacular as it has continued throughout the crisis.

The debt brake is a rule, with an escape clause that involves the parliament. In the Swiss version, the rule specifies that the overall federal budget must be balanced over the cycle. This is achieved as follows. Any imbalance, positive or negative, is credited into a control account. If the cumulated amount is negative, it must be brought to balance "over the next few years." No requirement applies when the cumulated amount is positive. This clever arrangement implies that, over time and at the government's discretion, deficits must be compensated for by surpluses. The stipulation is flexible enough not to put the government in a procyclical straitjacket. It can lead to prolonged slippages, however. In a country very sensitive to the rule of law, like Switzerland, such slippages are highly unlikely.[20] During the crisis, the debt brake figured prominently in policy debates and quite clearly shaped the policy response.

The arrangement includes an escape clause. In case of exceptional circum-

18. Expenditures had crept up to almost 60 percent of GDP by the early 1980s. They went down to less than 45 percent before the crisis.

19. It was initially planned to implement it in 2011 but this date has been pushed back because of the crisis. Interim arrangements start in 2011, however. A variant will apply to the Laender as of 2020.

20. It remains to be seen whether it will be as effective in Germany once it is implemented.

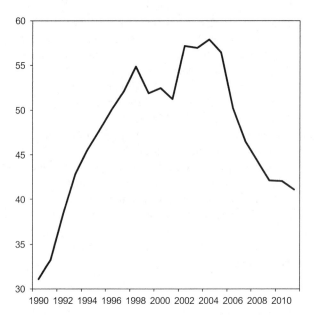

Fig. 12.3   Swiss public debt (percent of GDP)
Source: Economic Outlook, OECD.

stances (deep recession, natural disasters, and the like) the implied spending ceiling can be raised but this requires a qualified majority (three-fifths) in both chambers. An amendment stipulates that any such slippage must be added to the control account, which means that, even if exceptional, bygones shall not be bygones.

The success of the Swiss debt brake (so far) derives from the simplicity of the rule. As previously noted, it remains to be seen what would happen should a negative balance in the control account not be corrected "over the next few years." Presumably, the case could be sent to the Higher Court. That the debt has continued to decline throughout the crisis is surprising since deficits are expected in bad years, even without invoking exceptional circumstances (which would not have applied since the GDP declined by only 2 percent in 2009). One reason is that Switzerland is a small open economy closely integrated with the European Union so that it benefitted from fiscal expansions implemented elsewhere. Another reason is that the debt brake only concerns the federal government, which spends about one-third of total public outlays. The rest of the spending is carried by the cantons (about 40 percent of the total), municipalities, and the social security system. Many, but not all, cantons have adopted since the early 1980s—and some much earlier—various forms of budget rules. As a result, with one exception,[21] their debt levels are low. The same applies to municipalities in a similar fashion.

21. The exception is the Geneva canton, which has no budget rule.

Chile

Chile is an early fiscal rule adopter. Adoption came at the end of a long period during which the public debt was reduced from 165 percent in 1985 to 20 percent of GDP by 2000. The intention was to solidify and codify the emerging fiscal discipline tradition.[22] Maybe because of its pioneering aspect, the rule is technically complex (for noneconomists) and not quite complete.[23] Initially introduced informally, the rule was written into law in 2006 (Fiscal Responsibility Law).

The rule requires that the cyclically adjusted primary budget be in surplus. The target was 1 percent from 2001 until 2008, when it was reduced to 0.5 percent, and further to 0 percent in 2009 to allow for a countercyclical response to the global crisis. In practice, the procedure is to estimate cyclically adjusted government revenues and to then derive total maximum spending. There is no escape clause, but the target can be changed, as already noted. While the budget must be ex ante in conformity with the rule, there is no sanction when the realized budget differs, presumably because underlying assumptions proved to be too optimistic, which happened twice, in 2002 and 2009.

The calculation of the ex ante structural revenues is therefore the lynchpin of the rule. Beyond the usual complexity of taking into account cyclical effects, Chile's rule is highly sensitive to copper price fluctuations because tax revenues from copper production can represent a quarter of total public income. Given the volatility of copper prices, it is essential but highly challenging to correct ex ante for these fluctuations. This is where an institution is needed to operate the rule. A committee of independent experts is in charge of providing the government with assumptions regarding GDP and the long-run price of copper. It follows that forecast errors concerning the GDP cannot be the result of government's manipulation. It also follows that in any given year the actual price of copper is likely to differ from the long-run estimate. It is expected that the independent experts are not biased, so that forecast errors must cancel out over time, thus imparting no bias to the rule.

The surplus rule implies that eventually, the government must be a net creditor, which occurred in 2005, as figure 12.4 shows. This was an objective of the rule, in fact. It was recognized that copper resources would eventually disappear and that Chile needed to build up a welfare system. As a result, Chile operates two Sovereign Wealth Funds.

The success of the Chilean rule may be surprising given its incompleteness. There is no limit to the possibility of changing the target, nor even any standard procedure to do so, and there is no sanction for not achieving the target. Part of the reason for the success is the existence of an expert group, which is involved in the budgetary process, as it produces cyclically adjusted figures, an arrangement that is remindful of the Dutch case. Another reason

22. This is a clear case of reverse causality in the sense of Debrun and Kumar (2009).
23. Dabán (2011) offers a recent review.

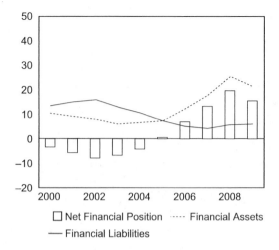

Fig. 12.4   Chile's central government (percent of GDP)
Source: Dabán (2011).

is the transparency of the process. The calculations of the cyclically adjusted budget, which have been refined over time, are presented and explained in great detail to the broad public. The two recent target changes, for instance, have been carefully and candidly explained.

Equally important is the relationship between government and parliament. The power to set the budget is entirely in the hands of the president. The parliament is not allowed to reduce taxes or raise spending. This fits well with the delegation model of Hallerberg, Strauch, and von Hagen (2009) since the presidential system delivers de facto a single party majority.

Britain's Office for Budget Responsbility

In 1997, the British Chancellor of the Exchequer adopted two fiscal rules: (1) the budget deficit may only finance public investment (a golden rule); (2) the debt-to-GDP ratio may not exceed 40 percent. The rule was to be monitored by the chancellor himself, based on forecasts by HM Treasury. The Treasury was also requested to produce long-run forecasts (forty years) to gauge long-run sustainability. As figure 12.5 shows, the rule was met for a few years but then slippage set in after 2002. The idea that a public commitment with no enforcement mechanism would work was disproved. This has led the newly elected British government to pass in 2011 the Budget Responsibility and National Audit Act.

The new act combines a set of rules and an independent fiscal policy committee.[24] The rules are similar to the previous ones: the cyclically adjusted

---

24. For details, see Wren-Lewis (2011b). This arrangement bears similarity to the Swedish independent council, described in Calmfors (2010).

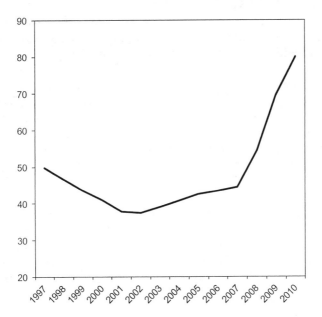

Fig. 12.5   Public debt in Great Britain
Source: AMECO, European Commission.

budget must be balanced—or in surplus—over the following five years, the debt-to-GDP ratio must be declining by the end of the legislature, and long-run forecasts must show that public finances are sustainable. The main difference is the replacement of the golden rule—a shaky concept since deciding what is public investment is open to manipulation—by the balance requirement over a rolling five-year horizon, which is essentially calling for balanced budgets, on average, over time.

The real innovation is the creation of the Office for Budget Responsibility (OBR). This independent body takes over the forecasting tasks so far carried out by the Treasury. This arrangement is a clear response to the fact that many of the slippages over the 2000s were predicted by optimistic forecasts regarding both macroeconomic variables and the budget figures. A Budgetary Responsibility Committee that includes five members runs the OBR. The first committee includes widely respected economists. The staff is small (fifteen persons), under the assumption that the OBR has full access to the Treasury resources.

Much like the US Congressional Budget Office (CBO), the OBR is restricted to produce forecasts only on the basis of government policy. This implies that the OBR cannot look at "what if" questions; that is, to make policy suggestions. On the other hand, it has the monopoly of official forecasts and policy evaluations. Importantly, the OBR has only an advisory role in the sense that the chancellor can carry out any policy that he wishes, but under the constraint that he cannot challenge the OBR's macroeconomic and budgetary implications since the Treasury has given up the possibility to use its technical expertise to that effect. Since the chancellor is also bound by the rules, the room for undisciplined behavior is narrow, but it still exists.

It will obviously take time to evaluate whether this arrangement is effective. It rests on delegation of fiscal discipline to the chancellor; Hallerberg, Strauch, and von Hagen (2009) argue that this is the correct arrangement for single-majority governments, which often occurs in the United Kingdom but not currently. Delegation also characterized the 1997 arrangement, when a single-majority government was in place, but it failed when the chancellor single-handedly decided to overlook his self-imposed rule. The new arrangement combines a reasonable set of rules with an institution that is intended to act as a whistle-blower. This is in line with the view by Jonung and Larch (2006), which considers that delegating forecasting to an independent agency is a key ingredient to achieve fiscal discipline. Interestingly, in the autumn of 2011, the OBR has warned that the fiscal retrenchment efforts were too strong at a time when a recession is likely. The chancellor promptly announced a set of expansionary policies.[25]

12.5.2   Subcentral Government Rules and Institutions

The additional common pool problem that arises in federal states requires special treatment to avoid that subcentral government indiscipline undermines adequate policies carried out at the central level. A textbook example of this problem is Argentina in the late 1990s.

Belgium

In the late 1980s, following years of internal strife and rapidly rising public debt, Belgium shifted from a centralized to a federal state. It created a complex overlapping system of regions and communities to which many central functions were transferred. By the mid-1990s, it set up an arrangement designed to establish overall budget discipline. The key characteristic was the adoption of institutions, without any numerical rule. The main element was a reform of the High Finance Council (HFC), entrusting this body with the task of monitoring regional governments and of suggesting budget balances for the various levels of government, with the objective of achieving debt sustainability. These suggestions shape formal agreements (called budgetary conventions) between the federal and the subcentral governments. These agreements are coherent with the Stability and Growth Pact's stability programs.[26]

The HFC is composed of high-level experts from ministries, the National

25. A similar situation arose in Sweden earlier in the year.
26. Macroeconomic forecasts are proposed by the National Accounts Institute, which pools resources from various institutions.

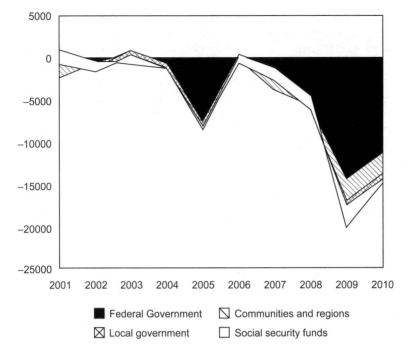

Fig. 12.6   Budget balances of various Belgian authorities (€ mn.)
Source: Belgostat.

Bank, the Federal Planning Bureau, and academia. It is therefore not an independent body, rather a coalition of the willing whose task is to find acceptable proposals in a system that is not politically harmonious.

The arrangement has worked well, as total public debt went down from 140 percent of GDP in 1993 to 88 percent in 2007. Since the crisis started, however, deficits have grown again and the overall debt is expected to reach 104 percent in 2011. Figure 12.6 shows that the relapse is mostly occurring at the federal level, even though slippages occur across the board. This reflects the working of the automatic stabilizers but also the need for the federal authorities to recapitalize banks to the tune of 6 percent of GDP. More worrisome is the recent deterioration. It may be the consequence of an ongoing and protracted political crisis that has left the country for months running with interim governments. It may also be a consequence of the common pool inherent to the overlapping of the federal system. This system gives rise to a severe vertical imbalance, whereby spending powers are extensively devolved, whereas tax policy and collection remain in federal hands. This leads to massive implicit transfers to the Walloon and undermines accountability at the regional level.

In a country with multiple and partly overlapping layers of governments, each one itself a coalition, the arrangement has emphasized contracts among parties and among governments. The HFC is generally credited for having played an important role, outlining consensus solutions that respect fiscal discipline.[27] However, Coene and Langenus (2011) argue that the HFC had influence when government's preferences and HFC's mandate were well aligned, yet another case of reverse causality. The absence of any numerical rule did not seem to have hampered the arrangement. Similarly, the fact that the HFC is not independent but instead brings together the traditional "culprits" of the deficit bias, points to the advantage of well-structured negotiations. In brief, the Belgian experience conforms to the view, developed by Hallerberg, Strauch, and von Hagen (2009), that arrangements well-adapted to the political situation may deliver fiscal discipline, in contrast to the view, presented here, that favors combining numerical rules and independent bodies.

Canada and the United States

Both countries share the absence of any constraining rule imposed by the federal on to subfederal entities, compensated by the adoption by most subfederal governments of self-imposed rules. In both countries, federal spending about matches in size subcentral spending with significant transfers from the federal level, some of which are conditional on policies in place.

In Canada, a spending limit was adopted at the federal level from 1992 to 1996. During this period six provinces adopted balanced budget rules that remain in effect. These rules differ from one province to the other (see Tellier and Imbeau 2004). Figure 12.7 shows that these changes came at a time when fiscal discipline was seriously under threat. The figure also shows that, since then, both levels of governments have stabilized their debts. The overall public debt level peaked at 102 percent of GDP in 1996 and declined to 67 percent in 2007. Not all provinces, however, have been fiscally disciplined: the aggregate performance conceals the combination of large surpluses in resource-rich provinces and sizable deficits elsewhere, notably in Ontario, the largest province.

In the United States too, all states but one have adopted various forms of balanced budget rules. These rules started in the middle of the nineteenth century and have been evolving since.[28] The federal government is subject to a nominal debt ceiling that is regularly raised by Congress, a procedure that can be conflictual when the president and the Congress majority are from different parties. In 1985, Congress passed the Gramm-Rudman-Hollings Act, which introduced the notion of budget balance paths, aiming at a balance in 1991. The Act was modified—including after being declared uncon-

27. For a recent appraisal, see Aneja et al. (2011).
28. Interestingly, Tejedo (2007) notes that these rules originated when US states faced sudden debt increases following bailouts of private banks. For a recent description of the situation, see NCSL (2010).

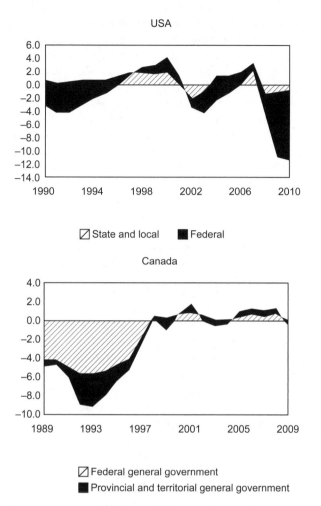

Fig. 12.7   Federal and subfederal budget balances in Canada and the United States (percent of GDP)
Source: Office of Management and Budget and Statistics Canada

stitutional by the Supreme Court—until it was abandoned in 1990, replaced by the Budget Enforcement Act, which introduced a rule of unchanged deficits at the margin. As Figure 7 shows, this act did not prevent a serious deterioration of the federal budget until it was left to expire in 2002. This is a good example of a rule that failed, because it was too tight and because the polity did not support it.

Figure 12.7 also shows that the federal budget has been strongly countercyclical while state budgets were very moderately countercyclical. This observation confirms that the state-level rules are binding while the federal arrangements are not. It is likely that state governments have little incentive to deviate from their rules because the fiscal multiplier is bound to be low given the integration of the US markets, while the federal government can expect its own fiscal policy to be more effective. Countercyclical transfers from the central level also reduce the pressure on state governments.

One interpretation of the contrasted experiences of Canada and the United States is that the common pool problem among subcentral governments is relatively weak. This may be due to the small multipliers, which matches Musgrave's view that countercyclical policy is better contracted out to the central government. Still, it remains to be understood why the common pool problem has been relatively benign at the subfederal level (California being a counterexample). The existence of rules is one interpretation. Yet another one is the role of market-imposed discipline. The evidence is that financial markets impose risk premia on government bonds that is related to debt size and also to budgetary arrangements.[29] This provides both a gauge and an incentive for state governments to be fiscally disciplined.

The Euro Area

The euro area is a very special case that combines national sovereignty, as far as fiscal policy is concerned, with some elements of federalism, the common currency. Further complicating the situation is the Stability and Growth Pact, which is designed to influence national fiscal policies but cannot override national sovereignty. The sovereign debt crisis has further erased the separation between a common currency and independent fiscal policies after the de facto abandonment of a treaty-level no-bailout rule that prevented governments and the central bank from helping out countries unable to borrow to serve their debts and pay for their deficits.

The European Commission can be seen as the equivalent of a central government but its budget, about 1 percent of the EU GDP, is far too small to play any macroeconomic role. In contrast to real federations, any countercyclical policy must therefore rest with the "subfederal" member states. In addition, the commission's budget must be ex ante in equilibrium. Furthermore, both the size and the use of the commission budget must be approved by the European Council that brings together the heads of state and government. In a nutshell, the commission budget is subject to a rigorous equilibrium rule and is under the control of member states.

The Stability and Growth Pact can be seen as a "federal" rule inasmuch as it commits—in theory—the member countries. In practice, however, the pact has not been effective. Over the first thirteen years of existence of the euro, the twelve initial member countries together have satisfied the 3 percent

29. For the United States, see Poterba and Rueben (1999) and for Canada see Booth, Georgopoulos, and Hejazi (2007). For the role of budgetary institutions, see Schuknecht, von Hagen, and Wolswijk (2008).

Table 12.3   **Number of years with budget deficit in excess of 3 percent of GDP: 1999–2011**

Austria	Belgium	Finland	France
4	3	0	7
Germany	Greece	Ireland	Italy
5	13	4	8
Luxembourg	Netherlands	Portugal	Spain
0	4	10	4

Source: AMECO, European Commission.
Note: All tests apply the Newey-West procedure to determine the bandwidth.
***Significant at the 1 percent level.
**Significant at the 5 percent level.
*Significant at the 10 percent level.

budget deficit limit only 60 percent of the time. The number of years when the limit has been exceeded is shown for each of these countries in table 12.3. Even if the rule may have had a moderating influence, the frequency of its violation is so high that its credibility is low, at best.[30]

On the other hand, the member countries have adopted a variety of budgetary arrangements, which are presented in European Commission (2006), although this tally is now partly outdated. The number of these arrangements is impressive but the devil hides in the details and most of these arrangements are effectively soft. Furthermore, few of them are directly tied to the Stability and Growth Pact, a discrepancy that is to be reduced with the adoption in 2011 of the "European Semester." This new procedure aims at tightening the macroeconomic assumptions to be used subsequently in national budget laws by allowing the commission to evaluate them early on. Yet, as with the Stability and Growth Pact, final authority rests with national authorities so that the effectiveness of this new procedure remains to be seen.

The lack of discipline at the national level (with notable exceptions, see table 12.1) and the inherent inability of the center to promote debt sustainability has been well-known for some time. The sovereign debt crisis illustrates the dangers of this situation. The loss of the no-bailout rule (see section 12.3.4) has considerably weakened an already feeble arrangement. Current efforts focus on strengthening and widening the Stability and Growth Pact, which has repeatedly failed.

The euro area experience shows that numerical rules—the deficit and debt limits of the Stability and Growth Pact—that are neither supported

30. An escape clause allows the limit to be exceeded, but an escape clause must be exceptional for the rule to be meaningful.

by hard legislation nor endorsed by the political system are not sufficient to deliver fiscal discipline. One could see the European Commission as a sort of advisory fiscal council dedicated to establishing discipline. The lesson here is that, in a politically heterogeneous situation (in contrast with the Dutch case) the council must be politically independent, which the commission is not, as its members are known to receive "informal" instructions from their governments, and as the commission has its own vast and complex agenda. Alternatively, following the Belgian example, the council must be ad hoc, with a narrow fiscal discipline agenda, and include policymakers and non-policymakers with the explicit objective of seeking agreements along the contract principle of Hallerberg, Strauch, and von Hagen (2009).

12.5.3   When Do Rules Actually Work?

Fiscal rules are rather brutal instruments and they suffer from time inconsistency. When they bind, policymakers are likely to try and evade them. Policymakers can look for loopholes, they can just ignore the rule, or they can change them. Rules can be made less brutal through the adoption of escape clauses, but then they are unlikely to be effective. The nature of the common pool problem is that policymakers often find it politically rewarding not to be fiscally disciplined. As long as the political costs of ignoring the requirements of fiscal discipline outweigh the political benefits of letting the public debt grow, a government will choose the latter over the former. Rules are useful if they significantly raise the political costs of fiscal indiscipline. The implication is that, to be effective, rules must be embedded in institutional arrangements.

The range of possible institutional arrangements is vast. They must be well-adapted to each country's political system. Electoral laws shape the type of government: single-party, coalition, or minority. As argued by von Hagen and Harden (1994), single-party governments make it possible to delegate power while the other forms of governance rely instead on contracts. Ethnic or ideological diversity results in worse common pool effects and calls for "wise men" arrangements, whereby independent bodies can achieve a reputation for truth telling. In all cases, transparencies, not just concerning accounting accuracy but also about the budgetary assumptions and their implications, are required to maintain the integrity of the rules.

Many countries operate several rules such as deficit and debt ceilings, spending ceilings, and tax floors. The multiplicity of rules offers opportunities for the government to escape them: rule arbitrage allows a government to argue that it meets some rules and cannot possibly meet all of them, and to pick those that are less constraining at any moment of time. Likewise, complex rules are a source of opacity that makes them understandable only to a small group of experts, chiefly government officials and interest groups that can capture them.

Because deficits and debts are endogenous—to cyclical conditions, to occasional financial turmoil, and other one-off events—the rules can never be completely simple and mechanical. If the goal is to achieve sustained deficit reduction, then judgment cannot be dispensed with and independent bodies such as fiscal councils can play an important role. These bodies appear to be most effective in reducing deficit bias when they validate the adequacy of budget assumptions and the ensuing calculations, and when they are given a formal and transparent advisory role.

12.6   Conclusions

In many developed countries, the financial crisis has merely added a layer of public debt to already impressive stockpiles. In these countries, fiscal policy has lacked discipline for several decades, for well-known reasons. The power of interest groups in most democracies creates externalities that lead to a deficit bias. The current public debt crisis in several nations has led to calls to reverse the long-standing deficit bias, which seems unlikely to occur without a change in the budgetary process, specifically designed to reduce the bias.

Fiscal rules have attracted increasing attention and many countries have adopted some rules. Evidence is now being accumulated on what rules can and cannot do. In line with these results, this chapter argues that rules are neither necessary nor sufficient to achieve fiscal discipline. Yet they can and do help. The chapter argues that rules can usually be dismissed all too easily when they clash with broad political objectives: discipline is pushed back to tomorrow just when it is needed most. This means that lasting rules cannot be too tight, but they become useless if they are too soft. The fine line between tight and soft is extremely hard to determine and may change as circumstances change. This difficulty can be alleviated through the setting-up of institutions that support the rule.

In a symmetric fashion, fiscal institutions are neither necessary nor sufficient to achieve fiscal discipline, but they help. Here again we face a delicate balance. Institutions must bind the policymakers without violating the democratic requirement that elected officials have the power to decide on budgets. This argues against assigning wide discretionary powers to fiscal institutions, but it is fully compatible with giving them either the authority to apply legal rules or to act as official watchdogs.

References

Abbas, S. Ali, Nazim Belhocine, Asmaa ElGanainy, and Mark Horton. 2010. "A Historical Public Debt Database." IMF Working Paper 10/245. Washington, DC: International Monetary Fund.

Alesina, Alberto, Ignazio Angeloni, and Federico Etro. 2001. "Institutional Rules for Federations." NBER Working Paper no. 8646. Cambridge, MA: National Bureau of Economic Research, December.

Alesina, Alberto, and Allan Drazen. 1991. "Why Are Stabilizations Delayed?" *American Economic Review* 81:1170–88.

Alesina, Alberto, and Roberto Perotti. 1995. "Fiscal Expansions and Adjustments in OCED Countries." *Economic Policy* 10:207–48.

Aneja, Sumit, Kevin Cheng, Yingbin Xiao, and Irina Yakadina. 2011. *Belgium: Selected Issues*. Washington, DC: International Monetary Fund.

Bohn, Henning. 1998. "The Behavior of US Public Debt and Deficits." *The Quarterly Journal of Economics* 113:949–63.

Booth, Laurence, George Georgopoulos, and Walid Hejazi. 2007. "What Drives Provincial-Canada Yield Spreads?" *Canadian Journal of Economics* 40:1008–32.

Bos, Frits. 2007. "The Dutch Fiscal Framework History, Current Practice and the Role of the CPB." CPB Document no. 150. CPB (Central Planbureau) Netherlands Bureau for Economic Analysis.

Calmfors, Lars. 2010. "The Swedish Fiscal Policy Council—Experiences and Lessons." Unpublished Paper. Swedish Fiscal Policy Council and Stockholm University.

Calmfors, Lars, and Simon Wren-Lewis. 2011. "What Should Fiscal Councils Do?" CESifo (Group Munich–Ifo Institute, Center for Economic Studies) Working Paper Series no. 3382.

Coene, Luc, and Geert Langenus. 2011. *Promoting Fiscal Discipline in a Federal Country: The Mixed Track Record of Belgium's High Council of Finance*. National Bank of Belgium.

Dabán, Terersa. 2011. "Strengthening Chile's Rule-Based Fiscal Framework." IMF Working Paper 11/17. Washington, DC: International Monetary Fund.

Debrun, Xavier. 2011. "Democratic Accountability, Deficit Bias and Independent Fiscal Agencies." IMF Working Paper. Washington, DC: International Monetary Fund.

Debrun, Xavier, David Hauner, and Manmohan S. Kumar. 2009. "Independent Fiscal Agencies." *Journal of Economic Surveys* 23 (1): 48–81.

Debrun, Xavier, and Manmohan S. Kumar. 2007. "Fiscal Rules, Fiscal Councils and All That: Commitment Devices, Signaling Tools or Smokescreens?" In *Fiscal Policy: Current Issues and Challenges,* edited by Banca d'Italia, 479–512. Rome: Bank of Italy.

Eichengreen, Barry, and Charles Wyplosz. 1998. "The Stability Pact: Minor Nuisance, Major Diversion?" *Economic Policy* 26:67–113.

European Commission. 2006. "Public Finances in EMU." *European Economy,* 3.

———. 2009. "Ageing Report." *European Economy,* 2.

Galí, Jordi, and Roberto Perotti. 2003. "Fiscal Policy and Monetary Integration in Europe." *Economic Policy* 37:533–72.

Guichard, Stéphanie, Mike Kennedy, Eckhard Wurzel, and Christophe Andre. 2007. "What Promotes Fiscal Consolidation: OECD Country Experiences." *OECD Economics Department Working Papers* 553. Paris: OECD.

Hallerberg, Mark, Rolf Rainer Strauch, and Juergen von Hagen. 2009. *Fiscal Governance in Europe*. Cambridge: Cambridge University Press.

International Monetary Fund (IMF). 2005. "Promoting Fiscal Discipline—Is There a Role for Fiscal Agencies?" SM/05/263.

———. 2009. *Fiscal Rules—Anchoring Expectations for Sustainable Public Finances*. Fiscal Affairs Department.

———. 2010. "A Historical Public Debt Database." http://www.imf.org/external /pubs/ft/wp/2010/data/wp10245.zip.

Jonung, Lars, and Martin Larch. 2006. "Improving Fiscal Policy in the EU. The Case For Independent Forecasts." *Economic Policy* 47:491–534.

Kopits, George. 2001. "Fiscal Rules: Useful Policy Framework or Unnecessary Ornament?" IMF Working Paper 01/145. Washington, DC: International Monetary Fund.

Kopits, George, and Steven Symanski. 2001. "Fiscal Rules: Useful Policy Framework or Unnecessary Ornament." IMF Working Paper WP/01/145, Fiscal Affairs Department. Washington, DC: International Monetary Fund.

Krogstrup, Signe, and Charles Wyplosz. 2010. "A Common Pool Theory of Supranational Deficit Ceilings." *European Economic Review* 54 (2): 273–81.

Kydland, Finn E., and Edward C. Prescott. 1977. "Rules Rather Than Discretion: The Inconsistency of Optimal Plans." *Journal of Political Economy* 85 (3): 473–91.

Larch, Martin. 2010. "Fiscal Performance and Income Inequality: Are Unequal Societies More Deficit-Prone? Some Cross-Country Evidence." Unpublished Paper. European Commission.

National Conference of State Legislatures (NCSL). 2010. "State Balanced Budget Provisions." NCSL Fiscal Brief, October.

Organization for Economic Cooperation and Development (OECD). n.d. *Economic Outlook*. http://www.oecd.org/eco/economicoutlook.htm.

Persson, Torsten, and Guido Tabellini. 2000. *Political Economics: Explaining Economic Policy.* Cambridge, MA: MIT Press.

Pisauro, Giuseppe. 2003. "Fiscal Decentralization and the Budget Process: A Simple Model of Common Pool and Bailouts." Italian Society for Public Economics Working Paper 294.

Poterba, James, and Kim Rueben. 1999. "State Fiscal Institutions and the US Municipal Bond Market." In *Fiscal Institutions and Fiscal Performance,* edited by J. Poterba and J. von Hagen, 181–208. Chicago: University of Chicago Press.

Roubini, Nouriel, and Jeffrey Sachs. 1989. "Political and Economic Determinants of Budget Deficits in Industrial Democracies." *European Economic Review* 33:903–38.

Schuknecht, Ludger, Juergen von Hagen, and Guido Wolswijk. 2008. "Government Risk Premiums in the Bond Market, EMU and Canada." Working Paper 879, European Central Bank (ECB).

Tejedo, Maria. 2007. "State Fiscal Institutions: An Evolution." PhD diss. University of Maryland at College Park.

Tellier, Genevieve, and Louis M. Imbeau. 2004. "Budget Deficits and Surpluses in the Canadian Provinces: A Pooled Analysis." Unpublished Paper. University of Ottawa.

von Hagen, Juergen. 2002. "Fiscal Rules, Fiscal Institutions, and Fiscal Performance." *The Economic and Social Review* 33 (3): 263–84.

von Hagen, Juergen, and Ian J. Harden. 1994. "National Budget Processes and Fiscal Performance." *European Economy Reports and Studies* 3:311–408.

Wren-Lewis, Simon. 2011a. "Comparing the Delegation of Monetary and Fiscal Policy." Discussion Paper 540. Department of Economics, Oxford University.

———. 2011b. "Fiscal Councils: the Office for Budget Responsibility." *CESifo DICE Report* 3:50–53.

Wyplosz, Charles. 2005. "Fiscal Policy: Institutions versus Rules." *National Institute Economic Review* 191:70–84.

———. 2006. "European Monetary Union: The Dark Sides of a Major Success." *Economic Policy* 46:207–62.

Comment   Lucio R. Pench

The chapter by Charles Wyplosz provides a fairly comprehensive, clearly written, and overall balanced overview of the role of fiscal rules and institutions in helping ensure fiscal discipline. I agree with its main conclusions, which I read as follows: fiscal policy is affected by a serious deficit bias, the dangers of which have been exposed by the financial crisis; fiscal rules and institutions, while no panacea, are complementary instruments toward correcting deficit bias; in binding policies and their makers, rules and institutions are themselves subject to time-consistency problems, which can be mitigated by careful design exploiting their complementarity. My discussion is organized as follows: after touching on the technical issue of the empirical definition of fiscal discipline, I briefly review the broad concept of fiscal governance, which includes but is not limited to the dichotomy rules versus institutions, and in this connection I briefly elaborate on the complementarity between the different elements of fiscal governance; I then point to recent findings that lend support to the effectiveness of fiscal rules. Some considerations on the state of the play in the euro area conclude.

At the outset the chapter defines fiscal discipline in terms of the "[debt] ratio [being] stationary over a sustained period" and presents for a number of industrial countries the result of two methodologies testing the null hypothesis of, respectively, nonstationarity and stationarity. My basic point is that such tests are a way of helping one read the corresponding tie series, but not too much should be read into them. This is illustrated by the profile of the corresponding debt ratios over the period considered (figure 12C.1).

With most profiles exhibiting a hump-shaped pattern, with the debt ratio typically peaking in the late 1980s and early 1990s (before resuming an upward trend since the start of the explosion of the financial crisis in 2008), it is not surprising that the tests tend to reject stationary but rarely, if ever, reject nonstationarity. Moreover, if a trend is nonstationary, its mirror image must be equally nonstationary: this is the reason why Norway, where the debt has been in overall decline since the early 1980s, is classified as nonstationary, while few would probably argue that the country has a fiscal discipline problem.

Stationarity tests, moreover, do not take into account the level around which stationarity is tested, while clearly this matters for overall perception of sustainability of a country's fiscal policies, a point underscored by the recent strand of empirical literature finding significant threshold effects in

Lucio R. Pench is director of fiscal policy in the Directorate-General for Economic and Financial Affairs at the European Commission.

I would like to thank Matteo Salto and Ombeline Gras for useful exchanges. The views expressed remain mine and do not necessarily correspond to those of the European Commission. For acknowledgments, sources of research support, and disclosure of the author's material financial relationships, if any, please see http://www.nber.org/chapters/c12657.ack.

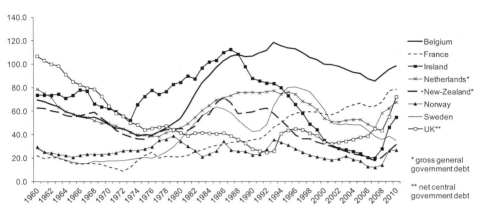

Fig. 12C.1   Evolution of gross central government debt levels (in percent of GDP) in selected countries (1960–2010)

the relationship between government debt and growth (Reinhart and Rogoff 2010; Kumar and Woo 2012).

The chapter focuses on the dichotomy rules versus institutions. I broadly agree with the definitions that are given of fiscal rules and fiscal councils (a particular type of institution), but I think that the discussion would gain from integrating other elements. For example, the chapter highlights the role of a "better budgetary process" in improving budgetary discipline, but does not elaborate on the dimensions conducive to a better quality of the budgetary process. Likewise, it mentions the time dimension of fiscal rules but does not discuss the role of medium-term budgetary frameworks; namely, the fiscal arrangements whereby the horizon of fiscal planning is extended beyond the annual calendar. Taking into account these different elements it may be preferable to elaborate the different institutional dimensions of fiscal policy under the encompassing concept of fiscal governance rather than in terms of rules versus institutions. This would include four main dimensions: numerical fiscal rules, independent fiscal medium-term budgetary frameworks, and budgetary procedures (European Commission 2010). In the same vein, while I fully agree that fiscal rules and institutions should be seen as complements rather than substitutes to each other, I would carry the argument further so as to encompass the four dimensions and their interconnections: for example, a budget balance rule is best seen as providing a medium-term objective, which needs to be operationalized through binding expenditure ceilings based on a multiannual expenditure rule; in turn, to be effective, expenditure ceilings need to be supported by top-down budgeting and the expenditure rule needs to be inscribed in a medium-term framework constraining the annual budgetary process.

The chapter stresses that the outcomes associated with fiscal rules are often disappointing and acknowledges that the econometric evidence on

528 Charles Wyplosz

their impact on budgetary discipline is not overwhelming. While I certainly agree with the first proposition and could not contest the second, I would like to point to a couple of recent empirical studies that strengthen the case for an independent effect of fiscal rules on budgetary discipline. Using a unique data set for the EU summarizing the quality of numerical fiscal rules and medium-term budgetary frameworks, Iara and Wolff (2010) estimate the impact of enhancing the quality of the budgetary framework in a structural model of sovereign spreads in the presence of different level of risk aversion: after controlling for the effects of debt and deficit and fixed countries effects, the time-varying fiscal governance quality is found to have a significant effect on risk premia, which is greater depending on the overall level of risk aversion and deficit and debt level (owing to the log-linear specification of the model). The main argument against the evidence on the effect of fiscal rule revolves around reverse causality; that is, a high-quality fiscal framework may be simply a characteristic of polities that care about fiscal discipline and do not have an independent effect on it. An interesting testing field in this respect is provided by the experience of Swiss cantons, which is studied by Feld et al. (2011): while sharing common institutional and cultural characteristics, Swiss cantons differ remarkably in terms of presence and strength of fiscal rules, and these are shown to contribute significantly to cantonal spreads; moreover, the "natural experiment" of a 2003 court decision relieving cantons from responsibilities toward lower municipal entities in financial distress—equivalent to the establishment of a credible no-bailout rule—is shown to have been effective in severing the link between cantonal risk premia and municipal financial situations.

Perhaps not surprisingly, I find the section on the fiscal arrangements in the euro area to be the least satisfying. My dissatisfaction is not so much with the employment of usual and dubious shortcuts (i.e., "[t]he European Commission can be seen as the equivalent of a central government"), which do not do justice to the admittedly complex and unique nature of the European Union. Nor would I contest that the Stability and Growth Pact has been less effective than its early proponents perhaps naively believed (Stark 2001). Rather, I would to have seen a better recognition of the evolving nature of fiscal governance in the euro area and the EU and the acceleration imparted by this evolution of the financial crisis. While this is not the place for even summarily charting the course of the reform of fiscal governance (see European Commission 2011, 2012), I would simply like to stress that one criticism that the chapter, not without some reason, levels at the European fiscal surveillance arrangements—namely, that they are "neither supported by hard legislation nor endorsed by the political system"—arguably no longer holds true. Acknowledging the complementarity between supra-national and domestic arrangements, and the necessity of political ownership of the former through some form of incorporation in the latter, the reform of economic governance that has entered into force at the end of 2012 (so-called "Six-Pack") includes for the first time a European directive setting out standards for domestic budgetary frameworks in a number of key areas, to ensure minimum quality as well as consistency with the European framework. This trend has received a further decisive impulsion with the signing early in 2012 of the Treaty on Stability, Coordination and Governance, which obliges its parties to incorporate in their constitution or in other legislation binding the budgetary process the medium-term objectives of the Stability and Growth Pact, including provision for corrective mechanism in case of deviations and for independent fiscal institutions for monitoring observance of the rules. While it is clearly too early to pass judgement on the effect of these far-reaching reforms, they attest to the euro area ability to learn from its experience with fiscal rules.

References

European Commission. 2010. *Public Finances in EMU—2010, European Economy,* no. 4/2010. Brussels: European Commission.

———. 2011. *Public Finances in EMU—2011, European Economy,* no. 4/2011. Brussels: European Commission.

———. 2012. *Public Finances in EMU—2012, European Economy.* Brussels: European Commission, forthcoming.

Feld, Lars, Alexander Kalb, Marc-Daniel Moessinger, and Steffen Osterloh. 2011. "Sovereign Bond Market Reactions to Fiscal Rules and No-Bailout Clauses: The Swiss Experience." Paper presented at Directorate General Economic and Monetary Affairs, European Commission Public Finances Workshop, Public Finances in Times of Severe Economic Stress: The Role of Institutions. November 30, Brussels.

Iara, Anna, and Guntram B. Wolff. 2010. "Rules and Risk in the Euro Area: Does Rules-Based National Fiscal Governance Contain Sovereign Bond Spreads?" *European Economy—Economic Papers,* 433. Directorate General Economic and Monetary Affairs, European Commission.

Kumar, Manhoman, and Jaejoon Woo. 2012. "Public Debt and Growth." Paper presented at the Bank of Italy's 14th Public Finances Workshop, Fiscal Policy and Growth. March 29–31, Perugia (S.A.Di.Ba).

Reinhart, Carmen, and Kenneth Rogoff. 2010. "Growth in a Time of Debt." *American Economic Review* 100 (2): 573–78.

Stark, Juergen. 2001. "Genesis of a Pact." In *The Stability and Growth Pact: The Architecture of Fiscal Policy in EMU,* edited by Anna Brunila, Marco Buti, and Daniele Franco, 77–105. Basingstoke: Palgrave.

The Electoral Consequences of
Large Fiscal Adjustments

Alberto Alesina, Dorian Carloni, and Giampaolo Lecce

13.1   Introduction

The conventional wisdom regarding the political consequences of large reductions of budget deficits (which we label "fiscal adjustments") is that they are the kiss of death for the governments that implement them: they are punished by voters at the following elections. In certain countries spending cuts are very unpopular, in others tax increases are politically more costly, but everywhere, the story goes, fiscal rigor is always unpopular.

The empirical evidence on this point is much less clear cut than the conviction with which this conventional wisdom is held. In this chapter, in fact, we find no evidence that governments that reduce budget deficits even decisively are systematically voted out of office. We also take into consideration as carefully as possible issues of reverse causality, namely the possibility that only "strong and popular" governments can implement fiscal adjustments and thus they are not voted out of office "despite" having reduced the deficits. Even taking this possibility into account we still find no evidence that fiscal adjustments, even decisive ones, systematically, on average, imply electoral defeats.

In this chapter our focus is large fiscal adjustments, which are currently at the center of attention in many Organization for Economic Cooperation and Development (OECD) countries. As a motivation we begin by examin-

Alberto Alesina is the Nathaniel Ropes Professor of Political Economy at Harvard University and a research associate and director of the Political Economy Program at the National Bureau of Economic Research. Dorian Carloni is a second-year PhD student in economics at the University of California, Berkeley. Giampaolo Lecce is a PhD student in economics and finance at Università Bocconi.

For acknowledgments, sources of research support, and disclosure of the authors' material financial relationships, if any, please see http://www.nber.org/chapters/c12654.ack.

ing the evidence on the ten largest multiyear fiscal adjustments in the last thirty years in OECD countries. We find no evidence that the turnover of governments in those periods was significantly higher than the average of the entire sample. In fact, it was lower.[1] We then explore more systematically all cases of large adjustments (defined as a reduction of at least 1.5 percent of GDP of cyclically adjusted deficits). Once again we find no evidence of a negative effect on election prospects. Contrary to the conventional wisdom, we find some evidence that fiscally loose governments tend to lose election more often than average, a result that is consistent with Brender and Drazen (2008). Next, we present a battery of regressions that show that indeed these results are quite robust and the data do not exhibit any correlation between deficit reduction and electoral losses.

But what about reverse causality? Perhaps weak governments, knowing their vulnerability, do not implement adjustments, but then, precisely because they are weak, they lose at polls, and the reverse holds for strong governments. This would explain the lack of correlation between fiscal adjustments and reelection. Unfortunately, measuring the "strength" of a government is not easy; often such strength or weakness depends on personalities involved, leadership style, and so forth, which are impossible for the econometrician to observe and measure. For instance, in principle a coalition government may be weaker and more unstable than a single-party government, but certain coalitions may be especially cohesive and certain single-party governments may hide strong division within the same party. The margin of the majority of the government in the legislature may be another indicator, but that too could be imperfect, due, for instance, to divisions within the government coalition even though the latter may have a large majority of seats. We find no evidence of a different behavior in terms of fiscal adjustments of coalition versus single-party governments. At the very least we can conclude that many governments can decisively tackle budget deficits without electoral losses. Perhaps not all, but a good portion can.[2]

If it is the case that fiscal adjustments do not lead systematically to electoral defeats why do they often seem so politically difficult? We can think of two explanations. The first one is simply risk aversion. Incumbent governments may be afraid of "rocking the boat" and follow a cautious course of actions and postpone fiscal reforms. The second and perhaps more plausible one is that the political game played around a fiscal adjustment goes above and beyond one man, one vote elections. Alesina and Drazen (1991) present a model in which organized groups with a strong influence on the polity manage to postpone reforms, even when the latter are necessary and unavoidable, to try to switch the costs on their opponents. The resulting

---

1. Obviously there is some arbitrariness in how to define the ten "largest" adjustments, but the result on their political consequences hold regardless of which (reasonable) definition is used.

2. See Bonfiglioli and Gancia (2010) for a model based upon politicians' competence in which certain but not all governments implement fiscal reforms and those which do are reelected.

wars of attrition delays fiscal adjustments. Strikes, contributions from various lobbies, and press campaigns are all means that can enforce (or block) policies above and beyond voting at the polls. For example, imagine a public sector union that goes on strike to block reduction in government spending on the public wage bill. They may create disruptions and may have consequences that may be too costly to bear for a government. Not only that, but public sector unions may have connections with parts of the incumbent coalition and block fiscal adjustments. Similar considerations may lead to postponements of pension reforms. In many countries pensioners developed a strong political support even within workers' unions. The latter would then water down the adjustment to placate this particular lobby even though the "median voter" might have been favorable to the tighter fiscal policy. To put it more broadly, voting in elections is not the only way in which various lobbies and pressure groups can influence the political process. Alesina, Ardagna, and Trebbi (2006) present a battery of tests on electoral reform in a large sample of countries, which are consistent with the empirical implications of the war of attrition model.

The paper closest to the present chapter in spirit is Alesina, Perotti, and Tavares (1998). These authors, using data up to the mid-1990s, found inconclusive evidence on the effects of fiscal adjustments on reelections in OECD economies. Buti et al. (2010) find that chances of reelection for the incumbent governments are, controlling for other factors, not significantly affected by their record of promarket reforms.[3] A related literature is the one on political budget cycles, which asks the question of whether incumbent governments increase spending or cut taxes before elections in order to be rewarded at the polls, an argument that implies budget deficits are popular and budget cuts are not.[4] Persson and Tabellini (2000) suggest that only in certain types of electoral systems are political budget cycles present. However, Brender and Drazen (2005) show, in fact, that while political budget cycles are common in new democracies (like in Central and Eastern Europe) they are not the norm in established ones, where increases in deficits tend to reduce the electoral success for the incumbents.

The rest of the chapter is organized as follows. In section 13.2 we briefly describe our data. Section 13.3 presents some suggestive qualitative evidence on the largest multiyear fiscal adjustments in the OECD countries in the last thirty years. Section 13.4 discusses more formally the correlations between deficit reduction policies and electoral results. Section 13.5 addresses the

---

3. In Buti et al. (2008) the empirical evidence also suggests that well-functioning and developed financial markets positively affect the reelection probability of reformist governments. It seems to suggest that financial market reforms facilitate reforms in product and labor markets.

Buti and van den Noord (2004a) and (2004b) also found the empirical evidence of a political business cycle in the early years of EMU. These results suggest that electoral manipulation of fiscal policy in EU countries has not been curbed by EMU's fiscal policy rules.

4. See Rogoff and Sibert (1988), Persson and Tabellini (2000), and Drazen (2000).

question of potential reverse causality. In section 13.6 we look at some case studies to further illustrate the link between fiscal adjustment and reelection prospects. The last section concludes.

13.2   Data

Our data sources are standard. For economic variables we use OECD Economic Outlook database no. 84. For political-institutional variables we use the Database of Political Institutions (DPI) 2009. In particular, we focus on the period 1975 to 2008. The countries are the members of the OECD that have been such for the entire period; the ones we analyzed in our work are: Australia, Austria, Belgium, Canada, Denmark, Finland, France, Germany, Greece, Ireland, Italy, Japan, Netherlands, Norway, Portugal, Spain, Sweden, United Kingdom, and United States.

The precise definition of all our variables is extensively described in the appendix, but for ease of exposition we also redefine them as we encounter them in the chapter. Specifically, all the variables corrected for the cycle are calculated using the cyclically adjusted variables of the OECD Economic Outlook database, and variation of cyclically adjusted variables are calculated over the potential output of total economy. In particular we used OECD reviewed and revised estimation methods. In order to provide a single measure of potential output, the chosen measure is "one which represents the levels of real GDP, and associated rates of growth, which are sustainable over the medium term at a stable rate of inflation" (Giorno et al. 1995). Our results are virtually identical if instead by dividing by potential GDP we divide by actual GDP. Fortunately the qualitative nature of our results is unaffected by the definition used.

13.3   The Ten Largest Fiscal Adjustments

We begin with some suggestive evidence regarding the ten largest fiscal adjustments in our sample. In table 13.1 we report (in order of cumulative size) the ten largest ones identified as follows: the ten cases in which the cumulative cyclically adjusted deficit reductions obtained by summing consecutive years of deficit reductions is the largest. Obviously, one could think of alternative definitions but our qualitative results do not change. For instance, we obtained very similar findings using a classification of the largest multiyear fiscal adjustments used by Alcidi and Gros (2010).

Many of the episodes listed in table 13.1 have been made "famous" by a lively literature that has investigated the economic characteristic and degree of success of these episodes.[5] In addition to the size of the adjustments in

---

5. See the original contribution by Giavazzi and Pagano (1990). The most recent paper in this line that also summarizes the previous literature is Alesina and Ardagna (2010).

Table 13.1   Ten periods with largest cumulative fiscal adjustment (cyclically adjusted variables)

Country	Years	Number of years	Yearly change in cycl. adj. deficit (COCHDEF)	Yearly change in cycl. adj. expenditures (COCHEXP)	Yearly change in cycl. adj. revenues (COCHREV)	Cumulative fiscal adjustment	% of fiscal adj. due to cut in expenditures	Term	Change in ideology
Denmark	1983–1986	4	−2.43	−0.85	1.58	−9.74	35.03	2	0
Greece	1990–1994	5	−1.88	−0.50	1.38	−9.39	26.38	2	1
Sweden	1994–2000	7	−1.20	−0.81	0.38	−8.38	67.91	3	0
Belgium	1982–1987	6	−1.26	−0.96	0.30	−7.57	76.50	2	0
Canada	1993–1997	5	−1.36	−1.25	0.11	−6.80	91.80	1	0
United Kingdom	1994–1999	6	−1.12	−0.66	0.47	−6.72	58.45	2	1
Finland	1993–1998	6	−1.04	−0.81	0.23	−6.23	78.13	2	1
Portugal	1982–1984	3	−1.89	−1.14	0.75	−5.67	60.16	2	2
Italy	1990–1993	4	−1.24	0.13	1.36	−4.95	−10.21	2	1
Ireland	1986–1989	4	−1.21	−1.54	−0.33	−4.82	127.50	2	1

Source: Authors' calculations on OECD Economic Outlook database no. 84 and DPI 2009.

terms of deficit reduction, we also report measures of the composition of the adjustment arising from spending cuts and tax increases over GDP. We calculate this variable by dividing the share of spending cuts over the reductions of fiscally-adjusted deficits (in shares of potential GDP). Note that the spending share can be greater than 100 if taxes were actually cut during the adjustment, or can be negative if spending was increased. We focus on this variable since the evidence shows that spending-based fiscal adjustments have been more long lasting and more successful in achieving fiscal balance with lower costs in terms of lost growth.[6] With "termination" we imply that there was an election in the period of the adjustments and/or in the two years following the end of it. We include the two years after the end of the fiscal adjustment because the results of an election within two years after the end of the period of deficit reduction could be affected by the tight fiscal policy quite directly. Beyond two years, too much time may have elapsed to attribute reelection (or defeat) mainly to the fiscal adjustment. In any event, our results do not quantitatively change if we include all terminations following the last year of the fiscal adjustments, even beyond two years. The last column, labeled "change in ideology," indicates how many changes in the political orientation occur during the fiscal adjustment and in the two years that followed its end.

Table 13.1 shows that government changes occurred in seven cases out of nineteen terminations, thus they were about 37 percent of the total. But if we look at the five largest adjustments in cumulative size, the ratio decreases considerably, as changes in government occurred only in one case out of ten. On the contrary, there were about 40 percent of government changes over the total number of terminations from 1975 to 2008 for the countries sampled in the table, indicating that periods of large fiscal adjustments were not associated with systematically higher government turnover.

In addition, the table allows us to make some preliminary observations about the link between cabinet change and the composition of fiscal adjustments. Considering the percentage of the adjustment due to cut in expenditures, and comparing the five fiscal adjustments for which the value was highest with the remaining adjustments, we find that the cases in which the expenditure share of the adjustment was higher were associated with less frequent change in government. In the table, if we pool together data for Ireland (1986 to 1989), Canada (1993 to 1997), Finland (1993 to 1998), Belgium (1982 to 1987), and Sweden (1994 to 2000), we get that government change occurred only in 20 percent of cases. Instead, for the rest of the countries considered, government changed in 56 percent of cases. This first evidence seems to suggest that tax-based adjustments make it more difficult

---

6. A long list of papers on fiscal adjustments has reached this conclusion. The latest in this series is Alesina and Ardagna (2010). This paper also includes a review of the previous literature. Using a different methodology (IMF 2010) also shows that spending-based adjustments are less costly than tax-based ones.

for incumbent governments to be reappointed when they implement large fiscal adjustments.

13.4   Deficit Reductions and Elections

13.4.1   Simple Statistics

We now turn to a more systematic analysis of deficit reduction policies in OECD countries. We define a year of "large fiscal adjustment," one in which the cyclically adjusted deficit over potential GDP ratio fell by more than 1.5 percent of GDP, while a year of "fiscal adjustment" is one in which the cyclically adjusted deficit over potential GDP ratio falls by any amount. Thus, large fiscal adjustments are a subset of all the adjustments. Fiscal expansions are defined identically to fiscal adjustments, but with the opposite sign.

With the definition of a "large fiscal adjustment," and given that the deficit is cyclically adjusted, one tries to capture years in which fiscal policy was decisively contractionary with (most likely) active discretionary fiscal policies that were not business as usual or the result of the cycle. When we use the cyclically adjusted definition of primary deficit (COCHDEF), we find 294 years (over 646 total) of fiscal adjustments and sixty years of "large" fiscal adjustments in our sample. We have more years of large fiscal adjustments if we consider not potential but actual GDP at the denominators of the ratios, but our results on the electoral consequences are completely unchanged.[7]

In this section, we examine the link between the timing of fiscal adjustments and the timing of changes in government. In order to measure "changes of government" we use two variables: one is all changes of a prime minister (ALLCH), the other one is change of the prime minister and in the party composition of the government (IDEOCH).[8] The first variable may overestimate "change," since a new prime minister with the same party or coalition may simply be a routine personnel replacement in a stable and reelected government. The variable IDEOCH may underestimate political turnover because even without a change in the party composition of the government, a prime minister may be changed because he or she may have become unpopular, possibly as a result of a fiscal tightening.

Another data complication relates to the timing of government change. The issue can be summarized as follows: if the government termination occurs in the first part of year t, should we consider the fiscal variable at time t as before or after the termination? If, for example, we were associating a change in government in the first part of year t with a reduction in

7. This explains why, with this method of dividing by potential GDP, we identify slightly fewer large adjustments than in Alesina and Ardagna (2010).

8. Excluding from the count of ALLCH the cases in which term limits were binding, like the second term of an American president, leave our results unchanged.

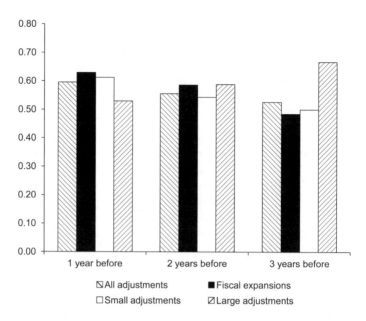

Fig. 13.1   Frequency in cabinet changes and fiscal adjustments
Source: Authors' calculations on OECD Economic Outlook database no. 84 and DPI 2009.

deficit over GDP in year *t*, we could erroneously conclude that the change in government occured as a result of the fiscal adjustment, although the fiscal adjustment could have been largely implemented in the second half of year *t*, after the elections. Hence, we adopt the same rule used in Alesina, Perotti, and Tavares (1998): every termination that occurs between July 1 of year *t* and June 30 of year *t* + 1 is considered to fall in calendar year *t* and is thought as contemporaneous to the fiscal outcomes of year *t*. Terminations that occured in the first part of each year are instead considered as contemporaneous to the fiscal variables of the previous year.

In figures 13.1 and 13.2 we plot the frequency of ALLCH and IDEOCH in the election year against cyclically adjusted deficit reductions of different sizes and fiscal expansions in the three years before the election, and we do not find evidence that fiscal adjustments are associated with more frequent changes in government or prime minister. Figure 13.1 investigates the frequency of change in government and/or prime minister (ALLCH). The left-hand set of bars in the figure indicates the frequency of change when the adjustment takes place one year before the election. The first two bars from the left show the average value of ALLCH when there is a fiscal adjustment and a fiscal expansion. There is a slightly higher propensity for a government turnover after a fiscal expansion, even though the difference is not statistically significant; the third and fourth bar show equivalent statistics but divide fiscal adjustments by size. They seem to show that large adjust-

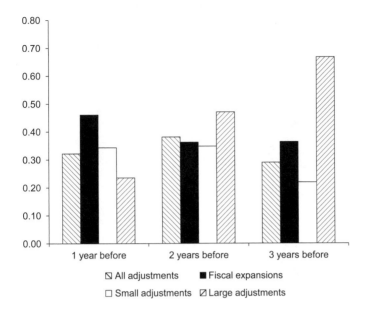

Fig. 13.2   Frequency in changes of cabinet ideology and fiscal adjustments
Source: Authors' calculations on OECD Economic Outlook database no. 84 and DPI 2009.

ments one year before the elections are associated with lower propensity to government changes. The same picture emerges when we consider adjustment two years before the elections.

In figure 13.2 we consider only government changes, defined as changes in the political orientation of the government (IDEOCH). Figure 13.2 provides comparable results to figure 13.1, except for the fact that the dependent variable is now IDEOCH instead of ALLCH. This figure does not show that incumbent governments are systematically voted out of office when they implement deficit reductions. The results we get in figure 13.2 are similar to those we got in figure 13.1, as they show that fiscal expansions (i.e., increases in deficits) are on average associated with higher government change than fiscal adjustments.

Figure 13.3 sheds some light on the relationship between the composition of the adjustment and government turnover. We label large adjustments as expenditure-based when spending cuts are greater than the median spending cut of all large fiscal adjustments. They are tax-based if the increase in tax revenues is greater than the median tax increase of all large fiscal adjustments. Consistently with the preliminary evidence provided in the first part of this chapter, figure 13.3 shows that if a large fiscal adjustment is expenditure-based, it is less likely that there will be a government change than if the deficit reduction is tax-based. This result holds both when we look at ALLCH and IDEOCH.

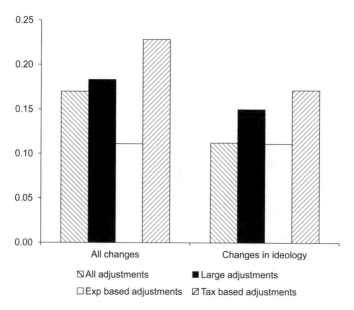

Fig. 13.3   Frequency in changes of cabinet ideology and cabinet changes given expenditures/tax-based adjustments

Source: Authors' calculations on OECD Economic Outlook database no. 84 and DPI 2009.

13.4.2   Regression Analysis

In this section we ran several regressions that try to predict the likelihood or reappointment of an incumbent government as a function of several political and economic variables, including changes in the deficit, taxes, and spending. The bottom line of these regressions is that it is difficult to find any economic variable (with the possible exception of inflation) that is systematically and robustly correlated with the probability of a government defeat in an election. This holds as well for fiscal variables: we find no evidence that spending cuts, tax increases, and deficit-reduction policies make it more likely for incumbents to lose.

Our interpretation is that political change is the result of a complex political game and it is hard to pinpoint stable correlations between economic variables and electoral results.[9] The important point of our purpose here is precisely that a fiscal adjustment is only one of the many components of such political dynamics and it is not a "deal-breaker," so that no matter what else is happening it implies an electoral defeat. If that were the case we

9. For the case of the United States, in a series of papers Fair (1978, 1982, 1988) argued that the rate of growth of the economy a few quarters before the election is a critical determinant of presidential elections. For a discussion of this evidence see Alesina and Rosenthal (1995).

should find a correlation between the occurence of fiscal adjustments and electoral losses.

We have tried many specifications of our probit regression in which the left-hand side variables are measures of government changes. We first adopted the same specification by Alesina, Perotti, and Tavares (1998) and then we explored many others. We first report probit regressions with the variable measuring cabinet change (IDEOCH) as our dependent variable. To study the impact of fiscal adjustments on cabinet change, and to test for the robustness of our results, we use three different measures: the change in noncyclically adjusted deficit (CHDEF), the change in cyclically adjusted deficit (COCHDEF), and the average change in deficit during the tenure of the current cabinet (TOTCHDEF). In our baseline specification, we also include macroeconomic variables such as the change in real GDP (dGDP), the change in unemployment rate (dUNR), and the inflation rate (INFL). We then use political variables to control for three different characteristics of the cabinet: the number of years the cabinet has been in power (DURAT), whether it is composed of a coalition of parties (COAL), and whether it has the majority in the parliament (MAJ).

Table 13.2 presents the results of our baseline specification. It shows that the deficit variables are not statistically significant irrespective of the measure we use, suggesting that governments implementing fiscal tightening are on average not penalized at the following election. The INFL (the inflation rate) is statistically significant in all regressions. It seems that voters are especially averse to inflation. Brender and Drazen (2008) find a similar result for a different (larger) set of countries and a different (earlier) time period. The coefficients on the other macroeconomic variables are of the sign one would expect, but they are not statistically significant in many specifications. They show that an increase in the growth rate of real GDP reduces the probability of a government change, whereas the unemployment rate has a really small coefficient. The signs of the coefficients on political variables are also generally consistent with conventional wisdom, although only DURAT is statistically significant. As we would expect, the probability of government change increases with the length of its tenure.

In table 13.3 we extend this baseline specification by including variables in deviation from the weighted average of G7 countries.[10] Thus we use GDP growth, inflation rate, and unemployment rate in deviations from G7 average in every year. The motivation is clear: we test whether voters punish government, not for their performance per se, but with respect to its performance relative to the "world average." As before, we do not find evidence of a statistically significant relation between the change in fiscal deficit and government change in the direction predicted by the conventional wisdom. No coefficients on deficit variables are statistically significant, as in table

---

10. Weights for each country are calculated using real GDP.

Table 13.2 **Probit coefficients (full sample)**

Variables	IDEOCH (1)	IDEOCH (2)	IDEOCH (3)	IDEOCH (4)	IDEOCH (5)
CHDEF[a]	-0.0627				
	(0.052)				
COCHDEF[b]		0.0039			
		(0.056)			
TOTCHDEF[c]			-0.0100		
			(0.067)		
CHEXP[d]				-0.0344	
				(0.063)	
CHREV[e]					0.0551
					(0.061)
DGDP	-0.0471	-0.0439	-0.1039**	-0.0499	-0.0320
	(0.042)	(0.044)	(0.048)	(0.044)	(0.042)
DUNR	0.0009	-0.0030	-0.0066	-0.0007	-0.0005
	(0.005)	(0.005)	(0.006)	(0.005)	(0.005)
INFL	0.0266**	0.0342**	0.0309**	0.0301**	0.0265**
	(0.013)	(0.014)	(0.013)	(0.013)	(0.013)
DURAT	0.2265***	0.2273***	0.2295***	0.2246***	0.2256***
	(0.050)	(0.052)	(0.051)	(0.050)	(0.050)
COAL	0.0547	0.0493	0.0450	0.0626	0.0644
	(0.150)	(0.154)	(0.152)	(0.150)	(0.150)
MAJ	0.0039	-0.0154	-0.0467	-0.0083	0.0084
	(0.178)	(0.182)	(0.179)	(0.178)	(0.178)
Constant	-1.7700***	-1.8006***	-1.6166***	-1.7657***	-1.8195***
	(0.230)	(0.242)	(0.237)	(0.234)	(0.230)
Log-likelihood					
Observations	613	591	613	614	613

Source: See appendix.

Note: Standard errors in parentheses.

[a]Change in public deficit: percentage point change in the ratio of public deficit to GDP.

[b]Change in the primary deficit (CHDEF), corrected for the cycle.

[c]Average change in deficit during tenure: average percentage point change in the deficit over the years that the current cabinet has been in power, up to the current year.

[d]Change in public expenditures: percentage point change in the ratio of primary expenditures to GDP.

[e]Change in public revenues: percentage point change in the ratio of public revenues to GDP. When TOTCHDEF is used, given variables are replaced by dTOTGDP, dTOTUNR, and TOTINFL. The coefficients on DGDP, DUNR, and INFL are the coefficients on these variables.

***Significant at the 1 percent level.

**Significant at the 5 percent level.

*Significant at the 10 percent level.

Table 13.3   **Probit coefficients (full sample), with additional controls**

Variables	IDEOCH (1)	IDEOCH (2)	IDEOCH (3)	IDEOCH (4)	IDEOCH (5)
CHDEF	−0.0663				
	(0.053)				
COCHDEF		0.0125			
		(0.058)			
TOTCHDEF			−0.0210		
			(0.070)		
CHEXP				−0.0325	
				(0.068)	
CHREV					0.0619
					(0.062)
DGDP	−0.0857	−0.0688	−0.1545**	−0.0820	−0.0603
	(0.060)	(0.062)	(0.061)	(0.064)	(0.059)
DUNR	0.0010	−0.0026	−0.0075	−0.0007	0.0000
	(0.005)	(0.006)	(0.006)	(0.005)	(0.005)
INFL	0.0308*	0.0425**	0.0302*	0.0344**	0.0332**
	(0.017)	(0.017)	(0.017)	(0.017)	(0.017)
DURAT	0.2241***	0.2259***	0.2236***	0.2221***	0.2231***
	(0.050)	(0.052)	(0.051)	(0.050)	(0.050)
COAL	0.0688	0.0666	0.0648	0.0787	0.0789
	(0.152)	(0.156)	(0.154)	(0.152)	(0.152)
MAJ	0.0001	−0.0282	−0.0428	−0.0125	0.0017
	(0.179)	(0.183)	(0.180)	(0.179)	(0.179)
DGDPg7	0.0520	0.0369	0.0640	0.0439	0.0420
	(0.055)	(0.058)	(0.049)	(0.055)	(0.054)
UNRg7	0.0128	0.0199	0.0131	0.0144	0.0151
	(0.022)	(0.023)	(0.022)	(0.022)	(0.022)
INFLg7	−0.0056	−0.0141	0.0107	−0.0052	−0.0138
	(0.031)	(0.032)	(0.032)	(0.032)	(0.031)
Constant	−1.6840***	−1.7501***	−1.5306***	−1.7003***	−1.7466***
	(0.260)	(0.271)	(0.266)	(0.265)	(0.257)
Log-likelihood					
Observations	613	591	613	614	613

Source: See appendix.

Note: See notes for table 13.2.

13.2. Once again, this result is fully consistent with those found by Brender and Drazen (2008). Also when we look at macroeconomic and political variables, our results do not vary substantially from the ones obtained in the previous specification.

In table 13.4 we use the same specifications as before but run the regressions only on deficit reduction years. Regressions on this restricted sample allow us to check for the robustness of the results we obtained while considering the full sample, and to assess if the sample of fiscal adjustment years differs significantly. The estimated coefficients on the variables mea-

Table 13.4		Probit coefficients (using only observations with CHDEF < 0)			
Variables	IDEOCH (1)	IDEOCH (2)	IDEOCH (3)	IDEOCH (4)	IDEOCH (5)
CHDEF	−0.1454				
	(0.108)				
COCHDEF		−0.0570			
		(0.105)			
TOTCHDEF			0.0281		
			(0.130)		
CHEXP				0.0608	
				(0.101)	
CHREV					0.2104*
					(0.109)
DGDP	−0.0249	−0.0515	−0.0701	−0.0077	0.0166
	(0.060)	(0.066)	(0.068)	(0.063)	(0.063)
DUNR	0.0098	−0.0035	0.0070	0.0078	0.0061
	(0.009)	(0.011)	(0.009)	(0.009)	(0.009)
INFL	0.0232	0.0331*	0.0273	0.0295	0.0191
	(0.019)	(0.020)	(0.019)	(0.018)	(0.019)
DURAT	0.1666**	0.1550**	0.1182	0.1624**	0.1691**
	(0.072)	(0.077)	(0.079)	(0.072)	(0.073)
COAL	0.1158	0.0903	0.1036	0.1374	0.1236
	(0.214)	(0.217)	(0.216)	(0.213)	(0.214)
MAJ	−0.0443	−0.0557	−0.0944	−0.0554	−0.0003
	(0.268)	(0.270)	(0.268)	(0.266)	(0.267)
Constant	−1.8521***	−1.6941***	−1.4695***	−1.7634***	−1.9791***
	(0.351)	(0.389)	(0.378)	(0.341)	(0.364)
Log-likelihood					
Observations	325	316	325	325	325

Source: See appendix.
Note: See notes for table 13.2.

suring the change of public deficit are not substantially different from those obtained in the previous set of regressions. They are not statistically significant except for CHREV (change in public revenues), whose effect on IDEOCH is positive, meaning that a positive change in the size of the public revenue increases the probability of government change. Thus, even when we restrict the analysis to deficit reduction years, there is no evidence that fiscal tightening harms incumbent governments by reducing the probability of their reelection. Coefficients on macroeconomic and political variables do not differ from the previous set of regressions either, showing that in most regressions only the duration of tenure (DURAT) has a statistically significant positive effect on IDEOCH. As before, the results are robust to the inclusion of variables measuring deviations of macroeconomic variables from G7 countries' weighted average values.

In table 13.5 we include the variables that control for the composition of

Table 13.5   **Probit coefficients (full sample, noncyclically adjusted variables)**

Variables	IDEOCH (1)	IDEOCH (2)	IDEOCH (3)	IDEOCH (4)
CHDEF[a]	−0.0907	−0.0444	−0.0812	−0.0697
	(0.057)	(0.060)	(0.056)	(0.059)
DGDP	−0.0450	−0.0438	−0.0463	−0.0478
	(0.042)	(0.042)	(0.042)	(0.042)
DUNR	0.0016	0.0007	0.0014	0.0010
	(0.005)	(0.005)	(0.005)	(0.005)
INFL	0.0251*	0.0255*	0.0252*	0.0266**
	(0.013)	(0.013)	(0.013)	(0.013)
DURAT	0.2256***	0.2277***	0.2254***	0.2270***
	(0.050)	(0.050)	(0.050)	(0.050)
COAL	0.0530	0.0479	0.0532	0.0557
	(0.151)	(0.151)	(0.150)	(0.150)
MAJ	−0.0041	0.0033	0.0002	0.0035
	(0.178)	(0.178)	(0.178)	(0.178)
PEXP[b]	−0.4227			
	(0.340)			
PTAX[c]		0.1798		
		(0.292)		
PTRF[d]			−0.3040	
			(0.347)	
PCGW[e]				−0.0753
				(0.297)
Constant	−1.7427***	−1.7839***	−1.7468***	−1.7655***
	(0.232)	(0.231)	(0.232)	(0.231)
Log-likelihood Observations	613	613	613	613

Source: see appendix.

Note: Standard errors in parentheses.

[a]Change in public deficit: percentage point change in the ratio of public deficit to GDP.

[b]Spending-based adjustment: dummy variable equal to 1 when following two conditions hold: (a) there is a large adjustment (CHDEF < −1.5); (b) CHEXP is less than its median across all years in which a large adjustment occurs.

[c]Tax-based adjustment: dummy variable equal to 1 when following two conditions hold: (a) there is a large adjustment (CHDEF < −1.5); (b) CHREV is more than its median across all years in which a large adjustment occurs.

[d]Transfer-based adjustment: dummy variable equal to 1 when following two conditions hold: (a) there is a large adjustment (CHDEF < −1.5); (b) CHTRF is less than its median across all years in which a large adjustment occurs.

[e]Government wage-based adjustment: dummy variable equal to 1 when the following two conditions hold: (a) there is a large adjustment (CHDEF < 1.5); (b) CHCGW is less than its median across all years in which a large adjustment occurs.

***Significant at the 1 percent level.

**Significant at the 5 percent level.

*Significant at the 10 percent level.

the fiscal adjustment. Also we check whether adjustments based on cuts in transfer payments or in government wage consumption are associated with a higher probability of cabinet changes. We focus on large adjustments (such that deficit to GDP is cut by more than 1.5 percentage points, from $t - 1$ to t), and add four variables to control for the composition of the adjustment, namely PEXP, PTAX, PTRF, and PCGW: the share of adjustment on total expenditure, total revenues, transfers, and government wages, respectively. We focus on transfers and wages because results by Alesina, Perotti, and Tavares (1998) suggest that these were the most successful adjustments in terms of a long lasting stabilization of the debt/GDP ratio. They may also be the least popular, at least according to conventional wisdom.

Although we get statistically insignificant coefficients for all variables of fiscal composition, it is worth spending some more time on the sign of the coefficients associated with the variables. The sign of the coefficient on PEXP, a dummy variable equal to one if the adjustment is large and expenditure-based, is negative, meaning that if an adjustment is large and expenditure-based it is associated with a reduction in the probability of a change of government. Similarly, if we look at PTAX, a dummy variable equal to one if the adjustment is large and tax-based, we get a positive coefficient, meaning that it is more likely that there will be a government change if the deficit reduction is based on an increase in taxes. We then analyze PTRF and PCGW, dummy variables associated with large adjustments based on cuts in transfer payments and government wage consumption, respectively. For both variables we get negative and statistically insignificant coefficients, which suggests that if the adjustment is based on cuts in these categories of expenditure, it is less likely that the government will change. When we repeat the analysis using cyclically adjusted deficit (COCHDEF) we obtain similar results.[11]

Finally, if we repeat the same analysis with ALLCH as the dependent variable, we find very similar evidence for variables measuring the change in fiscal deficit. All these results are available from the authors. While the coefficients on macroeconomic and political variables are left unchanged in most of the cases, there are small differences in the coefficients on fiscal deficit variables. When we run the same specification of table 13.2 on ALLCH, results are analogous as before. Similarly, when we run the same regressions only on fiscal adjustments years (as we did in table 13.4), we get that only the coefficient on TOTCHDEF is different: although it is positive as before, it is not statistically significant.

We have also explored whether or not there is a difference between the reaction to deficit reduction policies between right-wing or left-wing governments—that is, whether or not one type of government is punished (or rewarded) more than the other for reducing deficits. We find some very weak

---

11. These estimates are not reported in this chapter but they are available on request.

Table 13.6   Logit fixed effects model coefficients (full sample)

Variables	IDEOCH (1)	IDEOCH (2)	IDEOCH (3)	IDEOCH (4)	IDEOCH (5)
CHDEF	−0.1260				
	(0.100)				
COCHDEF		−0.0084			
		(0.109)			
TOTCHDEF			−0.1304		
			(0.135)		
CHEXP				−0.0997	
				(0.137)	
CHREV					0.1047
					(0.119)
DGDP	−0.1638	−0.1224	−0.3396***	−0.1728	−0.1159
	(0.114)	(0.116)	(0.125)	(0.124)	(0.112)
DUNR	0.0034	−0.0022	−0.0095	−0.0004	0.0016
	(0.010)	(0.010)	(0.012)	(0.009)	(0.010)
INFL	0.0113	0.0407	−0.0034	0.0168	0.0284
	(0.047)	(0.046)	(0.048)	(0.048)	(0.045)
DURAT	0.5246***	0.5401***	0.5410***	0.5244***	0.5221***
	(0.101)	(0.106)	(0.105)	(0.101)	(0.101)
COAL	0.0497	0.1209	−0.0311	0.0320	0.0269
	(0.406)	(0.415)	(0.410)	(0.406)	(0.407)
MAJ	−0.3609	−0.3537	−0.4716	−0.3877	−0.3539
	(0.433)	(0.435)	(0.435)	(0.434)	(0.434)
DGDPg7	0.0716	0.0681	0.0909	0.0589	0.0630
	(0.104)	(0.110)	(0.091)	(0.103)	(0.103)
UNRg7	0.0252	0.0784	0.0067	0.0237	0.0435
	(0.059)	(0.063)	(0.059)	(0.061)	(0.058)
INFLg7	0.0484	0.0368	0.0917	0.0535	0.0212
	(0.072)	(0.074)	(0.076)	(0.077)	(0.072)
Log-likelihood					
Observations	580	558	580	581	580
Number of countries	18	18	18	18	18

Source: See appendix.

Note: See notes for table 13.2.

evidence that left-wing governments are rewarded more than right-wing governments when they reduce deficits. The evidence is not very robust (available from the authors). Perhaps this evidence hints at the fact that left-wing government may follow types of adjustments that are less "unpopular" in terms of their redistributive consequences.

Lastly, to check the robustness of our results, we run a battery of regressions using a logit model and logit fixed effects model, in which we control for country fixed effects (table 13.6). The estimations we get are not substantially different from the ones we get in our probit specification. In particular, using the same specification of table 13.2 and table 13.3, the estimations obtained using a logit fixed effects model are consistent with previous results. The evidence suggest that DURAT is positive and statistically significant while INFL is almost always positive but not statistically significant in all the specifications. Once again, none of the deficit variables are statistically significant.

13.5   Reverse Causality

Thus far we have uncovered no evidence suggesting that governments that engage in even large fiscal adjustments are systematically voted out of office. A question that comes to mind is one of a sort of "reverse causation." Perhaps those governments that are strong are those that can safely engage in fiscal adjustments, and they are then reappointed despite having been fiscally responsible. Note that the question is not whether or not stronger governments implement more fiscal adjustments (an issue studied by Alesina, Ardagna, and Trebbi 2006), but whether stronger governments that implement fiscal adjustments are more likely to be reelected than weaker governments that implement fiscal adjustments. In other words, a weaker government may have a harder time breaking some impediment to implement reforms, but once it does, the question is whether it suffers more at the polls than a stronger government.

The difficulty is how to define, ex ante—that is, before reelection (or loss)—what a strong government is, in a way that is measurable by the econometricians. Our first measure of strength is whether or not the ruling government is formed by a coalition of parties. The idea is that coalition governments are more likely to suffer from internal disagreements (for decisions that include the nature and size of fiscal adjustments to be implemented), and they may be more likely to fall. The evidence does indeed suggest that the average duration of coalition governments is slightly shorter than single-party government. In our sample coalition governments last on average 4.12 years, while single-party governments last 4.20 years. Besides, if we look at the frequency of government change, we find that the probability of cabinet change is slightly higher (0.38) when a coalition government is in power at election time than when a single-party government in charge (0.34). Results are consistent when we analyze the "strength" of a government in terms of the share of votes they received at the election and not in terms of the composition of the executive. Obviously the duration of a government is endogenous to policy choices, therefore coalitions may choose certain policies that are less likely to be unpopular, which is precisely the point debated here.

Our second measure of government stability is a dummy variable equal to one if the party of the executive has an absolute majority in the house(s) with lawmaking powers. This measure seems reasonable since one would expect a government to last longer if it has the majority in all houses. In fact, we find that when this is the case (as measured by the variable MAJ), the government lasts on average 4.41 years, whereas for the rest of the observations the average duration is 4.17 years. However, differently from the evidence

Table 13.7   **Fiscal adjustments using different definitions of executive**

	No. of observations (1975–2008) (a)	No. of fiscal adjustments (1975–2008) (b)	No. of large fiscal adjustments (1975–2008) (c)	(b)/(a) %	(c)/(a) %	Average COCHDEF (1975–2008)
No absolute majority	465	229	47	49.2	10.1	–0.00794
Absolute majority	127	62	13	48.8	10.2	0.1465567
Single party	253	130	26	51.4	10.3	0.0291018
Coalition of parties	347	164	34	47.3	9.8	0.0296184

Source: Authors' calculations on OECD Economic Outlook database no. 84 and DPI 2009.

presented for the coalition variable, we get that governments holding the majority in the houses are more likely to change than the rest (45 percent of cases versus 34).

We can then proceed and use the variables previously defined to investigate the main issue of this section: are more stable governments more likely to implement fiscal adjustments? Do they do so because they are more likely to be reappointed despite that they have been fiscally responsible?

Our results show that coalition governments implemented 164 fiscal adjustments, corresponding to roughly 47 percent of total observations for which we had a coalition government, whereas single-party governments implemented 130 fiscal adjustments; that is, they did it in 51 percent of the years in which they were governing. If we only look at "large" fiscal adjustments results are similar with previous ones. Coalition governments implemented thirty-four large fiscal adjustments, corresponding to roughly 9.8 percent of total observations for which we had a coalition government, whereas single-party governments implemented twenty-six fiscal adjustments; that is to say, 10.3 percent of the years in which they were governing. If we then look at the stability of the government as measured by the majority in the houses, we find similar differences between governments with an absolute majority and government without an absolute majority in the houses when we look at large fiscal adjustments. The former implemented large adjustments in 10.2 percent of cases, the latter in 10.1 percent of cases. When instead we look at all adjustments the difference is not so clear-cut. Governments with the majority implemented sixty-two fiscal adjustments, which represent 48.8 percent of the years where a government with an absolute majority was in charge. Government without the majority implemented 229 fiscal adjustments, about 49.2 percent of the total (the results are reported in table 13.7). So according to our, admittedly imperfect, measure of "strength" it seems that "strong" governments implement fiscal adjustments only slightly more often than average.

Moreover, the evidence provided in figures 13.4 to 13.7 does not always

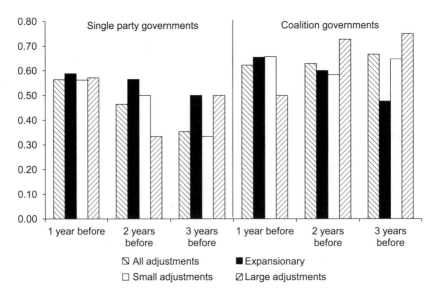

Fig. 13.4   Frequency in cabinet changes and fiscal adjustments (single party/coalition)
Source: Authors' calculations on OECD Economic Outlook database no. 84 and DPI 2009.

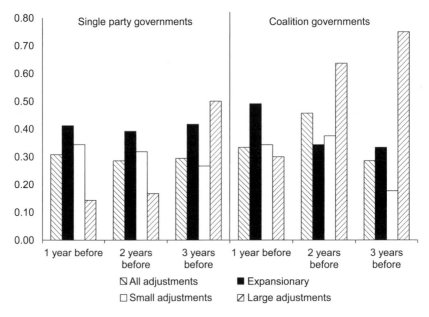

Fig. 13.5   Frequency in changes of cabinet ideology and fiscal adjustments (single party/coalition)
Source: Authors' calculations on OECD Economic Outlook database no. 84 and DPI 2009.

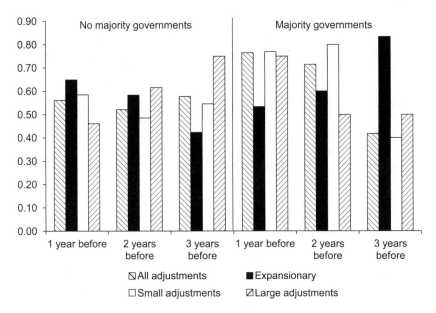

Fig. 13.6   Frequency in cabinet changes and fiscal adjustments (majority/ no majority)

Source: Authors' calculations on OECD Economic Outlook database no. 84 and DPI 2009.

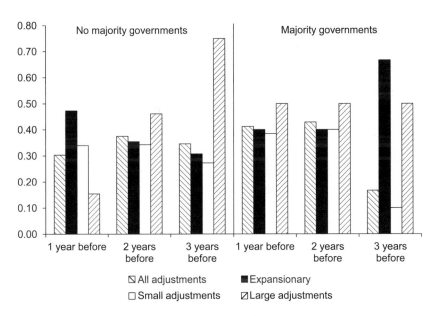

Fig. 13.7   Frequency in changes of cabinet ideology and fiscal adjustments (majority/no majority)

Source: Authors' calculations on OECD Economic Outlook database no. 84 and DPI 2009.

suggest that more stable governments implementing fiscal adjustments before the election were more likely to be reappointed. For example, figure 13.5 shows that if single-party governments implemented fiscal adjustments (in particular small ones) three years before the election, they were more likely not to be reelected than if coalition governments did so. Similarly, governments with an absolute majority in the houses were associated with government change in 41 percent of cases if they implemented fiscal adjustments one year before the election, compared to 30 percent in the rest of our sample (see figure 13.7).

The idea that more stable governments are not more protected from government change after they perform a fiscal adjustment is also supported by the set of regressions we show in tables 13.8 and 13.9. We add interaction variables to the baseline specification described before and try to capture the specific effect on government change associated with more stable governments implementing fiscal adjustments. Even in this specification, there is no statistically significant difference between coalition and single-party governments implementing fiscal adjustments on the prospect of being reelected. In column (4) of table 13.8, where we use a cyclically adjusted deficit variable, we do not find a statistically significant difference between coalition and single-party governments. Similarly in column (6), when we construct a variable interacting TOTCHDEF and COAL, we do not find any statistically significant effect of this variable on the dependent variable IDEOCH.

The evidence that stronger governments are not necessarily more protected from electoral turnover is also supported by our results in table 13.9. In all specifications where we include an interaction variable between the deficit variable and a dummy for the government having majority support in the parliament, we do not get statistically significant estimates for the coefficients on the interaction variable.

13.5.1   Discussion

If it is the case that certain types of fiscal adjustments are not necessarily costly in terms of lost output or lost votes, why are they often delayed and politicians reluctant to implement them?

There are two possible, related reasons. The first is that "vote-counting" is not the only political factor at play. Certain constituencies may be able to "block" adjustments to continue receiving rents from government spending because they have enough political energy (time, organization, money). This is sometimes referred to as an issue of diffuse benefits and concentrated costs. For example, in some cases strikes of public-sector employees may create serious disruptions. Pensioners' lobbies may be able to persuade politicians not to touch their pension systems, even when future generations will suffer the costs of delayed reforms. Lobbyists for certain protected sectors use campaign contributions for continued protection.

Table 13.8 Probit coefficients (coalition interaction term)

Variables	IDEOCH (1)	IDEOCH (2)	IDEOCH (3)	IDEOCH (4)	IDEOCH (5)	IDEOCH (6)
CHDEF[a]	-0.0627	-0.0817				
	(0.052)	(0.077)				
CHDEF*COAL[b]		0.0311				
		(0.093)				
COCHDEF[c]			0.0039	-0.0321		
			(0.056)	(0.083)		
COCHDEF*COAL[d]				0.0652		
				(0.110)		
TOTCHDEF[e]					-0.0100	-0.0284
					(0.067)	(0.094)
TOTCHDEF*COAL[f]						0.0321
						(0.116)
DGDP	-0.0471	-0.0470	-0.0439	-0.0426	-0.1039**	-0.1032**
	(0.042)	(0.042)	(0.044)	(0.044)	(0.048)	(0.048)
DUNR	0.0009	0.0010	-0.0030	-0.0028	-0.0066	-0.0066
	(0.005)	(0.005)	(0.005)	(0.005)	(0.006)	(0.006)
INFL	0.0266**	0.0269**	0.0342**	0.0347**	0.0309**	0.0313**
	(0.013)	(0.013)	(0.014)	(0.014)	(0.013)	(0.013)
DURAT	0.2265***	0.2286***	0.2273***	0.2299***	0.2295***	0.2314***
	(0.050)	(0.050)	(0.052)	(0.052)	(0.051)	(0.051)

Table 13.8 (continued)

Variables	IDEOCH (1)	IDEOCH (2)	IDEOCH (3)	IDEOCH (4)	IDEOCH (5)	IDEOCH (6)
COAL	0.0547	0.0562	0.0493	0.0483	0.0450	0.0450
	(0.150)	(0.150)	(0.154)	(0.154)	(0.152)	(0.152)
MAJ	0.0039	0.0059	-0.0154	-0.0107	-0.0467	-0.0477
	(0.178)	(0.178)	(0.182)	(0.182)	(0.179)	(0.179)
Constant	-1.7700***	-1.7789***	-1.8006***	-1.8141***	-1.6166***	-1.6266***
	(0.230)	(0.232)	(0.242)	(0.244)	(0.237)	(0.240)
Log-likelihood						
Observations	613	613	591	591	613	613

Source: See appendix.

Note: Standard errors in parentheses.

[a] Change in public deficit: percentage point change in the ratio of public deficit to GDP.

[b] Interaction variable interacting CHDEF and a dummy variable controlling for coalition governments.

[c] Change in the primary deficit (CHDEF), corrected for the cycle.

[d] Interaction variable interacting COCHDEF and a dummy variable controlling for coalition governments.

[e] Average change in deficit during tenure: average percentage point change in the deficit over the years that the current cabinet has been in power, up to the current year.

[f] Interaction variable interacting TOTCHDEF and a dummy variable controlling for coalition governments. When TOTCHDEF is used, given variables are replaced by dTOTGDP, dTOTUNR, and TOTINFL. The coefficients on DGDP, DUNR, and INFL are the coefficients on these variables.

***Significant at the 1 percent level.

**Significant at the 5 percent level.

*Significant at the 10 percent level.

Table 13.9   Probit coefficients (majority interaction term)

Variables	IDEOCH (1)	IDEOCH (2)	IDEOCH (3)	IDEOCH (4)	IDEOCH (5)	IDEOCH (6)
CHDEF[a]	-0.0627 (0.052)	-0.0400 (0.057)				
CHDEF*MAJ[b]		-0.1122 (0.121)				
COCHDEF[c]			0.0039 (0.056)	0.0469 (0.065)		
COCHDEF*MAJ[d]				-0.1696 (0.129)		
TOTCHDEF[e]					-0.0100 (0.067)	0.0414 (0.075)
TOTCHDEF*MAJ[f]						-0.2348 (0.156)
DGDP	-0.0471 (0.042)	-0.0453 (0.042)	-0.0439 (0.044)	-0.0413 (0.044)	-0.1039** (0.048)	-0.0971** (0.048)
DUNR	0.0009 (0.005)	0.0005 (0.005)	-0.0030 (0.005)	-0.0033 (0.005)	-0.0066 (0.006)	-0.0075 (0.006)
INFL	0.0266** (0.013)	0.0273** (0.013)	0.0342** (0.014)	0.0346** (0.014)	0.0309** (0.013)	0.0321** (0.013)
DURAT	0.2265*** (0.050)	0.2310*** (0.050)	0.2273*** (0.052)	0.2328*** (0.052)	0.2295*** (0.051)	0.2355*** (0.051)

Table 13.9 (continued)

Variables	IDEOCH (1)	IDEOCH (2)	IDEOCH (3)	IDEOCH (4)	IDEOCH (5)	IDEOCH (6)
COAL	0.0547	0.0550	0.0493	0.0446	0.0450	0.0580
	(0.150)	(0.150)	(0.154)	(0.154)	(0.152)	(0.153)
MAJ	0.0039	0.0101	−0.0154	−0.0050	−0.0467	−0.0400
	(0.178)	(0.178)	(0.182)	(0.182)	(0.179)	(0.181)
Constant	−1.7700***	−1.7879***	−1.8006***	−1.8216***	−1.6166***	−1.6638***
	(0.230)	(0.232)	(0.242)	(0.244)	(0.237)	(0.240)
Log-likelihood						
Observations	613	613	591	591	613	613

Source: See appendix.

Note: Standard errors in parentheses.

ᵃChange in public deficit: percentage point change in the ratio of public deficit to GDP.

ᵇInteraction variable interacting CHDEF and a dummy variable controlling for governments with majority support in parliament.

ᶜChange in the primary deficit (CHDEF), corrected for the cycle.

ᵈInteraction variable interacting COCHDEF and a dummy variable controlling for governments with majority support in parliament.

ᵉAverage change in deficit during tenure: average percentage point change in the deficit over the years that the current cabinet has been in power, up to the current year.

ᶠInteraction variable interacting TOTCHDEF and a dummy variable controlling for governments with majority support in parliament. When TOTCHDEF is used, given variables are replaced by dTOTGDP, dTOTUNR, and TOTINFL. The coefficients on DGDP, DUNR, and INFL are the coefficients on these variables.

*** Significant at the 1 percent level.

** Significant at the 5 percent level.

* Significant at the 10 percent level.

A second and related problem is what Alesina and Drazen (1991) modeled as a "war of attrition" political game. Political conflicts over the allocation of costs of the budget cuts or tax increases, for example, lead to a stalemate that requires time to be resolved. Postponing an adjustment may be costly, but all sides hope to be able to shield themselves from such costs, and the war continues until one side gives in. Thus, more polarized political systems and fractionalized societies, where deals and compromises are more difficult to reach quickly, should have a harder time stabilizing. Another implication is that a political consolidation of a stable and secure cohesive majority may be a precondition for a fiscal consolidation. Finally, this model is consistent with the crisis hypothesis; namely, the idea that a sharp deterioration of the economic situation may lead to reforms. In this case, a fiscal consolidation occurs simply because it becomes too costly to continue to postpone.

13.6   Case Studies

There is great variety of politico-economic features in large fiscal adjustments. They are the result of complex interactions between fiscal, macroeconomic, structural reforms, and political variables. In this section we again focus on episodes of large fiscal adjustments, and try to isolate some "interesting" cases. We consider different political environments in order to guarantee the appropriate variety. First we look at Canada in the 1990s, as it can be taken as an example of strong government implementing fiscal adjustments. The Liberal Party's share of votes in 1993 was really high, with more than 40 percent of the electors voting for the party. The second case we look at is Finland between 1993 and 1998. This case is completely different given the proportional and very fragmented political system, in which the government in charge is often a coalition. Third, we focus on Sweden between 1994 and 2000. The Sweden case has some macroeconomics analogies with the Finnish one, as both Sweden and Finland went through a severe financial crisis at the beginning of the 1990s. They also present some differences. In Sweden, the Social Democratic Party (SDP) had a consensus that lasted longer than in Finland: it took office in 1994 and started the fiscal consolidation right after the election, holding the majority until the 2006 elections. Our fourth case study considers the United Kingdom in the 1990s, which gives us a good example of a situation in which fiscal adjustments were implemented but the government was not reelected.

The empirical evidence suggests that in the cases of reelections, the government suffers a small decrease in the share of votes in the election following the consolidation program, but this does not prevent them from staying in charge (for example, in Finland). In some cases the voters seem to appreciate the consolidation as time goes by, and after a small decrease in the share of votes, a bigger increase follows (as in Canada).

13.6.1   Canada 1993 to 1997: Expenditure-Based Adjustment with Government Reelection

Canada experienced a severe economic downturn in the early 1990s, which had a significant impact on the country's budget balance. In 1992 public spending rose well above 50 percent of GDP and the budget deficit increased from 4.6 percent of GDP in 1989 to 9.1 percent in 1992. As a consequence, the public debt-to-GDP ratio grew sharply, to above 100 percent of GDP. The worsening of the overall general government deficit originated in the deficit of the provinces (Hauptmeier, Heipertz, and Schuknecht 2006). Moreover, other key elements contributed to this, such as the substantial competitive disadvantages that Canada faced because of high labor costs, low productivity growth rates, and a pronounced exchange rate appreciation that began in the mid-1980s.

In reaction to these events, in 1993 the Canadian government started an ambitious austerity program. The success was particularly based on three elements: low and stable inflation, structural reforms, and substantial expenditure reductions. By 1997, the budget had been balanced. More than 90 percent of the fiscal adjustment was due to spending cuts. The main expenditure measures included "cuts in wages (in particular, public employee compensation), unemployment benefits, defense spending, health care services, agricultural and business subsidies, and transfers to provinces and households" (Leigh, Plekhanov, and Kumar 2007, 13). As a result, total and primary expenditures declined by around 3.5 percent of GDP within the first two years. In the following years the consolidation path continued, and led to a total spending decrease by more than 11 percent of GDP over seven years, compared to the peak it reached in 1992.

On the revenue side, some reforms lowered the tax burden and improved the fairness of the tax system, reducing personal income taxes at the provincial level, increasing corporate income tax rates, and broadening the base of both. Other measures included a wide use of privatizations and a reformation of transfer systems, which benefited both the budget balance and the supply side of the economy. Some major reforms were also introduced to increase labor market flexibility and to make the financial sector more competitive and efficient. For instance, the financial services sector policy was reviewed and reformed in the late 1990s.

Traditionally, Canada had a two-party system, with the Conservative and Liberal parties dominating the political scene.

Beginning in the 1990s, Canadian national politics became more like a multiparty system, even though the Liberal and Conservative parties kept a relatively dominant role. But in 1993 a total of five main political parties competed for electoral support, and an erosion of the command was enjoyed by the Liberal and Conservative parties. In 1993 the Liberal Party took office, running its election campaign explicitly on a platform of addressing

Canada's fiscal issues (the so-called "Red book"). The party was able to win a strong majority, one of the best results in Canada's history, after being out of power since 1984. In the 1993 elections, the party won 177 seats and achieved the third-best performance in its history, and its best performance since 1949. The Liberal Party was reelected with a considerably lower majority in the following general election in 1997, but nearly tied their 1993 result in the subsequent 2000 election (see table 13.10). Chretien became the only Canadian prime minister to win three consecutive majority governments.

13.6.2   Finland 1993 to 1998: Expenditure-Based Adjustment with Government Reelection

During the 1980s Finland went through a financial liberalization process that led to a lending boom. The boom was followed by a recession, partially due to the banking crisis of 1991, and partially due to the deterioration of the terms of trade following the fall of the Soviet Union, which accounted for 15 to 20 percent of Finland's foreign trade. Finland's real GDP dropped by about 14 percent between 1990 and 1993. By 1994 unemployment had reached nearly 20 percent.[12] Government spending over GDP reached a staggering 65 percent and the deficit exceeded 7 percent. At the same time, bailout costs for the banking sector further accelerated the increase in the public debt ratio.

The government reaction was to enact a substantial fiscal adjustment over six years, between 1993 and 1998: the debt over GDP ratio went down a cumulative 6.2 percentage points between 1993 and 1998. We estimate that about 78 percent of the adjustment was due to expenditure cuts. According to Hauptmeier, Heipertz, and Schuknecht (2006) there was a 5 percent of GDP reduction in total expenditures over the first two years of the fiscal adjustment and expenditures were reduced by 15 percent to 49 percent of GDP over seven years. Furthermore, in the same period, the fiscal balance improved substantially to achieve a 7 percent surplus by the end of the 1990s. The main expenditure measures included cuts in social benefits, particularly unemployment benefits, transfers to municipalities, subsidies, wages, and capital spending. For instance, contractual pay increases were frozen for four years starting from 1991, and those measures were accompanied by moderate wage agreements in the public sector and reductions in public sector employment levels. The government also implemented broadly revenue-neutral tax reform, raising user fees in health and education, along with increases in payroll taxes and in employee compensation for social security. Complementary reform measures also helped the fiscal adjustment. For instance, "incomes policy agreements" were implemented on a biannual basis, contributing to wage stability and low levels of inflation. A devaluation of the exchange rate in 1992 also helped improve the budget balance by

12. For more details, see Honkapohja and Koskela (1999).

Table 13.10   Vote shares and seats by election in Canada, 1993–2000

	1993		1997		2000		Change in share 1997–1993	Change in share 2000–1997
	Percentage share of votes	Seats	Percentage share of votes	Seats	Percentage share of votes	Seats		
Liberal Party of Canada	41.3	177	38.5	155	40.8	172	-2.8	2.3
Bloc Québécois	13.5	54	10.7	44	10.7	38	-2.8	0
Reform Party of Canada	18.7	52	19.4	60	25.5	66	0.7	6.1
New Democratic Party	6.9	9	11	21	8.5	13	4.1	-2.5
Progressive Conservative Party of Canada	16	2	18.8	20	12.2	12	2.8	-6.6
Others	3.6	1	1.6	1	2.3	0	-2	0.7

Source: Elections Canada.

benefitting the tradable sector. Furthermore, inflation targeting at 2 percent contributed to the overall stability and renewed growth of the economy in the following years.

Finland can be classified as a case of expenditure-based fiscal adjustment with reelection if we look at the 1999 elections. The result is not as clear-cut as it was for Canada since there was a change in the Finnish government in the 1995 elections, after the austerity program had already started. The Finnish political background in the 1990s can be illustrated as follows. The Centre Party and the Social Democratic Party were the two main political parties between 1993 and 1998, and both implemented austerity policies during that period. In 1992, the Centre Party government elected in 1991 started a fiscal consolidation program based on a new medium-term framework. It lost the following elections, in April 1995, when the SDP won with 28.3 percent of the votes and immediately introduced an austerity package. In particular, the new social democratic government was formed by a five-party "Rainbow Coalition" and Paavo Lipponen, the SDP leader, was appointed prime minister. The SDP was reelected in 1999, although by a very narrow majority, having lost a significant share of the votes (5.4 percent) relative to the previous election. According to election results, there was a strong political competition among three parties between 1995 and 2003: the SDP, the National Coalition Party, and the Centre Party, with the latter taking office again after the 2003 elections. As in Canada, from electoral results we can see a decrease in votes for the leading political party during the fiscal adjustment. Still, the SDP, which had the majority in 1992, again had the relative majority in the 1999 elections (see table 13.11).

13.6.3   Sweden 1994 to 2000: Expenditure-Based Adjustment with Government Reelection

The boom of the 1980s in Sweden was followed by a recession, which was triggered by the banking crisis of 1991, after the collapse of a real estate bubble. The public expenditure ratio had increased to 73 percent of GDP in 1993 and public debt had risen rapidly, to over 70 percent of GDP. The budget deficit was at 11.2 percent of GDP and the unemployment rate at 7.5 percent. In response to these events, the Swedish government started a fiscal consolidation program, which, according to our estimates, led to a cumulative fiscal adjustment of 8.4 percent over seven years mainly because of substantial cuts in expenditures. By the end of the year 2000 there was a 3 percent of GDP surplus.

Around 70 percent of the adjustment was based on cuts in expenditures. Central features of the new budget process, implemented in January 1997, were also a budgetary process with multiyear expenditure ceilings and a medium-term target for the government's net lending. An expenditure ceiling was imposed in 1996, which limited central government expenditures and expenditures for the pension system outside the budget (but did not include

Table 13.11   Vote shares and seats by election in Finland, 1995–2003

	1995		1999		2003		Change in share 1999–1995	Change in share 2003–1999
	Percentage share of votes	Seats	Percentage share of votes	Seats	Percentage share of votes	Seats		
Social Democratic Party of Finland	28.3	63	22.9	51	24.5	53	-5.4	1.6
Centre Party	19.8	44	22.4	48	24.7	55	2.6	2.3
National Coalition Party	17.9	39	21	46	18.6	40	3.1	-2.4
Left Alliance	11.2	22	10.9	20	9.9	19	-0.3	-1
Swedish People's Party	5.1	11	5.1	11	4.6	8	0	-0.5
Green League	6.5	9	7.3	11	8	14	0.8	0.7
Christian League of Finland	3	7	4.2	10	5.3	7	1.2	1.1
Progressive Finnish Party	2.8	2	1	0	—	—	—	—
Finnish Rural Party	1.3	1	—	0	—	—	—	—
Others	4.1	2	5.2	3	4.4	4	1.1	-0.8

Source: Statistics Finland.

interest expenditures). The adjustment covered approximately two-thirds of the total Swedish general government expenditures and substantially reduced government transfers, such as pensions, early retirement benefits, housing subsidies, and social and unemployment insurance. Moreover, cuts across a broad range of spending programs were implemented between 1994 and 2000. Some revenue measures were also introduced, including increases in social security fees, full taxation of dividends and capital gains, and increases in personal income tax rates. Hauptmeier, Heipertz, and Schuknecht (2006, 20) report that since mid-1995, "the government gradually implemented a pension reform and introduced a funded pillar, besides pursuing a privatization program and a higher degree of labour market liberalization."

Sweden, as was the case for Canada and Finland, is a case of expenditure-based fiscal adjustment with reelection. In the September 1994 general election the Social Democratic Party won most seats, although not an overall majority, and Ingvar Carlsson returned to power at the head of a minority government after a center-right minority government had won the previous elections in the early 1990s. In August of 1995 Carlsson announced that he would step down as prime minister in March 1996, once his party had chosen a replacement. In the meantime, a referendum was passed in November 1994 supporting Sweden's application for entering the European Union (EU), and in January 1995 Sweden became a full EU member.

Göran Persson, Sweden's former finance minister, replaced Carlsson as prime minister in March 1996 and continued the austerity measures that started at the beginning of the 1990s. Although the fiscal adjustment was quite significant, as discussed earlier, Persson's Social Democrats finished ahead in the September 1998 general election, although its share of votes decreased by 7 percent to 38 percent. The votes for the Social Democratic Party were lost to the ex-communist Left Party, which doubled its vote to 12 percent between 1994 and 1998, and which supported the government conditional on it raising welfare spending and holding a referendum to join the Euro. Between 1998 and 2002, the economy started growing again, which enabled tax cuts and led to the Social Democratic victory in the following general elections in 2002. The Social Democrats held office until 2006 (see table 13.12).

13.6.4 United Kingdom 1994 to 1999: Expenditure-Based Adjustment without Government Reelection

On September 16, 1992, the prime minister major was forced to withdraw the pound from the European Exchange Rate Mechanism because the British government could not maintain the value of the currency at agreed-upon levels. In early 1993, there was positve growth driven by an increase in private consumption. Unemployment fell over the following years, while inflation remained relatively low. At the same time, austerity measures were implemented, mostly through expenditure cuts. Using our data, we estimate that

Table 13.12   Vote shares and seats by election in Sweden, 1994–2002

	1994		1998		2002		Change in share 1998–1994	Change in share 2002–1998
	Percentage share of votes	Seats	Percentage share of votes	Seats	Percentage share of votes	Seats		
Moderate Party	22.4	80	22.9	82	15.3	55	0.5	-7.6
Centre Party	7.7	27	5.1	18	6.2	22	-2.6	1.1
Liberal Party	7.2	26	4.7	17	13.4	48	-2.5	8.7
Christian Democratic Party	4.1	15	11.7	42	9.1	33	7.6	-2.6
Green Party	5	18	4.5	16	4.6	17	-0.5	0.1
Social Democratic Party	45.3	161	36.4	131	39.9	144	-8.9	3.5
Left Party	6.2	22	12	43	8.4	30	5.8	-3.6
Others	2.3	—	2.6	—	3.1	—	0.3	0.5

Source: SCB–Statistics Sweden.

Table 13.13   **Vote shares and seats by election in the United Kingdom, 1992–1997**

	1992		1997		
	Percentage share of votes	Seats	Percentage share of votes	Seats	Change in share 1997–1993
Labour	34.4	274	43.2	418	8.8
Conservative	41.9	343	30.7	165	−11.2
Liberal Democratic	17.8	18	16.8	46	−1
Others	5.9	24	9.3	30	3.4

Source: UK Parliament.

the United Kingdom experienced a cumulative decline in the ratio of deficit to GDP of 6.7 percentage points between 1994 and 1999, and that almost 60 percent of the fiscal adjustment was due to expenditure cuts. Expenditure measures mainly consisted of sustantial cuts in government consumption, public employment, and transfers. They also implemented cuts in defense, transport, and social benefits (by setting tighter eligibility criteria). On the revenue side the austerity program included increases in indirect taxes and some duties. However, "[t]he VAT was lowered on some items for equity reasons, advanced corporation tax rebates were abolished, and there was a small reduction in the corporate tax rate" (Leigh, Plekhanov, and Kumar 2007, 14). Complementary measures were also implemented, and they included establishing the independence of the Bank of England, reforming the tax systems (in particular in the area of corporate taxation), and social contributions, especially in the low-wage sector. Moreover, legislation on corporate governance and competition was improved, and the utilities sector was substantially reformed by changing regulations.

In the election of 1997 the Conservative Party lost and the Labour Party took office. It should be remembered that after three consecutive victories, the Conservative Party won again in 1992, but this time by a narrower margin: the Tory majority in 1992 was reduced from over a hundred seats to below thirty (see table 13.13). In addition, the economic credibility of the government was seriously undermined a few months after the election, when major was forced to withdraw the pound from the European Exchange Rate Mechanism.

13.7   Conclusion

In this chapter we have examined in some detail the evidence supporting the conventional wisdom that fiscally "tight" governments lose popularity and elections and fiscally expansionary ones win. We found surprisingly little evidence supporting this conventional wisdom, given the strength with which this view is held by politicians, commentators, political scientists, and economists. More precisely, we found no evidence that even large reductions of budget deficits are always associated (or most of the time) with electoral losses.

The biggest counter-argument is one of reverse causation, namely, strong and popular government can implement fiscal adjustments and be reelected despite such policies, thus only these governments do so. Our attempts to uncover this reverse causation does not provide convincing evidence that our results are only driven by this effect. Needless to say, it is difficult to measure "strength" of a government, ex ante, and therefore our test should be taken cautiously. But we believe that a cautious conclusion is warranted: reasonably solid governments not on the verge of losing an election can engage in fiscal adjustments, even aggressive ones, and survive the next election.

Three case studies of sharp fiscal adjustments (Canada, Finland, and Sweden) show a decline in political support for the government, but a strong recovery later on. In the case of the United Kingdom the political revival did not occur and a very unpopular John Mayor lost. The reader may note that the three governments that were reelected after major fiscal adjustments were left-leaning, and the one that lost was right wing.[13] One may wonder whether there is a pattern here. As we discussed before, we did explore whether this is a statistical regularity. The evidence is very weak but not fully inconsistent with this hypothesis; namely, that left-wing governments are rewarded more that right-wing governments when they implement a fiscal adjustment. If this is true it may have to do with the composition of the adjustment and its redistributive consequences. This is a very important area for future research—one could investigate more precisely the nature and the detailed composition of the adjustment in relation to its electoral consequences for the incumbent.

Appendix

National Accounts Data

Fiscal and macroeconomic data are taken from the OECD Economic Outlook database no. 84. In our analysis we focus on the period 1975 to 2008. Variables we use in our study are defined as follows:

CHEXP: Change in public expenditures: percentage point change in the ratio of primary expenditures to GDP. Primary expenditures are com-

---

13. We are especially grateful to Tom Romer for pointing us in this direction.

puted as government current disbursements less gross government interest payments.

CHREV: Change in public revenues: percentage point change in the ratio of public revenues to GDP. Public revenues are computed as government current receipts less gross governemnt interest receipts.

CHDEF: Change in public deficit: percentage point change in the ratio of public deficit to GDP. Calculated as CHEXP less CHREV.

CHTRF: Change in transfers to households: percentage point change in the ratio of transfers to households to GDP.

CHSUB: Change in subsidies: percentage point change in the ratio of subsidies to GDP.

COCHEXP: Change in government expenditures (CHEXP), corrected for the cycle: percentage point change in the ratio of cyclically adjusted primary expenditures to potential GDP.

COCHREV: Change in government revenues (CHREV), corrected for the cycle: percentage point change in the ratio of cyclically adjusted government revenues to potential GDP.

COCHDEF: Change in the primary deficit (CHDEF), corrected for the cycle: calculated as COCHEXP less COCHREV.

TOTCHDEF: Average change in deficit during tenure: average percentage point change in the deficit over the years that the current cabinet has been in power, up to the current year. That is the average of CHDEF for the years from the last termination up to the current year.

ΔGDP: Rate of growth of real GDP, percent. Computed as the percentage change of the variable "Gross domestic product, volume, at 2000 ppp."

ΔTOTGDP: Average growth during tenure: average growth rate from the time when a cabinet came to power, up to current year, percent.

ΔGDPG7: Growth of G7 countries: weighted average growth rate of the G7 countries, percent. Weights for each country are calculated using real GDP.

ΔGDPg7: Growth relative to the G7 countries: calculated as ΔGDP less ΔGDPG7.

UNR: Unemployment rate, percent.

ΔUNR: Growth of the unemployment rate, percent: $[(UNR_t/UNR_{t-1}) - 1] * 100$.

ΔTOTUNR: Average unemployment growth during tenure: average annual growth rate of unemployment rate from beginning of cabinet's tenure to current year, percent.

UNRg7: Unemployment rate relative to the G7 countries: unemployment rate less the GDP-weighted average of the G7 unemployment rate, percentage points.

INFL: Inflation: rate of change of the GDP deflator, percent. It is constucted using the variable "Gross domestic product, deflator, market prices."

TOTINFL: Average inflation during tenure: average rate of inflation from the beginning of cabinet's tenure to current year, percent.

INFLg7: Inflation rate relative to the G7 countries: inflation rate less the GDP-weighted average of the G7 inflation rate, percentage points.

PEXP: Spending-based adjustment: dummy variable equal to 1 when following two conditions hold:
1. There is a large adjustment (CHDEF < –1.5).
2. CHEXP is less than its median across all years in which a large adjustment occurs.

PTAX: Tax-based adjustment: dummy variable equal to 1 when following two conditions hold:
1. There is a large adjustment (CHDEF < –1.5).
2. CHREV is more than its median across all years in which a large adjustment occurs.

PTRF: Transfer-based adjustment: dummy variable equal to 1 when following two conditions hold:
1. There is a large adjustment (CHDEF < –1.5).
2. CHTRF is less than its median across all years in which a large adjustment occurs.

PCGW: Government wage-based adjustment: dummy variable equal to 1 when the following two conditions hold:
1. There is a large adjustment (CHDEF < 1.5).
2. CHCGW is less than its median across all years in which a large adjustment occurs.

NINTRTg7: Relative nominal interest rate: long-term nominal interest rate (ten-year treasury notes) of a given country less the GDP-weighted average of long nominal interest rates in the G7 countries, percentage points.

RINTRT: Real interest rate: ten-year interest rate minus the growth rate of the GDP deflator, percent.

RINTRTg7: Relative real interest rate: ten-year real interest rate of a given country less the GDP-weighted average of real interest rates in the G7 countries.

Cabinet Data

For cabinet data we use the Database of Political Institutions (DPI) 2009. Again, we cover the period 1975 to 2008. The cabinet variables we focus on are defined as follows:

TERM: Government termination: dummy variable equal to 1 in any year in which a government ends, regardless of the reason. A termination may or may not involve a "change" in cabinet ideology or prime minister.

DURAT: Duration: integer number of years that a cabinet has been in power, up to the current year. A cabinet that falls during its first year in power is counted as 1. Every time there is a government termination (TERM = 1), DURAT is reset to 1 the year after the termination.

SING: Single party: dummy variable equal to 1 if a single-party cabinet is in power.

COAL: Coalition: dummy variable equal to 1 if a coalition cabinet (including ministers from two or more parties) is in power.

MAJ: Majority: dummy variable equal to 1 if the cabinet has majority support in parliament.

IDEOCH: Change in ideology of cabinet: dummy variable equal to 1 if there is a change in the ideology index between the current year and the next. It is constructed by exploiting the change in the value of variable EXECRLC (describing the ideology of the chief executive's party) in the DPI data set.

ALLCH: Change of ideology or prime minister; dummy variable equal to 1 if either IDEOCH or PMCH is equal to 1.

References

Alcidi, Cinzia, and Daniel Gros. 2010. "The European Experience with Large Fiscal Adjustments." www.voxeu.org, April 28.

Alesina, Alberto, and Silvia Ardagna. 2010. "Large Changes in Fiscal Policy: Taxes versus Spending." In *Tax Policy and The Economy,* vol. 24, edited by Jeffrey R. Brown, 35–68. Chicago: University of Chicago Press.

Alesina, Alberto, Silvia Ardagna, and Francesco Trebbi. 2006. "Who Adjusts and When? On the Political Economy of Reforms." IMF Staff Papers. Washington, DC: International Monetary Fund.

Alesina, Alberto, and Allan Drazen. 1991. "Why Are Stabilizations Delayed?" *American Economic Review* 81:1170–88.

Alesina, Alberto, Roberto Perotti, and Josè A. Tavares. 1998. "The Political Economy of Fiscal Adjustments." Brookings Papers on Economic Activity, Spring. Washington, DC: Brookings Institution.

Alesina, Alberto, and Howard Rosenthal. 1995. *Partisan Politics, Divided Government, and the Economy.* Cambridge: Cambridge University Press.

Bonfiglioli, Alessandra, and Gino Gancia. 2010. "Politicians, Uncertainty and Reforms." Unpublished Manuscript.

Brender, Adi, and Allan Drazen. 2005. "Political Budget Cycles in New versus Established Democracies." *Journal of Monetary Economics* 52 (7): 1271–95.

———. 2008. "How Do Budget Deficits and Economic Growth Affect Reelection Prospects? Evidence from a Large Panel of Countries." *American Economic Review* 98 (5): 2203–20.

Buti, Marco, and Paul van den Noord. 2004a. "Fiscal Discretion and Elections in the Early Years of EMU." *Journal of Common Market Studies* 42 (4): 737–56.

———. 2004b. "Fiscal Policy in EMU: Rules, Discretion and Political Incentives." *Moneda y Crédito* 218:265–331.

Buti, Marco, Alessandro Turrini, Paul van den Noord, and Pietro Biroli. 2008.

"Defying the 'Juncker Curse': Can Reformist Governments Be Re-elected?" *Empirica* 36 (1): 65–100.
———. 2010. "Reforms and Re-elections in OECD Countries." *Economic Policy* 25:61–116.
Drazen, Allan. 2000. *Political Economy in Macroeconomics.* Princeton, NJ: Princeton University Press.
Fair, Ray C. 1978. "The Effect of Economic Events on Votes for President." *Review of Economics and Statistics* 60:159–72.
———. 1982. "The Effect of Economic Events on Votes for President: 1980 Results." *Review of Economics and Statistics* 64:322–25.
———. 1988. "The Effects of Economic Events on Votes for President: 1984 Update." *Political Behavior* 10:168–79.
Giavazzi, Francesco, and Marco Pagano. 1990. "Can Severe Fiscal Contractions Be Expansionary? Tales of Two Small European Countries." *NBER Macroeconomics Annual 1990,* vol. 5, edited by Olivier Jean Blanchard and Stanley Fischer, 75–111. Cambridge, MA: MIT Press.
Giorno, Claude, Pete Richardson, Deborah Roseveare, and Paul van den Noord. 1995. "Potential Output, Output Gaps, and Structural Budget Balances." *OECD Economic Studies* no. 24, 167–209.
Hauptmeier, Sebastian, Martin Heipertz, and Ludger Schuknecht. 2006. "Expenditure Reform in Industrialised Countries: A Case Study Approach." European Central Bank Working Paper Series no. 634, May.
Honkapohja, Seppo, and Erkki Koskela. 1999. "The Economic Crisis of the 1990s in Finland." *Economic Policy* 14 (29): 399–436.
International Monetary Fund. 2010. *World Economic Outlook,* September. Washington, DC: IMF.
Leigh, Daniel, Alexander Plekhanov, and Manmohan S. Kumar. 2007. "Fiscal Adjustments: Determinants and Macroeconomic Consequences." IMF Working Papers no. 07/178. Washington, DC: International Monetary Fund.
Persson, Torsten, and Guido Tabellini. 2000. "Political Economics: Explaining Economic Policy." Cambridge, MA: MIT Press.
Rogoff, Kenneth, and Anne Sibert. 1988. "Elections and Macroeconomic Policy Cycles." *Review of Economic Studies* 55:1–16.

Comment   Thomas Romer

There are few robust results in the large empirical literature that attempts to discover the determinants of electoral outcomes. Bad economic conditions are bad for incumbent governments. And usually the longer the government has been in office, the higher the likelihood of its defeat. Both of these patterns emerge in the data explored in the chapter by Alesina, Carloni, and Lecce (henceforth, ACL). But the main goal of the chapter is to see whether certain policy choices—large fiscal adjustments—are systemati-

Thomas Romer is professor of politics and public affairs and director of the Research Program in Political Economy at Princeton University.
For acknowledgments, sources of research support, and disclosure of the author's material financial relationships, if any, please see http://www.nber.org/chapters/c12655.ack.

cally related to the electoral fortunes of governments that undertake them. And the answer, at least in the econometric results presented here, appears to be that large fiscal adjustments are not "extra costly" politically in ways that are not already captured by the aggregate economic growth and government duration variables.

In trying to understand the connections between economic policies and political behavior by the electorate, it is useful to focus on the inference problems that voters face. A voter who wants to assess a government's economic performance needs to answer (at least) two very difficult questions: Does the economic situation warrant significant policy change? Will the incumbent government's policy turn out to be a good one (for whoever the voter thinks is relevant)? Big shifts in fiscal policy of the type that ACL are looking at tend to come after fairly prolonged economic pressures and lots of political maneuvering by interest groups, both domestic and international. Even economics professors can disagree about the need for large fiscal adjustments, how they should be implemented, and what their effects are likely to be.

To the extent that a voter relies on arguments by politicians, whether from those in power or their opposition, there will always be the issue of credibility. Leave aside the obvious point that incumbents always defend their policies and opponents attack them. There may nevertheless be useful information that comes from the ideological reputation of the incumbent government. Loosely speaking, governments on the right are more likely to push for policies that shrink the size of the public sector in good times and bad, for purely ideological reasons. Left-wing governments will usually resist reducing public expenditures. A right-wing government that implements a large fiscal adjustment may just be using the cry of "economic crisis" to adopt its ideologically preferred policy. By contrast, a left-wing government will almost certainly be going against its core ideological position to engage in large fiscal adjustment. Its claim that the painful policy shift was really necessary will be more credible. More voters are likely to tolerate (at least for a while) the costs of the adjustment implemented by the left-wing government.

The panel data estimates of the ACL chapter consider changes in government but do not distinguish between left and right governments. The "Nixon goes to China" argument of the previous paragraph suggests that, other things equal, a left government that undertakes a large fiscal adjustment is more likely to survive than a right government. Because there is no control for government ideology in the specification, we cannot tell from the large-N results whether this is so. Since the data include a mix of left and right governments, the results only tell us that on average the probability of government survival is not affected by large fiscal adjustments.

The brief narratives about specific cases do bear out my conjecture. In three of the four countries (Canada, Finland, and Sweden), center-left governments made major reductions in cyclically adjusted deficits (mostly by big reductions in spending). Though in each case they endured some heavy political weather, they survived. By contrast, in the United Kingdom, the center-right government lost the election after it undertook a large fiscal adjustment.

A slightly closer look at the Canadian case reinforces my point about the importance of credibility.[1] The national government was not alone in having to confront a deteriorating fiscal situation. The provincial governments of Ontario and Saskatchewan were under particular pressure from debt markets to rein in their spending. In both provinces, New Democratic Party (NDP) governments—ideologically to the left of the center-left liberals, who formed the national government—undertook big expenditure reductions. The liberals were not in any case identified ideologically as "small government" types. In light of the provincial experience, when the liberals made big cuts in the national budget, the further-left opposition NDP was in no position to accuse them of using the crisis to achieve ideological fiscal goals.

In the version of the ACL chapter that appears in this volume (revised after the Milan conference), the authors say that they went back and did find "some very weak evidence that left-wing governments are rewarded more than right-wing governments when they reduce deficits [though] the evidence is not very robust." I of course agree with their later conclusion that this is worth pursuing further, particularly since it provides an avenue for bringing a bit more politics into the study of the political effects of economic policy. Such further analysis will need to control for the possibility that a right government is *more likely* to undertake a large fiscal adjustment than a left government, even though it risks a higher probability of punishment than would a left government.[2]

Finally, on a narrower point, I note that in some situations, a government can lose considerable support and still squeak through an election. Instead of casting the analysis in terms of the 0–1 outcome of government turnover, it would be interesting to look at a more continuous measure of political support, such as vote shares or seat shares. The specific cases already do this to some extent, but it would be worth looking at the full sample in a more systematic way to get a finer measure of the political cost of large fiscal adjustments.

Reference

Redish, Angela. 2011. "Canada's Fiscal Turnaround." Unpublished Manuscript, November. University of British Columbia.

---

1. I am indebted to Redish (2011) for her highly informative account of the Canadian episode.
2. Because adopting the ideologically preferred policy provides benefits to the right-wing party (and its supporters) that offset the increased risk of losing power.

Contributors

Alberto Alesina
Department of Economics
Harvard University
Littauer Center 210
Cambridge, MA 02138

Alan J. Auerbach
Department of Economics
530 Evans Hall, #3880
University of California, Berkeley
Berkeley, CA 94720-3880

Axel H. Börsch-Supan
MEA at Max Planck Institute
Amalienstrasse 33
80799 Munich, Germany

Pierre Cahuc
Laboratoire de Macroéconomie,
  CREST
15 Boulevard Gabriel Péri
92245 Malakoff Cedex, France

Stéphane Carcillo
OECD
2 rue André Pascal
75775 Paris Cedex 16, France

Dorian Carloni
Department of Economics
530 Evans Hall, #3880
University of California, Berkeley
Berkeley, CA 94720-3880

Lawrence J. Christiano
Department of Economics
Northwestern University
2001 Sheridan Road
Evanston, IL 60208

Ruud de Mooij
International Monetary Fund
700 19th Street, NW
Washington, DC 20431

William Easterly
New York University
Department of Economics
19 West 4th Street, 6th floor
New York, NY 10012

Douglas W. Elmendorf
Director, Congressional Budget Office
US Congress
2nd and D Streets, SW
Washington, DC 20515

Richard W. Evans
Department of Economics, 167 FOB
Brigham Young University
Provo, UT 84602

Jordi Galí
Centre de Recerca en Economia
    Internacional (CREI)
Ramon Trias Fargas 25
08005 Barcelona, Spain

Francesco Giavazzi
Università Bocconi and IGIER
Via Guglielmo Rontgen, 1
20136 Milan, Italy

Yuriy Gorodnichenko
Department of Economics
530 Evans Hall #3880
University of California, Berkeley
Berkeley, CA 94720-3880

Robert E. Hall
Hoover Institution
Stanford University
Stanford, CA 94305-6010

Michael Keen
International Monetary Fund
Fiscal Affairs Department
700 19th Street, NW
Washington, DC 20431

Laurence J. Kotlikoff
Department of Economics
Boston University
270 Bay State Road
Boston, MA 02215

Philip R. Lane
Economics Department
Trinity College Dublin
Dublin 2, Ireland

Giampaolo Lecce
Department of Economics
Università Bocconi
Via Roentgen, 1
20136 Milan, Italy

Eric M. Leeper
Department of Economics
304 Wylie Hall
Indiana University
Bloomington, IN 47405-7104

Michael McMahon
Department of Economics
University of Warwick
Coventry CV4 7AL, United Kingdom

Lucio R. Pench
European Commission
Economic and Financial Affairs DG
Avenue de Beaulieu 1/Beaulieustraat 1
1160 Brussels, Belgium

Roberto Perotti
Università Bocconi and IGIER
Via Guglielmo Roentgen, 1
20136 Milan, Italy

Kerk L. Phillips
Department of Economics, 166 FOB
Brigham Young University
Provo, UT 84602

Paolo Pinotti
Università Bocconi
Via Guglielmo Roentgen, 1
20136 Milan, Italy

James M. Poterba
Department of Economics
MIT, E52-350
50 Memorial Drive
Cambridge, MA 02142-1347

Indira Rajaraman
Indian Statistical Institute
Shahid Jit Singh Marg
New Delhi 110016 India

Valerie A. Ramey
Department of Economics, 0508
University of California, San Diego
9500 Gilman Drive
La Jolla, CA 92093-0508

Thomas Romer
Woodrow Wilson School
306 Robertson Hall
Princeton University
Princeton, NJ 08544-1013

Mathias Trabandt
Board of Governors of the Federal
    Reserve System
20th Street and Constitution Avenue
    NW
Washington, DC 20551

Harald Uhlig
Department of Economics
University of Chicago
1126 East 59th Street
Chicago, IL 60637

Jaume Ventura
Centre de Recerca en Economia
    Internacional (CREI)
Ramon Trias Fargas 25-27
08005-Barcelona, Spain

Todd B. Walker
Department of Economics
Indiana University
100 S. Woodlawn
Bloomington, IN 47401-7104

David A. Wise
John F. Kennedy School of
    Government
Harvard University
79 John F. Kennedy
Cambridge, MA 02138

Charles Wyplosz
The Graduate Institute of International
    and Development Studies
P.O. Box 36
1211 Geneva 21, Switzerland

Author Index

Subject Index